The world atlas of
Whisky

DAVE BROOM

Glenfiddich Award-winning author

2ND EDITION: FULLY REVISED AND UPDATED

The world atlas of
Whisky

More than 200 distilleries explored and 750 expressions tasted

Mitchell Beazley

Dedication

In memory of my beloved mother, Isobel Broom, who sadly didn't live to see this work completed, but whose constant and loving support over the years got me to where I am. I hope you'd be proud.

An Hachette UK Company
www.hachette.co.uk

First published in Great Britain in 2010 by Mitchell Beazley, an imprint of Octopus Publishing Group Limited, Endeavour House, 189 Shaftesbury Avenue, London WC2H 8JY

www.octopusbooks.co.uk
www.octopusbooksusa.com

This revised edition published in 2014.

Distributed in the US by Hachette Book Group USA, 237 Park Avenue, New York, NY 10017, USA

Distributed in Canada by Canadian Manda Group, 664 Annette St., Toronto, Ontario, Canada M6S 2C8

ISBN: 978 1 84533 942 5

Set in Garamond and Futura.

Printed and bound in China.

Publisher's Credits for the 2nd Edition
Senior Editor: Leanne Bryan
Copy-editor: Jamie Ambrose
Proofreader: Hilary Lumsden
Americanizer: Constance Novis
Indexer: Cathy Heath
Executive Art Editor: Juliette Norsworthy
Designer: Bounford.com
Picture Research Manager: Giulia Hetherington
Assistant Production Manager: Caroline Alberti

Cartography
Heritage Editorial, heritage2ed@aol.com
Digital mapping by Encompass Graphics Ltd,
Hove, UK, www.encompass-graphics.co.uk

Acknowledgment
I particularly want to thank Davin de Kergommeaux and Bernhard Schäfer, who helped significantly in the writing of the Canadian and Central Europe sections, respectively.

Opposite: Whisky sleeping in the vaulted warehouses at Deanston distillery, Stirling, Scotland.

Contents

FOREWORD

Welcome to the new edition of Dave Broom's *The World Atlas of Whisky*. Since its original publication four years ago, the need for this book has only increased. We are currently experiencing a true whisky renaissance. Everything I originally said below remains true, and this book is your guide to getting the most out of your whisky experience.

If there ever was a time for a comprehensive book on whisky, it's now. The whisky world is more dynamic than at any other time in recent history. Why? One reason is that we are in the middle of a whisky boom. More and more people around the globe are beginning to realize the quality, individuality, and value of whisky. Even with the recent increase in whisky prices, whisky's value—especially bourbon—can't be beaten by any other distilled spirit. The whisky industry has responded to increased demand by increasing its output, expanding its capacity, and even building new distilleries.

Another reason is the proliferation of new artisan whisky-distillers. Gone are the days when nearly all whisky producers were from Scotland, Ireland, the USA (predominantly Kentucky and Tennessee), and Canada. Japan has proven that its distillers deserve just as much attention and respect by producing whisky that is as good as Scotch.

That's saying a lot! There have never been more Scotch whiskies to choose from—both from the distillery owners themselves, and also from the myriad independent bottlers. Hundreds, actually. And, thanks to enhancements in distilling and maturation over the past decade or two, the quality of the whisky has never been better.

Additionally, new small craft distillers now make whisky across Europe, throughout the USA, and beyond. In the USA alone, there are over 400 artisan distillers making whiskey that didn't even exist 15 years ago. That's about four times more than established bourbon distillers, and the growth rate of these new distillers is increasing.

What does all this mean to you, the whisky enthusiast? You can look forward to many new whiskies—both from established distillers and the new artisan distillers peppered across the globe—which will continue to proliferate well into the future.

This brings us to *The World Atlas of Whisky*. What I like about it is its comprehensiveness. The book defines whisky, how it's made (from grain to glass), where it's made, and why one whisky tastes different from another. It explains how to best appreciate whisky, gives a great synopsis of the new releases along with providing tasting notes to help guide you. The photography accompanying the text is beautiful, even breathtaking at times. It really benefits those who don't have the means to travel to the various distilleries and distilling countries.

Perhaps the most useful and innovative component of the book is the use of "Flavor Camps" when describing the flavor personality of whiskies. While I enjoy the thorough tasting notes provided for the whiskies profiled, the Flavor Camp concept is a great resource when trying to capture the general flavor profile of a given whisky. This is an extremely useful guide for all whisky enthusiasts, but I think it will be especially helpful for those just beginning to explore the somewhat daunting and overwhelming array of whiskies to choose from.

Most importantly, *The World Atlas of Whisky* captures the essence of what's happening right now. Dave Broom is one of the very few whisky writers with the ability to do this in such a comprehensive manner. He is one of the most respected independent authorities on whisky, worldwide. And justly deserved, I might add. I am particularly captivated by Dave's engaging writing style and colorful tasting notes. It's understandable why his writing is in such demand.

Thanks to Dave, this book is both informative and entertaining to read, regardless of where you are in your whisky journey. His knowledge, passion, and integrity shows in everything he writes. *Slainte*!

John Hansell
Publisher & Editor,
Whisky Advocate magazine

Left: A grain of truth. All single-malt whisky starts with barley.

Right: Every glass tells a story. Whisky is the most complex spirit of all.

INTRODUCTION

It is hard to believe that, only five years after the *Atlas* was first researched, the map of whisky has changed so significantly that another edition was required. Isn't whisky the spirit that was the epitome of the conservative and conventional? Whisky just *was*. It wasn't exciting; it didn't dress itself up in age-inappropriate clothing in an effort to convince people to try it. It was just always there: unchanging, stubborn (*thrawn* in Scottish parlance). People found whisky when they felt it was right. Whisky didn't demean itself by finding them. Or so we were told.

In fact, whisky has always been in a state of flux. It has been dynamic from the moment it started trickling out of alchemists' stills in the fifteenth and sixteenth centuries. It has been flavored, drunk long and short, unaged and wood-matured; it has leaped boundaries, and shifted shape constantly because of demand, climate, war, politics, and economics. The need for this new edition is because this process of change has accelerated like never before.

We are now living in the exciting reality of World Whisky. The established heartlands of Scotland, Ireland, the USA, Canada, and Japan are seeing a level of success like never before. New distilleries

The often forgotten element in whisky-making around the world, people; here at the Murree distillery in Rawalpindi, Pakistan.

are opening in all of these countries, with more planned. Many of these distilleries are also part of the burgeoning craft movement.

In addition, whisky-making has taken root around the globe. There are said to be 150 distillers making whisky in German-speaking Europe alone; there are five distilleries in England, more than 20 in France, the same number in the Nordic countries. Australia is booming, and South America is starting on its whisky journey, as is Asia. It isn't just that there is a spread of countries, but a spread of techniques. These are new whiskies in more than one sense. They had to be mapped.

Why are they appearing now? Interest is being driven by a new generation of drinkers who are interested not just in whisky's history and provenance, but also in its flavors and possibilities. There is an open-minded attitude on the part of the drinker that wasn't there before, one replicated by the approach of distillers old and new.

This has to be tempered with a note of caution. It is easy to become wildly enthusiastic over the numbers, easier now to start up a distillery, but it should never be forgotten that whisky, like all things, moves in cycles. It goes in and out of fashion. To survive, and hopefully to prosper, all distillers need to realize that it is a long-term business (in fact, many must first realize that it is a business) and that they are all competing in an area where there are many other options.

Today's whisky drinker is also a rum drinker, a gin drinker, a tequila drinker, a craft-beer drinker, and a wine drinker, though hopefully not all on the same night. Male or female, these are people with high standards who appreciate craft and, because of the increased choice, can adopt and reject brands.

How do the new whiskies break though? Not by being too clever (consumers are savvy), but by having integrity.

Whisky is "slow." It speaks of place, craftsmanship, and a timeless approach to taking an ingredient and magically extracting its essence. It is also slow in its ability to make you pause and consider what is happening to your senses when you take a sip. At the same time, it is moving rapidly.

One reason for this book is to give some frame of reference in this increasingly cluttered world. What are the flavors? What do they mean? Where do they come from? Who crafted them?

It will, hopefully, give you waypoints on your journey. This book is for you, the whisky-lover. The success of the new distillers and this new whisky world is in your hands.

HOW THIS BOOK WORKS

With such a wealth of information available, this book includes a number of text and visual devices to enable the reader to get the most out of reading about all the whisky-producing countries, regions, and distilleries. These include: maps, tasting notes with flavor ratings, and details about the individual distillery itself. Below is a guide to how these work.

MAPS

Main Key A number of methods are used to show where each distillery is located. In the case of distilleries that have the same name as the nearest place, only the distillery name is given (e.g. Lagavulin). Where there is room and scale allows, the nearest place is shown using a white dot. Where scale or space are an issue, the place name is given after the distillery name using a comma: Jim Beam, Clermont.

Elevation/Topography Key This relates to all maps and is included on those maps where it is felt that the scale allows for clear definition of the topography.

Regions Within each country, the distilleries are ordered by region, apart from the USA, where Kentucky and Tennessee appear separately from other US distilleries. This is because the distinctly different production process used to make these whiskeys results in its own subcategory.

Distilleries All the distilleries that have been written about appear on the maps. Where there are a large number of other distilleries of note (for example, the new whisky-producers in Europe or the craft distilleries in the USA), these are also included on the map although there may be no reference to them in the text.

Grain Distilleries, Maltings & Other Whisky-related Features Where feasible and useful, distinctions have been made to clarify what sort of distillery is specified, as well as the inclusion of a number of maltings.

DISTILLERY PAGES

Details Every distillery page gives details of the nearest village, town, or city, and (where available) a website or page related to that particular site for those featured in the tasting notes. On pages where there is more than one distillery, the details are divided by "/".

Visits Where the distillery is open for visits, details given are correct at the time of writing. If you are thinking of visiting a distillery, make contact in advance to check current opening details. If you are making an appointment or plan on taking a specific tour, never underestimate the time allowed for winding roads, sheep on the road, etc.

Sourcing Rare Malts Please note that although many distilleries are not able to open to the public, their products are available. For these, the best way to find out more is to make contact with a specialist whisky retailer, or refer to specialist whisky websites.

Mothballed This term defines those distilleries that have been taken out of production but which may be brought back into production at some date in the future. At the time of writing, the information given as to which plants are mothballed is as accurate as possible.

New/Planned There are a huge number of new distilleries opening and in the process of being built globally. The aim for this atlas is to be as comprehensive as possible, but there might be cases where we have not had the opportunity to include new distilleries on the maps.

TASTING NOTES

Selection I have chosen a selection of whiskies that best illustrate the breadth of each distillery's offering, looking at new spirit, young, teenage, and older releases where appropriate.

Order They have been ordered in a similar fashion for each country to allow easy comparison. The ordering follows one of two approaches: either by age, or, if more than one brand name is produced at a single distillery, in alphabetical order.

Age Definitions Usually the age statement forms part of the name of the whisky. "NAS" refers to those with no age statement on the label.

Independent Bottlings Where possible I have tasted whiskies from the distillery's owner but on some occasions, when these have not been available, I have tasted examples from independent bottlers.

Cask Samples Where possible, I have tasted bottled products but on some occasions, when these have not been available, the distiller has kindly supplied a cask sample. These are marked as such.

ABV/Proof The strength of all whiskies is written as a percentage of alcohol by volume (abv), i.e. 40%, apart from US whiskeys where US proof is also indicated (80°/40%).

Japan For its more specialist bottlings, Japan includes the year when the whisky was laid down, its series, and often a cask number, too.

Flavor Camps Every tasting note, except for new makes and cask samples, includes a Flavor Camp. Please *see* pp.26–7 for the full explanation of these. There is also a comprehensive listing of all the whiskies in their appropriate Flavor Camps on pp.324–6. If you like one whisky style in particular, this will give you an idea of other whiskies you might also like to try. Many of the younger whiskies are still evolving and may drift from one flavor camp to another as they mature. Take these analyses as their state of being at the time of writing.

Where Next? This feature is a quick cross-reference to another whisky you might like to try. It appears with all tasting notes except for "new makes" and "cask samples," which are often either works in progress or "snapshots" that are not commercially available, blends and grains.

TERMINOLOGY

Glossary There's lots of fun language associated with whisky and much of it changes around the world. If there's ever a term you are not sure about, check the Glossary on pp.327–8.

Whisky/Whiskey I have used the spelling "whisky" throughout the book because this is the legally recognized spelling to describe the whiskies from everywhere in the world except for Ireland and the USA. In those two exceptions the spelling "whiskey" has been used.

WHAT IS WHISKY?

This is an atlas. That means that there are maps, which is handy since they tell you where the distilleries are. However, that physical location is only a small element within a whisky's story. The map will tell you how to get to the distillery and what is nearby. It won't tell you everything you need to know about the whisky itself.

For this atlas to work, it also had to create a map of flavors, so you could see which whiskies are similar, which are different, and which challenge the conventional wisdom of the existence of broad regional styles. In doing so, we arrive in a world where the distiller and the site itself become the prime driving forces in the creation of flavor. In this way our Flavor Map allows us to discover why each distillery in, say, Scotland (or Kentucky), which effectively operates in the same way as its neighbor, makes a spirit unique to that specific site.

To begin our quest to find the heart of whisky, the book outlines what the shared production processes are for the four main styles of whisky—single malt, grain whisky, traditional Irish pot-still, and bourbon—looking at the main decision points available to the distiller which enable him or her to create that unique distillery character.

There isn't a separate history section because the story of each distillery adds its own voice to that map. By looking at flavor, we can see how whisky has evolved over time. In nineteenth-century Scotland, for example, although the motivation for making a specific style may have initially been driven by location (such as the use of peat), as the century progressed, the demands of the market and the development of blends also impacted on the flavors of whiskies being produced. Looking at single-malt Scotch from this angle suggests that instead of regional styles being dominant, whisky taste has evolved in a series of "Flavor Ages," which have, in simple terms, gone from heavy to light.

Each distillery is therefore examined not just as a producer of a brand, but as a living entity with its own story to tell—and the people who make it are here to help tell it. It was also important that the spirit itself was tasted from birth onward if the book was to look at the singularity of each distillery. If this is a map that takes us through the world of whisky, then its starting point has to be when the spirit is born. You cannot talk about distillery character if all you are looking at is the result of that actual distillery character's complex interaction with oak.

By tasting the new make and then the whisky at older increments, we can tease out how the flavors created in the distillery evolve: watch green fruits as they ripen and then dry; see grass turn to hay, observe sulfur drifting off to reveal purity behind; and note any oak influence.

The mature spirits are then grouped into Flavor Camps so that you can easily see similarities and differences (often one distillery will occupy more than one camp as its whisky matures); this also offers other potential routes through the great whisky maze. Whisky-making is a living, evolving, creative art, driven by people who want to accentuate their distinctiveness, and it is this multiplicity of individual personalities that are the waypoints on our map.

Continuity and consistency: two of the bywords of high-quality whisky-making.

A WHISKY WORLD

What is whisky? The answer given in the first edition still holds: a spirit that has been made by mashing a cereal, fermenting it into a beer, distilling that, and then aging the result. However, the variations on that simple principle have never been greater. Distillers around the world are asking the same question: why should whisky always conform to what has been handed down?

Speaking to new distillers is always fascinating. Many started because they loved single-malt Scotch (never blends, sadly) or bourbon. Almost all of them would then add, "But I wanted to make something that was mine." Why replicate what is out there? Can you really compete with Glenfiddich or Jack Daniel's? If not, then what are the other opportunities? Perhaps the cereal, for example. These days rye is no longer a Canadian or Kentuckian specialty. You can get ryes from Denmark, Austria, England, the Netherlands, and Australia. Why stop there? Why not try wheat whisky? Or what of oats, spelt, or quinoa? If you are using barley then why not take a leaf from a brewer's manual and use different roasts? Instead of using peat, why not try different woods—or nettles, or sheep manure?

If you are using different grains and smokes, then why not blend them together? Why stick to the standard distiller's yeasts when there are ale and wine yeasts to play with? Why not control the temperature of fermentation? Why stick to Scottish pot-stills or bourbon's column/doubler setup? What of Cognac stills, pots with plates in the neck? Hell, why not just design your own?

Today's new whisky-maker is facing exactly the same issues faced by Japanese distillers in the 1920s and '30s, which wasn't just how to make whisky, but how to make their whisky Japanese. The answer doesn't come from a marketing manual, but from heart and brain, meaning that the answers these distillers have given to that "What is whisky?" question are fascinating and often compelling. By successfully challenging convention, they are widening whisky's remit.

Yes, there is a place for Scotch single malt, bourbon, single pot-still Irish, and Canadian rye, but there is also now space for Swedish, Taiwanese, Australian, Dutch, and American craft alternatives, and more. Should the old countries be worried? Not yet, but they should be aware. Are they? Probably not.

That's not to say starting a distillery is easy. Maybe you are thinking of doing just that. Pause and listen to Francis Cuthbert of Daftmill Distillery, in Fife: "Have all your funding in place before starting. The costs of laying down stock will be ten times more expensive than the build. If you think that opening a coffee shop will offset these costs, then open a coffee shop and forget about the whisky."

Once you get started, what then? Here's Jean Donnay of Brittany's Glann ar Mor and Islay's Gartbreck: "Distillation is a lot more complicated than you think. You read, you visit distilleries, you ask questions, you think you have the figures, but the more I do it, the more subtle and complex it becomes. I always thought there was alchemy involved, something which cannot be explained, and I believe that even more now. Distillation is trickier than you think. Every day is different, and so every day you learn something different. If I were a distiller for 200 years I would still learn something new every day."

This is a sentiment that would meet with agreement from all distillers, old and new. No one is an expert. You never stop discovering as long as you continue to ask questions and be humble about what you are doing.

What is whisky? It is whatever you want it to be.

Fields of potential: Speyside remains one of Scotland's main producers of malting barley.

MALT PRODUCTION

While the world's single-malt distilleries follow the same process, each one will have its own particular take on how this is done. It is this individual approach, specific to each distillery, that gives each single malt its distillery character: its DNA. The distiller makes decisions throughout the process; the key decisions are shown in this diagram.

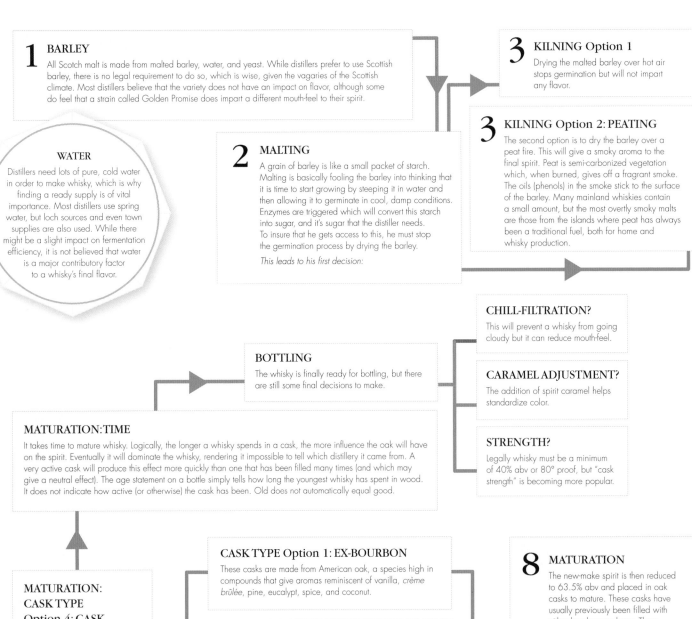

1 BARLEY

All Scotch malt is made from malted barley, water, and yeast. While distillers prefer to use Scottish barley, there is no legal requirement to do so, which is wise, given the vagaries of the Scottish climate. Most distillers believe that the variety does not have an impact on flavor, although some do feel that a strain called Golden Promise does impart a different mouth-feel to their spirit.

WATER

Distillers need lots of pure, cold water in order to make whisky, which is why finding a ready supply is of vital importance. Most distillers use spring water, but loch sources and even town supplies are also used. While there might be a slight impact on fermentation efficiency, it is not believed that water is a major contributory factor to a whisky's final flavor.

2 MALTING

A grain of barley is like a small packet of starch. Malting is basically fooling the barley into thinking that it is time to start growing by steeping it in water and then allowing it to germinate in cool, damp conditions. Enzymes are triggered which will convert this starch into sugar, and it's sugar that the distiller needs. To insure that he gets access to this, he must stop the germination process by drying the barley.

This leads to his first decision:

3 KILNING Option 1

Drying the malted barley over hot air stops germination but will not impart any flavor.

3 KILNING Option 2: PEATING

The second option is to dry the barley over a peat fire. This will give a smoky aroma to the final spirit. Peat is semi-carbonized vegetation which, when burned, gives off a fragrant smoke. The oils (phenols) in the smoke stick to the surface of the barley. Many mainland whiskies contain a small amount, but the most overtly smoky malts are those from the islands where peat has always been a traditional fuel, both for home and whisky production.

CHILL-FILTRATION?

This will prevent a whisky from going cloudy but it can reduce mouth-feel.

CARAMEL ADJUSTMENT?

The addition of spirit caramel helps standardize color.

STRENGTH?

Legally whisky must be a minimum of 40% abv or 80° proof, but "cask strength" is becoming more popular.

BOTTLING

The whisky is finally ready for bottling, but there are still some final decisions to make.

MATURATION: TIME

It takes time to mature whisky. Logically, the longer a whisky spends in a cask, the more influence the oak will have on the spirit. Eventually it will dominate the whisky, rendering it impossible to tell which distillery it came from. A very active cask will produce this effect more quickly than one that has been filled many times (and which may give a neutral effect). The age statement on a bottle simply tells how long the youngest whisky has spent in wood. It does not indicate how active (or otherwise) the cask has been. Old does not automatically equal good.

CASK TYPE Option 1: EX-BOURBON

These casks are made from American oak, a species high in compounds that give aromas reminiscent of vanilla, *crème brûlée*, pine, eucalypt, spice, and coconut.

CASK TYPE Option 2: EX-SHERRY

These casks are made from European oak, which imparts aromas of dried fruit, clove, incense, and walnuts. European oak is also richer in color and higher in mouth-drying tannin.

CASK TYPE Option 3: REFILL

Whisky distillers can use casks many times, and the more they are used, the less effect the species of oak has on the whisky. These "refill" casks are important in allowing distillery character to be shown. In practice, most distillers use a mix of all three options since this adds complexity to the palette of flavors.

MATURATION: CASK TYPE Option 4: CASK FINISHING

Distillers can give the flavor of their whisky a final twist by "finishing" it. This involves taking a whisky aged in ex-bourbon or refill casks and giving it a short period of secondary aging in a very active cask that has previously held sherry, port, Madeira, wine, etc., imbuing the whisky with some of the cask's character.

8 MATURATION

The new-make spirit is then reduced to 63.5% abv and placed in oak casks to mature. These casks have usually previously been filled with either bourbon or sherry. Three processes take place here.

1. Removal: The cask helps to remove the aggressive new-spirit character.
2. Addition: The flavor compounds in the cask are extracted by the spirit.
3. Interaction: The flavors from the wood and the spirit meld together to increase complexity.

Time, the freshness of the cask, and the type of oak all have a part to play.

4 MILLING

The malt is taken to the distillery, where it is ground into a rough flour called grist.

MASHING Option 1: CLEAR WORT

If a distiller pumps the wort slowly from the mash tun he obtains what is known as clear worts. This tends to produce a spirit with no great cereal character.

5 MASHING

The grist is then mixed with hot water (at 146.3°F/63.5°C) in a large vessel called a mash tun. As soon as the hot water strikes the grist, the conversion from starch to sugar takes place. The sweet liquor, known as "worts," is then drained through the perforated bottom of the mash tun. The process is repeated an additional two times in order to extract as much of the sugar as possible. The final "water" is then retained as the first water of the next mash.

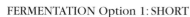

MASHING Option 2: CLOUDY WORT

If a distiller wants to produce a malty spirit with a dry, nutty, cereal character he will pump the worts quickly and pull some solids through from the mash tun.

6 FERMENTATION

The worts are then cooled and pumped into a fermenting vessel known as a washback. These can be made from either wood or stainless steel. Yeast is added and fermentation begins.

FERMENTATION Option 1: SHORT

In fermentation, yeast eats sugar and converts it into alcohol (wash). This process is completed in 48 hours. If a distiller takes this "short" option, his final spirit will have a more pronounced malty character.

YEAST

Because the same type of yeast is used throughout the Scotch whisky industry, it is not considered to have an impact on flavor. Japanese distillers, however, will use different strains to produce desired flavors in their malt whiskies.

FERMENTATION Option 2: LONG

A long fermentation (over 55 hours) allows esterification to take place. This produces lighter, more complex, and fruity flavors.

COPPER

Copper is hugely important in creating whisky's flavor. Because copper holds on to heavy elements, distillers can either prolong or restrict the length of the "conversation" between the alcohol vapor and the copper to create a desired character.

7 DISTILLATION A

The wash has a strength of 8% abv. This is then distilled twice in copper pot stills. The first distillation in a "wash still" produces "low wine" of 23% abv, which is then redistilled in a "spirit still." This time the distillate is divided into three: foreshots, heart, and feints. Only the heart is retained for maturation. The foreshots and feints are recycled with the next batch of low wines.

DISTILLATION B: CONDENSING

The alcoholic vapor is turned back into liquid by passing it through a condensing system containing cold water. Once again, the distiller has options that will impact on flavor.

DISTILLATION Option 1: LONG CONVERSATION

The longer the conversation between alcohol vapor and copper, the lighter the final spirit will be. This means tall stills are more likely to produce light spirit than small ones. Also, running a still slowly can extend the conversation.

DISTILLATION Option 2: SHORT CONVERSATION

Conversely, the shorter the conversation, the heavier the resulting spirit will be. Small stills or quick distillation tend to give this characteristic.

CONDENSING Option 1: SHELL AND TUBE

This is a tall cylinder containing a mass of small copper pipes filled with cold water. When the alcohol vapor hits the cold pipes, it turns back to liquid. Because there is a large area of copper, shell-and-tube condensers help to "lighten" a spirit.

CUT POINTS Option 1: EARLY

As a spirit is distilled, its aromas change. The first to appear are light and delicate. If a distiller wants to make a fragrant whisky, he will cut off spirit early.

DISTILLATION C: CUT POINTS

When the condensed spirit from the second distillation arrives in the spirit safe, the stillman must divide it into three: foreshots, heart, and feints. The point where he cuts from foreshots into spirit and from spirit to feints will also have an effect on flavor.

CONDENSING Option 2: WORM TUBS

This, the traditional method of condensing, involves a long copper pipe coiled in a tank of cold water. Because there is less copper at play here, worm tubs tend to produce a heavier spirit.

CUT POINTS Option 2: LATE

As distillation continues, the aromas deepen becoming more oily and rich: smokiness is one of these. A distiller who wants to make a heavy spirit will therefore cut late.

GRAIN PRODUCTION

Though often overlooked as a whisky style (and rarely seen bottled) grain whisky does make up the bulk of the whisky produced in Scotland and it performs an extremely vital function within blends. Its production is every bit as complex as any other type of whisky, as the graphic on this page illustrates.

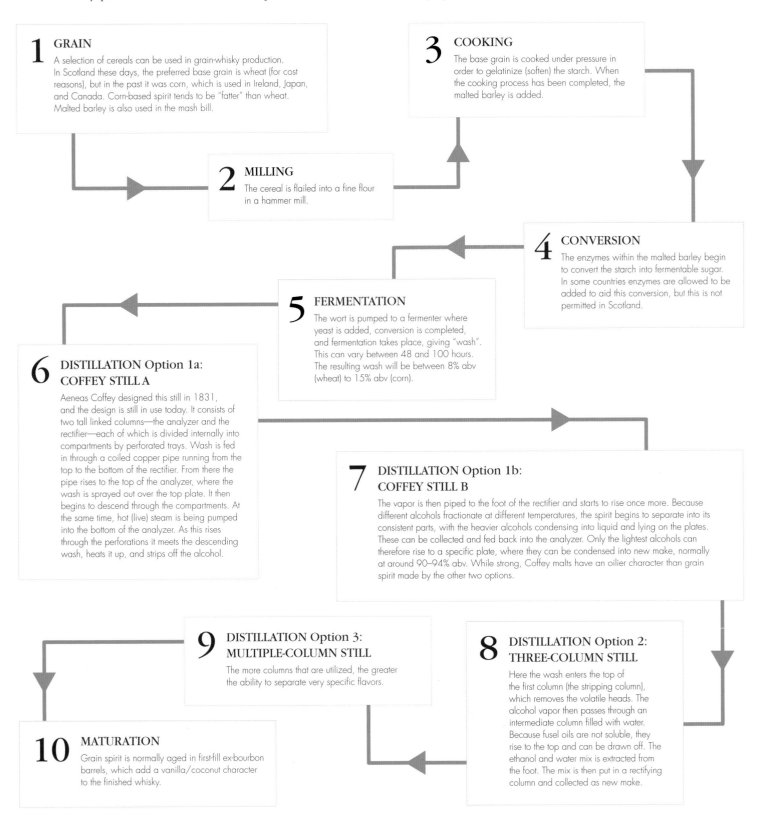

1 GRAIN

A selection of cereals can be used in grain-whisky production. In Scotland these days, the preferred base grain is wheat (for cost reasons), but in the past it was corn, which is used in Ireland, Japan, and Canada. Corn-based spirit tends to be "fatter" than wheat. Malted barley is also used in the mash bill.

2 MILLING

The cereal is flailed into a fine flour in a hammer mill.

3 COOKING

The base grain is cooked under pressure in order to gelatinize (soften) the starch. When the cooking process has been completed, the malted barley is added.

4 CONVERSION

The enzymes within the malted barley begin to convert the starch into fermentable sugar. In some countries enzymes are allowed to be added to aid this conversion, but this is not permitted in Scotland.

5 FERMENTATION

The wort is pumped to a fermenter where yeast is added, conversion is completed, and fermentation takes place, giving "wash". This can vary between 48 and 100 hours. The resulting wash will be between 8% abv (wheat) to 15% abv (corn).

6 DISTILLATION Option 1a: COFFEY STILL A

Aeneas Coffey designed this still in 1831, and the design is still in use today. It consists of two tall linked columns—the analyzer and the rectifier—each of which is divided internally into compartments by perforated trays. Wash is fed in through a coiled copper pipe running from the top to the bottom of the rectifier. From there the pipe rises to the top of the analyzer, where the wash is sprayed out over the top plate. It then begins to descend through the compartments. At the same time, hot (live) steam is being pumped into the bottom of the analyzer. As this rises through the perforations it meets the descending wash, heats it up, and strips off the alcohol.

7 DISTILLATION Option 1b: COFFEY STILL B

The vapor is then piped to the foot of the rectifier and starts to rise once more. Because different alcohols fractionate at different temperatures, the spirit begins to separate into its consistent parts, with the heavier alcohols condensing into liquid and lying on the plates. These can be collected and fed back into the analyzer. Only the lightest alcohols can therefore rise to a specific plate, where they can be condensed into new make, normally at around 90–94% abv. While strong, Coffey malts have an oilier character than grain spirit made by the other two options.

8 DISTILLATION Option 2: THREE-COLUMN STILL

Here the wash enters the top of the first column (the stripping column), which removes the volatile heads. The alcohol vapor then passes through an intermediate column filled with water. Because fusel oils are not soluble, they rise to the top and can be drawn off. The ethanol and water mix is extracted from the foot. The mix is then put in a rectifying column and collected as new make.

9 DISTILLATION Option 3: MULTIPLE-COLUMN STILL

The more columns that are utilized, the greater the ability to separate very specific flavors.

10 MATURATION

Grain spirit is normally aged in first-fill ex-bourbon barrels, which add a vanilla/coconut character to the finished whisky.

SINGLE POT-STILL IRISH WHISKEY

This process describes how single pot-still Irish whiskey is made, primarily at IDL's Midleton distillery, where it is used in brands such as Jameson, Powers, the "Spot" series, and Redbreast. At the moment, Bushmills and Cooley both run operations similar to Scottish single-malt production,

albeit with Bushmills using a complex form of triple-distillation, (*see* pp.200–1 for more details). In addition, Cooley uses heavily peated barley for its double-distilled brand Connemara. Grain whiskey is also produced by Irish Distillers and Cooley.

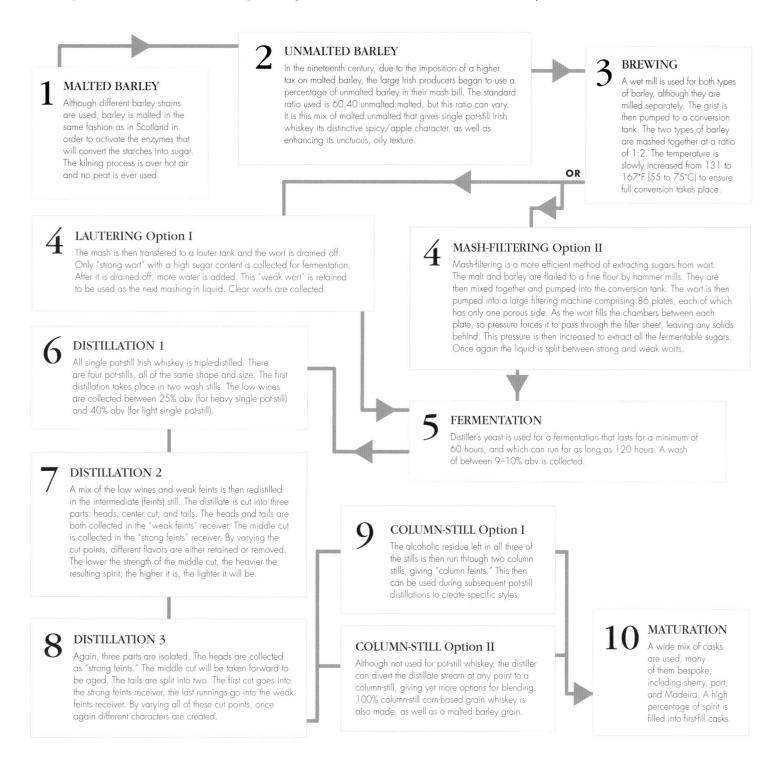

1 MALTED BARLEY
Although different barley strains are used, barley is malted in the same fashion as in Scotland in order to activate the enzymes that will convert the starches into sugar. The kilning process is over hot air and no peat is ever used.

2 UNMALTED BARLEY
In the nineteenth century, due to the imposition of a higher tax on malted barley, the large Irish producers began to use a percentage of unmalted barley in their mash bill. The standard ratio used is 60:40 unmalted:malted, but this ratio can vary. It is this mix of malted:unmalted that gives single pot-still Irish whiskey its distinctive spicy/apple character, as well as enhancing its unctuous, oily texture.

3 BREWING
A wet mill is used for both types of barley, although they are milled separately. The grist is then pumped to a conversion tank. The two types of barley are mashed together at a ratio of 1:2. The temperature is slowly increased from 131 to 167°F (55 to 75°C) to ensure full conversion takes place.

OR

4 LAUTERING Option I
The mash is then transfered to a lauter tank and the wort is drained off. Only "strong wort" with a high sugar content is collected for fermentation. After it is drained off, more water is added. This "weak wort" is retained to be used as the next mashing-in liquid. Clear worts are collected.

4 MASH-FILTERING Option II
Mash-filtering is a more efficient method of extracting sugars from wort. The malt and barley are flailed to a fine flour by hammer mills. They are then mixed together and pumped into the conversion tank. The wort is then pumped into a large filtering machine comprising 86 plates, each of which has only one porous side. As the wort fills the chambers between each plate, so pressure forces it to pass through the filter sheet, leaving any solids behind. This pressure is then increased to extract all the fermentable sugars. Once again the liquid is split between strong and weak worts.

6 DISTILLATION 1
All single pot-still Irish whiskey is triple-distilled. There are four pot-stills, all of the same shape and size. The first distillation takes place in two wash stills. The low wines are collected between 25% abv (for heavy single pot-still) and 40% abv (for light single pot-still).

5 FERMENTATION
Distiller's yeast is used for a fermentation that lasts for a minimum of 60 hours, and which can run for as long as 120 hours. A wash of between 9–10% abv is collected.

7 DISTILLATION 2
A mix of the low wines and weak feints is then redistilled in the intermediate (feints) still. The distillate is cut into three parts: heads, center cut, and tails. The heads and tails are both collected in the "weak feints" receiver. The middle cut is collected in the "strong feints" receiver. By varying the cut points, different flavors are either retained or removed. The lower the strength of the middle cut, the heavier the resulting spirit; the higher it is, the lighter it will be.

9 COLUMN-STILL Option I
The alcoholic residue left in all three of the stills is then run through two column stills, giving "column feints." This then can be used during subsequent pot-still distillations to create specific styles.

8 DISTILLATION 3
Again, three parts are isolated. The heads are collected as "strong feints." The middle cut will be taken forward to be aged. The tails are split into two. The first cut goes into the strong feints receiver, the last runnings go into the weak feints receiver. By varying all of these cut points, once again different characters are created.

COLUMN-STILL Option II
Although not used for pot-still whiskey, the distiller can divert the distillate stream at any point to a column-still, giving yet more options for blending. 100% column-still corn-based grain whiskey is also made, as well as a malted barley grain.

10 MATURATION
A wide mix of casks are used, many of them bespoke, including sherry, port, and Madeira. A high percentage of spirit is filled into first-fill casks.

KENTUCKY & TENNESSEE PRODUCTION

Bourbon distillers are faced with an equally large number of decision points in the creation of their own individual style. With a relatively small number of distilleries making a wide number of different styles and brands, they express their individuality by looking at the ratio of the cereals used, the types of yeast, the amount of sour mash used, the distillation strength, the barrel strength, and where in the warehouse the barrel is located.

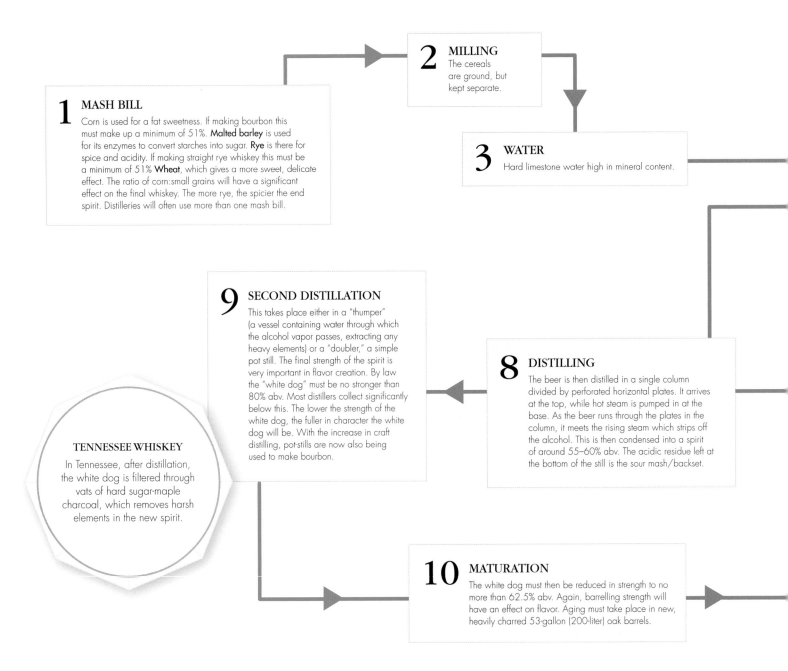

2 MILLING
The cereals are ground, but kept separate.

1 MASH BILL
Corn is used for a fat sweetness. If making bourbon this must make up a minimum of 51%. **Malted barley** is used for its enzymes to convert starches into sugar. **Rye** is there for spice and acidity. If making straight rye whiskey this must be a minimum of 51% **Wheat**, which gives a more sweet, delicate effect. The ratio of corn:small grains will have a significant effect on the final whiskey. The more rye, the spicier the end spirit. Distilleries will often use more than one mash bill.

3 WATER
Hard limestone water high in mineral content.

9 SECOND DISTILLATION
This takes place either in a "thumper" (a vessel containing water through which the alcohol vapor passes, extracting any heavy elements) or a "doubler," a simple pot still. The final strength of the spirit is very important in flavor creation. By law the "white dog" must be no stronger than 80% abv. Most distillers collect significantly below this. The lower the strength of the white dog, the fuller in character the white dog will be. With the increase in craft distilling, pot-stills are now also being used to make bourbon.

TENNESSEE WHISKEY
In Tennessee, after distillation, the white dog is filtered through vats of hard sugar-maple charcoal, which removes harsh elements in the new spirit.

8 DISTILLING
The beer is then distilled in a single column divided by perforated horizontal plates. It arrives at the top, while hot steam is pumped in at the base. As the beer runs through the plates in the column, it meets the rising steam which strips off the alcohol. This is then condensed into a spirit of around 55–60% abv. The acidic residue left at the bottom of the still is the sour mash/backset.

10 MATURATION
The white dog must then be reduced in strength to no more than 62.5% abv. Again, barrelling strength will have an effect on flavor. Aging must take place in new, heavily charred 53-gallon (200-liter) oak barrels.

4 COOKING

A The corn/water mix is heated almost to boiling, then cooked either under pressure or in open cookers to gelatinize its starch.

B Because rye and wheat can clump at high heats, they are only added when the temperature drops to 171°F (77°C). After they are cooked, the mix is cooled once more to 146°F (63.5°C).

C At this point malted barley is added to convert the starch into fermentable sugars. Two more ingredients must then be added before fermentation can take place.

5 BACKSET/SOUR MASH/SETBACK

This is the acidic spent liquid at the end of distillation, which is added to the fermenter. This adjusts the pH of the fermentation and prevents bacterial infection. The amount of sour mash used affects the percentage of sugars in the mash, so for a fresher bourbon you'll use less sour mash. Every bourbon is sour-mashed.

6 YEAST

Each distillery will have its own strain or strains of proprietary yeast. These are jealously guarded because the character of the yeast will have a significant effect on the flavor of the final spirit, helping to promote specific congeners (aka flavoring elements).

7 FERMENTING

Generally this will take up to three days, at the end of which the distiller has a beer of around 5–6% abv.

11 WAREHOUSING

The warehousing will have a further effect on the spirit's character. The hotter the temperature in the warehouse, the more intense the interaction between the spirit and the oak. Conversely, the cooler the environment, the slower this process will be. This means that the location of the warehouse, the number of floors, and what they are made out of (brick, metal, wood) are all important in flavor creation. Equally, the location of the barrel within those warehouses will have an impact. Some distillers will rotate barrels to get an even maturation; some "scatter" their barrels across different warehouses; others set aside warehouses or floors within warehouses for specific brands. By law, maturation must be for a minimum of two years.

The start of the Lincoln County Process—making charcoal at Jack Daniel's.

TERROIR

Terroir was folded into the notion of regionality when Scotch whisky firms tried to find a way to explain the fact that whisky was made across the country. The problem with that laudable aim was that it couldn't stand up to scrutiny. The boundaries weren't geographical, but political. The areas were also too large. Are we really to believe that every whisky in the Highlands, from Glasgow's outskirts to Orkney, tastes the same? Does every spirit in the village of Dufftown taste the same? No. Does every whisky in the three distilleries owned by William Grant in that town taste the same? No.

Whisky is about individuality. It is about singularity (the forgotten word in single-malt whisky). So if regionality is actually a political and economic discussion—Speyside was created as much by blenders as by geology—does that mean we dismiss *terroir*? No. We try to extricate it and examine it more deeply.

Terroir encompasses pedology (that's soil to you and me), geography, edaphology, microbiology, solar radiation, meteorology, and much more. It is about the importance of place, the significance of the spot on the Earth where something comes from, be that a vine or an individual distillery site. To go back to Dufftown: Glenfiddich, The Balvenie, and Kininvie all have their own *terroir*, as do Mortlach and Glendullan. Forests have *terroir*. Swiss oak and Spanish oak are the same species but contain different flavors. Trees on a shaded slope will be different in flavor to those on a sunny slope opposite. Barley varieties have *terroir*.

Terroir is also about man's interaction with all of this. From a drinker's point of view, a deeper and conscious understanding of an environment will give deeper appreciation of the whiskies. Take Islay: the liquid isn't necessarily leaching the smells of the island, but they are

Lagavulin on Islay is one distillery whose spirit seems to distill its surroundings.

Below: The most overt link between Scotland's earth and its whisky is in the use of peat.

identifiably there if you open your mind to a deeper reading of the island. That honeyed, flowery smell of meadowsweet is Bruichladdich; the windblown beach and seaweed bestrewn Machir Bay is Caol Ila; you get oyster brine in Kilchoman and herbal woodland notes in Bunnahabhain. Ardbeg's minerality is like salt-washed wet rocks and earth, while Laphroaig's pitch and dried seaweed, Lagavulin's bog myrtle and rock pools, and Bowmore's a mix of flowers and salt. Then there's Islay's smoke, which is different because of the island's climate and geology. *Terroir*. There is this sense of a linked, layered, overlapping cultural *terroir*, an expression of people and place in harmony.

Japanese whisky is "Japanese" not just because of climate, oak, and yeast, but because of a Japanese cultural aesthetic that underpins the whiskies in the same way it influences food, art, flower arranging, or poetry. All of the questing distillers here said something along the lines of "We want our whisky to reflect where we come from": the fields, the ground, the crops they support; the effects of air, wind, and rain; the past.

According to Fred Revol at France's Domaine des Hautes Glaces, "*Terroir* can be misinterpreted as being hands-off, that the soil gives everything and man is irrelevant. It's not true. It's not just soil and altitude, but process and know-how. It is something made by being in a place at a time." Rene Redzepi of Copenhagen's Noma restaurant defines his approach as coming from "a basic understanding—time and place: the season and where one is situated."

That should apply to *all* whisky. Those who distill mindfully will make a better product. And whisky is more than a product; it is a distillate of time and place, and the person making it. That's *terroir*.

FLAVOR

How then do we make sense of it all? Through flavor. By sticking our noses in the glass and inhaling. Every time we nose a whisky a picture appears, an olfactory hallucination that offers up clues as to the character of the whisky. The picture is, if you like, a map in itself, telling you about distillation, oak, and time. As fragrance specialist Givaudan's Dr. Roman Kaiser writes in his *Meaningful Scents Around The World*, "The sense of smell gives us a sense of other living beings."

We smell our way through our lives. Aromas help us to make sense of the world, but we do it without consciously realizing this. Kaiser argues that there was a deliberate relegation of the sense of smell in the eighteenth and nineteenth centuries when philosophers and scientists argued that sight was the superior sense, whereas smell was "a primitive, brutish ability associated with savagery and even madness." It is also the case that we simply forget to consciously smell things as we get older. We know what a flower smells like, so why differentiate between a daffodil and a freesia? The fact that so many of the pictures that appear in our mind when we concentrate on a glass of whisky come from our childhood shows that at some point in our lives we did take the trouble to inhale.

Flavor—by which I mean aroma and taste—is ultimately how we differentiate between whiskies. We might be tempted by the pack, or find the price attractive (or repellent), we might be led astray by the region, but the prime reason for buying a shot or a bottle of whisky is because we like the flavor. It appeals to us, it speaks to us, it hits a trigger in us.

But what does the picture mean? That aroma of vanilla, *crème brûlée*, coconut (1970s suntan oil), and pine says that the whisky has been matured in an American oak cask. Those pictures of dried fruits, and clove? They suggest that an ex-sherry cask has been used. The images of spring meadows—all green grass and blossom—speak of long slow distillation with lots of time for the vapor to talk to the copper. That aroma that brings to mind roasted meat? Short conversation, maybe the use of worm tubs. Is there an intense yet ordered aroma? The whisky could well be Japanese.

Pick up a glass of bourbon and taste it. Does it suddenly get spicier and more acidic toward the back of the tongue? That's rye kicking in; the more spice, the more rye is likely to be in the mash bill. Get that oiliness in the Irish whiskey? Unmalted barley. The sootiness in that whiskey from Tennessee? Charcoal-mellowing. Each of these flavors is natural. It has been created in the distillery, comes from the cask or, in the case of the leathery, fungal "rancid" richness of older examples, from a long interaction between the two.

Having trouble? Shut your eyes and think of what season the whisky reminds you of. Not only will the aromas suddenly snap into focus, but they will give you a clue as to how best to enjoy the whisky. A spring-like whisky? Have it cold, maybe with ice before a meal. Rich and autumnal? After dinner and slowly.

No spirit has such a complex array of flavors. No other spirit spans the aroma spectrum from whisper-light to heavily peated and all points in between. Don't look at a whisky as being a brand, look at it as a flavor package. If you understand flavor, you understand whisky. Now, let's explore.

Olfactory hallucinations: a whisky's character is expressed through the pictures in the noser's mind.

Left: A kaleidoscope of aromas is contained within whisky—from spice and fruit to honey, smoke, and nuts. These both anchor it to the real world and speak of our own memories.

HOW TO TASTE

We all know how to taste. If I were to put a plate of food in front of you, you would have an immediate (and strongly held) opinion about it. Were I to put a glass of whisky in front of most of you, however, you would find that the words to describe the aromas and taste wouldn't come as easily. Why? It's not that you can't taste whisky; it's simply that no one has taken the time to explain the language of whisky, to make it simple to understand.

Whisky is currently in the same position that wine was 20 years ago: there is a latent desire to try it, but the consumer doesn't have the language with which to describe what he or she wants. Instead of helping, words have become a barrier. To "understand" malt whisky it is thought you have to become part of a secret society, be given the codes. That's no way to encourage new drinkers. How, then, to talk without getting tangled up in adjectives, ensnared by nouns, mired in overcomplicated technical details? The answer is to keep things simple. We don't so much need a new language as to start talking in more simple terms about flavor: where it comes from, what it means.

Each of the entries in this book includes tasting notes for a representative selection of whiskies, which have then been subdivided into Flavor Camps. This will allow you to compare and contrast whiskies of a similar type, and also to see how a distiller can shift a whisky from one camp to another through maturation and/or the use of different wood types. Find a whisky you already know and find another you've never encountered before in the same camp. Now compare the two. What is similar and what are the differences? You don't have to overcomplicate matters by using fancy descriptors: simple terms like "fruity" or "light" or "smoky" are enough. Now find another whisky and repeat. And repeat. And repeat!

Right: Distillers use their noses to ensure that their whisky is maturing properly.

Below: Using the right glass is crucial in assessing whiskies.

FLAVOR CAMPS

The process of tasting is simple. Take a small measure of the whisky in a nosing glass. Look at the color, certainly, but, more importantly, get your nose in the glass. What aromas are you picking up? What pictures are in your head? Which of the following Flavor Camps does the whisky belong to? Now taste. You'll detect many of the aromas you've already noticed, but concentrate on how the whisky behaves in your mouth. What does it feel like? Thick, tongue-coating? Mouth-filling, light? Is it sweet, or dry, or fresh? It should be like a piece of music or a story with a beginning, middle, and end. Now, add some water—just a splash—and repeat.

Fragrant & Floral
The aromas found in these whiskies bring to mind fresh-cut flowers, fruit blossom, cut grass, light green fruits (apple, pear, melon). On the palate they are light, slightly sweet, and often with a fresh acidity. Ideal as aperitifs, or treat them like white wine: pop the bottle in the fridge and served chilled in wine glasses.

Malty & Dry
These whiskies are drier on the nose. Crisp, cookie-like, sometimes dusty with aromas that remind you of flour, breakfast cereal, and nuts. The palate is also dry but is normally balanced by sweet oak. Again, these are good aperitifs or breakfast whiskies.

Fruity & Spicy
The fruit we're talking about here is ripe orchard fruit, such as peach, apricot, maybe even something more exotic like mango. These whiskies will also show the vanilla, coconut, custard-like aromas of American oak. The spiciness is found on the finish and tends to be sweet, like cinnamon or nutmeg. With a little more weight these are versatile drams that can be enjoyed at any time.

Rich & Round
There is fruit here too, but now it is dried: raisin, fig, date, white raisin. This shows the use of European oak ex-sherry casks. You might detect a slightly drier feel; that's the tannins from the oak. These are deep whiskies, sometimes sweet, sometimes meaty. Best after dinner.

Smoky & Peaty
The smoke comes from burning peat when the malt is being dried. This gives a whole range of different aromas from soot to lapsang souchong tea, tar, kippers, smoked bacon, burning heather, wood smoke. Often sightly oily in texture, all peaty whiskies must have a balancing "sweet spot." Young peaty whiskies are a great wake-up as aperitifs; try them mixed with soda. Older richer examples are for later in the evening.

KENTUCKY, TENNESSEE & CANADIAN WHISKEYS
Soft Corn
The main cereal used in these whiskeys, corn, creates a sweet nose and a fat, buttery, and juicy quality on the palate.

Every bottle of whisky, such as these at Yamazaki in Japan, contains a whisky with its own individual, distinct character. Grouping them into Flavor Camps makes life easier.

Sweet Wheat
Wheat is occasionally used by bourbon distillers in place of rye. This affects flavor by adding a gentle, mellow sweetness to the bourbon.

Rich & Oaky

All bourbon must be aged in new-oak barrels, which is where the whiskey picks up all those rich vanilla-accented aromas, along with coconut, pine, cherry, sweet spice. This richness of extract is increasingly powerful the longer the bourbon remains in the cask, leading to flavors such as tobacco and leather.

Spicy Rye

Rye can often be picked up on the nose in the shape of intense, slightly perfumed, and sometimes slightly dusty aromas—or an aroma akin to freshly baked rye bread. It appears late in the palate, however, after the fat corn has had its say. It adds an acidic, spiced zestiness that wakes the palate up.

THE SINGLE-MALT WHISKY FLAVOR MAP

The Flavor Map™ was created to help consumers baffled by the volume of single malt Scotch on the market. Each whisky is an individual. We cannot rely on a regional definition as a guarantee of flavor. We can't leave it to retailers or bars: both tend to arrange whiskies alphabetically or by region. So how can we agree on a term to describe that individual?

Part of my job is to teach people—consumers, bartenders, and retailers—about how to taste whisky, and I used to find that it was very easy to slip into complex language, but considerably more difficult to try and explain flavor in a simple fashion.

One day I was discussing this issue of simplifying the language to allow people to make a considered choice with Jim Beveridge, master blender at Diageo. His response was to draw two lines on a piece of paper. "This is what we use in the lab," he said. "It allows us to plot the different components in a blend and also to compare Johnnie Walker with other blends." I have since found out that this method is used not just by whisky blenders but throughout the spirits and perfume industries. Jim, his colleague Maureen Robinson, and I then sat down to try and produce a consumer-friendly version of the Blender's Chart.

And here it is. This Flavor Map™ is simple to use. The vertical axis starts at the "Delicate" end with whiskies that are clean and pure. The more complex the whisky the higher up the line it sits. As soon as any smoke is discernible, then the whisky moves across the central line. The smokier it is, the higher up the line it is positioned.

The horizontal axis moves from "Light" to "Rich," starting with the lightest and most fragrant flavors and as you head toward the center, you move through grassiness, malt, soft fruit, and honey. As soon as you cross the central line heading toward "Rich," the influence of the cask becomes more important: American oak's vanilla and spice to begin with, before the dried fruit of ex-sherry casks become the dominant character toward the right-hand end.

It is important to underline that this map is not saying that any whisky is better than any other. It simply says what the dominant flavor characteristic is. There is no one good place to be, nor is there an area where whiskies could be seen to be inferior. It is a generic tool for categorizing single-malt Scotch whisky. And you won't find every whisky on the market on this map either—there just wouldn't be room. Instead, we have selected a large number of the most popular examples, many of which you will find within the pages of this book.

We keep the Flavor Map™ under review to take account of new expressions and changing styles. We hope it gives you an idea of similarities between whiskies—and differences. If you don't like peatiness then be careful of going too high up the smoky line. If you see a brand you know and like, then this map allows you to find an alternative which you could explore. Enjoy using it.

The Flavor Map™ is the result of a joint collaboration between Dave Broom and Diageo Scotland Limited. The map features brands of single-malt Scotch whisky, some owned by Diageo Scotland Ltd, and some owned by others. The latter may be registered trademarks of third parties. Copyright © 2010.

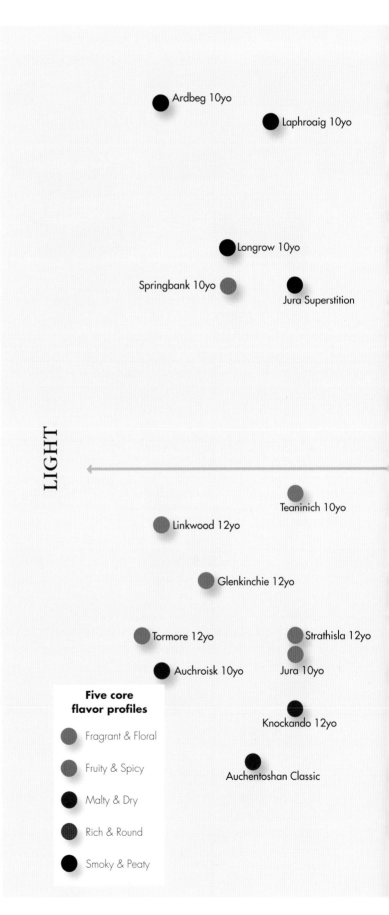

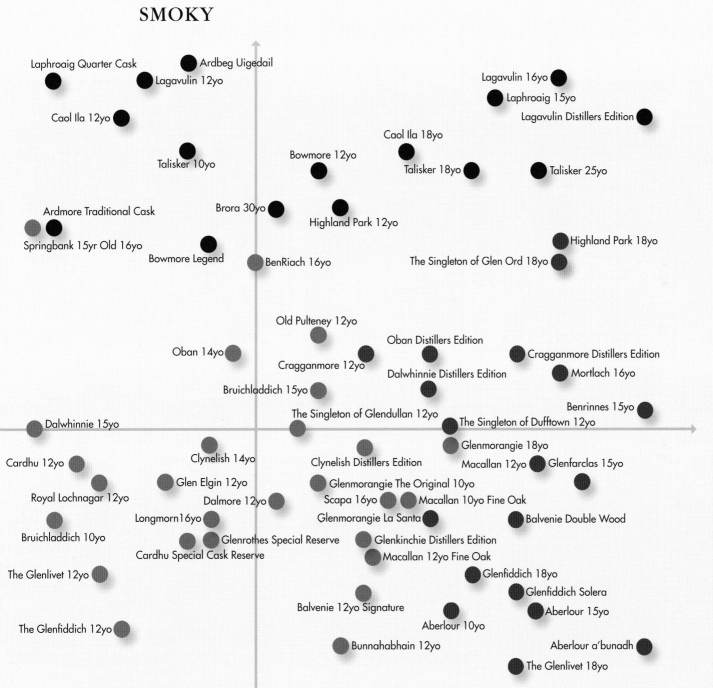

SMOKY

Laphroaig Quarter Cask

Ardbeg Uigedail

Lagavulin 12yo

Lagavulin 16yo

Caol Ila 12yo

Laphroaig 15yo

Lagavulin Distillers Edition

Talisker 10yo

Bowmore 12yo

Caol Ila 18yo

Talisker 18yo

Talisker 25yo

Brora 30yo

Ardmore Traditional Cask

Highland Park 12yo

Springbank 15yr Old 16yo

Highland Park 18yo

Bowmore Legend

BenRiach 16yo

The Singleton of Glen Ord 18yo

Old Pulteney 12yo

Oban Distillers Edition

Oban 14yo

Cragganmore Distillers Edition

Cragganmore 12yo

Dalwhinnie Distillers Edition

Mortlach 16yo

Bruichladdich 15yo

The Singleton of Glendullan 12yo

Benrinnes 15yo

Dalwhinnie 15yo

The Singleton of Dufftown 12yo

RICH

Glenmorangie 18yo

Cardhu 12yo

Clynelish 14yo

Clynelish Distillers Edition

Macallan 12yo

Glenfarclas 15yo

Glen Elgin 12yo

Glenmorangie The Original 10yo

Royal Lochnagar 12yo

Dalmore 12yo

Scapa 16yo

Macallan 10yo Fine Oak

Longmorn16yo

Glenmorangie La Santa

Balvenie Double Wood

Bruichladdich 10yo

Glenrothes Special Reserve

Glenkinchie Distillers Edition

Cardhu Special Cask Reserve

Macallan 12yo Fine Oak

The Glenlivet 12yo

Glenfiddich 18yo

Glenfiddich Solera

The Glenfiddich 12yo

Balvenie 12yo Signature

Aberlour 15yo

Aberlour 10yo

Bunnahabhain 12yo

Aberlour a'bunadh

The Glenlivet 18yo

Auchentoshan Three Wood

Auchentoshan 12yo

The Glenlivet 15yo

DELICATE

SCOTLAND

Scotland dominates the whisky world. It has even given its name to the style. Once, in Tunisia, tired of trying to explain where "*Ecosse*" was, I blurted out "Whisky!" and everyone immediately understood that this foreigner was from "Scotch-land." Scotch is both a style of whisky but also a signifier for a country. It's a country, however, whose geography forces you to take detours—going around the heads of lochs, not over a bridge; sailing to islands rather than flying; walking into remote hills because there is no road. It is a discursive landscape, a property shared by its whiskies. Scotland is also wildly contradictory. In 1919, the critic G. Gregory Smith argued that Scottish literature (and by extension, the Scottish psyche) was defined by a "zigzag of contradictions," which he called "the Caledonian antisyzygy." Whisky shares that, too.

Previous page: Enigmatic and lonely, but two of the elements of whisky-making are here—peat and water.

Scotland's whiskies distill the aromas of their land: the coconut of hot gorse, wet seaweed lying on hot sand, the delicacy of "gean blossom" (wild cherry). Then there's the perfumed headiness of heather, the oiliness of bog myrtle, cut grass, and the myriad aromas of peat: smokehouses and bonfires on the beach, and oyster shells and brine. Then there are aromas from overseas: tea and coffee, sherry, raisin, cumin, cinnamon, and nutmeg. There are chemical reasons for all of these, but there are also many cultural reasons.

Every malt-whisky distillery does the same thing. They malt, they grind, they mash, they ferment, they distill twice (occasionally three times), and then they age in oak casks. There are 112 distilleries doing this as I write and there are more than 115 different results.

In the definition "single-malt whisky," the most important word is SINGLE. Why does one distillery do the same as its neighbor but get a different result? In the following pages we'll try to pick out some clues, starting with the new spirit. You cannot understand a whisky fully by only looking at the end product. With that you are inhaling the story of 12 years or more of interplay between the spirit, wood, and air. The reference point has been lost. If you want to find the uniqueness of each single malt you have to go to the source: the clear spring of knowledge that flows into the spirit safe, that flows from the whisky-maker's mind. The same also applies to grain whisky. Only by trying to understand each whisky's DNA can you go on this journey of flavor.

Don't expect absolute answers; don't rely on figures and charts. That singularity could be the microclimate of warehouses, maybe the type of warehouses, or the atmospheric pressure in the mashhouse, the shape and the size of the stills, the nature of the fermentation. Yes, the following pages contain talk of reflux and purifiers and wort density, of setting temperatures and oxidation, but ultimately every distiller agrees that no matter how much knowledge they amass, the distillery does its own thing. Whether they are on an island, in pasture lands, or up a mountain, they shrug and say, "Flavor? To be honest, I don't know. It's just something about the place." It's Scotland.

The remote and wildly beautiful landscapes of Scotland contain many hidden whisky secrets.

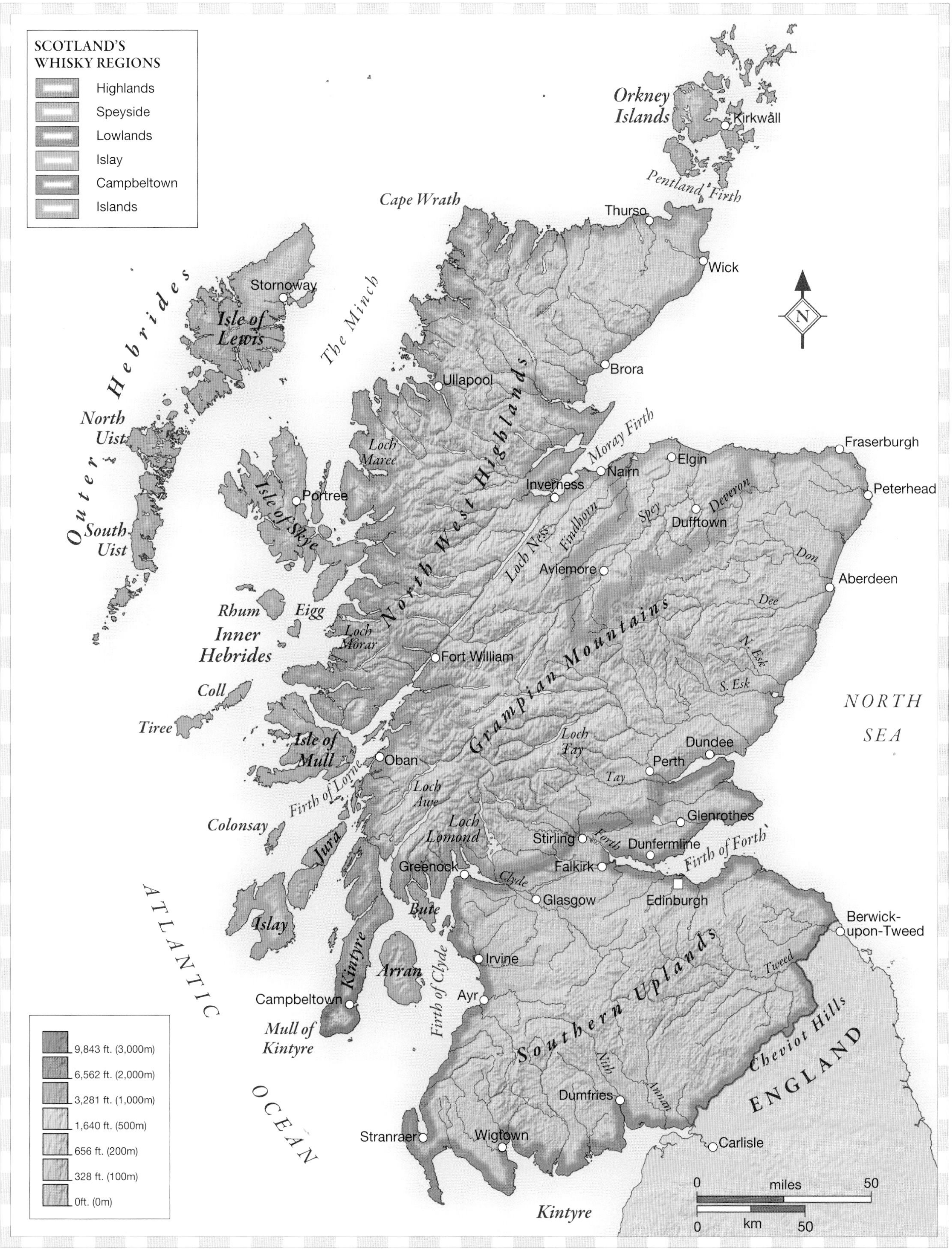

SCOTLAND'S
WHISKY REGIONS

- Highlands
- Speyside
- Lowlands
- Islay
- Campbeltown
- Islands

Orkney Islands
Kirkwall
Pentland Firth
Cape Wrath
Thurso
Wick
Brora
Ullapool
Isle of Lewis
Stornoway
The Minch
Outer Hebrides
North Uist
South Uist
Loch Maree
Isle of Skye
Portree
Moray Firth
Nairn
Elgin
Fraserburgh
Inverness
Peterhead
Spey
Deveron
Dufftown
Findhorn
Loch Ness
Aviemore
Don
Rhum
Eigg
Inner Hebrides
Loch Morar
Dee
Aberdeen
Coll
Fort William
N. Esk
Tiree
Grampian Mountains
S. Esk
NORTH SEA
Isle of Mull
Oban
Loch Tay
Dundee
Firth of Lorne
Loch Awe
Tay
Perth
Colonsay
Jura
Loch Lomond
Glenrothes
Stirling
Forth
Dunfermline
Greenock
Clyde
Falkirk
Firth of Forth
Bute
Glasgow
Edinburgh
Islay
Berwick-upon-Tweed
Kintyre
Arran
Firth of Clyde
Irvine
Campbeltown
Ayr
Tweed
Cheviot Hills
Mull of Kintyre
Southern Uplands
ENGLAND
Nith
Annan
Dumfries
ATLANTIC OCEAN
Stranraer
Wigtown
Carlisle
Kintyre

North West Highlands

- 9,843 ft. (3,000m)
- 6,562 ft. (2,000m)
- 3,281 ft. (1,000m)
- 1,640 ft. (500m)
- 656 ft. (200m)
- 328 ft. (100m)
- 0ft. (0m)

0   miles   50
0   km   50

SPEYSIDE

What is Speyside? It is a legally delimited region, but all that tells you is what (or where) Speyside isn't. It has long been the heartland of malt-whisky production and because of this it is easy to assume that its makes all fall within the same group. It's not so. There is no single Speyside style, just as there is no uniform Speyside landscape.

Seemingly impassable mountains offered moonshiners safe haven and smugglers secret routes.

How can one compare the rough lands of the Braes and Glen Livet with the fertile flatlands of the Laich O'Moray, or the distilleries that cluster around Ben Rinnes, with those of Keith or Dufftown? How, when you delve deeper, can you even assume there is some commonality in the makes from Dufftown, the self-proclaimed capital of whisky-making?

The "clusters" found in the following pages show the geographical proximity of distilleries, but are explorations of the different individualities existing within them. Speyside is about distillers finding their style, testing new ideas, and remaining true to tradition. It is about modernity and the belief in the microclimate that sets one site apart from the next.

Strathspey (if it was ever called that by its inhabitants) was a place of farm distillers who, with the ban on home distilling in 1781, then the prohibition on exporting below the Highland Line in 1783, and the restriction of the number (and size) of stills in each parish, found legal distilling virtually impossible. It was considerably cheaper to produce whisky illicitly, yet at the same time demand was rising in the Lowlands—the result of poor-quality whisky being made in that region itself. Moonshining was endemic in the late eighteenth and early nineteenth centuries, before changes in the law in 1816 and, more significantly, in 1823, removed the restrictions, encouraging commercial distilling to take place.

How did this affect Speyside's flavors? From 1823 onward you can observe it being pulled in two directions: between the old ways and the new; between the heavy makes of the sma' still and the lightness achievable from larger stills—and by the end of the century the desire of the blenders. Maybe this shift toward the light by some of those original distillers was as much a mental response—a liberation—while others held on to their tradition. The result is an interplay of light versus dark, the fragrant and sunlit against the chthonic, earthy malts whose character speaks of the hiding places; dank, crepuscular *bothies* (huts) and caves. In Speyside we still meet them both.

You can imagine a Speyside distiller looking across at Ben Rinnes mulling over the options and coming to similar conclusions as Thomas Hardy's narrator in *The Return of The Native*: "To recline on a stump of thorn … to know that everything around and underneath had been from prehistoric times as unaltered as the stars overhead, gave ballast to the mind adrift on change and harassed by the irrepressible New."

Speyside is all about diversity, not commonality. Speyside's journey—and therefore the journey of Scotch malt whisky too—has been, as we shall see, this development of site-specific individuality. Speyside doesn't exist, its distilleries do.

A land of mountain, plain, and river. Speyside is as varied as the flavors of its whiskies.

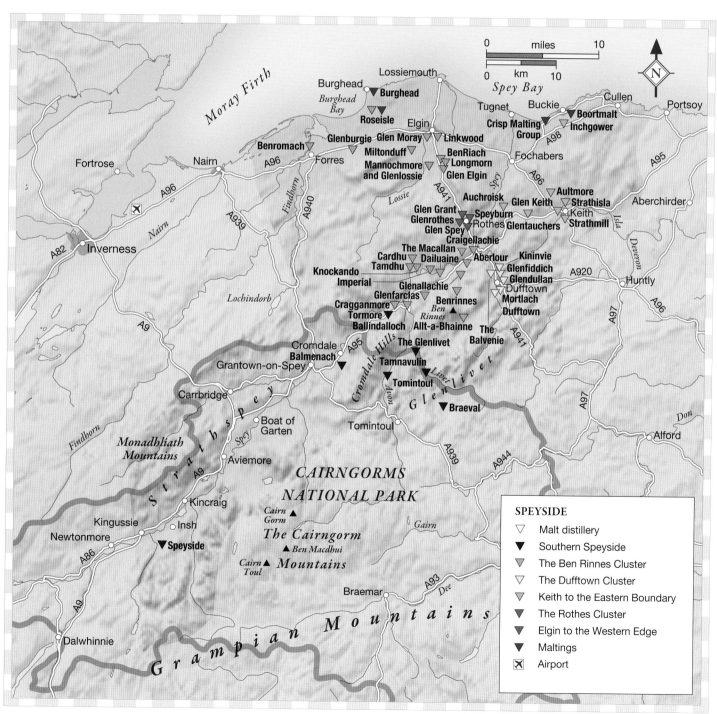

Moray Firth

Burghead
Burghead Bay
▼ Burghead
▽ Roseisle
Elgin
Spey Bay
Tugnet
Buckie
Cullen
Portsoy
▼ Boortmalt
Crisp Malting Group
▼ Inchgower
Lossiemouth

Fortrose
Nairn
A96
Forres
Benromach ▽
Glenburgie ▽
Glen Moray ▽
▽ Linkwood
Miltonduff ▽
BenRiach ▽
▽ Longmorn
Mannochmore and Glenlossie ▽
Glen Elgin ▽
Fochabers
A98
A95
Aberchirder

Inverness
A82
A96
A939
Findhorn
Lossie
A941
Spey
A96
Auchroisk ▽
Glen Keith ▽
Aultmore ▽
Strathisla ▽
Keith
Strathmill

Lochindorb
Glen Grant ▽
Glenrothes ▽
Speyburn ▽
Rothes
Glentauchers ▽
Deveron
Isla
Glen Spey ▽
Craigellachie ▽
The Macallan ▽
Aberlour ▽
Kininvie ▽
Cardhu ▽
Dailuaine ▽
Glenfiddich ▽
A920
Huntly
Tamdhu ▽
Glendullan ▽
Knockando
Dufftown ▽
Imperial
Glenallachie ▽
Mortlach ▽
Glenfarclas ▽
Benrinnes ▽
Dufftown
Cragganmore ▽
Ben Rinnes ▲
Tormore ▼
Allt-a-Bhainne ▲
The Balvenie
Ballindalloch
A97
A96

Cromdale
Balmenach ▼
A95
The Glenlivet ▼
Grantown-on-Spey
Tamnavulin ▼
Carrbridge
Tomintoul ▼
Glenlivet
Livet
Cromdale Hills
Braeval ▼
A97
Don
Alford

Boat of Garten
Spey
Avun
Tomintoul
A9
Monadhliath Mountains
Strathspey
Findhorn
Kincraig
Kingussie
Newtonmore
A86
Insh
▼ Speyside
CAIRNGORMS NATIONAL PARK
Cairn Gorm ▲
The Cairngorm
Gairn
A939
A944

Ben Macdhui ▲
Cairn Toul ▲
Mountains
A9
Dalwhinnie
Braemar
A93
Dee

Grampian Mountains

SPEYSIDE	
▽	Malt distillery
▼	Southern Speyside
▼	The Ben Rinnes Cluster
▽	The Dufftown Cluster
▼	Keith to the Eastern Boundary
▼	The Rothes Cluster
▼	Elgin to the Western Edge
▼	Maltings
⊠	Airport

miles 0 — 10
km 0 — 10
N

SOUTHERN SPEYSIDE

Our journey starts here, in the southern parts of Speyside, once the haunt of moonshiners and smugglers and also where the modern Scotch-whisky industry was born. Here are to be found whiskies from every point of our Flavor Map—yes, even peaty. Speyside is not so much a unified single style as a cross section of single-malt Scotch.

The River Avon snakes its way past Tomintoul in southern Speyside.

Speyside
AVIEMORE

It seems almost arrogant that the newest distillery in Speyside should take the name of the region itself. However, its owners could claim (with some legitimacy) that there was a distillery of that name in the same town of Kingussie at the end of the nineteenth century, although it only ran until 1911.

The building that now bears the Speyside name has only been operating since 1991, having been painstakingly planned and built by George Christie over a period of three decades. Christie had previously been the owner of the Strathmore/North of Scotland grain distillery in Clackmannanshire—a plant that produced "patent still malt" from column stills (*see* p.16).

Speyside takes a more conventional approach to its whisky-making. Two small stills, obtained from the old Lochside distillery, make what is a light, honeyed malt. "The stills were too big," said former manager Andy Shand, "so we had to lop a foot off the top and reweld them in order to make them fit."

Small stills can tend to make a heavy spirit, thanks to a shorter conversation between the alcohol vapor and the lightening properties of copper, so Shand has to have a light touch in order to create his light, new-make spirit. "We're very traditional," he said. "The fermentation is 60 hours long to build up esters and distillation is slow-paced. A lot of big firms fall into the trap of changing the setup and running too fast in order to make more spirit, and then lose their

character. We're also manual. Whisky-making today is too sanitized, too industrial. It's not left to people to do their own thing."

Though new, it's easy to believe that the Speyside approach, with its reliance on intuition, links the distillery with the early days of the region's story—not just because of the fact that it was built, slowly, by hand, but also that the architecture and the materials root it in the landscape. The Speyside distillery could have been there for centuries, and in some ways it has: the skills and attitude contained within its dry-stone walls are nothing if not timeless.

In 2013, the distillery was bought by Harvey's of Edinburgh, with the aid of Taiwanese backing.

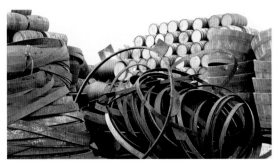

Barrels ready for repair: the destination for future Speyside whisky.

THE SPEYSIDE TASTING NOTES

NEW MAKE
Nose: Very fragrant and intense with sour plum, green apple notes.
Palate: As nose suggests: light and sweet. Fizzy with a green melon lift toward the back.
Finish: Lightly floral.

3YO CASK SAMPLE
Nose: Gold. Lots of nuttiness and a slight earthy note. Toasty, charred oak. Dried apple/apple juice, burlap, and sweet graham cracker.
Palate: Plenty of fresh wood, pancake batter, and a malty crispness. Fruit slightly hidden.
Finish: Softens.
Conclusion: In the additive stage of maturation. The spirit is absorbing rather than giving out.

12YO 40%
Nose: Pale straw. Distinctly earthy. Wheat chaff, geranium leaf. In time an herbal note akin to wild garlic and sorrel.
Palate: Spicier than the nose suggests; drier, too: the dusty earthiness carries through.
Finish: Light and short.
Conclusion: A refill cask hasn't woken the spirit up yet.

Flavor Camp: Malty & Dry
Where Next? Auchroisk 10yo

15YO 43%
Nose: Rich gold. Some sweetness and some coconut alongside apple peel, light candied florals, and angelica.
Palate: Plenty of sweet oak. Delicate fruits and a hit of cut flower. Oak gives a crisper structure.
Finish: Clean and sweet.
Conclusion: Clear resemblance to new make. An easygoing and understanding malt.

Flavor Camp: Fragrant & Floral
Where Next? Bladnoch 8yo

Balmenach

CROMDALE • WWW.INTERBEVGROUP.COM/GROUP-INVER-HOUSE-DISTILLERIES.PHP#BALMENACH

If The Speyside distillery is this simulacrum of an old site, then the next stop is the real deal. Not that it shouts about it. Indeed, its location a mile outside the village of Cromdale gives a clue to its origins. Old distilleries, the ones that sprang up from illicit sites at the start of the nineteenth century, were on farms or the sites of black *bothies* (huts)—places away from the beaten track.

In the late eighteenth and early nineteenth centuries, small-still distilling was effectively banned, with the result that a rural population who relied on it for its income was criminalized. In those days, making whisky involved subterfuge. Being hidden in the Cromdale Hills gave Balmenach's moonshining founder, James MacGregor, a positive advantage.

Speyside, the region, may exist in a legal sense, but it is far from being a single entity. Instead, it is a contrast between the old and the new, the dark and the light. Balmenach, with its small stills, wooden washbacks, and worm tubs belongs to the former style, and it is these pieces of equipment that help give it its heavy, brooding, power.

In simple terms, "light" is achieved through lots of copper contact in the still: the longer the conversation between vapor and copper, the lighter the spirit will be, so condensers, higher distillation temperatures, as well as cutting higher in the run all help produce a light character.

Using the ancient condensing technique of a copper pipe immersed in a bath of water (i.e. a "worm tub") results in less conversation between vapor and copper, hence a heavier style, and one which, at new-make stage, will normally have a sulfury note. It's important to stress that this sulfur acts as a marker for background complexities and is not in the mature spirit.

"We have worm tubs at Balmenach, anCnoc [Knockdhu], Old Pulteney, and Speyburn," says Stuart Harvey, master blender at Inver

Close to the wild Cromdale hills, Balmenach is a classic old-style distillery.

House, Balmenach's owner. "We don't pick up a lot of copper during the process, but preserve the sulfur compounds produced during fermentation. This results in the cooked vegetables, meaty, struck-match character you find in these new makes.

"During maturation, the sulfur compounds interact with the char layer of the cask," he adds. "This produces the toffee and butterscotch aromas and flavors in the mature whisky. Once the different sulfur compounds mature, the rest of the new-make character can shine through. The heavier the sulfur compounds, the longer it will take to mature."

Balmenach is in this last camp. Meaty when new, rich and heavy when mature—and perfectly built for long-term maturation in ex-sherry casks. Sadly though, it's rarely seen. Inver House has chosen to keep this distillery hidden as far as single-malt bottlings go, but search among the independent bottlers for a taste of the old ways.

BALMENACH TASTING NOTES

NEW MAKE

Nose: Robust and deep with meaty, leathery notes. There are notes of mutton stock and ripe apple. Here is evidence of the guts and depth given by the traditional worm tubs coming into play. This power will remain with the spirit as it matures.

Palate: Very heavy and dense in the mouth with an exotic sweetness. It is this sweetness that balances Balmenach: mature in a sherry cask and the meatiness is enhanced, refill or ex-bourbon and it is this more aromatic aspect that comes to the fore.

Finish: Long. A little smoke.

1979, BERRY BROS & RUDD BOTTLING
(BOTTLED 2010) 56.3%

Nose: Full gold. Full and very sweet, with lots of heavy chocolate, toffee, and cacao cream before moving into stewed Assam tea. Weighty. Wet earth. With water, there's milk chocolate and creamy toffee, damp earth, and a shoe-shop note.

Palate: Spicy start with good intensity. Burning leaves (seems to be a touch of smoke). Heavy mid-palate where stewed orchard fruits rest. Walnut whip. With water becomes more savory.

Finish: Firm and long. Lightly drying. Dried apple peel, then, after ten minutes, dried honey.

Conclusion: The sweet nature of American oak cask cannot hide Balmenach's bear-like qualities.

Flavor Camp: Fruity & Spicy
Where Next? Deanston 28yo, Old Pulteney 30yo

1993, GORDON & MACPHAIL BOTTLING 43%

Nose: Light gold. Dry leather/new leather belt, suggesting it's still at the early stages of interaction with the oak. Hard toffee and graham crackers, freshly varnished wood; with water, earthiness.

Palate: Thicker than the nose suggests. Chewy. Just a hint of cereal then a charred smokiness, beech leaves, green tobacco leaf. With water a previously hidden growly note adds further depth.

Finish: Wood.

Conclusion: Still coming together but distillery character is there.

Flavor Camp: Fruity & Spicy
Where Next? The Glenlivet 1972

Tamnavulin & Tormore

TAMNAVULIN • BALLINDALLOCH / TORMORE • CROMDALE • WWW.TORMOREDISTILLERY.COM

While Balmenach has retained a belief in the old ways, the next pair of stills shows that while it is wrong to believe that there is a unified Speyside style, it is possible to argue that there is a shared flavor among distilleries built across Scotland in the 1960s, a period when rising demand for Scotch in the USA led to a rash of new buildings. It seems beyond coincidence that all of these produce whiskies that are light and quite often malty.

Tamnavulin, built on the side of the Livet River in 1965, was, amazingly, only the second legal still to exist in Glen Livet. Its six stills produce a high-toned, quite simple new make, which, when followed through its evolution in cask, shows itself to be a whisky that is happy to do the blender's bidding. In essence, it is one where the cask rather than the whisky takes center stage.

This has its own dangers; it's easy to lose Tamnavulin in an oak forest. "You have to be careful not to overdress it," says Whyte & Mackay's master blender Richard Paterson. "It's very good in American oak, light sherry, even in tired wood, but heavy clothes will weigh it down." It is now part of Diageo.

Tormore, part of the Chivas Brothers portfolio, shares this 1960s iteration. Located eight miles northwest of Balmenach, it couldn't be more different from its neighbor. While the latter seeks refuge in the Cromdale moorland, the massive Tormore sits boldly beside the A96 highway, looking like a modernist homage to a Victorian hydropathic hotel. It was designed by Sir Albert Richardson, president of the Royal Academy, who, for all his qualities as an architect, had clearly never built a distillery when he was commissioned by Long John Distillers in 1959.

Its sheer size is a manifestation of the confidence of blenders at that time and its eight stills have always produced the light, dry style that the 1960s' North American market demanded: no peat in the malt, quick mashing, and short fermentations to get a cereal note, plus condensers to help lighten the spirit (although it can be rather rigid as a single-malt bottling).

TAMNAVULIN TASTING NOTES

NEW MAKE
Nose: Clean and dry with some dusty cereal notes. Grappa-like.
Palate: Light with notes of violet and lily. Crisp and bone-dry.
Finish: Nutty, short.

12YO 40%
Nose: Pale in colour. Very light. Toasted rice. Some vanilla, then felt.
Palate: Light and dry. Slightly rubbery with barley/malt crunchiness, lemon.
Finish: Quick.
Conclusion: A straight line from the new make. Lightness personified.

> **Flavor Camp: Malty & Dry**
> **Where Next?** Knockando 12yo, Auchentoshan Classic

1973 CASK SAMPLE
Nose: Greenish rim. Clean, sherried notes, roasted nut, brown banana skin, and nut oil. Light dried flower.
Palate: Sweet and light-bodied. Has a nutty mid-palate with subtle sweetness. Balanced.
Finish: Clean and medium.
Conclusion: Here a sherry cask has picked up the maltiness and made it nutty while also adding sweetness.

1966 CASK SAMPLE
Nose: Mahogany in colour. Rich and mature. Cracked old leather. Plum and prune with a heavy sweetness. Akin to Brandy de Jerez.
Palate: Light grip. Brazil nut and a fairly dense mid-palate. Dried herbs.
Finish: Nuts.
Conclusion: Maybe a little overdressed, but a demonstration of how malty whiskies need oak.

TORMORE TASTING NOTES

NEW MAKE
Nose: Full, with fresh corn tones and a slight farmyard (cow breath) note.
Palate: Pure and sweet with very light fruit.
Finish: Dusty, then light citrus.

12YO 40%
Nose: Slightly hard nose, then some oak shavings. Dry and nutty.
Palate: Tobacco leaf, dry spiciness (coriander powder) with an herbal/heathery note. With water, increasingly bourbon-like.
Finish: Crisp and nutty.
Conclusion: Active oak giving considerable support.

> **Flavor Camp: Fruity & Spicy**
> **Where Next?** Glen Moray 12yo, Glen Garioch 12yo

1996, GORDON & MACPHAIL BOTTLING 43%
Nose: Pale. Light maltiness and crab apple. Hint of flowers behind. Quite firm.
Palate: Apple tart. Gorse. Orange-blossom water. When diluted remains fresh with an added grassiness and a little oiliness.
Finish: Short and slightly bitter.
Conclusion: Has the distillery's very angular focus.

> **Flavor Camp: Fragrant & Floral**
> **Where Next?** Miltonduff 18yo, Hakushu 18yo

Tomintoul & Braeval

TOMINTOUL • BALLINDALLOCH • WWW.TOMINTOULDISTILLERY.CO.UK / BRAEVAL • BALLINDALLOCH

Two other 1960s' plants conform to the lighter template. The first, Tomintoul, was built in 1965 on the banks of the Avon River by whisky-broking firms W. & S. Strong and Haig & MacLeod, and is now part of Angus Dundee's stable. Why build here, though? Probably due to the water supply: three springs feed the plant. Or maybe the original owners tapped into the fact that there's an old whisky-making pedigree here; a cave behind a nearby waterfall was once home to an illicit still.

Tomintoul is sold as "The Gentle Dram" which, while accurate, seems to infer that it has a slightly bland nature; this would be doing the malt a disservice. This is malty, but "maltiness" is a broad category, stretching from the anorexic and bone-dry to an almost burnt richness.

Tomintoul sits in the middle, its cereal-like center reminiscent of a warm mash tun and the sweet breath of cattle in the barn. There's an intensity to the new make, which opens into soft fruit, which in turn acts as a counterpoint to the crispness of the cereal. There's enough there to cope with long-term aging in active casks. Older expressions show a lush, tropical fruitiness, typical of relaxed maturation.

A smoky expression (using local peat) is also produced, which gives our first example of how the location of the peat bog is key in the creation of specific aromas. Because of its composition, mainland peat gives a smoky effect more akin to wood smoke rather than the heathery, marine, or tarry notes from peat cut on the islands.

The illicit era is also the backdrop to Scotland's joint-highest distillery, Braeval, built in 1973 in the remote Braes of Glenlivet. This hidden flagon-shaped valley is bounded by the Ladder Hills and stoppered at its entrance by the Bochel Hill. Scattered around are ruins of old *shielings* (shelters), evidence of the seasonal cattle migration; *braes* is dialect for high pasture. By the time the valley was settled in the eighteenth century it was producing whisky, though it wasn't until 1972 that Braes got its first legal distillery. Braeval, too, conforms to the "late Speyside" light style. There's lots of copper in the system, but the make is heavier than you'd expect with a geranium note.

TOMINTOUL TASTING NOTES

NEW MAKE

Nose: Light cereal, oatmeal, sweet underneath. Touch of mash tun. Appetizing and sweet.
Palate: Focused, high-toned and sweet with a clean green character in the center. Quite intense.
Finish: Malty.

10YO 40%

Nose: Copper. Crisp and slightly malty. Hazelnut, mixed peel. Ovaltine with water. Seems young.
Palate: Sweet with lots of white raisin, licorice. Very smooth.
Finish: Ripe and sweet.
Conclusion: Sherried components give a dried fruit softness.

Flavor Camp: Malty & Dry
Where Next? Auchentoshan Classic

14YO, NO CARAMEL, NON-CHILL-FILTERED 46%

Nose: Pale straw. Very light and clean with a floral (daffodil/freesia) and white fruit lift. Delicate oak and a touch of flour/just-baked white bread.
Palate: Immediate floral lift with some pear juice. A fuller feel than the 10yo with a knob of melting butter in the center. Grows in the mouth.
Finish: Sweet and long.
Conclusion: Here's where Tomintoul's hidden qualities begin to emerge.

Flavor Camp: Fragrant & Floral
Where Next? Linkwood 12yo

33YO 43%

Nose: Thick and syrupy, with lots of dried tropical fruits and a hint of waxiness. Long and sumptuous, with a little charred oak with water.
Palate: Chewy and layered. All of the fruits bursting forward are given a dry/marzipan edge by some almond. With water, the oak moves to crème anglaise and patisserie.
Finish: Ripe and long.
Conclusion: A classic example of the tropical-fruit notes given by long maturation.

Flavor Camp: Fruity & Spicy
Where Next? Bowmore 1965

BRAEVAL TASTING NOTES

NEW MAKE

Nose: An estery start with a background heavy Marmite-like character; just a whiff of sulfur.
Palate: Soft with good weight then lifted to the back.
Finish: Dark grains.

8YO 40%

Nose: Nutty. Pistachio with some apple wood, the roasted cereal note now softened and giving an extra layer. Lighter than you'd think from the *clearic* (new make). Russet apples.
Palate: Scented and lifted. Some jasmine and lavender. Delicate.
Finish: Clean and quite simple.
Conclusion: Freshness is enhanced.

Flavor Camp: Fragrant & Floral
Where Next? Tomintoul 14yo, Speyburn 10yo

The Glenlivet

BALLINDALLOCH • WWW.GLENLIVET.COM • OPEN APR–OCT, MON–SUN

Contrary to popular belief, there were plenty of legal distilleries operating before the date most people believe ushered in legal whisky distilling. The passing of the 1823 Excise Act was, however, the signal for the emergence of what we now recognize as today's Scotch-whisky industry. The new legislation was aimed at stamping out illicit distilling by encouraging conditions for capital to be released into small-scale production facilities in the Highlands.

What is also overlooked is that this piece of legislation also expanded the options for distillers and, in doing so, changed whisky's flavors. There's a telling paragraph on this point in Michael Moss and John Hume's rigorously researched history of the Scotch whisky industry: "The new regulations [in 1823] allowed each distiller to choose his own methods of working—the strength of the wash, the size and design of the still, and the quality and the flavor of his whisky."

That's what was at the back of George Smith's mind when he was leaned upon by his landlord to take out one of the new licenses. This was not surprising, given his landlord was the Duke of Gordon, who had helped initiate the change in law by saying in the House of Lords that landowners would stop turning a blind eye to illicit distillation.

Smith had been moonshining since 1817 at the Upper Drumin farm high in the wilds of Glen Livet, one of many such operations in this hard-to-police area. Although his neighbors resented his new legal status—and Smith had little option but to go legit—it is what he did next that is intriguing.

He could have taken the same route as the MacGregors of Balmenach and stayed heavy. Smith and his sons, however, seem to have been liberated not just from the illegal ways of old, but from the old flavors. Smith moved into the light, embracing the possibilities of a new style. No more *bothies* and smoke-filled caves, but technology, capital, and, by the middle of the nineteenth century, proto-branding. Despite his being the only legal distillery in Glen Livet, it was Smith's style of whisky that became the shorthand for a specific flavor and, because every other distiller appended the appellation onto their name, Smith's distillery was permitted to call itself THE Glenlivet.

The old Drumin distillery closed in 1858 when Smith built a larger plant nearby at Minmore, where the current distillery still stands. Considerably expanded since those days, in 2009–10 it was given its most dramatic facelift yet. A new mash tun, eight new wooden washbacks, and a further three pairs of stills (making seven pairs in total), all with the same pinched waist of Smith's 1858 design, can make up to 2,641,721 gallons (ten million liters) a year. "The new Briggs mash tun has a monitor and viewing glass to check wort clarity; we don't want anything cloudy to give heavy cereal," says Alan

The quality of its wood management has enabled The Glenlivet to become one of the world's top-selling single malts.

Winchester, The Glenlivet's master distiller. "Then we give it a 48-hour ferment, while those stills give good copper contact to get fruity, floral esters, which will then undergo further esterification in the cask."

According to nineteenth-century records, Smith aimed for a pineapple character in his whisky. Today, for me, it is apples that are the defining character along with a gentle floral note when young. It has guts, however, The Glenlivet building in finesse as it matures—especially in refill casks (*see* pp.14–15).

High in the cool air of Minmore, The Glenlivet's warehouses have their own microclimate.

Equally important, though, is the design of the new stillhouse. Glenlivet was for many years a gray industrial-looking unit on a hill. Now with its panoramic window and dressed stone it has become part of the landscape once more, looking back as it does to the Braes and ahead to Ben Rinnes.

THE GLENLIVET TASTING NOTES

NEW MAKE

Nose: Medium weight. Clean with some floral notes, a little banana, ripe apple, and a touch of iris.
Palate: Soft, gentle fruits. Light, appley. Fresh zucchini.
Finish: Crisp and clean.

12YO 40%

Nose: Light gold. Scented, with lots of apple (fruit and blossom), jasmine tea, and a touch of toffee.
Palate: Delicate start, then sudden lift of chocolate. Apples flood into flowers, honey, poached pear.
Finish: Clean and soft.
Conclusion: Light and aromatic.

> **Flavor Camp: Fragrant & Floral**
> **Where Next?** Glenkinchie 12yo, anCnoc 16yo

15YO 40%

Nose: Coppery gold. Intensely spiced: sandalwood, rosewood, turmeric, cardamom. Rose petal.
Palate: Apples first. Flower stall. Gentle, light; grippy oak.
Finish: The spices return. Cinnamon and ginger.
Conclusion: French oak usage has upped the spiciness.

> **Flavor Camp: Fruity & Spicy**
> **Where Next?** Balblair 1975, Glenmorangie 18yo

18YO 40%

Nose: Full gold. Baked apple, light-brown sugar, antique shop, lilac. Light aniseed.
Palate: Richer than the 12yo with more sherry cask. Cedar, almond blossom, amontillado, and dried orange peel.
Finish: Apple and allspice.
Conclusion: Richer and more evolved, with a good line back to new make.

> **Flavor Camp: Rich & Round**
> **Where Next?** Auchentoshan 21yo

ARCHIVE 21YO 43%

Nose: Here, the apples have dried and slipped back a little, allowing other fruits (peach, cooked plum) to come through alongside an exotic, resinous oakiness. Water makes it akin to panettone with some almond.
Palate: Sweet and typically The Glenlivet. Now apples cooked in thick demerara sugar. Water brings out spice with an apple-led sugariness.
Finish: Gingery and long.
Conclusion: Elegant and mature, and still showing distillery character.

> **Flavor Camp: Fruity & Spicy**
> **Where Next?** Clynelish 14yo, Balblair 1975

THE BEN RINNES CLUSTER

Ben Rinnes is Scotland's whisky mountain—there's even a toposcope on its summit showing all the distilleries that can be seen from there. In its shadow, the play between the old, traditional ways and the modern, lighter aesthetic reaches its fullest expression. Here, distilleries that make heavy, meaty styles sit alongside those where flowers are the order of the day.

Cardhu (background) looks down to the riverside buildings of Knockando.

Cragganmore & Ballindalloch

BALLINDALLOCH • WWW.DISCOVERING-DISTILLERIES.COM/CRAGGANMORE • OPEN APRIL–OCT; SEE WEBSITE FOR DAYS & DETAILS

Ben Rinnes is the nexus point of Speyside. The most northerly outlier of the Cairngorm massif, it dominates the central part of the region. From its summit, the landscape of the area can be discerned; south to the Cromdales and Glenlivet, north to Rothes and Elgin, east into Dufftown and Keith. The cluster of distilleries that fall within its immediate shadow are further evidence of Speyside's development of its triple-faceted style.

One of the issues facing the post-1823 distiller was how to get his wares to market. Mountain tracks may have been a distinct advantage in the smuggling days, but poor communication with the new markets was a hindrance to many of the new start-ups and by the 1860s distilleries were struggling.

Their fortunes were to change in 1869 with the building of the Strathspey Railway which linked Dufftown with Boat of Garten and the line to Perth and the central belt. The first distiller within the Ben Rinnes cluster to take advantage of this was John Smith who built his Cragganmore distillery next to Ballindalloch station in 1869.

John Smith was a large man. In some ways, his size has diminished him, with all the attention paid to his girth detracting from his genius as an innovative distiller. He was related to George Smith of The Glenlivet and he was manager there, as well as at Dailuaine and Macallan before heading south to Clydesdale (Wishaw). He then returned to Speyside, briefly holding the lease on Glenfarclas before finally taking the lease on a piece of land beside the Spey.

Though there are now computers in the stillhouse, Smith's approach to whisky-making remains intact. The reason he built here was practical, but inside, it is his creativity as a distiller that is striking. He'd already worked at a diverse selection of other people's stills: The Glenlivet in its journey to light, Macallan and Glenfarclas (heavier), the triple-distilled Clydesdale. This was his chance to make his own whisky.

Cragganmore starts normally enough: lightly peated malt that's given a long fermentation in wooden washbacks. It is in the stillhouse however that Smith's genius is most apparent.

The wash stills are large with a sharply angled lyne arm leading into a worm tub. The spirit stills have a flat top with a long, gently sloping lyne arm stuck onto the side. The key word here is reflux (*see* pp.14–15).

What style of spirit was Smith trying to make? The longer you look the more confusing and contradictory it seems. The wash stills are huge, suggesting lots of reflux and therefore a light spirit, but the lyne arm is steeply angled downward, which stops that conversation from being too prolonged. The fact that it then leads into a cold worm tub

Although hidden from sight, and somewhat off the beaten track, Cragganmore was one of the first distilleries to take advantage of the railway.

A slow evolution in barrel will be one of the factors that adds further layers to this complex single malt.

BALLINDALLOCH: THE LAIRD'S DRAM

The Macpherson-Grant family has lived in Ballindalloch Castle since 1546. It was on their lands that the first Aberdeen Angus cattle were bred, and they leased the site to John Smith for Cragganmore. In 2014, an old farmstead next to (their) golf course was converted into a distillery. "The idea has been there lurking for a number of years," says Guy Macpherson-Grant, "and it became more obvious that this was a sensible thing to do while diversfying a traditional Highland estate."

This will be a "single-estate single malt." The barley is grown, distilled, and aged on the estate; the draff feeds the cattle. The most interesting decision has been the deliberate creation of "a robust, after-dinner whisky." This harking back to an older Speyside has meant worm tubs being installed, small stills, and a wood mix that includes first-fill barrels and hoggies, refill and ex-sherry, all overseen by the highly experienced Charlie Smith.

suggests the end result would be heavy. The spirit still is even more confusing. The alcohol vapor pings off the flat top and is refluxed back into the roiling mass of low wines. Because the lyne arm is offset from the top, it means that only certain flavors will come across. The long gentle declination of that lyne arm means there's a longer copper conversation taking place. It all points to extending the copper conversation—until you factor in the small stills and cold worms! The answer? He was a master of distillation who wanted to

make as complex a spirit as he could. Cragganmore may be confusing, but it is also inspiring. Guys like Smith were not uneducated men simply boiling up beer; they were innovators, experimenters, pioneers.

Today, Cragganmore is making a sulfury/meaty new spirit all year.

Hidden behind that sulfur in the new make, there is the glimmering of the complex mature character, all autumn fruits and flashes of late sun through the leaves in Ballindalloch's dark woods.

CRAGGANMORE TASTING NOTES

NEW MAKE

Nose: Concentrated. Meaty (lamb stock). Sulfur. Sweet citrus and fruits behind. Hint of nut.
Palate: Big and strong with some smoke, then the meat/sulfur tone comes through. Huge and dense. Thick, oily, and old-style. Has weight and suppleness.
Finish: Black fruits and sulfur.

8YO, REFILL WOOD CASK SAMPLE

Nose: Integrated and fruity. Touch of roast meat/roasting pan. Lots of mint, autumn leaves, and moss, even some pineapple and bramble. Sulfur with water.
Palate: Ripe and silky. Character has emerged. Complex and heavy. Fruit-led with backing of wood.
Finish: Closes down. Touch of peat.
Conclusion: The mature character is already emerging.

12YO 40%

Nose: Complex mix of ripe autumn fruits, cassis, some leather, heavy honey, chestnut. Light smoke.
Palate: Full-bodied and fruity. Stewed soft fruits, touches of walnut. Deep. Silky feel. Opened.
Finish: Light smoke.
Conclusion: Sulfur has totally gone and the meat has merged into a rich general fruitiness.

> **Flavor Camp: Rich & Round**
> **Where Next?** The GlenDronach 12yo, Glengoyne 17yo

THE DISTILLERS EDITION, PORT FINISH 40%

Nose: Rounded, sweet, and rich, with concentrated fruits and hedgerow jam tones. Sloe berries. Mildly exotic.
Palate: Generous and slightly fat, with a meaty underpinning. Off-dry, with dense fruits. Complex with water.
Finish: Very light smoke.
Conclusion: The autumnal elements within Cragganmore have a natural affinity with port.

> **Flavor Camp: Rich & Round**
> **Where Next?** The Balvenie 21yo, Tullibardine Port Cask

The Best of Speyside

CRAGGANMORE

12 YEARS OLD

Scotch Whisky

SINGLE SPEYSIDE MALT

AN ELEGANT, SOPHISTICATED SPEYSIDE WITH THE MOST COMPLEX AROMA OF ANY MALT. ASTONISHINGLY FRAGRANT WITH SWEETISH NOTES AND A SMOKY MALTINESS ON THE FINISH

40% vol 70cl e

CRAGGANMORE DISTILLERY BALLINDALLOCH, BANFFSHIRE

Knockando

KNOCKANDO • WWW.MALTS.COM/INDEX.PHP/EN_GB/OUR-WHISKIES/KNOCKANDO/INTRODUCTION

The contrast between Cragganmore and Knockando could not be more extreme. Whereas the former is hidden away in a leafy glen, the latter sits proudly, blond-stoned, beside what used to be the Strathspey railway line and is now the Speyside Way long-distance hiking path. There is an airiness to the layout, which somehow reflects this light-bodied malt whose character is reminiscent of motes of dust on a sunlit afternoon.

Knockando is firmly in the light camp. In fact, it is one of the precursors of the skeletal crew that came onto the scene in the 1960s. Here, cloudy wort and short ferments give an overriding malty new make character (*see* pp.14–15). As a result, the oak touch needs to be whisper light, just sufficient to provide some sweetness to that dusty palate.

Like John Smith, its original owner, John Thompson built Knockando on this site to take full advantage of the railway, but things had moved on since Smith's day. By the time Knockando was built, in 1890, blends were in the ascendency and, therefore, the blender was in charge of dictating what styles were needed. If the early distillers made, to a great extent, what they wanted—whisky as extension of personality and inclination—by the end of the nineteenth century a more hard-nosed pragmatism was taking over.

Distilleries were producing what the blenders wanted, and the blenders in turn had to be cogniscent of what the drinking public craved. What these distilleries from Speyside's last wave of building

The pale buildings of Knockando sit beside the Spey River.

in the nineteenth century show is the widening of the Scotch whisky template, the need for an ever-greater range of flavors with which to fashion blends.

Knockando became part of Gilbey's in 1904, one of the London-based blender's portfolio of Speysiders, all of which were on the delicate side. It was eventually to become a major player within J&B, one of the most fragile drams on the market, blended to suit the lighter American Prohibition-time palate.

KNOCKANDO TASTING NOTES

NEW MAKE

Nose: Mashy and clean with hazelnut. With water becomes dusty: sofa stuffing, felt.
Palate: Light and tight with some lemon. Very dusty. Simple.
Finish: Short, dry.

8YO, REFILL WOOD CASK SAMPLE

Nose: The new-make character is still there: dust and mouse. Old flour. Bone dry.
Palate: Powdered wheat breakfast cereal. There seems to be sweetness but it is well hidden. Crisp and dry.
Finish: Malty.
Conclusion: A dry nutty character that needs light sweet wood to bring it to life.

12YO 43%

Nose: Light and more nutty. Dry straw (the dust has gone). Hints of esters behind a soft, if light, vanilla note.
Palate: Light and fluffy with some milk chocolate, lemon. With water a dry malty character. Very light.
Finish: Short and dry.
Conclusion: A little longer in cask has filled out the center a little.

Flavor Camp: Malty & Dry
Where Next? Tamnavulin 12yo

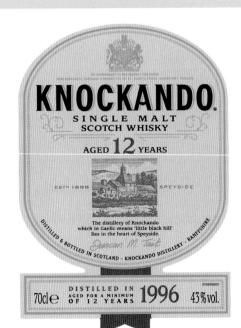

Tamdhu

KNOCKANDO • WWW.TAMDHU.COM

A few yards along the old railroad track sits Tamdhu, whose genesis was similar to that of its neighbor. Built in 1896 by a consortium of blenders, which sold it a year later to Highland Distillers (now Edrington), in its day it typified the late Victorian era, a manifestation in heavy stone, iron, copper, and wood of whisky's—and distilleries'—changing function.

Distilleries were no longer adapted farms but were designed as businesses: self-sufficient, with large maltings; close to good transportation for goods and waste, and with a substantial workforce housed on site. Tamdhu wasn't built in the hope that its whisky might sell. It was built because its owners knew it would.

Until recently, its claim to fame as far as whisky geeks were concerned was as the site of the last operational Saladin maltings in Scotland; they provided Highland Park's unpeated malt. As to the whisky? In terms of philosophy, little had changed since 1897. This was always a whisky destined for blends: The Famous Grouse, Cutty Sark, and the little-seen but excellent Dunhill. Yet like many distilleries with this primary function, this caused the Tamdhu name to slip from a wider consciousness. No matter how solid your construction or important your make, if you're not in single malt's front line, you're invisible—a ghost plant.

Edrington mothballed Tamdhu in 2010, but two years later it was snapped up by Ian MacLeod, blender broker and owner of Glengoyne, another former Edrington plant. The transformation has been total. There are new washbacks, new warehouses, and new people. The place has energy. It has life.

Wooden washbacks are believed to add to Tamdhu's character.

Yet lack of visibility means people don't realize your size. Tamdhu is a big site. It has six stills. It has volume. More significantly, now it also has presence. It's wraith-like existence used to manifest itself in a somewhat underwhelming occasional release, that inherent lightness not given any great assistance by oak. Now, thanks to Edrington's enlightened late-period policy of only using ex-sherry casks, the 10-year-old released by Ian MacLeod is a revelation. Oak adds a mature depth of resin and leather to Tamdhu's fragrant honey-apple character. Sherried but aromatic, weighty yet subtle, now you know why blenders love it, and now we have an idea of what it was like in 1897.

TAMDHU TASTING NOTES

NEW MAKE 69%

Nose: Very sweet and lily-like with hints of strawberry and raspberry. Clean, supple, and, with water, there are touches of young rhubarb and pea pod.

Palate: Sweet again with a light touch of citrus fruit and a hint of cereal. Good weight.

Finish: Substantial, with a delicate floral lift.

10YO 40%

Nose: The sherry-cask influence is apparent from the start, along with quince, apple, beeswax, and chocolate. With water, some Darjeeling tea and raisin.

Palate: Massed sweet fruit and a lot of cherry. Sweet with good grip. Its relative youth shows with some banana and layered fruit.

Finish: Light spice.

Conclusion: On the cusp between fruity and rich: an excellent example of an older style of Speyside.

Flavor Camp: **Rich & Round**
Where Next? Benromach, Glenfarclas

18YO EDRINGTON BOTTLING 43%

Nose: Bigger and more sherried, quite plump raisins. Like most light whiskies it picks up the cask influence easily.

Palate: Sherried character to the fore. Huge and raisined with a cereal dryness underneath. Balanced.

Finish: Clean and drying. Cookie-like.

Conclusion: Plenty of cask, with distillery character just holding on.

Flavor Camp: **Rich & Round**
Where Next? Arran 1996

32YO CASK SAMPLE

Nose: Open. Nutty and slightly smoky. A previously unseen honeyed note has emerged along with cinnamon.

Palate: Very spicy with ripe integrated soft/dried fruit.

Finish: Light and clean.

Conclusion: Sweet and balanced. Here, a slow maturation has benefited this light spirit well.

Cardhu

KNOCKANDO • WWW.DISCOVERING-DISTILLERIES.COM/CARDHU • OPEN ALL YEAR; SEE WEBSITE FOR DAYS & DETAILS

One major omission from the standard history of whisky distilling in Scotland has been the role played by women. Seduced by Sir Edwin Landseer's romantic depiction of the illicit distiller—a Highland chieftain, foot on stag, relaxing in his heather-roofed *bothy*—we forget about the careworn crone beside him. She's probably his wife. And she's the distiller.

When their husbands were out in the fields, tending the beasts (rather than hunting stags), the women would have been at home working on an endless succession of duties, including distilling. Such was the case at Cardhu. It may have been John Cumming who took the tack of Cardow Farm on Mannoch Hill above the Spey River in 1811, but evidence suggests that it was his wife, Helen, who made the whisky—illegally to begin with.

Cardow Farm acted as an early warning station for the moonshiners further south in Glenlivet. Stand at George Smith's original site at Minmore and a great bowl of land is laid out in front of you. There, high on a hill is Cardhu distillery. According to legend, the *gaugers* (taxmen) would arrive at Cardow Farm and Helen Cumming would invite them in for a wee cup of tea and a scone. As they were being entertained, so a red flag would be hoisted up a flagpole, warning the Livet moonshiners that the law was on its way.

In 1824 however, the Cummings took out one of the new licenses (conceivably the first to do so), but this change in legality made no difference to the way the distillery was run; the female hand remained on the tiller. After Helen's death, her daughter-in-law, Elizabeth, took charge of the plant, rebuilding it, before, in 1893, selling it to long-time client John Walker & Sons (on the agreement that the family would still operate the distillery). It was expanded again under its new owner in 1897, while a futher expansion in 1960 saw two more stills added to the original quartet.

Cardhu today is grassy and precise, a keenly focused new make whose orange and chocolate tones emerge later in life. It is, in other words, light, thereby not conforming to the loose theory that the older the distillery the heavier the style tends to be. "To the best of my knowledge the grassiness isn't a new development," says Douglas Murray, Diageo's master distiller and blender (aka "The Guru"). What we do know is that the character is the result of a

Originally installed by Elizabeth Cumming, Cardhu's stills help create its fresh character.

A large site with long-established links to Johnnie Walker, Cardhu is a perfect illustration of the rise of blended Scotch.

specific type of fermentation and distillation regime with the extra copper given by condensers taking it away from fruity (à la Glen Elgin) and more into the grassy camp.

Yet, when whisky's first great chronicler, Alfred Barnard, visited in the late 1880s, he found something quite different. Enjoying the "well-known hospitality of Mrs. Cumming," Barnard saw the old farm distillery with buildings that were "straggling and primitive," as well as Helen's brand-new site: "a handsome pile." Unusually for him, he actually comments on the whisky itself, "[It is] of the thickest and richest description and admirably suited for blending purposes."

In other words, it was an old-style, robust Speysider. The question is, when did it go light? Maybe under Walker's ownership as part of the general shift to a lighter character at the turn of the twentieth century. Conceivably it was happening when Barnard was visiting.

This is when Helen sold her old stills, mill, and waterwheel to William Grant, who was building his Glenfiddich distillery. Glenfiddich's stills are small. Cardhu's today are large. Maybe that's when the lighter make started. Though that's just conjecture, what's clear is that if Ben Rinnes is the focal point, then Cardhu is where this cluster starts to turn and embrace the new.

CARDHU TASTING NOTES

NEW MAKE
Nose: Green fruit pastille, wet grass, turmeric powder, Parma Violets, laurel.
Palate: Light and needle-fresh. Tight with some white flour, blueberry.
Finish: Light citrus.

8YO, REFILL WOOD CASK SAMPLE
Nose: Has softened from new-make stage. Mown grass, perfumed soap, and light cereal (the flour). Violet and then mandarin orange.
Palate: More green grass with lots of light aromatics bunched up behind. Has surprising weight. The wood has added a white chocolate effect.
Finish: Still citric.
Conclusion: Beginning to blossom.

12YO 40%
Nose: The grassiness is now drying (maybe from the attentions of the wood). Hay and some wood oil. A developing mix of orange, milk chocolate, and stawberry. Light cedar and mint with water.
Palate: Medium-bodied. The grassines is now crisp leaving the sweetness to be given by wood interaction and a developing orange note.
Finish: Short, spicy, and chocolate.
Conclusion: It will continue to develop but, as with most light spirits, has reached a balanced integration relatively early.

> **Flavor Camp: Fragrant & Floral**
> **Where Next?** Strathisla 12yo

AMBER ROCK 40%
Nose: Fresh, vibrant, and clean with the citric note typical of the distillery (sweet orange/ mandarin/lemon balm). Barley-sugar notes mix with light chocolate. It takes on some oxidative tones with water.
Palate: A sweet and assertive start is followed by fresh oak, lemon, and a vinous quality on the mid-palate, which moves into fruit syrups. Melting milk chocolate shows on the back.
Finish: Very spicy, with cherry and unrefined-sugar tones. Bittersweet (marmalade peel).
Conclusion: Shows good distillery character. Quite thick, with more spice on show. Balanced between citrus and spice.

> **Flavor Camp: Fruity & Spicy**
> **Where Next?** Oban 14yo

18YO 40%
Nose: Fruit-and-nut chocolate bars (hazelnut and raisin) move into some savory touches. There are little hints of chocolate orange as well. In character.
Palate: Super-ripe but mellow, then the typical Cardhu perkiness comes through. Lightly acidic and lemon-fresh (particularly with water), this is almost yuzu-accented. It deepens into caramel toffee in the center.
Finish: Lightly gripping, with a little oiliness.
Conclusion: It has retained its distillery character but taken on added weight and succulence.

> **Flavor Camp: Fruity & Spicy**
> **Where Next?** Yamazaki 12yo

Glenfarclas

BALLINDALLOCH • WWW.GLENFARCLAS.CO.UK • OPEN ALL YEAR, MON–FRI; SEE WEBSITE FOR DAYS & DETAILS

The dichotomy between heavy and light, old and new, which pervades the whole of Speyside, is at its most noticeable in the shadow of Ben Rinnes. Three miles to the south of Cardhu, hard on the lower slopes of the mountain, is Glenfarclas, whose heavily sweet, brooding new make immediately identifies it as a member of the former camps.

There is a feeling of permanence, of the past solidifying in your mouth when you taste it. Just as whisky has been pulled in many directions by commercial necessity, so Glenfarclas has stayed rooted. Yet a glance at its stills, the biggest in Speyside, would lead you to believe that here is a distillery making a lighter style. The secret to its new make's depth lies in the blazing fires beneath the stills themselves.

"We tried steam in 1981," says George Grant, whose family has owned the distillery for six generations. "But we pulled it out after three weeks and went straight back to direct fire. Steam might be cheaper, but here it just made the spirit flat. We want a spirit that has weight to it, we want to age it 50 years."

And where it is aged makes a difference. All of Glenfarclas is matured in "dunnage": (low, slate-roofed, earth-floored warehouses). These days distilleries often tanker new spirit off-site to palletized or rack warehousing in different parts of Scotland. If a whisky's character is about the accretion of small details, then could even this slight change in temperature have an effect? Grant believes so.

"There's a huge difference in temperature inside palletized warehouses, which are effectively tin sheds, and that is bound to affect the maturation cycle. Here, our losses are 0.05% a year. I've seen some in palletized sites where it's as high as 5%, the industry average is 2%. Here, the whisky is oxidizing slowly, not evaporating and that makes a difference." In these warehouses on the foothills of "The Ben," a *snell* (bitter) wind blowing there is regarded as a microclimate. It is site specificity at work and there's an almost Burgundian approach to whisky-making: knowing your plot, accepting what it gives you.

The wood type has a significant contribution to the Glenfarclas style; it's predominantly first-fill sherry cask (from Jose-Miguel Martin) with no first-fill bourbon. It's not just that Glenfarclas can cope with sherry casks; it *needs* sherry casks, and it absorbs the oak's power binding it in.

There are few families in Scotch with this lineage of distilling, giving the Grants an almost psychic link with place. "We have continuity," says Grant. "We don't have to answer to anyone so we can do it our way and because we have been doing it for six

Situated on the flanks of Ben Rinnes, there has been whisky made on the Glenfarclas site since the eighteenth century.

generations we're better placed than most. You either have your money in the bank or your money in stock. We have both. This is our twenty-second recession! We've learned only to make what we can afford and we never borrow money to make it."

And is this one of the few remnants of an older Speyside? "We don't even call ourselves Speyside!" laughs Grant. "We say that we are a Highland malt. This whole 'Speyside' idea is new [which is true: the region was known both as Strathspey and Glenlivet in the past] and it does confuse people. The Spey runs a long way." He pauses. "Right enough, 'Highland' is even more impossible to define. We are just Glenfarclas. I have a painting from 1791 showing a distillery on this site. We've been here legally for 175 years. People know what Glenfarclas is."

Ex-sherry casks are a major part of Glenfarclas' distinctive flavor profile.

GLENFARCLAS TASTING NOTES

NEW MAKE

Nose: Big, heavy, and fruity. Quite earthy and deep. Powerful with a touch of peat smoke.
Palate: Dry start, quite closed and tight, with that earthy note continuing. Ripe and dense. Old style.
Finish: Hint of fruit. Brooding.

10YO 40%

Nose: Sherried (amontillado pasada); toasted almond, chestnut. Ripe fruits, mulberry but also smoky edge: autumn bonfire. Sweetens into English sherry trifle, larch.
Palate: Clean and quite crisp with good heat in the mid-palate. Ripe and full. Damson jam. Still has the earthiness of the new make and that intriguing burnt note. Water sweetens it considerably.
Finish: Thick and long. Length, grip, and power.
Conclusion: Immediate acquisition of cask influences, but this has more to give.

Flavor Camp: **Rich & Round**
Where Next? Edradour 1997

15YO 46%

Nose: Amber. Deep and rich with date and dried fruit. Still has the edginess of youth but picking up complexity. The earthiness is lightening as things begin to sweeten up: chestnut purée, cedar, hazelnuts on a campfire, fruitcake.
Palate: Tight grip and not so much opening as bulging. Farclas just amasses weight as it matures. Woods. More grip than the 10yo but the spirit is so big that it simply shrugs it aside.
Finish: Powerful and long.
Conclusion: A sense of ever growing power.

Flavor Camp: **Rich & Round**
Where Next? Benrinnes 15yo, Mortlach 16yo

30YO 43%

Nose: Mahogany. Lots of dark chocolate and espresso. Still edgy. Now raisin but also molasses and prune and old leather. In time there's leaf mulch (a development of the earlier earthiness). Even a meaty touch.
Palate: Bosky and mysterious. Dense and crepuscular. Bolivar cigar and sweet dark fruits. Some tannic grip.
Finish: Coffee.
Conclusion: There might be big cask influence here, but even after three decades in an active cask the distillery is holding its own.

Flavor Camp: **Rich & Round**
Where Next? Ben Nevis 25yo

Dailuaine & Imperial

DAILUAINE • ABERLOUR

Despite Dailuaine being one of the most-spotted distilleries in Speyside, few know that's what they have seen. Heading toward Aberlour from Glenfarclas there will usually be clouds of steam billowing from a hidden valley on the river-side of the road. These are rising from Dailuaine's dark-grains plant, where the pot ale and draff from Diageo's central Speyside sites are processed into cattle feed.

Dailuaine itself is an interesting mix of old and new. An 1852 distillery, it was rebuilt in 1884 and was for a time the largest malt distillery in Speyside, featuring a kiln which Alfred Barnard commented on as having a roof, "of the steepest pitch in Scotland… [which] gives the malt a delicate aroma without having to use coke to prevent the flavor being too pronounced." This was further refined with the installation of the first distillery pagoda in Scotland: clear evidence that Dailuaine was trying to reduce smokiness to meet *fin-de-siècle* market demands.

Once the largest distillery in Speyside, Dailuaine continues to make a big, beefy dram.

For all of that, today Dailuaine remains in the heavy, old-style camp, though it is sweeter at heart with less of the meaty pungency of other members of that club.

While other Diageo plants such as Cragganmore, Mortlach, and Benrinnes find this character relatively easy to make, thanks to worm tubs (*see* pp.14–15), Dailuaine has to work against type to get this sulfury new make from its condensers. As we've seen, sulfuriness is down to a lack of copper interaction, but condensers are packed full of the metal. Solution here? Stainless-steel condensers. It seems only appropriate that this old distillery, which has always been at the forefront of innovation, should find a creative solution to maintain itself within the crepuscular world of older-style whisky.

Since 1897, it had a neighbor in the valley, the ill-starred Imperial distillery which, despite a high reputation of making the softest, cream-soda/floral malt, only operated intermittently, finally closing its doors in 1983. In recent years its stillhouse was targeted by copper thieves and was so cannibalized that when Chivas Brothers decided to restart production, it was easier to demolish and rebuild, although it has been decided under what name. Will the Empire strike back? I hope so.

DAILUAINE TASTING NOTES

NEW MAKE

Nose: Light meatiness, leathery. Some cereal and a partially hidden sweetness.
Palate: Big. Meaty. Sweet and thick, almost toffee-like. Heavy.
Finish: Long, with that hint of sweetness.

8YO, REFILL WOOD CASK SAMPLE

Nose: The meat has receded, leaving that sweetness to dominate. Light leather, black fruits, old apples.
Palate: Big heavy with damson and mulberry cut with leather. Rich and full.
Finish: The meatiness only shows now.
Conclusion: A heavy, rich, sweet spirit. A powerhouse.

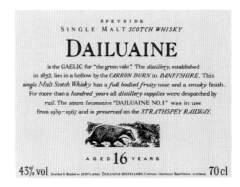

SPEYSIDE
SINGLE MALT *SCOTCH WHISKY*

DAILUAINE

is the GAELIC for "the green vale". The *distillery*, established
in 1852, lies in a hollow by the *CARRON BURN* in *BANFFSHIRE*. This
single Malt Scotch Whisky has a *full bodied fruity* nose and a *smoky* finish.
For more than a *hundred years* all *distillery supplies* were despatched by
rail. The *steam locomotive* "DAILUAINE NO.1" was in use
from 1939~1967 and is preserved on the *STRATHSPEY RAILWAY*.

AGED **16** YEARS

43% vol   70 cl

16YO, FLORA & FAUNA 43%

Nose: Red amber. Deep, earthy sherried. Funky with a light sulfur lift. Highly concentrated. Olde English marmalade. It remains slightly meaty, with molasses, rum and raisin, clove.
Palate: Huge and very sweet. Almost PX/Brandy de Jerez-like. Walnuts and chestnuts. An assault on the tongue.
Finish: Gripping, then slowly sweetens.
Conclusion: Sherry casks are needed to tame this beast. Distillery character still strong despite the attentions of oak.

Flavor Camp: Rich & Round
Where Next? Glenfarclas 15yo, Mortlach 16yo

Benrinnes & Allt-a-Bhainne

BENRINNES • ABERLOUR / ALLT-A-BHAINNE • DUFFTOWN

Finally, after skirting round "the Ben," now is the time to start climbing its slopes. This granitic outcrop is alive with springs, home to mountain hare, snow bunting, ptarmigan, and deer. Its lower reaches are thickened with peat, its summits a scrabble of pink granite. Though only a mile from the green Spey Valley, close to towns, BUT you are in the wild. It certainly spooked chronicler, Alfred Barnard, a man clearly best-suited for travel at sea level. "… no more weird or desolate place could be chosen", he wrote of its location.

This weirdness is a fair descriptor of the Benrinnes approach to whisky-making. One sniff of the new make and you are confronted with the Stygian qualities that define so many of Speyside's oldest sites. This is meaty with sulfur, a strange mix of the savory, and a little sweetness. That meatiness is its defining feature: a feral mix of tanned hides and cauldrons.

The character comes from its partial triple distillation. There are two sets of three stills, each working as a trio. The spirit from the wash still is split into "heads" and "tails." The former, high in strength, goes to one receiver, the latter, weaker, is redistilled in the intermediate still with the foreshots and feints from its previous run. The middle cut is collected and mixed with the "heads" from the wash still and the foreshots and feints from the previous run of the spirit still. Outside, chilled worm tubs help to cut down any copper contact. The sulfur comes from the worms, the meatiness from that intermediate still.

It is hard to think of a greater contrast to "The Ben" than the distillery on the mountain's eastern flanks. Built by Seagram in 1975, Allt-a-Bhainne and its slender stills with upward-angled lyne arms give a whisky with a delicacy typical of its era and its owner's house style.

BENRINNES TASTING NOTES

NEW MAKE
Nose: Dense. Hoof glue. Gravy. Lea & Perrins. Big meatiness.
Palate: Big and bruised. Heavy and full-bodied with some smoke. Good weight. Dry and powerful.
Finish: Sulfury.

8YO, REFILL WOOD CASK SAMPLE
Nose: Beef stock cubes, steak gravy. Very earthy and rooty.
Palate: Thick and concentrated with a tamarind-like sweetness in the center. Licorice and chocolate.
Finish: Meaty/sulfury.
Conclusion: A big bruiser, needs time to open to full maturity.

15YO, FLORA & FAUNA 43%
Nose: Red amber. Meaty. Toffee and still stock-cube dry meatiness. More time adds dried cep liquor. With water a smoky heathery lift.
Palate: Robust. Roasted meat and a fair grip of tannin. Long and ripe but the water helps to loosen the tannic grip, as does the inherent richness of the spirit. Hints of emerging leatheriness.
Finish: Bitter chocolate and coffee.
Conclusion: Now begining to enter mature stage.

> **Flavor Camp: Rich & Round**
> **Where Next?** Glenfarclas 21yo, Macallan 18yo Sherry

23YO 58.8%
Nose: Deep mahogany. Prune (Armagnac-like) with a light steak note behind. This interplay between muscularity and rippling sweetness continues all the way through. Bergamot, tomato paste, touch of allspice, and a slightly carbonized *jus* note, caramel apple, roast chestnut, coffee, earthiness.
Palate: Big, powerful, and assertive but not astringent because the concentrated sweetness remains. Raisin (PX) and lots of date. The feral beast has been semi-tamed. Softens as it slowly moves across the tongue. Water lightens the grip and adds a slight smoked character. Beefy in all senses.
Finish: Molasses.
Conclusion: Even after 23 years in a first-fill sherry cask, it is identifiably Benrinnes.

> **Flavor Camp: Rich & Round**
> **Where Next?** Macallan 25yo, Ben Nevis 25yo

ALLT-A-BHAINNE TASTING NOTES

NEW MAKE PEATED MALT
Nose: Very light smoke to start with. Plain, very clean, light base spirit with wisps of slightly grassy smoke coming across. Garden bonfire.
Palate: The smoke hits with full effect here. Wood smoke. Dry.
Finish: Drying.

1991 62.3%
Nose: Grassy and estery. Cooperage aromas. Oak. Light and clean. Quite simple.
Palate: Perfumed and floral note. Lots of freshly charred oak. Hint of barley sugar. High-toned and estery.
Finish: Clean and short.
Conclusion: Very much on the house style of the lighter side of Speyside.

> **Flavor Camp: Fragrant & Floral**
> **Where Next?** Glenburgie 12yo, Glen Grant 10yo

High on the slopes of The Ben, where Barnard feared to tread.

Aberlour & Glenallachie

ABERLOUR • WWW.ABERLOUR.COM • OPEN ALL YEAR APR–OCT DAILY; NOV–MAR, MON–FRI / GLENALLACHIE • ABERLOUR

Turning your back on the mountain and heading towards the Spey and the town of Aberlour, the whisky traveler first comes across Glenallachie. Although its location, out of sight from the road, away from the railway, suggests that this started life as an illicit site, it's another of the Ben's modern plants. Built in 1967 by Charles Mackinlay, it's a classic 1960s distillery, made specifically to provide light (and in this case cereal-accented) spirit for the growing North American market. That maltiness is on the sweeter side of the scale along with a latent fruity note.

The influence of Ben Rinnes itself may yet have an influence, however. One reason why the Benrinnes distillery makes a meaty spirit is because of the very cold water that flows from the mountain into its worms. Glenallachie also draws its water from the mountain, but here the cold temperature can cause problems with achieving character.

"These big Jura-like stills are made to make light [new make]," (see pp.14–15) says Alan Winchester, distilleries manager at owners Chivas Brothers. "But it can go sulfury if the process water gets too cold. The key to keeping the style is running things a wee bit warmer."

The mountain has finally relinquished its grip by the time you reach the neat little town of Aberlour. The tendency of distillers to secrete their plants up side alleys however seems still to be in force. The town's eponymous (and large) plant is some distance from the main road, only a rather smart Victorian gatehouse betrays its existence.

There has been a licit distillery in Aberlour since the 1820s, when two local farmers, John and George Graham, tried out their luck with one of the new licenses. The plant we see today was however originally built by James Fleming in 1879, and it is he who is considered its true founder. It's unlikely he would recognize the plant today as it was rebuilt in the 1970s and, like Glenallachie, is a good example of the open-spaced, clean, and efficient design prevalent at the time.

It's more intriguing to wonder if Fleming would recognize the make. Because he was building at the start of the lightening process of the 1880s, it's quite possible that he would. "The key for me in the new make is blackcurrant and a little green apple," says

Winchester, previously a manager here. "There's also an absence of cereal." Certainly, while Aberlour fits into the fruitier side of the Chivas Brothers house style, it is Winchester's currant leaf that gives Aberlour an intriguing, almost herbal fragrance as it matures. The fruitiness meanwhile, adds mid-palate softness, and there's sufficient weight to the spirit to allow it to sit happily in a sherry cask.

The "local" for workers, managers, and visitors to Aberlour. The Mash Tun is one of Speyside's finest pubs.

One of Scotland's hidden distilleries, Glenallachie is a classic 1960s site.

A flavor akin to malt (rather than cereal) in the new make is possibly the start of the whisky's signature mature note of toffee. While it might not be as beefy as some of the Ben's drams, neither is it as light as others. Rather, this supple character seems to bridge the stylistic gap between heavy and delicate. "What intrigues me," Winchester adds, "is how it is so close to Glenallachie in terms of location, yet the make is so different. We'll never know all the answers."

ABERLOUR TASTING NOTES

NEW MAKE

Nose: Sweet with blackcurrant leaf, some heavy florals, malt and, with water, some burlap.
Palate: Clean with citrus-fruit flesh, behind which you will find apple. Has presence.
Finish: Herbal.

10YO 40%

Nose: Copper. Intense malt note. Fruity, rounded with oak overlay. With water, becomes scented.
Palate: A positive nutty start, pecan pie. Toffee richness, then scented leaf quality seen on new make.
Finish: Assam tea, mint.
Conclusion: The oak adds volume and heft.

Flavor Camp: Rich & Round
Where Next? Ardmore 1977, Macduff 1984

12YO, NON-CHILL-FILTERED 48%

Nose: Big and substantial, with lots of marzipan, black banana, toffee, currant, maraschino cherries. Becomes scented with water, adding rosewater and a little leafy note.
Palate: Ripe and soft. The higher strength adds sparkle and lift, and there's a light cumin note. It's long on the tongue, and water pulls out ripe fruits.
Finish: Fresh and fruity.
Conclusion: This non-chill-filtered version has added weight and intensity.

Flavor Camp: Fruity & Spicy
Where Next? The BenRiach 12yo, Glengoyne 15yo

16YO, DOUBLE CASK 43%

Nose: More American-oak and refill-cask influence, allowing Aberlour's freshness to come through along with cereal, malty elements, balsa wood and linoleum. Water adds a little sherry touch.
Palate: Shows an immediate spicy attack with good liveliness. Needs water to calm things down. Much sweeter than the nose, with a little butteriness.
Finish: Good length.
Conclusion: An interesting mix of the Aberlour lightness but with subtle shadings of oak.

Flavor Camp: Fruity & Spicy
Where Next? Inchmurrin, Glen Moray 16yo

18YO 43%

Nose: Similar to the 12yo, but with added mint chocolate, cremino mushroom, and polished oak. With water, it gains notes of damson jam.
Palate: Strong and grippy, with plenty of plummy depth to carry.
Finish: Long and elegant.
Conclusion: A richer, deeper Aberlour with good balance.

Flavor Camp: Rich & Round
Where Next? The GlenDronach 12yo, Deanston 12yo

A'BUNADH, BATCH 45 60.2%

Nose: A big alcohol hit leads into a burnt molasses-like edge. Savory, with black cherries and an aroma akin to hot motorcycles.
Palate: Huge and quite tight. Heavily sherried, with masses of black fruit and a little drying cereal to add structure. Water allows a softer and more generous side to develop.
Finish: Big, bold, and robust.
Conclusion: The ongoing full-strength sherried blockbuster of a series continues.

Flavor Camp: Rich & Round
Where Next? Glenfarclas 15yo, Glengoyne 23yo

GLENALLACHIE TASTING NOTES

NEW MAKE

Nose: Light and sweet. Mashed fresh corn. This is aromatic and light.
Palate: Clean and precise. Soft and sweet.
Finish: Dry and clean.

18YO 57.1%

Nose: Amber. Clean and sherried with notes of fireworks, plum jam, raisin, light chicory, marmalade. Rich and expressive with Brazil nut.
Palate: Ripe and slightly dry with plenty of mature leathery notes. Nutty. Shows hints of its light floral character with water.
Finish: Long, sweet, and balanced.
Conclusion: The cask in charge but lending a degree of sophistication.

Flavor Camp: Rich & Round
Where Next? Arran 1996, The Glenrothes 1991

The Macallan

CRAIGELLACHIE • WWW.THEMACALLAN.COM • OPEN ALL YEAR EASTER–SEPT, MON–SAT; OCT–EASTER, MON–FRI

In the early days of single malt being commercialized, it was common practice to compare the drink to another wood-aged spirit with a high reputation. "This is as good as Cognac," marketeers would say. In The Macallan's case they'd add terms like "first growth," which is apposite. The Macallan's HQ, the whitewashed baronial Easter Elchies House, does give the whole estate the somewhat refined air of a château.

Although The Macallan's approach to whisky-making links it directly with the older distilleries in this cluster, and adds weight to the theory that the earliest ones (the distillery was founded in 1824) tend to make the heaviest whiskies, the manner in which it has sold its whisky has always seen it exist slightly off-center from the rest of the industry. One suspects that it doesn't mind that much.

This connection with the old ways is manifested most clearly in the stillhouse (or at the time of writing, stillhouses; a second one was brought back on stream in 2008), where tiny spirit stills hunker over their condensers like *Nibelungen* dwarves.

Reflux is a bad word here. The emphasis is on producing a spirit with guts. The new make (which you can taste as one of the many strokes of genius on its innovative tour) is oily, malty, and deep, but importantly, sweet. It's opinionated, making it clear from day one that this is not a spirit that will be pushed around.

That weight is vital since The Macallan has always allied itself with ex-sherry casks. Such is the symbiotic relationship with sherry that owner Edrington has casks made to its exacting specifications by the Tevasa cooperage in Jerez.

As has been traditional, a mix of European oak (*Quercus robur*), with its high tannin and aromas of clove and dried fruit, and American (*Quercus alba*), all vanilla and coconut, is used, giving whisky-maker Bob Dalgarno two very different main streams of flavor with which to work, and there are many variations within those two.

In sherry casks, the oiliness of the new make is both a facilitator of the flavors seeping from the oak, and a barrier to aggressive tannins, preventing them from grabbing the palate like a terrier with a rabbit. Old Macallan is smooth, not grippy. American oak (seen also in some ex-bourbon) reveals more of the cereal and soft fruity notes.

When I was speaking to him for the first edition, Dalgarno was putting together a vatting of sherry-oak 12-year-old from a range of whiskies, each with a different hue. His deep understanding of how there is a correlation between a color and a flavor spectrum has now borne fruit in the newest Macallan range: the four-strong 1824 Series.

This was his solution to an issue facing most producers: tightness of stock. Scotch's rapid expansion in the early part of the twenty-first century caught distillers on the hop. Memories of the whisky loch of the 1980s and subsequent distillery closures had meant that industry production levels remained cautious for decades. The inevitable result was a shortage of mature stock when the market exploded. The solution? No Age Statement (NAS) whiskies, which free the whisky-maker from the often restrictive nature of age statements, allowing them to explore flavor and distillery character.

Dalgarno's response was to look at how color could be used as an indicator of character. The irony (not lost on the firm's accountants, you feel) is that the new range is more expensive to produce than the whiskies its members have replaced.

It is unlikely that the stock shortage will occur again. Huge warehouses the size of aircraft hangars have been built and a new much-expanded distillery is currently under construction.

Meanwhile, The Macallan straddles the world, for many the epitome of whisky as luxury, for others a manifestation of old-style single malt, with a modern twist.

Secreted away in The Macallan's many warehouses are ex-sherry casks, whose contents whisky-maker Bob Dalgarno turns into one of this iconic distillery's many releases.

MACALLAN TASTING NOTES

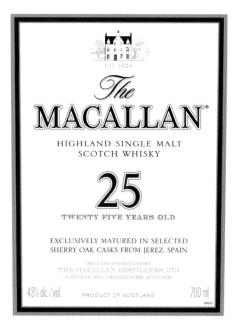

NEW MAKE

Nose: Clean. Some green fruit. Quite fat/oily, malty. Light sulfur.

Palate: Fat and oily and tongue coating. Heavy. Green olive. Unyielding.

Finish: Rich and long.

GOLD 40%

Nose: A warm, yeasty freshness mixes with freshly baked white bread, almond butter, hay, and vanilla.

Palate: There's substance behind the light, "open" nose, as well as a thickness, tongue-clinging oils, and a vibrant lemon note, with hard candy.

Finish: Dry and malty.

Conclusion: A lighter introduction to The Macallan but full of distillery character.

Flavor Camp: Fruity & Spicy
Where Next? Benromach 10yo

AMBER 40%

Nose: Soft fruit, stewing green plums, and fruit syrup. There's a hint of white raisin, then a hint of beeswax.

Palate: Earthy (damp sand) yet sweet, with semi-dried fruit and a hint of vanilla. Delicate almond notes behind.

Finish: Long and lightly malty.

Conclusion: Savoriness building.

Flavor Camp: Fruity & Spicy
Where Next? The Glenrothes 1994

15YO, FINE OAK 43%

Nose: Gold. Orange peel and ripe melon, mango, vanilla bean. Hot sawdust, hazelnut, and wax polish.

Palate: Nutty oak, cooked orchard fruit, black banana. Caramel toffee, bracken, malt, and dark chocolate.

Finish: Complex and fruity.

Conclusion: The distillery character and "Fine Oak" casks in balance.

Flavor Camp: Fruity & Spicy
Where Next? Glenmorangie 18yo, Glencadam 15yo

18YO, SHERRY OAK 43%

Nose: Dark amber. Fruitcake, plum pudding, rich moist cake, walnut, and gingerbread, then a touch of molasses and dried berries.

Palate: Rich and mouth-filling. Chewy. Raisin and fig. Very ripe and oily/rich.

Finish: A singed note adding to the complexity.

Conclusion: Balance struck between the bold distillery character and rich oak.

Flavor Camp: Rich & Round
Where Next? Dalmore 1981, Glenfarclas 15yo

SIENNA 43%

Nose: Stewed black cherries, red plums, and blueberries abound, but with purity and freshness.

Palate: Earthy and thick, with candlewax, resin, allspice, clove, peels, perfumed fruit, and the whiff of an artist's palette. Supple tannins.

Finish: Long and raisined.

Conclusion: A country house in autumn.

Flavor Camp: Rich & Round
Where Next? Yamazaki 18yo

25YO, SHERRY OAK 43%

Nose: Rich amber. Full-on Brandy de Jerez notes: dark sweet fruit, toasted almond, dried herbs. Almost fruit-compote sweetness, the sweetness of the spirit now in its fullest expression along with resin from the oak.

Palate: Very sweet. Into red-wine notes. Fine grip, mulberry, cassis, smoke, earthy, then a full hit of raisin.

Finish: Long and rich.

Conclusion: The sherry oak seems to link to the oil and play variations on that theme.

Flavor Camp: Rich & Round
Where Next? The GlenDronach 1989, Benromach 1981

RUBY 43%

Nose: Prunes mix with dried cherries, and with a sweet/savory edge akin to Barolo. Robust, yet sweet. Chocolate-covered Turkish delight.

Palate: Oloroso notes rub alongside Assam-like tannins. This is one to have with water on the side. Rich.

Finish: Long and deep.

Conclusion: Classical in structure and aromatics, with added vinous sweetness.

Flavor Camp: Rich & Round
Where Next? Aberlour A'Bunadh

Craigellachie

CRAIGELLACHIE • SPEYSIDE COOPERAGE • WWW.SPEYSIDECOOPERAGE.CO.UK • OPEN ALL YEAR MON–FRI

There is an element of resolution in this struggle between the old and the new, the light and the heavy, when we reach the final member of this, the largest of the Speyside clusters. Craigellachie looks both ways. It is a railway distillery, a late Victorian arrival, but it is one that has also retained older, traditional whisky-making ways. One of a number of distilleries built in the 1890s by a consortium of blenders and brokers, it was located here purely because of Craigellachie's transport links. This was the major rail junction in the days of the whisky trains and, by 1863, it was the station that linked Dufftown, Keith, Elgin, and Rothes with the Strathspey Railway.

If it took whisky out, it also brought raw materials and vistors to the area: the imposing Craigellachie Hotel was built in 1893 as a railway hotel. One of the blenders who had a stake in Craigellachie from the outset was Sir Peter Mackie, owner of White Horse Scotch Whisky and Lagavulin, and it was he who bought Craigellachie outright in 1915. Though the distillery has been extended and enlarged, it is the retention of older features that creates Craigellachie's singularity.

Nose the new make and there are the sulfury notes that have followed us across our Speyside journey. Instead of the meatiness seen elsewhere, however, there's a waxiness (waxed fruit?) on the nose, which then coats the tongue. Everything suggests that this is a weighty whisky, but one that is hiding another aspect of its personality. It's not so much shy, as sly.

"We use a sulfuring process in the malting stage," explains Keith Geddes, assistant master blender at present owner John Dewar & Sons. This is then enhanced in Craigellachie's large stills (allowing reflux) with a long spirit run ("just a trickle"), that directs the vapor into those worm tubs (*see* pp.14–15). "Copper removes sulfur," says Geddes, "and Craigellachie's worm tubs have less available copper.

Located in the middle of the village, Craigellachie is another of Speyside's many distilleries to be found close to the railway.

SPEYSIDE COOPERAGE

Located on a hill above Craigellachie, next to a field of Highland cows is a field filled with ziggurats of whisky casks. This is the Speyside Cooperage, which has been operating on this site since 1947. Now owned by French cooper Francois Frères, more than 100,000 casks are either repaired, recharred, or coopered from scratch here. There's also a visitors' center that affords people a rare insight into what remains a little-seen, yet vital, craft.

The sulfury new make character is always there and is a Craigellachie signature. We couldn't replicate this on any of our other sites, because they're all shell and tube sites."

As ever with sulfury sites, the question is: what lies beneath? "We could push it further if we wanted," says Geddes, "and take it into meaty territory, but we are looking for balance." That gravy-like depth in Dailuaine and Benrinnes isn't here. As it matures, Craigellachie moves into a world of exotic fruit, with that waxy feel on the tongue adding an extra textural element, which seems to enhance the very light smoke in older bottlings.

It is, in a strange way, like walking in reverse through the distillery, from the overcooked, cabbagey stench of the worms to the sweetness of the washbacks. This multifaceted complexity, this weight and fruit, this heavy/fragrant juxtaposition is a godsend to a blender, and one reason why Craigellachie is another malt that has remained in the chorus line. It was (unsurprisingly) a significant element within White Horse and is widely used by other blenders. Now, however, this most characterful of malts, this weird anomaly, the Janus of Strathspey, is taking center stage as part of John Dewar & Sons' belatedly welcome entry into the single-malt market.

Craigellachie is the perfect point at which to leave the Ben Rinnes cluster, a group of distilleries in which the entire history of Scotch can be seen. It would be easy to think that the spirit's journey has been one in which it has moved inexorably toward the big and the modern and the light, but this cluster shows that, throughout Scotland, the past is alive,

Wooden washbacks are just one of many traditional touches that help to maintain Craigellachie's singular character.

the old ways have been retained, and the link with the land, whether physical or emotional, has resulted in a collection of whiskies for which the uniqueness of site is the major factor in the creation of character.

CRAIGELLACHIE TASTING NOTES

NEW MAKE

Nose: Waxy. Vegetable. Radish. Boiled potato/starch. Light smoke.
Palate: Nutty and sweet with heavy beeswax and some sulfur notes. Heavy and full.
Finish: Deep and long. The vegetable returns.

14YO 40%

Nose: Pale gold. Waxed fruit. Quince. Fleshy, then apricot alongside light smoke and sealing wax and red currant. With water, there's wet reed, squash ball, and olive oil.
Palate: Light coconut before the feel takes over. Unctuous and glycerine-like. Jellied fresh fruits. Sweet yet solid.
Finish: Quince and then flour.
Conclusion: A blender's dream. A textural single malt.

Flavor Camp: **Fruity & Spicy**
Where Next? Clynelish 14yo, Scapa 16yo

1994, GORDON & MACPHAIL BOTTLING 46%

Nose: Gold in colour. Typically oily/waxy nose. Old saddle soap and soft tropical fruits with an added jag of citrus fruit.
Palate: Like eating waxed fruits. Rounded and palate-clinging. A little more estery with water, and a gentle honeyed/syrupy quality toward the finish.
Finish: Lightly spiced with touches of sweet dried tropical fruits.
Conclusion: Balanced and opening out. Expressive.

Flavor Camp: **Fruity & Spicy**
Where Next? Old Pulteney 17yo

1998 CASK SAMPLE 49.9%

Nose: Just emerging from its sulfury new-make shell, this is quite firm when neat. Light, fresh plum, and, with water, daffodils mix with purple fruit and then some honey.
Palate: Delicate smoke threads through a thick, rich mid-palate, where there is some mint and signature pineapple. Chewy and mouth-filling.
Finish: Long and thick.
Conclusion: Showing its mature potential.

THE DUFFTOWN CLUSTER

The self-proclaimed whisky capital of Speyside with its six distilleries on its fringes, Dufftown is little older than its first distillery, having been constructed in 1817 when James Duff built it as an improved town. Home to the world's biggest-selling single-malt brand and conceivably the world's biggest single malt (in terms of weight), this is a fine place to test the notion of *terroir*.

Steam rises into chilly winter air over the pagodas of The Balvenie.

Glenfiddich

DUFFTOWN • WWW.GLENFIDDICH.COM • OPEN ALL YEAR MON–SUN

As the world's best-selling single malt and the first distillery to open its doors (in 1969), it would be easy for a first-time visitor to Glenfiddich to expect a somewhat clichéd recreation of whisky-making, but instead they get the opposite. With 35 acres, this is a huge working site with its own cooperage, coppersmith, bottling line (all Glenfiddich is bottled on site), warehousing … and three distilleries. Glenfiddich is both a modern single-malt brand, but also a distillery where, despite the scale, traditional ethos of self-sufficiency has been retained.

Built by William Grant in 1886 and still owned by his descendants, the first spirit ran from its small stills (bought from Cardhu) on Christmas Day the following year. You can't help but feel that even in those early days, the founder had an eye on marketing.

Glenfiddich is about lightness of character, but walking into the stillhouse you'd think it would produce a similar style to Macallan. The stills are tiny, and science tells us, small stills will tend to produce a heavy, often sulfury new make (*see* pp.14–15). Nose Glenfiddich, however, and it's all grass, green apple, and pear. "We cut at high strength which is how we get this estery, clean spirit," says William Grant's master blender Brian Kinsman. "If we ran any deeper and cut later it would be much heavier and potentially sulfury."

So is this a case of a distillery running against type? "Not as far as we can tell," says Kinsman. "Glenfiddich, from our records, has always been light. The stills have always been that shape, and as demand grew we just built more of them." If they'd stuck at four stills and tried to cope with increased sales they'd have had to widen the cut in order to get more liquid—and changed the style. Building new stills was the only option in order to retain character. The fact that there are 28 stills in two stillhouses shows how big that demand is.

This lack of sulfur is also advantageous, Kinsman says, "because you don't have to overcome something before you start getting additive maturation." Even at three years of age, Glenfiddich is picking up wood notes: oak shavings in refill; ripe pineapple and creamy vanilla in first-fill bourbon; marmalade and white raisins in first-fill European … all cut with that green freshness.

A significant improvement in wood management and a rejigging of the wood mix has resulted in a much more coherent range. Whereas in the past Glenfiddich had a somewhat frustrating randomness about it, now there's a thread given by European oak, which is increased slowly with each age expression (bar the 21yo rum finish). As age takes hold, so the green apples of youth ripen, the cut grass dries, and a chocolate note slowly develops. For a light whisky, it manages to hold its own—even at 40 and 50 years. "The new make is light on the nose but it matures incredibly well," says Kinsman. "I think that freshness and intensity belies how much complexity is in there." For me, it seems to ride on a wave of oak, buoyed up by it but always remaining identifiably Glenfiddich.

The integration of oak and spirit is best personified by the pioneering establishment in 1998 of a *solera* vat for the 15yo. This Jerezano technique of fractional blending involves only removing 50% of the vat's contents for each bottling. This is then replaced with a mix

A large and complex distillery, Glenfiddich distils, matures, and bottles on site.

Glenfiddich is one of the last distilleries to have its own cooperage.

comprising of 70% from refill bourbon, 20% from European oak, and 10% in virgin oak. *Solera* blending not only adds depth (some whiskies have been there since 1998) but a different, softer mouth-feel. A similar technique is employed with the 40yo whose never-emptied vat contains remnants from the 1920s. Three new *solera* vats have recently been installed for its new "Cask" range.

It is this general amenability that holds the key to Glenfiddich's long-term aging ability—and, one might guess, is also the secret of its commercial success as well.

GLENFIDDICH TASTING NOTES

NEW MAKE

Nose: Crisp, clean, grassy, green apple, and in time ripe pineapple. Very pure and fresh.
Palate: Pears, grass, and esters. Light cereal background.
Finish: Light and fresh.

12YO 40%

Nose: The aroma is led by vanilla, then red apple, and a little white raisin in the background adding sweetness. With water some milk chocolate.
Palate: Sweet with plenty of vanilla, then a little Christmas pudding mix and mixed fruit. Gentle and smooth.
Finish: Buttery, but grassy.
Conclusion: The green notes of new make have now deepened and ripened. Some European oak has added depth.

Flavor Camp: **Fragrant & Floral**
Where Next? The Glenlivet 12yo, anCnoc 16yo

15YO 40%

Nose: Ripe and very soft with a character akin to plum jam and baked apple.
Palate: Soft and silky. Thicker than 12yo with stewed black fruit, coconut notes, and dried grass.
Finish: Ripe and full.
Conclusion: *Solera* adds a richer depth and feel.

Flavor Camp: **Rich & Round**
Where Next? Glencadam 1978, Blair Atholl 12yo

18YO 40%

Nose: More overt sherried notes: raisin and sherry-soaked dried fruit, mulberry, dark chocolate, and hay.
Palate: Concentrated dark fruit, more grip than the 15yo. Cacao, cedar.
Finish: Smooth, long, and still sweet.
Conclusion: The midpoint of the range as the freshness of youth gives way to the dark mysteries of age.

Flavor Camp: **Rich & Round**
Where Next? Jura 16yo, Royal Lochnagar Selected Reserve

21YO 40%

Nose: Deep amber. Sweet and oaky with coffee/cacao and a touch of cedar. Barley sugar and caramel toffee. Some black banana.
Palate: Rich and sweet with good length. Mocha, bitter chocolate and forest floor. Light tannins.
Finish: Dry oak. Leafy.
Conclusion: Has maturity, this has been given a finishing period in rum cask.

Flavor Camp: **Fruity & Spicy**
Where Next? Balblair 1990, Longmorn 16yo

30YO 40%

Nose: Resinous and thick. Ripe, rich, *rancioed*. Cigar humidor, nuttiness, and a surprisingly energetic lift.
Palate: Very smooth and silky. Flows over the tongue with a slight mossiness. Chocolate and coffee grounds now in charge.
Finish: Fading, but has residual sweetness.
Conclusion: The fruit has now been fully concentrated but that dry grassiness is retained giving a vestigial freshness.

Flavor Camp: **Rich & Round**
Where Next? Macallan 25yo Sherry Oak, Glen Grant 25yo

40YO 43.5%

Nose: Oily and resinous. Herbs, damp moss. Deep, rich. Whisky *rancio* but grassiness comes back, even at this advanced age. Beeswax. Slightly herbal.
Palate: Big and rounded with elegant chocolate notes: plum, espresso, mulberry. Oak is balanced because of the richness of the spirit. Relaxes to allow spices to come through. Light nutty, sherry.
Finish: Herbal and long.
Conclusion: A *solera*-style system used here with some of the original batch, containing whiskies from the 1920s to the 1940s, kept in the vat.

Flavor Camp: **Rich & Round**
Where Next? Dalmore, Candela 50yo

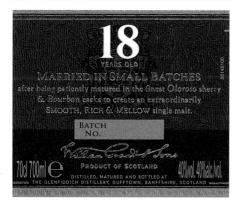

The Balvenie & Kininvie

THE BALVENIE • DUFFTOWN • WWW.THEBALVENIE.COM • OPEN ALL YEAR MON–FRI; BOOKING ESSENTIAL / KININVIE • DUFFTOWN

The second of the trio of distilleries on William Grant's Dufftown site, The Balvenie is no longer the little sister, the overlooked companion, the guarded cult, but a front-line single-malt brand in its own right. It also offers a good test for the notion of a Dufftown *terroir*. Three distilleries using the same water, identical malt, and virtually the same mashing, fermentation, and distillation regime yet producing three identifiably different malts. "The basic process is the same," says William Grant's master blender Brian Kinsman. "The only difference is the stills."

So where does that leave the importance of location as a contributor to flavor? "It will have some influence," he replies. "The ambient conditions within a plant will have an impact, somehow, on the character. You can tell this because even if you replicate a distillery in a different location—as we have done with Ailsa Bay (*see* p.148) you will not automatically get the same result. You need to change some elements in order to get the closest replication." And, as has been shown many times, that replication, while close, will never be identical. What we are talking about here therefore is not a regional (or even subregional) *terroir* but a site-specific *terroir*. The Balvenie, rather than the Dufftown site—or by extension Dufftown. Or Speyside.

Built in 1892, The Balvenie has retained its own malting floor, although it produces only a tiny percentage of the distillery's needs adding a small amount of peat. Anyone at The Balvenie will tell you, the key to its character is its fat, short-necked stills. These give a new make that is nutty and malty, but which has the sensation of a massing of fruit underneath, a glimpse of potential.

Even at seven years in refill cask, that nutty shell has cracked open allowing the sweet honeyed fruit to emerge. All through its aging this cereal note continues to shift down a gear, giving just a whisper of a dry structure as those fruits grow and expand.

If Glenfiddich is supported by wood, The Balvenie seems to absorb oak into itself, integrating the flavors from the oak and adding them to its honey-colored tapestry of taste. The Balvenie is never overwhelmed by wood—it's too big and fruity a dram for that.

It is this quality that prompted David Stewart, Grant's former master blender, to choose it as arguably the first "finished" whisky. Since then, the Balvenie range has expanded to include expressions finished in Madeira, rum, and port casks, while there is also a single-barrel range. In many ways it is the opposite to the slow build of Glenfiddich. At The Balvenie the whisky simply takes on board the new flavors introduced by different oaks and turns them to its advantage. The result is a wider range of flavors, but an equally strong identity.

In 1990, with demand for Glenfiddich growing, Grant's built yet another distillery on the site. Kininvie's function was to provide fillings for the (also expanding) Grant's blends. It has been misunderstood since Day One: a Glenfiddich copy, a Balvenie copy, a shed. None are true. Yes, mashing and fermentation take place within The Balvenie but, by law, Kininvie's production equipment has to be separate. Anyway, the fermentation regime is different. In the stillhouse (not a shed) there are nine stills, which give a floral new-make spirit that is light, sweet, estery, and different to its sisters. Not that many knew. Kininvie had to wait until 2013 for the first official bottling under its own name. Who knows? More may now follow.

The Balvenie still malts a small percentage of its own barley and dries it in its own kiln.

THE BALVENIE TASTING NOTES

NEW MAKE

Nose: Heavy. Nutty cereal, but great solid concentration of fruits behind. Very clean and sweet.

Palate: Cereal, robust, ripe. Nutty/muesli. Sweet.

Finish: Nutty and clean.

12YO, DOUBLE WOOD 40%

Nose: Sweet but in a mixed-peel way. Beeswax and pollen alongside light Scottish fruitcake. Touch of struck match.

Palate: Fatter than Signature with softer fruit. Chewy and juicy. Light grip from a combination of sherry cask and nuttiness. Cut peels and honey.

Finish: Long and with a little dried fruit.

Conclusion: A balance struck between evolving character and cask.

> **Flavor Camp: Fruity & Spicy**
> **Where Next?** The BenRiach 16yo, Longmorn 16yo

14YO CARIBBEAN CASK (RUM FINISH) 43%

Nose: Shows big, honeyed fruit typical of the distillery, but here with more banana, *crème brûlée*, thick Greek yogurt, stewed peaches, light corn syrup, and mint.

Palate: Thick and unctuous. Flavor oozes across the palate with ripe tropical fruits.

Finish: Long and sweet, with a touch of cereal.

Conclusion: Very Balvenie, but in tropical guise. The sweetest of the range.

> **Flavor Camp: Fruity & Spicy**
> **Where Next?** Glenmorangie Nectar d'Or

17YO, DOUBLE WOOD 43%

Nose: Deep and rich, with notes of Phoenix Honey Orchid (oolong) tea, and a little touch of malt and toasted oak. Chestnut honey this time.

Palate: Fine-textured and sweet, with a shift toward mellow mature wood. A little cacao.

Finish: Long and gentle.

Conclusion: The richest of the range.

> **Flavor Camp: Rich & Round**
> **Where Next?** Cardhu 18yo

21YO, PORTWOOD 40%

Nose: Full concentration. Cherry, rosehip syrup, planed oak, with wood smoke behind.

Palate: Unctuous, but honeyed. The fruit seems fresher than the 17yo Madeira, more mixed red and black with integrated oak. Powerful but sweet.

Finish: Long and sweet.

Conclusion: Though this is growing in weight, there's a clear line to the 12yo.

> **Flavor Camp: Fruity & Spicy**
> **Where Next?** Strathisla 18yo

30YO 47.3%

Nose: Masses of coconut and cooked orange peel. Luscious and soft.

Palate: Gentle, oozing, long, and ripe and, yes, honeyed. Ripe sweet orchard fruit, light oak, and a hint of sweet spice.

Finish: Sweet and full.

Conclusion: Has the languorous length of a slow-matured whisky.

> **Flavor Camp: Fruity & Spicy**
> **Where Next?** Tamdhu 32yo

KININVIE TASTING NOTES

NEW MAKE

Nose: Light and predominantly flowery and perfumed. Estery and clean.

Palate: Hay. Floral, leafy, and crisp. The lightest but also driest of the Dufftown trio.

Finish: Clean and short.

6YO CASK SAMPLE

Nose: Hugely floral. Fresh bouquet with vanilla bean.

Palate: Light, fragrant (hyacinth), lifted, sweet, and effusive.

Finish: Short and sweet.

Conclusion: A quick maturing style.

BATCH NUMBER ONE, 23YO 42.6%

Nose: Shows fruit blossom, wildflower meadow, sugared plums, and an old-fashioned candy shop. Water brings out grass and pineapple.

Palate: The oak is very restrained, allowing the palate to build in sweetness. There are notes of star fruit and white peaches.

Finish: Light citrus fruit.

Conclusion: Hidden depths and substantially different to its siblings.

> **Flavor Camp: Fruity & Spicy**
> **Where Next?** Craigellachie

Mortlach, Glendullan & Dufftown

MORTLACH • DUFFTOWN
GLENDULLAN • DUFFTOWN • WWW.MALTS.COM/INDEX.PHP/OUR-WHISKIES/THE-SINGLETON-OF-GLENDULLAN
DUFFTOWN • WWW.MALTS.COM/INDEX.PHP/OUR-WHISKIES/THE-SINGLETON-OF-DUFFTOWN

There's a hidden side to Dufftown's half-dozen malts, one that taps into that older, more mysterious Speyside and it's fittingly found in Mortlach, the name both of the original settlement and the town's oldest distillery, which was built in 1823 by James Findlater, Donald Mackintosh, and Alex Gordon, probably on the site of an older illicit operation.

If you can split Speyside into three—malty, fragrant, and heavy—then here's a member of the last group, perhaps the heaviest of them all. Mortlach's robust, meaty whisky is another which talks of older times, of woods and hollowways, of times when the soul needed serious, belly-filling fortification.

Where does the meaty style come from? "We don't know when it originated," says Diageo's master distiller and blender, Douglas Murray. "We inherited it." Perhaps it came from the illicit days, certainly in its use of worm tubs and a complex distillation regime, which on first glance seems somewhat improvised.

In a similar way to Benrinnes, Mortlach uses partial triple-distillation in order to build up the meaty element. Mortlach, Murray says blithely, "is distilled 2.7 times." Everything revolves around what happens in the stillhouse, where a seemingly random collection of stills have been assembled. There are half a dozen of these weird beasts: one triangular, some thin-necked, and a tiny afterthought in the corner, which is known as "the Wee Witchie."

The easiest way to try and understand the distillation regime here is to think of Mortlach as having two stillhouses. Two stills work as normal. Then wash stills Numbers 1 and 2 work in tandem. The first 80% of the run is collected as the charge for the Number 2 spirit still. The remaining (weak) 20% is destined for the Wee Witchie. This is charged, run, and all the spirit is collected. This is repeated twice with the middle cut only being collected on the third run. It's from the Wee Witchie that Mortlach's meatiness comes, but to get meaty you also

need sulfury, which means no copper. Mortlach therefore runs flat out with condensing done using cold worm tubs.

At its best in European oak, Mortlach was a little-seen cult malt. This throwback to the old days, to days before Dufftown even existed, is at the foundation of many famous blends. With the building of a new stillhouse, production has doubled and Mortlach is finally a front-line malt, combining this dark reduction of whisky with a new, refined, pleasure.

Mortlach, on its steep-sided hill, overlooks Dullan Water and the two distilleries sheltering there. Glendullan itself started in 1897, though the current box plant was built in 1962. It was here that billeted troops in World War II, who, overcome with fumes (or desire), rammed the warehouses with a gun carriage. The "dull" in the name somewhat detracts from the whisky itself, whose aromatic grapey lift in youth develops into a sloe-berry sweetness by the time it is a 12yo, and a member of Diageo's Singleton range, which also includes Dufftown and Glen Ord.

The glen is also home to Dufftown distillery, one of many former mills that have been converted into distilleries. Built the year before Glendullan, it is another whose destiny has always been inextricably linked with blends. If Mortlach is a representative of an ultra-traditional style, then Dufftown is a shape-shifter. A nutty/malty site in its days as a member of the Bell's estate, these days the new make is in the grassy camp. It, too, is a Singleton brand.

One town, six distilleries and every Flavor Camp (bar smoky) covered. Maybe that "Capital of Whisky" moniker is justified.

In the glen outside Dufftown sit three distilleries each making its own very distinct whisky.

MORTLACH TASTING NOTES

NEW MAKE

Nose: Dry, sulfury smoke. Powerful, meaty, and heavy. Beef-stock-like density.

Palate: Feral. Old woods, meat stock, fireworks. Muscular.

Finish: Thick and hot.

RARE OLD 43.4%

Nose: Ripe, deep fruit with nut-bowl sherried notes mix with game pie. In time there's quince, dried apple, licorice, and dark chocolate. Water brings out marmalade, chestnut, and praline.

Palate: Chewy and sweet. Dives deep quickly with oxidative notes before shifting into dark, inky, light Scottish fruitcake (almond and dried fruit). Thick and rich.

Finish: Dried fruit.

Conclusion: Not as meatily sherried as the old 16yo, but clearly Mortlach.

> Flavor Camp: **Rich & Round**
> Where Next? Dalmore 15yo

25YO 43.4%

Nose: Refined, with an aroma akin to the leather interior of a vintage car. A surprising note of mint adds freshness. Earthy and slightly meaty.

Palate: Grippy, dense, and mature with elegant bruised fruit, chestnut, sandalwood, and cigar-box tones. An interesting mix of meat and cream.

Finish: Long and fruity. Rich.

Conclusion: Elegant and long.

> Flavor Camp: **Rich & Round**
> Where Next? Macallan Sienna

GLENDULLAN TASTING NOTES

NEW MAKE

Nose: Perfumed, light, and floral (freesia); grape-like blossom. Becomes green grassy.

Palate: Quite dry, then delicate patisserie fruit. Very soft and gentle.

Finish: Light, clean, and quick.

8YO, REFILL WOOD CASK SAMPLE

Nose: Aromatic and lifted. Dessert apple. Sharp and slightly perfumed. Light lemon. Floral/aniseed. Bouquet-like.

Palate: All fresh and delicate. The freesia still there along with lemon and light acidity.

Finish: Clean and sharp.

Conclusion: Freshness. Impression is it will be best in a refill cask since it's easily dominated by active oak.

12YO, FLORA & FAUNA 43%

Nose: Light and gentle with some wood influence and a touch of sawdust. Apple continues to show, now with added custard from the wood.

Palate: Delicate, almost transparent to start then a twang of acidity halfway in bursts it open. Fragrant.

Finish: Lemon.

Conclusion: A slow development from the 8yo with just a little uptake of oak.

> Flavor Camp: **Fragrant & Floral**
> Where Next? Linkwood

THE SINGLETON OF GLENDULLAN, 12YO 40%

Nose: Full gold. Sherried with Moscatel-like sweetness and dusky sloe berry. Still aromatic but now the dried fruit is taking charge. Firm wood.

Palate: Light fruit. Black grapes and fruit sugars, then comes a mellow European-oak richness. The aromatic intensity is still there though the acidity has gone.

Finish: Gentle. Sweet almost jammy.

Conclusion: Still (just) Glendullan but cask now in charge.

> Flavor Camp: **Fruity & Spicy**
> Where Next? Glenfiddich 15yo, Glenmorangie Lasanta, Fettercairn 16yo

DUFFTOWN TASTING NOTES

NEW MAKE

Nose: Slightly bready, pineapple, estery, touch of wheat chaff.

Palate: Clean, estery fruitiness. High-toned and sharp with some cereal behind.

Finish: Nutty and clean.

8YO, REFILL WOOD CASK SAMPLE

Nose: Very clean. Malty, wheat breakfast cereal, touch of farmyard, malt bin.

Palate: Dry and quite crisp. Nutty, then a sweet hit that sinks very slightly onto the tongue.

Finish: Sesame.

Conclusion: Clean and nutty—a good example of old-style Dufftown.

THE SINGLETON OF DUFFTOWN, 12YO 40%

Nose: Sweet and figgy with a nut-shell undertow. Opens into sawn oak, draff, then marshmallow, and a touch of apple and fig relish.

Palate: Nut oils. Quite cookie-like and rich. Leafy.

Finish: Crisp, short.

Conclusion: European oak taking the (old) dry Dufftown character into a sweeter realm.

> Flavor Camp: **Rich & Round**
> Where Next? Jura 16yo

THE SINGLETON OF DUFFTOWN, 15YO 40%

Nose: Rich, with a cereal underpinning. Bran flakes and muesli with warm milk. Sweet. More lifted with water. Moist autumn woods.

Palate: Sweet and quite gentle. It firms just slightly in the center, but is all very approachable and eager to please.

Finish: Rich fruit emerges, then the oak dries.

Conclusion: The sweet Singleton signature is here allied to Dufftown in its nutty guise.

> Flavor Camp: **Rich & Round**
> Where Next? Singleton of Glendullan

KEITH TO THE EASTERN BOUNDARY

The importance of the blenders is seen clearly in the distilleries that surround the small town of Keith. Here are distilleries whose life has been spent in their service.

The Auld Brig at Keith has carried whisky over the Isla River for centuries.

Strathisla

KEITH • WWW.MALTWHISKYDISTILLERIES.COM • OPEN APR–OCT, MON–SUN; JAN–MAR, MON–FRI

Although it is unofficially recognized as the prettiest distillery in Scotland, Strathisla's whisky is surprisingly less well-known. In fact, none of the Keith cluster is a front-line single-malt brand. In this part of Speyside, whisky-makers keep their heads down and produce their spirit for blends—no matter how attractive their distilleries may be.

At Strathisla, this blend connection runs deep. This is a malt-whisky distillery that is a tourist attraction—people are rightly drawn to its cobbled courtyard, manicured lawns, and waterwheel—but it subsumes its own individual personality to act as the spiritual home of a blend: in Strathisla's case, Chivas Regal. While this is perfectly common practice, it obscures Strathisla's main claim to fame: this is the oldest licensed malt distillery in Scotland.

Some form of alcohol has been made on this site for 700 years. A monastic brewery stood on the site in the thirteenth century, while the Milton distillery (as Strathisla was known until 1953) took out a license in 1786, right at the start of the whisky-smuggling era.

Its spirit, however, doesn't conform to the old/heavy template, though the merest touch of sulfur in the new make suggests that there's some desire on the part of the plant to cleave to these older ways. The key lies in the stillhouse where the necks of the small stills rise into the rafters. "What's strange about Strathisla is that it's trying to make the light Speyside style, but these small stills can end up giving that wee touch of sulfur, and an aroma like pot ale," says Chivas Brothers' distilleries manager, Alan Winchester. "But there's a fruitiness that's sitting behind that."

It takes time for that to come to the fore. Strathisla seems to be made up of three distinct pieces: a mossy-woods note, the soft fruit, and

A candidate for Scotland's prettiest distillery, Strathisla has been making whisky since 1786.

floral top notes. As it matures, these rise and fall: mossiness when young; fruits and orange when aged. That's great blending material.

STRATHISLA TASTING NOTES

NEW MAKE

Nose: Clean with sweet mash, damp hay, and moss. Lightly floral, then a little burnt/sulfury note.
Palate: Very pure. Sweet, fine-bodied with very gentle fruit in the middle.
Finish: Cereal at the end.

12YO 40%

Nose: Copper, sweet oak, plenty of light coconut; green moss, citrus pulp, quince. Singed note at back.
Palate: Sweet vanilla, white chocolate. Very clean, with a cashew-like flavor, dry grass, and light fruits.
Finish: Toasted. Lightly perfumed.
Conclusion: Strathisla starts its life light and almost fragile—but watch what happens.

Flavor Camp: **Fragrant & Floral**
Where Next? Cardhu 12yo

18YO 40%

Nose: Copper. Wood-driven, with a toasted nuttiness. The moss has changed to green fern. Now comes more soft white fruit, a hint of honey, deeper florals, and dried apples.
Palate: Rounder than the 12yo with a more solid middle palate. Green plum then crisp wood.
Finish: Bone dry and spicy.
Conclusion: In its teens the fruits begin to build in strength.

Flavor Camp: **Fruity & Spicy**
Where Next? Glengoyne 10yo, Benromach 25yo

25YO 53.3%

Nose: Bigger (sherry) cask influence. Some *rancio*, dried mushroom, vetiver. Deep and sweet, with fruitcake batter.
Palate: Full, soft, and light with some orange peel. Then its full ripeness shows, once again, in the middle of the tongue, where it deepens finally into orange-blossom honey. Succulent.
Finish: Long, soft, and clean.
Conclusion: It has finally emerged from the woods.

Flavor Camp: **Rich & Round**
Where Next? Springbank 18yo

Strathmill & Glen Keith

STRATHMILL • KEITH / GLEN KEITH • KEITH

Keith itself has a long history of mills, most powered by the Isla River, which snakes its way through the town. These grew in importance during the eighteenth century when the Earl of Findlater built "New Keith." The water powered woolen mills, while locally grown cereal crops were also ground here. In 1892, one of these cereal mills was converted into a distillery: Glenisla-Glenlivet. There was considerably more money to be made in whisky than in bread.

Glenisla was soon sold to the gin producer W&A Gilbey, who changed its name to Strathmill and in time the make became an integral part of J&B. It's worth noting that all of the distilleries within this little cluster provide spirit for lighter-bodied blends.

Strathmill has an intriguing olive-oil note, which adds a slick texture to its inherently light character. The oiliness, as in Glenlossie, is the result of a purifier pipe on the lyne arm of the spirit still, which increases reflux—a lightening technique. It was installed in 1968.

This search for the delicate through the use of different distillation techniques was also found at the Glen Keith distillery, built behind Strathisla in 1958. As former owner Seagram's test plant, in its time it has made triple-distilled malt, "Bushmills"-style whisky, even peated. The six slender stills, with their upward lyne arms looking like elephants' trunks testing the air, fell silent in 1999. Now it has been retro-fitted with a new, larger mash tun and extra washbacks, and is running again. Keith has its third still back.

The Glen Keith distillery has now reopened.

STRATHMILL TASTING NOTES

NEW MAKE
Nose: Olive oil, fresh corn with butter. Has a discreet substance. Fresh yeast and a hint of red fruit.
Palate: Needle-sharp, quite hot. Evaporates on the tongue. With water, it shows its weight and the raspberry leaf emerges.
Finish: Zingy and hot.

8YO, REFILL WOOD CASK SAMPLE
Nose: Rounded and buttery moving into honey, plus a hint of old-fashioned talcum powder and delicate rose. Still hard.
Palate: Grassy and quite clean with a little violet and that red-fruit acidity seen in new make.
Finish: Clean and still tense.
Conclusion: Light, but that buttery quality gives the weight to cope with aging.

12YO, FLORA & FAUNA 43%
Nose: Dry and reminiscent of oatmeal with light-brown sugar. Toasted corn and hint of honey.
Palate: The honeyed quality comes through strongly. The red fruit has gone and given way to an intense coriander-seed spiciness.
Finish: Clean and lifted.
Conclusion: Another which develops interestingly... and relatively quickly.

Flavor Camp: **Fragrant & Floral**
Where Next? The Glenturret 10yo, Yamazaki 10yo

GLEN KEITH TASTING NOTES

NEW MAKE
Nose: Very clean and quite fruity, with hints of light apricot and canned tomato soup/tomato vine. Chalky with water.
Palate: Clean and very pure, with good weight and some sweetness. Thickens into violets.
Finish: Clean and sharp.

17YO 54.9%
Nose: Perfumed and estery with verjus, a little wisteria, and frangipane, cooking apple, and fresh plum. With water, a little starchy cereal and some cookie notes show their hand.
Palate: Gentle and softly spreading, with light tangerine and cool melon tones. A burst of lemon enlivens the mid-palate.
Finish: Crisp and clean, with a little flour.
Conclusion: Delicate and fresh.

Flavor Camp: **Fragrant & Floral**
Where Next? Kavalan Classic

Aultmore & Glentauchers

AULTMORE • KEITH / GLENTAUCHERS • KEITH

The Keith cluster's willingness to play a supporting role is repeated at Aultmore. Built in 1896 to take advantage of the blend boom, it has played a central role within John Dewar & Sons since 1923. Indeed, the deal-breaker when Dewar's was bought by Bacardi from UDV was over who would hold on to Aultmore. It's another forgotten jewel. A modern plant, it stands strangely isolated on a bluff looking south toward Keith, the sea wind at its back.

Its slightly anonymous interior is more than compensated for in the new-make spirit coming from its small stills with their downward-looking lyne arms. Its penetrating, grassy intensity with subtle depth gives energy and drive to a blend. Now, however, it is finally getting the single-malt treatment as part of Dewar's new range. The prized asset may yet be finally understood.

Heading west toward Rothes from Keith you pass by yet another one of those "What's its name again?" distilleries. Unseen as a major malt brand, Glentauchers' six stills have been producing whisky since 1898, originally for James Buchanan's Black & White blend. For a short period at the start of the twentieth century it distilled malt whisky through a column still (a technique that the Scotch Whisky Association recently deemed "nontraditional").

Mothballed in 1985, it became part of Allied Distillers (now Chivas Brothers) which, since its purchase in 1989, have removed any peatiness in the barley used and balanced the distillation of its six stills. "We wanted to bring this into the fruity/floral camp," explains distilleries manager Alan Winchester. His enthusiasm for the spirit is shared by blenders, such as Chivas Brothers' Sandy Hyslop, who uses its grassy/floral character in blends such as Ballantine's.

Keeping an eye on the spirit. Collecting the right flavors in the middle cut is the most important part of a stillman's job.

AULTMORE TASTING NOTES

NEW MAKE

Nose: Sweet. Scallion. Grassy.
Palate: Sweet but firm. Full weight. A bit burnt. Rounded.
Finish: Strawberry and melon, which again may develop into something interesting.

16YO, DEWAR RATTRAY 57.9%

Nose: Rich and heavily sherried. Fig rolls, fruitcake, bitter orange, and light, almost tarry note. Sweeter with water: sweet coffee, some perfume on top.
Palate: Ripe with tomato leaf, black cherry, walnut, and seemingly, smoke. Good grip balances a silky feel.
Finish: Long and generous.
Conclusion: Heavily influenced by cask but that floral quality just discernible on the nose.

Flavor Camp: Rich & Round
Where Next? Royal Lochnagar Selected Reserve, Aberlour 16yo

1998 CASK SAMPLE 50.9%

Nose: Light and lifted, with delicate fruit. Very precise. Light, buttery oak gives a creamy substance. With water, it shows a hint of canola oil and sesame, poached pear and apple.
Palate: Clean, with fresh acidity. There's a central sweetness, and good length for something that initially appears light. Subtle weight.
Finish: Fragrant and soft.
Conclusion: Aultmore is all about control. This has it.

GLENTAUCHERS TASTING NOTES

NEW MAKE

Nose: Grassy, light. An unusual note of chocolate-coated graham crackers, then tea leaf and florals.
Palate: Light and pure. Slightly fizzy, light, and ethereal.
Finish: Clean.

1991, GORDON & MACPHAIL BOTTLING 43%

Nose: Pale gold. Typical of the light and floral distillery character. High-toned with hyacinth, bluebell, and a little rose. Clean, sweet oak. Still delicate.
Palate: Fresh and whisper-light. Little hint of ripe red apple then some lemon verbena.
Finish: Short and light.
Conclusion: A little more substance than the oak but gently handled so as not to drown this fragile whisky.

Flavor Camp: Fragrant & Floral
Where Next? Bladnoch 8yo, anCnoc 16yo

Auchroisk & Inchgower

AUCHROISK • KEITH / INCHGOWER • BUCKIE

Just as mature spirits can be placed on a flavor wheel or map, so new-make character has an industry-shared list of descriptors. If two distillers were talking about a similar character but one called it "cereal," while the other said "hamster cages," then there could be confusion. If they both agree to call it nutty/spicy then things become considerably easier.

That's not to say that all nutty/spicy sites make identical whisky. The final two members of the Keith cluster belong to this new-make family, but are in fact at either ends of the spectrum.

"Nutty/spicy is in fact two camps," says Douglas Murray, Diageo's master distiller and blender, aka The Guru. "If you mash quickly and pull solids through, that's nutty/cereal. If you mash at a higher temperature on the second water you can take out the cereal note and end up with spicy. In the fermenter that cloudy wort will give nutty/spicy if you ferment for 45 to 50 hours. Ferment for longer and the character changes. The danger is that if you speed up production and cut

ferment times and get cloudy wort, then you lose your character and make nutty/spicy," (*see* pp.14–15).

Auchroisk is a modern, angular white-rendered distillery on the Keith to Rothes road. Here the new-make style has a heavy, almost burnt nuttiness created by overboiling the wash still and allowing some solids to come over. Once in wood this singed note dies off and is replaced by sweetness.

Inchgower on the other hand is intensely spicy, which may account for this coastal distillery in Buckie seemingly having a saline edge and a new-make aroma that's akin to tomato sauce. "There are lots of tanks at Inchgower," says Murray, "and lots of tanks in the system pushes that spiciness toward waxiness. Remember, all sites do not make one flavor descriptor but a unique mix of flavors and intensity. Small changes give big character variations."

AUCHROISK TASTING NOTES

NEW MAKE

Nose: Burnt. Heavy cereal. Bran flakes. Pot ale.
Palate: Firm crisp, wheat germ. Quite hard. Beneath there's a nodule of sweetness.
Finish: Dry.

8YO, REFILL WOOD CASK SAMPLE

Nose: Cookies, light citrus fruit. Singed grass. Carpet shop, a little rubber.
Palate: Dry but clean. Assam tea. Chalky.
Finish: Still firm.
Conclusion: Is purified but still needs time to sweeten fully.

10YO, FLORA & FAUNA 43%

Nose: Considerably sweeter with more nuttiness. Sugary with cashews and macadamia nuts, hints of wild herbs (lemon balm). The burnt note has receded into a roasted depth.
Palate: The suggestion of sweetness in new make and 8yo is now brought out by coconutty, sweet-cask influence, which has the effect of riding over the wheat-chaff maltiness.
Finish: Still dry.
Conclusion: It has taken a decade of slow maturation in refill to start to reveal its full and pretty, sweet personality.

Flavor Camp: **Malty & Dry**
Where Next? Speyside 12yo

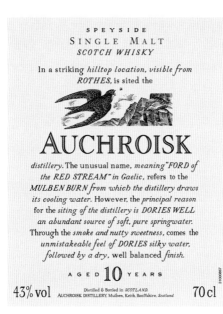

SPEYSIDE
SINGLE MALT
SCOTCH WHISKY

In a striking *hilltop location, visible from ROTHES,* is sited the

AUCHROISK

distillery. The unusual name, *meaning "FORD of the RED STREAM" in Gaelic,* refers to the MULBEN BURN *from which the distillery draws its cooling water.* However, the *principal reason for the siting of the distillery is DORIES WELL an abundant source of soft, pure springwater.* Through the *smoke and nutty sweetness,* comes the unmistakeable feel of *DORIES silky water,* followed by a *dry,* well balanced *finish.*

AGED **10** YEARS

43% vol   70cl

INCHGOWER TASTING NOTES

NEW MAKE

Nose: High-toned and very intense. Tomato sauce, green malt, cucumber. Slightly saline. Touch of geranium.
Palate: Acidic, nutty. Spritzy, sea-spray feel. Tingling, spicy.
Finish: Salted nuts.

8YO, REFILL WOOD CASK SAMPLE

Nose: Still intense now with added lemon and lime (almost young/fermenting Sémillon). The fruit is restrained, hard, and green. Green jelly.
Palate: Retained that salinity. Light and clean with the nuttiness taking charge late on.
Finish: Spicy.
Conclusion: A hard nut to crack. Still coming together.

14YO, FLORA & FAUNA 43%

Nose: Still intensely spicy—and it might be that spice that gives the impression of saltiness. Lemon puffs, vanilla ice cream, and wood smoke.
Palate: The highly focused spicy distillery character dominates at start and toward the back, effectively squeezing any sweetness into a small spot in the center of the tongue.
Finish: Energetic and salty.
Conclusion: A once-only example with such a powerful distillery character that you doubt if it will ever be dominated.

Flavor Camp: **Fruity & Spicy**
Where Next? Old Pulteney 12yo, Glengoyne 10yo

THE ROTHES CLUSTER

Although it could give Dufftown a run for its money for the title of Speyside's whisky capital, Rothes seems to prefer to draw a veil over its whisky-making activities. Yet here they range from the world's leading producer of pot-stills, through a selection of top-class distilleries, to a dark-grains plant that processes all the residue, turning it into cattle feed. All whisky is here.

Slumbering in the crepuscular warehouses at Glen Grant.

Glen Grant

ROTHES • WWW.GLENGRANT.COM • OPEN ALL YEAR; SEE WEBSITE FOR DAYS & DETAILS

John and James Grant moved to Rothes to establish its first distillery in 1840 after some experience of distilling in Aberlour. John was a gentleman distiller, James an engineer and politician. The year after the distillery appeared, James proposed to the Elgin and Lossiemouth Harbour Co. that a railway should be built, linking the Lossiemouth port to Elgin, and that it should be extended to Craigellachie, via Rothes. Eventually it was, but only thanks to the Grant brothers bankrolling it to the tune of £4,500 ($6,793).

While James was machinating, John was creating not just a distillery but an estate. Distilleries are, by nature, functional, and while their locations may be spectacular or their architecture aesthetically pleasing, they are essentially industrial sites. Glen Grant is an exception and as such it speaks volumes about not just the remarkable family which ran it until 1978, but the arrival of the gentleman distiller. No other distillery can quite match the extravagances of John Grant and, more significantly, his son John (aka The Major) who took over in 1872.

Extravagantly mustachioed, seemingly never without a rod or gun, The Major was the epitome of Victorian sensibilities: a big-game hunter, a playboy, interested in engineering and innovation. He was the first man to have a car in the Highlands, the first man there to have an electric light (powered by water turbines in the distillery). Rothes is an unlikely place to find grapes and peaches (even today, a lemon in the local shop is unusual), yet all grew in the Major's stately pleasure dome next to where the Spey did run.

Glen Grant remains a manifestation of The Major's restlessness. It started as a two-stiller, then expanded to four, but one pair

THE SAD TALE OF CAPERDONICH

In 1898, The Major set up another distillery next to the railway line. Caperdonich promptly closed in 1902, reopened in 1965, and closed again in 2003. "Why did it fail?" asks Malcolm. "It had the same water, the same yeast—even the same manager. But they had a different shape of still, though even when they put in the German helmet it still didn't make Glen Grant." The site is now part of coppersmith Forsyths' workshops, which, with order books bulging, certainly need the space!

comprised a large wash still and a small spirit, "Wee Geordie." When a new stillhouse was built in the 1960s, it ran on gas fires while the old stillhouse was on coal.

Today, there are eight massive, steam-driven stills, the wash ones with a "German helmet" bulge at the base of their bull necks. All of the lyne arms then take a dip into purifying tanks. "The purifiers have been here since the Major," says Dennis Malcolm, Glen Grant's master distiller. "It's clear that he wanted to make a lighter spirit." These days, the new make is whistle-clean, all green grass, apple,

The distillery's water runs beside the woodland paths of "The Major's" famed Victorian garden, a visitor attraction in its own right.

The new and ultra-modern visitors' center features "help yourself" dramming.

and bubblegum. The process started by The Major has been constantly tweaked in order to get to this point. Wee Geordie ("which gave a heavier style") was retired in 1975; coal went, then gas; the final wisps of peat disappeared in 1972; while sherry casks have been replaced primarily with ex-bourbon.

It was its lightness that endeared Glen Grant to the Italian market—this was the biggest-selling single malt for many years thanks to its dominance there—a link that was finally cemented when Gruppo Campari bought Glen Grant, brand and all, for £170 million ($256 million) in 2006. Since then, millions more have been spent by Malcolm, helping to bring the distillery and The Major's gardens back to life.

In the tranquil garden—alive with birdsong and the smell of privet hedges, brown foaming water rampaging over the rocks—sipping a dram from The Major's safe in a cliffside cave, looking back into the sun, a golden haze over the garden, you are for a second back in whisky's gentlemanly interlude, with raked paths, peaches in your greenhouses, your Rolls-Royce in the garage.

GLEN GRANT TASTING NOTES

NEW MAKE

Nose: Very clean and sweet. Green apples, flowers, and bubblegum with a hint of yeast behind. Lifted and high-toned.
Palate: Immediate fruity/estery notes of apple and pineapple. Pure and clean.
Finish: Lightly floral.

10YO 40%

Nose: Pale gold. Light and floral with a vanilla undertone. Estery. The fruits have been ripened and, in the pineapple's case, canned. With water, cupcakes, hyacinth.
Palate: Light with a sappy quality. Good wood here, giving lots of creaminess while adding a subtle sweet spice.
Finish: Soft with a hint of green grape.
Conclusion: Clean, light, and refreshing.

Flavor Camp: **Fragrant & Floral**
Where Next? Mannochmore 12yo

MAJOR'S RESERVE 40%

Nose: Clean and quite zesty, with crisp apple, a touch of mint, cucumber, kiwi fruit, and a delicate, drying barley note.
Palate: Effervescent and delicate. White-wine notes, some greengage jam, strawberry, gooseberry.
Finish: Tight and clean.
Conclusion: The light, fresh introduction to the Glen Grant range. Have with ice and soda as an aperitif.

Flavor Camp: **Fragrant & Floral**
Where Next? Hakushu 12yo

V (FIVE) DECADES 46%

Nose: Classic Glen Grant lift and energy: green apple, fruit blossom, pear and yellow fruit; lemon-butter frosting and nettles with water.
Palate: Vibrant and energetic, but holds to the middle of the tongue, where some luscious oak develops.
Finish: Long, mellow, and sweet.
Conclusion: Created by legendary distillery manager Dennis Malcolm to celebrate his half-century at Glen Grant, this uses casks from each of his five decades.

Flavor Camp: **Fragrant & FLoral**
Where Next? The Glenlivet XXV

The Glenrothes

THE GLENROTHES • ROTHES

In the old Rothes graveyard, its tombstones covered with what look like mourning weeds, stands a grave-watcher's house where, in the eighteenth century, mourning relatives would station themselves immediately after committal. Here they would remain until the decomposition of their beloved's corpse eliminated any chance of body-snatching taking place. Their morbid vigil, one imagines, would have required regular fortification with illicit hooch brought down from the neigboring hills.

The body-snatching era had long gone by the time the new Glenrothes distillery was established in 1878. The graveyard returned to being a place of peace rather than desecration, the fumes from the distillery triggering the slow growth of the black crepe-like fungus that festoons the tombs. The siting of the distillery, graveyard apart, is further evidence of how the liberalization of distilling laws in 1823 brought about a physical change to Speyside's distilleries. No longer did they have to be secreted in peat sheds, *shielings*, and remote farms. Now, as distillers moved from the moonlight into daylight, they also moved into the area's towns, though old habits appear to have died hard. All of this whisky town's distilleries still remain a discreet distance from the main street.

The Glenrothes however almost failed to become a Rothes plant. Soon after its establishment it immediately ran into financial difficulties when the Glasgow Bank went belly-up. It was only saved a year later thanks to a cash injection from the unlikeliest source, the United Free Presbyterian Church of Knockando, who put aside its teetotal beliefs when it saw a sound business opportunity.

The congregation would be surprised by what sits on the site today. The Glenrothes has expanded dramatically from its old core. Today there are 10 stills (five wash, five spirit) producing its whisky.

A quick mashing cycle gives worts which are pumped into either stainless steel or wooden washbacks. While debate continues over the benefits of one type over the other, very few distilleries have this halfway house. This suggests to the casual observer that The Glenrothes' distillers feel there is no difference in character between the two; that's not necesarily true. Each charge of the wash still is from two wooden to one steel. Changing over entirely to stainless steel might just have changed the character.

A combination of long (90-hour) and short (55-hour) fermentations also necessitates a slight tweak in order to preserve character. These are set at different temperatures (both in steel or wood) and depend on the length of ferment to iron out any differences in flavor.

It's in The Glenrothes' cathedral-like stillhouse that the true character is created. Here the stillman sits, framed between the ten pots. All are

The Glenrothes, a late nineteenth-century distillery, soon transported its A-listed whisky south to the blenders.

The Glenrothes pack is modeled on old sample-room bottles and each is signed by its whisky-maker.

big, with boil bulbs to increase reflux and a very slow distillation to tease out the rich, soft fruitiness that sits at The Glenrothes' heart.

The new make is filled mostly into ex-sherry casks—the distillery itself is owned by that great sherry-lover, the Edrington Group. Until recently most of it went to blends—not just Grouse but Chivas and other top makes. Its hidden location, one feels, wasn't just physical but philosophical. It did its work out of sight, behind the scenes.

Recently, however, it has come into the new world of single malt thanks to its brand owner, the London wine merchant, Berry Bros. & Rudd, which has taken its 300 years of expertise in fine wine and applied it to single malt. The Glenrothes doesn't conform to the standard approach of age statements but is released in vintages to show different facets of this most elegant of malts.

The Glenrothes is a slow whisky, its complexities taking time in the glass, on the nose, and mostly in the mouth to develop. Rich but not heavy, sherried, but never overly so, it plays variations on a theme between oak, fruits, spice, and honey with, in older expressions, a dazzling spice on the back palate. Understated rather than bold, elegant rather than brash, it seems to symbolize its discreet location.

THE GLENROTHES TASTING NOTES

NEW MAKE

Nose: Clean. Vanilla, Chanel No 5, white-fleshed fruit, cainned pear, touch of cereal, buttery.
Palate: Buttery and fat but rather than Macallan-like oiliness, there's a lifted spicy quality. Intense.
Finish: Creamy.

SELECT RESERVE NAS 43%

Nose: Rain-moistened tweed. Cereal/cookie-like. Malty and slightly tense with a little touch of fresh black plum behind. Butter.
Palate: Nutty to start then a shift into damson giving extra mid-palate weight (which is very Edrington), with that vanilla note seen in the new make adding a softness.
Finish: Long and nutty.
Conclusion: In youth still.

Flavor Camp: Fruity & Spicy
Where Next? The Balvenie 12yo Double Wood, Glen Garioch 12yo

EXTRAORDINARY CASK, 1969 42.9%

Nose: Elegant and highly complex, with masses of tropical fruit. Multifaceted and dazzling, with mango, beeswax, tobacco, chestnut honey, and then blackberry and cedar.
Palate: Subtle and almost lacy to start, but with classic Rothes weight. Multilayered and soft. Light shiitake mushroom, polished wood, dried tropical fruit.
Finish: Fruity and Cognac-like.
Conclusion: Superbly elegant. Classic old Rothes.

Flavor Camp: Fruity & Spicy
Where Next? Tomintoul 33yo

ELDER'S RESERVE 43%

Nose: Full-bodied and typically elegant. Refined, with hints of barley, creamy oak, oxidative depths. Sweet with stewed plums and red fruit.
Palate: Unctuous, with hints of geranium, bitter orange, and honeycomb. Nicely funky and mature with water.
Finish: Long and gentle.
Conclusion: A No-Age-Statement whisky, but the youngest component is 18yo.

Flavor Camp: Fruity & Spicy
Where Next? The Balvenie 17yo

Speyburn

SPEYBURN • ROTHES • WWW.SPEYBURN.COM

The only sight you get of Speyburn as you drive on the road to (or from) Elgin is a pagoda roof poking out of a tight little glen, giving it the impression of an old secret illicit site. In fact, like all of Rothes' distilleries, this is from the late nineteenth century and, rather than being hidden from sight, it is located right next to the Rothes–Elgin branch line, built at the instigation of John Grant. This change of angle also makes it seems as if the distillery runs back from the road, only slowly revealing its conglomeration of buildings. From the railway side however, you'll see a frontage of pagoda-topped distillery, warehouses, and malting plant. It's our perspective that has changed, not Speyburn's.

The strong spirit of innovation that Rothes seems to attract was alive here as well. Not only does Speyburn sit opposite the first purpose-built dark-grains plant in Scotland, which turns the waste grain into animal feed, but it was the first distillery in Scotland to try pneumatic (aka drum) malting on site. Speyburn's drums continued until 1968, two years after the railway stopped carrying freight. With this, Speyburn sank back into relative obscurity.

It's worth discovering. This is another of Inver House's worm-tub sites, making a new spirit that's full of struck match and town gas. It behaves, however, like its stablemate anCnoc (Knockdhu), shedding its sulfur early on and revealing its true fruity, fragrant/floral character.

"It's easy drinking," says Inver House's master blender Stuart Harvey, "but it has more body than anCnoc—that's the difference." The difference in production might be subtle, but the effect is noticeable. "It's impossible to fix precisely what makes each character different," says Harvey. "You can run

Being almost wholly obscured from view seems to suit the subtle Speyburn style.

everything in exactly the same way in an identical distillery and you'll get different characters," he adds. "Whisky is site-specific. You can only make our character at our distilleries."

SPEYBURN TASTING NOTES

NEW MAKE

Nose: Wet leather. Light bran/oat. Touch of Jamaican pot-still rum. Plenty of citrus fruit. Struck match/gassy sulfuriness.
Palate: Big and slightly bready with some meaty notes, but a delicate quality is hiding. Has depth.
Finish: Freshens.

10YO 40%

Nose: Pale gold. Light and floral with barley sugar and light lemon. Clean, fresh, and soft. Stewed rhubarb. Cherry blossom.
Palate: Creamy vanilla, steamed sponge pudding, then comes flowers. Good mid-palate weight yield a succulent feel.
Finish: Lightly acidic.
Conclusion: Another of those where sulfur lifts to reveal esteriness and also palate weight.

Flavor Camp: **Fragrant & Floral**
Where Next? Glenkinchie 12yo, Glencadam 10yo

21YO 58.5%

Nose: Rich, sherry notes: cake, nut, and prune. Bitter chocolate and a charred, meaty note.
Palate: Powerful European-oak punch: orange, sweet spices, molasses scones with some sweet spirit. The charred notes lend an intriguing balance.
Finish: Licorice.
Conclusion: Big cask influence and maybe that meatiness indicates a heavier style being made in the past?

Flavor Camp: **Rich & Round**
Where Next? Tullibardine 1988, Dailuaine 16yo

Glen Spey

GLEN SPEY • ROTHES

At the opposite end of the town from Speyburn is the gated entrance to Glen Spey, the final member of this reticent whisky hub. Rothes may prefer to keep its business to itself, but within these streets the whole whisky-making process takes place. It was no coincidence that Rothes was chosen by early distillers. There are multiple water sources, there was the railway, and it was also both on the southern limits of the barley-growing plains and had access to peat. The situation, in other words, was vital.

Each distillery would have had its own maltings (Glen Grant and Speyburn each had drum maltings into the 1960s), and local coppersmiths (Forsyths continues to supply stills to the whole whisky industry), and, with Speyburn's dark-grains plant, Rothes was the perfect example of self-sufficiency.

Glen Spey is, like its neighbors, a late nineteenth-century plant, having been established in 1878 when a local grain merchant, James Stuart, saw an opportunity to extend his mill in Rothes to include a distillery.

Typical of the Rothes distilleries, Glen Spey prefers the quiet life out of the public glare.

After expanding the distillery footprint and changing its name to Glen Spey, in 1887 he sold it to the gin distiller W&A Gilbey, the first of that firm's Speyside interests (in time it also owned Knockando and another old grain mill that rejoiced under the name of Strathmill).

Still retaining an air of Victorian rectitude, Glen Spey conforms to the light Gilbey/J&B style. Here, as at Strathmill, there's a purifier on the tall reflux-inducing wash stills, which—who knows?—may have appeared after a neighborly visit to Glen Grant. This has the effect of introducing an oily element to the nutty character, which manifests itself (to this writer, at least) as an almond note.

Rothes at first glance may not seem like a whisky town—but it is.

GLEN SPEY TASTING NOTES

NEW MAKE

Nose: Fat. Popcorn/butterscotch-like with sweet fruit behind. Slight saltiness then green almond/almond oil.

Palate: Clean and green. Light nut/flour. Dry overall. Simple.

Finish: Dry and crisp.

8YO, REFILL WOOD CASK SAMPLE

Nose: Slightly immature but lifted. Toasted wood/roasted malt; peanuts and almond. White rum. Behind there's baked apple.

Palate: Very intense then at the halfway point comes hazelnut flour. Light and clean.

Finish: Nutty.

Conclusion: Not yet integrated and a little twiggy.

12YO, FLORA & FAUNA 43%

Nose: Malty but scented with a hint of lavender and earthiness. Dusty chalk (school blackboards) and then that signature almond note.

Palate: Peanuts and almond flakes. Clean with a soft sweet spot in the center. Lilac and iris on the back palate.

Finish: Crisp and clean.

Conclusion: Fully developed into a balanced mix of malt and fragrance.

> **Flavor Camp: Malty & Dry**
>
> **Where Next?** Inchmurrin 12yo, Auchentoshan Classic

ELGIN TO THE WESTERN EDGE

The Bermuda Triangle of whisky lies just outside Speyside's largest town. Here are cult distilleries whose whiskies are revered by blenders and aficionados, but which seem to have disappeared from the general drinker's consciousness. There are some surprises in store: the epitome of fruitiness, of fragrance—and the heaviest peated spirit in Speyside.

Sandstone cliffs illuminated by low evening sunlight at Burghead.

Glen Elgin

GLEN ELGIN • ELGIN • WWW.MALTS.COM/INDEX.PHP/EN_GB/OUR-WHISKIES/GLEN-ELGIN/THE-DISTILLERY

In what appears to be a Speyside characteristic, even the region's largest conurbation keeps its local distilleries somewhat hidden. Apart from two front-line single-malt brands, Glen Moray and The BenRiach, these are stills whose work is done behind the scenes, absorbed into a multiplicity of blends. The result of this is that they are often overlooked as being nothing more than fodder for fillings, whereas the opposite is in fact the case. The reason that the bulk of this cluster's distilleries are little seen is because blenders prize their idiosyncratic singularities.

Glen Elgin is a classic case. Hidden up a narrow road off the A941 highway, its character is the definition of fruitiness— almost absurdly so—since its fleshy ripeness brings visions of peach juice dribbling down your chin. This seems surprising if you give the distillery no more than a cursory glance. Six small stills plus worm tubs equals sulfury new make, right? No. Here is one of three worm sites owned by Diageo that works against type.

"Provided you run the stills to ensure the sulfur is removed during distillation then you can make an intense light spirit," explains Douglas Murray, Diageo's master distiller and blender. That sulfury new-make character seen elsewhere is avoided here by allowing the vapor a more relaxed relationship with the copper in the still. Equally, the fermentation is important. "In Glen Elgin, the bulk of the character is created before it goes to the still," he continues. This erotically charged fruitiness is generated by a relaxed regime: longer and slightly cooler ferments, and a slow and copper-rich conversation in the still.

Then there's the worms. "Worm sites have increased complexity and give a more intense character," says Murray. "There's actually not that much difference between Cardhu and Glen Elgin in terms of process." There is however a huge difference in character. The succulent versus the grassy, the lush versus the sharp.

Old coopering equipment that has seen long service sitting in the warehouses of Glen Elgin.

GLEN ELGIN TASTING NOTES

NEW MAKE

Nose: Ripe. Juicy Fruit chewing gum. Red apple, baked banana, green peach. Silky.
Palate: Light smoke. Clean but ripe and rich. Silky mouth-feel.
Finish: Luscious and long.

8YO, REFILL WOOD CASK SAMPLE

Nose: The fruit has softened and ripened and now ranges from canned to fresh. Lots of canned peach, fresh melon, seemingly creamy. Sweet, plump, and juicy. Light smoke.
Palate: Very sweet and concentrated. Pools in the center of the tongue. Apricot. Very juicy and sweet. Peach nectar.
Finish: Soft and, yes, fruity.
Conclusion: Sweet and rich and almost in need of some control from cask.

EST. 1900

GLEN ELGIN™

SPEYSIDE SINGLE POT STILL MALT WHISKY

HAND CRAFTED

AGED **12** YEARS

43%vol   GLEN ELGIN DISTILLERY, ELGIN, MORAYSHIRE   70cl ℮

North of *Scotland's mountainous Cairngorm region* the arable land is rich, the climate cool and dry. Here, where the River Lossie meanders toward the ancient Royal Burgh of Elgin, is the fine old distillery that bears its name. House martins, which have returned each April for as long as can be remembered, swoop among the now rare *worm tubs*. The distillery maintains *traditional* practices like these, in order to maintain its whisky's elusive fruity character. To this day, Glen Elgin stands out from the crowd for its HAND-CRAFTED approach to whisky making.

DISTILLERY MANAGER *Andrew C Cant*

12YO 43%

Nose: Full gold. The fruit is now sharing the top slot with a sweet and slightly dusty spiciness. Some nutmeg and cumin. More integrated oak adding some grip to the fresh fruit.
Palate: Soft tropical fruit to start, then changes suddenly halfway through into those spices that slowly become fragrant woods.
Finish: Fruity but drying.
Conclusion: The cask has added complexity to the whole package, but distillery character is still clearly visible.

Flavor Camp: Fruity & Spicy
Where Next? Balblair 1990, Glenmorangie The Original 10yo

Longmorn

LONGMORN • ELGIN • WWW.LONGMORNBROTHERS.COM/HTML/DISTILLERY.HTM

Glen Elgin's near neighbor has also tended to keep its own counsel. Longmorn is one of those malts that, like some underground musician, builds a reputation among an obsessive fan base who then somehow resent the fact that their hero might just be becoming better known.

Longmorn was established in 1893 by John Duff who was born in the nearby town of Aberchirder. Duff had previously designed Glenlossie before heading to the Transvaal to try and start the South African whisky industry. When this failed, he headed home to the Lossie to design and build Longmorn, here in the rich farmlands of the Laich O'Moray, near to the peats from the *foggie loans* (peat moss) of the nearby Mannoch Hill.

Duff's business went bust at the end of the nineteenth century and Longmorn passed into the hands of James Grant. Soon, it was elevated to A1 status by blenders.

"Longmorn is a real gem," says Colin Scott, master blender at owner Chivas Brothers. "It is a true friend to a blender as it has the power to influence and the elegance to harmonize the other whiskies in the blend." It's those blenders who were the jealous fans. Even when it became part of The Glenlivet Distilleries group, unlike its stablemates, Glen Grant and The Glenlivet, Longmorn was never promoted to single-malt brand status.

What the blenders are guarding is a soft, rich, complex new make produced in fat, plain stills. It is sweet, it is fruity, it has depth, it has breadth. It is fragrant yet powerful. It is gentle and honeyed in

Longmorn's complex new make runs into one of the most ornate spirit safes in the industry.

American oak barrels, richer and spicily expansive in hogsheads, darkly rich and powerful in ex-sherry butts. It has the ability to perform a multiplicity of functions.

As a keystone of many blends, it is also one of the foundations of Japanese single malt. The original still shapes served as the model for the Yoichi distillery in Japan because it was here that one of the fathers of Japanese whisky, Masataka Taketsuru, first experienced hands-on distilling. The word spreads, but other than an expensively packaged official 16yo, Longmorn remains in the hands of its original fans.

LONGMORN TASTING NOTES

NEW MAKE
Nose: Soft and fruity: almost fruitcake. Ripe banana, pear. Rich and round with a soft meat-like note at the back.
Palate: The fruit continues. Ripe and long.
Finish: A little floral touch.

10YO CASK SAMPLE
Nose: Pale gold. The fruit is ripening, but has a slight green peach character, then comes vanilla and cream.
Palate: The central fruitiness is now rising: apricot and mango, then with water, melted milk chocolate, and mace.
Finish: Lightly spiced.
Conclusion: For all the soft power, the impression is that this is still slightly asleep.

16YO 48%
Nose: Old gold. Fruitcake. There is still soft fruit but also a hint of dusty spice, fried banana, citrus fruit. Diluted, there's cream toffee, peach, and plum.
Palate: Thick. Chocolate again. Ripe tropical fruit, fruit sugars.
Finish: Ginger snaps.
Conclusion: Ripe and complex.

Flavor Camp: Fruity & Spicy
Where Next? Glenmorangie 18yo, The BenRiach 16yo

1977 50.7%
Nose: Banana chips; jungle mix; given depth by cereal. Peachy, scented. Chinese tea, stewed fruit, citrus.
Palate: Deep. Rich. Opens into sandalwood, vetiver, damson, and sweet, stewed fruit.
Finish: Full and long. Cinnamon in butter.
Conclusion: Goes into lusciousness. An absorbing whisky.

Flavor Camp: Fruity & Spicy
Where Next? Macallan 25yo Fine Oak

33YO, DUNCAN TAYLOR BOTTLING 49.4%
Nose: Even after over so long this retains the distillery character's fruitiness. Cooked quince, guava with a light crystallized ginger in syrup. Little smoke.
Palate: Gentle, sweet, and fruity. Lies on tongue. The tingling gingeriness/ginseng? adds a lift to back palate.
Finish: Fruit returns, now semi-dried.
Conclusion: The oak is balanced, allowing the distillery character to show its fullest expression.

Flavor Camp: Fruity & Spicy
Where Next? Glenmorangie 25yo, Dalwhinnie 1986

The BenRiach

ELGIN • WWW.BENRIACHDISTILLERY.CO.UK • PRIVATE TOURS AVAILABLE; SEE WEBSITE FOR DETAILS

Britain was luxuriating in an economic boom at the end of the nineteenth century. Industrial output was rising and a side effect of this was an increased investment in new distilleries. Boom, inevitably, is followed by bust, and, perhaps triggered by the collapse of blending and broking house Pattison in 1898, the industry began to slither into a decline. Although exports for blends were growing, sales in the domestic market (upon which Scotch was still heavily reliant) began to fall, leaving the stocks out of balance and with the possibility of worse to come as the large plants built at the tail-end of the nineteenth century began to come on stream.

Some of those were bailed out by blending firms looking to extend their own estate (and control more of their own inputs). Others closed, considered surplus to requirements. There were 161 distilleries (including grain) open in Scotland in 1899. By 1908, this number had fallen to 132. Many of those that closed were large-scale enterprises built in the last days of wild optimism, silenced before they had had a chance to open their mouths. Caperdonich, built in 1898 as Glen Grant Mark II, closed in 1902, Imperial built as Dailuaine II in 1897, closed in 1899. Another new plant, which had the shortest of lives, was the last of the Fogwatt Triangle, The BenRiach, which started off as Longmorn's sister plant in 1898 and closed in 1900. It was 65 years before it began to distill whisky again.

In the intervening years, Longmorn used malt from The BenRiach's malting floors, but it wasn't until the middle of another boom in whisky sales and a buoyant mood among blending firms that spirit began to run from its four stills once more.

It remained in a supporting role, a quiet whisper within blends, adding some spicy fruitiness, perhaps at times adding a heavy peated character when stocks of Islay were running low. While occasionally officially bottled as a single malt, even those releases seemed to indicate a whisky that, while decent, was never as startling as the other two members of this triumvirate: Glen Grant and Longmorn.

When it closed in 2003 it looked at if The BenRiach's jinxed life was continuing. This time, however, there was a white knight, in the shape of former Burn Stewart managing director, Billy Walker. Eyebrows were raised on news of the purchase—and then the whiskies started appearing. Complex, spicy, and, in older examples, showing the dazzling, dancing quality on the palate that is only ever discerned in whiskies of this style that have had a long, relaxed maturation in refill casks. In other words, a revelation to drinkers, if not to blenders.

These days production is flat-out and the world of single malt is very much the focus. "It's taken us five years to get everything balanced properly," says manager Stewart Buchanan. "A lot of equipment had been removed, so there was plenty to be replaced and then rebalanced. As we had no records of new make before the takeover, we did numerous trials of cut points and we think it's pretty much spot-on.

"What we look for is a perfumed, fruity sweetness; you can even get some of those fruits in the tun room where the smell becomes really appley. I think any whisky-making is about looking after the barley, and because we have a broad cut, we're capturing a good spread of flavors, from this early sweetness to those cereal notes from later in the run."

It might have been a latecomer on the scene, but The BenRiach is breaking free of the blend-oriented focus of this part of Speyside. And who knows? It could be leading some of these quiet but often spectacular performers into a new arena.

Right: A quiet supplier of fillings for blends for many years, The BenRiach now has the capacity to become a significant single-malt brand.

Left: Mashing in at The BenRiach: the moment in the early stages when the barley's starches are turned into fermentable sugars.

THE BENRIACH TASTING NOTES

NEW MAKE

Nose: Sweet, cake-like, fruity, zucchini, fennel. Lemon then a sweet cookie note, chalk.

Palate: That highly concentrated, slightly waxy, soft fruitiness leads the way, then comes a dusky/dusty perfumed quality. Chewy.

Finish: Crisp and clean. Malt. Then lots of spice.

CURIOSITAS 10YO PEATED 40%

Nose: Raffia/wheat breakfast cereal to start, then dried wood smoke/charred sticks moving into bitumen and baked fruit behind.

Palate: Hugely smoky, then sweet oak and a lightly fruity palate. Good feel.

Finish: Still smoked with a light cereal note.

Conclusion: A curiosity indeed. Originally made to provide peaty component for Chivas Brothers' blends.

Flavor Camp: **Smoky & Peaty**
Where Next? Ardmore Traditional Cask

12YO 40%

Nose: Full gold. Spicy start with some perfumed/waxy exotic florals (frangipani), confectioners' sugar, and sawdust. Fresh fruit with more fresh oak with water.

Palate: Remains lightly waxy, with a clinging fruit syrup quality. Apricot, banana, and cinnamon.

Finish: A burst of spice, then a quick end.

Conclusion: A slow build with American oak an ideal partner.

Flavor Camp: **Fruity & Spicy**
Where Next? Longmorn 10yo, Clynelish 14yo

16YO 40%

Nose: Full gold. Everything has deepened and the spice has receded as the fruit emerges as the dominant partner. Touch of woodsmoke. Dried banana and ripe melon. Little nuttiness. Retains the exotic edge.

Palate: More dense and less fresh fruit, more baked/semi-dried. Bigger, chewier and more intense with some cumin. With water there's a touch of sherry, then sherried notes.

Finish: Dry oak and white raisin.

Conclusion: Flexing its muscles.

Flavor Camp: **Fruity & Spicy**
Where Next? The Balvenie 12yo Double Wood

20YO 43%

Nose: Relaxed, mature character: dazzling spices led by mace and some subtle cumin. Sweet and sour play off each other, then there are dried peels and apricot tones.

Palate: Ripe and soft, with lots of fresh orchard-fruit juices becoming more nectarine-like in time.

Finish: Sweet spices. Long.

Conclusion: Elegant, with distillery character given extra substance by the restrained oak.

Flavor Camp: **Fruity & Spicy**
Where Next? Paul John Select Cask

21YO 46%

Nose: Gold. Smoke and damp hay, bay leaf/laurel, autumn leaves, and pear. Melon remains but the spices have moved to a light dusting in the background.

Palate: Smoky and nutty. Walnut shell. Sage but still with that chewy quality. Oak has moved into sandalwood and camphor. Restrained with good oak support.

Finish: Ginger and light peat.

Conclusion: Moving into the third stage of its evolution.

Flavor Camp: **Fruity & Spicy**
Where Next? Balblair 1975, Glenmorangie 18yo

SEPTENDECIM, 17YO 46%

Nose: Backyard bonfire, with balanced sweetness adding a counterpoint: cinnamon-dusted apples baking in the fire.

Palate: The continuing interplay between fruit and grassy smoke continues on the palate alongside toffee, nougat, peach syrup, and salty licorice.

Finish: Smoke returns.

Conclusion: Balanced, smoky, and with identifiable distillery character.

Flavor Camp: **Smoky & Peaty**
Where Next? Independent bottlings of Ardmore

AUTHENTICUS, 25YO 46%

Nose: Smoke once more. Wood smoke: alder and fruit woods, with a light aromatic lift akin to smoked meat.

Palate: The distillery character begins to come through with plump, soft, orchard-fruit sweetness. The beeswax you get from age and smoke above.

Finish: Smoldering.

Conclusion: Mature, perfectly harmonized, and balanced.

Flavor Camp: **Smoky & Peaty**
Where Next? Independent bottlings of Glen Garioch and Ardmore

Roseisle

ROSEISLE • BURGHEAD

When Diageo announced the plans for a distillery next to its maltings at Roseisle, the reaction was both hostile and doom-laden. According to the skeptics, the 2.6-million-gallon (10-million-liter) capacity plant, which opened in 2010, would mean the closure of Diageo's smaller sites, and the death of artisan distilling. Nothing would ever be the same. Allegedly.

But the 14-still plant was only the first part of a £1-billion ($1.7-billion) investment by Scotland's biggest whisky distiller to increase capacity at all of its sites. Nothing closed. In fact, new distilleries were built.

Located next to the large maltings of the same name, Roseisle was built to be as green as possible. A biomass plant helps it generate much of its own energy, while waste heat is circulated in a loop, helping to run the maltings at Roseisle and at Burghead.

The distillery is also set up to produce different style of whisky for blending requirements, and while this is not unusual, the techniques used are novel. Six of the seven pairs of stills have two shell and tube condensers: one stuffed with copper pipes as per usual, the other made of stainless steel. If heavy spirit is needed, then the vapor is directed into the latter, where the lack of copper imitates a worm-tub effect. Conversely, if a light spirit is required then the standard, copper-rich condensing system is the one used.

So far, barring a short period after opening when it made "nutty/spicy," Roseisle has been on the light, grassy side of things. There's been inevitable fine-tuning.

Ferments have been extended to 90 hours, the stills are run slow, and given air rests after each distillation to refresh the copper. In addition, each still is fully cleaned once a week, which gives it an extra six or seven hours to breathe.

All of this means that production is limited to 22 mashes a week. "Once you are on light, you have to slow things down," says manager Gordon Winton. "We're hitting all the targets, and the blenders are saying that the Roseisle style is different to the other grassy sites."

And what of making heavy style? "It will happen when they need some." Which means starting to fine-tune all over again? Winton laughs. "Aye, but that's whisky for you! You can never fully relax."

The stillhouse at Diageo's remarkable Roseisle Distillery.

Glenlossie & Mannochmore

GLENLOSSIE & MANNOCHMORE • ELGIN

If The BenRiach has emerged fully formed from its sequestration, then the next two appear content to remain hidden from view (although the newest member will find it hard). Glenlossie and Mannochmore share a site; in fact, Mannochmore lies inside Glenlossie's bounds, somewhat protected by its considerably older brother. Both are in the lighter end of the flavor spectrum but, importantly, make different variations on that theme.

Glenlossie is a good example of the search for lightness that took place in the late nineteenth century. Built in 1876 by John Duff, a former manager of The GlenDronach, its stills are equipped with purifiers, clever design being used to supply this more delicate character.

Reflux is the key here: that prolonged, intentional redistilling of condensing vapors inside the still (*see* pp.14–15). Glenlossie is more than just light, however. A nose of the new make shows an oiliness that adds both aroma to the basic, delicate grassy fragrance and a slickness to the mouth-feel. "If you run the fermentation in such a way as to make things grassy and then increase the reflux, you'll get that added oiliness," says Douglas Murray, Diageo's master distiller and blender. "Oiliness is lots of active copper on a potentially grassy spirit."

It's possible that Glenlossie has been saved by its purifier pipe. It certainly has, quietly, had a fair amount of attention lavished on it, extended from four to six stills in 1962. It is quite common for one of the members of a double site to close. It's what happened at Clynelish, for example, when Brora disappeared, while Teaninich and Linkwood's old stillhouses are also no longer producing. Not so here.

In 1971, the six-still Mannochmore was built at Glenlossie (along with a dark-grains plant) and started to produce its own variation on the light theme. No oil here; this is all about a sweet floral freshness when new that develops a fleshy quality when mature. It needs careful handling: the boisterousness of first-fill sherry would obliterate its discreet nature.

This makes it all the more surprising that it was chosen as the malt beneath the thick black molasses that made up Loch Dhu, the notorious "black whisky," that briefly appeared in the 1990s. Dismissed out of hand on release, Loch Dhu is now highly collectable. Mannochmore, meanwhile, has drawn the covers over its head once again.

MANNOCHMORE TASTING NOTES

NEW MAKE

Nose: Sweet, carrot, fennel, flower stems straying into stone fruit. Grappa-like.
Palate: Light and clean. Floral, gentle, and fresh.
Finish: Quick, discreet.

8YO, REFILL WOOD CASK SAMPLE

Nose: A deeper fragrance with a touch of wet earth and jasmine. Vanilla, still some immature grappa-like edginess; slightly chalky.
Palate: Fat and quite broad. Unripe peach, then vanilla, and that flower-shop character.
Finish: Still hot.
Conclusion: Seemingly light in aroma but is taking its time to build up momentum. A dark horse.

12YO, FLORA & FAUNA 43%

Nose: Clean. Vine flower with some peach juice developing along with dessert apple.
Palate: Lightly oily and slightly spicy. A mandarin-like freshness. Very delicate and uncluttered.
Finish: Fresh and slightly citric.
Conclusion: Still light and perfumed.

Flavor Camp: Fragrant & Floral
Where Next? Braeval 8yo, Speyside 15yo

18YO, SPECIAL RELEASE 54.9%

Nose: Beeswax, nuts, and an intense cinnamon lift. Freshly polished oak dominates at the start but underneath is a soft fruitiness: banana, stewed rhubarb, that characteristic peachiness, and some coconut.
Palate: The lush nature of the nose confirmed on the palate along with apricot, orange peel, vanilla, and a light grip from the oak. Good acidity. Sinks onto the mid-palate where a shift to spiciness takes place before, surprisingly, the fruit reappears along with macaroon.
Finish: Soft to start then a slight oaky grip. Clean and fine.
Conclusion: Here's a whisky that, while light at new-make stage, benefts hugely from the attentions of American oak (on evidence, European oak dominates it).

Flavor Camp: Fruity & Spicy
Where Next? Craigellachie 14yo, Old Pulteney 17yo

GLENLOSSIE TASTING NOTES

NEW MAKE

Nose: Melting butter, quite broad. White currant, wet chamois. Green and oily, canola oil.
Palate: A show of oil, unripe fruit, sweet cardboard.
Finish: Strawberry (unripe).

8YO, REFILL WOOD CASK SAMPLE

Nose: More floral with a peachy note. Similar elderflower cordial note to Linkwood, light mint, lime, and pink grapefruit. The fruit is ripening.
Palate: Intense and aromatic with a clinging quality.
Finish: Fresh and light.
Conclusion: At a mid-point in its evolution. Needs time to ripen. Again, the texture is key.

1999, MANAGER'S CHOICE, SINGLE CASK 59.1%

Nose: Wood rubbed with linseed oil, grapes, jasmine, Amalfi lemons. Very up and direct but not immature. There's an intriguing antiseptic note with water along with toasted marshmallow.
Palate: Peppery, lemon-zesty, grassy; the oak delivers a menthol/eucalypt hit. Light and perfumed.
Finish: Clean fragrant and lifted.
Conclusion: Another lesser light that's shining brightly.

Flavor Camp: Fragrant & Floral
Where Next? Glentauchers 1991, anCnoc 16yo

Linkwood

LINKWOOD • ELGIN

Speyside's hidden narrative is the pursuit of the light. The distillers who joined in the hunt found themselves in varied places within this new flavor world. Occasionally, some pursued light with such relentless drive that character was close to being sucked out of their whiskies. Others headed down a grassy track; some went dusty with vampiric vigor; others lay in floral bowers. All were faced with the reality that light whiskies need to be handled with care and discretion: refill casks, a little hint of first fill, but don't overload with oak if you wish to retain that carefully crafted distillery character.

The other issue facing these distillers is that, as new drinkers have come to single malt, so they have pursued bolder flavors. In this way single malt is no different from wine: the new wine-drinker cuts his or her teeth on fruit bombs. In this new market, what space is there for the subtle, the discreet?

What if there were a single malt somewhere in the world that managed to combine a delicacy of aroma with palate weight; that was as fresh as a late spring day but wasn't as wispy as a chiffon dress? Not many single malts manage to achieve this tricky balancing act, but the one made by Linkwood does.

This style of whisky, Douglas Murray, Diageo's distilling and blending guru, says is the most testing type to make because it appears to do something that seems to run counter to what whisky is about: it suppresses flavors. Even its new-make definition ("clean") seems to drag it closer to the world of vodka and neutrality rather than the congener-rich complexities of single malt. Fear not. Linkwood's new make smells of the skin of peaches, of light apple blossom falling

Situated in farmland on the outskirts of Elgin, Linkwood is among the most aromatic Scotch.

Light it may seem, but Linkwood blooms with age.

in an orchard; in the mouth it sticks and seems to spin in a ball in the middle of the tongue. It's a conjuring act. You expect one thing and get another. It starts early in the process with a different grind being given to the malted barley in order to give a thick filter bed in the mash tun. No cereal-producing solids are wanted in the low-gravity wort, which is given a long fermentation. "The whole issue here is to stop characters forming," says Murray.

The stills are rounded and Rubenesque and unusual (though not unique) in the fact that the spirit stills are larger than the wash still. They're filled low and given a long distillation in order to maximize the time that the vapor can dribble back down the inside of these great copper bellies, stripping away more unwanted characters.

Condensers are used to extend this copper interaction, though the old Linkwood distillery, which sits on the other side of the courtyard, has worm tubs. Old Linkwood, however, still shows this spring-like quality. (It was in old Linkwood, incidentally, that much of Diageo's research into copper and worm tubs was tested).

It's a whisky that is in demand by blenders (it has recently doubled capacity) offering both texture and top notes to a blend. While it can stand up to sherry casks (that fragrance and feel are retained), it shows at its best in refill casks, allowing the drinker to set out different ages and experience a liquid version of time-lapse photography: as the blossom of youth fruits, falls, and lies on a bed of dried flowers.

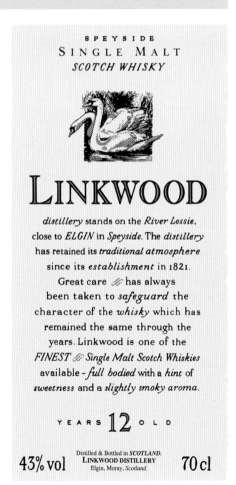

LINKWOOD TASTING NOTES

NEW MAKE
Nose: Perfumed. Pineapple, peach blossom/peach skin, quince. Some weight.
Palate: Incredibly fresh. Pastries, apple. Lightly oily/chewy in feel.
Finish: Clean and surprisingly long.

8YO, REFILL WOOD CASK SAMPLE
Nose: Straw. Green apple, elderflower, white fruit. Amazingly fresh. With water, there's pear.
Palate: Good weight. Apples and gently poached pear, then elderflower cordial. Tongue-coating.
Finish: Fresh, light, and zesty.
Conclusion: An intriguing mix of fragrance and body.

12YO, FLORA & FAUNA 43%
Nose: Big, fragrant. Camomile and jasmine mixed with apple. Quite scented and heavy. Picks up weight as it goes.
Palate: Rounded. The oily character in the center is now adding extra depth allowing the ripe fruits and touches of grass to revolve around it.
Finish: Tropical fruit and grass.
Conclusion: A perfumed clean whisky that deepens with age.

Flavor Camp: **Fragrant & Floral**
Where Next? Miltonduff 18yo, Tomintoul 14yo

SPEYSIDE
SINGLE MALT
SCOTCH WHISKY

LINKWOOD

distillery stands on the *River Lossie*, close to *ELGIN* in *Speyside*. The *distillery* has retained its *traditional atmosphere* since its *establishment* in 1821. Great care ⅍ has always been taken to *safeguard* the character of the *whisky* which has remained the same through the years. Linkwood is one of the *FINEST* ⅍ Single Malt Scotch Whiskies available – *full bodied* with a *hint* of *sweetness* and a *slightly smoky aroma.*

YEARS 12 OLD

43% vol   Distilled & Bottled in *SCOTLAND*.
LINKWOOD DISTILLERY
Elgin, Moray, *Scotland*.   70cl

Glen Moray

ELGIN • WWW.GLENMORAY.COM • OPEN ALL YEAR OCT–APR, MON–FRI; MAY–SEPT, MON–SAT

Hidden beside the Lossie River and surrounded by a housing estate, Glen Moray's low profile (in both senses of the term) is a surprise given the size of the site. Originally a brewery, this was another distillery built in the late nineteenth-century whisky boom, which fell foul of the change in economic circumstances at the start of the new century and closed in 1910. However, unlike The BenRiach, its silent period was relatively short: it reopened in 1923. The stillhouse, small and compact, seems out of proportion with the rest of the buildings, which used to house the distillery's own Saladin maltings.

The fruitiness, which is a constant thread through this Elgin grouping, reappears here with an added buttery quality lending the palate a gently soft quality, which is married with American oak. If you like fruit salad and ice cream then Glen Moray is your whisky.

It's the distillery's microclimate that manager Graham Coull zones in on when describing Glen Moray's DNA. "The slightly warmer Moray climate and the location of the distillery in this low level really helps to suck the spirit into the wood, heightening the oak's effects on flavor. In addition the low-lying dunnage warehouses with a low water table (they've flooded on numerous occasions) create what we feel is a greater mellowing to the product. Add the high proportion of first-fill casks, and you create a whisky with a wonderful sweet/spicy balance."

Some fresh oak barrels have also been tested here. A cask bottled by the Scotch Malt Whisky Society was generous with its flavors but while the whisky showed an intense *crème brûlée*/butterscotch effect, the deep fruitiness of Glen Moray showed through. The below-the-radar properties extend to the marketing, too. Despite its evident

The flatlands beside the Lossie River are home to this huge whisky-making site.

qualities, Glen Moray was sold as a loss-leader by previous owner Glenmorangie; while good for volume, this did little for its image, or for that of the category. Soon after the LVMH takeover of Glenmorangie, Glen Moray was sold to French distiller La Martiniquaise.

GLEN MORAY TASTING NOTES

NEW MAKE
Nose: Very clean and (fresh) fruity with a buttery note and a touch of slightly spicy cereal.
Palate: A lightly waxy feel, then comes the ripe pulpy fruits with some dessert apple.
Finish: Clean.

CLASSIC NAS 40%
Nose: Light gold. Like most no-age-statement (NAS) brands, the wood is the dominant partner. Crisp and oaky with that butteriness and a little green fruits. Apple.
Palate: Gentle and creamy. Soft feel.
Finish: Gentle soft and clean.
Conclusion: All slightly suppressed. Slightly sleepy.

Flavor Camp: Fruity & Spicy
Where Next? Macallan 10yo Fine Oak, Glencadam 15yo

12YO 40%
Nose: The soft fruit returns. Fruit chews, pear followed by blond tobacco and vanilla. Mint in time.
Palate: Quite bourbon-like, new oak, pine sap. Light apple.
Finish: Spice and the nuts in cream toffee.
Conclusion: First-fill influence adds another soft layer.

Flavor Camp: Fruity & Spicy
Where Next? Bruchladdich 2002, Tormore 12yo

16YO 40%
Nose: Gold. Resinous note often found in older whiskies. Still syrupy sweetness, creamed coconut, suntan oil.
Palate: Wood is fairly grippy, but sufficient of the distillery character seeps in toward the finish to balance.
Finish: Clean and silky.
Conclusion: Amenable.

Flavor Camp: Fruity & Spicy
Where Next? Macallan 18yo Fine Oak, Mannochmore 18yo

30YO 40%
Nose: Mature and autumnal. Spices now come through. Again there's tobacco—this time Dominican Republic cigar—and a touch of light varnish.
Palate: Smoky wood. Hickory. Deck oil.
Finish: Soft and finally fruity.
Conclusion: Big, sweet, wood influence here.

Flavor Camp: Fruity & Spicy
Where Next? Old Pulteney 30yo

Miltonduff

MILTONDUFF • ELGIN

By the start of the 1930s, a collection of global circumstances were conspiring against the Scotch whisky industry. Falling demand in the UK, partly triggered by the economic effects of the Great Depression, had dramatically lowered production. The only bright spot was the continuing solidity of exports to Canada. The fact that many (if not most) of the cases of blends headed straight from the warehouses of Canadian importers into bootlegger's trucks and the still-dry American market was of no concern to the Scots. It was also clear that Prohibition was entering its end game and, with the anticipation of a boom in sales in the USA, there was considerable positioning behind the scenes.

Sales did not rise immediately after Repeal in 1933, the result of a $5-a-gallon import duty. After this was halved in 1935, Canadian distiller Hiram Walker-Gooderham & Worts went on a spending spree, buying its second Scotch distillery, Miltonduff, the blending firm of George Ballantine, and starting work on the Dumbarton grain distillery, which would go on to produce the most "Canadian" of Scotland's grains.

In buying Miltonduff, Hiram Walker had a distillery which, legend has it, was originally the mill for neighboring Pluscarden Abbey and which had been licensed since 1824.

It wasn't unused to innovation either. "Miltonduff was triple-distilled in the late nineteenth century and for a time it's believed that it was trying to make something akin to Highland Park," says Alan Winchester, Chivas Brothers' distilleries manager. "Hiram Walker changed that, for whatever reason, to what we have now." In 1964 it was also to add a pair of Lomond stills, producing a malt called Mosstowie.

Winchester's "reason" lies with Ballantine's and the changing North American palate which, during Prohibition, had gone light. The Canadians brought not just capital but a new sensibility

Miltonduff is alleged to be located on the site of an ancient monastic brewery.

to whisky-making. The days of the delicate and gentle, building since the start of the twentieth century, were now here. This is shown when you take a whiff of its floral, green, oily new make with a lifted complexity that, with a light touch when it comes to cask management, blooms.

MILTONDUFF TASTING NOTES

NEW MAKE

Nose: Sweet, with cucumber. Green/oily with some lime blossom and vine flower.
Palate: Intense but balanced, with a lightly buttery center.
Finish: Crisp. Peanut.

18YO 51.3%

Nose: Rounded but still that characteristic purity. Camomile, elderflower. Very fragile and delicate. Blossom-like.
Palate: Though there's oak, it is still sweet with slightly heavier florals, hyacinth, rose petal. Precise, it holds well on the tongue.
Finish: Clean, perfumed.
Conclusion: Rock candy.

Flavor Camp: Fragrant & Floral
Where Next? Linkwood 12yo, Speyburn 10yo, Hakushu 18yo, Tormore 1996

1976 57.3%

Nose: Light and scented: heather and cannabis, pot pourri, vanilla, coconut, and orchid.
Palate: Rounded and oaky, but retains the intensity of new make. Almost like a flower jelly. There's a lot going on.
Finish: Clean and light.
Conclusion: The retention of fragrance is the key here.

Flavor Camp: Fragrant & Floral
Where Next? Tomintoul 14yo

Benromach

FORRES • WWW.BENROMACH.COM • OPEN ALL YEAR; SEE WEBSITE FOR DAYS & DETAILS

Benromach is a conundrum. When independent bottler Gordon & MacPhail (G&M) bought it in 1994 it was a blank canvas. Closed since 1983, another victim of the Great Crash of the early 1980s, it was a shell. Everything you now see inside—mash tun, wooden washbacks, the stills with their external condensers—is new. The question facing G&M was: do we start from scratch and make a new whisky, or try to replicate what went before? Interestingly, they have managed to do both.

As we've seen, the distilleries of the 1960s and 1970s can mostly be grouped within a similar Flavor Camp. Benromach is different. In the new make you can detect echoes of an older Speyside, when even its lighter whiskies had mid-palate depth and a smoky edge. Not as heavy as Mortlach, Glenfarclas, or Balmenach perhaps, but certainly fuller than the super-light brigade. "There has been a gradual lightening of Speyside in the last 40 years as changes were made to raw materials and production processes," says Ewen Mackintosh, whisky supply manager at G&M. "When we set about re-equipping Benromach, we made the decision to create a single malt that was typical of a Speyside whisky found pre-1960s."

The end result was, however, more mysterious. The stills, for example, are a different shape and smaller than the originals, yet, as Mackintosh explains, when they compared new make from the previous and current regimes there was a shared fingerprint. "The only factors that remain the same are the water source and some of the wood used to build the washbacks," he says. "There is also a little mystery surrounding Scotch whisky, which suggests that where the characteristics of a single malt are derived from will never be fully explained." In other words, despite changing everything, something about Benromach will always make it "Benromach."

It would be wrong to think that this is simply a replica. New Benromach comes in wine finishes, new oak is used, there's an organic variant, a wood-smoke-rich, heavily peated one, and the fat and creamy Origins which uses 100 percent Golden Promise barley. From a period of silence, Benromach is now pretty noisy—or as noisy as the gentlemanly Gordon & MacPhail ever gets.

BENROMACH TASTING NOTES

NEW MAKE

Nose: Very sweet with banana and maltiness. Medium to full, white mushroom, and light smoke.
Palate: Chewy and quite thick with a little touch of soft fruitiness.
Finish: Clean with a little peatiness.

2003 CASK SAMPLE 58.2%

Nose: An intriguing mix of the fruity and the slightly oily (rapeseed). Very light smoke comes through, along with some heavy lily and cut-flower notes.
Palate: Smoky to start with, but this is balanced by the oily floral character seen on the nose. Some semi-dried fruit.
Finish: Long and gentle.
Conclusion: There is a sense here of Benromach being a slow-maturing whisky.

10YO 43%

Nose: Light gold, some cedar notes and fresh oak character. Moves into pineapple and buttery malt, whole-wheat bread and banana skin.
Palate: Light grip, mouth-filling. Light dried apricot on top of that malty core. Has relaxed into an expansive character. Seems slightly oilier than the new make.
Finish: Wood smoke. Length.
Conclusion: Wood has added a new dimension, enhancing the basic richness of the spirit. A new old-style Speysider.

Flavor Camp: Fruity & Spicy
Where Next? Longmorn 10yo, Yamazaki 12yo

25YO 43%

Nose: A similar cedary note to 10yo; hints of leathery maturity. In time, citrus fruit, custard, nuts. Grassy for its age. Freshens with water. Light peatiness.
Palate: Very sweet and direct giving a line to the 10yo, but this shows the extra spiciness of age. Light powdered ginger and a stewed-fruit character.
Finish: Grassy and quite dry.
Conclusion: Although the stills have changed since this was made, somehow it remains the same.

Flavor Camp: Fruity & Spicy
Where Next? Auchentoshan 21yo

30YO 43%

Nose: Relaxed and lightly smoky, with warm driftwood, supple leather, candied fruit, and spices. Also an oily richness.
Palate: Quite waxy and mouth-filling/tongue-clinging. Apricot to the fore. Has freshness still.
Finish: Energetic and long.
Conclusion: Although from the DCL era when the stills were different, you can see how contemporary Benromach will mature when in relaxed casks.

Flavor Camp: Fruity & Spicy
Where Next? Tomatin 30yo

1981, VINTAGE 43%

Nose: Mahogany. Big, resinous. Black fruits, significant sherried impact. Moving into a sweet/savory character and some wood. Substantial weight and a dried mulchy undertow. Black banana, Seville orange, and toasted marshmallow.
Palate: Big and intense. Varnish and slightly oily texture. Cookie-like/nutty. In time a tingle of allspice.
Finish: Smoke and dense fruit.
Conclusion: It has the weight to cope with the close attentions of sherry casks.

Flavor Camp: Rich & Round
Where Next? Springbank 15yo

Glenburgie

GLENBURGIE • FORRES

Like Miltonduff, eight miles away, Glenburgie was another of the distilleries into which then owner, Hiram Walker, installed Lomond stills. Invented by Alastair Cunningham in 1955, the still's design contained moveable baffle plates in its thick neck. The continuing belief that this was in order to make a heavier whisky is however overly simplistic. Cunningham's brief was to try and widen the range of distillates coming from one still. The adjusting of the plates, as well as the fact that they could be water cooled or left dry, would, the theory went, produce different types of reflux and thereby allow different flavors to be created.

The trouble was, they didn't work particularly well. When run as wash stills the plates became coated with solids, thereby cutting back on copper availability as well as potentially producing a burnt note in the final spirit. Quietly the Lomonds were retired, scrapped, or cannibalized. Today, there are just two left. Scapa's, with its plates removed, runs as a normal wash still, while Bruichladdich has just installed one called "Ugly Betty" (Lomonds are not the most aesthetically pleasing of designs— more of a copper oil drum than an elegant swan), which ran in the Inverleven distillery.

In some ways, Miltonduff and Glenburgie can be seen as a mirror image of Diageo's Glenlossie and Mannochmore. "We always swapped between those," confirms Chivas Brothers' distilleries manager Alan Winchester, whose firm acquired the first pair when it bought Allied Distillers, "though I'd say Glenburgie was more of what I'd call a sweeter, grassier style."

Today there's no signs of the "Glencraig" Lomonds at Glenburgie, whose slightly brutal open-plan layout shows how far whisky has come since the 1823 revolution. The only suggestion of the distillery's nineteenth-century origins is a tiny stone cellar that sits somewhat

The sole remaining original building contains some of Glenburgie's most precious stocks.

incongruously in the middle of the distillery's busy roadway. Its presence here takes on a symbolic air as we bid farewell to Speyside, this heartland of malt distilling, this land of river, moor, and coastal plain; of boldness and understatement; of tradition and innovation; of origins and future possibilities; whose broad range of aromas, techniques, and philosophies have so influenced the direction of Scotch whisky.

GLENBURGIE TASTING NOTES

NEW MAKE

Nose: Very clean and light with a touch of grassiness, linseed oil, and sweetness.
Palate: Delicate and fragrant, but also oily on the tongue.
Finish: Nutty and intense.

12YO 59.8%

Nose: Pale gold. Grassy but being in a fairly active cask allows coconut to become the stronger personality.
Palate: When diluted (it's too hot and intense when neat) this is sweet and gentle. Vanilla bean from the cask. The gentle tongue-sticking quality adds interest.
Finish: Grassy. Chinese white tea.
Conclusion: Assertive wood matches the intrinsic sweetness of the spirit.

Flavor Camp: **Fragrant & Floral**
Where Next? anCnoc 12yo, Linkwood 12yo

15YO 58.9%

Nose: Gold. Lots of acetone, almond milk. Light and sweet. Clean.
Palate: The grass has both dried into raffia and added a slight bison-grass-like fragrance, then comes a pleasant agricultural note akin to cowpats.
Finish: Light spice. Clean.
Conclusion: Gentle and attractive.

Flavor Camp: **Fragrant & Floral**
Where Next? Teaninich 10yo

HIGHLANDS

If Speyside illustrates the absurdity of the belief that two distilleries next to each other should make a similar style, how is it possible to link the malt distilleries that stretch from the housing schemes of northern Glasgow to the Pentland Firth? Legally, in whisky terms the Highlands are everything north of the Highland Line that isn't Speyside, but even that boundary is a political one, abandoned in 1816, rather than the geological boundary that separates the "Low Land" from the "High Land."

This "High Land" has a powerful appeal. It is what most visitors think Scotland really is: a place of mountain and moor, of lochs, castles, soaring eagles, and stags at bay. In other words, Scotland as cliché. The Highland distilleries and their whiskies reveal a richer, living landscape. These whiskies exist because of the battle between man and his environment; they speak of folk wisdom and technology, of clearance and repopulation, and a stubborn (in Scots, *thrawn*) refusal to conform. They exist because they offer something that is outside the norm, beyond the gravitational pull of Speyside.

In the Highlands it is wise to expect the unexpected. Here we find grass, smoke, wax, tropical fruit, and currants, austerity and voluptuousness. Again there is no unity, but there are flavor trails that can be followed: the honey that runs from Deanston to Dalwhinnie, the different fruits of the northeastern coast, the unexpected blast of peat smoke in the Garioch.

Sometimes it is what *isn't* there that intrigues. Why are the surviving Perthshire distilleries clustered together in such a small area of such a fertile county and why are they all so wildly different in terms of flavor? Why couldn't the equally rich arable lands of the eastern coast support whisky-making? Why are there no distilleries in Aberdeen or Inverness?

Even the seemingly coherent mini-region of the northeastern coast, where every train station seems to have a distillery next to it, confounds expectations: from the barley fields of the Black Isle just north of the Moray Firth where Scotland's first whisky "brand" was born and died, to the startling sight of snow-dusted hills on one side of the road and a moored oil rig in the deep firth on the other. In truly paradoxical Highland style, it is both a place of Pictish stones and heavy industry, of creation myths and the birth of geology; oil, and whisky, flow land and herring fleets, and a succession of distilleries that seem to try deliberately to outdo each other in terms of weird alchemy. As you head ever farther north in the ever-changing light of this forgotten coastline, the Caledonian antisyzygy is distilled.

Most of Scotland is "High Land" and this multifaceted area of hill and moor gives a disparate range of whisky styles.

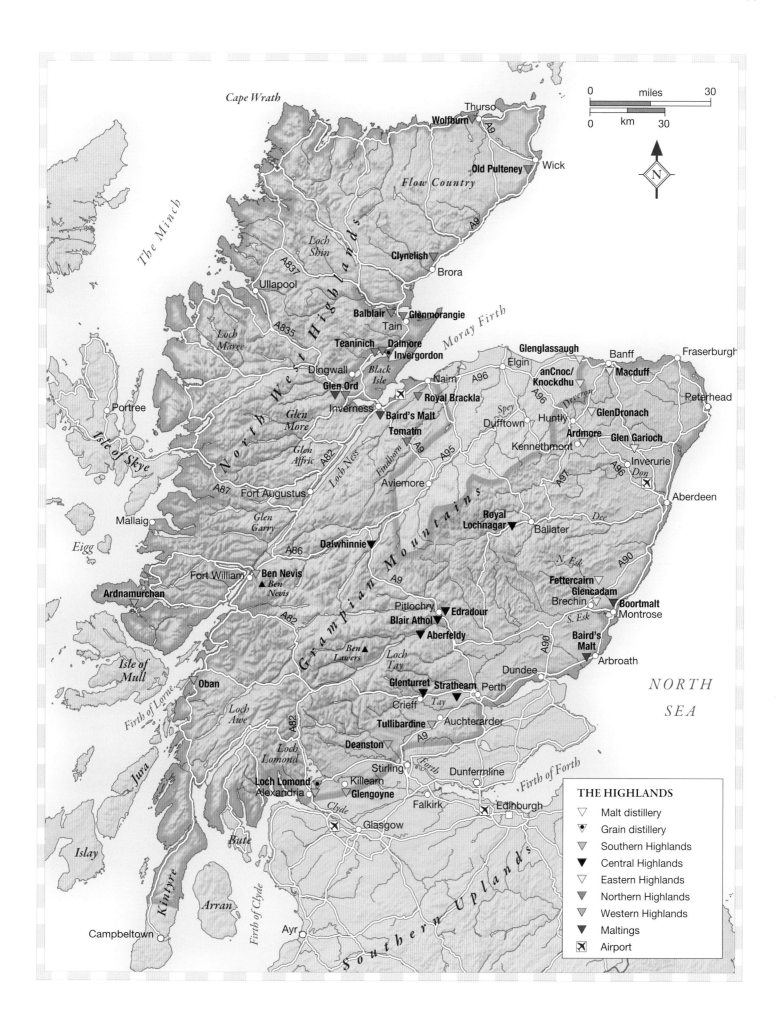

Cape Wrath

Thurso

Wolfburn ▽

A9

Wick

Old Pulteney ▽

Flow Country

miles 0 — 30

km 0 — 30

N

The Minch

Loch Shin

A837

Ullapool

Clynelish ▽

Brora

Loch Maree

A835

Balblair ▽

Tain

Glenmorangie ▽

Moray Firth

Glenglassaugh ▽

Banff

Fraserburgh

Teaninich ▽

Dalmore ▽

Invergordon ●

Elgin

anCnoc/ Knockdhu ▽

Macduff ▽

North West Highlands

Dingwall

Black Isle

Nairn

A96

Spey

Dufftown

Huntly

Deveron

GlenDronach ▽

Peterhead

Glen Ord ▼

Inverness

Royal Brackla ▽

A96

A96

Ardmore ▽

Glen Garioch ▽

Glen More

Baird's Malt ▼

Kennethmont

A97

Inverurie

Don

A96

Aberdeen

Glen Affric

Tomatin ▼

A9

A95

Findhorn

Aviemore

Loch Ness

A82

Fort Augustus

Grampian Mountains

Royal Lochnagar ▼

Ballater

Dee

A90

Glen Garry

A86

Dalwhinnie ▼

A9

N. Esk

Mallaig

Glen Garry

Ardnamurchan ▽

Fort William

▲ *Ben Nevis*

Ben Nevis ▽

A82

Fettercairn ▽

Glencadam ▽

Brechin

S. Esk

Boortmalt ▽

Montrose

Pitlochry

Edradour ▼

Blair Athol ▼

Aberfeldy ▼

Ben Lawers ▲

Loch Tay

Baird's Malt ▼

Arbroath

Isle of Mull

Firth of Lorne

Oban ▽

Loch Awe

Glenturret ▽

Stratheam ▼

Perth

Crieff

Tay

Dundee

NORTH SEA

Eigg

Isle of Skye

Portree

A87

Tullibardine ▽

Auchterarder

A9

Deanston ▽

Loch Lomond

Stirling

Forth

Dunfermline

Firth of Forth

Jura

Loch Lomond

Loch Lomond ●

Alexandria

Killearn

Glengoyne ▽

Falkirk

Edinburgh

Islay

Bute

Clyde

Glasgow

Arran

Firth of Clyde

Kintyre

Campbeltown

Ayr

Southern Uplands

THE HIGHLANDS

▽ Malt distillery

● Grain distillery

▼ Southern Highlands

▼ Central Highlands

▽ Eastern Highlands

▼ Northern Highlands

▼ Western Highlands

▼ Maltings

✗ Airport

SOUTHERN HIGHLANDS

Close to the northern suburbs of Glasgow they may be, but the distilleries in this part of Scotland have their own identities. Less unified in character, they are more a collection of intriguing personalities: an old farm site, a little-known distillery where innovation is the byword, Scotland's greenest site, and a resurrected plant.

Ben Lomond dominates the landscape of the Southern Highlands.

Glengoyne

KILLEARN, GLASGOW • WWW.GLENGOYNE.COM • OPEN ALL YEAR MON–SUN

No matter which way you cut it—defining the Highlands as the "High Land" above the geological fault that cuts diagonally across Scotland, or by an arbitrarily drawn line by nineteenth-century politicians for tax purposes (the way in which the regions are now legally defined)—Glengoyne is a Highland distillery.

A neat, white-painted farm-style plant, it's wedged into a small valley under the volcanic plug of Dumgoyne, the most westerly end of the Campsie Fells. To the south are green fields and then the outskirts of Glasgow.

It's an intriguing distillery, small in scale (a perfect place for the whisky newbie to learn about distillation). The new make, however, is light and intense with grassy notes and a smooth, fruity, middle palate that stretches out slowly during maturation. For manager Robbie Hughes, the key is the combination of time and copper, starting with fermentation. "The minimum 56-hour fermentation time ensures most of the energy has been removed from the wash and reduces carry-over on the wash still, which can produce a nuttier note."

Distillation is equally prolonged; again it's time—and copper. "We try and have maximum copper contact," says Hughes. "Slow distillation runs, maximizing the copper contact and thus increasing the estery notes. We distill very slowly, never overheating the stills. This aids reflux so many of the heavier compounds won't get the energy to get over the neck and into the middle cut. We also have copper pipes all the way to the spirit safe."

It's this mix of vigor and central fruitiness that allows Glengoyne to enjoy long maturation and gives it sufficient intensity of character to cope easily with first-fill sherry butts. A distillery that has tended to be overlooked in the past, it's now making a strong case for future inclusion in the top ranks.

The mash tun at Glengoyne.

GLENGOYNE TASTING NOTES

NEW MAKE

Nose: Very intense and lifted. Grassy (sweet hay) with a light fruity note.
Palate: Sweet with a solid mid-palate. Good bite.
Finish: Tight and pent-up. Instant coffee granules. Spicy.

10YO 40%

Nose: Pale gold. Immediate sherried notes. Cookie dough with a little butter, then moorland/green bracken.
Palate: Light clean and quite dry before central sweetness comes through. With water, cake-like.
Finish: Tight and drying, becoming spicy.
Conclusion: The assumption from the new make is this is light but there's depth within this vibrant character.

Flavor Camp: Fruity & Spicy
Where Next? Strathisla 18yo, Royal Lochnagar 12yo

15YO 43%

Nose: Shows an elegant, sherried character, with Glengoyne's signature spiciness adding freshness. Estery with undercurrents of hazelnut, white raisin, and subtle oxidative notes rather than overt sherry cask.
Palate: Ripe, with gentle, sweet spices. The layered palate offers some very pure, sweet fruit. Elegant with water.
Finish: Complex and long.
Conclusion: A slow-maturing single malt. Here Glengoyne begins to enter its second phase.

Flavor Camp: Fruity & Spicy
Where Next? Craigellachie, The Glenrothes Quercus Robur

21YO 43%

Nose: Even more dense. Mushroom and a touch of saddle oil, fruitcake, and a hint of allspice. Dried black cherry. Still has that central solidity seen in the new make. Fruitcake batter.
Palate: Earl Grey tea and dried rose petal. Espresso coffee. Sweetness is a little hidden and the maltiness is now malt extract. Water allows some dried raspberry to show.
Finish: Tannic.
Conclusion: The cask is now in charge but the distillery character continues to evolve underneath.

Flavor Camp: Rich & Round
Where Next? Tamnavulin 1963, Ben Nevis 25yo

Loch Lomond

ALEXANDRIA • WWW.LOCHLOMONDDISTILLERY.COM

One of Scotland's most remarkable (and probably its least-known) distilleries lies in Alexandria, near the southern banks of Loch Lomond. This is a strange interzone between the industrial Lowlands and the romantic Highlands, an undecided borderland that's home to housing schemes and golf clubs, mountains and urban sprawl. The distillery reflects this multiple (and slightly confusing) environment. Is it Highland? Lowland? Both? Loch Lomond is a grain and a malt distillery on the same site. This is a self-sufficient whisky plant making blends, single malts, and whiskies that have legislators tied in knots.

The malt distillery has four sets of stills of three different designs: the original stills from 1966, a set of standard pots from 1999, plus a new set, which are larger replicas of the originals whose design is intriguing. Often wrongly described as Lomond stills, they are pots with a rectifying column in the neck.

The spirit can be taken off at different plates, so the distiller is lengthening or shortening the neck, which has a direct effect on character. The eight different malt types produced here (including peated) provide the base for single-malt expressions and, with grain from the distillery's other plant, all the components for its High Commissioner blend.

Innovation is the key ingredient here. Take yeast. Scotch whisky is peculiar in its dependency on the same strains of yeast. Not Loch Lomond. It has been using wine yeasts for about a decade. The negative side is that they are twice as expensive as distiller's yeast, but the belief is that it brings something to the whisky, adding extra lift and fragrance.

The controversy lies in the production of a malt spirit that is produced in a column still (see p.16). The firm claims it should be a malt whisky, the Scotch Whisky Association says it's not traditional—despite this being a nineteenth-century technique. Not that Loch Lomond seems to care. It has always done things its own way. It might just be a model for the future.

In 2014 Loch Lomond distillery was sold to a private equity firm.

LOCH LOMOND TASTING NOTES

SINGLE MALT NAS 40%

Nose: Gold color. Vetiver. Malt bin, geranium, and lemon. With water, vegetal notes, and sweet wood phenols.
Palate: An herbal/nutty and slightly oat-like crispness, then a lightly clinging mid-palate. Brass.
Finish: Oily.
Conclusion: Light spirit and fresh oak working together.

Flavor Camp: **Malty & Dry**
Where Next? Glen Spey 12yo, Auchentoshan Classic

29YO, WM CADENHEAD BOTTLING 54%

Nose: Fluffy and light: marshmallow, floury hamburger buns, confectioner's sugar in an apple sponge cake. Then hardens into green fern, cucumber.
Palate: Malty and sweet to start. Nicely soft.
Finish: Clean and short.
Conclusion: A very slow maturation. Summer fresh.

Flavor Camp: **Fragrant & Floral**
Where Next? Glenburgie 15yo

SINGLE MALT, 1966 STILLS 45%

Nose: Dark gold color. Masses of oak extract. Suntan oil, sauna. Very sweet and bourbon-like. With water, fruit chews, and red plum.
Palate: Intense. Wood oils and pine. Touch of fresh oregano. Lemon zest.
Finish: Drying.
Conclusion: Clean, light spirit, and active oak.

Flavor Camp: **Fruity & Spicy**
Where Next? Maker's Mark, Bernheim Original Wheat, Glen Moray 16yo

INCHMURRIN, 12YO 46%

Nose: Mealy and sweet, with a pleasant freshness and cleanliness. There's light lemon in the background, alongside custard apple and white chocolate.
Palate: Fresh and fruity, with real impact, length, and good oak balance. Water relaxes it, bringing out some lemongrass and cooked pear.
Finish: Gentle, clean, and medium-length.
Conclusion: Balanced, gentle, and approachable.

Flavor Camp: **Fruity & Spicy**
Where Next? Bruichladdich 10yo

RHOSDHU (GRAIN/MALT HYBRID) 48%

Nose: Sweet barley, hay loft with a crisp fresh pear note almost *eaux de vie* in intensity. Clean and light.
Palate: Quite perfumed with lots of fruit blossom and a silky, aromatic feel. Orgeat and light nut.
Finish: That essence note.
Conclusion: Made from malted barley which has been run through a column still.

Flavor Camp: **Fragrant & Floral**
Where Next? Nikka Coffey Malt

12YO, ORGANIC SINGLE BLEND 40%

Nose: Sweet barley, hay loft with a crisp, fresh Williams pear note that is almost eau de vie in intensity. Clean and light.
Palate: Quite perfumed, with lots of fruit blossom and a silky, aromatic feel. Almond syrup notes mix with light nut tones.
Finish: That essence note.
Conclusion: Made from malted barley that has been run through a column still.

Flavor Camp: **Fragrant & Floral**

Deanston

DEANSTON • STIRLING • WWW.DEANSTONMALT.COM • OPEN ALL YEAR MON–SUN

Deanston, it must be said, doesn't look like a distillery. Neither should it really. It was, after all, originally an eighteenth-century mill, which at one time boasted the largest waterwheel in Europe and was home to the development of the Spinning Jenny. The mill was here because of the water. The Teith River was harnessed to provide power and today 5,283,441 gallons (20 million liters) of water an hour pass through the distillery turbines, meaning that it is not only self-sufficient in power, but sells the excess back to the National Grid. Green is the word.

Deanston is a relative newcomer, dating from just 1964 when the old mill finally closed. Once owned by Invergordon, it's now part of Burn Stewart, whose general distilleries manager, Ian MacMillan, is based here.

It's also one of Scotland's more surprising sites. The turbines are unusual, for starters, but so, somehow, is the size (the 11-ton open-topped mash tun) and the little details like the brass chokers around the necks of the four fat stills, and the upward angle of the lyne arms.

The biggest surprise, for those who haven't tried Deanston recently, is the new make: all snuffed candles and beeswax, the latter easing itself into honey as it matures. It's miles away from the simple, dry style of the recent past.

"That waxiness was the original house style," says MacMillan, "but during Invergordon's stewardship [1972–90] it got lost and I made it my task to get it back on track." So how has he achieved this? "By changing things bit by bit, but mainly by reintroducing lower gravities (ie. less sugar) in the worts to help promote esters. The ferments are longer and we're distilling slowly and giving the stills air rests. I believe in the old-fashioned ways."

This waxy style is now a rare commodity in whisky, resulting in Deanston's make being highly prized by blenders.

In the extraordinary vaulted warehouse lie casks of organic whisky, while all the single-malt bottlings are now at 46 percent and non-chill-filtered. "Chill-filtering means you lose aroma and flavor," says MacMillan. "It has taken 12 years to develop these flavors. Why take them straight out? I want people to taste them!"

Deanston: a surprise at every turn.

DEANSTON TASTING NOTES

NEW MAKE
Nose: Heavy. Snuffed candle/beeswax and, in time, wild garlic. Wet reeds and a hint of cereal underneath.
Palate: Clean and very thick on the tongue. Tongue-coating. With water a touch of bran but mostly it's candle wax.
Finish: Lightly clinging.

10YO CASK SAMPLE
Nose: Gold. Big American oak influence with masses of coconut. The waxiness seems to have gone, but a new honeyed aspect is emerging. Suntan lotion. Light chocolate.
Palate: Big wood influence with masses of sweetness. Very honeyed and gentle. Feel is similar to new make.
Finish: Soft, with light butterscotch.
Conclusion: Flavors show integration between wood and that waxy character, which is now becoming more honeyed.

12YO 46.3%
Nose: Light gold. Clean and sweet. Light corn syrup. Some toffee, canned peach as it opens, along with melting milk chocolate. Sweet cereal in the background along with clementine.
Palate: Very sweet and concentrated. Honeyed, canned rice pudding and slightly waxy with a touch of crisp oak toward the finish.
Finish: Tingling and lightly spiced.
Conclusion: Now at 46.3% and non-chill-filtered, it has revealed a softer and juicier heart than the older expression.

Flavor Camp: Fruity & Spicy
Where Next? Aberfeldy 12yo, The BenRiach 16yo

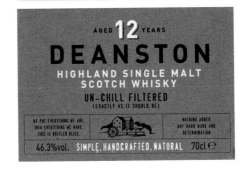

28YO CASK SAMPLE
Nose: Gold/amber. Classic mature character. Lots of spices and also a hint of soapiness, then lightly polished furniture—we're almost back to the beeswax of the new make, cut with caramel and pecan.
Palate: Drying. Slightly faded but with a strawberry note (that is also in the 16yo release). The waxiness is back. Fragile.
Finish: Tingling, clean, cinnamon.
Conclusion: Deanston's been on a roller-coaster.

Tullibardine

AUCHTERARDER • WWW.TULLIBARDINE.COM • OPEN ALL YEAR MON–SUN

It's little wonder that Tullibardine was built in Blackford, at the northern edge of the Ochil Hills. This is a site with plentiful supplies of water. Highland Spring is bottled here, while beer has been brewed since 1488. The first Tullibardine was established in 1798, but the current site was constructed in 1949 during the postwar boom—again, on the site of a brewery. Owned and designed by the famous distillery architect William Delmé-Evans, it was a tiny operation that was refitted when new owner Brodie Hepburn took over in 1953; the original mash tun and washbacks heading eight miles north to The Glenturret.

Tullibardine ended up with Whyte & Mackay, and in 1994 the distillery was mothballed. It was reopened in 2003 by a consortium who, to offset costs, leased out some of the old warehousing as a shopping development.

In 2011, Tullibardine changed hands once again when it was bought by French wine and spirit group Picard, owner of the Highland Queen and Muirhead's brands. "When Picard took over, they told us that they saw themselves as custodians, not owners," recalls international sales manager James Robertson. "They are looking long-term." The shopping development is in the process of being converted back into its original purpose, the distillery is running at full capacity, and there is investment in equipment. More significantly for the drinker, the range has been rationalized, repackaged, and relaunched.

The issue with buying any mothballed distillery is managing the hole in stock, and, in Tullibardine's case, also managing whisky that had been put in tired casks to be a young, fresh component in blends. The needs for single malt are diametrically opposed to that. A plethora of finishes was initially one way to get over the issue of wood, but the old range was too large, and lacked coherence and an identifiable distillery character.

Thankfully, all that has changed. The enlightened wood policy that started with the last owner is finally bearing fruit. The make

The gates at Tullibardine were locked for nine years but the distillery is now happily up and running once more.

had also been tweaked under the previous regime by the legendary John Black, who, with 57 years in the industry, was Scotland's oldest distiller. Sadly, he died in 2013, but his legacy is now guaranteed.

Tullibardine is a case study of how whisky is not an instantaneous spirit, and how turning any distillery around takes time. Here, however, it has definitely happened.

TULLIBARDINE TASTING NOTES

SOVEREIGN 43%
Nose: Like creamy, light sweet oatmeal topped with light-brown sugar, with soft fruit behind. Becomes fragrant with less maltiness than in the past. Delicately perfumed and, with water, fresh green leaves.
Palate: Soft and fresh, with a lacy feel. With water, it becomes sweeter and slightly more silky. The floral notes are brought forward.
Finish: Touch of malt.
Conclusion: A more flowery and forward Tullibardine than in the past.

Flavor Camp: **Fragrant & Floral**
Where Next? Linkwood 14yo, Glen Keith

BURGUNDY FINISH 43%
Nose: Tight, with the light distillery character given weight by wine casks that shift things into raspberry jam skimmings and hard candy.
Palate: Unctuous feel, dominated by lightly stewed fruit.
Finish: Tayberry and blueberry. Long.
Conclusion: Strikes a good balance among all the different elements (distillery/refill/wine cask).

Flavor Camp: **Fruity & Spicy**
Where Next? Glenmorangie Quinta Ruban

20YO 43%
Nose: Woody and mealy, with touches of freshly baked whole-grain bread. Shows the light oiliness that's typical of age.
Palate: The oak adds richness to the mix, but it retains a fat cereal note. Hints of snuffed candle.
Finish: Nutty.
Conclusion: Quite different in character to the younger examples, with much more cereal accents.

Flavor Camp: **Malty & Dry**
Where Next? Glen Garioch

CENTRAL HIGHLANDS

Clustered around central Perthshire, with two outliers, here we find distilleries with stories that speak of secrets, smuggling, millers, farmers, royalty, and blenders being drawn back to their family roots. This once was a center of distilling activity, only these few have survived. The reason? Quality and individuality.

The countryside watered by the River Tay has long been whisky country.

The Glenturret & Strathearn

CRIEFF • WWW.THEFAMOUSGROUSE.COM • HOME TO THE FAMOUS GROUSE EXPERIENCE • OPEN ALL YEAR MON–SUN
STRATHEARN • METHVEN • WWW.FACEBOOK.COM/STRATHEARNDISTILLERY

With the exception of its two outliers, the Central Highland's distilleries are clustered together in central Perthshire, as if to draw on a sense of mutual support. There would be no surprise if they did. While there are only half a dozen Central Highland stills left today, Perthshire alone was once home to more than 70. The majority were opened in the post-1823 get-rich-quick boom, when farmer-smugglers, in the spirit of Isaiah 2:4, turned away from the illegal and embraced a new lawful and peaceable life.

Many quickly discovered that there was a difference between producing small amounts of variable-quality whisky for back-door sales, and selling larger amounts of consistent quality through the front. Couple this with the economic depression of the 1840s and most had gone by the mid-nineteenth century.

Three distilleries in this region do, however, give an idea of what these old farm sites might have looked like. The first is The Glenturret distillery, on the outskirts of Crieff. The mash is a mere one ton, the stills are basic and angular, and the overall impression is of barns and outbuildings being put to secondary use.

The Glenturret is actually an exercise in re-creation. Dismantled in 1929, it lay derelict for three decades. Now part of the Edrington Group, it's home to The Famous Grouse Experience. In some ways, the big bird has deflected attention from the fact that The Glenturret makes a delightful dram—although this itself has been re-created. "John Ramsay [Edrington's former master blender] re-engineered The Glenturret when we bought it in 1990, adjusting flow rates and cut points and being more consistent in their application," says his successor, Gordon Motion. There's also now a heavily peated variant that is used for The Black Grouse.

Re-engineered it may be, but is it still recognizably The Glenturret? "We couldn't change the stills, so we can only make a certain type of whisky," Motion explains. "Any distillery is a balance between what you inherit and what it will give you."

STRATHEARN DISTILLERY: WHISKY IN MINIATURE

The address says it all: Bachilton Farm Steadings. Scotland's smallest distillery opened in old farm buildings in the village of Methven in 2013. Everything is done in miniature here: the wash still takes 211 gallons (800 liters), the charge for the spirit still is only 118 galons (450 liters), the make is being filled into 13-gallon (50-liter) casks. There's flexibility, however. A gin is already on the market, and there are plenty more ideas floating around, including DIY distilling days. Small perhaps, but Strathearn's ideas are huge.

Whisky-making in miniature, The Glenturret is one of Perthshire's few remaining farm distilleries.

THE GLENTURRET TASTING NOTES

NEW MAKE
Nose: Green bitter-orange, curaçao, some sulfur, and fresh corn with a little enamel paint behind.
Palate: Quite nutty and jalapeño-hot. The texture is creamy, and there's a touch of sulfur on the back palate. Lightness and freshness behind will emerge in cask.
Finish: Clean.

10YO 40%
Nose: Light gold. Sweet, with notes of proving bread, linoleum, orange blossom.
Palate: Floral but quite fat and creamy on the tongue. With water, there's pollen and dried flowers, garden twine and pink rhubarb. Lifted and citric.
Finish: Fragrant and fresh.
Conclusion: Light in aroma, but with enough weight to stand long-term maturation.

Flavor Camp: Fragrant & Floral
Where Next? Bladnoch 8yo, Strathmill 12yo

Aberfeldy

ABERFELDY • HOME OF DEWAR'S WORLD OF WHISKY • WWW.DEWARS.COM • OPEN ALL YEAR; APR–OCT, MON–SUN; NOV–MAR, MON–SAT

Perthshire is Scotland caught in two minds. If you stick to the main roads you'd believe it was a landscape of relaxed grassy hills. Deviate from that crowded route, however, and you'll find a countryside that is Highland, a place of 3,000-foot (920-meter) peaks: Ben Lawers, Meall Garbh, Schiehallion. The last was where, in 1774, the Earth's weight was calculated and, as a consequence, where contour lines and modern mapping were invented.

It's an interzone, unsure of whether it is wilderness or manicured farmland, a place where the past seeps in. Driving along Glen Lyon from Aberfeldy you pass Fortingall where, hunched and dark in the churchyard, is a yew tree estimated to be 5,000 years old; follow the glen west and you end up in the peat bogs of Rannoch Moor.

It was into this borderland that John Dewar was born in 1805, on a croft in Shenavail, two miles outside Aberfeldy. Apprenticed as a carpenter aged 23, he headed to Perth to join a distant relative's wine-merchant business. By 1846 he had his own business and had began dealing in whisky. By the end of the century, Dewar's blend was selling over half a million cases worldwide. The firm needed a distillery and in 1898 they opened one at Aberfeldy.

Why here? John's sons, John Alexander and Tommy, could have built their distillery anywhere. By the end of the nineteenth century, Speyside would have been the most logical place for it. Instead, they built it within sight of their father's humble birthplace, where he walked bare-footed as a child, carrying peats for the fire as payment for his education. They built in Aberfeldy because of an emotional link.

The Aberfeldy distillery was built by John Dewar's sons two miles from their father's farmhouse.

The beeswax/honey note is triggered in the long fermentation and concentrated during slow distillation in the tight-necked, onion-shaped stills. Cutting high in the run preserves a delicacy of aroma, seen best in maturation in refill or first-fill American oak, while the waxiness adds a thickness to the palate, allowing long maturation.

It may have been set up to produce a style that suited a blender's requirements, but its location speaks of a psychic link to place. Aberfeldy's pragmatic and emotional reasons come together.

ABERFELDY TASTING NOTES

NEW MAKE

Nose: Sweet with a lightly waxed note, white fruit.
Palate: Clean focused. Highly sweet, waxy texture, clean.
Finish: Long and slowly drying.

8YO CASK SAMPLE

Nose: Gold. Sweet. Clover honey, malty notes, pear.
Palate: Sweet and silky and surprisingly spicy. Tries to attack but is restrained by a central thick sweetness.
Finish: Lean.
Conclusion: Still evolving.

12YO 40%

Nose: Amber. The honey on the 8yo is much deeper but also more scented. The green pear has gone and a floral note—the estery notes in new make—emerges with ripe apple. Fresh oak and raspberry jam.
Palate: The oak leads but has also now been bound into the sweetness developing a butterscotch accent. Rounded. Tablet and peach juice.
Finish: Long and sweet.
Conclusion: Firing on all cylinders now.

Flavor Camp: Fruity & Spicy
Where Next? Bruichladdich 16yo, Longmorn 10yo, Glen Elgin 12yo

21YO 40%

Nose: Amber. Medium to heavy with more smoke, light corn syrup, macadamia nut. Supple. Oak is now just a support. Touch of beeswax and coconut cream. With water, heather honey and peat.
Palate: Surprisingly, smoky, which adds a fragrant (but also dry) layer on top of the sweet silky and lightly minty/waxiness.
Finish: Long and softly spiced. Oak comes through.
Conclusion: Intriguing.

Flavor Camp: Fruity & Spicy
Where Next? Glenmorangie 25yo

Edradour & Blair Athol

EDRADOUR • PITLOCHRY • WWW.EDRADOUR.COM • OPEN APR–OCT, MON–SAT
BLAIR ATHOL • PITLOCHRY • WWW.DISCOVERING-DISTILLERIES.COM/BLAIRATHOL • OPEN ALL YEAR; SEE WEBSITE FOR DAYS & DETAILS

Pitlochry is a prosperous looking wide-streeted Victorian town, but in the eighteenth and nineteenth centuries the center of commerce lay three miles to the north in the village of Moulin. While there is some debate over the meaning of the name, it's close to the Gaelic *muileann* (mill) and where there's a mill there's usually a distillery. In Moulin's case, there were four. One remains.

Whether Edradour is still Scotland's smallest distillery is a moot point. Any that are smaller are recent builds. The most important element is that it has survived from the Victorian era and, more significantly, that it is still producing whisky. Want an insight into the old days of Perthshire distilling? The clues are all here.

"Essentially it's the same kit," says Des McCagherty of Signatory Vintage, which bought Edradour in 2002. "Open-topped rake mash tun, Morton's refrigerator, wooden washbacks, and tiny stills with worm tubs. We've only changed things because we had to: the worm had to be replaced and we've put in a new stainless-steel Morton's refrigerator." The traditional kit gives an oily, sweet new make, which is deeply honeyed, with some roasted-cereal notes and a ripe thickness on the palate. This robust character is now going mostly into traditional wood. "The final thing is that Edradour is now all single malt [rather than going into blends] and we are filling into first- or second-fill wood," says McCagherty. "The bulk of Edradour goes to sherry [casks] and Ballechin [the new heavily peated variant] mainly into first-fill bourbon. Edradour lends itself to a good sherry cask."

It's another of a small but growing band of independent distillers who McCagherty sees as keeping alive techniques that would have died, and "distilleries that would have disappeared".

Pitlochry is also home to Diageo's Blair Athol distillery, producing legally since 1798 and part of the Bell's stable since 1933. Bell's was a distiller that ran most of its sites in a similar fashion: cloudy worts, short ferments, condensers, resulting in a nutty/spicy style. Blair Athol is at the extreme heavy end of this. Controlled carry-over in the wash still gives an agriculturally pungent new make that leads into a richly fruited maturity. Like Edradour, it is at its best in ex-sherry casks.

BLAIR ATHOL TASTING NOTES

NEW MAKE

Nose: Heavy malt-extract character. Cattle feed/dark grains. Seeds and nuts, then carbolic soap.
Palate: Charred and malty. Heavy and powerful.
Finish: Bone-dry.

8YO, REFILL WOOD CASK SAMPLE

Nose: Muesli: black grapes, flaked oats. Rich and broad, the fruit emerging.
Palate: Hot, full-bodied, and slightly earthy. Weighty and still burnt/dry. Powerful potential.
Finish: Dry and long.
Conclusion: This heavyweight needs time and active casks to pull out its hidden secrets.

12YO, FLORA & FAUNA 43%

Nose: Dark amber. Roasted malt, violet. Malted loaf, some raisin. Slightly waxy with light prune. Sweetens with water.
Palate: Heavy and sweet. Dry malty/nutty depth with raisin on top. The charred note is now integrated into the oak, adding depth and richness. Malted milk with water.
Finish: Bitter chocolate.
Conclusion: European oak gives this big malty spirit the extra layers it needs to balance out.

Flavor Camp: Rich & Round
Where Next? Macallan 15yo Sherry, Fettercairn 33yo, Glenfiddich 15yo, Dailuaine 16yo

EDRADOUR TASTING NOTES

EDRADOUR NEW MAKE

Nose: Heavy. Clean. Honeyed and lightly oily with black fruits, banana skin, meadow hay/hayloft. Barley.
Palate: Sweet start then linseed oil and currranty fruit. Chewy and muscular. Mouth-coating with firm cereal support.
Finish: Long. Drying.

BALLECHIN NEW MAKE

Nose: As heavy as Edradour with a little more cereal and wood smoke (birch logs).
Palate: Immediate smoke but the deep fruit and oils balance.
Finish: Oily but fruity. A big spirit but balanced.

1996, OLOROSO FINISH 57%

Nose: Full gold. Hazelnut oil, dry grass, touch of spice. Light earth. Roast nuts. With water, herbs, almond.
Palate: Nutty start then the oiliness carries it forward, becoming sweet in the center. Mouth-coating and generous.
Finish: Light anise.
Conclusion: Interestingly, a bit akin to Lepanto brandy.

Flavor Camp: Fruity & Spicy
Where Next? Dalmore 12yo

1997 57.2%

Nose: Copper. More restrained than the 1996. Lightly stewed fruit. Plum and fruitcake. With water, a hint of graphite and poached pears in red wine.
Palate: The honeyed sweetness is in control. Fresh red fruit, dried raspberry, strawberry, chocolate hint.
Finish: Sweet.
Conclusion: Like many Edradours, intriguing vinous quality.

Flavor Camp: Rich & Round
Where Next? Dalmore 15yo, Jura 21yo

HIGHLAND
SINGLE MALT
SCOTCH WHISKY

BLAIR ATHOL

distillery, established in 1798, stands on *peaty moorland* in the *foothills* of the *GRAMPIAN MOUNTAINS.* An ancient source of *water* for the *distillery, ALLT' DOUR BURN~'The Burn of the Otter',* flows close by. This *single MALT SCOTCH WHISKY* has a *mellow deep toned* aroma, a *strong fruity* flavour and a *smooth* finish.

AGED **12** YEARS

43% vol   Distilled & Bottled in SCOTLAND. BLAIR ATHOL DISTILLERY, Pitlochry, Perthshire, Scotland.   70cl

Royal Lochnagar

BALLATER • WWW.DISCOVERING-DISTILLERIES.COM/ROYALLOCHNAGAR • OPEN ALL YEAR; SEE WEBSITE FOR DAYS & DETAILS

The next central distillery lies in Deeside, an hour north of Moulin, over the high pass of Glenshee. Coming into this landscape of heavy, dark-green forests and neat towns festooned with royal warrants can lull the visitor into believing this is an easily read area of middle-class respectability, but this has always been a hideaway. Its high mountain passes gave grazing and soft passage to the drovers taking their cattle to the central markets—the same routes plied by whisky smugglers heading south from Speyside, or from Deeside's own black *bothies* (huts). Queen Victoria and Prince Albert built Balmoral Castle here because of the area's isolation; it would be here the mourning queen would sequester herself.

The surrounding back country is scattered with fine lodges, *shielings, bothies,* and old distilleries. A secret, hermetic, landscape in which you can easily lose yourself. Nothing is quite what it seems. The first distillery in Upper Deeside was allegedly burned down by illicit distillers after its owner James Robertson, himself a moonshiner, set up a legal site beside the river at Crathie.

By 1845, Royal Lochnagar (it was given the accolade by Queen Victoria who liked a tipple mixed with claret) was built. Given the nature of this part of the world, it is, inevitably, hidden above the Dee on a mini-plateau, its thick walls made of local granite whose flecks of mica and feldspar make it glister in the sun after rain.

The tiniest of Diageo's plants, your assumption when looking at Royal Lochnagar's two small stills and its worm tubs is that this is a heavy site. And yet this is a distillery which, rather like Glen Elgin (*see* p.86) works against type, using techniques that hyper-extend the copper conversation.

A relaxed approach is taken here. The stills are run only twice a week and are given an air rest between distillations to allow the copper to rejuvenate. The worm tubs are kept warm, again to increase copper availability. What should be sulfury is instead grassy, but Lochnagar's inbuilt character means this grass isn't green, but dry, offering a minor echo of its location and in its (yes, inevitably, easily overlooked) mid-palate solidity, the clues to its suitability for long-term maturation. In Upper Deeside, nothing is quite what it seems.

ROYAL LOCHNAGAR TASTING NOTES

NEW MAKE

Nose: Dry hay, light pear, and ripened fruits with just a hint of smoke. Heavy, grassy.
Palate: Fresh and clean with distinct smokiness in a solid center. Dips on the tongue.
Finish: Clean.

8YO, REFILL WOOD CASK SAMPLE

Nose: Picked up some vanilla/white chocolate from the cask. Still the hay/straw character but the fruit is now softening. Light smoke.
Palate: A surprising citric, appley note to start, then comes the sweet straw. Retains good palate richness that is beginning to develop flavor.
Finish: Pear-like. Dry grass again.
Conclusion: Worm tubs have given this grassy malt extra depth.

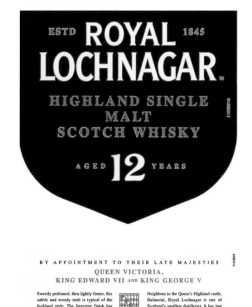

12YO 40%

Nose: Clean. Grass clippings, with a touch of cereal behind. Quite fresh with a crisp nature. In time there's dry hay, hazelnut, light cumin seed, and lemon.
Palate: Sweeter than you expect. Light to medium-bodied, but a balance has been struck between the dryness (malt/hay) and sweet (praline/light fruit) notes. Cinnamon.
Finish: Gentle and clean.
Conclusion: Fresh and appealing.

Flavor Camp: **Fruity & Spicy**
Where Next? Glengoyne 10yo, Yamazaki 12yo

SELECTED RESERVE NAS 43%

Nose: Big sherried influence. Sweet dried fruits (making Christmas pudding), some rum and raisin, and a little molasses.
Palate: Fruitcake with a light tingle of allspice. The grassiness has gone but the depth of the spirit allows it to cope with the oak.
Finish: Long and sweet.
Conclusion: A bold expression in which the distillery character plays a seconary role.

Flavor Camp: **Rich & Round**
Where Next? Glenfiddich 18yo, Dailuaine 16yo

Dalwhinnie

DALWHINNIE • WWW.DISCOVERING-DISTILLERIES.COM/DALWHINNIE • OPEN ALL YEAR; SEE WEBSITE FOR DAYS & DETAILS

After the Deeside detour, the final distillery in this central region sits, isolated, on a high plateau between the Cairngorm and the Monadhliath mountain ranges. The location, while spectacular, is initially at least surprising. This is an exposed site: the joint-highest distillery in Scotland (an honor it shares with Braeval), situated in the coldest settlement in the UK. The distillery used to have a bunkhouse that served as a billet both for workers unable to get home— because of the weather naturally—and stranded motorists.

Why build here? The answer lies at what most visitors arriving by road think is the back of the distillery (it's actually the front): the railway line. Here is another late Victorian distillery (it was constructed in 1897) built to take advantage of the blending boom and easy access to the central belt. Whether distilling took place here prior to this is unclear. Certainly its situation as a meeting point of drove roads suggests that plenty of illicit stuff must have passed through over the years.

That honeyed thread, which runs through some of these central Highland distilleries, here reaches its most concentrated expression. Rich, thick, and sweet, Dalwhinnie's texture, appropriately enough given its location, allows it to be a single malt that takes on a new dimension when frozen. Honey is however not immediately apparent when the new make is nosed. Dalwhinnie's secret lies at the road entrance, the large circular wooden tubs containing the worm tubs for its pair of stills (*see* picture, far right).

The new make, starved of copper contact, ends up leaving those worms as sulfury as car exhaust fumes. It seems a strange way to go about making whisky. Why, with all the technology at their disposal, doesn't Diageo simply make it without the sulfur? "It's the price you pay at this stage for wanting the real distillery character," says Diageo's distilling and blending guru, Douglas Murray. "If you ran it to take out the sulfur, as we do at Royal Lochnagar, the new make would be grassy or fruity. If you run things to make sulfury [spirit], the building blocks that give that grassy/fruity character don't get together, so you end up with a light and delicate character. Sulfur is simply a marker when it is new, the real character lies underneath."

It lies there for a long time. Dalwhinnie slumbers under this blanket for many years, one reason for the main expression being bottled at 15yo. The other advantage of this longer maturation is that the honeyed note, just discernible in new make, has a chance to concentrate, which begs another question: where does the honey come from?

"I think honey is a halfway house," says Murray. "To simplify things we talk about waxy, or grassy, or fruity in new make, but if you run the distillery in order to make waxiness, but don't push it to the extreme (as we do at Clynelish) you end up with a pleasant, sweet butteriness." Sweetness combined with waxiness can be perceived as beeswax when young and honey when mature, the same character that you pick up at Aberfeldy or Deanston.

And here, in the tundra, surrounded by nothing but moor and mountain, time seems to slow. As the visitor takes deep breaths to calm the city-tuned heart, he is mirroring Dalwhinnie's whisky with its steady, relaxed thickening, its accretion of density, its real personality.

Dalwhinnie new make flows through worm tubs into the spirit safe.

WORMS V CONDENSER

Although the original method of condensing, these days worm tubs are a rarity. "Shell and tube" condensers were introduced throughout the industry during the twentieth century. Though more efficient, they also fundamentally altered character, removing depth. The proof of this was discovered here at Dalwhinnie when the old worms were removed. With them went "Dalwhinnie." They were quickly replaced and Dalwhinnie reappeared.

Scotland's joint-highest distillery, Dalwhinnie is also the coldest settlement in Britain.

DALWHINNIE TASTING NOTES

NEW MAKE

Nose: Pea soup, sauerkraut. Masses of sulfur. Heavy and with some peat smoke. Exhaust fumes.

Palate: Dry and deep with sweetness underneath. Heavy.

Finish: Sulfur.

8YO, REFILL WOOD CASK SAMPLE

Nose: Leafy notes, some wood, and still some sulfur (broccoli) but also runny honey and hot butter.

Palate: The sensation is of dimly seen potential flavors. A soporific heaviness with glimpses of honey, heather, and soft fruit.

Finish: Dumb and smoky.

Conclusion: Sleeping still. Interesting to compare this at the same age to other sulfury new makes such as Speyburn, anCnoc, and Glenkinchie. Just needs time for its mature character to emerge fully.

15YO 43%

Nose: Mellow with rich sweetness and lots of American oak/*crème brûlée* character. Whisper of smoke. Honeyed with lemon zest. Becomes more pollen-like with water. Good weight.

Palate: Immediate and quite thick start. Smoke is light but noticeable. Good mix of dessert-like sweetness/Greek yogurt with acacia honey and crisp wood.

Finish: Long and soft.

Conclusion: Now fully awake, it has shaken off its sulfury overcoat to reveal itself in its honeyed guise.

Flavor Camp: **Fruity & Spicy**

Where Next? The Balvenie 12yo Signature

DISTILLER'S EDITION 43%

Nose: Deep gold. Fat and creamy with a new tangerine marmalade note. More fragrant and smooth than the 15yo with an added nuttier note as well, while the smoke has gone. Dessert apple and sweet pear mixing with the discreet honey.

Palate: Rounded and sweet and the grilled nut has given extra grip and interest to the palate. Orange blossom honey and almonds.

Finish: Longer and slightly thicker.

Conclusion: Slightly juicier and more interesting. Balanced.

Flavor Camp: **Fruity & Spicy**

Where Next? Glenmorangie The Original 10yo, The Balvenie 12yo Signature

1992, MANAGER'S CHOICE, SINGLE CASK 50%

Nose: Bright gold. Saddle soap that's gone a bit hard and tacky. Behind that are some heavy florals (think lily), currant leaf, and a touch of sulfur.

Palate: Ripe and fruity, it's reminiscent of the wee packs of breakfast spreads you get in a Scottish B&B, a hint of apricot, some tangerine marmalade, a bee's worth of honey. Light.

Finish: Whipped cream, but short.

Conclusion: A slightly less active cask and the sulfur is still there.

Flavor Camp: **Fruity & Spicy**

Where Next? Aberfeldy 12yo

1986, 20YO SPECIAL RELEASE 56.8%

Nose: Glowing amber. Rich and ripe. Light moor-burn notes drift in immediately, alongside dry bracken. Then it deepens: cooked autumn fruit, dried peach, heather honey running over hot crumpet, peach tart. With water, the impression is of caramelized fruit sugars and moist light-brown sugar.

Palate: Soft, with light smoke and a previously hidden spiciness. Time seems to slow it, deepen, and sweeten the flavors: spices, bitter orange. Cake-like richness, toffee.

Finish: Generous and long. Ripe fruit.

Conclusion: The depth of character is now revealed.

Flavor Camp: **Fruity & Spicy**

Where Next? Balblair 1979, Aberfeldy 21yo

EASTERN HIGHLANDS

Fertile it may be, this is a relatively sparsely populated part of Scotland, distillery-wise. The reasons for this are complex and surprising—as are the whiskies. As ever, though, you can't make broad assumptions about regional style. Even the smokiest example from the Eastern Highlands is also one of the most fragrant.

The Deveron River snakes into the Moray Firth at Macduff.

Glencadam

BRECHIN • WWW.GLENCADAMDISTILLERY.CO.UK

The Eastern Highlands are littered with the memories of failed plants. Brechin's North Port; Glenury-Royal in Stonehaven; all of Aberdeen's distilleries. Our story starts, however, in Montrose, which once boasted three distilleries: Glenesk (aka Hillside), which also made grain whisky and had its own drum maltings; Lochside, another joint malt/grain plant; and Glencadam. When all three shut it seemed as if the east coast's distilling history had been consigned to the past. Then, in 2003, Glencadam was bought by Angus Dundee. Little known in the days of being a provider of juice for Ballantine's and Stewart's Cream of the Barley blends, its whiskies have proved to be a revelation.

The fact that Glenesk and Lochside both made grain (and the former had its own maltings) shows how rich in raw materials this part of the country is. Why then were distilleries decimated? Some argue that there was a lack of water, although the truth might be more business-led.

Malt whisky is all about individuality. The question at times of stock surplus is, is this whisky individual enough? All the east-coasters were small sites owned by large blending firms and the brutal reality was that they were surplus to requirements in flavor terms. The grain whisky could be made elsewhere; the make

coming from the malt plants was close enough to that coming from larger distilleries. At times of crisis (such as the late 1970s) you trim at the margins of the estate. Whisky is rarely romantic. There's precious little room for sentiment.

Glencadam, however, has survived. Its fragrant floral style of whisky isn't that far from Linkwood (*see* pp.92–3) with which it shares a clinging quality in the center of the tongue. This lightness of character, Angus Dundee's blender Lorne MacKillop believes, comes from the fact that the stills' lyne pipes are at an upward angle, thereby increasing reflux. "It wasn't known as a single malt," he says. "And we wanted to accentuate this floral style, so decided to bottle it non-chill-filtered with no caramel added." The east coast may not be exactly rising but at least it is alive.

GLENCADAM TASTING NOTES

NEW MAKE

Nose: Fragrant/floral with some *eaux de vie* (Poire William), green grape, a little popcorn underneath.

Palate: Very sweet. Green with a pooling effect in the middle of the tongue. Becomes more floral to the finish.

Finish: Clean and light.

10YO 46%

Nose: Light gold. Delicate with flowers then fresh apricot, just-ripe pear, lemon.

Palate: Gentle and smooth. Sweet with vanilla, nutmeg, then cappucino. Again the fruits settle and sit in the center before the floral lift.

Finish: Apple blossom.

Conclusion: Delicate yet with substance.

Flavor Camp: Fragrant & Floral
Where Next? Glenkinchie 12yo, Speyburn 10yo, Linkwood 12yo

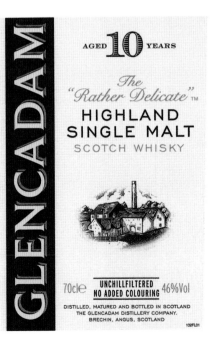

15YO 46%

Nose: Gold. Sweet and slightly restrained with just a little more dry-leaf character. The flowers are a little heavier, the wood has added a balanced nuttiness.

Palate: Firmer than 10yo, but still tongue-coating. Nuts, a hint of light date, ripe fruits.

Finish: Fruit now pulls free.

Conclusion: Crisp with positive bite, but such sweet concentration the wood doesn't dominate.

Flavor Camp: Fruity & Spicy
Where Next? Scapa 16yo, Craigellachie 14yo

1978 46%

Nose: Dark amber. Full and sherried with some *rancio*. The fruits now heading into late-autumn ripeness. The green apple is now caramel apple. Lots of chocolate, then cigar box/humidor.

Palate: Firm but smooth. Again rich chestnut and chocolate but still that inherent ripeness. Highland toffee.

Finish: Soft and nutty.

Conclusion: Has held up well for what seems a light spirit.

Flavor Camp: Rich & Round
Where Next? Glengoyne 17yo, Glenfiddich 15yo, Hakushu 25yo

Fettercairn

FETTERCAIRN • WWW.FETTERCAIRNDISTILLERY.CO.UK • OPEN MAY–SEPT, MON–SAT

The Howe of the Mearns is the setting for Lewis Grassic Gibbon's *Scots Quair* trilogy, which recounts the changes in Scotland as it moves from a golden age of agriculture to twentieth-century industrialization. Though written in the twentieth century, it can be seen as a late Romantic book, which both celebrates a mythical link to the land and meditates on loss: of roots, of faith, of political belief. Its narrative arc covers the same period as the rise of whisky and it is centered on the part of the world where Fettercairn sits.

The distillery sits on the flatlands looking out toward the coast, just outside a pretty town that could have acted as a model for Gibbon's Seggie, but its backdrop is mountainous. It is only a short (if hilly) trek to Royal Lochnagar.

Inside, the setup speaks of traditional ways of whisky-making, maybe with some echoes of the moonshining days when the smugglers would descend from Deeside with their wares. There's an open-topped mash tun, stills with soap grinders on the sides—soap was used as a surfactant to reduce frothing in the wash still—although it's in the dunnage warehouses where a more modern side is revealed.

This acts as one of the experimental sites where Whyte & Mackay's master blender Richard Paterson investigates wood, here most notably virgin oak, and for a specific reason: to try and surmount the burnt/vegetable note in younger Fettercairn. "It is a fight," says Paterson. "There were stainless-steel condensers here from 1995 until 2009, which gave that burnt note and made the malt a bit hard. This is a whisky that needs American oak to sweeten it and that's why I started using virgin oak—just to give it that sweet start."

The lush lands of the Mearns surround this one-time farm distillery.

Fettercairn, it strikes me, is an awkward delinquent that takes a long time to lose its youthful sulkiness. When it does, finally, reach maturity it appears to have learned from its somewhat aggressive past and become a whisky to sit down with. Whatever you do, don't dismiss it.

FETTERCAIRN TASTING NOTES

NEW MAKE
Nose: Floury, vegetable, light sulfur, hinting at sweetness.
Palate: Firm, slightly fruity, and with weight. Seems closed.
Finish: Crisp and short.

9YO CASK SAMPLE
Nose: Preserved lemon and turnips. Slightly singed. Lots of cask influence. Vanilla hit and oak shavings.
Palate: Better than the nose with sweet cardboard, some red apple.
Finish: Nuts.
Conclusion: Still absorbing the oak, still resisting. Even now, this Fettercairn seems to be refusing to grow up.

16YO 40%
Nose: Light amber. Bigger and sweeter with a coconut/white raisin mix and a little smoke. Better balance.
Palate: Some wood smoke drifts through along with Assam-like tea notes, some raisin, Brazil nut.
Finish: Toffee, quite rounded.
Conclusion: It needs sweetness and direction.

Flavor Camp: **Rich & Round**
Where Next? Dalmore 15yo, The Singleton of Glendullan 12yo

21YO CASK SAMPLE
Nose: Light balsamic vinegar tone. Lightly juicy. Touch of pot ale.
Palate: Big tannins. Akin to Manzanilla *Pasada*. Almond, then burning grass. With water, a little smoke.
Finish: Firm and tight.
Conclusion: Plenty of cask influence trying to prise open a tough customer.

30YO 43.3%
Nose: Amber. Very soft to start, touches of cream, but an earthy, leathery quality develops. Fruits. Smoke.
Palate: Black fruits, fruitcake, cigar. Very leathery.
Finish: Shows slight fragility but balanced.
Conclusion: The teenage rebel has grown up, showing an avuncular nature from a leather armchair.

Flavor Camp: **Rich & Round**
Where Next? Benrinnes 23yo, Tullibardine 1988

Glen Garioch

OLD MELDRUM, NR ABERDEEN • WWW.GLENGARIOCH.COM • OPEN ALL YEAR OCT–JUN, MON–SAT; JUL–SEPT, MON–SUN

At the tap o' the Garioch, in the lands o' Leith Hall, a skranky black farmer in Earlsfield did dwell... This ballad, first sung at the start of the agricultural revolution, speaks of the hard lives of seasonally hired workers in the Garioch (pronounced *geerie*), the 150 square miles of fertile land centered around Inverurie running northwest to Strathbogie that was "improved" during the late eighteenth/early nineteenth centuries. It's a fecund place, dominated by the mother hills of Tap O'Noth and the Mither Tap. Maybe at the end of his servitude to his *skranky* (thin, mean) master the singer would have tried the whisky made at one of the Garioch's trio of distilleries.

If so, perhaps it would have been the eldest, Glen Garioch. Founded in 1798, by the twentieth century it had been absorbed into DCL (the precursor to Diageo) and was piling on the local peat, along with its neighbor Ardmore, resulting in that unusual style, the smoky Highlander. In 1968, DCL needed increased production of smoky whiskies for its blends but claimed there was insufficient water to expand Glen Garioch, so they closed the plant and looked elsewhere—a move that resulted in the reopening of Brora in the Northern Highlands.

Lack of water in this area of springs? Bowmore's owner Stanley P. Morrison thought otherwise. He bought Glen Garioch, hired a local water diviner (there's a link to ancient wisdom), and found a new and plentiful water source.

Today, this tiny distillery whose stillhouse reminds you of a conservatory makes a peat-free spirit, but the richness of its make remains. These small stills produce a powerful punch. "What I look for in new make is a meaty, tallow character, which has gone by the time it's being used in Founder's Reserve, leaving a rich depth," says Iain

Glen Garioch's stills sit in a conservatory stillhouse and produce a richly sweet make.

McCallum, master of malts at Morrison Bowmore Distillers. "To me, Glen Garioch is boisterous and robust." It's clearly not in any way *skranky*.

After years of languishing on the sidelines, Glen Garioch has a new pack, new expressions, and there's potential for more to come. "It's almost silently efficient," says McCallum. "One of those undiscovered gems." How true is that of this part of the world?

GLEN GARIOCH TASTING NOTES

NEW MAKE
Nose: Cooked vegetable: cabbage, stewing nettles. Gravy, then whole-grain bread dough. With water, sweet; cow barn.
Palate: Meal-like, sweet and long. Has a rich weight and a sulfury note.
Finish: Nutty.

FOUNDER'S RESERVE NAS 48%
Nose: Light gold. Sulfur has gone, revealing sandalwood and a lightly herbal/heathery rootiness. Becoming a little honeyed, with the oak comes hints of orange *crème brûlée* and pine sap.
Palate: Dry crunchy start. The solidity of the spirit gives good feel now that the wood has done its softening act. With water, butter cookies.
Finish: Long. Friable.
Conclusion: Substantial but sweet.

Flavor Camp: **Malty & Dry**
Where Next? Auchroisk 10yo

12YO 43%
Nose: Full gold. Toasted cereal. The sweetness carries through here. Fleshy with a touch of nutmeg and that heathery note.
Palate: Brazil nut, some pepper. A chunkily fruity rich mid-palate. With water, showing a light beeswaxy note then the herbs come back.
Finish: Long and lightly nutty.
Conclusion: Bold and generous.

Flavor Camp: **Fruity & Spicy**
Where Next? The Glenrothes Select Reserve, Tormore 12yo

Ardmore

KENNETHMONT • WWW.ARDMOREWHISKY.COM

The second of the Garioch distilleries is another that came into existence as major blenders looked to own their own production facilities; Dewar's at Aberfeldy, Johnnie Walker with Cardhu, and here, just outside Kennethmont in 1898, the Glasgow-based blender Teacher's built Ardmore. Its size speaks of the way in which blenders had acceded to the landed gentry. Adam Teacher discovered the site when he went to visit Colonel Leith-Hay in Leith Hall (echoes of the *"skranky black farmer"*) and it is named after the Teacher's own country pile on the Firth of Clyde.

The reason for its location was threefold: access to raw materials (locally grown barley and peat from Pitsligo), plentiful water, and the fact that Kennethmont was on the Great North of Scotland Railway, which linked Inverness to Aberdeen. It is a big site, once home to a Saladin maltings plant, and its heavy, industrialized air seems somewhat out of place in this rural setting. Its links with its Victorian past remained until 2001, when the coal fires were finally removed.

Ardmore is a paradoxical whisky that somehow manages to be both heavily peated and fragrant. This bonfire in the apple orchard character has set it apart and made it prized by blenders. You cannot imagine such a now-isolated site would have survived if it did not offer something significantly outwith the norm.

While its wooden washbacks may give an influence, it's the stillhouse where Ardmore's secrets are to be found. "The coal fires had to come out because of the law," says manager Alistair Longwell. "The difficult thing for us to do was to retain that coal-fired character, which gives heaviness, when we switched to steam. It took seven months to get the flavor back, by adjusting cut points and creating hot spots inside the stills."

Although an unpeated version (Ardlair) is made these days, it's the smoke that sets Ardmore apart. "But the rest of the industry moved away from us," says Longwell. "This was the character that made Teacher's." He pauses. "It's the last bit of Teacher's that's left. It's a labor of love." Here in the farmlands, the paradox carries on a lost tradition.

ARDMORE TASTING NOTES

NEW MAKE

Nose: Wood smoke and light oiliness, with a light grassy note behind. In time, apple skin, lime, and very light cereal.
Palate: Sweet and smoky. Positive weight and oiliness with a touch of citrus fruit and dried flower providing lift. A complex new make with many avenues of potential approach.
Finish: Light smoke. Clean.

TRADITIONAL CASK NAS 46%

Nose: Full gold. Sweet oaky notes, burning leaves, dried grasses, slightly exotic. Incense, apple purée, grass clippings on a bonfire. New wood.
Palate: Fruitier than new make, the smoke in check but when it comes there's a hint of smoked ham, then pepper. Same oily feel, becoming sweeter and more vanilla-led.
Finish: Peppery wood smoke.
Conclusion: Finished in quarter casks, this young whisky shows the fusion of light fruit and smoke that typifies Ardmore.

Flavor Camp: **Smoky & Peaty**
Where Next? Young Ardbeg, Springbank 10yo, Connemara 12yo, Bruichladdich Port Charlotte PC8

TRIPLE WOOD (A WORK IN PROGRESS) 55.7%

Nose: Big oak-driven, creamy vanilla, cut with wood smoke and fruitcake. Smoke well integrated, then a lime cordial blast.
Palate: The casks here seem to have pulled out the oily character and accentuated the hints of citrus fruit on the new make.
Finish: Only now does the smoke show itself.
Conclusion: Despite a triple-wood maturation (five years in ex-bourbon, three and a half in quarter, then three in European-oak puncheon) it can cope.

25YO 51.4%

Nose: Pale gold. Dry smoke, apple wood, some earth, cedar, nut bowl, heavy peat then garam masala. Very lifted.
Palate: Classic Ardmore: the top notes now released, the green apple skin now old fruit, the smoke fully integrated. Seems delicate but the heaviness of the center pulls the complex strands together.
Finish: Long and smoky.
Conclusion: Pale due to it being aged in a refill cask. A clear line to new make.

Flavor Camp: **Smoky & Peaty**
Where Next? Longrow 14yo

1977, 30YO OLD MALT CASK BOTTLING 50%

Nose: Cow breath and sweet hay with a hint of scented smoke. Lemon. Mature. Becomes fresher and greener in time. Privet.
Palate: Clean, leafy with an acidic energy. Orchard fruits, then hazelnut and light smoke. Balanced.
Finish: Tight and smoky.
Conclusion: Mature and balanced. Though smoky the fragrance tips it into the fragrant camp.

Flavor Camp: **Fragrant & Floral**
Where Next? Hakushu 18yo

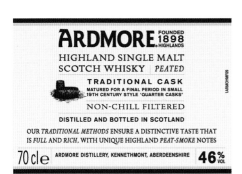

The GlenDronach

FORGUE, BY HUNTLY • WWW.GLENDRONACHDISTILLERY.COM • OPEN ALL YEAR OCT–APR, MON–FRI; MAY–SEPT, MON–SUN

The last of the Garioch trio lies in the village of Forgue and was built in 1826 by a consortium of local farmers. Unusually, in an industry where consolidation has always been the norm, The GlenDronach remained in private hands until 1960 when it became part of Teacher's, the blending house that also owned nearby distillery Ardmore.

Teacher's is a muscular blend and The GlenDronach was a good fit. This is a big spirit whose new make is weighty with a buttery effect that spreads over the tongue. It's built to cope with prolonged aging—and ex-sherry casks. Though one-time owner Allied tried to make it a single-malt brand like its Garioch neighbors, The GlenDronach seemed destined to be a cult until it was bought in 2006 by The BenRiach's Billy Walker (*see* p.88). The focus is now single malt.

Its muscularity, believes manager Alan McConnochie, lies in an adherence to traditional methods, such as a rake system in the mash tun. "It's a funny thing," he says. "We get the same malt as The BenRiach, but if you stick your head in the mash tun here, the smell is totally different. They say water doesn't make a difference? I'm not so sure."

Long ferments in wooden washbacks take the wash to a slow distillation. "There's little reflux," says McConnochie. "There's no stress here, none of that running up and down the inside of the still." Neither did he notice a difference when the coal fires were extinguished in 2005.

The GlenDronach reminds me a little of former British Prime Minister Gordon Brown. It is a malt of serious mien whose brief show of youthful exuberance in the 12yo version soon deepens, becoming serious as it does, seemingly being drawn back into the heavy earth of its birth. The new owner is now giving the whisky

Deep in color, rich in aroma, The GlenDronach's rich style is made for ex-sherry casks.

five years in ex-bourbon casks before re-racking into oloroso sherry and sometimes from there into Pedro Ximénez sherry casks.

"People associate The GlenDronach with sherry," says McConnochie. "It's a lot harder to overpower it with wood, which is a nice problem to have!" The muscularity of the farmlands shows through once more.

THE GLENDRONACH TASTING NOTES

NEW MAKE
Nose: Heavy but sweet and rich. Slightly earthy fruitiness.
Palate: Robust but at the same time buttery in texture adding weight and suppleness.
Finish: Very long and fruity. Plum.

12YO 43%
Nose: Deep gold. Sweet and sherried. Tweedy with a little plum stone, dusty cereal note.
Palate: Big, rich with dried fruits, already good concentration. Unctuous feel, then damson. Water gives it a sudden spark of lift where grassiness develops.
Finish: Earth and sooty smoke.
Conclusion: Already full and deep with a spark of adolescent cheekiness.

Flavor Camp: **Rich & Round**
Where Next? Glenfiddich 15yo, Cragganmore 12yo, Glenfarclas 12yo

18YO ALLARDICE 46%
Nose: A serious, classically sherried nose. Layered and velvety with massed dried red fruits, musk, raisins, and depth of distillate. Molasses toffee. Turns feral with water.
Palate: Molasses toffee, licorice-root sweetness, and depth. Light grip.
Finish: Long and sweet, with concentrated fruit.
Conclusion: This is unreconstructed, old-style single malt.

Flavor Camp: **Rich & Round**
Where Next? Karuizawa (1980s), The Macallan 18yo

21YO PARLIAMENT 48%
Nose: Wood oil, yew trees, lightly dusty. Big, layered dried fruits, raisins, figs, and dates. Hints of coffee grounds, mocha, and molasses.
Palate: Ripe, full, and quite firm to start with. Needs some water to allow the deep, sightly smoky sweetness to be revealed. Takes on a gamey edge with water.
Finish: Baked fruit, length, and heft.
Conclusion: Powerful and complex.

Flavor Camp: **Rich & Round**
Where Next? Karuizawa (1970s), Glenfarclas 30yo

anCnoc & Glenglassaugh

ANCNOC • KNOCK • WWW.ANCNOC.COM / GLENGLASSAUSGH • PORTSOY • WWW.GLENGLASSAUGH.COM • OPEN MAY–SEPT, MON–SUN; OCT–APR, MON–FRI

Here's an anomaly. A distillery that can't make up its mind what it is called and in which region it belongs. Confused? Knockdhu distillery, in the village of Knock, was built in 1893 by the then mighty blender John Haig & Co. When it was launched as a single malt its new owner Inver House felt its name was too close to Knockando, so it became anCnoc.

It lies close to the Speyside boundary but as we have seen, this is a line that follows a parliamentary boundary rather than possessing any geographical logic, so Knockdhu is a Highlander. Just to confuse matters further, it produces a whisky which, Inver House's master blender Stuart Harvey says, "is typical of what most people think of as a 'Speyside.' In fact, it might actually be more 'Speyside' than most Speysides!" Those drinkers used to an appley fragrant, light dram, may be surprised at the new make: a member of the sulfury brigade. The background is intense and citric and it is this underlying character that is fully expressed in the bottle.

"It's actually slightly heavier than Old Pulteney," says Harvey, "because there's less reflux in the stills, while the worm tubs add that vegetable note to the new make. The biggest change in Scotch whisky's character came when distilleries took out worm tubs and installed condensers. They might be more efficient but because they strip out sulfur they can also remove underlying weight and complexity." Here the sulfur is a marker for what lies beneath. A heavily peated variant is now being produced, but for the moment it's only used for blending. Just as well; we're confused enough!

Glenglassaugh, on the sea cliffs next to the pretty village of Portsoy, is potentially the luckiest distillery in Scotland. It was built in 1878, during the nineteenth-century blend-led boom, and was soon absorbed into Highland Distillers.

Like many of these late-era plants, it failed to survive the first crisis it encountered. Blenders, faced with the need to bring stock levels into balance, chose to close newer distilleries that were unproven and with less depth of aged stock.

Glenglassaugh closed in 1907, and spent some time as a bakery before the US-led increase in demand started in the 1950s. In 1960 it was reopened.

Its future was far from secure, however. Glenglassaugh was seen as a being a "difficult" make: an awkward individual that resisted the collegiate atmosphere of a blend. Had the single-malt market existed, its story might have been very different, but when another crisis forced a cull of distilleries in the 1980s, it was an inevitable candidate for the axe. In 1986 it closed again, seemingly for the last time.

Then, in 2007, it was saved and started to produce a year later. Managing such a huge gap in stock was always tricky, but the range has cleverly balanced releases of works in progress (Revival, Evolution) and selective releases of older, top-quality casks. In 2013 it changed hands once more, joining the the portfolio of The BenRiach Distillery Company, which, with The BenRiach and The Glendronach, has made a reputation of reviving old, forgotten distilleries. It the ideal fit.

ANCNOC TASTING NOTES

NEW MAKE
Nose: Cabbage/broccoli-like sulfury notes but with an intense lift of grapefruit and lime.
Palate: Sulfur again. Middle weight, then comes the citrus peel along with fragrant notes.
Finish: Clean and long. Surprising weight.

16YO 46%
Nose: More obvious oak, but the aromas seem to be growing at the same pace. Apple blossom, cut flower, lime, and a little mint.
Palate: Sweet and slightly fuller with more oak extract. Green grape, fresh (more Sancerre than absinthe).
Finish: Dusty/chalky before return of green herbs of 12yo.
Conclusion: Freshness is the key here, but allied to a supple feel.

Flavor Camp: **Fragrant & Floral**
Where Next? The Glenlivet 12yo, Teaninich 10yo, Hakushu 12yo

GLENGLASSAUGH TASTING NOTES

NEW MAKE 69%
Nose: Very juicy, with fruit-juice tones, almost like fruit chews. Has power behind its clean, sweet drive. A little blackcurrant juice and hothouse aromas.
Palate: Off-dry. There's a tight bite to it. With water, it's clean, with a little greengage.
Finish: Creamy and lightly malty. Tense.

EVOLUTION 50%
Nose: Has picked up some clean oak. Sweet, with hot sawdust. The greengage continues, with more vanilla to balance. Shows currants with water.
Palate: Cask-driven, with lots of vanillins, but there are bananas and fresh, ripe fruit.
Finish: Juicy and tight.
Conclusion: Appropriately named, this is a direct line from the new make.

Flavor Camp: **Fruity & Spicy**
Where Next? Aultmore, Balblair 2000

REVIVAL 46%
Nose: Has an oaky, oxidative note. Amplifies the new make's malt. A touch of dates. Water freshens it.
Palate: Ripe, with a touch of sherry cask (used for finishing). An almost lactic/condensed-milk note.
Finish: Slightly numb and tight.
Conclusion: Lovely mid-palate feel. Distillery character.

Flavor Camp: **Fruity & Spicy**
Where Next? The Glenrothes Select Reserve

30YO 44.8%
Nose: Robust, with almonds and dried-fruit aromas. Mature, leaf-mulch notes; profound concentration.
Palate: Very ripe and rich with candied peels. Length.
Finish: Shows its age slightly.
Conclusion: Has mix of fruitiness and tightness still.

Flavor Camp: **Rich & Round**
Where Next? Kavalan Solist, Glenfarclas 30yo

Macduff

MACDUFF • PORTSOY

The Eastern Highlands finally peter out on the Moray coastline with another seaside distillery, Macduff, which, like Knockdhu, appears to suffer from a minor personality crisis since it has been bottled under a different name, Glen Deveron and, now in its new guise, The Deveron. The name is appropriate enough. Macduff, after all, is where the Deveron River debouches into the sea. In the other direction come the salmon and sea trout that make this one of the pre-eminent fishing rivers of the Highlands, with beats stretching back to its rising in the heathery wilds of the Cabrach.

A seven-arched stone bridge spans the river's mouth, separating Macduff from its immediate neighbor, Banff, which also used to have its own plant. The latter finally closed its doors in 1983, after what must be the most jinxed history of any distillery. It caught fire twice, was bombed, and in a separate incident, exploded. Even after it closed, its warehouses caught fire. The hoodoo doesn't appear to have crossed the Deveron, because Macduff has had considerably better luck.

Needless to say, there is considerable rivalry between the two towns, with the Royal Burgh of Banff considering itself more sophisticated than its younger neighbor, which was built in 1783 as a model town by James Duff, Earl of Fife (*see* p.62). Thanks to its sheltered harbor, Macduff became a significant herring port.

Built on the former garden of Duff House, this is a surprisingly large site, with warehouses (now sadly empty) straggling up the length of a hill. The plant itself, painted in the cream and red of Dewar's livery, is modern, having been built in 1962–3 by Brodie Hepburn, a Glasgow-based whisky-broking firm that also had interests in Deanston and Tullibardine. Its aim? To benefit from the new age of blended whisky. Appropriately enough it chose modernist distillery designer William Delmé-Evans (*see* box, below) to create the new coastal plant.

Macduff then passed through the hands of several brokers such as Block, Grey & Block, and Stanley P. Morrison before, in 1972, becoming part of Wm. Lawson, which needed a core malt for its eponymous blend. In 1980, it became part of Martini, which a dozen years later merged with Bacardi in its pre-Dewar's incarnation. A lot of owners, certainly, but importantly, unlike Banff, it survived.

DESIGNER EXTRAORDINAIRE: WILLIAM DELMÉ-EVANS

William Delmé-Evans (1929–2003) is recognized as being the pre-eminent distillery designer of the twentieth century. All of his distilleries were constructed in order to conserve energy in both architecture and the use of modern equipment. His whisky life started when he bought an abandoned brewery in Blackford in 1949 and built Tullibardine, which he then sold to Brodie Hepburn. He went on to design Jura (1963), learning to fly in the process, and Macduff, ending his career with his most modernist design: Glenallachie (1967).

As Lawson's was building itself into a multimillion-case blend (its biggest market today is Russia), Glen Deveron, meanwhile, was being promoted as a budget malt in France.

It is everything that a 1960s distillery should be: highly engineered, with lauter tun, stainless-steel washbacks, condensers, steam-driven stills, all of which lead you to believe it is going to be light and inoffensive. But Macduff has depth—and weirdness.

The mashing is quick, the ferments short, but it's the stills that make you scratch your head. For starters, there are five of them: two wash and three spirit. The fifth was installed in 1990, when under the Wm. Lawson stewardship. It is unclear whether a sixth was planned, or whether triple-distillation was to be tested, but its absence leaves Macduff one of only two distilleries with this odd setup. The other is Talisker.

All the stills have slightly upward-angle lyne arms which, halfway along, take an abrupt right-angled handbrake turn. That kink isn't the result of Delmé-Evans' elbow being jogged, but a deliberate design to try and promote specific flavors. The angle of the condensers will also have an effect; the shell and tubes attached to the spirit stills lie horizontally and have after-coolers, allowing condensers to be kept warmer, extending copper conversation. This is a malty spirit—no doubt the about that—but instead of being in the light, cookie camp, it has weight but also fruit. Complexity, in other words.

When they are put in cask, spirits such as this seem to return to their origins, as if the malt husk needs to be cracked once more to allow the sweetness and fruitiness contained within to be revealed fully. That takes time.

There's also the difference between the needs of a blender and that of a single-malt bottler. The heavy nutty/spicy characters of the youthful make can be highly desirable in a blend, but are exposed in a single malt.

Macduff can also throw out some pretty weird aromas as it matures: residual sulfur from distillation, beans, cannabis. It needs help from active casks. The new bottlings under The Deveron name shows that this lesson has been learned.

Macduff's sheltered harbor made it a major herring port.

MACDUFF TASTING NOTES

NEW MAKE
Nose: Green, malty. Peanut oil and fava bean with a heavy cereal note behind.
Palate: Fat and thick with a whiff of sulfur, then intense cassis tones.
Finish: Dries suddenly.

1982, THE DEVERON CASK SAMPLE 59.8%
Nose: Chewy and sweet, with dried fruits and Brazil nut tones. Moves into heavy, roasted maltiness. Dry bracken with water and lots of ginger and nutmeg spiciness.
Palate: Thick, chewy, sweet maltiness that brings to mind chocolate-hazelnut spread on toast. Light tannins.
Finish: Ripe and long.
Conclusion: A massive, malty mouthful.

1984, BERRY BROS & RUDD BOTTLING 57.2%
Nose: Mahogany. Aniseed and malt. The currant leaf has moved into skunk/cannabis.
Palate: A touch paradoxical since it starts quite dry but then the fat fruit bunches together in the center.
Finish: Very nutty with a little dusting of white pepper.
Conclusion: Idiosyncratic to the last.

Flavor Camp: **Malty & Dry**
Where Next? Deanston 12yo

NORTHERN HIGHLANDS

Scotch whisky's forgotten coast stretches from north of Inverness to Wick, and although it is home to one of the biggest malt brands, the majority of its malts remain less well-known. Here, though, you will find some of Scotland's most idiosyncratic and individual distilleries. This is an area where aroma, flavor, and texture are pushed to the extreme.

Northern lands. Whisky's forgotten coast ends here at Thurso Bay, but the journey continues to the horizon—and Orkney.

Tomatin

TOMATIN • INVERNESS • WWW.TOMATIN.COM • OPEN ALL YEAR MID-APR–OCT, MON–SUN; OCT–MAR, MON–FRI

If you want to see a physical manifestation of the changing moods of the Scotch whisky industry, then head to Tomatin. The distillery was built in 1897 with two stills. This number was doubled in 1956. It rose to six in 1958, ten in 1961, 14 in 1974. Then, just as the rest of the industry was closing distilleries in the early 1980s, Tomatin increased to 23 stills in 1986. By then it had been bought by Takara Shuzo, a Japanese distillery that needed fillings for its blends.

These days there are six pairs of stills and production, which peaked at 3.2 million gallons (12m liters) per year, is now 528,344 gallons (2m liters). Not that Tomatin is complaining. "I would say that there has been a definite improvement over the years," says sales director Stephen Bremner. "This has come about due to a change in strategy, from producing a malt for blending, to a good-quality single malt." This, when you reflect on it, is a fair reflection of the market as well. The make is fragrant and intense, with estery fruits and a little spice—

the result of long fermentations and distillation in small but long-necked stills, whose condensers sit in the chill air. One of the main improvements has come as a result of a tightening of wood policy (Tomatin is one of the few distilleries with its own cooperage), with an increase in first-fill bourbons and sherry butts.

The result is a new range of single malts amplifying what the public has been missing out on for decades. The guiding hand comes from master distiller Douglas Campbell, who joined Tomatin in 1961. The fruity signature is the constant, given different hues by oak, ripening fully after decades into lush topicality. This soft heart is even seen in Cù Bòcan, a lightly peated variant named after a mythical local hellhound; though it greets you with a growl, it's soon happily licking your face.

TOMATIN TASTING NOTES

NEW MAKE

Nose: Intense. Fruit *eaux de vie*. Floral.
Palate: Slightly vegetal, suggesting there's some weight to come out but overall high-toned and sweet.
Finish: Hot.

12YO 40%

Nose: Typically intense distillery character with a vibrant attack. Young and still slightly tight, with yellow fruit and oak still in the additive stage.
Palate: Very light and clean, with a delicate silkiness to the mid-palate moving into honey and caramelized sugars.
Finish: Whittled sticks.
Conclusion: A light, clean apéritif.

Flavor Camp: **Fragrant & Floral**
Where Next? Teaninich 12yo

18YO 46%

Nose: Identifiably Tomatin, with a mix of ripe apple, light honey, black grape, chestnut honey, and a light drift of fragrant wood smoke.
Palate: Mature oxidized depth. Hints of peach, Oolong tea, the honeyed richness, then some coffee.
Finish: Chocolate orange.
Conclusion: 18yo whiskies, from refill casks, are then married in ex-sherry butts, which adds a subtle depth.

Flavor Camp: **Fruity & Spicy**
Where Next? The Glenrothes 1993

30YO 46%

Nose: Tropical fruit, passion-fruit, overripe mango, guava; a little cream and relaxed oak. With water, some ginger and even a little dry grass.
Palate: Soft fruit all the way, with a tingling spiciness. Clean and long, with good complexity.
Finish: Oak tightens and gently dries.
Conclusion: Classical notes of gentle, mature old whisky.

Flavor Camp: **Fruity & Spicy**
Where Next? Tomintoul 33yo

CÙ BÒCAN 46%

Nose: Gentle wood smoke. Drier than the standard expressions, with a peppery, earthy character. Light balsam with water.
Palate: Immediate hot embers and sweet oak. Green leafiness. Sweetness with water.
Finish: Delicate smoke.
Conclusion: This peated variant is balanced, light but with distillery character.

Flavor Camp: **Smoky & Peaty**
Where Next? The BenRiach Curiositas

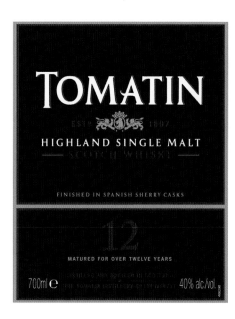

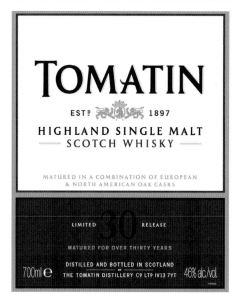

Royal Brackla

ROYAL BRACKLA • NAIRN

You are deep in a bloodied landscape by the time you reach Royal Brackla. The Culloden battlefield is nearby, as is Cawdor Castle, where, according to Shakespeare, Macbeth committed regicide. The blasted heath therefore cannot be far away, either. Thankfully, the lasting impression of Royal Brackla is not one of death, hauntings, and murder, but tranquillity.

To enter the stillhouse from the tun room, you slide open a heavy safety door in order to reveal a view of the swan-dotted distillery loch, framed between two of the company's quartet of stills. The scent of this year's barley harvest mingles with the heady fumes from the spirit safe.

Clearic, or new-make spirit, has been running in this idyllic spot since 1812, back when Captain William Fraser established his distillery (much to the dismay of the locals, who were then making a fine living from moonshining). Fraser's whisky, however, began to build a name for itself and, in 1835, it became the first to be given a royal warrant, by King William IV. From that moment on, the reputation of the distillery was guaranteed.

An advertisement for Royal Brackla in 1836 reported that "The King's Own Whisky, distilled expressly for the use of His Majesty at Fraser's Royal Brackla distillery, is perhaps the only malt spirit that proves alike congenial to the palate and constitution of connoisseurs of every country. It is peat-flavored, but far from rank—strong, but not fiery, and produces the most exquisite Punch or Toddy."

Sadly, the knowledge of its quality has rarely escaped the confines of blender's laboratories. Here's another top-quality single malt that has selflessly given of itself to add complexity to blends, such as Dewar's (which owns the distillery). Quite why none of its owners saw the tourism potential of such a site, however, is amazing.

To make its intense and estery new make, (there's no peat used these days) the whisky-making is as gentle as the location. Slow mashing for clear wort, long fermentation, and then relaxed distillation to encourage dribbles of reflux combine to make this estery, lifted, intense make, although it is one with presence rather than flimsiness. Royal Brackla can cope with the attentions of European oak.

The good news is that the tourists are now being allowed in, and The King's Own Whisky (with touches of sherry) is once again available as an official bottling.

Captain Fraser and his patron would surely approve.

Royal Brackla is the site of some of the most idyllic stills in Scotland.

ROYAL BRACKLA TASTING NOTES

NEW MAKE
Nose: Fruity/oily with porcelain-like coolness. Cucumber.
Palate: Needle-sharp. Pineapple, green apple, and unripe fruits. Very clean and slightly oily.
Finish: Grassy.

15YO, REFILL WOOD CASK SAMPLE
Nose: Assertive spiciness from the cask. Ripe apple and cinnamon/mace. The cucumber remains.
Palate: Has retained its purity. Light and floral/lilac. Concentrated in the center of the tongue with a hint of *crème brûlée* as it goes. In time a hint of Calvados and burnt wood sugars.
Finish: Ripe, with cream toffee, then a fresh, acidic end.
Conclusion: Has developed secondary and tertiary aromas. Needs gentle handling.

25YO 43%
Nose: Sandalwood, sweet malt, cherry, spices, and peanut shell. *Crème pâtissière*.
Palate: Sweet fruits: melon, apricot. The sweet vanilla custard takes charge with some nuttiness beneath. Oak is firm.
Finish: Dry and nutty.
Conclusion: A little maltier than new make style but the sweetness dominates.

Flavor Camp: Fruity & Spicy
Where Next? Macallan 18yo Fine Oak

1997 CASK SAMPLE 56.3%
Nose: Light straw. Intense and estery. Quite tight with lime and pine needles/spruce buds mixed with green apple. Fresh and vibrant.
Palate: Pure, with some kiwi fruit, even a hint of cucumber. Ultra-fresh. Water makes a little fleshy note emerge and some gentle flow develops.
Finish: Tight. Clean. Acidic.
Conclusion: Very Brackla in its intensity.

Glen Ord & Teaninich

GLEN ORD • MUIR OF ORD, NR INVERNESS • WWW.DISCOVERING-DISTILLERIES.COM/GLENORD • OPEN ALL YEAR; SEE WEBSITE FOR DAYS & DETAILS / TEANINICH • ALNESS, ROSS-SHIRE

The Black Isle is neither an island nor, come to think of it, is it black. This promontory, which lies between the Moray and Cromarty Firths is, however, fertile and the ideal conditions for cultivating barley helped make it the site of one of the most remarkable early distilleries. Ferintosh was established in the late seventeenth century by landowner, Duncan Forbes. As a reward for the support he gave to the Protestant King William of Orange in his battle with the Catholic King James I, Forbes was granted the privilege of being allowed to distill whisky made from grain grown on his own land duty-free. Eventually he had four distilleries on his estate, netting the family £18,000 ($26,435) in profit per annum (£2m/$2.9m in today's money). Ferintosh, it is believed, accounted for two-thirds of the whisky sold in Scotland by the end of the eighteenth century before the privilege was withdrawn in 1784.

The sites of the original Ferintosh plants have long gone. Today its successor is Glen Ord, whose position here has all to do with the quality of the malting barley. This is a self-sufficient plant, malting all of its own requirements thanks to the drum maltings on site, which also supply malt for six other Diageo sites, including Talisker.

Surrounded by verdant fields, it is only apposite that Glen Ord makes a green, grassy spirit with a drift of peat running through it. Various attempts have been made to market it as a single malt: the latest finds it joining Diageo's Singleton series and draped in sherry casks.

This grassiness links Glen Ord to the first distillery on the coastal strip that we now follow on the way to Wick. Teaninich is slightly oilier thanks to a mash filter giving ultra-clean wort and bulky stills maximizing copper contact. A weird exoticism pervades its aromatics: green tea, lemongrass, and a perfume akin to bison grass.

While medium-bodied Ord melds amenably into wood, Teaninich stands apart: aloof, rapier-like, cutting through any attempts by wood to tame it. As part of owner Diageo's production expansion, both distilleries have seen their capacities doubled. An entire new "Roseisle-style" distillery is also planned next to Teaninich.

GLEN ORD TASTING NOTES

NEW MAKE
Nose: Freshly cut green grass and light smoke. With water, it's just-cut hedges.
Palate: Good weight again with that grassy/privet note. Like chewing spring leaves, green pea-shoots. With water, some smoke emerges.
Finish: Fermenting white wine.

THE SINGLETON OF GLEN ORD 12YO 40%
Nose: Deep amber. Green-fig jam, fresh date, garden twine, garden bonfire in the distance. Brazil nut. Sweet and plummy with a gingerbread note when diluted.
Palate: Fruit compote, light on the palate until the center when smoke and cashew appear. White-raisin cake. Vanilla toward the back. Thick.
Finish: Lightly grassy.
Conclusion: The distillery character is (just) there but this is a big sweet variation on the theme.

> **Flavor Camp: Rich & Round**
> **Where Next?** Macallan 10yo, Aberlour 12yo, Aberlour 16yo, Glenfarclas 10yo

TEANINICH TASTING NOTES

NEW MAKE
Nose: Scented, aromatic, privet hedge, lawnmower, Japanese green tea, and green pineapple.
Palate: Intense and very green and acidic. Softens slightly with water. Has substance.
Finish: Privet. Short and hot.

8YO, REFILL WOOD CASK SAMPLE
Nose: Intense, clean, now Chinese white tea, bison grass, lemongrass. With water, a hint of gum tree.
Palate: Needle-sharp and slightly austere. Daffodils and grass. Wet bamboo. With water, a softer texture.
Finish: Clean and smoothly minty.
Conclusion: Highly individual and "Asian."

10YO, FLORA & FAUNA 43%
Nose: Still has exotic lemongrass but now it's Chinese green tea. The austerity remains with a little more creaminess than the 8yo. With water, green anise.
Palate: A soft start with herbs and spices. The soft center is guarded but water smooths things considerably.
Finish: Herbal.
Conclusion: Light but complex.

> **Flavor Camp: Fragrant & Floral**
> **Where Next?** Glenburgie 15yo, anCnoc 16yo, Hakushu 12yo

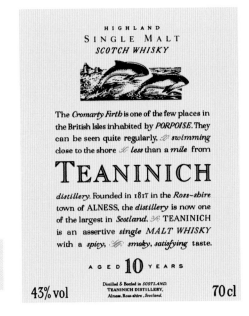

HIGHLAND
SINGLE MALT
SCOTCH WHISKY

The *Cromarty Firth* is one of the few places in the British Isles inhabited by *PORPOISE*. They can be seen quite regularly, swimming close to the shore less than a mile from

TEANINICH

distillery. Founded in 1817 in the *Ross-shire* town of ALNESS, the *distillery* is now one of the largest in *Scotland.* TEANINICH is an assertive *single MALT WHISKY* with a *spicy*, smoky, *satisfying* taste.

AGED **10** YEARS

Distilled & Bottled in *SCOTLAND.*
TEANINICH DISTILLERY,
Alness, Ross-shire, *Scotland.*

43% vol   70cl

Dalmore & Invergordon

ALNESS • WWW.THEDALMORE.COM • OPEN ALL YEAR APR–OCT MON–SAT; NOV–MAR, MON–FRI / INVERGORDON • MILTON

A heightened sense of individuality is the key to all the whiskies from this northeastern coast and Dalmore couldn't be any further from Teaninich's steeliness. This is a whisky that revels in its richness and depth. If Teaninich seems to speak of an eternal cold spring, at Dalmore, hard on the shores of the Cromarty Firth, it's as if it is autumn all year round. You leave with berry juice filling your mouth.

Established in 1839, Dalmore's distillation regime seems to have been born out of some manic episode on the part of the founder. The wash stills have flat tops and lyne arms sticking out of the sides, the spirit stills have water jacket mufflers round their necks. To make matters more complicated, they're all different sizes.

Dalmore has two stillhouses. The two wash stills in the old stillhouse differ in size to each other; the two in the new stillhouse match in size, but differ to those in the old stillhouse. Result? Different strengths and character of low wines. The design similarity but size discrepancy is repeated in the spirit stills. At Dalmore, the strength of this charge will vary because the stills are all different shapes and sizes. At any point there might be high-strength feints arriving from the spirit-still side along with high-strength low wines from the wash-still side; equally there might be low-strength feints and low-strength low wines; or high-strength feints and low-strength low wines, etc. That's a myriad different flavors in the new make.

This weight also helps dictate Dalmore's wood policy. This is a spirit that revels in the close attentions of ex-sherry casks, which add structure but also pick up the sweetness and take it deep into mysterious areas. At 5 years it seems to be absorbing wood but keeping its counsel; even at 12 there's a feeling the forces of darkness are massing behind the oaken gates. Only at 15 years does the sleek Dalmore begin to step out.

In recent years this forgotten giant has been relaunched, propelling itself into the luxury arena with a number of ultra-aged, ultra-expensive expressions. Sirius, Candela, and Selene all have in excess of 50 years in cask and are filled with exotic concentrated *rancio* scents of maturity.

Three miles up the coast, a different scent pervades the air: one of cooking cereal. This is the site of Scotland's most northerly grain distillery, Invergordon. It may seem unusual to find a type of whisky considered to be urban in such a rural setting, but Invergordon has a long industrial history. An aluminum smelter ran until 1981, while a deep-water harbor resulted in the building of a naval yard. Today, wind turbines and oil rigs are manufactured and repaired here and on the other shore of the firth at Nigg Bay.

When the naval yard closed in the late 1950s, a new source of employment was needed, and building a distillery seemed a perfectly sensible idea. There were crops from the fertile surrounding farmlands, a port, and a workforce. It was the perfect fusion of agriculture and manufacturing heritage.

Invergordon started producing from a Coffey still in 1960, the number soon rising to four sets. Today, it alternates between wheat and corn to produce in the region of 9.5 million gallons (36 million liters) a year, a make that is spicy and slightly lactic. It's most widely used in owner Whyte & Mackay's blends, but will be used by other non-group blenders. There was, briefly, a single-grain bottling, The Invergordon, targeted at women in the early 1990s, and a malt distillery, Ben Wyvis, ran for 12 years from 1965–77. Its stills are now at Glengyle (*see* p.189).

DALMORE TASTING NOTES

NEW MAKE

Nose: Sweet black fruit with a squeeze of orange juice/kumquat. Curranty.
Palate: Ripe and heavy, with underlying cereal.
Finish: Freshens into citrus-fruit tones.

12YO 40%

Nose: Quite restrained and crisp to start. This is more malt driven. Some dried fruit.
Palate: Clean, then lots of Christmas cake, orange peel, and currant leaf.
Finish: Long and fruity.
Conclusion: Already sweetening but still finding its way.

Flavor Camp: **Fruity & Spicy**
Where Next? Edradour 1996 Oloroso Finish

15YO 40%

Nose: Sweet, with heavy sherry influence. Jammy, with wild fruit and leaf. Substantial and weighty.
Palate: Soft and gentle. Dried fruit, orange pekoe tea.
Finish: Kumquat.
Conclusion: A mix of bold sherry casks; the distillery and wood have achieved an equilibrium at this age.

Flavor Camp: **Rich & Round**
Where Next? The Singleton of Dufftown 12yo

1981 MATUSALEM 44%

Nose: Round and rich with mulberry, coffee, a touch of cheese-like *rancio*, walnut. Seville orange.
Palate: Long, soft, and powerful. Robusto cigar, leaf mulch.
Finish: Long with light grip.
Conclusion: Intense, powerul thanks to sweet-sherry cask.

Flavor Camp: **Rich & Round**
Where Next? Aberlour 25yo, The Macallan 18yo Sherry

INVERGORDON TASTING NOTES

INVERGORDON 15YO CASK SAMPLE 62%

Nose: Sweet, sour, and slightly vegetal. Notes of flower stalls, light cheese rind, grass clippings.
Palate: Akin to a Trinidadian rum. Sweet but also lightly phenolic (not smoky). Has a firm, cereal character with an interesting burnt edge.
Finish: Bitter chocolate.
Conclusion: The most individual of Scotland's grains.

Glenmorangie

TAIN • WWW.GLENMORANGIE.COM • OPEN ALL YEAR; SEE WEBSITE FOR DAYS & DETAILS

In a field outside the village of Hilton of Cadboll stands a re-creation by sculptor Barry Grove of the largest Pictish carved stone ever found. Around its twining animals, bosses, and knotwork is a scroll of stylized birds, each of which sits slightly off-center from its partner on the opposite side. "The Picts liked asymmetry," says Grove, "out of which they achieved balance."

The bottom panel of the stone is the source of Glenmorangie's signet trademark, a whirling maze of linked patterns that seems to both link it to this locus, and also replicate the asymmetric whorls that you see when water is added to whisky (aka vyscimetry). This is echoed in the water bubbling through the sandy base of Glenmorangie's Tarlogie Springs.

This hard water, rich in magnesium and calcium, might have an effect on Glenmorangie's character. "If all of Glenmorangie's flavors equal 100%, then the water might be 5%—at max," says Dr. Bill Lumsden, head of distilling and whisky creation at Glenmorangie.

Originally a brewery, Glenmorangie's Old Red Sandstone buildings cascade down the hill to the Dornoch Firth, a practical gravity-fed nineteenth-century design, allowing barley to enter at the top of the hill and emerge, transformed, into clear spirit at the bottom.

The start of the Glenmorangie process is contained within functional stainless-steel tuns and washbacks but, as with any distillery, you have to find the line of flavor and try and tease it apart, just like tracing one of the strands on the Cadboll Stone.

The first part of the teasing apart of Glenmorangie's knots comes in the stillhouse where tall, slender stills stand like supermodels, their necks arcing dismissively into condensers. Masses of copper is at play here in these, the tallest stills in the industry.

The spirit cut starts very high-toned, filled with nail polish and cucumber, then it freshens to citrus, banana, melon, fennel, and soft fruit. Aromatic, lifted, and clean, there's also a discreet cereal note adding a crisp undercurrent and preventing things from getting too lush and fruity, all the result of Lumsden's narrowing of the cut when he was manager here.

Constructed out of the local Old Red Sandstone, Glenmorangie was originally the site of Tain's brewery.

The flavor line then runs to the warehouses. While all distillers these days appreciate the importance of oak, with Lumsden it's an obsession. He only uses casks twice and the make-up is mostly American oak. In one dank, earth-floored warehouse he explains why he keeps all the second-fill casks in this environment: "There's much more cask-driven oxidation in second fill. You get a greater range of complexities and this environment is perfect for that to take place."

The Original (as the 10yo has been renamed) is 100 percent American oak: an assemblage of first-fill ("giving the coconut and vanilla"), and these dunnage-aged second-fills ("giving those honey and minty characters"). While the Glenmorangie character is interacting slowly, becoming sweetly fruited, there's a third element in the mix, a portion of whisky aged in Glenmorangie's bespoke casks made from slow growth, air-dried, American oak. These expensive babies are seen in full light in Astar—"Original on steroids,"—as Lumsden puts it; all popcorn, eucalyptus, and *crème brûlée*.

Lumsden was a pioneer of finishing, the technique of giving a second period of maturing in an active cask. When it works well it gives a new twist to the line of flavor, but it can easily be overdone. "The wood makes the whisky, but wood can ruin whisky as well,"

Bespoke casks resting in one of Glenmorangie's many warehouses. The firm is one of the leading researchers into wood management.

he says. As ever, balance is key. In many ways Glenmorangie operates like that Pictish scrollwork: an asymmetrical balance in which distillery character and cask play off each other. The wood gently squeezes the fruits, the juices run, oak reveals itself but always underneath runs the original character, like a Pictish pattern leading you back to the start.

GLENMORANGIE TASTING NOTES

NEW MAKE

Nose: Intense. Floral. Crystallized fruit. Citrus fruit chews. Citrus fruit and bananas, fennel.
Palate: Sweet and intense with pure fruit. Flowers with a light nuttiness behind. Chalk and cotton candy.
Finish: Clean.

THE ORIGINAL 10YO 40%

Nose: Pale gold. Soft fruit, sweet sawdust, white peach, nettle, light mint, vanilla, banana split, coconut ice cream, mango sorbet, tangerine.
Palate: Light oak touches. Vanilla and cream, then cinnamon. Light touch of passion-fruit.
Finish: Minty and cool.
Conclusion: Oak is giving a very subtle and aromatically harmonious support.

Flavor Camp: Fruity & Spicy
Where Next? Glen Elgin 12yo, Aberfeldy 12yo

18YO 43%

Nose: *Crème brûlée*, light chocolate, eucalyptus, pine resin, raspberry, honey, *crème caramel*, and jasmine.
Palate: Dried fruit, mint. Ripe and palate-thickening with light plum and hard toffee.
Finish: Allspice and long pepper. Vetiver.
Conclusion: Age has added a deeper layer of flavor; wood is integrated but still distillery character shining through.

Flavor Camp: Fruity & Spicy
Where Next? Longmorn 16yo, Glen Moray 16yo, Yamazaki 18yo, Macallan 15yo Fine Oak

25YO 43%

Nose: Mature deep and sweet. Honeycomb, wax, and citrus peel with some marzipan, nut, and cigar wrapper. Red fruit cut with herbs and peach pit. Hint of clove. Those passion-fruits reappear. Luscious toffee. Sweet orange peel.
Palate: Mouth-coating. Honey. Nutmeg, red pepper flakes. Starts sweet, then deepens in the center with light oak structure. Orange *crème brûlée*, strawberry, orange-blossom water. Complex.
Finish: Toffee, raspberry leaf, and spiced honey. Hot toddy.
Conclusion: Layered.

Flavor Camp: Fruity & Spicy
Where Next? Longmorn 1977, Aberfeldy 21yo, The Balvenie 30yo

Balblair

EDDERTON, TAIN • WWW.BALBLAIR.COM • OPEN APR–SEPT, MON–SAT; OCT–MAR, MON–FRI

As you move north of Tain, so the black-earthed fields, which have accompanied you since Dingwall, become squeezed between mountain and shore. The light, constantly changing, glancing off the firth, throws shadows across worn-down, heather-covered hills. These are Balblair's surroundings. Known as "The Parish of the Peats," the evidence is there in the encroaching heather moor. There's been a distillery in the village of Edderton since 1798, but production shifted here, next to the railway in 1872.

Small and solid, there's a feeling of permanence about Balblair that is reflected in the whisky-making philosophy at work inside. As at Glenmorangie (which employs 20 people), staffing levels at Balblair are high by today's standards where sometimes you can walk round a distillery without seeing a soul. "We've got nine working here," says assistant manager Graeme Bowie. "I prefer the manual way of making whisky. I can see why people have moved to automation, but surely a distillery is at the heart of a community? For me, the traditional way is best."

Traditional is an apposite word here. This is one of those cuddly old distilleries, a collection of rooms and low lintels, a place of energy, heat, and building in of aromas. "You can run a distillery like a modern brewery," says Stuart Harvey, master blender at Balblair's owner Inver House. "But it can become too sterile and then you lose the character, which is exactly what you want."

The washbacks are wooden, but it's the stills where the Balblair DNA lurks. Bowie explains: "In Balblair you get that natural spiciness coming through. There's a deep bed in the mash tun and a bright wash, therefore we're encouraging floral/citric esters, but also want depth and fruit". That's where the stills come into play. Short and squat like inverted mushrooms, there are three in the stillhouse but only two are in use.

"It's the only one of our sites with condensers," says Harvey. "But these stills make a complex and full-bodied spirit. We burst the yeast cells in the distillation, which is where fruits come from: it is the equivalent of *bâttonage* in Burgundy, and these short fat stills will capture it. We want a meaty/sulfury spirit so that when you put it in cask it will react with the wood and produce butterscotch and toffee."

This heavier new make takes longer to interact with wood. Although you could describe both Balbair and Glenmorangie as "fruity," they are different types of fruit: Glenmorangie is light, carried along on a wave of oak, while Balblair is fuller and richer, needing time.

It was patient insofar as becoming a front-line malt. This was another make ring-fenced by blenders and whose rebranding (a modern bottle with a Pictish symbol; vintage rather than age-statement releases) was revelatory to malt consumers. The fruit and toffee are always present but, as it matures, the exotic, heady spices come more to the fore. A slow developer, it also behaves slowly in the mouth. A very different style.

"There's this individuality to northern malts," says Harvey. "They have more unique identities than whiskies from Speyside, which is a bit of a maze." It chimes with the comments of author (and whisky-lover) Neil Gunn, who was born locally. Speaking of Old Pulteney, he said he could "recognize some of the strong characteristics of the northern temperament" —a phrase that could apply to any whisky from this northeastern coast.

BALBLAIR TASTING NOTES

NEW MAKE
Nose: Vegetable (cabbage) sulfur with fruity, hot, weighty notes; dry leather. With water, creamy.
Palate: Little nut but dominated by spice and fruit.
Finish: Spicy.

2000 CASK SAMPLE
Nose: Pale gold. Clean, sweet, and spicy with prickles of ginger and mace alongside light coconut and marshmallow. Very sweet. With water, talcum powder and lemon.
Palate: Hugely spicy start, *ras el hanout*. Light and dancing on the tongue. Unripe fruit underneath. Sweet and softening. Lots of distillery character.
Finish: Zingy. Massed spiciness.
Conclusion: Although it needs a little more time for the fruit to soften, the full Balblair spiciness is on show.

1990 43%
Nose: Full gold. Tropical fruit and light cereal. Luscious with some just-ripe apricot, sandalwood. Fragrant.
Palate: More oak interaction allowing a thicker feel as well as more grip. Vanilla bean and masses of sweet spice. The fruit is now baked and there's less citrus fruit. With water, *crème brûlée*, rose petal.
Finish: Fenugreek. Dry oak.
Conclusion: The cask is both melding with the fruit, softening them and, with the light cereal, adding grip and a toasty background.

Flavor Camp: Fruity & Spicy
Where Next? Longmorn 1977, Glen Elgin 12yo, Miyagikyo 1990

1975 46%
Nose: Rich amber. Deep, slightly resinous, and complex. The spice is in charge: cardamom, coriander seed, butter. The leathery note of age with heavy jasmine. A little smoky. Varnish with water.

Palate: Big and smoky. Resin, molasses, cardamom, and ginger, almost Japanese in its intensity. Best neat. Light cigar, lead, and antique-shop notes.
Finish: Still the spice. Cedar and rose dust.
Conclusion: The key here is following the spice and seeing how it interplays with the fruit.

Flavor Camp: Fruity & Spicy
Where Next? The BenRiach 21yo, Glenmorangie 18yo, Tamdhu 32yo

BALBLAIR
Established in 1790
VINTAGE
19 **75**
Highland Single Malt
Scotch Whisky
70cl.℮ 46%vol.

Clynelish

BRORA • WWW.DISCOVERING-DISTILLERIES.COM/CLYNELISH • OPEN ALL YEAR; SEE WEBSITE FOR DAYS & DETAILS

Caithness is sliced by broad valleys (*straths*) which run far into its interior. Man's footprints are hard to discern: there are a few piles of stones, and some lines in the turf indicating old field workings. Yet until 1809 this was once pasture. On the road to Brora you pass Dunrobin Castle, the seat of the Duke and Duchess of Sutherland. It was they and their estate manager, Patrick Sellar, who cleared this land, replacing families with sheep and game, forcing their tenants onto the coast, housing them in crofts with insufficient land to cultivate crops for their own needs. Some went to sea, hunting the herring; others were put to work in the Duke's new coal mine at Brora, in the parish of Clyne.

Coal transformed Brora. There were a brick works, a tile works, tweed mill, salt panning—and, in 1819, a distillery that could use the grain the crofters grew, the coal they dug, and make the duke a handsome profit. By the end of the nineteenth century, Clynelish's whisky was the most expensive on the market and on allocation. This popularity (it became part of the Johnnie Walker stable) resulted in a new distillery being built in 1967.

The old plant was given a reprieve in 1969, however. A dry period on Islay had stopped production and DCL (Distiller Company Ltd) needed supplies of heavily peated malt. Old Clynelish's (now renamed Brora) two pots were fired up once more. This heavy peated phase lasted until 1972 when, with Islay up and running, peating levels dropped off. They continued to fluctuate for the rest of Brora's late renaissance until it closed in 1983.

Brora is (usually) smoky, oily, and peppery with an undertow of grass. Clynelish, meanwhile, moved in a different direction. Its new make smells of a just-snuffed candle and wet oilskins. Here, the effusive, upfront aromatics of its neighbors have been subsumed in favor of texture. That waxiness is quite deliberate and created in the feints and foreshots receiver where a natural precipitation of oils builds up over the year. In most distilleries this is removed, but not here.

From its panoramic stillhouse window, you can look out to the old Brora, lichen-festooned and decaying. The industrial equivalent of the ruined *sheilings* (cottages) in the *straths*.

CLYNELISH TASTING NOTES

NEW MAKE

Nose: Sealing wax, sour orange. Very clean. Snuffed candle and wet oilskins.

Palate: Distinctly waxy feel with a clinging quality. Mouth-filling. Broadens and deepens. This is about texture rather than flavor at this stage.

Finish: Long.

8YO, REFILL WOOD CASK SAMPLE

Nose: The heavy wax on the nose seems to have gone, revealing apricot jam, pine, sweet citrus peel, and then with water, a scented candle re-emerges.

Palate: Clean and soft. Still that textural quality now with more sweet fruit, cocoa, and masses of orange. Some oak.

Finish: The wax returns.

Conclusion: Has opened already, but will continue to develop.

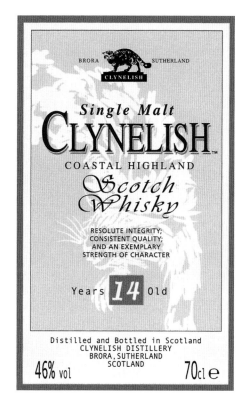

14YO 46%

Nose: The snuffed candle (orange-scented) notes remain. Oily and clean with some scented grass and sealing wax. Open and fresh. Ginger. With water, coastal freshness.

Palate: Good feel. More about sensation than specific flavors. In time a waxy lift that's slightly floral, slightly citric. Hint of brininess.

Finish: Long and gentle.

Conclusion: Small change aromatically from 8yo, more a slow oak integration and a deepening of flavor.

Flavor Camp: **Fruity & Spicy**
Where Next? Craigellachie 14yo, Old Pulteney

1997, MANAGER'S CHOICE, SINGLE CASK 58.8%

Nose: Bright gold. Aromatic and slightly herbal: sage and marjoram with lifted citric notes; kumquat plus lemon; then ripe summer fruit (apple, quince).

Palate: Very spicy start, alongside soft and gentle fruits and a touch of the sea. Water allows buttery oak to show alongside *crème brûlée*.

Finish: Long and smooth with citrus-fruit tones.

Conclusion: A really waxy example, with the quince note, which seems to be part of the style as well.

Flavor Camp: **Fruity & Spicy**
Where Next? Old Pulteney 12yo

Wolfburn

THURSO • WWW.WOLFBURN.COM

There is something immensely satisfying at reaching the end of a road. The sky seems to get larger, the horizon opens up. Symbolically, it is a place of possibilities, a place to look out from, not back to. Such it is with Thurso, the most northerly town on the British mainland. Stand on its cliffs and across the chaotic currents of the Pentland Firth are the sunset-red cliffs of Hoy. It is a place of smugglers and wreckers, of fishermen, surfers, and distillers.

A subtle change has also taken place as the utter north has been reached. We've moved off the Pictish Trail and into Viking territory. Thurso's deep harbor was where their longships would have sheltered, and the town's name comes from the Norse *Thjórsá*, meaning "Bull's River."

The Vikings must have had something about naming waters after animals, because Thurso is also home to one of Scotland's newest distilleries, the evocatively named Wolfburn, whose name is not the product of some slightly fevered marketing meeting, but comes from the Wolf Burn from which the distillery takes its process water.

A distillery of that name ran here from 1821 until the 1860s, and was for that brief period the largest in Caithness. Its successor commenced production on January 25, 2013, almost unbelievably only five months after construction started.

The hand on the helm is Shane Fraser, who started his whisky life under Mike Nicolson at Royal Lochnagar before becoming manager at the mighty Glenfarclas. "Shane had very clear ideas about the character," explains business development manager Daniel Smith. "Clear worts, long fermentation to create complexity, and a distillation regime that has hints of malt behind the fragrant fruit. I've never seen a human being as happy as he was when he got the cut right on the very first run."

The new make is being filled into 85% ex-bourbon and 15% sherry butts. Small amounts of whisky will be released from 2016 onward, but 80% of the production is being laid down for long-term maturation. Judging by the enthusiastic reaction to the subscription of the first release, most of it will be consumed in Thurso.

This is not the end of the road, but the start of a journey.

WOLFBURN TASTING NOTES

WOLFBURN CASK SAMPLE 60%

Nose: Clean and sweet, with lightly poached fruit: hints of red apple and pear. Lightly herbal, with a little rose note in the background.

Palate: Full and luscious and lacking in aggression. Melon, pear, and, with water, a silkiness.

Finish: Barley-sugar sweetness.

Conclusion: A vatting of 90% ex-bourbon and 10% sherry. Young, obviously, but already showing good balance.

Shane Fraser (right) and Iain Kerr (left) are crafting a new chapter in northern whisky's heritage.

Old Pulteney

WICK • WWW.OLDPULTENEY.COM • OPEN ALL YEAR OCT–APR, MON–FRI; MAY–SEPT, MON–SAT

The town of Wick, where the most northerly mainland distillery is to be found, is effectively on an island separated from the rest of Scotland by the expanse of the Flow Country, a dun and tawny expanse of black pools, peat bog, and reed. Location is about more than just a place on the map, it is a psychological state. It's not unsurprising that, when it comes to whisky, Wick has its own approach. Whisky is here because of Wick and Wick is here because of the herring.

Fish called the men into existence. The distillery, in turn, takes its name from Pulteneytown, built by Thomas Telford, an urban distillery at the center of its community, producing spirit for a thirsty town. Pulteneytown is named in honor of Sir William Pulteney MP who, at the end of the eighteenth century, had lobbied for the creation of new fishing ports in the remote north. The new harbor that his vision built could hold larger vessels which, in turn, landed more fish. In the nineteenth century, Wick was like the Klondike, with men hunting the "silver darlings," instead of gold. They needed whisky. Enter James Henderson, gentleman distiller who had been making whisky at his family seat at Stemster. He moved production to the boom town.

Other distillers in this era took the opportunity to change their distilling kit. Not Henderson. His stills, Alfred Barnard would write in 1886 were: "of the oldest pattern known, similar to the old smuggler's kettle." A wash still with an exaggerated boil bulb and flat top, the spirit still with purifier and its looping lyne arm like a stylized Pictish animal. Both sink into worms. They speak of improvisation and extravagance, but they work. "The wash still is key to Pulteney's character," says Stuart Harvey, master blender at owner Inver House. "You get massive reflux

Wick harbor—and Old Pulteney—were both built to satisfy the demands of the town's herring fleet.

and capture those top-end esters, but you also get leather. Pulteney has less spice and more fragrance than Balblair, but it's got more oil." Idiosyncratic. What else would you expect from such a location?

OLD PULTENEY TASTING NOTES

NEW MAKE

Nose: Heavy. Struck match with an almost creamy oiliness. Linseed oil. Hint of salinity/spice. Citrus peel/orange crate.
Palate: Thick and oily with juicy soft fruit. Touch of vanilla.
Finish: Fruity.

12YO 44%

Nose: Fruit is now bulging out. Persimmon and peach. Slightly salty and oily. Melon.
Palate: Unctuous feel. A thick bubble of oil. Juicy but slightly green fruits.
Finish: Fragrant.
Conclusion: Thick and tongue-coating.

Flavor Camp: Fruity & Spicy
Where Next? Scapa 16yo

17YO 46%

Nose: Lightly bready (bread and butter) with quince and toasty wood. More cask driven.
Palate: Physically broader than 12yo. Touch more cream.
Finish: Juicy and long.
Conclusion: The cask has made more drive and cut down on the oiliness.

Flavor Camp: Fruity & Spicy
Where Next? Glenlossie 18yo, Craigellachie 14yo

30YO 44%

Nose: Amber. Big, resinous. Racing stable: saddle soap, hoof oil, sweet nuts. Cedar. Yeast hint. Clean.
Palate: Marzipan. Again the lift of citrus fruit, but now the oil has come back forcefully.
Finish: Thick.
Conclusion: A typically Pulteney weird complexity.

Flavor Camp: Fruity & Spicy
Where Next? Balmenach 1993, Glen Moray 30yo

40YO 44%

Nose: Amber. Hugely perfumed. Preserved lemon, cinnamon, that saddle-soap note again, light smoke, and dried flowers. A late blossoming. Oddfellows.
Palate: Rosemary. Intense and then typical Pulteney oiliness coats the tongue. The smoke adds a new dimension.
Finish: Fragrant and long.
Conclusion: Concentrated and reduced.

Flavor Camp: Fruity & Spicy
Where Next? Longmorn 1977

WESTERN HIGHLANDS

Welcome to Scotland's smallest whisky "region," which, although it stretches the length of the long, indented, western coastline, currently only boasts two representatives. The reason they have survived is not only down to their towns' good transportation links, but also because of their individual personalities and, maybe, a shared belief in an older way of making whisky.

Seil Island lies close to Oban, the gateway to the Western Isles.

Oban

Oban's distillery is jammed between a cliff and the harborside buildings, giving it the air of being a slightly furtive operation, as if the town were trying to put on a different face to the world. Respectability is an important element in Calvinist Scotland and drink is, for some, decidedly not respectable. Not that this would have bothered John and Hugh Stevenson who took advantage of a scheme in the late eighteenth century when the Duke of Argyll offered 99-year leases at nominal *tack* (rent) for anyone who would build a house. The Stevensons ended up effectively building a town and a brewery, which by 1794, had become a licensed distillery. As far as the Stevensons were concerned whisky was decidedly respectable. They, their son, and grandson ran the distillery until 1869.

Other whisky ventures have tried and failed on this coastline, the result of problems over transportation. Oban, however, was perfectly positioned. It remains a major hub: railway station, ferry port, the end (or the beginning) of the road between Glasgow and the Western Isles. It's another of those distilleries that today works against type. Its two small onion-shaped stills are linked to worm tubs, leading you to conclude, logically, that this should be a heavy and possibly sulfury new make. Far from it.

Instead, Oban has an intense fruitiness with a jag of citrus, the result of air-resting the stills between distillations to allow the copper to revive itself and get ready to grab the sulfury compounds as they try to sneak across the lyne arms. Warmer worms also help to prolong the conversation between the vapor and the copper, revealing the fruit behind and adding a spicy tingle to the new make, which could be interpreted as saltiness.

Fermentation kicking off in one of Oban's washbacks.

OBAN TASTING NOTES

NEW MAKE

Nose: Fruity. Touch of rooty smoke to start. Baked peach and high citrus fruit/orange crate. Perfumed and complex. Has depth.

Palate: Creamy and gentle. Then the orange peel arrives and spreads across the tongue.

Finish: Smoke.

8YO, REFILL WOOD CASK SAMPLE

Nose: Earthy, perfumed, green banana/green orange, osmanthus (oolong tea). Weighty and slightly saline.

Palate: Sweet and dense. Masses of citrus-fruit tones. Concentrated. Numb.

Finish: Tickle of smoke.

Conclusion: The impression is of freshness and weight. One that might need time but can cope with an active cask.

14YO 43%

Nose: Clean and crisp. Light vanilla, some milk chocolate and lots of sweet spice. Fragrant with just a touch of smoke. Dried peels. Firm oak.

Palate: Soft sweet start with a zesty character running all the way through. Very clean with orange notes, mint, and syrup.

Finish: Very spicy and tingling.

Conclusion: Clean and balanced and now open.

Flavor Camp: Fruity & Spicy

Where Next? Arran 10yo, The BenRiach 12yo

Ben Nevis & Ardnamurchan

FORT WILLIAM • WWW.BENNEVISDISTILLERY.COM • OPEN ALL YEAR; SEE WEBSITE FOR DAYS & DETAILS / ARDNAMURCHAN • GLENBEG

If we return to our loose theory that "old" stills tend to produce a heavier style of spirit, then Ben Nevis would be a prime example of this in action. It also seems only appropriate that a distillery close to the buttresses of Britain's highest mountain makes a powerful dram—something light and ethereal would simply seem wrong in these surroundings.

Founded (legally) in 1825, Ben Nevis (the distillery, that is) has had an intriguing career. At one point it had a Coffey still installed and was the only whisky in Scotland to marry together the grain and malt components for its blend in cask before maturation.

In 1989, when it was bought by Japanese distiller Nikka, many believed a new phase of modern-style whisky-making would be ushered in. If anything, the opposite has been true. Old-school beliefs help to produce this "old-style" whisky that is rich, fruity, and chewy, with an intriguing leathery note that deepens with age.

It is appropriate, too, that the long-serving manager, Colin Ross, is a proud traditionalist. "Having being brought up on the traditional distilling practices, I've tried rigorously to maintain these within our distillery. This adherence to time-honored values means, in Ben Nevis's case, a reversion to wooden washbacks and brewer's yeast specifically for flavor creation.

"It could well be that these two factors might have contributed to the character," says Ross. "My first manager always told me that fermentation was most important of all, but there are so many other contributing factors."

Physically remote it may be—in whisky terms—but this distillery stands at the heart of traditional whisky-making.

This tiny subregion received its third member in 2014 with the opening of Adelphi's Ardnamurchan distillery on the remote eponymous peninsula. It saw a return to distilling for a firm that, in the nineteenth century, had operated large plants in England, Ireland, and Scotland but, in recent, years had specialized as an independent bottler.

Ardnamurchan was chosen because two of the owners have land there, appropriately near the "rocky excrescence" of MacLean's Nose, whose name is shared by the firm's consultant, Charles. It may be remote (sailing there might be the easiest option), but with 132,086 gallons (500,000 liters) a year of peated and unpeated makes planned (using barley grown on the Fife estate of sales and marketing director Alex Bruce), the long-term possibilities are considerable.

BEN NEVIS TASTING NOTES

NEW MAKE

Nose: Rich and oily with a little meaty sulfur note. Fruity behind.
Palate: Thick and sweet. Heavy mid-palate. Very chewy and clean. Rich. Less meat on the palate and more red licorice and red fruit.
Finish: Thick.

10YO 46%

Nose: Full gold. A mix of coconut, even some soft suede. Has the fatness of the new make. Thick almost syrupy fruit-paste quality. The oak adds a nutty background.
Palate: Coconut again: coconut cream this time. The feel remains thick and sweet with toffee.
Finish: Long, lightly nutty.
Conclusion: A bold whisky that is welcoming the attentions of pretty active casks.

Flavor Camp: Fruity & Spicy
Where Next? The Balvenie 12yo Signature

15YO CASK SAMPLE

Nose: Pale gold. Lifted, clean, and lightly fragrant as if a new delicacy has emerged. Still, the leather is the dominant character. Heavy and sweet. Light peat smoke.
Palate: Thick and chewy, but now an added chestnut honey flavor. Quite creamy with water, and an added praline touch.
Finish: Supple and long.
Conclusion: Remains a substantial malt that simply continues to take whatever the cask throws at it.

25YO 56%

Nose: Dark amber. Rich with runny toffee, light dried fruit. The thread to follow here is leather: from soft suede to this old armchair.
Palate: Hugely concentrated. Bitter toffee, dark chocolate, black cherry. Akin to a very old bourbon.
Finish: Dry coconut. Sweet and long.
Conclusion: The thick sweet power allows this to mature well.

Flavor Camp: Rich & Round
Where Next? The GlenDronach 1989, Glenfarclas 30yo

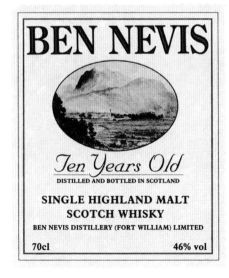

LOWLANDS

Drumchapel, Bellshill, Broxburn, Airdrie, Menstrie, Alloa. Not soccer teams
from the Irn-Bru Scottish Third Division, but a list of the hidden power bases
of Scotch whisky. All are in the Lowlands, where the bulk of Scotland's
whisky is produced, matured, and blended.

The mindset of the Lowland distiller has always been different
from that of his Highland counterpart. They have always thought
big, needing to satisfy a larger populace, and also for commercial
reasons. In the eighteenth century, while their northern and western
counterparts were distilling whisky to satisfy their immediate
communities, Lowland distillers, such as the Haigs and Steins, were
exporting to England. Their spirit was shipped south, rectified,
and poured down the gullets of the London denizens of Spitalfields
and Southwark as gin.

Export to England was a way to make money, but export licenses
were difficult to obtain and, because a high tax was levied on their
stills according to their capacity (peaking at an astounding £54/$80
per gallon), the only way in which to stay in business was to distill
more rapidly. In 1797, the Scottish Excise Board reported that a 253-
gallon still in Canonmills distillery "… worked at the rate of 47 charges
and discharges in the space of 12 hours …" Precious little time for
copper conversation there!

The spirit tasted burnt and was brimming with fusel oils. It might
have been acceptable after rectification into gin, but when taken
unadulterated by local Lowland drinkers? Even if the quality of
the illicit Highland malt was not up to today's standards, it was
significantly better than this.

When the new commercialized single malts arrived post-1823,
Lowland distillers once again began to up production, but this
time with a new design of still that gave both volume and quality.

In 1827, Robert Stein of Kilbagie invented a "continuous" still,
then, in 1834, Aeneas Coffey's patent still was installed at Grange
in Alloa. The Lowlands became the undeniable capital of grain-
whisky production.

It would be wrong, however, to think that the history of Lowland
whisky-making is solely about grain. Hundreds of malt distilleries
have opened (though most have closed) since the nineteenth century.
Despite that, the Lowlands remain, if not unknown, then certainly
underappreciated. Lowland malt just doesn't conform to the image
of mountains, heather, and wild spaces.

As a style they are too easily dismissed as being "light," when the
term is shorthand for bland. When you look closely, however, every
flavor camp is represented here; there is triple-distillation, the reek
of peat smoke.

In fact, the Lowlands is the fastest-growing malt region in Scotland.
Aisla Bay, Daftmill, Annandale, Kingsbarns are open, Inchdairnie is set
to follow, while there are proposals for a grain and malt plant in the
Borders, one in Glasgow, in Portavadie, and in Lindores.

All will approach whisky in their own way and learn what their
distilleries will give. Their emergence gives balance to the Lowlands
once more. Yes, it is large-scale. Yes it is home to the reality of
Scotch: blends. Yes, Glasgow remains as much of a whisky capital
as Dufftown. Yes, Lowland whisky is urban, but now it is also
regaining its rural roots.

Don't just head north. Stay and explore.

Border lands—looking across Wigtown Bay to Ben John and Cairnharrow from Carrick Point.

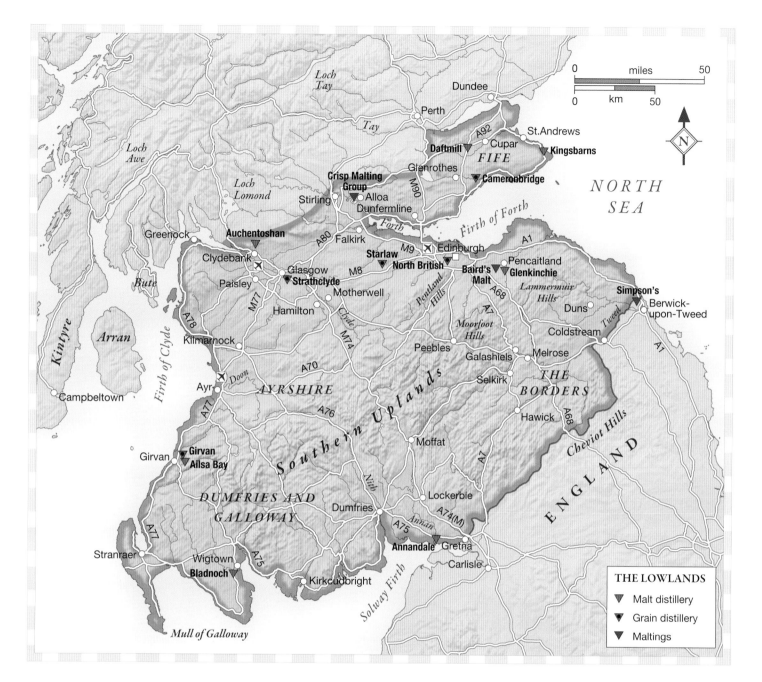

Placid and gentle—just like Wigtown's sole single malt.

Lowland grain distilleries

STRATHCLYDE • GLASGOW / CAMERONBRIDGE • LEVEN / NORTH BRITISH • EDINBURGH • WWW.NORTHBRITISH.CO.UK
GIRVAN • WWW.WILLIAMGRANT.COM/EN-GB/LOCATIONS-DISTILLERIES-GIRVAN/DEFAULT.HTML

There is a profound irony in the fact that Scotland's biggest volume-whisky style is its least well-known. Grain whisky was created in the nineteenth century when the country's large Lowland distillers needed to produce more whisky more efficiently, initially for export to England as the base for gin, and by the mid-century as a major component in blended Scotch.

Today, the Lowlands is home to six of Scotland's seven grain plants: Girvan, Loch Lomond, Strathclyde, Starlaw, The North British, and Cameronbridge, adding up to a total in excess of 79,251,615 gallons (300,000,000 liters) a year.

Grain is a high-strength spirit (*see* p.16), but it is not neutral. Equally, each grain distillery has its own character, derived from the type of grain used: wheat at Girvan, Strathclyde, and Cameronbridge; wheat and maize at Starlaw and Loch Lomond; corn exclusively at North British. Loch Lomond even runs a barley mash through its columns. Distillation also varies from Coffey-style two columns to Girvan and Starlaw's vacuum-distillation systems.

There are different approaches to maturation as well. Diageo tends to fill Cameronbridge into first-fill, whereas Edrington predominantly uses refill for North British, as does Grant for Girvan.

The result of all of these variations is a range of different new-make and mature characters (*see* tasting notes, below).

Grain, therefore, is a dynamic, flavorsome element in blends, not something that dilutes character. "Grain is the base flavor that gives our blends their character," says Brian Kinsman, master blender at William Grant & Sons. "It would be difficult if not impossible, to make Grant's without Girvan grain. In many ways the grain whisky will define the direction of the blend and the malts will create the style."

It's a belief shared by Kirsteen Campbell, master blender at Edrington. "Everyone wants to focus on the malts, but if you aren't using good-quality grain, then overall the blend is not going to hold up." Slowly they are beginning to be bottled on their own. Cameron Brig has long been available. Girvan's Black Barrel was discontinued, but in 2013 a range of new expressions appeared. Edrington has Snow Grouse, while in 2014, Diageo launched Haig Club in association with David Beckham. Grain is suddenly trendy. Seek out independent bottlers, such as Clan Denny, or blenders, such as Compass Box, whose Hedonism was the grain that made everyone sit up and take notice.

LOWLAND GRAIN DISTILLERIES TASTING NOTES

STRATHCLYDE 12YO 62.1%

Nose: Citric and intense, with a light-scented floral aroma behind. Firm and green, with a little marshmallow.
Palate: The same tight, slightly firm focus, with lemon and mandarin. Palate is sweet and supple.
Finish: Tight and firm.
Conclusion: A lot going on.

Flavor Camp: **Fragrant & Floral**

CAMERON BRIG 40%

Nose: Young, with a sweet-sour interplay. Apricot kernel, then creamy butterscotch. With water, a light earthiness.
Palate: A little chocolate and sweet coconut. The spirit has some fleshy, its oily weight allied to fresh American oak. Thick feel.
Finish: Tart and green.
Conclusion: Underrated brand—and style.

Flavor Camp: **Fruity & Spicy**

NORTH BRITISH 12YO CASK SAMPLE 60%

Nose: Gentle, but also the weightiest of the grains. Buttery and creamy, with a lift from some residual sulfur.
Palate: Bold and fat, thick and chewy. With water, you get more vanilla, ripe soft fruit, and a little touch of artichoke.
Finish: Medium dry.
Conclusion: The biggest and most complex of the grains.

GIRVAN "OVER 25YO" 42%

Nose: Fresh and delicate. Cool and precise, with a light floral/herbal element and light chocolate. Restrained wood and a little citrus.
Palate: Soft with white chocolate, vanilla, lemon butter frosting. Becomes slightly acidic.
Finish: Spicy.
Conclusion: Energetic and whistle-clean.

Flavor Camp: **Fragrant & Floral**

HAIG CLUB 40%

Nose: The sweetness is immediate. Limón and lemon zest, frying butter and mace. Then green apple and hard candies, wild flowers, charred/toasted oak and candy floss. Water brings out geranium leaf and light maple syrup.
Palate: Rum-like, with citrus fruit, frying plantain, and enough soft sweetness in the center to allow it to cling. Citrus fruit and fresh acidity.
Finish: Light cream and lemon.
Conclusion: Hugely versatile, typifyng the new approach to grain.

Flavor Camp: **Fruity & Spicy**

Daftmill & Fife

DAFTMILL • CUPAR • WWW.DAFTMILL.COM / KINGSBARN • ST ANDREWS • WWW.KINGSBARNSDISTILLERY.COM / INCHDAIRNIE • GLENROTHES / LINDORES ABBEY DISTILLERY • NEWBURGH • WWW.THELINDORESDISTILLERY.COM

My generation was intimately acquainted with the products of Fife when growing up. It produced coal for our fires, fish for our supper, linoleum for the kitchen floor, and leather belts for when we misbehaved at school. Today most of the engineering has gone, the mines long closed, the belts banned. All that's left for Fife are the dwindling fish stocks, agriculture, a burgeoning music community, and whisky. In recent years, all of it has come from the Cameronbridge distillery (*see* opposite) but, in the nineteenth century, there were 14 malt distilleries in the kingdom. In 1782, at the start of the smuggling era, 1,940 stills were seized.

Most of these distilleries (illegal and legal) would have started on farms. It was apt that, in 2003, two farming brothers, Francis and Ian Cuthbert, applied for permission to convert three of the buildings on their Daftmill farm into a distillery. (The name, by the way, is because the *burn* (watercourse) on the property appears to run uphill—and not only after you've had a couple of drams.)

In those days, starting a new whisky-making venture was deemed a bold, even insane, move. Nowadays the Cuthberts are seen as pioneers of a new movement within whisky-making, which has seen the art head back to its origins. The barley is their own, the draff feeds their beef herd, they make what they can afford to every year: on average 20,000 liters (5,283 gallons). It is whisky as it used to be.

At the time of writing, none has yet been released. "We did think of bottling in 2014," says Francis. "With all these new distilleries springing up, we better get our finger out!" There's something of a perfectionist streak in him. "We thought we'd cracked it when the spirit first ran off the still, but eight years down the line I still think

it can be tweaked to make it even better." Time has, however, allowed a distillery character to emerge. "I always pick out an herbal note in the background that only develops in maturation—that, and a creamy, buttery mouth-feel," he says. "Everything must take time to evolve."

The relatively small production isn't the result of a half-hearted approach. Speak to him and he is totally committed to his whisky. Rather, it is a knowledge that, to understand character, you have to wait. That's not just a farmer talking; that's a real whisky man.

In 2014, the Cuthberts were joined by the Kingsbarns distillery, which is owned by independent bottler Wemyss. Another converted farm using local barley (the Kings Barns were where Scotland's fourteenth-century King David I stored his grain) the aim is for a lighter-style single malt.

A third Fife malt distillery, Inchdairnie, is being built in Glenrothes by Indian distiller Kyndal. It will produce spirit for India and Asia. A final site, Lindores, is also planning to have its own distillery by 2016. Coal, linoleum, and belts may have gone, but golf, beaches, music, and whisky continue.

DAFTMILL TASTING NOTES

2006 FIRST-FILL BOURBON CASK SAMPLE 58.1%

Nose: Clean and sweet, like vanilla spongecake. Light fruit: strawberry, meadow flowers, sweet dessert apple. With water, lots of pear, cream, and elderflower.

Palate: Light, delicate, and sweet with no sign of immaturity. Gently soft mid-palate.

Finish: Sweet and long.

Conclusion: Already well-balanced and characterful.

2009 FIRST-FILL SHERRY BUTT CASK SAMPLE 59%

Nose: Sweetly mature (already!) with masses of raisin, toffee, vanilla, and *crème caramel*. With water, a perfumed violet/floral note.

Palate: Dense. Red fruit behind, alongside a little cinnamon. Light grip and very fruity underneath.

Finish: Sweet and elegant.

Conclusion: Precocious and already mature.

A model for all small-scale distillers, Daftmill understands the importance of time.

Glenkinchie

PENCAITLAND • WWW.DISCOVERING-DISTILLERIES.COM/GLENKINCHIE • OPEN ALL YEAR; SEE WEBSITE FOR DAYS & DETAILS

The Lowlands are nothing if not spread out in whisky terms. To find the next distillery you have to travel east to the edge of the Borders, and a similarly bucolic setting. Glenkinchie lies within arable farmland, meaning that there would have been little problem with raw materials when it was founded in 1825 on land that had belonged to the deQuincey family (hence "Kinchie").

Rebuilt in the 1890s, today Glenkinchie presents an air of solid bourgeois respectability. It's tall, brick-built, solid, and speaks of a feeling of prosperity and sureness of intent. This place was built to make whisky—alot of whisky, and its owners were going to make a lot of money out of it.

It's little surprise then that when you enter the stillhouse you look down on a pair of enormous pots: the wash still, with a capacity of 8,454 gallons (32,000 liters), is the largest in Scotch whisky. It is somewhat reminiscent of the style and size distillers in Ireland were building at roughly the same time as Glenkinchie was rebuilt. As demand rose, the stills got larger, and as the stills got larger, the style of whisky changed from heavy to light. The fact that the Lowlands make gentle whiskies has nothing to do with the environment; it is down to market forces.

Gentle is, however, not the descriptor you'd come up with if you were to nose the new make. Cabbage soup might be closer to the mark. The clue to this also lies in the stillhouse. Those fat country squires of stills have lyne arms that go through the wall into worm tubs. Like Dalwhinnie, Speyburn, and anCnoc, this is a light mature spirit that starts sulfury and, like those other distilleries, it's what lies beneath that is important.

An uphill struggle. Lowland whiskies are sadly overlooked by many.

The cabbagey notes fly off quicker than at Dalwhinnie, leaving a whisky that is clean and delicate with a background grassiness but that distinctive, worm-derived palate weight. A recent shift of the standard bottling from 10yo, where there was the occasional hint of vestigial sulfurousness, to 12yo has proved to be a sound move: those extra couple of years have helped to build weight and to reveal its full mature character.

GLENKINCHIE TASTING NOTES

NEW MAKE

Nose: Struck match and light cabbage water. Fragrant behind. Quite agricultural aromas.
Palate: Big sulfur hit then dry grass, cooked vegetable. What's hiding underneath?
Finish: Sulfur.

8YO, REFILL WOOD CASK SAMPLE

Nose: Damp hay, then, clover, washed linen. The sulfur is already almost gone. With water, jellied fuit: guava.
Palate: Intense sweetness. Pure and clean with a light dry floral edge, then comes the residual sulfur.
Finish: Gentle with a hint of struck match.
Conclusion: A butterfly emerging.

12YO 43%

Nose: Clean, meadow-like. Lightly floral, apple, orange.
Palate: Sweet with a little nut but generally a good silky feel. Direct and clean with a little vanilla.
Finish: Lifted. Lemon cake and some flowers.
Conclusion: Attractive, with substance. Butterfly takes wing.

> **Flavor Camp: Fragrant & Floral**
> **Where Next?** The Glenlivet 12yo, Speyburn 10yo

1992, MANAGER'S CHOICE, SINGLE CASK 58.2%

Nose: Early summer aromas of thyme, lemon balm, green melon, Muscat grapes, night-scented stocks.
Palate: Gentle, with those flowers once more along with some creaminess and fresh fig.
Finish: Lightly bitter. Lemon.
Conclusion: A light and perfumed example.

> **Flavor Camp: Fragrant & Floral**
> **Where Next?** Bladnoch 8yo

DISTILLER'S EDITION 43%

Nose: Gold. Fatter than 12yo, with riper, semi-dried fruit. Baked apple. Some dry oak. More substantial. Slightly more liquorous. Vanilla spongecake, white raisin in the background. No sulfur.
Palate: Less overtly sweet to start and wider on the tongue. Some barley sugar, dried apricot, heavier florals. Fleshy, slightly more tropical in character.
Finish: Light, sweet spice and citrus-fruit oils.
Conclusion: Here, the finish has added a new element while not killing the distillery character.

> **Flavor Camp: Fruity & Spicy**
> **Where Next?** Balblair 1990

Auchentoshan

AUCHENTOSHAN • CLYDEBANK • WWW.AUCHENTOSHAN.COM • OPEN ALL YEAR, MON–SUN

Although the fourth of the handful of Lowlanders may be less than romantically situated—between the Clyde River and the main road from Glasgow to Loch Lomond—it offers up another way of producing light: triple-distillation. In the nineteenth century, this was a fairly common method of production, especially in the Lowland belt, perhaps as a result of Irish immigration, or even as an attempt to copy what, at that time, was a more successful whisky style. Economics at work again. Today, however, Auchentoshan (aka "Auchie") is the only Scottish distillery that does it exclusively.

Here, triple-distillation is used to build strength and lighten character, ending up with a fresh, highly focused new make. The charge for the third (spirit) still is made up of high-strength "heads" from the intermediate. When this is distilled the spirit cut is taken between 82–80% abv (*see* pp.14–15). "It's on spirit for maybe 15 minutes," says Iain McCallum, blender at owner Morrison Bowmore. "Obviously that's giving us a light character, but I don't want neutrality. Auchentoshan should have sweetness, a malty note, citric fruit, and, as it matures, a hazelnut character." Auchie's inherent delicacy of character means that McCallum cannot be too heavy-handed with oak.

"It's such a light spirit that it could easily be swamped. I believe strongly in having the character of the spirit coming through the heart of the brand," says McCallum. "And with Auchie you have to take it easy with the oak."

A clever balancing act is therefore required to give the young spirit a sufficient boost from wood: enough to underpin its delicacy with layers of flavor. Equally, in older expressions the key is having a gentle oaken touch.

The lightness of the spirit also means Auchie has a greater degree of flexibility than bolder, stronger beasts. As a result, the firm has been working extensively with bartenders to develop Auchie as a base for long and mixed drinks.

They do things differently beside the Clyde. But it isn't blindly perverse, it is done for a reason: it works.

AUCHENTOSHAN TASTING NOTES

NEW MAKE

Nose: Very light and intense. Pink rhubarb, sweet cardboard, banana peel, leafy.
Palate: Tight and hot. Slightly biscuity, intense lemon lift.
Finish: Quick. Apple.

CLASSIC NAS 40%

Nose: Light gold. Sweet oak. Slightly dusty with a light floral note; touches of coconut matting from oak.
Palate: Sweet and nutty with plenty of vanilla that takes things into a chocolate realm. The high-toned notes of new make still in evidence.
Finish: Fresh.
Conclusion: Deftly handled oak allows character to show.

Flavor Camp: **Malty & Dry**
Where Next? Tamnavulin 12yo, Glen Spey 12yo

12YO 40%

Nose: Again the oak leads the way. Touches of hot cross bun, a paprika-covered roasted almond. Citric lift.
Palate: Soft and clean, the cereal note now drifting toward spice. Still that leafy quality.
Finish: Crisp and clean.
Conclusion: Identifiably Auchie.

Flavor Camp: **Malty & Dry**
Where Next? Macduff 1984

21YO 43%

Nose: Slightly funky maturity. Concentrated dark fruits, then come dry spices (coriander seed), roast chestnut but still that intense dustiness and freshness.
Palate: Rich and liquorous with a lavender-like flavor on the palate.
Finish: Perfumed.
Conclusion: Even at 21 years a light spirit holds its own.

Flavor Camp: **Fruity & Spicy**
Where Next? The Glenlivet 18yo, Benromach 25yo

Bladnoch, Annandale & Ailsa Bay

WIGTOWN • WWW.BLADNOCH.CO.UK • OPEN ALL YEAR; SEE WEBSITE FOR DAYS & DETAILS / ANNANDALE • ANNAN • WWW.ANNANDALEDISTILLERY.CO.UK / AILSA BAY • GIRVAN

A mile out of Wigtown on the banks of the meandering river from which it takes its name, Bladnoch is a big, rambling site whose considerable warehouse complex heads off up into the fields to the back of the distillery. A walk around the site leaves you with the distinct impression that every building you have entered has been accessed through the back door—there may not even be a front door.

Bladnoch is less a purpose-built distillery, more a random collection of dark-stoned, slate-roofed buildings, one of which happens to house whisky-making equipment. The others house a shop, a cafe, offices, a bar that doubles as a village hall, as well as an old kiln that can also double as a venue, and a campsite. Bladnoch is less a distillery and more a community, the focal point of the village since 1817.

This feeling that every room contains a surprise starts in the mash house (entered through the side door) where slightly cloudy worts go through to one of the half-dozen Oregon pine washbacks where it's allowed to ferment in a leisurely fashion for what owner Raymond Armstrong calls "four hours short of three days." The stillhouse is more of a stillroom. There's none of the usual bars, ladders, and guards around the stills that poke through the floor. Stillman John Herries controls things from a rickety table, next to which is a wooden box with switches and valves.

The fact that it's working at all is a surprise. It was closed from 1938 until 1956 and ran from then until 1992 (latterly as part of Bell's), before closing again in 1993. Armstrong, a Belfast-based chartered surveyor, bought it the next year, intending to convert the site into holiday homes, but then he fell in love with the place. The garrulous Ulsterman had to go back to Diageo to ask if he could re-start production.

Eventually they relented, allowing him to make 26,417 gallons (100,000 liters) of whisky a year. Spirit started flowing again in 2000, the interim period being taken up with legal issues and the need to re-engineer the plant.

AILSA BAY: THE NEWCOMER WITH A MISSION

An hour's drive north from Bladnoch on the Clyde coast is William Grant's Girvan grain distillery, which is home to one of Scotland's newest malt plants, Ailsa Bay. This wasn't, however, built as a new "Lowland" distillery but, as Grant's master blender Brian Kinsman explains, "as something flexible to take all the things we liked in our Dufftown site and replicate them." Modeled on The Balvenie, Ailsa Bay exists in order for the malt brand to grow. "The stills are Balvenie-shaped for the simple reason that it's growing as a single malt but is also a major component in blends so there is pressure on supply." Kinsman hasn't stopped there. Four styles: estery, malty, light, and heavy peat are all produced on the site.

"They were churning it out before they closed it down," recalls Herries. "Everything was just forced through. Now we're more relaxed again." That would explain the nutty character that you pick up on older expressions and why the Armstrong-era whiskies resemble nectar-heavy flowers.

"The trouble with the whisky business is a lot of enthusiasts don't appreciate the subtleties and elegance of Lowland malts," says this born-again whisky evangelist. "We just have to convince them." At the time of writing, Bladnoch has been put into administration. Several buyers have already expressed an interest.

David Thomson, former cereal-chemist-turned-researcher-into flavor-perception-turned-market-researcher, became a distiller in 2014,

Scotland's most southerly distillery comes complete with cafe, village hall, and campsite.

bringing the defunct Annandale farm distillery back to life, 93 years after it had closed its doors. Its rebirth gives whisky-lovers another reason to turn left when they cross the border. His varied experience has given him a clear long-term vision for his new baby.

"There are 100 other Scottish distilleries," Thomson says. "We have to make ourselves heard rather than just add to the noise. That means showing why we are different."

All that is known at the time of writing is that smoke will be involved. "We're in a peat bog," Thomson adds, "and it was a smoky whisky"—confounding people's expectations as to what Lowland malts should be, while at the same time underlining that this is as varied a region as any.

The distilleries speak their own language.

Resting the stills between distillations helps preserve Bladnoch's fragrant character.

BLADNOCH TASTING NOTES

NEW MAKE

Nose: Fresh and gentle with clean floral notes and light citrus fruit.
Palate: Clean and zesty with good acidity, blossom, and a little touch of honey.
Finish: Clean and short.

8YO 46%

Nose: Light gold. Marshmallow, cut flowers, and sweet apple with a light hint of beeswax. Lemon puffs. With water, a slow lift of clover honeycomb.
Palate: Clean and slightly buttery. Soft center with fragrant flowers and that honeyed note. Becomes lightly spiced on the finish.
Finish: Light and clean.
Conclusion: Fresh as a spring day.

Flavor Camp: Fragrant & Floral
Where Next? Linkwood 12yo, Glencadam 10yo, Speyside 15yo

17YO 55%

Nose: Light gold. Broader and more nutty with that sweet undertone still in evidence, although this is more mash-like than honeyed. Freshly baked bread and apricot jam. Hot buttered toast.
Palate: Slightly perfumed quality, then it settles into honeynut cornflakes.
Finish: Spicy and a little soapy.
Conclusion: Typical of the last days of the *ancien régime*.

Flavor Camp: Fragrant & Floral
Where Next? The Glenturret 10yo, Strathmill 12yo

AILSA BAY TASTING NOTES

No mature spirit has been released. Nor do the new makes have names. Here are six examples of the different spirit types being made.

1.

Nose: Light and estery. Sesame. Pineapple with a little brassy note. Dry.
Palate: Very pure, that estery pineapple, pear, bubblegum note along wth melon.
Finish: Soft and gentle.

2.

Nose: Clean, light, crisp with light cereal undertones.
Palate: Whistle-clean. Very pure with green grassiness. Has mid-palate fatness.
Finish: Crisp.

3.

Nose: Nutty with a hint of cooked vegetable sulfur. Pot ale. Heavier.
Palate: Fatter on palate. Ripe and heavy. Lentils.
Finish: Broad and ripe.

4.

Nose: Cereal and acetone. Green almond. Less roasted than the previous.
Palate: Pure. Big nut with fruits in the background. Light nuttiness/nutshell. Dry and clean.
Finish: A sudden sweetness. Will develop in an interesting fashion.

5.

Nose: Fragrant peat smoke. Rooty with cigar and light ham. Burning wood, pear, and new runners.
Palate: Dry smoke hits immediately. Solid but with a sweet core. A big hitter.
Finish: Smoke now lifts and floats gently away.

6.

Nose: Backyard bonfire with a hint of oils. Heavy and dry.
Palate: Powerful and sightly earthy. Clean but more of a foggy effect.
Finish: Long.

ISLAY

Flat calm off the south coast of Islay. The boat's wake is barely managing to lazily flop the bronze seaweed against the chain of islets that protect this channel from the sea. Seals gaze at us, big-eyed. White sand runs under the keel. Black letters scroll slowly across a white wall opposite. Journey's end. You can fly to Islay, but to fully appreciate the island you must sail there. After all, the sea as much as the land has dictated Islay's wider *terroir*. Islands behave differently from the mainland.

All Islay's distilleries are on the coast. This allowed raw materials in, and whisky out.

Sit on the top of Opera House Rocks on its west coast at sunset and look out. The sea is rolling in under a blue and turquoise sky, the wind riffling through the *machair* (plain), the world is suffused with a soft light. Everything glows as if lit from within. The next landfall is Canada. You are on the edge of the world.

Islay has been inhabited for 10,000 years, but its "modern" era starts on the coast, in places such as the tiny chapel of St. Ciaran (Kilchiaran). The monks from Ireland sought out this northern and western desert for their retreats.

It would be ideal if someone like St. Ciaran had brought distillation with him from Ireland, but it's unlikely. The art only passed into Western thought in the eleventh century. However, Islay could lay claim to being the spiritual home of distillation in Scotland thanks to the arrival of the MacBeatha family (aka Beaton) who knew the secret of distillation. In 1300, they became the hereditary physicians of the Lords of the Isles, the MacDonalds, landing as part of Aine O'Cathain's wedding party on her marriage to Angus MacDonald. This island therefore is the fulcrum around which distillation, and in time whisky, revolved. Islay isn't insular. It is part of the wider world.

By the fifteenth century, whisky was being made, although it was far from the spirit of today. It would have been made from a range of cereals, sweetened with honey and flavored with herbs, but it would have been smoky. You cannot escape peat on Islay. It is the DNA of its malts. Here, the geographical *terroir* doesn't just speak, it roars.

Islay's malts start life on the peat moss. Their aromas are the product of thousands of years of maceration, compression, decay, and transformation. Islay peat is different to mainland peat; maybe that's where the seaweedy, medicinal, kipper-like aromas originate.

I asked Mike Nicolson, a former manager of Lagavulin, what being an incomer on the island was like. "There's a tighter relationship between the managers and the community here. You begin to think further out when you make decisions. You know you're part of a community that has been there for a very, very long time indeed, and that takes you into that continuum thing where you're reminded that life is short and that you're following on from those who went before, who made an exceptional spirit in that place, for generations."

Loch Indaal. The shores of this shallow loch are the perfect place to sit with a sunset dram— or two—and contemplate the magic of Islay's location.

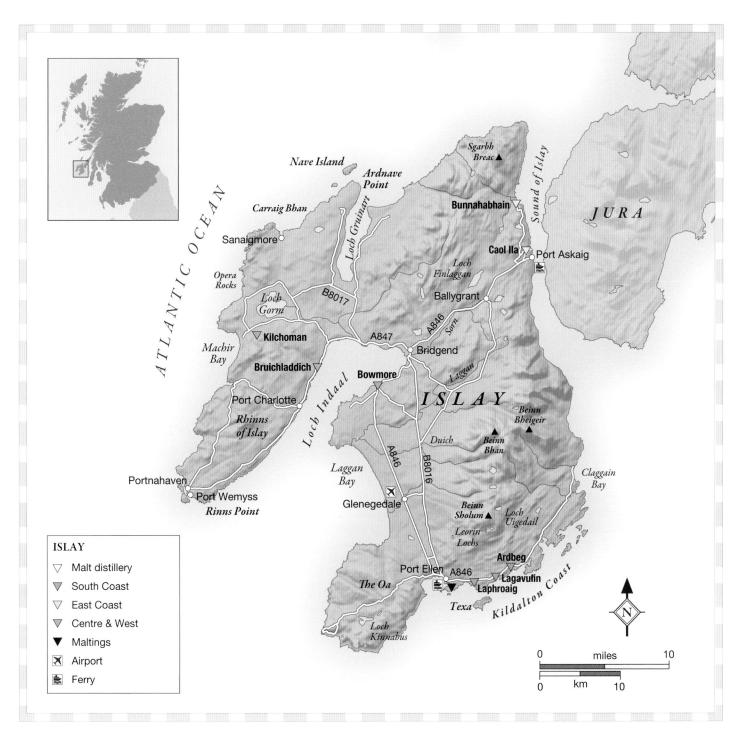

ISLAND

Nave Island

Ardnave
Point

Sgarbh
Breac ▲

Carraig Bhan

ATLANTIC OCEAN

Sanaigmore

Bunnahabhain

J U R A

Loch Gruinart

Caol Ila

Port Askaig

Opera
Rocks

Loch
Gorm

B8017

Loch
Finlaggan

Ballygrant

Kilchoman

A847

A846

Sorn

Machir
Bay

Bruichladdich

Bridgend

Port Charlotte

Rhinns
of Islay

Loch Indaal

Bowmore

Laggan

I S L A Y

Beinn
Bheigeir ▲

Duich

Beinn
Bhan ▲

Claggain
Bay

Portnahaven

Laggan
Bay

A846

B8016

Port Wemyss

Rinns Point

Glenegedale

Beinn
Sholum ▲

Loch
Uigedail

Leorin
Lochs

The Oa

Port Ellen

A846

Ardbeg

Lagavulin

Laphroaig

Kildalton Coast

Texa

Loch
Kinnabus

ISLAY

▽ Malt distillery
▽ South Coast
▽ East Coast
▽ Centre & West
▼ Maltings
☒ Airport
⛴ Ferry

0   miles   10

0   km   10

N

SOUTH COAST

Islay's south coast is a place of offshore reefs, tiny seal-haunted bays, and ancient Celtic Christian sites. It is also home to the Kildalton Trio, three legendary distilleries that make the biggest, peatiest whiskies of all. Don't be fooled by first impressions, though: beneath their smoky exteriors beat hearts filled with sweetness.

Islay doesn't just attract flocks of whisky-lovers; it is also a renowned bird-watching center.

Ardbeg

PORT ELLEN • WWW.ARDBEG.COM • OPEN ALL YEAR; SEE WEBSITE FOR DAYS & DETAILS

Soot. That's what comes at you. A chimney being swept, but there's a citric edge, is it grapefruit? Then there's dulse (local seaweed) on the rocks, a burst of violet, then banana, wild garlic in the spring woods. Ardbeg new make is a balancing act between the smoke and the sweet, between soot and fruit. The smell is with you all the way through the distillery, it's built into the bricks. But what of that sweet element? Go to the stillhouse.

There's a pipe linking the lyne arm of the spirit still to its belly, diverting any liquid that has condensed back into the still. This reflux not only helps build complexity, but will help to lighten the spirit by giving the vapor more contact with copper. Result? That sweetness.

Ardbeg's recent history mirrors perfectly the vicissitudes of the whisky industry. This is a long-term business, so stocks are laid down by a mixture of experience and optimistic market projections. In the late 1970s it was blind optimism. Sales fell, but stocks continued to be laid down. By 1982, the whisky loch resulted in a mass cull of plants. Ardbeg was one.

By the 1990s the place was forgotten, ghostly. When you turn the heat off in a distillery you're left with a coldness that seeps into your soul. The echo of cold metal makes you realize that distilleries have a spirit of their own.

The barrel-roofed warehouses of Ardbeg face onto the sea. It is interesting to consider what effect that might have on the character of its whisky.

PEAT AND SMOKINESS

That Ardbeg is heavily peated is true, but simplistic. Ardbeg, Lagavulin, Laphroaig, and Caol Ila all happen to be peated to more or less the same level, yet the nature of the smokiness in each is substantially different. Why? It's down to distillation, mostly. The shape and size of the still, the speed at which it is run, and, vitally, the cut points (see pp.14–15). Phenols don't just appear at the end of the spirit run, they drift across all the way through. Their concentration and composition change as well, meaning that those captured early in the run are substantially different from those that appear at the end. Cut points are set in order to retain—or reject—specific phenols.

But by the late 1990s malt was on the up and Glenmorangie bought the site and stock for £7.1m ($10.5m) in 1997. A further few million have since been spent getting it up and running again.

There's been a few changes. "We're running longer ferments," says Dr. Bill Lumsden, Glenmorangie's distilleries director and whisky creator. "Short ferments give you pungency from the smoke, but with long ferments you get creaminess and slightly more acidity. The stills are the same, the peating is the same, but the spirit run has been tweaked a little."

Islay peat—and lots of it. A key ingredient in the creation of Ardbeg's individual character.

A wood policy has been put in place with more first-fill American oak in the system. "The main change was that the quality of wood is now higher," says Lumsden. "Now we can flesh out the rawness."

It's been a long haul between purchase and the release of the first Glenmorangie-owned Ardbeg, a process charted by releases that marked the incremental progress of the spirit: "Very Young," "Still Young," "Almost There."

"My objective was to recreate the original house style," says Lumsden, "the 'Young' range was tongue-in-cheek, but it showed what we were doing. Old Ardbeg was sooty and tarry, but the quality was also inconsistent and every year was different. We needed consistency." The problem was, the cult of Ardbeg was built on these inconsistencies. Whisky-makers may hate vintage variations, whisky-nuts love them. Trying to keep both happy has involved a balancing act: a core range supplemented by a selection of "wonderful oddities" as Lumsden calls them. Examples such as the recent heavily peated Supernova.

Holes in the stock profile have also meant a need for creative blending, which in turn has liberated Ardbeg from age statements. "Uigeadail was to give an idea of the old style; Corryvreckan to show Ardbeg in French oak; Airigh nam Beist was my homage to the old 17yo," says Lumsden.

There's a swagger to Ardbeg these days as if the distillery itself has reclaimed its destiny. "It's difficult to talk empirically about how much a distillery dictates what it is going to make," says Lumsden, "but I'd reckon it's 30 percent us and the rest is the character of the place, the history. We've had to work sympathetically around what was there. Distilleries are somehow alive."

ARDBEG TASTING NOTES

NEW MAKE

Nose: Sweet and sooty touch of dulse and rock pools. Lightly oily then peat smoke, unripe banana, garlic, violet root, tomato leaf. With water, creosote and Chinese cough medicine, solvent.
Palate: Big, soot; intense, slightly peppery. Sweet-centered. Mossy peat, grapefruit.
Finish: Oatcake.

10YO 46%

Nose: Smoky but also sweet and citric, with estery notes lurking. Seaweed and ozone freshly mixed with wet moss, sansho pepper, and cinnamon.
Palate: Really sweet start. Lime chocolate; menthol/wintergreen/eucalyptus mixed with big, rich, sooty smoke.
Finish: Long and peaty.
Conclusion: Shows the required balance between dry smoke and sweet distillate.

Flavor Camp: Smoky & Peaty
Where Next? Stauning Peated

UIGEADAIL 54.2%

Nose: Mature and rich, with a concentrated black-fruit sweetness and an earthy note. Some lanolin and ink and lightly meaty. Water brings out green tea, water-mint, and molasses.
Palate: Huge and elemental. Sweet again, with the alcohol cutting through the thick smoke to clear the complex mix of rumbling peat, Pedro Ximénez sherry, shoreline, creosote, and dried fruit.
Finish: Long and raisined.
Conclusion: Ardbeg at its most massive.

Flavor Camp: Smoky & Peaty
Where Next? Paul John Peated Cask

CORRYVRECKAN 57.1%

Nose: Brooding, with a sense of power. Some charred oak, red fruit, spent fires. Less ozonic and more meaty.
Palate: Tarry, Latakia tobacco/pipe smoke, oils. Deep and tarry. Very thick, but in the center there's real fruit-lozenge sweetness. Water makes it more overtly smoky and shows a light acidity.
Finish: Refreshingly sour—and smoky.
Conclusion: Massive, smoky, but balanced.

Flavor Camp: Smoky & Peaty
Where Next? Balcones Brimstone

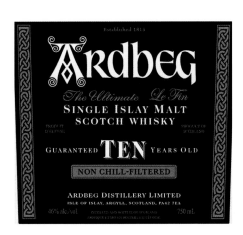

Lagavulin

PORT ELLEN • WWW.DISCOVERING-DISTILLERIES.COM/LAGAVULIN • OPEN ALL YEAR; SEE WEBSITE FOR DAYS & DETAILS

The Kildalton Coast is indented by small rocky bays, its rocks fracture the thin earth—a place of hideouts and hermetic practices. From here, you can see the other points of the cradle of distillation: Kintyre slumping opposite, the blue hills of Antrim on the horizon. Guarding Lagavulin Bay are the ruins of Dunyvaig Castle, the final destination of Aine O'Cathain's wedding flotilla in 1300 (*see* p.150).

If Ardbeg sprawls across its bay, then Lagavulin seems compressed by its location, the buildings forced upward, the present dominating the past, the sheer white-painted walls looking down on the black stumps of the ruined castle, the silent bell on the hill. The Lords' days are over, it seems to say, now is the time for whisky.

The scene wouldn't have been nearly as grand when the two legal distilleries, which once stood here, were established on Lagavulin Farm in 1816 and 1817. The bay was regarded as the center of production on the island with up to 10 small-scale (illicit) operations working here before the Islay *gaugers* (tax officers) and landlords clamped down on the practice. By 1835, there was a single plant, and it had into Islay's largest plant by the end of the century.

Water rushes in from hill lochs down the *lade* (channel) into the mash house as you enter what look like the original late Victorian offices, but are in fact the original malt barns given a sympathetic

PORT ELLEN MALT WHISKY: GONE BUT NOT FORGOTTEN

Lagavulin's owner, Diageo, also owns Caol Ila and the Port Ellen maltings, which supplies peated malt for some of the island's plants. Until 1983 it also had a third distillery whose shell now sits in the shadow of the maltings. Port Ellen was built in 1830 and had been exported as a single malt in the nineteenth century, but the combination of the expansion at Caol Ila in the early 1970s and the slump at the end of that decade sealed its fate. It is now a cult malt whose austere, pier-head aromas have become revered.

makeover. Breathe in. There's smoke once again. One previous manager, fresh from the mainland, hit the fire alarm when he first arrived here, thinking the place was on fire, but the smoke seems different to Ardbeg's. Yet all of Lagavulin's malt is peated at the same place, the Port Ellen maltings, and is also in the "high smoke" bracket.

The trail of smoke leads you through the prickling CO_2-laden tun room, past the hot cereal smells of the mash tun into a short,

Lagavulin's bay was originally the site of one of the castles occupied by the Lords of the Isles.

A very slow second distillation is one of the secrets of Lagavulin's complexity.

bonfire, but with an intense sweet core. Clearly then it's the stills that make the difference here. The wash stills are huge, but with acutely angled lyne arms that swoop into condensers (this is the only one of Diageo's old "Classic Six," without worms). Heaviness being built in? The spirit stills are significantly smaller, fat-based, and plain, looking like stylized elephant's feet. In these, the heat is turned down, allowing maximum reflux, polishing, removing; retaining smokiness but taking away sulfur.

It's a surgical dissection of heaviness, a slow revelation of the sweet core, which must be at the heart of any smoky spirit if it is to be a balanced, mature whisky.

They are aged, for single malt, in refill casks, which are overseen by Iain MacArthur, crofter, warehouseman, wit. Here, pulling samples

covered passageway. The smoke seems to billow out, but halfway the aroma changes, smoky still, but now with an overwhelming sweetness, a strange exotic pungency. Pour some of the new make on your hands and inhale. If Ardbeg is sooty, then Lagavulin is more like a beach

from a selection of casks he shows how the fieriness of youth is slowly tempered by oak, introducing a new complexity. Lagavulin is about peeling away layers, as it pulls you onto the pier looking out, past the castle, thinking of Aine and her bevy of boats, out into the cradle.

LAGAVULIN TASTING NOTES

NEW MAKE

Nose: Sooty smoke. Bonfire-like. Dense and foggy. Kiln-like. Gentian, fish boxes, seaweed. Sulfur hint.
Palate: Big, complex with lifted aromatics, almost floral but held in check by earthy/seashore smoke.
Finish: Long and peaty.

8YO, REFILL WOOD CASK SAMPLE

Nose: Complex. Drying crab creels, seaweed. Wet peat bank, little hint of rubbery immaturity, pipe smoke. Kilns. Sweet and smoky. Heavy and lifted.
Palate: Sooty. *Smoored* (smothered) fire. Ripe fruit. Heather and blaeberry, seaweed. Vibrant, deep.
Finish: Explosive. Peat. Spice, oatcakes, and seashell.
Conclusion: Ready to go.

12YO 57.9%

Nose: Straw. Intense smoke. Carbolic soap, lightly smoked haddock, but also sweet. Bog myrtle. Wasabi on fresh herring. Ozone. Light sootiness.
Palate: Dry, with intense smoke to start; smoked cheese, rolled in oatmeal. Tight yet effervescent. Hugely fragrant. Uncompromising but open. Water allows its sweet center to show, and also youth.
Finish: Firm smoked dry.
Conclusion: Intense, complex smokiness, and sweetness.

Flavor Camp: Smoky & Peaty
Where Next? Ardbeg 10yo

16YO 43%

Nose: Big, robust, and complex. Seriously smoky, pipe tobacco, kiln, beach bonfire, smokehouse all allied to ripe fruitiness. Touch of creosote and Lapsang souchong tea.
Palate: Lightly oily and defiantly smoky. Fruit comes first with medicinal touch alongside bog myrtle while smoke builds steadily toward the finish. Elegant.
Finish: Long and complex mix. Seaweed and smoke.
Conclusion: Opens quickly. Its effusive character starts to concentrate into an essence of shoreline peatiness.

Flavor Camp: Smoky & Peaty
Where Next? Longrow 14yo, Ardbeg Airigh nam Beist 1990

21YO 52%

Nose: Huge and complex, mixing saddles, dark chocolate, Pu-erh tea, and smoldering kiln, geranium, and velvet.
Palate: Gamey and molasses-like. The smoke is fully integrated, the fires ember-like, the oak there adding structure but not dominating. Massive, dense, layered, and complex.
Finish: Long, fruity, and smoky.
Conclusion: Aged in a first-fill sherry butt.

Flavor Camp: Smoky & Peaty
Where Next? Yoichi 18yo

DISTILLER'S EDITION 43%

Nose: Mahogany. Woodier than the 16yo and slightly vinous. The black fruit is now dried and there's generally less definition on the nose, as if all the almost paradoxical complexities have been tidied up. Almost discreet, it does open with time and water.
Palate: The smoke seems to have been shunted forward (if only because the finish is so much sweeter). A good mix of rich spirit, dried fruit, and a touch of cinnamon toast.
Finish: Thick and only lightly smoked. Generous and sweet.
Conclusion: Lagavulin with added sweetness.

Flavor Camp: Smoky & Peaty
Where Next? Talisker 10yo

Laphroaig

PORT ELLEN • WWW.LAPHROAIG.COM • OPEN ALL YEAR MAR–DEC, MON–SUN; JAN–FEB, MON–FRI

The final member of the Kildalton trio lies little more than a couple of miles from Lagavulin. It, too, is smoky, yet once again the character of that smoke is fundamentally different from that of its neighbors. Laphroaig is heavy and rooty, like walking down a freshly tarred seaside road on a hot day. It was a style that was envied by its neighbor at one time, Sir Peter Mackie, who owned Lagavulin and had lost the agency for Laphroaig in 1907. He built a replica called Malt Mill at Lagavulin, using the same water, same stills, and even (after financial inducement) the same distiller. The whisky was different. "It's something that scientists try to explain, but can't," says Laphroaig's manager, John Campbell. "Character is about location, maybe that's why distilleries are all across Scotland, rather than in one super-distillery. It could be down to altitude, it could be proximity to the sea, it could be humidity; I don't know, but it exists."

It does also lie within the creative process at the distillery. Laphroaig still operates its own floor maltings, which provide up to 20 percent of its requirements. For Campbell, the maltings aren't there as a sop for tourists, they certainly don't offer any savings in fixed cost, but they do provide a different character. "We get a different smokiness here than we get from Port Ellen [malt]. We kiln differently, we peat, and then dry at low temperatures. This gives us higher levels of cresol [a key phenol] and it's this that gives you that tarry note in the spirit. It wouldn't be there without the floor maltings."

The stillhouse is, inevitably, different. There are seven stills for starters, while on the spirit side there are two different sizes, with one twice the size of the other three. "We are effectively making two different spirits, which we then marry together before casking," says Campbell.

Ardbeg and Lagavulin both strive for an element of reflux to get sweeter estery notes. Laphroaig on the other hand, steers the other way. Here, Campbell wants to hold onto that heavy, tarry weight that means having the longest foreshot run in the industry (45 minutes) so that those sweet esters at the start of the run are recycled rather than collected (see pp.14–15). "We cut at 60 percent, which isn't as low as some, but because we get less of the estery notes there is a larger percentage of smokiness, so the spirit seems heavier."

The sweetness that does exist within Laphroaig is found from its virtually exclusive use of American oak barrels—all of which come from Maker's Mark. "For consistency," says Campbell. It's this vanilla character that smoothes away the more rugged edge of the new make and adds a subtle sweet drive to the mature spirit. A good example of this process is the Quarter Cask release in which young Laphroaig is given a short period of extra maturation in new tiny, "quarter" casks made from American oak. The vanilla and the smoke are here at their peak.

Low tide on the seaweed-strewn strand at the third of the mighty Kildalton malts, Laphroaig.

For Campbell, though, Laphroaig is more than just technology, it's people. "I'd say that we were the result of the people who have worked here. People have influenced the style and the attitude to making whisky, none more so than Ian Hunter [who owned it from 1924–54]. It was he who created the recipe that we have now. In the 1920s we were mucking around and it really wasn't until 1940, after Prohibition, that he began to source ex-bourbon casks and mature the whisky on site."

Laphroaig believes that its signature flavors come partly from its own floor maltings.

So, it comes back to location again. "A traditional warehouse gives more body to the whisky, maybe because you get more oxidation in a damp dunnage than the rack. We have both on site and I know that there is a difference." Maybe he should have told Sir Peter Mackie.

LAPHROAIG TASTING NOTES

NEW MAKE

Nose: Heavy, tarry smoke. Oilier than its neighbors. A light medicinal note (iodine, hospital) along with a crisp maltiness and gentian root. Has complexity.
Palate: Hot embers followed by the rich spread of smoke. Both dark and clean. Hot roads on a summer day by the sea.
Finish: Dry clean, smoky, Crisp.

10YO 40%

Nose: Rich gold. Smoke is being both restrained and manipulated by sweet oak. Wood oils, pine woods. Seashore, wintergreen. Nutty background and, with water, iodine.
Palate: Smooth, soft start with plenty of vanilla accents then a slow uptake of smoke, but the oak is balanced. Becomes tarry to the finish.
Finish: Long, lightly peppery smoke.
Conclusion: The key here is the balance between the dry (smoke) and the sweet (oak).

Flavor Camp: **Smoky & Peaty**
Where Next? Ardbeg 10yo

18YO 48%

Nose: Rich gold. Restrained and gentle. The smoke, having been given more time with the oak, is now mossy and has picked up a spicier edge alongside that creamy oak. Light iodine and that rootiness of new make.
Palate: Nutty start. Walnut, and whisky-soaked raisin. Little citric note rising above the slightly shy smoke.
Finish: Smoked salted cashew.
Conclusion: A toned-down example.

Flavor Camp: **Smoky & Peaty**
Where Next? Caol Ila 18yo

25YO 51%

Nose: The smoke has returned! Soy sauce, fishboxes, dried tar, heavy tobacco, burning lobster creels.
Palate: After the huge impact of the nose, this seems almost gentle. Age has thickened it. It has become coherent with full integration (and therefore complexity) of distillery character and oak plus new exotic flavors.
Finish: Still tarry.
Conclusion: Smoke doesn't disappear, it simply becomes more concentrated and absorbed into the overall flavor.

Flavor Camp: **Smoky & Peaty**
Where Next? Ardbeg Lord of the Isles 25yo

EAST COAST

Islay's East Coasters enjoy views across the fast-running tidal race of the Sound of Islay to the raised beaches of Jura and north to the shores of Colonsay and Mull. In some ways, their remoteness is surprising because this pair are the island's largest producers—and in some ways perhaps Islay's least known.

Gazing over to the raised beaches of Jura; Islay's East Coast distilleries have a spectacular outlook.

Bunnahabhain
PORT ASKAIG • WWW.BUNNAHABHAIN.COM • OPEN ALL YEAR; TOURS APR–SEPT BY APPOINTMENT ONLY

Islay's northeastern coast was deserted in the late nineteenth century when the Islay Distillery Company (IDC) started work on not just a new distillery but an entire village in what is now known as Bunnahabhain. With a road, a pier, houses, a village hall, as well as a substantial distillery, Bunnahabhain is a fine example of the optimism surrounding Scotch whisky in the 1880s and the paternalistic attitudes of the new distilling companies.

The Islay Distillery Company's endeavors certainly met with the approval of Alfred Barnard when he visited in 1886. "This portion of the island was bare and uninhabited," wrote whisky's first chronicler, "but the prosecution of the distilling industry has transformed it into a life-like and civilized colony," which was probably meant to be less patronizing than it now reads.

Bunnahabhain was built to provide spirit for blends. Six years after its founding, it merged with The Glenrothes to form Highland Distilleries, which undoubtedly saved this high-capacity site on a remote island when the downturns of the early 1900s and the 1930s came along.

Though launched as a single malt in the late 1980s, Bunna' has never received the backing it needed (and deserved). Its huge stills produced a clean, slightly ginger-accented new make, which was ignored by the peat freaks who flooded into Islay from the 1990s.

That situation is being addressed by new owner Burn Stewart, which took over in 2003. Heavily peated malt is now being used every year, a style that its previous owner denied was ever produced. "Rubbish!" says Burn Stewart's master blender Ian MacMillan. "Bunnahabhain was peaty until the early 1960s and only changed because they didn't need smoky [whisky] for their blends. I want to recreate what it would have been like in the 1880s and

Looking across to the cloud-shrouded Paps of Jura, it is not hard to believe that Bunnahabhain is Islay's most remote distillery.

show that it could be what people think of as an 'Islay' whisky." Islay permeates the gentle unpeated style as well.

"There's a difference in maturation cycles on the island," says MacMillan. "There will be a coastal influence. The Bunna' matured in Bishopbriggs is a different beast to the same whisky matured on Islay."

BUNNAHABHAIN TASTING NOTES

NEW MAKE
Nose: Sweet and full with slight oiliness and a little yeasty note and a hint of sulfur. In time an aroma akin to tomato sauce and when diluted, lots of malt.
Palate: Violet-like rootiness and sweet mid-palate weight before drying considerably.
Finish: Gingery spice.

12YO 46.3%
Nose: Lots of sherry, reminiscent of Brandy de Jerez. Black fruit and a lick of varnish and a glimmer of smoke. Fruitcake batter and nuts.
Palate: Rich and sweet, with crystallized ginger chocolate and coffee. Aromatic with liqueur chocolate.
Finish: Quite spicy.
Conclusion: Has a density that belies its age.

> **Flavor Camp: Rich & Round**
> **Where Next?** Macallan Amber

18YO 46.3%
Nose: Controlled; sherried depth. Marzipan, frosting, ginger root, and dried currants. Slightly earthy.
Palate: Molasse toffee; mossy, with polished wood and cold Assam tea. Oxidized notes prominent. Light grip.
Finish: Long, slightly cookie-like.
Conclusion: Bigger and sweeter than the 12yo.

> **Flavor Camp: Rich & Round**
> **Where Next?** Yamazaki 18yo

25YO 46.3%
Nose: Very sweet; toffee and sherry. Currants and dark fruit. Complex and voluptuous with real depth.
Palate: Layered sweetness, then raisined richness. Long.
Finish: Balanced and long.
Conclusion: Has more weight and body than in the past.

> **Flavor Camp: Rich & Round**
> **Where Next?** Mortlach 25yo

TOITEACH 46%
Nose: Off-dry with smoke quite restrained. A firm, toasty, vanilla note like young Sémillon with heathery smoke in the background.
Palate: Well-balanced with the sweet central core emerging fully before the smoke begins to come through. Soft fruit, light cereal notes.
Finish: Oatcake.
Conclusion: Part of an ongoing investigation into peating Bunnahabhain, the maturing stock is now beginning to add sweetness to balance.

> **Flavor Camp: Smoky & Peaty**
> **Where Next?** Caol Ila 12yo

Caol Ila

PORT ASKAIG • WWW.DISCOVERING-DISTILLERIES.COM/CAOLILA • OPEN ALL YEAR; SEE WEBSITE FOR DAYS & DETAILS

Although it sits little more than a stone's throw from Port Askaig, one of Islay's two ferry terminals, until you set sail you wouldn't know Caol Ila existed. It was built in 1846 by Hector Henderson, who, smarting after two other distilling projects had foundered, saw whisky-making possibilities in a cliff-backed bay next to one of the fastest tidal races in Scotland.

Islay was, as now, popular as a single malt and would grow in importance as the century progressed and blenders realized that a little touch of smoke in their blend added complexity and a touch of mysteriousness. Blends are Caol Ila's lifeblood. It's the largest distillery in terms of capacity on the island but in many ways the least known, the quiet man of an island on which some robust personalities vie constantly with one another for attention. Its manager, Billy Stitchell, is a perfect personification of this quiet calm.

Its importance in blending resulted in the old distillery being demolished in 1974 and today's new, larger, plant being constructed. Here, the Scottish Malt Distillers (SMD) stillhouse design, with its car dealership window, works to its greatest effect. Caol Ila has the finest panorama of any stillhouse in Scotland, looking across the Sound of Islay to the Paps of Jura, the view framed by its huge stills.

Caol Ila's malt sneaks up on you. There's smoke, but it is understated. The creosote and seaweed of the Kildalton Coast has been replaced by smoky bacon, seashells, and a grassy lift. It's less "peaty," yet the malted barley is exactly the same as that which goes to Lagavulin. Everything in Caol Ila is run differently: mashing regime, fermentation, and most importantly the size of those stills and the cut points. Knowing the phenolic parts per million (ppm) of malt

The huge Caol Ila is somehow wedged into a tiny coastal gorge.

(i.e. peatiness) might win a Trivial Pursuit quiz but it means nothing, since peatiness is lost during the whisky-making process.

You may even find Caol Ila with zero ppm because, since the 1980s, it has run for part of the year unpeated, and with a different distillation regime. Occasional releases show a malt with a fresh green melon character. The quiet ones always surprise.

CAOL ILA TASTING NOTES

NEW MAKE

Nose: Fragrant and smoky. Juniper and wet grass. Cod liver oil and wet kilt. Lightly malty with a seashore freshness.
Palate: Dry smoke then an explosion of oil and pine. Hot.
Finish: Grassy and smoky.

8YO, REFILL WOOD CASK SAMPLE

Nose: That grassiness continues. The oiliness is now bacon fat, the juniper continues. Fat and smoky: a mix of sweet, oily, and dry.
Palate: Oily and chewy. Saltier than the new make. Pear and ozone. Salty skin and fresh fruits.
Finish: Intense smoke.
Conclusion: All the components are there with smoke to the fore.

12YO 43%

Nose: Balanced mix of ozone freshness, smoked ham, and a little touch of seaweed. Very clean and lightly smoky with some sweetness behind. Angelica and seashore-fresh.
Palate: Oily and tongue-coating. Pears and juniper. Dries toward the finish though the smoke is a constant thread adding fragrance and a drying, balancing element.
Finish: Gently smoked.
Conclusion: Again it's all about balance here.

Flavor Camp: Smoky & Peaty
Where Next? Glan ar Mor, Kornog (France), Highland Park 12yo, Springbank 10yo

18YO 43%

Nose: Intense. Briny/seashore, smoked fish, bluebell, smoked ham. Sweet woods.
Palate: Soft and quite rich and less oily as well. The smoke has receded a little as the wood has combined with the fruits.
Finish: Lightly smoky and herbal.
Conclusion: A more active cask has calmed the peatiness down.

Flavor Camp: Smoky & Peaty
Where Next? Laphroaig 18yo

CENTER & WEST

A trio of distilleries are found in this final Islay cluster. Two sit on the shores of Loch Indaal, while the third is Scotland's most westerly, and one of its newest sites. Welcome to the Rhinns, with its round church, some of Scotland's most ancient rocks, restless innovation, and the place where Scotland's first distillers may have settled.

A picture of tranquillity; sunset on Loch Indaal. Now turn the page...

Bowmore

BOWMORE • WWW.BOWMORE.COM • OPEN ALL YEAR; SEE WEBSITE FOR DAYS & DETAILS

Bowmore's distillery walls form part of the sea defenses for this neat white-painted village on the shores of Loch Indaal, which itself only dates back to 1768, a time when the agricultural improvements that would significantly change the Scottish landscape were building in momentum. In 1726, "Great" Daniel Campbell of Shawfield used the £9,000 ($13,320) he received in compensation for his house being burned down during the Malt Tax riots in Glasgow to purchase Islay. His improvements were carried on by his grandson, Daniel the Younger, who built Bowmore. The island was being run like a business. There was flax for weaving into linen, a fishing fleet, and the introduction of two-row barley on newly enlarged farms, which, with its better yields and easier malt-ability, gave a chance to distill on a more commercial scale.

It means that, instead of being an isolated plant built because of access to the sea (or because its obscure location was perfect for moonshining) Bowmore's distillery sits in the heart of this small community. The waste heat warms the swimming pool (a former warehouse), the smoke from its kilns scents the air. It is rooted in its location.

The smoke issuing from the pagoda roof is evidence that Bowmore, like Laphroaig, has retained its own malting floors. "We're meeting 40 percent of our own needs," says Iain McCallum, master of malts at owner Morrison Bowmore Distillers (MBD). "As an industry, we always talk of heritage and tradition, but we actually do things traditionally; it's why people come to see us." There's a pragmatic reason as well, since floor maltings can allow the distillery to run if the barley supplies are held up from the mainland because of weather.

Bowmore's peaty note is different again. Though not the most heavily peated of the island's malts, it is the most overtly smoky, with the clearest peat reek. Just as sulfury new make sites on the mainland are hiding something, peaty new makes conceal background characters that only reveal themselves in maturation.

In Bowmore's case it is tropical fruit, which is there in the new make, but it can be obscured by peat when young, sat on by first-fill sherry casks. In refill casks, however, and with age, it suddenly and startlingly blossom, giving an exotic Caribbean edge to a whisky from a small, chilly Hebridean island. It's a character that Bowmore-lovers have always revered.

"Some of the 1970s coming through now are as good as the legendary 1960s," says McCallum. "We have fantastic whiskies; we've just not been good at telling people what we are good at. As a firm, we were blend, we were bulk, but now we're single malt, which allows us to focus on the portfolio, slim it down,

Storms on Loch Indaal frequently batter the Bowmore warehouses, which help to act as the town's flood defences.

Bowmore still malts a significant percentage of its own barley. Any that isn't dried over peat, however, will start to sprout!

and release some spectaculars." It takes time to change a whisky firm's fortunes but there is plenty of evidence that MBD's improved wood policy is now bearing fruit (if you pardon the pun) with casks from its Loch Indaal-backed warehouses.

"Effectively, all our single malt is matured at Bowmore," says McCallum. "We're right next to the water and the microclimate will be different. There's always a saltiness to Bowmore. Now, I'm a chemist and I know there's not actually salt in there, but I can discern that character in the whisky. Maybe there's some magic in those damp, low-roofed vaults."

BOWMORE TASTING NOTES

NEW MAKE

Nose: Hugely sweet, with fragrant peat smoke, broom/pea pod; a touch of wet grass, barley, vanilla. With water, dubbin and concentrated jellied fruit.
Palate: Dense, damp peat smoke blanketing the tongue. A nutty undertow. Sweetness with water. Hazelnut.
Finish: Fragrant smoke.

DEVIL'S CASK 10YO 56.9%

Nose: Bold. Prune, dried fig, salt toffee, shoe leather, rose petal, savory maritime edges. Smoke.
Palate: Retained sweetness, mixing black cherry, pipe tobacco, and cloves.
Finish: Smoky and deep.
Conclusion: Matured in first-fill sherry cask. Bowmore at its biggest.

> **Flavor Camp: Smoky & Peaty**
> **Where Next?** Paul John Peated Cask

12YO 40%

Nose: Rich gold. Toasty oak, some date. Thicker, with charred wood melding with peat reek. Touches of mango chews. Ripe and fleshy. Orange zest.
Palate: Deeper, with more fruitiness. Sweet herbs, toffee, lightly salty. The smoke shifts toward the back.
Finish: A build of smoke along with light chocolate malt.
Conclusion: Balanced and showing a steady integration.

> **Flavor Camp: Smoky & Peaty**
> **Where Next?** Caol Ila 12yo

15YO DARKEST 43%

Nose: Amber. Deep with significant sherry notes, moving into chocolate-covered cherry, molasses, orange zest, beach bonfire.
Palate: Concentrated, with a lavender hint. PX-like sherry, bitter/salted chocolate and coffee. The oiliness of the new make now returns thanks to the sherry casks.

Finish: Thick and long. Now the smoke is released, but the tropical fruit has gone.
Conclusion: Rich and powerful with balanced smoke.

> **Flavor Camp: Smoky & Peaty**
> **Where Next?** Laphroaig 18yo

46YO, DISTILLED 1964 42.9%

Nose: Hallucinatory intensity of tropical fruit: guava, mango, pineapple, grapefruit. Light touch of peat smoke.
Palate: Concentrated, even at low strength. Silky, heady, and haunting. This lasts forever in the dry glass.
Finish: Eleganty drying.
Conclusion: Classic old Bowmore.

> **Flavor Camp: Fruity & Spicy**
> **Where Next?** Tomintoul 33yo

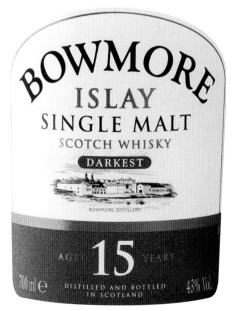

Bruichladdich & Kilchoman

BRUICHLADDICH • WWW. BRUICHLADDICH.COM • OPEN ALL YEAR; SEE WEBSITE FOR DAYS & DETAILS
KILCHOMAN • BRUICHLADDICH • WWW.KILCHOMANDISTILLERY.COM • OPEN ALL YEAR NOV–MAR, MON–FRI; APR–OCT, MON–SAT

We've come a long way since May 29, 2001, when the cast-iron gates of Bruichladdich distillery swung open once more after seven years of silence. Walking around the distillery 13 years later, you'd think initially that little has changed. The mill is the same Heath-Robinsonian model that was installed in 1881, the mash tun is still open, the washbacks are Douglas Fir, the stillhouse is wooden-floored, but then you notice a few details, such as the great lump of a Lomond still in the corner inside, from which the distillery's Botanist Gin is made.

You might also notice some French accents. In 2012, the Rémy Cointreau group splashed out £58m ($97.8m) for the distillery. If ever there were a sign of how high whisky's reputation had risen in just over a decade, this was it. Bruichladdich had been bought for £6m ($10m) just 11 years previously.

Rémy's vote of confidence not only meant better distribution arrangements, but a new focus. Bruichladdich is now financially secure, and money is available to invest. For years the team, especially the miraculous engineer Duncan MacGillivray, had somehow kept the place running. Now is the chance to make the Laddie vision a reality.

This is a place built on dreams that always seemed bigger than its size. The decision to bottle on site meant higher costs, but it also created jobs. Nine local farmers are planting barley for whisky (25 percent of the Laddie's requirements): something that hadn't happened since the tail-end of the nineteenth century. It's more expensive, but all part of a long-term, deep exploration of Islay's unknown, untapped *terroir*.

The base whisky remains honeyed, sweet, lemon-barley-sugar-like, while peated variants Port Charlotte and Octomore have shaken off their youthful punchiness and are maturing into thoughtful, if somewhat boisterous, teenagers.

The mass of expressions has been reduced. The wood is better (so less need to re-rack), and there is now a need to build an identifiable brand in volume. It doesn't mean, however, that the questing mind of Jim McEwan, brought back from the brink of retirement by the new owner, isn't coming up with exciting creations.

Like many "new" distilleries, Bruichladdich has looked at the big questions: "Who am I? What can I do?" Its response is "I am many things. I can do anything, and everything reflects Islay."

Something strange happened to me in autumn 2013. I had a sample of a new Kilchoman bottling, from 2007. After inhaling—and without thinking—I wrote: "Classic Kilchoman character." Even though there is a difference between age and maturity, it is fair to say that it can take a decade or more in decent casks for a distillery to settle fully into its mature guise. Kilchoman has reached that important marker quicker than most people would have imagined.

This, currently Islay's newest and smallest distillery (another is planned for Gartbreck, on the shores of Loch Indaal), has always been precocious, however. Its aim was to take whisky back to its farmstead roots.

Located away from the coast in the rich farmland parish of Kilchoman parish, where the Beatons settled in the fourteenth century, it overlooks the blue waters of Loch Gorm. In late summer, on either side of its long drive, barley rustles in the fields, which will then be taken, malted, distilled, and aged on site. This is a modern take on old-style farm distilling, with echoes of how Ileachs used to make only what their fields give them.

The distillery is now managed by John MacLellan, formerly of Bunnahabhain: another member of a generation of locals seemingly born with a valinch in their hand. He oversees the creation of a new make, which is smoky and shore-like, with hints of clove and soft fruit, but while it has been top-notch from the start, like any spirit it needs to be balanced and enhanced by wood.

The open-topped mash tun at Bruichladdich is one of the few still operational in the industry.

It's the quality of the casks that have already given mature spirit, which isn't just spirit plus oak but an integrated whole. Seashore notes move to brine and samphire; the fruits soften and ripen; herbs develop, and there's enough back-palate tightness to show there's plenty more to give.

The range is anchored by Machir Bay, a vatting of ex-bourbon casks, a percentage of which are finished briefly in oloroso casks. There are vintage bottlings and a yearly 100 percent Islay release. All are released in limited quantities since this is a distillery where the bulk of

Ribboned out along the shore next to the beach, Bruichladdich's buildings are now home to a huge number of whisky-making experiments.

stock is being laid down; proof lies in the building of a new warehouse at Conisby. That said, there are still some suitably eccentric touches that show the hands-on farm thinking hasn't wholly evaporated. On one visit I saw bottles for a single-cask bottling being filled from an old teapot. That, somehow, is 100 percent Islay as well.

BRUICHLADDICH TASTING NOTES

ISLAY BARLEY, 5YO 50%
Nose: Fresh. Agave syrup, lightly buttery, with touches of lily of the valley and lemon spongecake.
Palate: The cereal character is restrained, with a charred hint on the palate, along with banana, mandarin, cassia, and pink marshmallows.
Finish: Floral notes emerge late, with some white pepper.
Conclusion: Using barley grown on Rockside Farm.

Flavor Camp: **Fragrant & Floral**
Where Next? Tullibardine Sovereign

THE LADDIE, 10YO 46%
Nose: Very gentle and sweet, with characteristic distillery freshness. Floral, light vanilla, lemon peel, melon, and honey.
Palate: Creamy, with a drift of barley, this remains fresh but with a tongue-clinging quality. Soft fruit.
Finish: Sweet and gentle.
Conclusion: A landmark bottling for the new team.

Flavor Camp: **Fragrant & Floral**
Where Next? Balblair 2000

BLACK ART 4, 23YO 49.2%
Nose: Mature notes of beeswax-burnished church pews, a sprinkling of rosewater, dried mango, rosehip syrup, and potpourri.
Palate: Parma violets underpinned with light lavender, where fleshiness mingles with the exotic notes of manuka honey, dried lemon, pomegranate.
Finish: Apricot pits, dried lemon.
Conclusion: A mix of casks, finishes, and who knows what?

Flavor Camp: **Rich & Round**
Where Next? Hibiki 30yo, Mackmyra Midvinter

PORT CHARLOTTE SCOTTISH BARLEY 50%
Nose: Beach bonfire, hot sand, faint hint of balloons, olive oil, preserved lemon, and eucalyptus.
Palate: Thick, sweet with strawberry candies, which push back against the peat.
Finish: Campfire smoke.
Conclusion: Young but with substance.

Flavor Camp: **Smoky & Peaty**
Where Next? Caol Ila 12yo, Mackmyra Svensk Rök

PORT CHARLOTTE PC8 60.5%
Nose: Gold. A roasted peatiness. Wood smoke, burning leaves with dry grass. Scented. Young.
Palate: Intense, heathery character. A fog of smoke over the palate.
Finish: Hot embers.
Conclusion: Clean and developing interestingly.

Flavor Camp: **Smoky & Peaty**
Where Next? Longrow CV, Connemara 12yo

OCTOMORE, COMUS 4.2, 2007, 5YO 61%
Nose: Like standing beside a kiln. The distillery's sweetness has been retained, here in the guise of pineapple and banana.
Palate: Eucalyptus lozenges, with light maltiness before that Laddie thickness makes things even sweeter.
Finish: Long and smoky.
Conclusion: Powerful, yet balanced.

Flavor Camp: **Smoky & Peaty**
Where Next? Ardbeg Corryvreckan

KILCHOMAN TASTING NOTES

MACHIR BAY 46%
Nose: Smoke, samphire, and fleshy fruits; scallops and white peaches. Water shows sea-washed rock, light flowers, and hot sand.
Palate: Sweet, sour, and smoky with a chalky edge and a peppery palate. Water releases blossom and a little gunsmoke.
Finish: Lightly smoked. Sweet.
Conclusion: Fresh and smoky.

Flavor Camp: **Smoky & Peaty**
Where Next? Chichibu Peated

KILCHOMAN 2007 46%
Nose: A sparkling mix of seashell and fresh seaweed mixed with churned butter, driftwood, and fresh kilned peat.
Palate: Samphire, peat, sweet barley, and an herbal kick.
Finish: Lightly smoky. Light clove.
Conclusion: Full integration between oak and that distillery character.

Flavor Camp: **Smoky & Peaty**
Where Next? Talisker 10yo

ISLANDS

We are entranced by islands. The notion of somehow being cut off excites us, while getting there involves not just a physical transportation but a psychological one as well. We leave the familiar for "that land over there," and making that journey off Scotland's coasts involves traveling on some of the best sailing grounds in the world: a world of bright-jade seas, pink granites, ancient, gritty zebra-striped gneiss, and lava flows; a place of raised beaches, winds, and sheltered bays; a thrilling living landscape, home to orca, minke, dolphin, gannet, and sea eagle.

Its aromas are those of wet rope and salt spray, of heather and bog myrtle, of guano, seaweed, and sump oil, of drying crab shells, bracken, and fish boxes. Its secrets also lie below the ground, in the rock and what lies upon that rock: heather, or the windblown sand which has rooted the fertile *machair* (beach grass), and how both have been compressed into fragrant peat. And in Orkney's case, peat that's different from that of Islay.

Whisky would have been made on every one of these islands at some stage and in some form, whether that be farmers making it for their community or in a commercial fashion. Tiree, the westernmost Inner Hebridean island, had two licensed distilleries and was a whisky exporter in the eighteenth century. Mull and Arran, too, were noted whisky islands, and the Outer Hebrides was also whisky territory.

Now? Distilleries are scattered around the Hebrides, the exception rather than the rule. Yet the spaces are as interesting as those that have survived. The Clearances put paid to most farm distilling (157 moonshiners were arrested on Tiree alone and many were then evicted) as well as creating the larger sites, such as Talisker and Tobermory. Others tried and failed, many more simply didn't continue, the changed market demands of the nineteenth century made this an expensive place to distill on a commercial scale. It still is.

In our state of entrancement we overlook the realities of living on an island: communication, raw materials, higher fixed costs, the lack of things we take for granted on the mainland. "If I want to buy a new pair of trousers I have to drive to Inverness," said a former manager of Talisker to me once. Newcomers, who come here with their get-rich-quick schemes soon realize that getting rich isn't going to happen. Neither is quick. Island life works to a longer time frame—but time suits whisky. Island life may be wonderful, but it is hard.

Is there any surprise that the whiskies made out here on the fringed western coast, though generous in their nature, have something of this uncompromising landscape about them? You have to meet them on their terms. That is why they have been so successful. Island whiskies, with their scents that seem to drift in from the landscape, by and large haven't been steered by the requirements of the market; they are as they are. Take them or leave them.

Rugged and individualistic, the landscape of the Scottish islands is reflected in the uncompromising nature of its whiskies.

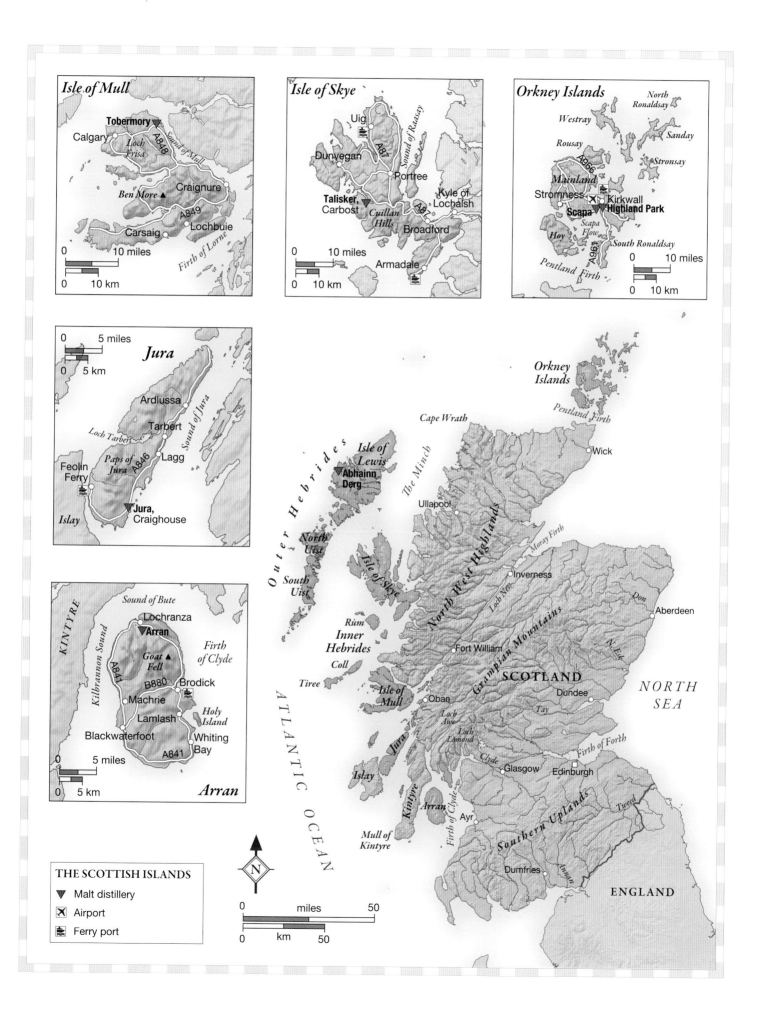

Isle of Mull

Calgary
Tobermory ▼
Loch Frisa
Sound of Mull
A848
Craignure
Ben More ▲
A849
Carsaig
Lochbuie
Firth of Lorne

0   10 miles
0   10 km

Isle of Skye

Uig
Dunvegan
A87
Portree
Sound of Raasay
Kyle of Lochalsh
Talisker,
Carbost
Cuillan Hills
A87
Broadford
Armadale

0   10 miles
0   10 km

Orkney Islands

North Ronaldsay
Westray
Rousay
Sanday
Stronsay
A966
Mainland
Stromness
Kirkwall
Highland Park ▼
Scapa ▼
Scapa Flow
Hoy
A961
South Ronaldsay
Pentland Firth

0   10 miles
0   10 km

Jura

0   5 miles
0   5 km

Ardlussa
Tarbert
Loch Tarbert
Sound of Jura
Paps of Jura
A846
Lagg
Feolin Ferry
Jura,
Craighouse
Islay

Arran

Sound of Bute
Lochranza
Arran ▼
KINTYRE
Kilbrannon Sound
Goat Fell ▲
A841
B880
Brodick
Firth of Clyde
Machrie
Lamlash
Holy Island
Blackwaterfoot
A841
Whiting Bay

0   5 miles
0   5 km

THE SCOTTISH ISLANDS

▼ Malt distillery
✕ Airport
⚓ Ferry port

N

0   miles   50
0   km   50

Orkney Islands
Pentland Firth
Cape Wrath
Wick
Outer Hebrides
Isle of Lewis
Abhainn Dearg ▼
The Minch
Ullapool
North Uist
North West Highlands
Moray Firth
Isle of Skye
Inverness
Loch Ness
Don
South Uist
Rum
Inner Hebrides
Fort William
Grampian Mountains
Aberdeen
Coll
N. Esk
Tiree
Isle of Mull
Oban
SCOTLAND
Dundee
NORTH SEA
Loch Awe
Tay
Jura
Loch Lomond
Firth of Forth
ATLANTIC OCEAN
Islay
Clyde
Glasgow
Edinburgh
KINTYRE
Arran
Firth of Clyde
Ayr
Southern Uplands
Tweed
Mull of Kintyre
Dumfries
Annan
ENGLAND

Loch Scavaig and the back door to the Cuillins. Behind these mighty peaks is Talisker.

Arran

LOCHRANZA • WWW.ARRANWHISKY.COM • OPEN ALL YEAR • DAYS VARY IN WINTER; MID-MAR–OCT, MON–SUN

Arran is hard enough to define as an island never mind a whisky. Split by the Highland Boundary Fault, it's a geologist's paradise: granite intrusions, Dalradian metamorphic rocks, sedimentary layers, glaciated valleys, raised beaches. Its northerly half is craggy and mountainous, the south is all undulating pasture. Highland or Lowland? Maybe simply Scotland distilled. In whisky terms, it's more complex. The distillery is sitated in Lochranza in the north, therefore legally it's Highland, but it's on an island so, surely it's an island dram? Maybe definitions mean nothing. It is the small-scale specificity of the site that matters. And it's the attitude of the people at the distillery that helps create its individuality.

Arran has always been both bewildering and revelatory. It was at Lochranza that the father of geology, James Hutton, discovered one of his "unconformities," where younger rocks sit horizontally on top of deeply eroded older ones that have been raised to the vertical, revealing the immense time over which geological processes take place.

The distillery was built in 1995—a very belated return to whisky-making for an island once famed for its moonshining. That just leads to another question. Why, after almost 160 years, was Arran's new distillery built in the north rather than in the south where, history shows, most distilling activity took place?

"They looked at a dozen sites," the original manager (and distilling legend) Gordon Mitchell says. They settled for Lochranza because of the water. "Loch na Davie gives us volume, a good pH to help with fermentation—and there's nae dead sheep in it either!"

Like most new-build distilleries, it is a one-room layout, which also features, somewhat incongruously, though appealingly, a large pot plant. Originally grist was brought in, but now a mill has been installed. "I want control over the whole process," says current manager James MacTaggart, a native Ileach with over three decades of whisky-making experience at Bowmore under his belt. Not surprisingly, there's some peaty make being produced every year.

Arran throws up an intense spray of citrus fruit from day one: a lifted element to the crisp, cereal bedrock. "It's hard to say exactly where it comes from," says MacTaggart, "but I run these wee stills very slow and give it lots of time for reflux. I guess that's where the citrus comes from."

The light character was a commercial decision. Arran was built just before the boom in young, peaty whiskies and there was a commercial necessity to make a relatively quick-maturing spirit. It's sometimes been described as "easy," but that is rather disparaging. Arran, now at its nineteenth birthday, is still growing. It's shown in recent years that it can deal with the attentions of sherry as part of the wood mix and, for this writer at least, the scaling back of the number of finishes has been a positive move, allowing the true Arran character to reveal itself. Arran has done that most difficult thing. It has survived.

Nonconformity might just be a neat enough descriptor for this distillery. Neither classic Highland, Lowland, or, indeed, what one would assume Island should be. But this is only right and proper because, as we have seen, Arran itself hardly conforms to any neat definition. Arran (the island and the whisky) is Arran.

ARRAN TASTING NOTES

NEW MAKE

Nose: Lifted and very citric: fresh orange juice, unripe pineapple undercut with a bran/oaty note. Green.
Palate: Tingling effect. Clean and masses of citrus fruit. Very focused and sweet. Cereal.
Finish: Clean and intense.

ROBERT BURNS 43%

Nose: Lifted and aromatic, quite estery with quetsche and mirabelle note. Arran's citric signature here shows itself as pomelo. Becomes perfumed with water.
Palate: In similar vein to the nose. A lift into fruit blossom and cut flowers. Effervescent, with a light chalkiness.
Finish: Lively and citric.
Conclusion: Young but already well balanced.

> Flavor Camp: **Fragrant & Floral**
> Where Next? The Glenlivet 12yo

10YO 40%

Nose: Shows a bit more cereal-led character, with tangerine, a little banana. Cream (with water) adds smoothness.
Palate: Restrained and a classic Arran mix of cereal and fruitiness. Water softens it.
Finish: Spicy: ginger and galangal.
Conclusion: Young but already self-assured.

> Flavor Camp: **Fruity & Spicy**
> Where Next? Clynelish 14yo

12YO, CASK STRENGTH 52.8%

Nose: Balanced, sweet. The Robert Burns chalky note is here with lemon pith and freshly sawn light oak.
Palate: Sweet and concentrated. Relaxed, yet with a balance of floral notes, citrus fruit, and a mature hazelnut element.
Finish: Lemon barley sugar.
Conclusion: Sufficient character depth to mask the alcohol.

> Flavor Camp: **Fruity & Spicy**
> Where Next? Strathisla 12yo

14YO 46%

Nose: Gentle, warm, and toasty oak. Light and green with a little fennel, lemongrass, and a sweetness.
Palate: Lightly sweet and maturing well with more of the balanced oak tones. Custard creams and yuzu.
Finish: Still slightly tense.
Conclusion: The tightness of the finish shows that there's still plenty more of the distillate to come.

> Flavor Camp: **Fragrant & Floral**
> Where Next? Yamazaki 12yo

Jura

CRAIGHOUSE • WWW.ISLEOFJURA.COM • OPEN MAY–SEPT, MON–SAT; ESSENTIAL TO CALL BEFORE

That there is a distillery on Jura is no mean achievement. This is hardly one of the most populous islands of the Hebrides and transport (everything must go via Islay) is hardly conducive to keeping control of fixed costs. When the distillery in Craighouse (called variously Caol nan Eilean, Craighouse, Small Isles, Lagg, and Jura) closed in 1910, it seemed likely that the locals would have to import their drams from neighboring Islay.

In 1962, however, two landowners, Robin Fletcher (George Orwell's landlord during his time on the island) and Tony Riley-Smith (uncle of the publisher of *Whisky Magazine*), worried at the decline in population, hired William Delmé-Evans to build a new plant.

There's one thing which Jura has plenty of and that's peat, but until recently there was none used in its whisky production. Whereas records show that Small Isles made heavily peated whisky, Fletcher and Riley-Smith's main client was Scottish & Newcastle who wanted light and unpeated for their blends. So, like most of the distilleries from the 1960s, that was the style it made, with huge stills installed to assist the process.

It's what lies above the island's peat that gives Jura one of its defining aromatic characteristics: fern, green in its humid summer woods, drying over time into bracken, all backed with a cereal rigidity. Jura is a tough one. "It has to settle before you put it into sherry," says Richard Paterson, master blender at owners Whyte & Mackay. "It's almost saying I'm happy in a suit, not a mink coat. Put me in sherry too early and I'll head off in another direction."

This slow process of coaxing takes the best part of 16 years to start and hits its peak at 21 (or older). The old "no peat" rule has gone, with heavily peated single cask bottlings showing a fog of

Jura, the singular island. One road, one village, one whisky.

pine alongside that bracken, while the turfy Superstition offers a different—and in some ways more complex—character. Embracing its environment rather than working against it may be the best for Jura in the long run.

JURA TASTING NOTES

NEW MAKE
Nose: Dusty, dry, green bracken. Light grassy note.
Palate: Intense and light with a touch of perfume in the mid-palate, then flour. Very tight.
Finish: Sweet as this is, it's a hard nut to crack.

9YO CASK SAMPLE
Nose: Gold. The flour/dust has now taken shape as green malt with a back note of hazelnut. Citrus fruit now coming through (lemon) and that green fern character remains along with a little nougat. Still crisp.
Palate: Very dry and firm. Flaked almond, unripe fruit, malt.
Finish: Begins to open at the very end, offering a nodule of sweetness.
Conclusion: Simple and a clear extension of the new make character. Still that firm undertow.

16YO 40%
Nose: Amber. Rich, extractive wood notes: vanilla, sweet dried fruit, prune, chestnut, and bramble jelly. Slight lactic touch. A dry character behind.
Palate: More rounded and soft compared with the 9yo. Silky feel and gentle. Ripe fruit cut with dry grasses (the evolution of that green bracken).
Finish: Mix of sweet sherry and firm spirit.
Conclusion: The active cask mix has helped to coax the underlying sweetness out.

Flavor Camp: Rich & Round
Where Next? The Balvenie 17yo Madeira Cask, The Singleton of Dufftown 12yo

21YO CASK SAMPLE
Nose: Mahogany. Mature: allspice, ginger, raisin, dried peels. Then comes molasses, a tweedy note (maybe the dryness finally disappearing). The beginnings of concentration.
Palate: Huge sherried influence: Palo Cortado. Sweet/savory character. Fruitcake and walnut. Mellow and long.
Finish: Ripe sweet fruits.
Conclusion: The intriguing spiciness is late to emerge in Jura's evolution.

Tobermory

TOBERMORY • WWW.TOBERMORYMALT.COM • OPEN ALL YEAR MON–FRI

Anyone who has sailed on Scotland's west coast appreciates that you have to balance being on one of the most spectacular cruising grounds in the world with having lots of challenging weather being flung at you. Tobermory, the capital of the Isle of Mull, is one of the main havens for spume-lashed yachties, weary after another day battling with the elements. As you stagger up from the anchorage heading for the Mishnish Hotel, the first building that greets you seems in a similar state to yourself: wave-blown and blasted. Tobermory distilllery, it must be said, is hardly one of Scotland's most beautiful.

Its story in some ways parallels the islands themselves. Starting life in the late eighteenth century as a brewery, it passed through a succession of owners who treated it like many absentee landlords treat their Hebridean tenants, while the wood policy prior to 1993 came straight from the, "If it's from a tree, we'll use it," era. Now in the care of Burn Stewart, it is another plant being brought back around by general distilleries manager Ian MacMillan. (*see* p.104, Deanston).

He has succeeded and, though the oily, vegetable-like new make is somewhat odd, there's an interesting mossy character that develops along with a red fruitiness. There is certainly something odd about the stills, which have an S-shaped bend at the top of the lyne arm. "The kink is the key here," he says. "It gives lots of reflux, which helps with that underlying lightness."

This lightness of character also lurks underneath the heavily peated version from this distillery, Ledaig (pronounced Lea-Chick), whose new make is full of mustard, limpets, and smoke, like a puffer's funnel. The release of 30yo+ versions of both, however, shows how refined this pair can become.

The gable end of the Tobermory distillery is a welcome sight for many a weary mariner.

In other words, both drams are highly individual and, like Jura, need time. "They do take a while to get going, but that's just the style," says MacMillan. "Who said whisky should just take five minutes?"

TOBERMORY TASTING NOTES

NEW MAKE

Nose: Oily, vegetable and, weirdly, licorice. When this clears, there's moss and brass, artichoke and bran.
Palate: Oily. Fat and solid to start, but bone-dry on the finish.
Finish: Hard and short.

9YO CASK SAMPLE

Nose: Very fruity (citrus-fruit chews and lime cordial), strawberry chews. Then wet cookies, fenugreek, oily, then a sherried note.
Palate: Linseed oil. Rather than the fruit, now a whole-wheat character emerges becoming sweeter as it moves. With water, there's some balsawood.
Finish: Crisp.
Conclusion: The sweet and dry characters seen on the new make are still tussling.

15YO 46.3%

Nose: Deep amber. Big sherried impact: white raisin on top of the green notes seen in the new make. Some minty chocolate and a mature jamminess developing.
Palate: Spicy, with some cherry (as well as sherry) showing, the red fruit developing in an interesting manner. Hazelnut.
Finish: Dry with a lick of molasses.
Conclusion: The cask has rounded things out but the feeling remains that this has a way to go.

Flavor Camp: **Rich & Round**
Where Next? Jura 16yo

32YO 49.5%

Nose: Deep amber. Mature, elderberry, raisin, slightly smoky, autumn woods, leaf mold, that moss once more.
Palate: Firm grip with assertive heavy sherry notes. Cedar and a gentle soft creaminess.
Finish: Lingering.
Conclusion: Finally it emerges.

Flavor camp: **Rich & Round**
Where Next? Tamdhu 18yo, Springbank 18yo

Abhainn Dearg

ABHAINN DEARG • CARNISH, ISLE OF LEWIS • WWW.ABHAINNDEARG.CO.UK • OPEN ALL YEAR MON–FRI

Anyone who has traveled to the Western Isles will know that there is a culture of enthusiastic consumption of Scotland's spirit going back many centuries, Surprising, then, that this long chain of outliers didn't produce their own spirit (legally at least) between 1840 and 2008. The last distillery to operate was the surreally named Shoeburn, which, records suggest, supplied considerable quantities to Lewis's capital Stornoway, but not much made it off the island. As I said…

In 2008 Marko Tayburn decided to do something about this. Building a distillery is a demanding exercise needing patience, vision, deep pockets, and, as Marko points out "…plenty of time sitting on your arse filling in forms."

Building one on the mainland is tricky. Building one on the northwestern coast of Britain's most westerly islands, bar St. Kilda, is a different prospect indeed. But he did it. He found an old fish farm on the Red River (*Abhainn Dearg*), designed the stills himself, used local barley, and got to work. The aim is self-sufficiency, which, after all, is the reality of life on the islands. If you find that something needs doing, you just do it.

"We always knew what we wanted," he says of his bold, peaty spirit. "It is different and it is identifiable, which is what you want. We make our whisky the only way we know how. It's the sum of all its parts. But," he pauses, "the thing is, it's also a slice of the Outer Hebrides: the machair, the peat, the sand, the water, the mountains.

"The big plants are fine," he adds, "but I like the small-scale distilleries that reflect different places and people." Any conversation with Marko will end up involving the landscape, the people, his palpable pride in being Hebridean. Abhainn Dearg, then, is more than just a product. Rather, it is an expression of a specific mindset.

Remote it might seem, but he has been taken aback by the number of people coming to Lewis expressly to see the distillery. The most remote distillery in Britain is not just true to itself, but linked to the wider whisky world.

Distilleries, it would seem, are now like London buses: you wait for hours and then three come along at once. At the time of writing, there are now advanced plans for long-promised distilleries on the islands of Harris and Barra. Is a new Hebridean whisky culture being born?

Abhainn Dearg has started a renaissance in distilling in the Outer Hebrides.

ABHAINN DEARG TASTING NOTE

SINGLE MALT 46%

Nose: Deep amber. Mature, with notes of elderberry and raisin. Slightly smoky, with a touch autumn woods, leaf mold; that moss once more.

Palate: Delicate smoke all the way through. A weighty distillate that sits on the tongue. Hot mustard oil, saddle soap.

Finish: Cereal.

Conclusion: Young, still, with this intriguing mix of weight and airiness. Will need time in active casks.

Flavor camp: Fruity & Spicy
Where Next? Kornog

Talisker

TALISKER • CARBOST • WWW.DISCOVERING-DISTILLERIES.COM/TALISKER • OPEN ALL YEAR; SEE WEBSITE FOR DAYS & DETAILS

Situated at the head of Loch Harport in the village of Carbost, Talisker is one of the most spectacularly situated distilleries in Scotland. This is a place of mountain and shore. Behind the distillery rise the Cuillins, their shattered and fractured ridge acting as a barrier to the south. Stand on the shore and inhale deeply: seaweed and brine. Then do the same with the new make: smoke, oysters, lobster shell. Talisker distills itself. But surely this is romantic nonsense, brought about by the extreme location, this island where you confront the insignificance of mortality?

Hugh MacAskill, "Big Hugh," didn't build a distillery here for any metaphysical reasons. The nephew of a Mull landowner (whose Mornish estate he would inherit) MacAskill took the control of Talisker in 1825 and applied the brutal economics of "improvement" upon his tenants—or those still there after the previous landlord Lauchlan MacLean had finished.

Talisker, like Clynelish (*see* p.133), is a Clearance distillery. The people had an option: stay in Carbost and work at the distillery or clear off to the Colonies. Skye's desolate beauty isn't just the effect of its geology, but the result of nineteenth-century capitalist economics. "Skye isn't empty," writes British author Robert MacFarlane. "It is emptied."

The whisky, too, doesn't initially appear to be about abstract connections. Talisker is about reflux, purifiers, and peat. It's about "process"… and yet that procession of flavors on the tongue still lead you back to the littoral. Skye's thin soils mean that there are 21 springs feeding into the distillery; the barley is peated

(and these days comes from Glen Ord); the ferments are long and in wood. All this gives a wash, which goes into two of the more intriguingly shaped stills in the industry.

Talisker's secrets start here in these tall pots whose lyne arms have a dramatic U-bend in them. Vapors will reflux here and can be led back into the still through a purifier pipe. The lyne arm rears back up to its original height, goes through the wall and coils around in a cold worm tub. These are pretty remarkable flavor-making machines. The low wines then go to two of three plain spirit stills (maybe a hangover from when Talisker was triple distilled) and give that complex new make.

There's smoke obviously, but also sulfur in here: that's the combination of worms plus exhausted copper, but also an oily sweetness from all of that reflux in that big wash still with its purifier. It's that sulfur note that eventually recedes to the back of the palate to give Talisker its giveaway peppery note.

Caught between the shore and the Cuillins, Talisker is one of the most spectacularly situated distilleries in Scotland.

So, is Talisker a factory making whisky or are these white-painted buildings a manifestation of the place itself? "Of course you can capture the place in the whisky," says Diageo's master distiller and blender, Douglas Murray. "You can't condense the spirit without capturing some of the essence of the location. There's something about this site that makes Talisker … Talisker. We'll never know how it happens, and we don't want to." Site-specific *terroir*.

In recent years the Talisker family has grown considerably, from powerful, peaty expressions such as 57° North, Storm, and Dark Storm to permanent members at 25 and 30 years old. All share this mix of land, sea, and shoreline. Skye distilled.

All of these island whiskies have survived because they are both pragmatic—whisky-making is one of the few businesses that work here—but also because their flavors (driven predominantly by peat) are uncompromising, as is the landscape. In this way the whisky reflects both where it is from and the people who make it. This is cultural *terroir* as well.

Checking the cratur. Talisker's peppery smoky style is in constant interplay with the subtle caresses of oak from its time spent in cask.

TALISKER TASTING NOTES

NEW MAKE

Nose: Light smoke to start. Very sweet with sulfur in the background. Oyster brine, lobster shell. Perfumed smoke at the end.
Palate: Dry smoky and sulfury. Light tar. New leather. Soft fruits. Salty.
Finish: Long, smoky, and peppery with sulfur underneath.

8YO, REFILL WOOD CASK SAMPLE

Nose: Scented. Heathery/earthy peatiness. White peppercorn, developing a medicinal edge. Still has the briny/oyster-like notes of new make. Iodine and dried mint. With water, bog myrtle, and larch.
Palate: Big white peppercorn hit. Marine. Solid thick texture with some oil. Complex.
Finish: Dry then sweet then dry and peppery again.
Conclusion: Already hitting its mature character.

10YO 45.8%

Nose: Gold. Smoky fires. Heather, licorice root, and bilberry. A mix of earthy smoke (bonfires), pork crackling, and a light seaweed touch. Sweetness runs underneath. Balanced. Light complexity.
Palate: Immediate. A rich complex mix of pepper flakes then a really sweet soft fruitiness, all linked by a sooty/mossy smokiness. Hint of sulfur. A mix of sea and shore, the sweet, the fiery, the smoky.
Finish: Peppery and dry.
Conclusion: Balance struck between seemingly contradictory elements.

Flavor Camp: Smoky & Peaty
Where Next? Caol Ila 12yo, Springbank 10yo

STORM 45.8%

Nose: Smoky and saline. Breaking waves and a lift from the sulfury new make. Water calms the storm slightly, allowing the syrupy, fruity sweetness to build, then the briny smoke returns.
Palate: Typically Talisker, lulling you into sweetness then bursting into powerful, assertive smoke.
Finish: Salty and peppery.
Conclusion: A No-Age-Statement Talisker that maximizes the peat element.

Flavor Camp: Smoky & Peaty
Where Next? Springbank 12yo

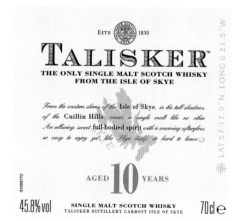

18YO 45.8%

Nose: Gold. Complex, burning heather, sweet tobacco, old warehouse, spent bonfire. Underneath is almond paste/nougat butter cookies, and a lightly herbal note. Plenty of smoke. Rich and complex.
Palate: A slow start, then pepper, a light smoked-fish note, but the key is the sweet fruit syrup, which gives a balancing element. Builds in stages to an explosive finish.
Finish: Red peppercorn.
Conclusion: Retains Talisker's identifiable attack but with a growing sweet center.

Flavor Camp: Smoky & Peaty
Where Next? Bowmore 15yo, Highland Park 18yo

25YO 45.8%

Nose: Scented, violet-like with wet rope, brine sat on canvas, green ferns, and light leather. Shore-like, bonfire embers.
Palate: Hugely complex. Strawberries with cracked black pepper, bay leaf, seaweed, and smoke.
Finish: Salty chocolate.
Conclusion: A balanced, mature, mysterious whisky. A classic Talisker.

Flavor Camp: Smoky & Peaty
Where Next? Lagavulin 21yo

ORKNEY ISLANDS

Orkney stands apart from the rest of Scotland. Here is a place of standing stones, Neolithic burial chambers, and ancient roundhouse forts. A place where the relentless sea beats at the cliffs and Viking sagas still appear contemporary. All seem to co-exist in this enchanted collection of islands whose two distilleries take different approaches to expressing their location.

Temporal simultaneity: Orkney's ancient past is palpably alive.

Highland Park & Scapa

HIGHLAND PARK • KIRKWALL • WWW.HIGHLANDPARK.CO.UK • OPEN ALL YEAR; SEE WEBSITE FOR DAYS & DETAILS
SCAPA • KIRKWALL • WWW.SCAPAMALT.COM

The propellers cut the cloud, revealing an undulating coastline, which from this height, looks more like a gentle waltz between land and sea than the drunken stagger of the Scottish west coast. Orkney is unlike the rest of Scotland, in landscape, in culture, in people—and in whisky. This archipelago of low green disks remains both an outpost of Norse culture, while not being Scandinavian, and in Scotland, but not Scottish. Again, here we have islands whose inbuilt insularity and self-sufficiency created their own solutions, and the islands' two distilleries, Highland Park and Scapa, represent two different creative approaches to whisky-making: one naturalistic, the other technological.

Highland Park, as the name suggests, sits on top of the hill above Kirkwall, its layered dark stonework making it look as if it sprang directly from the rock. Passing under its ornate gateway ("Estd. 1798") is like entering a strange other dimension, with flagged winding alleys, leading between buildings that seem to have grown organically as the distillery's needs increased.

It floor malts 20 percent of its own barley requirements on site, one day on peat, and one day on coke, giving a medium/heavy character. This is then blended with unpeated malt from the mainland. Dried yeast is used in a long ferment regime, distillation is slow. The result is a new make that mingles fragrant smoke and a citric uplift. "HP" is sweet from the word go, and this dance between smoke, sweetness, orange, and rich fruit continues through all its expressions. Sometimes peat has the upper hand, at others the sweetness eases itself forward, while age steadily draws both elements into a dense, honeyed compact. Balance is the key.

HP's DNA lies at the front and back ends of its creation. As part of the Edrington Group, its wood is under the eye of master of wood, George Espie, and since 2004 no bourbon casks have been filled

SCAPA: A VARIATION IN STYLE

Overlooking Scapa Flow and about a mile as the crow flies from Highland Park, Scapa's whisky couldn't be more different. Unpeated and juicily fruity, the key to its character lies in the stillhouse where a Lomond still stands. Though its baffle plates have been removed, its broad neck and the use of a purifier give a huge amount of copper conversation. Now renovated by new owner Chivas Brothers, this pretty distillery and its hugely drinkable make is finally becoming better known.

(neither, incidentally, does any caramel tinting take place). This is a whisky from ex-sherry casks made from four-year-old, air-dried seasoned European and American oak. "That wood policy gives consistency of character," says brand ambassador Gerry Tosh. "That's the biggest challenge when you have seven expressions ranging from

The steep paved alleyways of the Highland Park distillery give it the air of a self-contained medieval town.

12yo to 50yo, with no finishing." If Espie and whisky-maker Max MacFarlane have their hands on controlling unwanted surprises at the end, then the beginning is down to Orkney.

Walk onto Hobbister Moor, where Highland Park extracts 350 tons of peat a year, and you'll notice a change in the land's aroma: a pine-like, herbal fragrance that's replicated in the whisky. To get a true understanding of why HP is different, travel from there to the cliffs of Yesnaby, where that aerial illusion of a gentle coastal dance is blasted away. Here, on top of these wave-pounded multicolored strata, the winds reach more than 100 mph, 80 days a year. "It's Orcadian peat that makes Highland Park different," says Tosh, "and this is where it starts. The salt spray means there's never been trees on Orkney, leaving only heather and because of that the peat is different and because of that the aroma when it's burned is different … and that makes Highland Park."

A distillery character rooted in its place of birth.

HIGHLAND PARK TASTING NOTES

NEW MAKE
Nose: Smoke and citrus fruit. Very lifted and sweet. Fresh, kumquat peel, and light juicy fruit.
Palate: Light nut. Big spread of sweet citrus fruit then comes fragrant smoke.
Finish: Continues to sweeten with a touch of pear on the finish.

12YO 40%
Nose: Light gold. The fruit has come through, softening the peat. Still that big citric hit, moist fruitcake, berry fruit, and that olive oil. With water, there's baked fruit and gentle smoke.
Palate: Soft and gentle with hints of white raisin and peat creeping in slowly from the mid-palate. Everything concentrated in the center of the tongue.
Finish: Sweet smoke.
Conclusion: Already open and picking up complexity.

Flavor Camp: Smoky & Peaty
Where Next? Springbank 10yo

18YO 43%
Nose: Full gold. Ripe and fatter than the 12yo with fleshier fruit rather than the peels of the 12yo. Madeira cake, sweet cherry, and more spice. Fudge and light honey. The smoke is dying in the fireplace.
Palate: This more dense progression continues. Dried peach, honey, polished oak, walnut. Juicy with a little marmalade.
Finish: Integrated smoke.
Conclusion: A clear family resemblance, and picking up weight from oak.

Flavor Camp: Rich & Round
Where Next? The Balvenie 17yo Madeira Cask, Springbank 15yo, Yamazaki 18yo

25YO 48.1%
Nose: Amber. Luscious with masses of sweet dried fruit. More heathery smoke/heather honey than the 18yo. There's also the start of whisky *rancio* notes of furniture polish and moist earth.
Palate: Molasses and concentrated fruit sugars. Allspice and nutmeg, and remains sweet.
Finish: Dried orange peel and fragrant smoke. Darjeeling tea.
Conclusion: Beginning to enter its third age, but distillery character is there.

Flavor Camp: Rich & Round
Where Next? Springbank 18yo, Jura 21yo, Ben Nevis 25yo, Hakushu 25yo

40YO 43%
Nose: Mature. Light *rancio* touches. Highly exotic. Suede and a sexual, sweaty muskiness. There's smoke on the back and then a return of the fudge sweetness. Grows with water and keeps on giving for hours moving into perfumed smoke (moor burn) and light orris-like rootiness.
Palate: Dry start, then becomes oily and tongue-coating. The leather comes back alongside notes of bitter almond, raisin, and dried peels. In time the smoke emerges and eventually takes the upper hand.
Finish: Crisp then sweetens.
Conclusion: Mature and evolved but clearly Highland Park.

Flavor Camp: Smoky & Peaty
Where Next? Laphroaig 25yo, Talisker 25yo

SCAPA TASTING NOTES

NEW MAKE
Nose: Estery with banana, green pea, quince, plums. Some damp earth behind and a touch of wax.
Palate: Sweet and lighty oily. Fruit chews.
Finish: Clean. Short.

16YO 40%
Nose: Gold. Lots of American oak overlay. Banana and fruit chews. Light and aromatic with a hint of fresh thyme.
Palate: Light oiliness still. Quite a fat feel, yet somehow airy. Light toasty notes from the oak. The fruit anchors it to the center of the tongue.
Finish: Unctuous and ripe.
Conclusion: Bouncy and eager to please.

Flavor Camp: Fruity & Spicy
Where Next? Old Pulteney 12yo, Clynelish 14yo

1979 47.9%
Nose: Gold. More integrated character with light cacao, mashed banana/black banana. The quince returns. Full and vibrant.
Palate: Complex and rich. Guava. Toasted oak. Sweet.
Finish: Gentle spiciness. Fruit.
Conclusion: Still has masses of distillery character, but calmer than the puppy-like 16yo. Needs time to become serious.

Flavor Camp: Fruity & Spicy
Where Next? Craigellachie 14yo

CAMPBELTOWN

Campbeltown Loch, I wish ye were whisky went the old Scottish music-hall song. Well, at one point the singer's dream was reality. This small town at the foot of the Kintyre peninsula has been at some point home to at least 34 distilleries. Fifteen of those disappeared during the 1850s Depression, but by the end of the nineteenth century Campbeltown malt was a desirable commodity, its smoky, oily character an integral part of blends. Campbeltown was a boom town.

A deep and sheltered harbor enabled Campbeltown to become a major fishing port and whisky producer with quick access to the Lowland markets.

The villas on the east side of its bay are evidence of the wealth that existed here. It was whisky-making paradise: there was a deep natural harbor, a local coal seam, and 20 maltings in the vicinity working from a mix of local barley and grain from nearby Ireland and southwestern Scotland. Distilleries were crammed into its streets, up alleyways. Yet by the end of the 1920s only one, Riechlachan, was operational, and even that fell silent in 1934, when today's survivors, Springbank and Glen Scotia, reopened.

The question why the other 17 distilleries failed has never been fully answered. Various theories have been put forward: overproduction leading to a drop in quality (though we can dispense with the myth that the whisky was filled into herring barrels); an inability to get rid of effluent (an issue in the nineteenth century when "the free-ranging pigs of Dalintober relished pot ale and were frequently seen indulging that taste at the Pottle Hole"); the working out of the Machrihanish coal seam. All had a part to play, but there isn't a single answer to its decline. It was simply the most exposed region in a perfect storm.

By the 1920s, blenders had fixed on their most popular styles, thereby restricting the requirements of Campbeltown's predominantly smoky/oily style. They were also dealing with the consequences of a fall in consumption during World War I, and a decline in production, which had left stock levels even lower than this level of demand. In addition, UK duty had risen significantly in 1918 and 1920, but distillers weren't allowed to pass this on to the consumer, making it more expensive to replenish stocks.

At one point the produce of 34 distilleries would have been shipped from these waters. Today, there are just three left.

Export was equally difficult thanks to Prohibition in the USA and the Great Depression. Caught between rising costs and falling sales, whisky-making became uneconomic, especially for small, independent distillers.

We tend to forget that the entire industry was affected. Fifty distilleries across Scotland were closed in the 1920s and only two pot-still sites were operational in the whole country in 1933. When the crisis passed, the industry had been rationalized by the Distillers Company Ltd (an echo of the 1850s, a precursor of the 1980s cull). It was "leaner," maybe even "fitter." What is clear is that the (primarily) small distilleries of Campbeltown simply didn't fit into this new whisky world. This notion that Scotch whisky has lived a charmed life is false.

And yet, there is a happy ending. Today, Campbeltown has been reinstated as a whisky region in its own right and is home to three distilleries making five different whiskies. One of these producers acts as a template for the new wave of small, independent distillers; another has been brought back from the grave. The loch may not be filling with whisky, but Campbeltown is back.

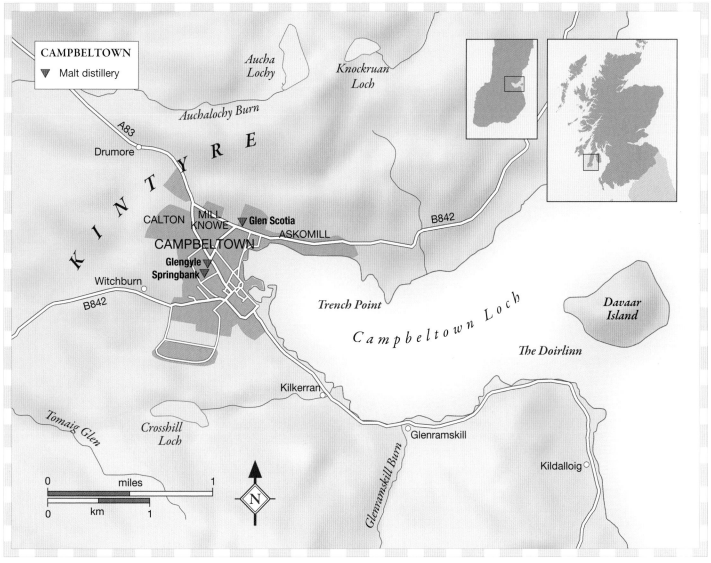

Springbank

CAMPBELTOWN • WWW.SPRINGBANKWHISKY.COM • OPEN ALL YEAR MON–SAT; ADVANCED BOOKING REQUIRED

Hidden up a narrow street behind a church, the Springbank distillery buildings have been owned by the same family since 1828, the longest such example in Scotch whisky. Self-sufficiency is the byword here. All the distillery's requirements are malted, distilled, matured, and bottled on-site: the only Scottish distillery to have everything under one roof. This total self-reliance is relatively new, however. Like any distilleries reliant on contracts for fillings, it found itself exposed during the 1980s crash and responded by going back to fundamentals. The message was clear: Springbank's destiny should lie in its own hands, not by being in hock to the majors.

It's this balance between retaining old ways while having an eye to the future that intrigues most. Take what happens inside the boatskin larch fermenters. "We always try to replicate conditions that existed as far back as records allow us to check," says production director Frank McHardy. That means low gravity worts (around 1,046°), extra-long (100-hour) ferments, and a low-strength wash (between 4.5–5% abv, the industry standard is 8–9% abv). "That lengthy fermentation in larch promotes loads of fruitiness, the lower OG helps create esters."

The distillery's three stills—a direct-fired wash still and two low wines stills, one of which runs into a worm tub—produce three distinct new makes. Springbank itself is 2.5 times distilled: the wash still giving low wines, the low wines still giving "feints" and the final mix in the second low wines still is a mix of 20 percent low wines and 80 percent feints (*see* pp.14–15). The new make is big, one of the most complex in Scotch, capable of prolonged aging and giving a sense that all of Scotland's styles are here compressed into one package.

"It's a method of production which has gone on for as long as we have records," says McHardy. "One thing we're pretty sure of is that Springbank distillery was the only one in Campbeltown to carry out this process." It could be the reason for its survival.

Springbank remains an upholder of traditional whisky-making customs, yet it is also the template for many new distilleries.

From barley to bottle. Springbank is the only distillery to malt, distill, mature, and bottle on the same site.

Of the other two styles, the fragrant, appley, unpeated, triple-distilled Hazelburn looks to the Lowlands or maybe, to Northern Ireland, where McHardy spent 13 years as manager of Bushmills. Meanwhile heavily peated Longrow is "normal," i.e. double-distilled, but maybe closer to the original "Campbeltown" template. Bold when young, it lacks any of the rubbery immaturity that can mar young peaty whiskies and can also grow in complexity (*see* p.188).

All three are defiantly non-linear. This is a distillery in which flavors jump through hoops, run against the norm, are nudged, boosted and refined. Don't, however, patronize Springbank by thinking it is some museum of whisky-making. Its calculated

belief in the old ways, but also of multiple streams, a tight wood policy, and self-sufficiency has made it a template for other newer (and often noisier) distillers. It's not just the past, it's A Future.

Ultimately, it's Springbank's ability to stay ahead of the times that has allowed it to survive over the years.

SPRINGBANK TASTING NOTES

NEW MAKE

Nose: Huge, luscious, and complex. Baked, soft fruit, some vanilla, touch of Brylcreem, and very light cereal. Sweet, rich, and heavy. With water, smoke and a little yeast.
Palate: Heavy, oily. Very full-bodied with rich smoke and a little briny tingle. Heavy, earthy, and ripe.
Finish: Earthy and full.

10YO 46%

Nose: Light gold. Light additive oak-shaving notes. Smoke, ripe fruits, extra virgin olive oil, and fragrant wood. Rich and charred. Toasty with a light citric lift.
Palate: Sweet start and then the black olive comes through before briny smoke builds. Still tense.
Finish: Smoke. Long.
Conclusion: A slow gentle development from new make. Like a young white burgundy or Riesling, it's hugely drinkable but with so much more to come.

Flavor Camp: **Smoky & Peaty**
Where Next? Ardmore Traditional Cask, Caol Ila 12yo, Talisker 10yo

15YO 46%

Nose: Smoky and briny: the smell of a beach after a storm. Black olives, a light grassiness, and then roasted almond, melon, sour plums, and a steady build of oily depth.
Palate: Balanced and rich. The higher strength adds impact to the smoke. Richly fruited, oily, and deep, with a citric edge.
Finish: Long, gently smoked.
Conclusion: Balanced, complex, and layered.

Flavor Camp: **Smoky & Peaty**
Where Next? Talisker 18yo

HAZELBURN TASTING NOTES

NEW MAKE

Nose: Clean and spicy. High-toned and limey with a little touch of starch behind. Intense and pure. Green apple.
Palate: Light and rapier-like intensity but good soft feel.
Finish: Green plum.

HAZELBURN 12YO 46%

Nose: Full gold. Sherried notes: amontillado-like nuttiness mixed with molasses, prune, and white raisin. Real lifted sweetness behind.
Palate: Soft. The wood's thickened the feel but the penetrating intensity cuts through the oak adding a zesty intensity to the top. Becomes more citric as it moves: orange and sweet dried fruits.
Finish: Clean.
Conclusion: Full, balanced integration of distillery and oak.

Flavor Camp: **Fruity & Spicy**
Where Next? Arran 12yo

LONGROW TASTING NOTES

NEW MAKE

Nose: Very sweet. Cassis. Earthy smoke. Wet slate.
Palate: Intense and sweet start before a huge purple cloud of smoke. Touch of tomato sauce spiciness.
Finish: Bone dry, smoke, and a hint of tingling salt.

14YO 46%

Nose: Rounded. The smoke is obvious but not dominant since more wood coming through—think moorland and chimneys, lilac and bracken. Bonfire and wet-slate character suggesting there's more.
Palate: Big and lightly malty. Dry wood smoke, then that ripe black fruit seen on the new make makes its move, mixing with some sweet date.
Finish: The smoke surges through and is sustained.
Conclusion: Now on a roll.

Flavor Camp: **Smoky & Peaty**
Where Next? Yoichi 15yo, Ardbeg Airigh nam Beist 1990

18YO 46%

Nose: Roasted barley, caramelized notes, then smoke and heavy sweetness. Water brings out creosote, hot driftwood, licorice, and sesame.
Palate: Eruptive smoke. Bold and earthy, with massed weight of fruits.
Finish: Lengthy, oily, and rich.
Conclusion: The combination of direct-fire worm tub and peat has produced a rich, powerful malt.

Flavor Camp: **Smoky & Peaty**
Where Next? Yoichi 15yo

KILKERRAN TASTING NOTES

NEW MAKE

Nose: Clean. Wet hay. Bakery and light sulfur. Yeasty and a slippery weight.
Palate: Similar weight to its neighbor but fatter and more marshmallow-like. Starts fruity, then drier and malty.
Finish: Perfumed.

3YO CASK SAMPLE

Nose: Rich gold. Precocious. Lots of additive coconutty notes. Sweet damp hay/raffia and patisserie.
Palate: Ripe and sweet with mango balanced by oak and that cereal grip. Mouth-filling.
Finish: Long and sweet.
Conclusion: Been given a big leg up by an active cask, but moving speedily.

WORK IN PROGRESS NO 4 46%

Nose: Clean and sweet. Good presence, with sweet citrus fruit, cooked rhubarb, and canned peaches.
Palate: Very light bran notes. Thick and chewy. Orange peel and vanilla. Scotch tablet. Has an acidic jag on the back palate.
Finish: Light tarragon. The sweetness continues.
Conclusion: The sweet, fruity distillery character is now fully established.

Flavor Camp: **Fruity & Spicy**
Where Next? Oban 14yo, Clynelish 14yo

Glengyle & Glen Scotia

CAMPBELTOWN • WWW.KILKERRAN.COM • CONTACT DISTILLERY FOR VISIT

The decline of Campbeltown's whisky is written upon its architecture. Tantalizing glimpses of old sites remain—a cracked and faded sign, the shape of the windows on an apartment building, the incongruous sight of a supermarket with a pagoda roof. It's a fascinating but sobering experience that exposes the fragility of the whisky industry. Yet dwelling on its past is to do the town's distillers a disservice. Campbeltown is not a place for whisky-archeologists, but whisky-lovers.

In 2000 Hedley Wright, whose family has owned Springbank since its founding in 1828, bought a distillery next door. This had been Glengyle, closed for 80 years.

The shell of a building was refitted into a neat single-level design and its pair of stills were salvaged from Frank McHardy's first distillery, Ben Wyvis, which operated briefly in the Invergordon grain distillery. "These were subjected to some changes when installed here," McHardy explains. "We got the coppersmith to reshape the ogee and also sweeten the angle of the pot's shoulders. The lyne arm was also angled upward to give the still some reflux qualities." The early releases show a lightly peated, medium-bodied character.

The whisky is called Kilkerran as the brand name, Glengyle is owned by Campbeltown's third distillery: Glen Scotia. When Alfred Barnard arrived in Campbeltown he wrote that this plant, then just called Scotia, "seems to have hidden itself away out of sight, as if the art of making whisky ... was bound to be kept a dark secret."

Not a lot has changed. Glen Scotia remains one of Scotland's more elusive distilleries, famed for its alleged haunting by former owner Duncan MacCallum. Now owned by Loch Lomond Distillers it's been in full production since 1999, though never with the aid of people from Springbank. At the time of writing, it is being reformulated, repackaged, and rebranded, with 10 and 12 year old expressions.

GLEN SCOTIA TASTING NOTES

10YO 46%

Nose: Lightly minty with gentle, fresh pear behind. In time, some daffodil, and with water, a mineral note.
Palate: Soft and lightly oily, with some central sweetness. Supple. The florals return, lily-like.
Finish: Soft, if short.
Conclusion: A restrained and balanced introduction.

Flavor Camp: **Fragrant & Floral**
Where Next? Chichibu Almost There

12YO 46%

Nose: Robust and earthy, with aromas of nuts, cereal (draff), and old coins. With water, some wet stone, and a vegetable/turnip note.
Palate: Full, cereal-driven, and oily. Needs water to soften and allow some nuttiness to come forward.
Finish: Chalky.
Conclusion: Old-style Glen Scotia.

Flavor Camp: **Malty & Dry**
Where Next? Tobermory 10yo

Back from the dead. Glengyle was reopened in 1999 after 80 years of silence.

Left: The nose knows. Edrington's master blender, Gordon Motion, at work.

Right: Though the personnel may have changed, the process of blending remains the same.

SCOTCH BLENDS

Scotch single malt may link the spirit with the land, but the majority of these distilleries would not exist were it not for blended Scotch, which accounts for over 90 percent of the Scotch whisky sold throughout the world. When the world talks of "Scotch" they are talking blends. And blends have their own story to tell.

Blends are less about place, but more about occasion, and flavor lies at the heart of it. Scotch whisky has faced numerous crises through its history. Each time it has reinvented itself by looking at flavor.

In the 1830s, whisky distilling was seen as a get-rich-quick scheme, but within two decades the industry was over-capacity. Rum was Scotland's preferred spirit, while Irish whiskey was outselling Scotch in Scotland. "Chiefly on account of its uniformity of style," as William Ross, MD of key player, Distillers Company Ltd (DCL), recalled to the Royal Commission on Whisky and Potable Spirits, set up in 1908, which formalized the legal definition of Scotch whisky.

A change in law in 1853 had allowed whisky of different ages from the same distillery to be blended "in bond" (prior to tax being paid), which allowed the mixing of different ages and enabled more experimentation in a bid to achieve flavor consistency. Within a year, Usher's Old Vatted Glenlivet (initially a vatted malt) appeared. The blending houses we know today developed in 1860, in tandem with the first issuing of "grocers' licenses," a move that enabled a wider range of retailers (especially grocers) to sell directly to the public.

It was the grocers (aka "Italian warehousemen") who took advantage of this opportunity, people like John Walker and his son Alexander, the Chivas brothers, and wine merchants like John Dewar, Matthew Gloag, Charles Mackinlay, George Ballantine, and William Teacher.

Understanding the principles of bringing together different flavors and textures to create a uniform and consistent whole was familiar to them. The significant shift wasn't just the liquid, in which light patent-still grain calmed the rambunctious temperaments of the single malts, but in the merchants putting their names on the bottle as a personal guarantee of quality. From this point on, blends were the future of Scotch and the blender become the arbiter of style.

By the end of the nineteenth century, new malt distilleries were being built specifically to tap into the blended market or at the behest of blenders themselves. This happened particularly in Speyside as the blenders tried to give their blends a gentler character. Why? The market.

The genius of blenders such as the Walker and Dewar families and James Buchanan was that they went to the English market, saw what the middle class wanted to drink, and fitted a blend around those requirements. The same process happened around the world. Blends were being made to suit a serving style (whisky and soda) and an occasion (pre-dinner, pre-theatre). Scotch became a signifier of success.

This process has continued through the lightening years of Prohibition and postwar times to today's market, moving from the cut-glass tumblers of London to the beach bars of Brazil, the nightclubs of Shanghai, or the *shebeens* of Soweto. Blends by their nature are fluid, they shift in accordance with changing tastes, they live in the real world.

The Art of Blending

CHIVAS BROTHERS • WWW.CHIVAS.COM • SEE ALSO WWW.MALTWHISKYDISTILLERIES.COM
DEWAR'S • ABERFELDY • WWW.DEWARSWOW.COM • OPEN ALL YEAR MON–SAT
JOHNNIE WALKER • WWW.JOHNNIEWALKER.COM / WWW.DISCOVERING-DISTILLERIES.COM/CARDHU •
OPEN ALL YEAR; SEE WEBSITE FOR DAYS & DETAILS
GRANT'S • DUFFTOWN • WWW.GRANTSWHISKY.COM • WWW.WILLIAMGRANT.COM

The idea that history is written by the victors doesn't hold water (pardon the pun) with Scotch whisky. As far as an English-speaking audience is concerned, whisky's history has been that of how single malts were temporarily usurped by those inferior creatures called blends, and of how the natural order of things has been restored. However, 90 percent of the Scotch sold in the world is blended, and its sales continue to grow. Blends remain the victor.

That, however, is the wrong way to look at things. Blends and malts co-exist happily. They need each other and they occupy different places in the world of whisky. One isn't better than the other. They're different.

Malts are about intensity of character. Single-malt bottlings are about maximizing this singularity. Blends are about creating a totality.

In principle, the creation of a blend is a simple one. You take some grain whiskies and some malt whiskies and mix them together to give an acceptable final flavor. We can all do this as a one-off and make maybe one bottle that we find satisfying. But what if you are making millions of bottles every year? Each time you make your blend it must be the same, but the component parts will vary because each cask is different. Blenders must have an intimate knowledge of their palette of flavors. They must know not just what whisky A tastes like, but what it tastes like when put with whisky B, C, and D. They need to build in as many options for themselves as possible in order to retain consistency. At all times they have to be true to the house style.

Because of the perceived victory of single malts, when faced with a blend, drinkers want to know what malts are used, how many of them are in the blend, and how old they are. The simple answer to that is: the right ones, the right number, and at the right level of maturity. Blends are based around flavor and consistency. How you get there isn't important.

The malts used are chosen because of the way they interact with the other whiskies: some are used for top notes, others for grip; some for smoothness, others for richness; some for smoke. Some might be in relaxed casks to enhance vibrancy, while other might be overwooded (in malt terms) to provide grip.

Their number is the right one to achieve that flavor profile, as is the level of maturity, which is different from how old they may be. Age is a statement of time, while maturity is concerned with how wood, spirit, and air have interacted. Different levels of maturity equal different flavors. Blending is not a numbers game; it is flavor game, and by having a range of distillery characters, woods, and aspects of maturity you get complexity.

Then there's grain. Jim Beveridge, Johnnie Walker's master blender, always emphasizes the transformative power of grain, the manner in which it not only adds its own flavor, but helps tease out new flavors from the different malts in the mix. It isn't a filler or a diluting element, but it contributes texture and gives a greater unity and coherence to the blend. When you taste a blend, it's grain that is providing the soft, tongue-clinging element that seems to pull the flavors along. It adds flavor and mouth-feel. Grains are a way to allow the hidden complexities within the malt—and by extension the blend—to be revealed.

"Sometimes one element within a malt's character can be dominant: smoke, for example," adds Brian Kinsman, master blender at William Grant & Sons. "What grain does is reduce that dominance, allowing other secondary and tertiary flavors to be revealed. The core distillery character is still there, but now there is more to work with.

"The key is the balance between malt and grain—not the percentage. A blend isn't poor if it has a lot of grain. It's poor because it is unbalanced. You could say the same with regard to a blend that has a lot of malt."

Each grain distillery will have its own character, and while blenders tend to base their blends around a single grain (usually their own if they own a distillery), they use others to support it because of their specific qualities.

"Because they use maize (corn), the North British new make typically has oily, buttery notes," says Kirsteen Campbell, master blender of Cutty Sark. "These notes become sweeter and more vanilla-like on maturation. That and the oiliness give a lovely, smooth mouth-feel. It's the sweet heart of Edrington's blends. Not using good-quality grain would be like using cheap flour to bake a cake. Most importantly, the grain gives smoothness, which complements the stronger flavors of the malts. Aged for longer, grain becomes very complex, taking on richer oaked flavors and subtle spice."

The key isn't just throwing different flavors and textures together, but having an understanding of how these apparently disparate elements work in harmony with one another, and then how they can be made to suit a serve or an occasion. Writing about blends in 1930, Aeneas MacDonald stated: "Blending made it possible to make a whisky that would suit a different climate and different classes of patrons. The great export trade in whisky is almost entirely due to the elasticity that blending brought to the industry."

This elasticity has remained true. A blender is not just thinking what goes into a blend but how that blend will be consumed. By and large, blends are not made to be drunk on their own. The majority of them are created to work at their best when drunk long or mixed in cocktails.

They are versatile. They are compelling. They are the reason why whisky is a world drink.

SCOTCH BLENDS TASTING NOTES

ANTIQUARY 12YO 40%

Nose: Sweet, with steamed syrup pudding, soft, peachy fruit, light vanilla, and popcorn-like grain.
Palate: Gentle but with depth. Grain shows light milk chocolate. Sweet spices.
Finish: Long and sweet.
Conclusion: Balanced and sophisticated.

Flavor Camp: **Fruity & Spicy**

BALLANTINE'S FINEST 40%

Nose: Vibrant and lifted. Patisserie notes; grassy and estery. Subtly sweet, with a green edge.
Palate: Fresh and perfumed. Light flowers, green fruits, and a succulent center.
Finish: Crisp and fresh.
Conclusion: Delicate and comes to life with ginger ale.

Flavor Camp: **Fragrant & Floral**

BUCHANAN'S 12YO 40%

Nose: Lushness: all mango and papaya with yielding grain and creamy oak.
Palate: Clean oak adds some structure and a little toasted edge. Light coconut. Remains fruity.
Finish: Lightly drying and spicy.
Conclusion: Soft and generous.

Flavor Camp: **Fruity & Spicy**

CHIVAS REGAL 12YO 40%

Nose: Light and cereal-accented. Dry hay, maple-syrup sweetness, and light vanilla.
Palate: Fresh. Pineapple and red fruit, while a little white raisin adds depth to the dry-grass elements.
Finish: Fresh and dry.
Conclusion: Seems delicate but has substance.

Flavor Camp: **Fragrant & Floral**

CUTTY SARK 40%

Nose: Bright and effervescent. Blanched almond, lemon cheesecake, vanilla, and some green pear/apple.
Palate: All that vibrancy plus some silky grain that adds to the depth.
Finish: Zesty.
Conclusion: Very up—and at its best mixed with soda or ginger ale.

Flavor Camp: **Fragrant & Floral**

DEWAR'S WHITE LABEL 40%

Nose: Very sweet: mashed bananas and melting white-chocolate ice cream. Gentle grain, some honey. Given just the right amount of spicy energy by cloves and mace on the finish.
Palate: Gentle and creamy. Greek yogurt, citrus fruit, and dessert apple.
Finish: Cloves and mace.
Conclusion: The sweetest of the major blends.

Flavor Camp: **Fruity & Spicy**

THE FAMOUS GROUSE 40%

Nose: Well-balanced: zesty orange peel, ripe bananas, a hint of green olive, and toffee.
Palate: Smooth, with a light nuttiness, ripe fruits, toffee, and then some raisin adding depth.
Finish: Lightly spicy, with sweet ginger.
Conclusion: Medium-bodied and elegant.

Flavor Camp: **Fruity & Spicy**

GRANT'S FAMILY RESERVE 40%

Nose: Freshness backed with silky grain, toasted marshmallows, and almond flakes, a light floral note.
Palate: More substance with waxiness, dark chocolate, red fruit and caramel.
Finish: Long, with some dried fruit.
Conclusion: Medium-weight, balanced.

Flavor Camp: **Fruity & Spicy**

GREAT KING STREET 46%

Nose: Cream soda, pears, lily of the valley, and gentle grain. Quite floral and lifted.
Palate: Luscious and soft with hints of green cardamom, anise, lemon, and nectarine.
Finish: Gentle and quite long.
Conclusion: Higher malt-to-grain ratio and more first-fill casks in use. Try as a highball.

Flavor Camp: **Fruity & Spicy**

OLD PARR, 12YO 40%

Nose: Leathery, rich, and ripe with raisin, date, and walnut cut by lilac, violet, and some citrus fruit with lightness and fragrance—here in the guise of flamed orange peel, caraway, and cilantro.
Palate: Thick, fruity blackcurrant chewiness, with added caraway and coriander seed. The leather returns.
Finish: Sherried and deep.
Conclusion: Old-style rich blend.

Flavor Camp: **Rich & Round**

JOHNNIE WALKER BLACK LABEL 40%

Nose: Dark fruit: blackberry, cooked plum, raisin, some fruitcake. With water, a light maritime smokiness.
Palate: Soft and rich, with sherried depths and some marmalade that adds zest to the dried fruit.
Finish: Lightly smoky.
Conclusion: Complex and rich.

Flavor Camp: **Rich & Round**

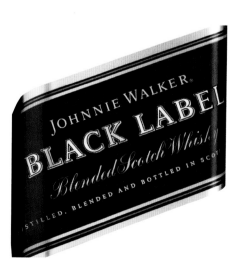

IRELAND

Until the past decade, Irish whiskey's one time pre-eminence had largely been forgotten. Yet this is a country that had conceivably made a barley spirit before Scotland, a country whose love of its make was so famed in the sixteenth century that Shakespeare wrote, "I would rather trust ... an Irishman with my *aqua-vitae* bottle ... than my wife with herself."

Previous page: **Until the nineteenth century** most of Ireland's whiskey was made by small farmers.

Below: **Whiskey-making** has been part of rural Ireland for centuries.

It wasn't *aqua vitae*, however, that made the Irish famous initially, but *usquebaugh*, described by one of the playwright's contemporaries, the gentleman traveler Fynes Moryson, as being "preferred before our own [English] *aqua vitae* because of the mingling of Raysons, Fennell seede and other things." This flavored whiskey-based distillate was a noted Irish specialty up to the nineteenth century.

Until then, whiskey in Ireland followed the same dynamic as in Scotland; the battle between the illicit mostly rural *poitín*, and the legal "Parliamentary whiskey" made in Cork, Galway, Bandon, Tullamore, and, most significantly, Dublin.

At that point, Dublin was becoming a significant trading port, where the industrious could make their fortune. Whiskey was one of those new enterprises. Men like John Jameson and his sons benefitted from the 1823 legislation, which encouraged investment in distilling and changed Dublin into the world's whiskey capital.

They took a different path to their colleagues (and relations) in Scotland. Not for them the lightness of Aeneas Coffey's patent still whiskeys, they worked with pot-still whiskeys made with malted and unmalted barley as well as rye and oats: a style that they ensured had a consistent flavor, and was available in volume. If you drank whisky in the mid-nineteenth century, the likelihood is it would have been Irish single-pot still.

It wasn't to last. Ireland suffered the most out of the main whiskey-distilling nations in the twentieth century. Not just from the economic woes that hit them all, but the triple whammy of independence

cutting off the British Empire trade: a refusal to work with bootleggers eliminating the US market; and an isolationist policy at home, which, by combining high domestic taxes with an export ban, led to a collapse in distilling. There were only six distilleries operational in the Republic in the 1930s. By the 1960s, the last three left standing joined forces to become Irish Distillers Limited (IDL).

With hindsight, it was with the launch of a new Jameson blend and the opening of the centralized distillery at Midleton County Cork in the 1970s that things began to change.

At the time of writing, there are 19 planning applications for distilleries being considered. "We've just had the first meeting of the new Irish Whiskey Association," says Noel Sweeney, master distiller at Kilbeggan Distilling (formerly Cooley). "We reckoned that it was the largest number of whiskey distillers in one room since the 1800s."

Ireland is taking control of its heritage. "It was a disgrace that we only had three distilleries and never made much of our whiskey heritage," says Oliver Hughes, owner of the new Dingle distillery. "Ireland? It's the most famous drinking culture in the world!"

So what is Irish whiskey in the twenty-first century? It is, simply, whiskey made in Ireland. Like the country, it is multifaceted. It is grain, malt, blend, single-pot still, unsmoked, and smoked. It is made by big distilleries and small; it is made across the country; it is served neat, hot, long, and shaken.

So, pull up a chair, pour a ball o' malt, and let Ireland come to you. Relax. There's time. In Ireland, there's always time.

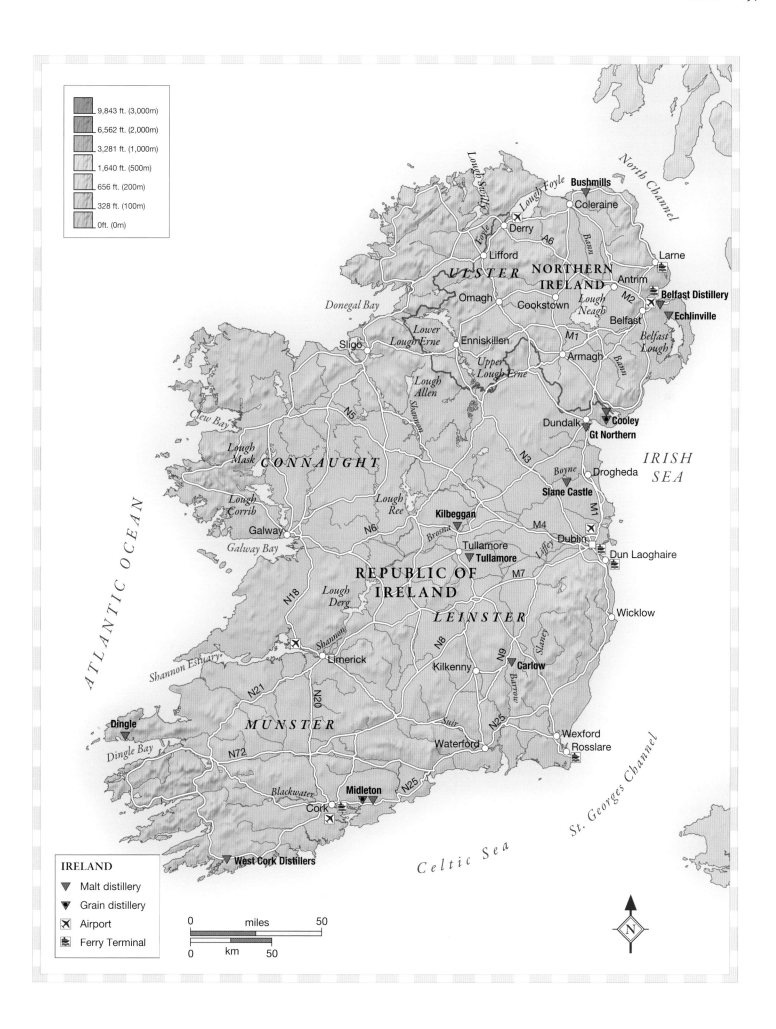

9,843 ft. (3,000m)
6,562 ft. (2,000m)
3,281 ft. (1,000m)
1,640 ft. (500m)
656 ft. (200m)
328 ft. (100m)
0ft. (0m)

Lough Swilly
Lough Foyle
Bushmills
North Channel
Coleraine
Derry
Foyle
A6
Lifford
ULSTER NORTHERN
IRELAND
Bann
Larne
Omagh
Cookstown
Antrim
M2
Belfast Distillery
*Lough
Neagh*
Belfast
Echlinville
Donegal Bay
Enniskillen
Armagh
*Belfast
Lough*
Bann
Sligo
*Lower
Lough Erne*
M1
*Upper
Lough Erne*
*Lough
Allen*
Shannon
Dundalk
Gooley
Gt Northern
*IRISH
SEA*
Clew Bay
N5
*Lough
Mask*
CONNAUGHT
N3
Boyne
Drogheda
*Lough
Corrib*
*Lough
Ree*
Slane Castle
M1
Kilbeggan
Brosna
M4
Dublin
Galway
N6
Tullamore
Tullamore
Liffey
Dun Laoghaire
Galway Bay
*REPUBLIC OF
IRELAND*
M7
ATLANTIC OCEAN
N18
*Lough
Derg*
LEINSTER
Wicklow
Shannon Estuary
N21
N20
Shannon
Limerick
N8
Slaney
N9
Dingle
Kilkenny
Carlow
Dingle Bay
MUNSTER
N72
Barrow
Suir
N25
Wexford
Rosslare
Blackwater
Midleton
N25
Waterford
Celtic Sea
St. Georges Channel
Cork
West Cork Distillers

IRELAND
▽ Malt distillery
▼ Grain distillery
✕ Airport
⛴ Ferry Terminal

0   miles   50
0   km   50

N

The art of distilling conceivably spread from Ireland's rocky coastline to Scotland.

Bushmills

BUSHMILLS • WWW.BUSHMILLS.COM • OPEN ALL YEAR; SEE WEBSITE FOR DAYS & DETAILS

The North Channel has long been a busy waterway between Ireland and Scotland. Years of shared tales, songs, and poetry, of politics and science, a great tidal flow of humanity and ideas. Whiskey is an integral part of this. Was it here that whiskey-making knowledge in the shape of the Beaton family left for the shores of Islay in 1300? This is the world Bushmills is part of, although this being Ireland, to get to the facts you first need to clear away the brush of half-truths.

For example, although a permit to distill in this vicinity was granted in 1608, the town's first distillery did not appear until 1784, complete with two small pot-stills. By 1853 it had been "improved" and had just had electric light installed, although two weeks after the power was switched on, the distillery was destroyed by fire. Whether the two are connected isn't clear.

When whiskey chronicler Alfred Barnard visited in the 1880s, he reported enthusiastically that the now enlarged distillery was "alive to all modern inventions." It wasn't making triple-distilled whiskey though. That only started in the 1930s, after Scotsman Jimmy Morrison was employed as manager to improve the make. His solution was to try "a triple type of pot still [distillation] not in use anywhere else" (*see* p.17). Oh, and it was peated until the 1970s.

Today, it makes a light, grassy triple-distilled malt as well as its own blends: the rich, fruity Black Bush and the fresh, gingery Original. It is both immediate and easy-sipping, but at the same time complex—more or less what you would expect from such a shape-shifting place.

Bushmills' heart is the spirit that comes out of its nine stills, scattered in seemingly random fashion in the stillhouse, whose slender necks have squeezed the vapor into an intimate conversation with the copper, increasing reflux.

Light is the desired flavor here, achieved by cutting the spirit from the intermediate stills into three. The heads are run into the low-wines receiver, then a middle cut is taken that goes into the strong feints receiver. The remainder, the weak feints, ends up in the low-wines receiver (*see* p.17).

The two stills being used for the spirit run are then each charged with 1,849 gallons (7,000 liters) of strong feints. Only a tiny cut (from 86% down to 83%) is collected as spirit. The distillation continues, however, with the rest of the distillate being collected as strong feints. Of course, the weak feints and the excess from the spirit still keep being redistilled, cut, redistilled, and topped off.

Rather than trying to work out the intricacies, it's much more satisfying to just stand in the stillhouse and watch, inhale, and listen. The stillman stands in the center surrounded by spirit safes, looking like the conductor in a concert hall, controlling the flavors. The music is the hiss of steam and echoes of valves, the melodies the aromas mingling, heavy and light, bass and descant. Bushmills is not linear and ordered; its flavors are streaming, in flux, overlapping, and being diverted and collected.

Today, the new make is matured in a high percentage of first-fill casks. "This whiskey is light, complex, but there's less fusel oil," says Egan. "If you have a delicate spirit you daren't put it into poor casks."

Everything about the distillery and its evolving whiskeys speaks of a place that has always been self-aware. It has taken what may appear

Whiskey on the rocks. The basalt columns of the Giant's Causeway are close to Bushmills distillery.

to be the unconventional route, the awkward path, but that decision, whether conscious or intuitive, has been the very reason why it has survived. It never quite made "Irish whiskey," it made Bushmills. The very thing that sets Bushmills apart: its flavor and the way in which that flavor is made, speaks of its heritage, its cultural *terroir*. This is a part of the world where whiskey-making is in the blood. Antrim's

A large, rambling site, Bushmills has been through a range of different incarnations in its long and varied history.

quiet lanes, its serrated coastline, have produced people who are born distillers, who revel in their questioning mentality and belief in an unconventional individuality.

BUSHMILLS TASTING NOTES

ORIGINAL, BLEND 40%

Nose: Light gold. Very fresh with a delicate herbal twinge. Hot clay and scented grasses.
Palate: Sweet with a little dustiness. Sweet centered with a little orange blossom, honey becoming grassy to the back.
Finish: Crisp and gingery.
Conclusion: Made for mixing—and that's a compliment.

Flavor Camp: **Fragrant & Floral**

BLACK BUSH, BLEND 40%

Nose: Full gold. Clean oak. Spice and Galia melon with a little date, black grape juice, then coconut and cedar. With water, it's plum clafoutis and stewed rhubarb.
Palate: Juicy, fruity, and ripe. Fruitcake, barley sugar. Deep. Pools in the center.
Finish: Creamy and long.
Conclusion: Serve with one rock of ice.

Flavor Camp: **Rich & Round**

10YO 40%

Nose: Gold. Green-grassy moving into light hay, malt bin, then fresh plaster, balsawood. Clover.
Palate: Crisp but with vanilla sweetness from ex-bourbon casks. Lightly fragrant.
Finish: Dry grasses and dusty spices.
Conclusion: Slightly fuller than in the past.

Flavor Camp: **Fragrant & Floral**
Where Next? Cardhu 12yo, Strathisla 12yo

16YO 40%

Nose: Deep amber. Big sweet sherry character, lots of concentrated black fruits, prune but also sweet oak. Has retained the juiciness of character. Raisins and teacake.
Palate: Ripe and vinous. Mulberry jam, currant. Just a little touch of tannin then black cherry before toffee.
Finish: Grapes again.
Conclusion: Maturation in three oak types, yet not grippy.

Flavor Camp: **Rich & Round**
Where Next? The Balvenie 17yo Madeira Cask

21YO, MADEIRA CASK FINISH 40%

Nose: Big and generous. Shifting into coffee cake with buttercream frosting. Water makes it reminiscent of a sherry bodega. Then come mint, citrus-fruit zest, and fresh tanned leather. Grist-like sweetness.
Palate: Sweet and gripping with dark dried fruits, molasses, red licorice.
Finish: Firm, nutty, and clean.
Conclusion: Double-cask treatment has added weight.

Flavor Camp: **Rich & Round**
Where Next? Dalmore 15yo

Echlinville & Belfast Distillery

ECHLINVILLE • KIRCUBBIN• COUNTY DOWN

Ever since the closure of Coleraine in 1978, Northern Ireland had only one distillery: Bushmills. Just as in the Republic, any broader whiskey-making heritage had been forgotten. As stills go cold, so memories disperse like aromas from a glass. Former household names like Belfast's Dunville's are no more than faded labels and slightly rusty pub signs.

It wasn't always this way. At the start of the nineteenth century, the north of Ireland was making significant volumes of pot-still whiskey. By the end it had become a significant producer of grain. That was to be its downfall. The fact that the price of northern Irish grain undercut Scotch was of significant frustration to the Distillers Company Limited (DCL), which had a virtual monopoly on grain production in Scotland.

In the 1920s, at a time of overproduction and low sales, DCL started on a series of purchases in the north. Between 1922 and 1929, it bought Avonviel and Connswater in Belfast, Waterside and Abbey in Derry, and closed them all down. By the mid-1930s, the only large producer left was the profit-making Royal Irish in Belfast (Dunville's home), which, inexplicably, closed down in 1936.

Now, in the former stableblock of a grand house in Echlinville on the Ards peninsula, a potential revival is starting. In 2013, Northern Ireland's second legal distillery started operations. It's the brainchild of local man Shane Braniff, who had already established his brands, Feckin Irish Whiskey and Strangford Gold, using stock from Cooley in 2005. When Cooley's sale to Beam cut off that supply, Braniff's solution was simple: he'd make his own.

"The aim was always to do that," he says. "I'd said when I was selling seven containers a year of the brands that we'd build a distillery." He's planted 100 acres of barley and is starting floor malting. "When you see 'field to glass' on the label it will be true," he says. It's an extension of his belief that the microclimate of the Ards peninsula is a perfect whiskey-making spot for barley cultivation and maturation.

"I'm a quality man through and through," he says, "but more and more in all businesses you see everything being brought down to price alone. I believe that if I can produce one of the best whiskeys in the world I'll get proper rewards."

He's not the only one. At the time of writing, an audacious new site for a distillery was opening. Peter Lavery has invested some of the money he won in the lottery in 2001 to build a malt distillery in Belfast's former Crumlin Road Gaol. The aim is to produce 7,9251 gallons (300,000 liters) per annum of a triple-distilled single malt.

He's aiming to create a new whiskey, Titanic, but with an eye on history has bought one of the defunct Belfast whiskey brands, McConnell's. With Shane Braniff's purchase of the Dunville's label, it's clear that not only is the north on the rise, but it is doing so with a renewed grasp of its whiskey history.

The grand home of Echlinville Distillery.

Cooley

COOLEY • DUNDALK • WWW.KILBEGGANDISTILLINGCOMPANY.COM

The Cooley peninsula in County Louth is not just home to a distillery, but one of the settings of *The Táin Bó Cúailnge*, the medieval Irish epic in which a king and queen battle over the ownership of a magical bull—a pretty neat analogy over what in 1988 seemed to start as the fight for the soul of Irish whiskey.

The firm was established by John Teeling, with the express intention of offering Irish-whiskey consumers a choice. Since 1966, the only distiller in the Republic had been IDL and, inevitably, its styles defined what "Irish whiskey" was: triple-distilled, unpeated. By the 1990s, Cooley was on the market with double-distilled malt, peated malt, single grain, and blends. Irish whiskey had rediscovered its original diversity.

The site wasn't chosen for its aesthetics. Its utilitarian collection of concrete boxes started life as one of five government-owned plants that had originally produced fuel from potatoes. It might not be the prettiest of places to look at, but it is to smell. Walk into its production side and the sweet aroma of cornbread and popcorn assails you, a scent that is captured in Greenore single grain: the luscious, corn-based spirit that has emerged from the 28-plate Barbet column.

There's also a pair of pots, whose upward-pointing lyne arms have cooling pipes inside to encourage reflux. Even the peated Connemara has at its heart this delicacy, which acts as a counterpoint to hefty, turf-like phenols.

Blending has been part of Cooley from the start; one reason double-distillation was used was that they needed some weight from their malt component. And, since its 2011 takeover by Jim Beam (and renaming as Kilbeggan Distilling Company), the focus has been on the Kilbeggan brand. "We got rid of own-label and non-contract supply," says master distiller Noel Sweeney. "We're now working at full capacity for Kilbeggan." Many of the new startups are former Cooley customers.

With a ready supply of fresh bourbon casks, Kilbeggan Distilling Company is in a better position than others, given the current shortage of wood. Even then, supplies are tight.

"You know," says Sweeney, "I said to the minister of forestry recently, 'Forget about all that spruce; you should be planting oak forests.' We'd be self-sufficient!"

That old Cooley spirit is still alive.

A serious investment in wood has been of huge benefit to Cooley.

COOLEY TASTING NOTES

CONNEMARA 12YO 40%

Nose: Scented, with cut-grass, bamboo leaves, dried apple, and a little peat. Like the new make, the peat seems shy...

Palate: ...but not on the palate where it now mingles among almond, fennel seed, and banana.

Finish: Smoked paprika. Turfy smoke.

Conclusion: Balanced.

Flavor Camp: Smoky & Peaty
Where Next? Ardmore Traditional Cask, Bruichladdich, Port Charlotte PC8

KILBEGGAN 40%

Nose: Hugely oily with masses of new oak, an aroma like box-fresh running shoes, and an intense, smoky, hickory perfume.

Palate: Thick, plenty of fresh oak. Sweet drive.

Finish: Light, soft fruits. Oak grip. Oily.

Conclusion: Big and bold.

Flavor Camp: Fruity & Spicy
Where Next? Chichibu Chibidaru

Kilbeggan

KILBEGGAN • TULLAMORE • WWW.KILBEGGANWHISKEY.COM • OPEN ALL YEAR; SEE WEBSITE FOR DAYS & DETAILS

A tour of Irish distilleries used to be little more than a trip around mausoleums. At the end of the tour you'd get a glass and pay your respects to the fallen. The Irish do history well, but no matter how interesting the visit, it remained a sad experience. Such was the case with Kilbeggan.

Matthew McManus was one of the first to realize that there might be money to be made in commercial distilling. In 1757, he built a distillery in this small town in the Irish Midlands. It was bought by John Locke in 1843 and it remained in the family's hands until the 1940s. Like most Irish distilleries, it suffered in the twentieth-century whiskey crisis, closing its doors in 1953 and lying pretty much derelict until it was reopened as a distilling museum in 1982.

It was both a fascinating and sad place to visit. On one hand, here was a perfectly preserved eighteenth-century distillery: a waterwheel turned two massive millstones; the mash tun was a wide, open-topped vat; a steam engine provided heat, and outside were three fat-bellied, verdigris-streaked stills. "This is what we were," it said.

Cooley bought the site in 1988, initially for its warehousing capacity and the brand names, but in 2007 the discovery of an ancient, tiny, ball-like pot-still allowed them to start distilling using low wines from their main plant. In 2010, the production side was fully revamped, a second still was installed, and Kilbeggan had its distillery back.

For a while the firm ran it as its pilot plant, testing single-pot still and rye, but now it is providing spirit for Kilbeggan and is that brand's home.

Jim Beam's aim for the brand is clear: to get it to sufficient volume so as to compete with the major players. It has been tweaked slightly, and repackaged, and a new focus on the US market is underway.

The change from Cooley—the odd player, the maverick, the one that overtly didn't play the game—to the new-look brand-focused Kilbeggan Distilling Company has been remarkable. The former wild boy is now part of the establishment.

What of the changes? "Mr Teeling has a lot to answer for!" jokes master distiller Noel Sweeney. "The attitude across Ireland has changed. Whereas the only people who were doing something different was us, now, as an industry, people are being proactive. There are new products, innovation, and diversification."

There is also a whole new raft of distillers starting out and asking the same questions as John Teeling and the team did in the 1980s: "What is Irish whiskey? What can it become?"

The good old days. Kilbeggan was a famous brand before the great collapse of the twentieth century.

Tullamore D.E.W.

TULLAMORE D.E.W. • WWW.TULLAMOREDEW.COM • OPEN ALL YEAR MON–SUN; SEE WEBSITE FOR DAYS & DETAILS

"Give every man his DEW"—a pun, and not a bad one in the world of drinks, which encapsulated the visions of Daniel Edmund Williams, the general manager (and eventually owner) of the Daly distillery in Tullamore. It was he who improved the distillery in 1887 and used his initials to create a new brand, Tullamore D.E.W., complete with slogan.

Tullamore remained in the Williams family through all the tribulations of the twentieth century, closing for 13 years between 1925 and 1937. The family installed a patent still in 1947 and began making a lighter blend to appeal to a changing American palate. This mix of single-pot still, malt, and grain was innovative for its time, but it was too late. The distillery closed in 1954, when the brand was bought by Powers (in 1994 it was sold to Cantrell & Cochrane) and produced by IDL (*see* p.207) to that original recipe.

So far, so typical. But then, in 2010, the brand was bought by William Grant & Sons, which immediately announced that it would build a distillery. In Tullamore. The whiskey's long-serving brand ambassador is John Quinn, who has been working on the brand since 1974.

"Since the time when C&C bought the brand, there's been talk of distilling, but when Grant's announced that it would happen the hairs stood up on the back of my neck. It's enormous for me, but it's also huge for the town. The sense of pride is incredible." Whiskey gives identity, and purpose. It's not just a drink.

A pot-still distillery (making malt and single-pot still) is operational with a grain plant to be installed in phase two, meaning everything needed for the blend is made on site. "The task is to make the same as we got from Midleton, though out of smaller stills, because consumers need consistency," Quinn says. "It would be exciting to just go and do something completely new, but you can't change the flavor."

There is also the issue of making single-pot still, for decades solely an IDL specialty. "William Grant knows how to make whisky. They have distilleries," is all Quinn will say, but you know there has been plenty of unmalted:malted being run through Scottish stills in anticipation.

The three styles also give the possibility of range extensions down the line. "We certainly couldn't have done that before," he laughs. "Now we can. Watch this space."

TULLAMORE D.E.W. TASTING NOTES

TULLAMORE D.E.W. 40%

Nose: Very fresh and grassy, with jags of lemon and some firm cereal tones. With water, some green olive, grape, and toasted oak.
Palate: Clean. Light to medium-bodied. Fairly firm, with red apple and milk chocolate.
Finish: Lightly acidic.
Conclusion: Fresh and made for drinking long.

Flavor Camp: **Fragrant & Floral**
Where Next? Lot 40

12YO SPECIAL, RESERVE BLEND 40%

Nose: Lush and generous. Fruity and creamy: mango, peach, and vanilla. American oak, toffee, light ginger, and buttered scones.
Palate: Ripe fruits, stewed rhubarb within a light oak frame. Water brings out blackcurrant and more pulped fruits.
Finish: Spicy and tight.
Conclusion: Has complexity among its elements: fruit, crispness, oak.

Flavor Camp: **Fruity & Spicy**

PHOENIX SHERRY FINISH, BLEND 55%

Nose: Mossy. Green fig jam, poached pear. Broad and complex with sherry, liqueur chocolate, blackberry.
Palate: The higher strength adds bite to what might have been too soft. Sherry adds some structure and oxidized nuttiness. Light Seville orange. Curranty.
Finish: Ginger, spice.
Conclusion: Has weight, heft, and class.

Flavor Camp: **Rich & Round**

SINGLE MALT, 10YO 40%

Nose: Fresh and green on the nose: Sauvignon Blanc-style gooseberry (fool), light sugar, and restrained oak. With water there's more tropical fruit, graphite, and some weighty, mature fruitiness.
Palate: Masses of fruit: hedgerow, currants, blueberries. Soft peachiness alongside white raisins. The wood is in check.
Finish: Rounded, long, and gentle.
Conclusion: A cornucopia of fruits.

Flavor Camp: **Fruity & Spicy**
Where Next? Langatun Old Deer

Dingle

DINGLE • WWW.DINGLEDISTILLERY.IE • VISITS BY APPOINTMENT; SEE WEBSITE FOR CONTACT DETAILS

Oliver Hughes, the owner of the Dingle distillery in Ireland's far southwest, is a trailblazer by nature. In 1996, he established Ireland's first brewpub, the Porterhouse, in Dublin's Temple Bar, but it's only been very recently that craft brewing has taken off in Ireland. "Maybe I'm always a bit too far ahead of the curve," he jokes. "Sometimes you feel like a pioneer, but remember: the pioneers got shot by the Indians, and the settlers then took their land!"

Now he's doing it again. Dingle was the first of a large number of new distilleries that are beginning to spring up across Ireland. "Distilling seemed the logical extension to brewing," he says. "There is an obvious demand for Irish whiskey, and having been going to Dingle for 30 years, I knew it as a fantastic location and a part of Ireland with its own identity. It deserved a distillery."

Dreaming about opening a distillery is one thing; making it a going commercial concern is another. The Irish category may be small compared to Scotch, but it has some serious players. "You have to differentiate, that's true," Hughes says. "That means not just in product—we're also making a gin and a vodka—but in the style of whiskey we're producing.

"When we started, I had several long discussions with our consultant, John McDougall, in various pubs in the peninsula. It was he who told me that as Irish whiskey tends to be sweeter than Scotch, we'd need boiling bulbs on our stills. Everything has been designed to produce specific flavors."

That flavor, for Hughes, means a whiskey with "a luxurious feel to it." As a result, when the first casks of whiskey were filled on December 18, 2012, there was a high percentage of ex-sherry and ex-port being used.

An exploration of this extreme westerly location is also starting. "I'd like to mature in different spots within the peninsula and outlying islands," Hughes explains, "and I've got other special releases planned."

Does having a craft-brewer's mentality help? "Yes, because you have to be innovative there as well. We did a 11% stout aged in whiskey barrels, so I'd like to take the same barrels and age whiskey in them again. I use different malts for stout, so what happens if I distill with them? Dark malts could be very interesting."

Dingle is set to be joined by any number of new plants. Kentucky-based Alltech has distilled in Carlow but is relocating to Dublin; the Teeling family has bought the ex-Heineken brewery in Dundalk and are planning a grain-and-malt plant there and a micro-site in Dublin; while a distillery is also on the way for Slane Castle.

The change in Ireland is quite remarkable.

Craft distilling in the Republic of Ireland started here, in Dingle.

DINGLE TASTING NOTES

NEW MAKE

Nose: Immensely sweet, with a custard element. Apple crisp and raspberry leaf. A little cereal with water.
Palate: Very fruity, then roasted cereal. Has guts, with an assertive feel. The butteriness remains.
Finish: Ripe fruits.

BOURBON CASK SAMPLE 62.1%

Nose: Immediate vanilla uptake. Caramel pudding. The sweet raspberry fruit is still there alongside banana notes.
Palate: A light cask influence brigs the citric top notes into play. Light and clean. Sweet.
Finish: Tight and green.
Conclusion: Clean, well-made, and quite precocious.

PORT CASK SAMPLE 61.5%

Nose: Redcurrant bush and leaf. Supple. In time, lots of cranberry and raspberry juice. Aromatic with water.
Palate: Berries, with that cranberry crunchiness. A hint of earthiness (maybe the oak). Delicate.
Finish: Young, fresh, and acidic.
Conclusion: The cask is giving plenty to the spirit, but it has the guts to cope. A distillery to watch.

IDL & West Cork Distillers

MIDLETON • WWW.JAMESONWHISKEY.COM/UK/TOURS/JAMESONEXPERIENCE • OPEN ALL YEAR MON–SUN; SEE WEBSITE FOR DAYS & DETAILS
WEST CORK DISTILLERS • SKIBBERREEN • WWW.WESTCORKDISTILLERS.COM

Whiskey and County Cork go together. The city remains home to some remarkable drinking dens, where you settle in for a long evening of good *craic* (loosely translates as "fun"), accompanied by any number of glasses of whiskey, washed down with fine, craft-brewed stout. It's a city that also has a great whiskey-making tradition. In 1867, four of its plants (North Mall, Watercourse, John Street, and The Green) merged with nearby Midleton to form Cork Distilleries Company (CDC). It was the last of these that would eventually become the country's focal point for whiskey-making.

The Old Midleton distillery was built on a colossal scale. Originally a woolen mill, it was bought by the enterprising Murphy brothers in 1825, and they invested heavily; soon, they were muscling their CDC colleagues out of the way. The reason? Quality and volume. By 1887, Midleton was producing a million gallons a year and had the largest pot-still in the world.

In the 1970s, when IDL (Irish Distillers Ltd) closed its last two Dublin plants (John's Lane and Bow Street), production switched to Midleton. Here is where the whiskeys that were to save Irish whiskey would be made. In 1975, IDL's new high-tech distillery opened in the fields behind the old site.

What happened at Midleton was a forensic examination of what IDL's whiskeys were—and what they could be. On one hand, the firm had to preserve the specific recipes and distillates that made up their brands. On the other, they now had a new distillery with infinite possibilities of creating new distillates.

Yes, the past had to be preserved in the guise of single pot-still whiskey, but this was also a time of creative possibilities, allied to an enlightened wood policy. At a time when the Scotch industry was still

IRISH INNOVATION: WEST CORK DISTILLERS

In 2013, the county's second distillery started producing. West Cork Distillers, located in Ireland's most southerly town, Skibbereen, is set up to produce a wide range of spirits, many under contract to bottlers to help with cashflow. A double-distilled single malt made in Holstein stills is being laid down as well, while they are also blending and bottling bought-in mature stock under the expert eye of Dr. Barry Walsh, IDL's former master blender. In co-owner, John O'Connell, whose previous career involved working for Kerry and Unilever, they have a man who sees the possibilities of using different yeasts and technology to establish a point of difference. "We have to innovate," he says. "One of the reasons for Irish whiskey's collapse in the twentieth century was a refusal to do that. We can't make the same mistake again."

of a mind that if the wood came from a tree, it would be okay, IDL was embarking on a bespoke-cask program.

Whiskey takes time. It had to be done patiently. And so, quietly, Barry Crockett, Barry Walsh, Brendan Monks, Dave Quinn, Billy Leighton, and others worked away. The new distillery could be

"New" Midleton is one of the whiskey world's most remarkable distilleries. Created out of a spirit of adversity, it kept the Irish-whiskey flag flying.

Masters of wood. IDL pioneered many approaches in wood management now accepted as the norm in the world of whisky.

glimpsed behind locked gates as you toured the atmospheric buildings of Old Midleton. The talk was of the golden age, the tour of a silent plant, when, in the next field, Irish whiskey's future was being crafted.

Now the fruits of those long years are being shared and, after a €100m ($136m) investment by owner Pernod-Ricard, those gates have been opened. Today we can see the new brewhouse, pot-stillhouse, and grain distillery that have upped Midleton's production capacity to a scarcely believable 16 million gallons (60 million liters) a year.

The pot-stills sit behind a huge panoramic window, the path leading from there back to the old site. The pieces have been joined, the past and present linked. Now, for the future.

To most drinkers around the world, Irish whiskey equals Jameson. The reformulation of the brand in 1972 as a new, light blend was the start of a long process, with the aim of nothing less than saving the style. To do that it had to change. This was no abandonment of principles, but a sensible repositioning of Irish whiskey in a global market that had turned away from heavy styles. If the world palate had altered, then there was little sense in trying to force people to drink single-pot still. Frustrating though it was for those of us who loved Power's, Green Spot, Crested Ten, and Redbreast, the single-brand strategy paid off. Long-term consistent advertising and steady backing turned Jameson from being a specialty into a global brand.

The key in its creation was finding a way in which to work with the possibilities the new Midleton distillery had opened up. The lauter mash tun gave clearer wort, meaning more estery notes could be enhanced. Single pot-still could now be made in different "weights," but for the new blend they also needed a light, clean, and aromatic grain; the new three-column setup provided that. Once again, grain is the secret weapon.

Then, slowly, the Jameson family began to grow and, with each addition, the palate weight increased. More single pot was in these older variants, as well as different woods: virgin oak for Gold; port pipes in Vintage; bespoke American casks for Select. Jameson was now also a bridge to single pot-still.

If it was aimed at the global palate, then the Irish one had remained true to Power's. This old Dublin brand has a higher percentage of single pot-still to standard Jameson (and less first-fill oak), and is a fatter, juicier, more hedonistic experience as a result. In Cork, people remained true to the local blend Paddy, named in honor of CDC's top salesman, Paddy Flaherty, who would go into pubs and buy everyone a drink of "his" whiskey. Soon everyone was clamoring for "a glass of Paddy's." The irony is he spent so much buying the whiskey that he never earned a bonus.

"We had to experiment," said Barry Crockett about the early days of Midleton. I disagree. They didn't *have* to; they wanted to. In doing so they laid the foundations for a new Irish whiskey market.

SINGLE POT-STILL

The beating heart of all of the new IDL blends remained single pot-still, the whiskey style that acts as a liquid barometer for Irish whiskey's fortunes (see p.17 for production details). Although Irish and Scottish distillers had been mixing malted and unmalted barley together for many years as well as rye and oats it was in 1852 that the style became formalized—the result of Ireland's large city distillers trying to avoid the high tax being levied on malted barley.

Changing the mash bill in this way meant a significant shift in flavor profile. The use of unmalted barley added an oiliness to the texture, a juicily thick quality, and a spicy, crisp finish. This was the whiskey style that made Irish. In fact, up until the 1950s, this was Irish whiskey.

The launches of new Jameson, and prior to that Tullamore D.E.W., were both attempts to get away from a type of whiskey that was deemed too heavy for the modern drinker.

Whiskey-lovers disagreed, but for years it was hard to get hold of. There would be sightings of Redbreast (originally made by Jameson for Gilbey's) or Green Spot (made by the same firm for Mitchell's of Dublin), or they would seek solace in the heavier pot-still blends like Crested Ten or Powers.

The style was still being made, however. Or rather, the *styles*, given that Midleton doesn't make single pot-still; it makes single pot-*stills*: a range of variations on the template of mouth-coating texture, apple, spice, and blackcurrant notes. By varying the mash bill and distillation regimes—fill levels, strength of distillate, cut points—four styles are produced: light, two medium (or "mod pot"), and one heavy. Add in different cask types from a wood regime that was the first in the world to use bespoke casks, and the possibilities widen, with new textures, flavor, and intensities being created. All were being fed into the growing IDL blend families.

Then in 2011 it all changed. Redbreast and a repackaged Green Spot were joined by Powers' John's Lane and Barry Crockett Legacy. Since then, two new Redbreast variants and Yellow Spot have been added; with the promise of at least one new release a year for the next decade. With this, the foundations of the Irish renaissance were complete.

This is an addictive style. It is seductive, asks you to linger, whispers "Just one more glass" in your ear. You succumb. Who couldn't?

IDL & WEST CORK DISTILLERS TASTING NOTES

JAMESON ORIGINAL, BLEND 40%

Nose: Full gold. Highly scented. Herbs, hot earth, amber, scented wood, and caramelized apple sugars. Mead-like. Fresh and zesty.

Palate: Soft with lots of vanilla. Succulent mid-palate then starts to dry, becoming slightly finer. The spices begin to creep in.

Finish: Cumin. Balsawood. Clean.

Conclusion: Balanced and aromatic.

Flavor Camp: Fragrant & Floral

JAMESON 12YO, BLEND 40%

Nose: Less perfumed than the "standard" with more honey, some sultana, toffee, and butterscotch. Cooked apple. Dried herbs and hot sawdust.

Palate: Juicier and fuller than standard with more coconut, vanilla, and a hint of dried fruit concentration. Succulent. Little hint of camphor.

Finish: Allspice.

Conclusion: More pot still adding weight and feel.

Flavor Camp: Fruity & Spicy

JAMESON 18YO, BLEND 40%

Nose: Full gold. Little closed to start but then heavier pot still begins to develop. The most polished and oiliest (linseed oil) of the trio. Some resin but also that lifted note now gone into dried herbs.

Palate: Chewy and full with more sherried notes. Raisin rather than sultana. With water, sweet gingerbread.

Finish: Again it's spicy, this time mace along with chestnut honey.

Conclusion: A clear family resemblance but a weightier proposition.

Flavor Camp: Rich & Round

POWERS 12YO, BLEND 46%

Nose: Big, succulent, blossom-like. More peachy. More freshly fruited and generally fatter than Jameson.

Palate: Massive shot of banana milkshake sweetened with peach nectar and honey. Thick texture before a cashew/pistachio note. Mouthfilling.

Finish: Ripe then coriander and turmeric.

Conclusion: Unctuous.

Flavor Camp: Fruity & Spicy

REDBREAST 12YO 40%

Nose: Rich, soft fruits. Supple and light, with wet chamois, cake mix, ginger, and tobacco. Nuttiness behind and a hint of custard powder before moving into currant leaf.

Palate: Clean. Cigar and black fruits, but fresh, light pot gives drive. Tongue-coating, with great presence.

Finish: Dry spices.

Conclusion: The benchmark single pot still.

Flavor Camp: Rich & Round
Where Next? Balcones Straight Malt

REDBREAST 15YO, 100% POT STILL 46%

Nose: Huge. Autumn fruits (red & black). Toffee and light leather, sandalwood, pollen. Polished oak. Rich.

Palate: Fat and rounded. Chamois leather then masses of spice. Layered effect of cumin, ginger, mixing with new leather, dried fruit, baked apple. Complex.

Finish: Long ripe, throat-clinging.

Conclusion: Like Jameson on steroids. Classic pot still.

Flavor Camp: Rich & Round
Where Next? Old Pulteney 17yo

POWERS JOHN LANE'S 46%

Nose: Fuller than Redbreast, with more overt oiliness alongside pepper, leather, and old rose petals. Chocolate-covered morello cherries alongside tanned hides, and a mix of sandalwood, humidor, and blackcurrant.

Palate: Ripe, fat, and oily with classic Powers peachiness (and some mango and passion fruit). Rich, unctuous, and deep with real boldness of character.

Finish: Coriander seed. Earthy dryness.

Conclusion: Mouth-coating and thick.

Flavor Camp: Fruity & Spicy
Where Next? Collingwood 21yo

GREEN SPOT 40%

Nose: Lively and sweet. Hint of oil immediately with light apple skin, pear, dried apricot, and banana chips. Touches of sweet oak.

Palate: Fresh start. Softens into currant, clove, and fennel. Becomes spicier with water. Sesame and rapeseed oils, then whitecurrant.

Finish: Curry leaves and star anise.

Conclusion: The lightest example.

Flavor Camp: Fruity & Spicy
Where Next? Wiser's Legacy

MIDLETON BARRY CROCKETT LEGACY 46%

Nose: Honey, sweet hazelnut, and fresh barley. Light hint of lime, grass, currant leaf, green mango, conference pear, vanilla, oak.

Palate: Silky, relaxed, and honeyed. Bergamot and fresh citrus to start. There's a mellow mid-palate, then big cardamom and nutmeg.

Finish: Long, with some coconut oak and black fruits.

Conclusion: Restrained and elegant.

Flavor Camp: Fruity & Spicy
Where Next? Miyagikyo 15yo

JAPAN

On a visit to Karuizawa distillery I saw a poster of a fierce-looking man, with pebble-thick glasses and jutting goatee beard. It turned out to be the *haiku* poet, Santoka. It was the perfect synchronicity. Santoka famously liked a drink and what is *haiku* if not a distillation of words into the essence of experience? Or, in Santoka's words, tapping "the deep breath of life." Whisky is a *haiku*. Its creation is concerned with the concentration of flavor, but behind its technical aspects it is a manifestation of a wider culture.

Though it is impossible for any *gaijin* (non-Japanese) to understand Japanese culture fully, some appreciation of the Japanese sensibility does make the creative processes behind its whiskies a little more understandable. Japan's whisky history has taken on the gloss of a folktale. The arrival of western spirits in the form of a case of Old Parr brought back in 1872 by the Iwakura trade mission; the subsequent creation of imitation foreign spirits in Japanese laboratories; the founding of Kotobukiya by the young Shinjiro Torii in 1899; the sending of young chemistry student Masataka Taketsuru to Glasgow to study chemistry in 1918; Taketsuru's seduction by Scotland. Add to that his marriage to Rita Cowan, his apprenticeships at Hazelburn and Longmorn; his subsequent hiring by Torii-san, who was by then casting around for a Japanese distiller for Japan's first dedicated whisky distillery at Yamazaki in 1923; how they worked together and then split: Torii founding Suntory, Taketsuru founding Nikka, which remain the two pillars of whisky-making in Japan.

There is an assumption that, because the Japanese have adhered to the Scottish template of whisky-making, their whisky is a copy. Nothing could be further from the truth. From the outset, the aim was to create a Japanese style. It's also widely believed that these are technological whiskies, disconnected from the land. Again, this belief is fundamentally wrong.

Yes, Japanese whiskymakers initially turned to science. What else were they to do? Wait for 200 years to build up a residue of folk wisdom? When Shinjiro Torii built the country's first dedicated whisky distillery, Yamazaki, in 1923, he and his distiller, Masataka Taketsuru, were starting from scratch. They were both visionaries whose companies, Suntory and Nikka, continue to dominate Japnese distilling, but their dreams were grounded in science.

But while Japanese whisky may have been born from research, it has evolved in the fashion it has because the influence of Japan the country came into play: its climate, its economics, its food, its culture, its psychology—a need for release after a day's work. These were (and remain) whiskies crafted to suit Japanese sensibilities.

Japanese whisky isn't necessarily lighter, but it possesses a heightened clarity of aroma. The absence of a cereal background note also differentiates it from Scotch, as does the use of the intensely aromatic Japanese oak. If Scottish single malt is a rushing mountain *burn* (watercourse), with all the flavors jostling for position, Japanese malt is a limpid pool where all is revealed.

Its creation is concerned with the concentration of flavor, but behind its technical aspects it is a manifestation of a wider culture. Though it is impossible for any *gaijin* to understand fully Japanese culture, the more I look at these whiskies the deeper the connection with a Japanese aesthetic becomes.

Japanese art, poetry, ceramics, design, and cuisine all share a purity and apparent simplicity. This underlying principle is called *shibusa*, an object that is simple, understated, yet deep and natural. Japanese whisky's "transparency" shows *shibusa*, and I don't think it's a coincidence.

Shibusa is closely linked to a deeper concept called *wabi-sabi*, which also reveres simplicity and naturalness, but praises the imperfections within things as being that which makes them beautiful. As Leonard Cohen sang, "There is a crack in everything, that's how the light gets in."

Where is whisky in this? Distillation is the technique of capturing an essence (a spirit), but not to the point of neutrality. Whisky has impurities. That's what its flavors are. It is these "flaws" that make whisky so compelling. They are its *wabi-sabi*.

These ideas are so deeply engrained in Japanese aesthetics that they become subconscious, but I believe they are behind the crafting of the Japanese style. In the deepest sense, Japan made these whiskies and that is a model for all new distillers.

As a result, Japanese whisky's emergence into Western markets has resulted in its style, methods, and flavors being rightly revered. And yet, of all the nations in this book, Japan is the only country not to have increased the number of its distilleries.

Suntory, Nikka, and tiny Chichibu are all in export, but Karuizawa and Hanyu's stocks will soon have gone. Eigashima only makes whisky for two months a year; Gotemba is virtually invisible, even in Japan; and Mars has only recently restarted. Japan desperately needs new distilleries. Only one in Okayama Prefecture has opened recently.

The world is moving fast. Japan's influence could easily wane.

Cool, calm, collected—yet also enigmatic. The world is now unraveling the secrets of Japanese whisky.

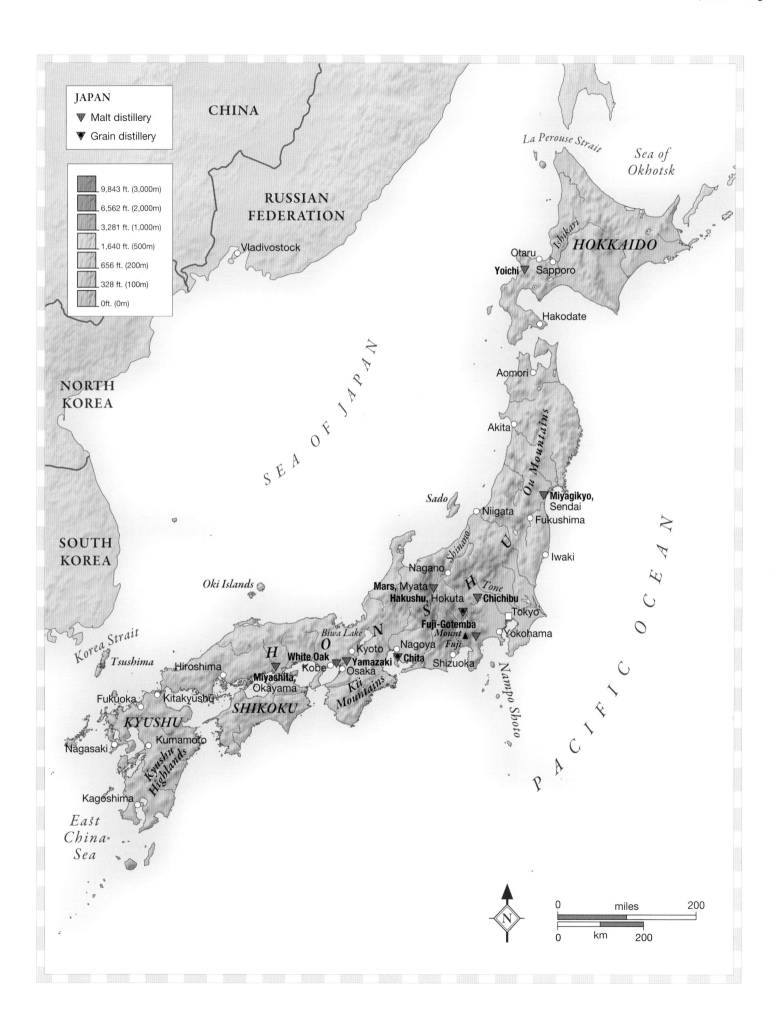

CHINA

RUSSIAN
FEDERATION

Vladivostock

NORTH
KOREA

SOUTH
KOREA

SEA OF JAPAN

Korea Strait

Tsushima

Hiroshima

Fukuoka
Kitakyushu

KYUSHU

Nagasaki
Kumamoto

*Kyushu
Highlands*

Kagoshima

*East
China
Sea*

La Perouse Strait

*Sea of
Okhotsk*

Ishikari
HOKKAIDO

Otaru
Yoichi ▼ Sapporo

Hakodate

Aomori

Akita

Ou Mountains

▼ **Miyagikyo,**
Sendai
Fukushima

Iwaki

Sado
Niigata

Shinano

Nagano

U

H *Tone*

Mars, Myata ▼ **Chichibu**
Hakushu, Hokuta
Tokyo

S

Fuji-Gotemba Yokohama

*Mount
Fuji* ▲ ▼

N

Nagoya

O Kyoto ▼ **Chita** Shizuoka

Biwa Lake

H **White Oak** Kobe **Yamazaki**
Osaka

Miyashita,
Okayama

SHIKOKU *Kii
Mountains*

Nampo Shoto

PACIFIC OCEAN

Oki Islands

N

0 — miles — 200
0 — km — 200

Yamazaki

OSAKA • WWW.THEYAMAZAKI.JP/EN/DISTILLERY/MUSEUM.HTML • OPEN ALL YEAR; SEE WEBSITE FOR DAYS & DETAILS

It starts here, next to the old road that linked Kyoto with the port of Osaka, across the railway where today bullet trains hurtle; a place of stifling summer humidity and winter chill. This is Yamazaki. Torii-san chose to build here in 1923 for a number of reasons. It made shrewd commercial sense to be situated between two important markets with good transportation links, and it was the meeting place of three rivers, meaning a plentiful supply of water. There's a deeper resonance, however. This was where Sen Rikyu, the sixteenth-century creator of what we know as the tea ceremony, built his first tea house because (some believe), of the water quality. This is more than just a convenient bit of flat land beside the railway tracks.

Yet this rootedness doesn't mean it is hog-tied by the past. Japanese distillers have an almost alarming willingness to scrap the old and start afresh. Yamazaki has been rebuilt three times, most recently in 2005. In this last renovation, the stillhouse was totally refitted, the stills replaced by smaller models, direct fire brought back in (naked flames at the base), and the styles changed. Note the plural. When you try to understand Japanese whisky it is wise to put Scotland to the back of your mind. The creation of styles is another example of Japan's fusing of the pragmatic and the creative.

Scotland has 118 malt distilleries, allowing its blenders to draw from a huge variety of styles that they exchange with one another. In Japan the Big Two (Suntory and Nikka) have four malt plants between them—and they don't exchange. If they want a variety of whiskies for their blends then they have to make them on site.

Yamazaki has two mash tuns, mashing low and heavily peated barley, giving startlingly clear wort (hence the lack of cereal notes in the spirit) that's fermented with a mix of two yeasts in either wooden (considered better for longer flavor-generating lactic fermentation) or steel washbacks. It's the stillhouse that takes the first-time visitor by surprise: eight pairs of stills, all different shapes and sizes. All the wash stills are direct-fired and one has a worm tub. Aging is in five different types of cask: sherry (American and European oak), ex-bourbon, new, and Japanese oak.

Located across the tracks from the ancient road between Kyoto and Osaka, Yamazaki was Japan's first purpose-built whisky distillery.

This allows a different approach to single malt. In Scotland, each distillery will tend to produce one style, meaning that the difference between an 18-year-old and a 15-year-old is, in simple terms, three years plus any tunes you play with wood. At Yamazaki, the constituent

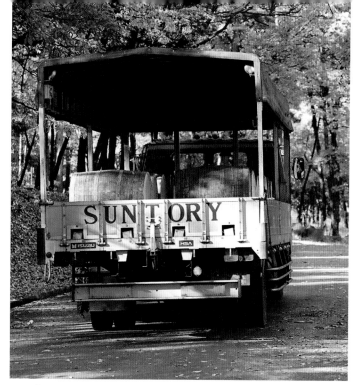

Going for a spin. A new maturation technique—or the result of the large scale of the distillery?

Multiple styles of whisky are made at Yamazaki.

parts of each age expression are diferent: Yamazaki 18yo isn't just six years older than the 12yo, it's made up of different whisky types, all of which are married together for six months prior to bottling.

What is fascinating, however, is that, for all its diversity, there is a unifying character to Yamazaki, a moment when the whisky dips and holds in the center of the tongue, when the fruit comes through. It can cope with the boldness of sherry and the incense-scented *mizunara* (Japanese oak), whose intense, acidic character acts as a counterpoint to the richness of the spirit. Thus it embodies the arc

of Japanese whisky's life: from its early days when Shinjiro Torii and his successors were searching for lightness to suit the needs of the Japanese consumer, to the new malt-centric consumer who wants more character.

For all its technological innovations (and there are many more hidden from sight), Yamazaki remains a place of tranquillity, a place where this Japanese fusion of opposing elements (which in the West might seem diametrically opposed)—the modern with the ancient, intuition and science—appears perfectly natural.

YAMAZAKI TASTING NOTES

NEW MAKE, MEDIUM STYLE

Nose: Gentle, sweet, fruity with heavy florals (lily) apple, strawberry.
Palate: Rounded, with the "Yamazaki dip" mid-palate (*see* main text). Fruity with a spicy edge. Vibrant.
Finish: Smooth and long.

NEW MAKE, HEAVY STYLE

Nose: Deep and rich with very light vegetable notes. Rich fruit.
Palate: Chewy and full, with a big vanilla hit. Clinging and ripe. Thick with hints of smoke.
Finish: A little closed.

NEW MAKE, HEAVY PEATED STYLE

Nose: Clean. Iris and artichoke. Smoke is solid and fragrant.
Palate: Sweet and thick (the dominating characters). Smoke confined mostly to the back palate. Beach bonfire.
Finish: Spiced.

10YO 40%

Nose: Light gold. Fresh with more of the spicy aspects on show. Toasty oak. Estery.
Palate: Clean and zesty, light citrus fruit, hint of *tatami* (Japanese reed mats). Green fruits.
Finish: Soft, then crisps up.
Conclusion: Delicate and clean. Suited to *soda-wari* style (on the rocks with soda). Spring-like.

Flavor Camp: **Fragrant & Floral**
Where Next? Linkwood 12yo, Strathmill 12yo

12YO 43%

Nose: Gold. The fruit begining to show. Ripe melon. Pineapple, grapefruit, and also some of the floral notes. The hint of *tatami* and a little dried fruit.
Palate: Sweet fruit. Has a succulent feel; syrupy, mid-apricot, and a hint of vanilla.
Finish: Lightly smoked with the dried fruit continuing.
Conclusion: Medium-bodied but packed with character. Summery.

Flavor Camp: **Fruity & Spicy**
Where Next? Longmorn 16yo, Royal Lochnagar 12yo

18YO 43%

Nose: Light amber. Autumn fruit. Ripened apples, semi-dried peach, raisin. Light leaf mulch. Little more smoke. Florals now deepened. More perfumed.
Palate: Woods. Fuller sherry notes, walnut, and damson. Lightly mossy. Still clings to the center of the tongue. Complex.
Finish: Sweet oak. Rich.
Conclusion: A further and deeper journey into the woods. Autumnal.

Flavor Camp: **Rich & Round**
Where Next? Highland Park 18yo, Glengoyne 17yo

THE
YAMAZAKI
SINGLE MALT
WHISKY
AGED **12** YEARS
The oldest distillery in Japan
YAMAZAKI DISTILLERY
PRODUCED BY SUNTORY
PRODUCT OF JAPAN
ウイスキー

山崎

"YAMAZAKI"

Hakushu

HOKUTO CITY • WWW.SUNTORY.CO.JP/FACTORY/HAKUSHU/GUIDE • OPEN ALL YEAR; HIT "ENGLISH" TAB FOR TOUR DAYS & DETAILS

There's a cool breeze blowing through the pines that stretch far up the granite slopes of Mount Kaikomagatake in the southern Japanese Alps. Dotted between the trees are warehouses and distillery buildings, although it is hard to comprehend the size of Suntory's Hakushu distillery until you climb to the air bridge: the glass corridor linking the two tower tops in its museum. This is a vast site—part national park, part distillery complex—that still holds upward of 450,000 casks. An indication of the scale of Japanese distillers' ambition in the 1970s when a booming economy, and a seemingly insatiable thirst for (blended) whisky led to the building of what, for a period of time, was the world's largest malt distillery.

It was water that led Suntory here. Soft mountain spring water (which the firm now bottles) in sufficient quantities to match the company's grand vision. Unfortunately, however, it wasn't to be. Japan's whisky boom ended in the early 1990s when the Asian financial crisis started the deflation through which the country continues to walk, zombie-like.

A clear manifestation of the effects of this decline in whisky's fortunes lies behind a pair of vast iron doors in the West distillery. Head blender Shinji Fukuyo pushes them open and we enter a chill mausoleum. Dwarfed by massive copper pots he speaks of how this distillery was making 7,925,161 gallons (30 million liters) of spirit a year from two stillhouses: East and West.

Now, production has shifted to the East site and has been reduced by one-third. Just as at Yamazaki, the vagaries of the market have resulted in Hakushu changing itself, with the biggest refit taking place in 1983. Before its closure, Fukuyo had experimented in the West site. One of the stills has a flat top. "Oh yes, I did that," he says blithely. "I wanted to make a different style so thought I'd see what would happen." It's very typical of the dramatic changes that Japanese distillers make, seemingly without a second thought.

If anything, Hakushu is even more radical than Yamazaki. Here, four types of barley, from unpeated to heavy peated, are used, and the clear wort is given a long ferment in wooden fermenters using a mix of distiller's and brewer's yeasts. "Wooden fermenters and the brewer's yeast help to encourage lactic bacteria," says Fukuyo. "It's this that helps to produce esters and a creaminess to the spirit." Or to be accurate, spirits. There are six pairs of direct-fired, golden-sheened stills in a mind-boggling variety of shapes and sizes: tall, fat, thin, minuscule; lyne

An almost obsessive control of wood is key to Japanese whisky's quality. **Left:** here a cask is recharred. **Right:** a sample is about to be drawn.

Idyllic location. Hakushu is situated in a nature reserve in the Japanese Alps.

arms go up, down, and can be detached and diverted into worm tubs or condensers. The permutations are baffling, but again as with Yamazaki, there seems to be a coherence to the variations in spirit type.

Hakushu, even in its heaviest and peatiest expression, has a focus and directness that sets it apart from Yamazaki's depth. In its youth it seems to encapsulate directly its location, a single malt that's filled with a green, leafy character: wet bamboo, fresh moss after rain, and, yes, that creaminess that is partly from the preference for American oak casks here and conceivably from this longer fermentation regime. The peat is there but almost as an afterthought.

The Hakushu style could also conceivably come from the ambient temperature. "Here the temperature range goes from 39–72°F (4–22°C)," says Fukuyo. "At Yamazaki it's between 50–81°F (10–27°C) and with greater humidity in summer." The pine-fresh 10yo gives no indication that Hakushu has the capability of extended aging. The 25yo is heavier, peatier, too, but always with this pebble-fresh directness and a touch of cool mint that ripples through, like the wind in the pines.

In 2010 a column-still was installed at the distillery, initially for experimental purposes. Corn has mainly been used but there have been trials with other grains, including wheat and barley.

HAKUSHU TASTING NOTES

NEW MAKE, LIGHTLY PEATED
Nose: Very clean. Cucumber, fruit chew. Touch of grassiness, white pear, plantain. Smoke, very subtle.
Palate: Sweet and intense. Green melon. High acidity. Fresh. The smoke drifts in the background…
Finish: … then comes through on the finish.

NEW MAKE, HEAVY PEAT
Nose: Robust and firm with a touch of nuttiness. Less "foggy" than Scottish peatiness. More clarity and lightly scented. Wet grass and lemon.
Palate: Zesty and citric with building smoke.
Finish: Recedes gently.

12YO 43.5%
Nose: Straw. Cool and green and lightly perfumed. Grassy and lightly floral, touch of pine and sage. Green banana.
Palate: Smooth and silky with a little mintiness and green apple. Bamboo and wet moss. Lime and camomile.
Finish: The merest touch of smoke.
Conclusion: Fresh and seemingly delicate but has substance. Focused.

> **Flavor Camp: Fragrant & Floral**
> **Where Next?** Teaninich 10yo, anCnoc 16yo

18YO 43.5%
Nose: Gold. Cookie-like with ginger and almond/marzipan. Lightly waxy, plums, and sweet hay. Marzipan, green grass, green apple. Currant leaf.
Palate: Medium bodied and clean (again, good acidity). Mango, ripe honeydew melon. Grassy still. Delicate wood smoke and toasty oak.
Finish: Clean and lightly smoky.
Conclusion: Poised. Still discrete with a little more smoke.

> **Flavor Camp: Fragrant & Floral**
> **Where Next?** Miltonduff 18yo

25YO 43%
Nose: Amber. Intense with lots of dried fruit and waxed furniture. Lightly caramelized fruits. Baked apple, white raisin, ferny/moss, and mushroom. Dried mint and smoke.
Palate: Big, ripe, and generous with the broadest spread of the range. Vinous and silky with light tannin. Praline.
Finish: Smoke drifts through the wood.
Conclusion: Bold, but still has the fresh acidity that typifies the distillery.

> **Flavor Camp: Rich & Round**
> **Where Next?** Highland Park 25yo, Glencadam 1978

THE CASK OF HAKUSHU, HEAVY PEAT 61%
Nose: Golden. Intense and appetizing with an ozone-like freshness. Carnation, scallion with smoke building in the background, released fully by water. Retains aromatics. Fleshy fruit and moist peat.
Palate: Equally intense—partly the alcohol, partly the distillery. Spreads across the tongue. Melon and huge smoke.
Finish: Green and long.
Conclusion: Balanced and typically idiosyncratic.

> **Flavor Camp: Smoky & Peaty**
> **Where Next?** Ardmore 25yo

Miyagikyo

SENDAI • WWW.NIKKA.COM/ENG/DISTILLERIES/MIYAGIKYO/INDEX.HTML • OPEN ALL YEAR; NO ENGLISH TOURS AVAILABLE

The first of Nikka's two malt distilleries lies in the northeast of Honshu, around 45 minutes west of the city of Sendai. This is a place of twisting roads and gnarled maple-covered hills, one of those secret parts of Japan that the stranger rarely visits. Hot water gushes from the earth, discreet old *onsen* (hot springs) are dotted around in the mountain valleys. Contrary to some reports, the distillery was not affected by the Tohoku tsunami disaster, or the subsequent fallout from the Fukushima nuclear plant.

Once again, water looms large in the story of the distillery's founding. By the late 1960s, Masataka Taketsuru, the legendary co-founder of Japanese whisky who had created Nikka in the 1930s, wanted another distillery site. If his first search had led him directly to the cold north (*see* Yoichi, p.224), this time the whole of Japan was considered as having potential. Company legend has it that it took him three years of traveling to find this spot in the Miyagi Valley (*Miyagikyo*) where the Nikkawa and Hirose rivers meet. He walked onto the rounded gray pebbles of the riverbank, drank the water, and pronounced it good. In 1969, the Sendai distillery was in production.

Taketsuru's concern about water quality is not unusual among distillers. Although water may not have a direct impact on flavor, distilleries need it in plentiful quantities, at the right temperature (cold), and the mineral content can have an effect on fermentation. When Taketsuru started his apprenticeship at Longmorn distillery in 1919 (*see* p.87), two of his 13 initial questions to his manager concerned water. After discovering the distillery's water source, he asked, "Have you ever analyzed the water?" The answer was in the negative. He then asked if there were any distilleries in Scotland where a microscope was used. The answer was, "I don't think so." One can guarantee that once he tasted Miyagikyo's water he also had it analyzed. Things are not left to chance these days.

Miyagikyo has subsequently been expanded twice and makes spirit in a malt and a grain plant. The malt side conforms to the Japanese multiple-stream approach to whisky-making, though the Nikka technique is different to Suntory's.

Mostly unpeated barley is used, but medium and occasionally heavy peat is also processed into either clear (mostly) or cloudy wort. The fermentation is with a combination of various different yeast types. The stills are all the same shape: large capacity with fat bottoms, a boil bulb, and fat necks—similar, in fact, to Longmorn's.

In a landscape of blunted hills, forests, and hot springs, the Miyagi Valley was chosen for the quality of its water.

When tasting Miyagikyo, Taketsuru's intentions become clear. At Yoichi, he created a heavy, smoky, richly textured single malt. Here, lightness of touch was the key. If Yoichi is a winter whisky, all smoke and leather armchairs, Miyagikyo is filled with the fruits of late summer. Here's the balance in the portfolio, the new element for the blends. The grain plant adds the final element and is further evidence of the way in which Japanese distillers, while always investigating new techniques, have retained those elements of the past that work.

As well as a modern column-still, it houses a pair of Glasgow-built Coffey stills that produce three different types of grain spirit: corn only, a corn/malted barley mix, and an all malt distillate. The last, which is bottled in small quantities as "Coffey Malt," has been (rightly) hailed for its quality—and also as a typical example of Japanese innovation. In fact, Coffey Malt was widely made across Scotland at the time when Taketsuru was studying. Maybe it was simply another technique he stored away waiting for the right moment … and the right location; maybe a place where crimson autumn leaves dance in the eddies of the river and children's shrieks of pleasure rise in the crisp air.

The four distinct seasons have their own influence on the way Miyagikyo evolves in the cask.

MIYAGIKYO TASTING NOTES

15YO 45%

Nose: Full gold. Soft and sweet. Lots of runny toffee, milk chocolate, and ripe persimmon.
Palate: The gentle and lifted character of the 10yo now given a little more peachy depth and spin with a touch of sherried elements. Light raisin, touch of pine again.
Finish: Long and fruity.
Conclusion: Sweet and easy drinking.

Flavor Camp: Fruity & Spicy
Where Next? Longmorn 10yo

1990, 18YO SINGLE CASK 61%

Nose: Oolong tea, preserved lemon, light, and clean. Hard caramel, then comes strawberries, oak lactone, little hint of oiliness. With water, it's chocolate cookies, fragrant oak.
Palate: Immediate and direct. Quite fat, jammy, and tongue-coating. Builds steadily to the back palate. Stewed apples and white currants. Opens into thyme, citrus fruit. Slightly acidic.
Finish: Lightly oaky.
Conclusion: Has a lovely pooling effect on the palate.

Flavor Camp: Fruity & Spicy
Where Next? Balblair 1990, Mannochmore 18yo

NIKKA SINGLE CASK COFFEY MALT 45%

Nose: Suntan lotion, latté. Macadamia nuts. Sweet with ripe tropical fruit. In time, fragrant wood and shoe leather. Water brings out a lightly floral touch alongside caramelized fruit sugars. Balanced with some complexity.
Palate: Almost creamy to start, then flambéed banana and white chocolate.
Finish: Long and unctuous.
Conclusion: Highly individual.

Flavor Camp: Fruity & Spicy
Where Next? Crown Royal

Karuizawa & Fuji-Gotemba

KARUIZAWA • NAGANO • WWW.ONE-DRINKS.COM
FUJI-GOTEMBA • MT FUJI • WWW.KIRIN.CO.JP/BRANDS/SW/GOTEMBA/INDEX.HTML • OPEN ALL YEAR; ENGLISH TOURS ON REQUEST

Karuizawa is a small, very chic, town which sits at an elevation of 2,625 feet (800 meters) in Nagano Prefecture. It has enjoyed a charmed life: from the seventeenth to nineteenth century as a post town on the Nakasendo Way, which ran between Kyoto and Edo; then as a refuge for Christian missionaries; as a spa for Japan's elite; now as a ski resort and home to top-end *onsen* (hot spas). Above it smolders Mount Asama, Japan's most active volcano.

Its distillery started life as a winery, which was converted in 1955 to whisky-making in order to tap into the start of Japan's whisky boom. Life as a single malt was never the intention of its makers. This was to be the provider of the bass line within a blend called Ocean.

One style was made. It used Golden Promise barley, plenty of peat, clear wort, long fermentation, and was distilled in small stills, then aged mainly in ex-sherry casks. Everything about it was directed toward heaviness, and yet in taste, Karuizawa could only be Japanese. The smoke is sooty, its older expressions have a resinous depth, with a whiff of the wild and feral. The spices are exotic (cardamom and allspice) and there are notes of soy, but all are framed within a very focused, intense, Japanese style.

In its later years, though mothballed, it was building a cult following and it was hoped that the buzz would convince owner Kirin to reopen it. Instead, the distillery was sold off to a real-estate

FUJI-GOTEMBA

Karuizawa might have been below an active volcano, but Fuji-Gotemba's situation is even more surprising, considering that it lies between Mount Fuji (which is due for another eruption) and a Japan Defense Force firing range. Stylistically, it couldn't be more different from Karuizawa. Built in 1973 as a joint venture between Kirin and Seagram, it makes malt and grain (the grain in this case being fuller) in a similar manner to Gimli (*see* p.275); it even has that distillery's kettle-and-column setup. Aged exclusively in American oak and made specifically to match with Japanese cuisine, the single malt should be a huge seller. Sadly, it is underpromoted—and therefore underappreciated.

developer. The only good news is that the stock was saved by the Number One Drinks Company, which is eking out the last remaining liquid as single-cask releases and a vatting called Mount Asama.

With Karuizawa's unnecessary death, one of the world's great whiskies has passed.

FUJI-GOTEMBA TASTING NOTES

FUJI SANROKU 18YO 40%

Nose: High-toned and estery. Quite restrained. Polished wood, peach stone, violet. With water, there are white flowers and grapefruit.
Palate: Sweet, fragrant, and honeyed. Very light grip with a little lemon and hot sawdust.
Finish: Gentle. Lychee.
Conclusion: Very clean and precise.

Flavor Camp: Fragrant & Floral
Where Next? Royal Brackla 15yo, Glen Grant 1992 Cellar Reserve

18YO, SINGLE GRAIN 40%

Nose: Gold. Very sweet and intense with a buttery fat character. Lots of honey and sesame and coconut cream.
Palate: Thick, soft, and sweet. The fat corn quality comes through along with baked banana.
Finish: Long and syrupy.
Conclusion: Gentle, mellow, and sweet. Very amenable.

Flavor Camp: Fragrant & Floral
Where Next? Glentauchers 1991, The Glenturret 10yo

KARUIZAWA TASTING NOTES

1985, CASK #7017 60.8%

Nose: Pigeon blood. Deep and slightly feral, turned earth with molasses, geranium, cassis, and cedar before prunes come through along with stewed Assam tea. With water, there's damp coal bunker, varnish, raisin, and sulfur.
Palate: Big, quite tarry, and smokiness with a slight rubbery note. Gripping and masses of eucalyptus reminiscent of an ancient expectorant. Again the sulfur becomes a little too obtrusive with water.
Finish: Sooty and long.
Conclusion: Classic Karuizawa. Uncompromising.

Flavor Camp: Rich & Round
Where Next? Glenfarclas 40yo, Benrinnes 23yo

1995 NOH SERIES, CASK #5004 63%

Nose: Resinous. Varnish, balsam/Tiger balm, geranium, shoe polish, prune, heavily oiled woods. Barberries and rosewood casket. Water makes it evergreen with coal smoke and leather.
Palate: Light astringency when neat, wood oils, teetering into bitterness. With water, there's eucalyptus. Strange things are going on, it could be a smoky Armagnac. Fragrance stops it from becoming too grippy.
Finish: Tight and exotic.
Conclusion: Do you drink this or rub it on your chest?

Flavor Camp: Rich & Round
Where Next? Benrinnes 23yo, Macallan 25yo, Ben Nevis 25yo

Chichibu

CHICHIBU • EIGASHIMA • KOBE • WWW.EI-SAKE.JP; OPEN BY APPOINTMENT ONLY

The ethics of sustainability as envisioned by the Lifestyles of Health and Sustainability movement is not a topic you normally find yourself discussing on a distillery visit. Things are different at Chichibu, but then again owner Ichiro Akuto is not your average distiller. His family has been making alcohol (sake, then shochu) in quiet Chichibu since 1625. In the 1980s, they started distilling whisky in the industrial town of Hanyu, trucking water in from Chichibu for mashing. The timing couldn't have been worse. The whisky market collapsed and, by 2000, Akuto-san was left with the ruins of a distillery and 400 casks of old stock whose final Card Series release was in 2014. In 2007, he went back home to Chichibu, bought a plot of land, two razorback ridges outside town, and within a year had a tiny distillery operational.

Staffed by a team of enthusiastic youngsters and under the tutelage of the former distiller at Karuizawa, Chichibu is tiny: the space, no more than a large room, is winery-clean. It is the only distillery I've been to where you have to change into rubber slippers before entering.

Akuto-san's vision of a distillery with strong links to local producers is forming. Ten percent of Chichibu's malt is now locally grown. While this might seem small, it is a major step in an industry that has long been totally reliant on imports. Local peat is also being used. The parallels with Kilchoman on Islay are strong (barring the slippers).

As the Chichibu concept coalesces, Akuto-san continues to experiment with different styles and maturation regimes. One bottling was made with barley that was floor-malted by him and his team in Norfolk (training for their own malting floor), and which is deliberately cereal-accented in a very non-traditional Japanese way. He is making three distillates (including heavy peat) by adjusting the temperature of the condensers: cold for heavy and hot for light. Chichibu's small size allows him to focus intently on each part of the process.

The make is aged in a wide mix of casks—everything from red oak, through the normal whisky selection to local *mizunara*, 132-gallon (500-liter) American oak casks, wine casks, and the cute *chibidarus* (quarter casks). The last of the Karuizawa casks in the warehouse also gives an interesting refill profile as they are slowly depleted. A cooperage is now also being built.

It is a holistic vision: that's what 385 years of perspective give you.

And what has surprised him most? "The interrelated cycle: forestry, farming, and distilling that you need to make good whisky. Community. I used to think the cask was everything. Now I know how important distillation is, but in reality it is a totality."

CHICHIBU TASTING NOTES

ICHIRO'S MALT, CHICHIBU ON THE WAY DISTILLED 2010 58.5%

Nose: Bamboo shoots and then pink rhubarb before floral notes develop alongside strawberry jam and cream. With water, some pineapple and melon.
Palate: Typical Chichibu feel: a quick but gentle thickening on the palate. Strawberry and vanilla appear once more before youthful chalkiness comes through.
Finish: Blossom-like.
Conclusion: Sweet and gaining in complexity.

Flavor Camp: **Fragrant & Floral**
Where Next? Mackmyra

THE FLOOR MALTED 3YO 50.5%

Nose: Malty, but it is more chaff-like than nutty. Chichibu's floral element is there, alongside grape must, verjus, and herbs.
Palate: A mix of the very sweet fruit with, unusually, some cereal dryness. Light, sour plum.
Finish: Fresh and tight.
Conclusion: Made from barley malted in Norfolk.

Flavor Camp: **Malty & Dry**
Where Next? St George EWC

PORT PIPE 2009 54.5%

Nose: Young, but the oak is apparent. Slightly hot when neat, with a distinct raspberry and cranberry fruitiness, nettles, grass, and, with water, chalk.
Palate: Sweet on the tip of the tongue. There are little glimpses of raspberry fool and some caramelized notes from the cask.
Finish: Tight. Slightly sappy.
Conclusion: Matured in 132-gallon (500-liter) ex-port pipes. Coming together.

Flavor Camp: **Fruity & Spicy**
Where Next? Finch Dinkel

CHICHIBU CHIBIDARU 2009 54.5%

Nose: Has the intensity of youth with some lemon meringue pie, pomelo, and hint of night-scented stocks.
Palate: Mouth-watering citrus character and soft-centered sweetness moving to mace and strawberry tones.
Finish: Popping candy.
Conclusion: *Chibidaru* is a Japanese slang term meaning "small," which is appropriate given the size of the cask: quarter-size.

Flavor Camp: **Fruity & Spicy**
Where Next? Miyagikyo 15yo

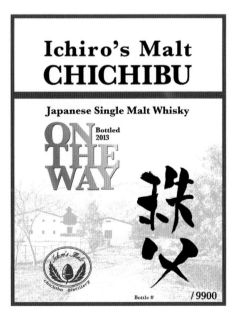

Mars Shinshu

MARS SHINSHU • MIYATA VILLAGE • KAGOSHIMA PREFECTURE • WWW.WHISKYMAG.JP/HOMBO-MARS-DISTILLERY

Not only does this distillery, which is set high in the Japanese Alps among mountains that seem to be made of crushed green velvet, have the most unusual name, its story is linked to the earliest days of Japanese whisky, whose telling makes you wonder "What if?" It's a tale that is also not just about one distillery, but three.

Its owner, Hombo, first took out a license to distill whisky in 1949, although it wasn't until 1960 that it started making whisky—and not here, but at a purpose-built plant in Yamanashi. This was run by Kijiro Iwai, who had been Masataka Taketsuru's immediate superior at the turn of the century. Both men had worked for a firm, Settsu Shozu, which had intended to build Japan's first whisky distillery. Sadly, when Taketsuru returned, the firm was in financial failure. He went to join Yamazaki, founded Nikka, and the rest is history. But what if Settsu's distillery had been built instead?

Iwai, it seemed, was a whisky-man, too, and when the plant in Yamanashi started, Iwai used Taketsuru's original report to make his whisky. It was, unsurprisingly, heavy and smoky. Yamanashi ran for nine years and when production there switched over to wine,

distilling moved to Kagoshima, located in the south of Kyushu, where two tiny pot-stills also made heavy, smoky whisky.

In 1984, production was switched to the current Mars site, which had been chosen because of its altitude (to encourage slow maturation) and the availability of soft, granite-filtered water. A style change was also brought in. This whisky was to be *light*.

The few casks from this period show it to be Japan's sweetest whisky, filled with soft, honeyed fruit. It should have gone well, but again, timing was bad. This was the start of Japan's great whisky crash and, with export not considered an option either, Mars closed in 1995.

Thankfully, though, Hombo has a clearer vision of whisky than the previous owner of Karuizawa. With whisky once again selling domestically and overseas, the distillery was reopened in 2012. Now two styles—unpeated and (with a nod to Iwai) peated—are made. Some of that new spirit is being vatted with old stock, while the occasional old cask is being bottled. There is life on Mars!

Located high in the Japanese Alps, Mars Shinshu has reopened after seventeen years.

MARS TASTING NOTES

NEW MAKE, LIGHTLY PEATED 60%

Nose: Green pear and light smoke. There's a hint of sulfur in the background.
Palate: Sweet, with lifted smoke. A touch of sulfur on the mid-palate, which will mature nicely.
Finish: Sugary.

KOMAGATAKE SINGLE MALT, 2.5YO 58%

Nose: Ridiculously fruity. Iced white peaches, melon rind, fruit syrup, and very delicate oak.
Palate: Hugely sweet. Young and spicy, but already you can see the balance developing.
Finish: Unripe fruit showing that time is still needed.
Conclusion: It's as if it never went away. Distillery character has been regained immediately.

Flavor Camp: Fruity & Spicy
Where Next? Arran 14yo

White Oak

EIGASHIMA • KOBE • WWW.EI-SAKE.JP

White Oak is an enigma. This distillery on the Akashi Strait near Kobe could have been where Japan's first whisky was made. It had a license to distill whisky in 1919, but only began to make the spirit—and then only occasionally—in the 1960s when it all went for blending. In similar fashion to the similarly sized Hanyu and Mars, it was exposed when the market went into decline. Although production has started up again, it has been limited.

Owner Eigashima Shuzo specializes in production of shochu, umeshu, wine, and brandy. As a result, whisky has to fight for its place within an already established portfolio and, one would imagine, a crowded distillation schedule. With such a range of spirits, whisky production is limited to two months a year (and that was upped from only one month). What is made is unpeated and predominantly filled into ex-Wild Turkey barrels and sherry casks.

A recent visit by Stefan van Eycken of the Nonjatta blog, however, revealed a more complex wood regime than had previously been thought. Whisky is aging in white wine casks from the firm's Yamanashi facility and, most intriguingly of all, some ex-shochu casks made from Konara oak (*Quercus serrata*). A limited release of Konara finish was made in 2013. In addition, independent bottler Duncan Taylor also has some White Oak maturing in Scotland.

Most of the releases in recent times have been of young whisky but I'm with the Japanese-whisky lovers who feel that this is a make that needs some gentle, lengthy coaxing from cask to fully open. Time is needed. Commercial needs, however, sometimes outweigh those of the demands of whisky geeks and it would appear that the policy of young releases will continue. So, sadly, is that of limited production. Shochu and sake are where the firm makes its money, and money talks.

Another shochu producer (and craft brewer), Miyashita began distilling whisky in its Okayama plant in limited quantities in 2012. It is currently aging in a mix of casks with the first release planned for 2015.

WHITE OAK TASTING NOTES

5YO BLEND (BOTTLED FOR NUMBER ONE DRINKS) 45%

Nose: Pale, light, and clean with a little waxiness. Opens with a scented, angelica-like lift, then gooseberry jam before it deepens into roasted tea. Water brings out yeastiness, cucumber, borage, and lime.
Palate: Sweet, with vanilla custard and a sweet gingery accented note leading to ripe pear.
Finish: Gentle and light.
Conclusion: Delicate but well balanced.

Flavor Camp: Fragrant & Floral

HANYU

Ichiro Akuto's family (*see* Chichibu, p.221) has been involved in the alcohol business since 1625, predominantly as sake-brewers. In the 1940s, they obtained a license for a new distillery in the town of Hanyu, on the banks of the Tone River, but it wasn't until 1980 that whisky was made there. Its bold style didn't find favor in a market that was looking for lightness. This, and the collapse of the Japanese whisky market in the 1990s, forced Hanyu's closure, and in 2000 it was demolished, but not before Ichiro managed to buy the 400 remaining casks. Its most prominent range has been the Card Series selection of single casks, each with the face of a playing card. Ichiro claims there is no significance for the apportioning of specific cards to a specific style, but malt-lovers of a conspiratorial nature still try to discern a pattern. The series ended in 2014, with two releases of The Joker.

Close to Kobe, the White Oak distillery was the first to be licensed for whisky-making in Japan.

Yoichi

YOICHI • WWW.NIKKA.COM/ENG/DISTILLERIES/YOICHI.HTML • OPEN ALL YEAR; SEE WEBSITE FOR DAYS & DETAILS; TOURS IN JAPANESE

Although spread out across central and northern Honshu, all Japan's malt distilleries are easily accessible from Tokyo. There's good reason for that: ease of transportation and access to the main markets. All of them, that is, bar one. Where is Yoichi? Your eyes finally head north to Hokkaido; you trace the line to the ferry crossing between Aomori and Hakodate, past Sapporo, then 31 miles west to the coast. This is the northlands, this is opposite Vladivostock. Why, when everyone concentrated on Honshu, would the co-founder of Japanese whisky head here?

Masataka Taketsuru always had a vision of making whisky in Hokkaido. It was his perfect location. While in Hazelburn, worrying (again) about water quality in Japan he wrote: "Even in Scotland there is occasionally a shortage of good water, therefore it is totally unreasonable to build a pot-still factory at Sumiyoshi [Osaka] where we cannot have water without digging a well.

"If we consider the geography of Japan, a place would be needed that would constantly supply good-quality water, where barley can be obtained, with a good supply of fuel, coal, or wood, with a railway link, and with water navigation."

All signs, he felt, pointed to Hokkaido but his boss, the pragmatic Shinjiro Torii, thought it was nowhere near the markets, so Yamazaki it was. No one knows the true story behind the foundering of the relationship between the two men, maybe it is simply coincidence that Taketsuru was moved to manage a brewery in Yokohama the same year as his whisky, Shirofuda, was launched—and flopped. It was too heavy, too smoky, not "Japanese" enough.

At the end of his contract in 1934 and with finance from backers in Osaka, Taketsuru and his Scottish wife Rita headed north, finally, to Hokkaido, ostensibly to make apple juice. In reality, he was

Scotland or Japan? Yoichi was Masataka Taketsuru's homage to his spiritual home, but also one of the sites where a uniquely Japanese character of whisky was created.

going to satisfy his vision, which he made reality in the small fishing port of Yoichi, encircled by mountains, next to the great, gray, chill Sea of Japan.

And the whisky that appeared in 1940? Big. Smoky. Not, in Torii's terms, "Japanese." Today, Yoichi's tall, red-roofed kiln is no longer puffing out clouds of smoke from Japanese peat, cut on the Ishikari plains. Like all Japanese distilleries, the malt comes from Scotland. Inevitably, a number of styles (Nikka remains politely opaque about how many) are made: there are different peating levels (unpeated to heavy), different yeast strains, fermentation times, and cut points.

The clear point of difference is the coal fires sitting under the quartet of hefty wash stills. It's an art running coal, the stillman always anticipating what is about to happen, getting ready to damp down, to boost heat, and to maintain control of a living flame. But the result is a density given to the final spirit. The worm tubs help, as might a maturation temperature profile running from 39°F (-4°C) in winter to 72°F (22°C) in summer.

Yoichi is big. It is oily, smoky yet fragrant. It has depth, but also the clarity of character that allows the complexities to be seen clearly. Its weight isn't the same as Karuizawa's four-square solidity; this has salty touches. At times there are glints of Ardbeg, but then a touch of black olive. And the smoke: it takes you not to Islay, but Kintyre. You look around to see a small fishing port, miles from the nearest main town and a cussedly different style of whisky-making. It could be Campbeltown, where Taketsuru worked, where he could have stayed to work. Yoichi is not a copy by any means, it can only be Japanese, but there's a psychic link.

Taketsuru remains an enigma. Pragmatist or romantic? Probably both? Was his move to Hokkaido for practical reasons only, or was there also a wish for a physical distancing from the past, a need for the sea air, the space to breathe?

YOICHI TASTING NOTES

10YO 45%

Nose: Light gold. Clean and fresh. Vibrant smoke. Sooty and slightly salty. Needs water to bring out its real depth and oily base.

Palate: That oiliness allows the flavors to cling to the tongue. Lightly oaky, the crisp apple notes behind the big smoke.

Finish: Once again an acidic edge.

Conclusion: Balanced and young: have it with soda water.

Flavor Camp: Smoky & Peaty
Where Next? Ardbeg Renaissance

12YO 45%

Nose: Full gold. Immediate briny-accented smoke with a touch of marzipan behind. Weightier than the 10yo with a heavy floral note, some baked peach, apple, and the start of a cacao note.

Palate: Oily with that baked apple character coming through. Sweet and cake-like, a little butter, then cashew and smoke.

Finish: Smokiness develops.

Conclusion: A balance between the pull of the shore and that of the orchard.

Flavor Camp: Smoky & Peaty
Where Next? Springbank 10yo

15YO 45%

Nose: Deep gold. Less overtly smoky and more of the deep rich oiliness that typifies the distillery's makes. Cigar, cedar, and walnut cake. Hint of black olive behind.

Palate: Has all of the distillery's density of character. Again the tongue-coating oiliness clamps the flavors to the tongue. Sherried notes: eugenol (clove-like) and the cacao note seen in the 12yo now moved to a full bitter chocolate.

Finish: Slighty salty.

Conclusion: Robust but elegant.

Flavor Camp: Smoky & Peaty
Where Next? Longrow 14yo, Caol Ila 18yo

20YO 45%

Nose: Amber. Intense and maritime. Drying fishing nets, wet seaweed, boat oil, lobster shell. Sandalwood and intense dense fruitiness. Tapenade and soy sauce. Becomes spicier with water: fenugreek, curry leaves.

Palate: Deep and resinous. The smoke now starts to build through the thick black oiliness. Light leather that's cut with a surprisingly fresh top note.

Finish: Linseed oil and a touch of spice before the smoke returns.

Conclusion: Powerful and contradictory.

Flavor Camp: Smoky & Peaty
Where Next? Ardbeg Lord of the Isles 25yo

1986 22YO, HEAVY PEATED 59%

Nose: Gold. Orange zest, incense, and peat smoke. Fleshy fruit, black olive with assertive smoke, buddleia, hard toffee, and roasting sweet spice. The balsamic note suggests age.

Palate: Big smoke and a solid mix of fruitcake and tarred twine. Substantial and complex, although needing a touch of water to show it's got a gentle and fruity side.

Finish: A smooth buildup of all the complexities on the palate.

Conclusion: Boldness remains in force.

Flavor Camp: Smoky & Peaty
Where Next? Talisker 25yo

Just one example of the multiplicity of styles produced at Yoichi.

Japanese Blends

NIKKA • WWW.NIKKA.COM/ENG/PRODUCTS/WHISKY_BRANDY/NIKKABLENDED/INDEX.HTML • SEE YOICHI & MIYAGIKYO
HIBIKI • WWW.SUNTORY.COM/BUSINESS/LIQUOR/WHISKY.HTML

Japanese whisky, like Scotch, was built on blends. It was the complex needs of the blended market that triggered the innovations in distilling at the single malt distilleries that so define Japanese whisky. Even today, with a boom in malt whisky among a new generation, blends make up the bulk of sales; blends lie behind the need for so many expressions from single distilleries. Yet, while the mechanics of blending are the same as in Scotland, Japan itself, its climate and its culture, has dictated what the style of those blends should be. Blends reflect society.

Japan's first blend, Shirofuda (White Label), released in 1929, was heavy and smoky. It wasn't a success. Shinjiro Torii went back to the drawing board and went light. His next release, Kakubin, remains one of Japan's top-selling whiskies. A lesson had been learned, one that would be fully exploited in the postwar period when the Japanese economy began to heat up.

Suddenly there were bars full of hardworking salarymen needing to relax and let off steam. What would they drink? In Japan, beer has much the same status as in Germany: a foodstuff... "breakfast beer" is served without any eyebrows being raised in business hotels. Whisky? Not neat, certainly. In humid Japan you needed something light and refreshing. The answer? Whisky *mizuwari*: blended whisky, ice, heavily diluted with water.

It might be politically incorrect to suggest this today, but the *mizuwari* serve meant that you could drink a lot. A LOT.

Blended Japanese whisky was enormous. In the 1980s, Suntory Old was selling 12.4 million cases in its home market. That's almost as much as all the Johnnie Walker variants sell globally today. "You can't compare it with today," says Suntory head blender Seiichi Koshimizu. "Our big sellers at that time were [Suntory] Red, White [aka Old], Kakubin, Gold, Reserve, and Royal. It was a pyramid with a unified 'Suntory' style. In society there was also a pyramid and if you were promoted, you would try a higher-level whisky; so as you moved up through that hierarchy, so you changed your whisky."

Who said blending was easy? An array of bottles—and flavor possibilities for the Japanese blender to play with.

Has that changed? "The idea of hierarchy has gone. Now you drink a 'higher' whisky because you want to try it! So, even as beginners, younger drinkers are trying premium and malt whiskies." It's a generational and social shift reflected in whisky.

Interestingly, it is currently moving in two ways. A young generation (including a higher than average percentage of women) that turned its back on their fathers' drink and drank shochu is now coming to whisky, either with the single malt style or through—guess what?—heavily diluted whisky highballs.

New, top-end blends are now being developed. Suntory's premium Hibiki range (launched in 1989) has a new member, a 12yo variant, which contains whiskies filtered through bamboo charcoal and a malt that's been aged in plum-liqueur casks. Nikka's From The Barrel is offering malt drinkers an entry into a world they had rejected, while the firm's Blender's Bar offers a snapshot of the possibilities afforded by blending, but featuring wildly different flavored whiskies made from different ratios of the same components.

Blending may seem coldly analytical, but it is creative. "We are artisans," says Shinji Fukuyo, another of Suntory's senior blending team. "We all strive to become artisans, but you cannnot lightly call yourself one. Artists aim to create something new, they are creators. We artisans are responsible for creation but also to sustain the quality in our products. We have a promise to keep."

Every whisky will be tasted, assessed, and noted.

JAPANESE BLENDS TASTING NOTES

NIKKA FROM THE BARREL 51.4%

Nose: A wood in springtime: bark, moss, and green leaves and a light floral underpinning along with rosemary oil. New car. Water makes it more dense. Coffee cake.
Palate: Discreet and soft with melon, peach, sweet persimmon. Dries towards the back where that mossy note reappears.
Finish: Tight oak.
Conclusion: Intense and balanced. A blend for malt lovers.

Flavor Camp: **Fruity & Spicy**

NIKKA SUPER 43%

Nose: Copper. Fleshy and crisp, light dried fruit, caramel and hints of smoke. Raspberry with a light, rooty, floral note.
Palate: Clean and lean with some slick grain helping the flow. Light citrus. More sweet than the nose.
Finish: Medium length. Clean.
Conclusion: A sound and mixable blend.

Flavor Camp: **Fragrant & Floral**

HIBIKI 12YO 43%

Nose: Spice (dusty, nutmeg). An intense green mango/Victoria plum note. Pineapple and lemon.
Palate: Gentle, sweet. Vanilla ice-cream, peach. Spicy.
Finish: Long pepper, menthol then coriander seed.
Conclusion: Highly innovative blending.

Flavor Camp: **Fruity & Spicy**

HIBIKI 17YO 43%

Nose: Soft and gentle fruits with touches of lemon balm and orange leaf, then comes cacao, apricot jam banana, and hazelnut.
Palate: Gentle grain giving a lush toffee-ed character. Dried fruit notes sit underneath. Black cherry and sultana cake. Long and ripe.
Finish: Smooth and honeyed.
Conclusion: A layered effect justifies the Japanese approach to whisky-making.

Flavor Camp: **Fruity & Spicy**

CHITA SINGLE GRAIN 48%

Nose: Buttery and needs water to allow a flow of fudge, orange peel, *crème brûlée*, and green banana tones.
Palate: Chewy toffee-cream sweetness is offset by tart red fruit.
Finish: Relaxed and sweet.
Conclusion: An alcoholic Danish pastry.

Flavor Camp: **Soft Corn**

17 Years Old
HIBIKI
SUNTORY WHISKY
A harmonious blend of
handcrafted select specially aged whiskies

THE USA

Distillers use what grows around them. A new country holds no fears for them; they just adapt to the change in circumstances, take a new base ingredient, and improvise on it. In Mexico, the settlers learned to turn agave into tequila, in the Caribbean, they did the same with cane and made rum. In the early days of the settling of the United States, it was apples and other fruits that were transformed into brandies. It wasn't until the mid-eighteenth century that whiskey began to be made in any quantity, mainly by *émigré* farmers from Germany, Holland, Ireland, and Scotland who settled in Maryland, Pennsylvania, West Virginia, and the Carolinas, and planted rye, the basis for America's first indigenous whiskey style.

Corn-based spirit had to wait until 1776, when "corn patch and cabin" rights were granted to new settlers in the virgin territory of Kentucky county. They took that "Indian corn" and distilled it. It made economic sense. A bushel of corn sold for 50 cents, whereas the five gallons of whiskey you could make from that bushel could net you $2. They used what grew around them.

By the 1860s, the industrial revolution had created a commercial whiskey industry. Distilleries grew in size, railroads allowed national distribution, and, importantly, the quality had improved, thanks to scientific advances spearheaded by James Crow at the Old Oscar Pepper distillery in Kentucky (*see* p.232, p.236–7).

It's interesting to speculate what today's whisky world might look like had America not fallen under the influence of temperance. It's quite likely it would have become the dominant player, not Scotch. We'll never know.

We do know that by 1915, 20 states were dry, including Kentucky. Whiskey production stopped in 1917 in order to produce industrial alcohol for the war effort. Three years later, on January 17, 1920, the Great Drought started. By 1929, the US was drinking less than in 1915, when states began to dry up, but Americans were sippin' stronger, switching from beer to spirits, halting a 75-year fall in whiskey consumption.

Although social historians point out that more spirits were drunk in the 13 years of Prohibition than before, this was little consolation to American whiskey-makers, who watched a new generation drinking Scotch and Canadian whisky. By the time of repeal in 1933, not only was there little stock, but the American palate had changed. Maybe drinkers could have been persuaded back to rye and bourbon were it not for World War II shutting the industry down again. When it restarted, postwar, it had been effectively closed for almost three decades. American whiskey was a stranger in its own country.

Its renaissance has been a long and patient one. In many ways, distillers had to wait for tastes to change; their attempts to go light simply diluted the essence of the American whiskey style. It was only when big flavor began to swing back into fashion, triggered by Californian wine as well as single malt, that there were signs that a new generation of American drinkers were ready to rediscover their own spirit.

Now rye is back and the bourbon industry is in a flurry of creativity. The craft-distilling movement has taken root, even in bourbon's spiritual home of Kentucky. Bourbon, corn whiskey, and rye and wheat whiskeys are being made across America. In addition, flavored whiskeys—honey, cherry, gingerbread, spice—are creating a new market, while there's been a nostalgic return to 'shine. That same question "What is whiskey?" is being asked here as well.

Kentucky's limestone bench is good not just for bourbon-making but horse-breeding as well.

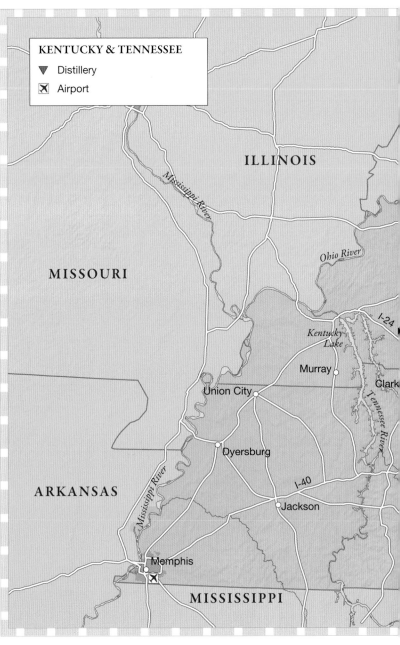

KENTUCKY & TENNESSEE
▼ Distillery
✖ Airport

Previous page: **Looking toward** the Rocky Mountains from Sweet Grass County, Montana.

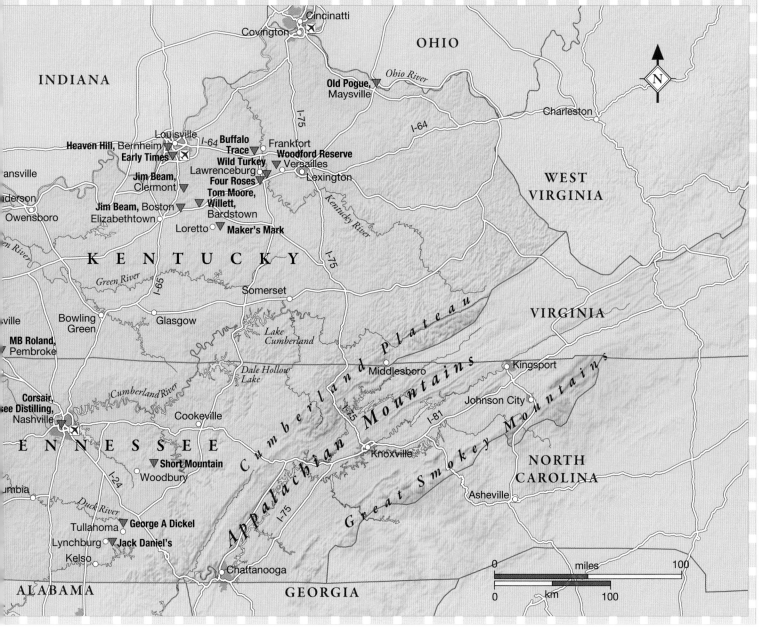

KENTUCKY

Although bourbon can be (and is) made anywhere in the USA, its homeland is Kentucky. All new distillers trying their hand at bourbon look here first, paying homage to the pioneers who crafted what has become America's signature style. But why Kentucky?

The free land given to eighteenth-century settlers on the understanding that they planted corn gave the Commonwealth of Kentucky a head start in whiskey production. Farmstead stills became small distilleries. By the start of the nineteenth century, whiskey barrels were being shipped down the Ohio to the Mississippi, and from there to New Orleans.

It was rough stuff, aged for as long as it took to get to market, but it can be argued that it was the first deliberately wood-aged whiskey style. It took a Scot, James Crow, to change things. From 1825 until his death 31 years later, he brought scientific rigor to whiskey-making: sour-mashing, saccharometers, pH testing. Crow created consistency.

With better spirit and a changing market, so aging and new charred barrels became the norm. No one knows who started this, although it could well have come from the Americas' first spirit, rum. Rum distillers knew about the transformative effect that wood had on a rough spirit and had been using charred barrels since the seventeenth century. Sour-mashing is also, probably, originally a rum technique.

With each development, the flavors of bourbon began to become fixed—even in law. Today, "Straight bourbon" is a whiskey distilled no higher than 160° (80% abv) and made from a fermented mash of not less than 51 percent corn, which is put in barrel at not more than 125° (62.5% abv), and aged in new charred-oak containers for a period of two years or more.

There's a certain flexibility: there's no restriction on cask size, nor does it say that American oak must be used; while the 51 percent allows plenty of variation in mash bills, the precise corn/grain proportions. Bourbon is a series of improvisations on these themes: upping and lowering the corn-to-rye ratio to bring out spice or corn fatness, substituting rye for wheat to smooth things out, utilizing different yeast types to produce specific aromas. Finally, there's Kentucky itself.

Bourbon was born in Kentucky and has survived in Kentucky because of Kentucky. Its hard limestone water requires sour-mashing, which in turn gives flavor. The wild yeasts in its air have helped generate distilleries' own strains, its soils give the corn and rye, and its climate impacts hugely on the final flavor of the bourbon. Finally, there's a cultural *terroir* in the shape of whiskey-making dynasties: the Beams, the Samuels, the Russells, the Shapiras. Bourbon is made by people.

Across Kentucky, distilleries are expanding, trying to keep pace with growing demand. Distillers are examining what bourbon can be, where its flavors come from, what the maturation cycles provide. Wood is a major focus, partly because of the naturally curious minds at work, but also because there are worries about whether there will be sufficient trees to sustain the need for new barrels. In parallel to this serious product development, flavored variants are appearing, seemingly every week. Never has Kentucky produced such a wide variety of whiskeys.

Bourbon Street, New Orleans: destination for the Mississippi-shipped whiskeys from Kentucky.

Maker's Mark

LORETTO • WWW.MAKERSMARK.COM • OPEN ALL YEAR MON–SAT; MAR–DEC, MON–SUN

In 1844, the *Nelson Record*, living up to its name, recorded that Taylor William Samuels' distillery in Deatsville, Kentucky, was: " … well constructed and equipped with all the modern improvements known in the distillery business." Taylor William, it would seem, was following in a family tradition. The Samuels family, Scots-Irish in origin, had apparently been turning their corn into whisk(e)y since 1780. Nothing's changed. They still are.

The Maker's Mark story is one of heritage and perseverence, shot through with the cussedness that permeates all of the distillers in this part of the world—but with an important twist. The tales that swirl around bourbon are drawn from family histories, half-truths, and suppositions, all stitched together like an old-time patchwork quilt. It may annoy historians, but it makes great marketing. One theme is that after Prohibition, the distiller picked himself up, dusted off the old recipe, and got down to business once more. It's very American, it's laudable, and it's often true.

When Bill Samuels Sr. decided to revive the family tradition in 1953 at Star Hill Farm, he deviated from this. He picked himself up, looked around, and said: "We're going to do it differently this time."

In other words, not just start a distillery from scratch, but go back to basics. To Bill Sr., the bourbons on the market were hard, harsh, low-priced, and, most importantly, being outsold by Scotch. If bourbon was to have a future, he mused, it would have to up its quality and change its flavor.

Here in the bosky hollow next to Hardin Creek, in a distillery that had been producing since 1805, he planned his single style of whisky (Bill Sr. stuck to the Scottish spelling). No rye in the mash bill, but wheat. Maker's, contrary to popular belief, is not the sole wheated bourbon on the market. Bill Sr. consulted with the greatest advocate of the wheated style, Pappy Van Winkle, and came up with a mash bill of 70 percent corn, 16 percent wheat, and 14 percent malted barley.

"He did lot of different things," says Maker's' brand ambassador, Jane Conner. "Things were bad, so he just did the opposite." These

Charred barrels are an essential element in the creation of the Maker's Mark character.

"different things" are seen today at the distillery: a roller mill to stop the grains from scorching, slow cooking in open cookers, "to get the essence of corn," the use of its own house jug yeast. Distillation to 130° proof (65% abv) in three copper beer columns with doublers. This gives a pleasantly focused white dog (the American term for new make).

"Maturation is key," says Conner. "Our oak is air-dried for 12 months and given a lighter char for flavor reasons. We don't want the sickly sweetness of other bourbons. What he wanted was a smoother bourbon. 'Easy-drinking' is a bad thing to say these days, apparently, but I don't see why. Surely it's nice to create something that's drinkable?"

Maturing its whisky in black-painted rick warehouses dotted around the property, Maker's still rotates its barrels: taking the slow-maturing casks from the cooler bottom floor and replacing them with the ones that have been baking on the top floor. Conner says that this is for consistency, but if only one bourbon is being made, wouldn't a cross-section be easier? "A cross-section might work if you just had one warehouse but we have 19 and every one is different. Rotating makes sense as maturation is just crazy in Kentucky."

Maker's had stuck with its gentle yet bright style since 1953, but in 2010 it released Maker's 46. Wood was key: to try to intensify the wood effect without damaging the balance. Working with Independent Stave, the solution was to sear (not char) French oak staves to restrict tannin yet amplify caramelization.

The finishing process starts with standard Maker's being removed from the barrel, the head taken off, ten staves inserted; then the barrel is refilled and allowed to rest for between three and four months. When John Glaser of Scotch company Compass Box previously tried a similar technique, his whisky was banned. A more open-minded approach seems to be the American norm.

Black and red. The slightly ominous-looking company livery of Maker's Mark couldn't be in greater contrast to this most open-hearted of bourbons.

MAKER'S MARK TASTING NOTES

WHITE DOG 90°/45%

Nose: Sweet, gentle, and pure with good corn oiliness. Touch of heavy florals, apple, and lint.
Palate: Fleshy and ripe with red summer fruit. Fragrant with a gentle texture. Very bright and dynamic.
Finish: Focused with a little fennel.

MAKER'S 46 94°/47%

Nose: Cinnamon toast, maple syrup, nutmeg, hint of cardamom. Danish pastry, cherry, vanilla.
Palate: Ripe and full. Thick caramel, candied orange zest, toffee, and soft red and orchard fruit.
Finish: Spicy and sweet.
Conclusion: Clean, sweet, concentrated with extra spice.

Flavor Camp: **Rich & Oaky**
Where Next? Four Roses Single Barrel

Maker's (S IV) Mark ®
KENTUCKY STRAIGHT BOURBON
WHISKY
Handmade

Distilled, aged and bottled by the
Maker's Mark Distillery, Inc.
Star Hill Farm, Loretto, Ky. USA
750mL   45% alc./vol.

MAKER'S MARK 90°/45%

Nose: Soft, with buttery oak. Creamy feel. Maraschino cherry, sandalwood, and upfront apple. Fruit now fully ripe. With water, more blossom-like. Balanced wood.
Palate: Smooth, sweet, and gentle. Quite chewy. Some laurel, syrup, coconut.
Finish: Soft.
Conclusion: Rather than rye acting as the gripping agent, here the oak is allowed to exert a gentle squeeze on the soft spirit.

Flavor Camp: **Sweet Wheat**
Where Next? W L Weller Ltd Edition, Crown Royal 12yo

Early Times & Woodford Reserve

EARLY TIMES • LOUISVILLE • WWW.EARLYTIMES.COM
WOODFORD RESERVE • VERSAILLES • WWW.WOODFORDRESERVE.COM • OPEN ALL YEAR

Louisville is a fascinating amalgam of the grand and the blue collar: a state capital with impressive brick buildings festooned with wrought ironwork, a museum to a baseball bat, and hotels with hidden passageways for bootleggers to escape through. It's also the birthplace of Muhammad Ali and a quiet revolution in American music. But in areas such as Shively are the shells of warehouses and old plants, once home to mighty whiskey producers.

Both of Louisville's two operational distilleries are situated around here: Heaven Hill's Bernheim, and Brown-Forman's Early Times. Operational since 1940, Early Times produces Early Times and Old Forester. "They are two very different whiskeys," says master distiller Chris Morris. "Early Times is relaxed, Old Forester is focused." That "old-fashioned country style" found in Early Times starts with a mash bill that is 79 percent corn, 11 percent rye, and 10 percent barley malt (see p.18). "We use the IA yeast strain, in use since the 1920s," says Morris. "This gives a low congener profile, which helps create that mild character. We also sour it to 20 percent [i.e. 20 percent of the mash is backset, whereby the acidic (i.e. "sour") spent lees from the bottom of the beer column are added to the fermenter]. Old Forester's mash bill has a higher rye-to-malt ratio, 18:72 percent, which helps to up the spiciness. It too has its own yeast and is soured only to 12 percent."

Sour-mashing can be a confusing issue, with many bourbon drinkers claiming to prefer "sour-mashed" brands over others simply because the term is on the label. In reality, all straight whiskeys are sour-mashed. Kentucky and Tennessee sit on a limestone bench meaning the water is mineral-rich, but also hard and alkaline. Adding backset helps acidify the mash, stop potential infection, and ease fermentation. The percentage of sour used has a significant impact on flavor, as Morris explains. "The more sour you use, the less sugar the yeast has to work with, so a 20 percent sour and a three-day ferment [as with Early Times] gives a lower congener level, while Old Forester's 12 percent sour and five-day ferment gives more flavor and a fresher beer as there's more material for the yeast to work with. Old Forester's beer smells like rose petals, Early Times' is nachos." Both are taken off the thumper at 140° (70% abv) and diluted to 125° (62.5% abv) and then barreled.

While Early Times is happy to stick as a down-home, easy-sipping bourbon (or, when aged in refill barrels, Kentucky whiskey), Old Forester has been moving into the area of special release with its Birthday Barrel selection of older bourbons (on average 10 to 14 years) taken from a single day's production. "It allows us to look for unusual profiles," says Morris. "Once, for example, a squirrel got itself in a junction box and blew the power—killed himself as well—and left us with a three-day ferment, which gave us different congeners."

The squirrel might have felt more at home at Brown-Forman's other distillery, Woodford Reserve, whch lies in the heart of horse-breeding territory, next to Glenn's Creek in Woodford Co. Here, in the 1830s,

Oscar Pepper hired the father of modern bourbon, James Crow. Today, these pale limestone buildings contain a unique bourbon distillery, which uses pot-stills (like miniaturized versions of Glemorangie's) to triple-distill.

"This distillery honors Pepper and Crow," says Morris, "but it isn't a recreation of nineteenth-century whiskey." Instead, Woodford Reserve is a continuation of Crow's exploration of what was possible. Made to the

Barrels fitting snugly behind the thick limestone walls of the Woodford Reserve distillery.

same mash bill as Old Forester but with only six percent souring and a different yeast, it has a week-long fermentation. The white dog comes off the third still at 158° (79% abv), but the less "efficient" pots build in more flavor than a spirit of the same strength out of a column. Barreled at 110° (54.5% abv) in air-dried oak, the Distiller's Select has bourbon from the Shively distillery blended in. The Double Oaked is a blend of standard barrels and uses a lightly charred, heavily toasted barrel.

Crow's "why not?" ethos extends to the Master's Collection limited-release program. "We have five sources of flavor in bourbon," says Morris: "grain, water, ferment, distillation, and maturation. Distillation and water are constants, so any innovation involves looking at the other three." Recent releases have included a four-grain mash bill, a sweet mash, a Chardonnay finish, a rye, a "four-wood" (bourbon-barrel matured, then finished in oloroso, port, maple wood), and two single malts (called Straight Malt) made from 100 percent malted barley, one aged in refill, the other in new charred oak. Crow's legacy lives on.

Originally the Old Oscar Pepper distillery, Woodford Reserve was where James Crow brought scientific rigour to the art of bourbon distilling.

EARLY TIMES & WOODFORD RESERVE TASTING NOTES

EARLY TIMES 80°/40%

Nose: Gold. Perfumed and honey-like with lots of spun sugar and sweet popcorn. Coconut and a lick of honey.
Palate: Medium weight and soft. The corn shows well mixing with vanilla fudge, with a deeper tobacco note behind showing an unexpected seriousness.
Finish: Gentle and long.
Conclusion: Sweet and easy drinking.

Flavor Camp: **Soft Corn**
Where Next? George Dickel Old No.12, Jim Beam Black Label, Hedgehog (France)

WOODFORD RESERVE DISTILLER'S SELECT
86.4°/43.2%

Nose: Dark amber. Waxy honeyed notes. Lemon-thyme and intense citrus fruit. Stewed apple, nutmeg, and lemon spongecake. The oak gives a syrupy/barley-sugar character. With water, there's charred wood, corn leaf, and wood oils.
Palate: Clean and light to start. Precise and almost angular. Zesty and tight. The thyme comes back along with the citrus peels. Rye eases in subtly.
Finish: Mix of citrus fruit and sweet spice.
Conclusion: Balanced and very clean.

Flavor Camp: **Spicy Rye**
Where Next? Tom Moore 4yo, Maker's Mark

LABROT & GRAHAM
WOODFORD RESERVE
DISTILLER'S SELECT

Wild Turkey

LAWRENCEBURG • WWW.WILDTURKEYBOURBON.COM • OPEN ALL YEAR MON–SAT, APR–NOV MON–SUN

Iron-clad and black-painted, sitting on the edge of a cliff above the Kentucky River, Wild Turkey's location was for a long time a physical metaphor of the past state of the bourbon industry. The fact that it has survived is down to the efforts of one man: Jimmy Russell, the master distiller who has been distiller here for 60 years. In fact, it could be argued that the values of old-time bourbon have only survived because of the distillers of Jimmy's generation who resisted change if it meant compromising on character and quality.

Jimmy and Wild Turkey have achieved a form of symbiosis: Wild Turkey is a big bourbon whose thick, rich physicality makes the drinker take his/her time. It represents a slower, less hectic time. He has an old-style distiller's polite contempt for scientists and expresses benign amusement when fielding questions about Turkey's DNA. I just do it the way I've always done it, he seems to say, the way I was taught and the way I've taught Eddie. (Eddie is Jimmy's son. He's also the distiller and in his 35th year at Wild Turkey.)

The Wild Turkey rationale is all about building in flavor, anchoring this bourbon in the mouth. "We're in the low-70s when it comes to corn and therefore close to 30 percent in small grains," says Jimmy. "Some of the other fellows are in the high-70s, some are mid-70s. A couple even use wheat. We're the lowest. We're traditional, with more body, more flavor, and more character."

Above: Two generations of genius. Eddie Russell (l) and Jimmy Russell (r), are the custodians of Wild Turkey. Below: Filling barrels at low strength is one of Wild Turkey's signatures.

That character starts with open-topped cookers and fermenting with a single yeast strain. "How old is the strain? Well I've been here for 55 years and it was here when I arrived!" says Jimmy. "It, too, has an effect on flavor. It's there to help promote that heavier flavor."

Collected off the still at 124–126° (62–63% abv) the white dog is barrelled at 110° (55% abv). Jimmy explains: "My feeling is that the higher percentage of alcohol, then the less flavor you'll have. Because we go into the barrel at a low proof and then bottle at 101° (50.5% abv), we're not losing much in terms of flavor, and that helps in making that older style."

It might even be a style recognizable to the Ripy brothers, who moved here in 1905 from their family distillery in Tyrone, Pennsylvania, which had been making bourbon since 1869. In the 1940s, the Ripy distillery was bought by Austin Nichols and renamed Wild Turkey after its bourbon became the favored drink at the directors' annual wild-turkey shoot. It ended up as part of Pernod Ricard, which never seemed to grasp its potential, and in 2009 was bought by Campari. Maybe the hands-off approach worked out for the best. Jimmy has kept on making his style of bourbon and now the market has gone full circle.

"I think the consumer is coming back to what they wanted years ago," he says. "It's not just the older generation drinking Wild Turkey, but new drinkers looking for a bourbon with flavor and body that they can sip and have a good time with. It's going back to pre-Prohibition times. Everything comes around." Even straight rye, a style which only a few distillers (including Turkey) perserved with, is back.

The sweetness of American oak mingles with the richness of corn and rye – and some magic – to make Wild Turkey.

Was he tempted to change when bourbon went light? "We couldn't have competed in that market, so I s'pose it was part economics on the part of the bosses and partly my philosophy. We wanted to stay true to what bourbon was all about, which is not watered down."

Campari has invested $100 million in the facility with a new visitor's center, a packaging unit, and a $55-million distillery expansion, which has more than doubled capacity.

The Turkey is flying. Bourbon has looked over the abyss and stepped back into a world of flavor. Jimmy Russell has been vindicated.

WILD TURKEY TASTING NOTES

101° (50.5%)
Nose: Toffee, caramel, and rich fruit. Quite succulent, with dried cherry, chestnut toffee, spicy rye, and good depth. Has a youthful freshness.
Palate: Burnt sugar and an almost leathery ripeness. Thick, long, and sweet. Light tannin.
Finish: Cocoa butter.
Conclusion: A more restrained Turkey than the old 8yo.

Flavor Camp: Soft Corn
Where Next? Buffalo Trace

81° (40.5%)
Nose: Approachable and quite delicate. Sweet, with maple-syrup notes, baked fruit, and a little heat from spicy rye.
Palate: Gentle. Still has distillery weight that anchors the mid-palate. Lemon and lifted fruit.
Finish: Gentle.
Conclusion: Turkey Lite.

Flavor Camp: Soft Corn
Where Next? Wiser's Deluxe

RUSSELL'S RESERVE BOURBON 10YO
90°/45%
Nose: Huge and sweet with vanilla, chocolate, caramel. Baked peach, fruit syrups, then the chestnut honey seen on the 101 with Greek pine honey. Thick, almost waxy feel. With water, more rye. Nutmeg.
Palate: As nose with added Turkish Delight and plenty of oak giving support to the liquorous thickness of the weight. Almond. Sweet.
Finish: Rye lift but balanced by the sheer weight. Cinnamon. Tobacco.
Conclusion: Complex and layered.

Flavor Camp: Rich & Oaky
Where Next? Booker's

RARE BREED 108.2°/54.1%
Nose: Deep amber/coppery glints. Less thick than Russell's Reserve and also a cleaner sweetness. Orange and allspice with a previously unseen leathery note. Fragrant and, for Turkey, subtle.
Palate: Overtly spicy. Varnish, that tobacco-leaf quality then spiky rye.
Finish: Long, mixing sweet toffee and jags of spice.
Conclusion: A small batch blend of bourbons between six and 12 years old and bottled undiluted.

Flavor Camp: Rich & Oaky
Where Next? Pappy Van Winkle Family Reserve 20yo

RUSSELL'S RESERVE RYE 6YO 90°/45%AV
Nose: Light gold. Intense rye to start with but very honeyed behind. Less dusty than some ryes but still bold with green fennel seed, spruce, and garden twine. With water, there's camphor, sourdough, and sweet oak.
Palate: Slow, honeyed start. Hard candy and then a dry rye character begins to change the sweetness to a clean acidity.
Finish: Fizzy spice.
Conclusion: Quite a gentle rye.

Flavor Camp: Spicy Rye
Where Next? Millstone Rye 5yo (Holland)

Heaven Hill

LOUISVILLE • WWW.HEAVEN-HILL.COM • HERITAGE CENTER: BARDSTOWN • OPEN ALL YEAR MON–SAT; MAR–DEC, MON–SUN

There are warehouses as far as you can see. Massive metal-clad tenements of whiskey spilling across the rolling Kentucky landscape looking a little like a housing project that's been dumped here by some stray tornado. The extent of the warehousing is testament to the volume of different whiskeys produced by the various Heaven Hill distillers. This, after all, is the American distiller with the largest roster of brands on the market.

There's a feeling of permanence about this scene. This is bourbon's heartland. Two of the Heaven Hill brands are named after legendary pioneers of distillation in this corn-rich land: Evan Williams and Elijah Craig. Yet the Heaven Hill story is a relatively recent one, starting from the distilling wasteland that was left by Prohibition. Only a tiny fraction of the hundreds of distillers who plied their trade before the Volstead Act came into force in the 1920s took up whiskey-making after the repeal. Some of these restarted operations.

There were also, however, some newcomers who sensed an opportunity. The Shapira brothers were in the latter camp. Storekeepers by trade, they bought a plot of land outside Bardstown in the 1930s and started distilling in 1935. They called their distillery Heaven Hill: not, as many imagine out of some romantic allusion, but after the original owner William Heavenhill. When the operation got going properly postwar, they hired a master distiller—and in Kentucky who better to get than a Beam? In this case Earl Beam, Jim's nephew.

THE BOURBON/SCOTCH DIVIDE

One way in which the bourbon industry differs from Scotch is in its intense personal crafting of whiskey styles. Because of Prohibition, American whiskey had to start afresh. The styles that emerged from its distilleries were very much the creations of the distiller. Parker learned from his father; he didn't follow an approach handed down for over a century, as is the case in Scotland. There is a direct physical and emotional attachment. Sometimes it isn't location but the personality of the people.

Earl's son Parker and grandson Craig, now rule the whiskey-making roost here while the Shapira family still owns the business.

Today the Heaven Hill Bardstown site contains the company HQ, a prize-winning visitors' center, and that warehousing, but there's no distillery. There's a reason for that. There used to be one, at the bottom of the hill. Then in 1995 a lightning strike on a warehouse

Not a Bardstown housing project, but just part of Heaven Hill's huge warehousing complex.

Full of color and life, the bourbon is now ready for the next phase of its life—a bottle—and your glass.

sent a river of flaming liquor straight into the distillery and it exploded.

Today, all the Heaven Hill brands are produced at what used to be United Distillers & Vintners' [now Diageo's] Bernheim distillery in Louisville, which the drinks giant had closed in 1999. Switching site is no easy task, and as Parker says with typical understatement, "There were some kinks in here which we had to iron out before we could get the Heaven Hill character right."

Bernheim was fully computerized, but Parker and Craig were used to a sleeves-rolled-up approach. "Whiskey is a hands-on business," Parker says. "You need to make it personal. That's the way in which we've always worked and I guess I just don't know any other way." He likes his whiskeys with age on them; even the Heaven Hill flagship, Evan Williams, is seven years old, a fair age for a bourbon.

Indeed, the father-and-son team craft whiskeys from across the American tradition songbook. There are corn and rye-based bourbons in Evan Williams and Elijah Craig; corn and wheat with Old Fitzgerald;

straight rye in Rittenhouse and Pikesville; and the most recent innovation is the straight-wheat Bernheim Wheat.

I see Parker and Craig's quiet personalities writ large in Parker's eponymous releases and across this calm, understated yet innovative portfolio.

HEAVEN HILL TASTING NOTES

BERNHEIM ORIGINAL WHEAT 90°/45%

Nose: Gentle, with butter and fresh baking, red fruit, and allspice. Clean and defined.
Palate: Tingle of freshly planed oak. Reminiscent of melted rock candy with a hint of toffee and a menthol note. Very fine.
Finish: A stunning glass, gentle yet exotic.
Conclusion: Gentle and dangerously drinkable. A new world of opportunity opens up.

Flavor Camp: **Sweet Wheat**
Where Next? Crown Royal Ltd Edition

OLD FITZGERALD 12YO 90°/45%

Nose: Complex earth tones with licorice, cigar smoke, leather, walnut spongecake.
Palate: A deep brooding bourbon with butterscotch and vanilla underpinnings showing lovely interplay between honey and chocolate. Wood has a presence, but nuttily so.
Finish: Oak, but lovely balance.
Conclusion: Deep and powerful. Demands a cigar.

Flavor Camp: **Rich & Oaky**
Where Next? W L Weller, Pappy Van Winkle

EVAN WILLIAMS SINGLE BARREL 2004 86.6°/43.3%

Nose: Light amber, with the brand's typical sweet spices, smoky citrus fruit, and immediate rye accents, balanced with a gently restrained, mature sweetness. With water, some wintergreen and honey.
Palate: Soft, sweet, and delicate, with orange-blossom honey. Sours toward the back palate, where the spices release. Water makes it almost effervescent.
Finish: Fresh and clean.
Conclusion: Mature but never overoaked. Remarkable series.

Flavor Camp: **Spicy Rye**
Where Next? Four Roses Yellow Label

RITTENHOUSE RYE 80°/40%

Nose: A teasing mix of sweet and sour. Camphor, turps, varnish, rich oak. Hugely spicy. With water, there are nuts, shaved wood, and flamed orange peel.
Palate: Intensely spicy, a firm grip and mouth-tightening tannins overtake surprising sweetness. Scented lemon, dried rose petal.
Finish: Long wonderfully bitter. Rye!
Conclusion: A great start for newcomers to the rye world.

Flavor Camp: **Spicy Rye**
Where Next? Wild Turkey, Sazerac

ELIJAH CRAIG 12YO 94°/47%

Nose: Sweet and dense. Apricot jam, stewed fruit, charred oak. Custard, cedar, and a little tobacco leaf.
Palate: Rounded. A very sweet start, licorice, before spiced apple takes over on the finish.
Finish: Sweet. Candy. Oak.
Conclusion: Sweet and rich. An approachable old-style bourbon.

Flavor Camp: **Rich & Oaky**
Where Next? Old Forester, Eagle Rare

Buffalo Trace

FRANKFORT • WWW.BUFFALOTRACE.COM • OPEN ALL YEAR MON–SAT; APR–OCT, MON–SUN

First there came the buffalo, finding a fording point on a bend in the Kentucky River on their annual migration. Then came the Lee brothers, who set up a trading post, Leestown, in 1775. Today, there's a massive distillery that seems to have acquired more names than most along the way: OFC, Stagg, Schenley, Ancient Age, Leestown—and now Buffalo Trace.

This is a university of straight whiskey distillation. Even the red-brick buildings add to that air. The polar opposite to Maker's Mark with its single recipe, here the aim is to be as diverse as possible: there's wheated bourbon (W L Weller); ryes (Sazerac, Handy); corn/rye bourbon (Buffalo Trace); and single barrels (Blanton's, Eagle Rare). The Pappy Van Winkle range is also made here.

In addition, there's an annual Antique Collection of limited releases and the occasional experimental bourbons. It's as if Buffao Trace is trying to single-handedly restore the number of bourbon brands to its pre-Prohibition level.

Given his multitasking responsibilities, master distiller Harlen Wheatley seems remarkably laid back. "We have five big recipes," he says, "but we only run one at a time. So we'll be on wheated for six to eight weeks, then rye/bourbon, and then one of the three different rye recipes. We like to have a bit of everything!"

Though the specifics are a secret, there's no addition of backset at the cooking stage, which takes place under pressure (*see* pp.18–19). "It is a better way to get all the sugars," says Wheatley, "and results in a more consistent ferment." Only one yeast strain is used, but the fermenters are different sizes creating different environments. The distillation for each brand is, however, totally different with varying degrees of reflux and distillation strength.

Distillation is only half the story. The complex range of differently flavored white dogs (*see* p.18) is matched by a complex range of maturation conditions. Each barrel is different, as is the microclimate within each warehouse. Understand that and you increase your complexity.

"We have 75 different floors in total," explains Wheatley, "split across three sites, and in brick, stone, heated, and rick [multistory, wooden-framed]. Because each floor and each warehouse is different, the location of barrels is important."

It's not just mash bill and distillation, but the physical placement of the barrel that makes the difference. "Weller is seven years old, so we're not going to put that on the top or the bottom floors. Pappy 23yo we have to watch very carefully—that's probably a second or third floor—while Blanton's has its own warehouse, which produces a very specific effect."

Diversity is a result of this human matrix of knowledge.

No distiller in the world has looked so forensically at wood and maturation. As well as building a new microdistillery and having ongoing experiments with recipes for barreling strength on rye and wheat, the distillery has been examining whether the top or the bottom of a tree has an effect. The complex wood chemistry is different at each part: the higher concentration of lignin at the base gives more vanillin; the higher tannins in the top produce more structure and aid esterification.

Buffalo Trace's mastery of a wide range of styles has made it the red-brick University of Bourbon.

So, 96 trees were felled and two barrels were made from each. These have been filled with the same mash bill but at two barreling strengths, and aged in two different warehouses. At the time of writing the experiment is continuing. A further radical development is Warehouse X, which came to being after a tornado ripped the roof off of a rickhouse, exposing the casks there to the open air and light for several months. The resulting bourbon was noticeably different.

Warehouse X holds 150 barrels in four chambers and one "breezeway." Each chamber has a different amount of light (artificial and controlled natural). The humidity in each is controlled, with the breezeway having natural air-flow. "The warehouse gives flavor," the late Elmer T. Lee said. Quite how much and in what way might be revealed in the next 20 years.

The final seal of approval at the distillery for bottles of Buffalo Trace.

BUFFALO TRACE TASTING NOTES

WHITE DOG, MASH NO 1

Nose: Sweet and fat. Cornmeal/polenta. Hot with lily, nutty roasted corn/barley. Hint, with water, of a vegetal *rhum agricole* note.
Palate: Lifted. Big Parma Violet hit then a spreading chewy corn.
Finish: Long and smooth. No harshness.

BUFFALO TRACE 90°/45%

Nose: Amber. Mix of cocoa butter/coconut and a scented violet/herbal note. Touch of apricot and spice. Clean oak. Spiced honey, butterscotch, and tangerine.
Palate: Spicy start with sweet citrus fruit then vanilla and eucalyptus, then Peychaud's Bitters. Fat and generous. Medium-bodied. In time lots of fresh grated nutmeg.
Finish: Light grip and rye spices.
Conclusion: Mature and rich. Balanced.

Flavor Camp: **Soft Corn**
Where Next? Blanton's Single Barrel, Jack Daniel's Gentleman Jack

EAGLE RARE 10YO SINGLE BARREL 90°/45%

Nose: Amber. Deeper than Buffalo Trace, this has more dark chocolate and dried orange peel along with that scented note, which is one of the distillery's signatures. Molasses and lively spices, some cherry cough medicine, star anise. Mellow oak. With water, polished wooden floors.
Palate: Soft and very thick. Quite a different feel to Buffalo Trace with more tannin and crisper oak. Vetiver.
Finish: Dry then an acidic hit.
Conclusion: All together a bigger prospect.

Flavor Camp: **Rich & Oaky**
Where Next? Wild Turkey, Ridgemont Reserve 1792 8yo

W L WELLER 12YO 90°/45%

Nose: Clean and light. Grated nutmeg, vellum, roasting coffee bean. Honeycomb and rose petal with a little hint of heavy florals.
Palate: A clean and very honeyed palate with crisp spice from the oak that softens into melted chocolate.
Finish: Sandalwood.
Conclusion: A wheated bourbon showing the characteristic gentle mellowness of that grain.

Flavor Camp: **Sweet Wheat**
Where Next? Maker's Mark, Crown Royal Ltd Edition

BLANTON'S SINGLE BARREL NO 8/H WAREHOUSE 93°/46.5%

Nose: Amber. More cooked fruit and caramel. Lots of vanilla bean, corn, and peach cobbler. Sweet, clean, and lightly spicy.
Palate: Starchy start then a floral lift—almost the jasmine/lily of the white dog. Wood begins to tighten but this is toffee-like. Almost smoky charred.
Finish: Turmeric and dry oak.
Conclusion: Rounded compared to the Eagle's talons.

Flavor Camp: **Soft Corn**
Where Next? Evan Williams SB

PAPPY VAN WINKLE'S FAMILY RESERVE 20YO 90.1°/45.2%

Nose: Rich amber. Ripe and oaked. Sweet fruit jams and heavy maple syrup. A little spice. With water has the funky/fungal qualities of wood-aged spirits.
Palate: Oak and dry leather. Cigar then mothballs before drifting to dried mint, dried cherry, and licorice.
Finish: Gentle bite and oak.
Conclusion: Old and wooded.

Flavor Camp: **Rich & Oaky**
Where Next? Wild Turkey Rare Breed

SAZERAC RYE & SAZERAC 18YO BOTH 90°/45%

Nose: The younger has a nose of dust, Parma Violet, and proving sourdough bread with orange bitters and red cherry jag. The 18yo is also scented, but the attack has lessened and moved to an integrated leathery/varnish note. Cherries are now black.
Palate: Flinty and intense. Lots of camphor. Classically zesty. The 18yo shows more oak and baked rye bread. Oily rather than flinty, but scented still.
Finish: Allspice and ginger. The 18yo retains the ginger, adds anise, and a throat-thickening sweetness.
Conclusion: Like peatiness in Scotland, the rye character isn't lost but absorbed into the spirit.

Flavor Camp: **Spicy Rye**
Where Next? Young: Eddu (France), Russell's Reserve Rye 6yo; Old: Four Roses 120th Anniversary 12yo, Four Roses Mariage Collection 2009, Rittenhouse Rye

BUFFALO TRACE
DISTILLERY

WHITE DOG
MASH #1

Corn, Rye and Malted Barley Recipe
62.5% Alcohol by Volume (125 Proof)

WHISKEY • DISTILLED & BOTTLED BY BUFFALO TRACE DISTILLERY
FRANKFORT, KENTUCKY • 375 ML

Jim Beam

CLERMONT • WWW.JIMBEAM.COM • OPEN ALL YEAR MON–SUN

Scottish distillers are rightly proud of their whisky-making tradition, yet to the best of my knowledge there's no dynasty in Scotland like the Beams. The family history claims Jacob Beam (originally Boehm) started distilling in 1795 in Washington County. In 1854, his grandson David M. Beam moved the operation near to the railroad in Clear Springs where his sons, Jim and Park, then learned their trade. So far, so normal. It's what happened after Prohibition that is remarkable.

Aged 70 in 1933, Jim applied for a license to distill and built a new distillery in Clermont, with Park and his sons making the whiskey. Jim handed over to his son Jeremiah, then his grandson Booker Noe took up the reins. Now Booker Noe's son, Fred, is there. When you consider that Parker and Craig Beam at Heaven Hill are Park's grandsons too, and that it was a Beam who started Early Times, you begin to wonder whether the state should be renamed.

It's only when you understand that lineage that you can begin to understand why an old man started up the family business again, at the age of 70. What else was James Beauregard Beam to do? Bourbon ran in his veins.

Did he change things? Yes and no. The sweet, hopped yeast, cooked up in the family home was a recreation of the original, but distillation was able to take advantage of twentieth-century developments. I well remember Booker Noe guffawing as I spluttered through a fusel-heavy glass of (another firm's) pre-Prohibition bourbon. "I like true bourbon," he rumbled, "but you know, some things just needed changing."

Beam's post-Prohibition story is very much a balance between the commercial necessities faced by a big brand in an ever-changing market and this adherence of Booker to his belief in Big Bourbon. It's a creative tension that gave the world its biggest-selling bourbon brand, but also saw, in 1988, the launch of the uncompromising "straight from the barrel" brand, Booker's, and then, four years later, the Small Batch Collection.

The downside of being a major brand is that aficionados can be dismissive of the whole range, yet there is as much creativity at Beam's two distilleries in Clermont and Boston as at any other plant. Not that there's any great emphasis placed on secret mash bills as being the main driver for flavor. "The yeast is obviously important," says brand ambassador Bernie Lubbers. "And yes we do have more than one recipe, but the first questions you should ask about any bourbon are what is the proof off the still, what's the barreling strength, and where are the barrels stored? Look at Scotch. It's just barley yet you get hundreds of different flavors. It's not just the recipe!"

The Beam range uses the flavoring potential of strength and location to its fullest. White and Black Label come off at 135° (67.5% abv), are barreled at 125° (62.5% abv), and the barrels are scattered around the warehouses: top, bottom, sides, and middle. Old Grandad is a high rye recipe but is otherwise the same as White and Black. The rye is lower strength: 127° (63.5% abv) and it's barrel led at 125° (62.5% abv).

Things have certainly changed in Clermont since the Beams first started distilling.

JIM BEAM TASTING NOTES

WHITE LABEL 80°/40%

Nose: Fresh and zesty. Has a youthful energy. Light rye lemon spiciness, then ginger and tea. Scented and vibrant.

Palate: After such a sassy nose, the palate starts very silkily with real menthol. Cool mint cigarettes. Butter toffee. Crisp.

Finish: Sweet.

Conclusion: Balanced and vibrant.

> **Flavor Camp: Soft Corn**
> **Where Next?** Jack Daniel's

BLACK LABEL 8YO 80°/40%

Nose: Soft with a little molasses, spiced orange, and a similar fresh spiciness to the White Label. Caçao and cigar ash.

Palate: The oaky notes continue: cedar and char balanced by the punchy spirit. More overtly spicy than the White Label.

Finish: Molasses.

Conclusion: Oak and energy.

> **Flavor Camp: Soft Corn**
> **Where Next?** Jack Daniel's Single Barrel, Buffalo Trace, Jack Daniel's Gentleman Jack

KNOB CREEK 9YO 100°/50%

Nose: Amber. Rich and sweet. Pure fruit. Caramelized fruit sugars, agave syrup. Light coconut and apricot. Cigar leaf.

Palate: Big, sweet, and luscious. Full bodied with lots of cinnamon, blackberry, and spun sugar.

Finish: Oak and butter.

Conclusion: Rich but has that Beam energy.

> **Flavor Camp: Rich & Oaky**
> **Where Next?** Wild Turkey Rare Breed

BOOKER'S 126.8°/63.4%

Nose: Huge and soft. Baked fruit with blackstrap molasses. Tropical fruit and black banana. Deep and powerful.

Palate: Sweet and almost liqueur-like. The spirit coping with the attack of the oak. Blackberry jam and burnt sugar. Orange-blossom honey.

Finish: Wood and heat.

Conclusion: A huge no-holds barred experience.

> **Flavor Camp: Rich & Oaky**
> **Where Next?** Russell's Reserve 10yo

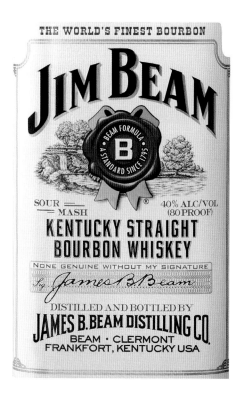

There's even greater variation with the small batches. Knob Creek is distilled to 130° (65% abv) and barreled at 125° (62.5% abv). "It's a 9yo product so we're not going to have any [barrels that] touch the sides or the top floors of the warehouses," explains Lubbers. Basil Hayden is high in rye but distilled and barrelled at 120° (60% abv) and aged in the center of the warehouses as is Knob Creek. Baker's is distilled and barrelled at 125° (62.5% abv) but is aged for seven years on the top floor, "that's why it's so intense." And Bookers is distilled and barreled at 125° (62.5% abv) and aged on the fifth and sixth floors.

"You know," says Lubbers, "Booker would go up there all the time, just stand there and see what was happening." Dreaming, working out. The human touch.

Four Roses

One of the first neon signs in Times Square in the late 1930s was a Four Roses advertisement. Having survived Prohibition, how then did it become invisible in America? Look north. In 1943, Four Roses became one of the five Kentuckian distilleries owned by Seagram. Its new parent then embarked on a peculiar strategy. Four Roses was to become export-led, but restricted in the US because (it is alleged) Seagram CEO Edgar Bronfman Jr. wanted to sell his Canadian whisky instead.

In 1960, it was replaced by a blended version that looked the same, but sure didn't taste like it. Its reputation, unsurprisingly, plummeted before being plucked from the wreckage of Seagram by Japanese brewer/distiller Kirin.

In reality, Four Roses was saved by a bourbon man. Like Jimmy Russell, Booker Noe, and Elmer T., Jim Rutledge believed in his bourbon, nurtured it, preserved it, and now was able to show it.

The one positive legacy from Seagram was its obsession with yeast. It had 300 strains in its Canadian HQ and each of its Kentucky sites used its own strain—all of which were retained at Four Roses when the other sites closed.

In some ways Rutledge has ten distilleries to play with, not one. Here there are two mash bills: OE (75 percent corn, 20 percent rye, five percent barley malt) and OB, where the rye element is upped to 35 percent, which Rutledge claims is the highest for any straight bourbon. Each of these is then fermented with five different yeasts:

K for spiciness; O for bold fruitiness; Q to get a floral, fruity effect; F for an herbal note; and V for light, delicate fruit. All 10 distillates are then aged separately, giving a huge range of flavor possibilities to work with when Rutledge is creating his blends.

With each barrel having its own personality—even with single-story warehousing there are variations between the bottom and the sixth tier—Rutledge has the flexibility to create a complex, consistent product, as well as multiple variations.

It also allows him to be able to have a different blend for each of the ranges. Yellow Label (which uses all ten variants) is completely different to Single Barrel (OBSV), while Small Batch is a blend of different ages of OBSK, OESK, OESO, and OBSO.

What's intriguing about each is how the rye manifests itself. Normally when you taste bourbon there's a step-change between the alluring soft corn and oak start and the spicy attack on the rye on the finish, as if a seemingly mild-mannered secretary has slugged you with a blackjack hidden in her purse. That doesn't happen here. There's rye aplenty, but the transition from sweetness to spiciness is a seamless one, the punch masked by a caress: less of a blackjack and more a stiletto blade. Rutledge finally has the world at his feet.

FOUR ROSES TASTING NOTES

BARREL STRENGTH 15YO SINGLE BARREL
104.2°/52.1%

Nose: Cotton-candy sweetness, green plum, eucalyptus, oak.
Palate: Perfumed, silky, and sweet with fizzing spices. Succulent flow balanced by spice and toffee apple.
Finish: Tight and spicy.
Conclusion: Balanced and fine-boned.

Flavor Camp: **Spicy & Rye**
Where Next? Sazerac 18yo

YELLOW LABEL 80°/40%

Nose: Gentle and lightly sweet, with those floral elements coming through. A hint of peach and then subtle, sweet spice.
Palate: The mellow character continues with some vanilla bean before it starts to tingle lightly with allspice and clove, and lemon peel. Soft fruit is then given a bite of apple.
Finish: Relaxes again with just a brief jag of rye.
Conclusion: Controlled and characterful.

Flavor Camp: **Soft corn**
Where Next? Maker's Mark, 157

BRAND 12 SINGLE BARREL 109.4°/54.7%

Nose: Masses of menthol/eucalyptus, powdered spices. High rye accents, then marzipan and coconut. Intense and high-toned.
Palate: Perfumed, hot, with lots of menthol once more. The oak has grip and gives structure. There are bitter notes of orange peel and dark chocolate, but there's enough sweetness to balance.
Finish: Sweet but bold.
Conclusion: Big flavor delivery.

Flavor Camp: **Spicy Rye**
Where Next? Lot 40

BRAND 3 SMALL BATCH 111.4°/55.7%

Nose: High rye spiciness: allspice, Chinese five-spice powder, intense camphor, and bruised red fruit with sweet oak behind. Intense and captivating.
Palate: Peppermint to start with, alongside cherry throat lozenges. There's a genuine head-clearing quality to this. Pleasant dustiness starts midway, while big citrus fruit and cooked fruit are massing behind.
Finish: Spiced apple. Oak.
Conclusion: Balanced. Bold but with finesse.

Flavor Camp: **Spicy Rye**
Where Next? Wiser's Red Letter

Barton 1792

BARDSTOWN • WWW.1792BOURBON.COM • OPEN ALL YEAR MON–SAT

Being hidden from sight in a ravine would bother most distillers, but for years it suited the guys at a site that has been known by a number of names in its time. If other distilleries were good at getting their distillers working on ever more innovative new expressions, then the fellows down in the hollow outside Bardstown just kept their heads down and got on with making damned good bourbon, which they then sold at a (very) fair price. If no one visited them, that was fine. Not that they were (or are) in any way unfriendly; they just didn't see the necessity of having to play the marketing game. In this respect, it's like the Kentuckian equivalent of one of the numerous Speyside distilleries that sit in the background.

Since Barton 1792's former parent company at one point owned both Loch Lomond and Glen Scotia distilleries, there is what you might call "previous." The 1876 site of Mattingly & Moore was located here before Tom Moore set up in 1899. Its post-Prohibition life started in 1944, when it was bought by Oscar Getz's Barton Brands (the same Getz who gave his name to the marvelous bourbon museum in Bardstown).

The 1940s red-brick distillery uses a number of mash bills (details are secret), its own yeast, and a copper-headed beer column, where the reflux is played and prolonged before the doubler does its work. Barton sold up to Constellation in 1999, which changed the name to Old Tom Moore, before flipping the company to Sazerac, which promptly changed it back to Barton, adding "1792" (the year of Kentucky's accession to the Union) to the moniker. More significantly, they also opened a visitor's center.

Turns out the guys wanted people to see them after all.

High-grade corn is the base of Tom Moore's range of bourbons, giving a broad platform upon which the rye and oak can play.

BARTON 1792 TASTING NOTES

WHITE DOG, FOR RIDGEMONT

Nose: Sweet, fat, and clean with a tight back note. Corn oil and a light dustiness.
Palate: Intensely spicy from the word go. Big impact, then a slow softening (almost works in reverse to normal). Intense.
Finish: Tight. Will need time in wood.

TOM MOORE 4YO 80°/40%

Nose: Fresh, young, and oak-driven. Post oak. Lumberyard. In time, geranium leaf and cedar and fresh-turned earth.
Palate: Aromatic, all rosewood and subtle sweetness. Light with popcorn.
Finish: Toffee.
Conclusion: Young and energetic. Made to mix.

Flavor Camp: Spicy Rye
Where Next? Jim Beam White Label, Woodford Reserve Distiller's Select

VERY OLD BARTON 6YO 86°/43%

Nose: Tea-like. Polished oak, rubbing spices. Vibrant fresh and dry: very much in the house style.
Palate: A sweet and soft entry to the palate. Nutmeg in butter, rose, grapefruit, and coffee.
Finish: Cigar box.
Conclusion: Crisp and clean.

Flavor Camp: Spicy Rye
Where Next? Evan Williams Black Label, Jim Beam Black Label, Sazerac Rye

RIDGEMONT RESERVE 1792 8YO 93.7°/46.8%

Nose: Has that deep, slightly oily note of the white dog but now polished by oak into a fine sheen.
Palate: Ripe with some fresh citrus fruit, a little touch of vanilla, and the tea note seen in the young. Weightier.
Finish: Cigar (now out of the box).
Conclusion: This is a bourbon with which to convince Scotch drinkers.

Flavor Camp: Rich & Oaky
Where Next? Eagle Rare 10yo Single Barrel

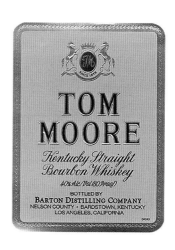

TENNESSEE

In some ways, the story of Tennesseean whiskey parallels that of Kentucky's: boom, Prohibition, and slow recovery. The difference is that while in Kentucky most of the major distillers came back after Prohibition in the 1930s, Tennessee had been dry since 1910 and had operated a smaller-scale industry even in those days. The result was that only one distillery started up immediately after repeal: Jack Daniel's. It would be 25 years before the state's second (legal) distillery, George Dickel, would be opened.

The word "legal" is used deliberately. Tennessee is a microcosm of America's ambivalent relationship with alcohol. Its hills and hollows continue to hide numerous moonshining stills, many of them close to fundamentalist churches preaching against the evils of drink. Its music (and this state is rich in musical heritage) both celebrates and castigates whiskey drinking. For as many songs as there are about the joys of drinking 'shine, there are more that use drink (usually whiskey) as a symbol of dissolution and despair, the refuge of the self-pitying, broken-hearted fool. George Jones, no stranger to booze, sums it up in "Just One More": "Put the bottle on the table and it stays right there/'til I'm not able to see your face in every place I go/ One drink, just one more/and then another."

This dichotomy is seen clearly in Lynchburg: conceivably the most famous small town in the world, home to the world's bestselling American whiskey—just don't expect to be able to wander into a bar in the town and order one. Lynchburg's dry. You won't even get a taste when you tour the distillery.

In other words, they do things a little differently in Tennessee and this extends to their whiskeys: the rye percentage in the mash bill is very low for example (*see* pp.18–19). Conforming to the same legal framework as straight bourbon, to become Tennessee whiskey the white dog (new make) must be put through the Lincoln County Process: filtration through a bed of sugar-maple charcoal, before being barreled. The result is a softer and slightly sootier spirit.

Is this wholly a Tennessean invention? There's evidence that filtration was being used in Kentucky as far back as 1815, but it appears to have been dropped soon after. As Jeff Arnett, master distiller at Jack Daniel's, points out, it's expensive.

The fact that it is known as the Lincoln County Process also points to it not only being a Tennessee specialty, but one fixed in a specific location: Cave Springs where the Jack Daniel's distillery is now situated. Before the distilling prodigy arrived, one Alfred Eaton was using Cave Springs' limestone water to make his whiskey—and using the charcoal-filtering method from 1825 onward. If Eaton didn't invent it, then he certainly exploited it to the full.

Quite where it came from no one has been able to say. Vodka was being charcoal-filtered by that time, but unless there was a Russian *émigré* distiller in the area, it's unlikely that the technique could have been directly passed on. It remains a mystery, just another one of Tennessee's many secrets.

Left: Charcoal filtration (here, at Jack Daniel's) is the key difference between Tennessee whiskey and bourbon.

Right: Jack Daniel's has always prided itself on its old-time charm.

Money to burn: every year, Jack Daniel's spends more than $1 million on making charcoal.

Jack Daniel's

LYNCHBURG • WWW.JACKDANIELS.COM • OPEN ALL YEAR MON–SUN

Iconic is a word too freely bandied around in the world of drink, but occasionally its use is appropriate. Jack Daniel's is one of those times. Clutched by numerous rock stars, the square bottle with the black and white label has become both a signifier for hedonistic rebelliousness and down-home, small-town values. Brand-building 101 starts with Jack Daniel's.

Its founding has all the hallmarks of a folktale. Born round about 1846, the young Tenesseean Jack Daniel argued with his wicked stepmother and ran away from home to live with an "uncle." By the age of 14 he was helping out a storekeeper and lay preacher called Dan Call who was running a still in Louse Creek. When Dan was away in the Civil War, Jack learned the art of whiskey-making from Nearest Green, an old slave, and when Jack moved from Louse Creek (maybe he already had an eye for marketing) in 1865, Green's sons, George and Eli went with him.

Jack moved to take up the lease of the old Eaton distillery in Cave Springs on the outskirts of Lynchburg where, it is generally agreed, the Lincoln County mellowing process originated (Lynchburg was in Lincoln County at the time). "Our uniqueness starts with that water," says Jack Daniel's master distiller Jeff Arnett. "It is 56°F (13°C) all year and it provides minerals and nutrients that become part of the distillery's character. If we had different water, the character would change." That water from the echoing cool cave is added to a low rye (eight percent) mash bill—to reduce any pepperiness in the final spirit, and the soured mash is fermented with the aid of the distillery's own yeast. Distillation is via a copper still and the doubler gives a 140° (70% abv) white dog, which then undergoes the process that makes Jack a Tennessee whiskey: charcoal mellowing through 10 feet of sugar-maple charcoal.

Hidden in the woods: just one of Jack Daniel's many warehouses.

Why, though, were Tennessee whiskeys mellowed in the first place? "I reckon that there were things in those old days that Jack couldn't control and mellowing got rid of them" says Arnett. "It evened things out and he could use fast-growing local sugar maple. He did a lot of things for purely practical reasons.

"If you taste the white dog coming off the still it's astringent, after mellowing there's a different mouth-feel, its clean and light," he adds. "Technically speaking we don't have the same issues as Jack faced, but without mellowing our character changes."

Why then, if it's so beneficial, wasn't the technique more widespread? "It's expensive! We have 72 vats and each has to have its charcoal changed every six months. That's $1 million a year."

The more you investigate Jack Daniel's, the greater the realization that it is all about wood, be that charcoal or barrels. "We make our own barrels," says Arnett. "We have our own wood buyer, our own drying process, our own toasting process. It all creates complex characters to give that toasty upfront sweetness that tells you it's Jack."

The long-running campaign—which has never exploited Jack's notorious party-animal side—has you believing this is some small-scale operation from Sleepy Hollow. Nothing could be further from the truth. The operation is vast, and all for one make, albeit with three expressions.

There have been some changes in recent years: the flavored-up Tennessee Honey and Tennessee Fire; Arnett's unaged Tennessee rye; and, in homage to one of its most famous drinkers, Sinatra Select, which uses barrels with deeply grooved staves to maximize the surface area available to the white dog. With a $103-milion expansion of capacity underway, maybe the next should be belated recognition of Nearest Green?

Copper, here in the beer still, helps to lighten the white dog.

JACK DANIEL'S TASTING NOTES

BLACK LABEL, OLD NO.7 80°/40%
Nose: Golden amber. Sooty with caramelized sugars and felt, then an iris note. Eucalyptus wood on a barbecue. Sweet.
Palate: Light sweet and clean with vanilla and marmalade sponge but young and firm underneath.
Finish: Touch of spice and a touch of balancing bitterness.
Conclusion: Easy sweet and mixable.

Flavor Camp: Soft Corn
Where Next? Jim Beam White Label

GENTLEMAN JACK 80°/40%
Nose: Less sooty and oaky than standard Jack with more creamy vanilla. Bonfire in the woods. More custard and ripe banana.
Palate: Very smooth and soft. Chewy and fleshy fruits with the rigidity of the standard underneath.
Finish: Spiced.
Conclusion: Softer and more gentle.

Flavor Camp: Soft Corn
Where Next? Jim Beam Black Label

SINGLE BARREL 90°/45%
Nose: Dark amber. More banana. Bigger and more estery. Wood. Pine-like. With water a charred note.
Palate: Has the energy of the standard and the sweetness of Gentleman with an added spicy attack. Balanced.
Finish: Clean and lightly spiced.
Conclusion: Takes the best points of the two styles.

Flavor Camp: Soft Corn
Where Next? Jim Beam Black Label

George Dickel

CASCADE HOLLOW, BETWEEN NASHVILLE & CHATTANOOGA • WWW.DICKEL.COM • OPEN ALL YEAR MON–SAT

The distillery in Cascade Hollow takes us back to the quilt of tales and the myths that have been bundled around brands. American whiskey's tempestuous history, with brands changing hands many times, distilleries disappearing then reappearing on another site and with a new name, not to mention the devastation wreaked by Prohibition, has meant that company archives have been shredded. In addition, what was normal behaviour in Tennessee in the nineteenth century might not seem too respectable in the twenty-first. The blanket is pulled over the truth.

Such is the case with George Dickel. The sanitized official version has him and his wife, Augusta, out for a horse-buggy ride in 1867, when they come to Tullahoma and decide to build a distillery there. The fact is, George Dickel never owned the Cascade distillery. Neither did he ever make whisk(e)y.

Dickel was a German immigrant who arrived in Nashville in 1853, and started off as a shoe retailer, before branching out into grocery and whiskey wholesaling, which, during the Civil War, meant the other sort of bootlegging. A profitable business ensued, with Dickel, his brother-in-law, Victor Shwab, and Meier Salzkotter going into business and selling whiskey through Shwab's Climax Saloon (a fairly appropriate name for one of Nashville's premier dens of iniquity). In 1888, Victor Schwab personally bought a two-thirds share in the Cascade distillery, which had been established in 1877, and granted Dickel exclusive rights to bottle and distribute the whiskey.

A decade later, Shwab had bought the distillery outright, where it was run by MacLin Davis—the real (and only) distiller. The Shwab family and Dickel's widow then switched production—complete with charcoal mellowing—of Cascade whiskey to the Stitzel distillery in Louisville in 1911, the year after Tennessee went dry.

The firm was sold in 1937 by George Shwab to Schenley Industries, which, in 1958, sent Ralph Dupps to Tennessee to start up production of George Dickel in a new distillery close to the original Cascade plant. Now that's a story. There's nothing wrong with George Dickel

being a successful wholesaler. After all, it's true to say that some of the greatest names in whiskey were just that.

Today, the George Dickel distillery is situated in a narrow tree-shaded valley on the highland rim of the Cumberland plateau, close to Normandy Lake. The grains and corn are pressure-cooked and fermented for three to four days with the aid of Dickel's own yeast. As this is a Tennessee whisk(e)y, it is charcoal-mellowed prior to barreling, but here the technique is different to the one at Jack Daniel's 18 miles to the southwest.

At Dickel, the white dog is chill-filtered prior to mellowing, to remove fatty acids. The vats have woolen blankets on their tops and bottoms; the former to allow an even distribution of the white dog, which floods the vat (no drip-feeding here) and the latter to stop any charcoal from being pulled through. Ten days later, it's barreled and then left to age in single-story hilltop warehouses.

Stylistically, it is totally different from Jack. Dickel is all about lush fruit and sweetness. Even though its rye (launched 2012) has 95 percent of the grain in its mash bill and is aged for a relatively short four years, this mild-mannered fruity character prevails.

The distillery was closed between 1999 and 2003, but is now in full production, with owner Diageo finally realizing that it has had a world-class whiskey on its books for years. Now all they need to do its get the history straight. Shwab—and MacLin Davis—deserve it.

The Cascade distillery has changed somewhat since the days when Victor Shwab owned it.

Sugar maple rick ready to be fired into charcoal...

... through which the white dog from this still will be filtered.

GEORGE DICKEL TASTING NOTES

SUPERIOR NO.12 90°/45%
Nose: Amber. Very sweet and slightly waxy. Apple pie and lemon. Light clove and light corn syrup.
Palate: Very smooth and lightly herbal notes: back to thyme and dried oregano, then ginger, lime blossom, and honey.
Finish: Clean and soft with baked apple and a final cinnamon twist.
Conclusion: Gentle and smooth but has real personality.

Flavor Camp: **Soft Corn**
Where Next? Early Times, Hudson Baby Bourbon

8YO 80°/40%
Nose: Really sweet and fruity, with plump apricot cobbler, some mashed banana, and peach. Subtle, with fruit syrups galore. Oak grows as it develops. Water brings out mandarin and some pink grapefruit alongside sweet spices.
Palate: Clean and heightened fruitiness. Light oak. There's a hint of char, but the wood is in check. Balanced and succulent.
Finish: Simple and short.
Conclusion: Luscious and long.

Flavor Camp: **Soft Corn**
Where Next? Jameson Gold

12YO 90°/45%
Nose: Mature. The fruit has receded and now some oak comes through. A little drier moves to oolong tea and caramelized nectarine.
Palate: Very precise, with lots of fresh cherries. Balance struck between middling oak grip and coconut and the Dickel signature of gentle, sweet fruit.
Finish: Dry-roasted spices.
Conclusion: Mature and elegant.

Flavor Camp: **Fruity & Spicy**
Where Next? The BenRiach 16yo

BARREL SELECT 80°/40%
Nose: Vanilla comes to the fore alongside mandarin, wisteria, and juicy fruit. Has the juiciness of the 8yo but with added cream and a little touch of butter-fried cinnamon and nutmeg.
Palate: Shows a light bite of fruit skin, light lemon zest, and some pepper.
Finish: Softens.
Conclusion: Polite and charming.

Flavor Camp: **Soft Corn**
Where Next? Forty Creek Copper Pot Reserve

RYE 90°/45%
Nose: This is rye in its most relaxed, avuncular guise. Gentle and in that typically sweet Dickel character. Persimmon and peach pit lighten into ointment and strawberry. With water, there is clove.
Palate: Gentle spices. Not a rye to scare you but woo you. More spices with water.
Finish: Perfumed.
Conclusion: A breakfast rye?

Flavor Camp: **Spicy Rye**
Where Next? Crown Royal Reserve

CRAFT DISTILLERS

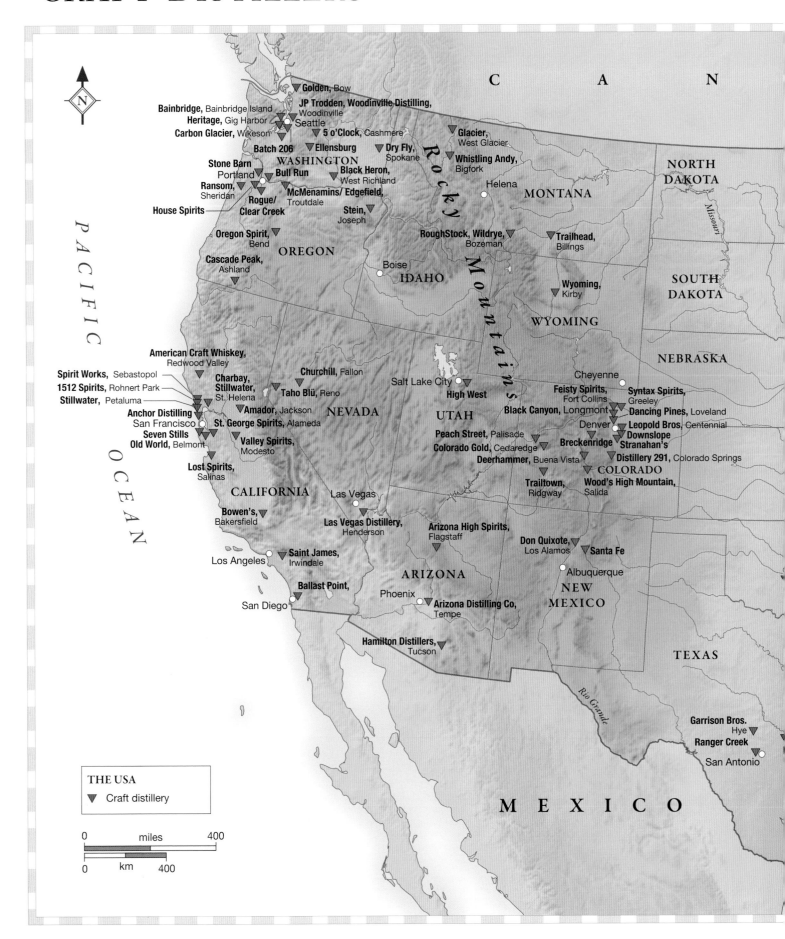

C A N A N

Golden, Bow

JP Trodden, Woodinville Distilling,
Woodinville

Bainbridge, Bainbridge Island
Heritage, Gig Harbor
Carbon Glacier, Wikeson
Seattle

5 o'Clock, Cashmere

Batch 206
Ellensburg
Dry Fly, Spokane

Glacier, West Glacier

Whistling Andy, Bigfork

Stone Barn
Portland
Bull Run
Black Heron, West Richland

WASHINGTON

Helena

MONTANA

NORTH DAKOTA

Ransom, Sheridan
Rogue/Clear Creek
McMenamins/ Edgefield, Troutdale

House Spirits

Stein, Joseph

Oregon Spirit, Bend

OREGON

RoughStock, Wildrye, Bozeman

Trailhead, Billings

Cascade Peak, Ashland

Boise

IDAHO

Wyoming, Kirby

SOUTH DAKOTA

WYOMING

Rocky Mountains

NEBRASKA

American Craft Whiskey, Redwood Valley

Churchill, Fallon

Cheyenne

Spirit Works, Sebastopol
1512 Spirits, Rohnert Park
Stillwater, Petaluma

Charbay, Stillwater, St. Helena
Taho Blü, Reno

Salt Lake City

High West

Feisty Spirits, Fort Collins
Black Canyon, Longmont

Syntax Spirits, Greeley
Dancing Pines, Loveland

Anchor Distilling
San Francisco
St. George Spirits, Alameda
Amador, Jackson

NEVADA

UTAH

Denver

Leopold Bros, Centennial
Downslope
Stranahan's

Seven Stills
Old World, Belmont
Valley Spirits, Modesto

Peach Street, Palisade
Colorado Gold, Cedaredge
Deerhammer, Buena Vista

Breckenridge
Distillery 291, Colorado Springs

Lost Spirits, Salinas

CALIFORNIA

Las Vegas

Trailtown, Ridgway
Wood's High Mountain, Salida

COLORADO

Bowen's, Bakersfield

Las Vegas Distillery, Henderson

Arizona High Spirits, Flagstaff

Don Quixote, Los Alamos
Santa Fe

Los Angeles

Saint James, Irwindale

Albuquerque

ARIZONA

NEW MEXICO

Ballast Point,
San Diego

Phoenix
Arizona Distilling Co, Tempe

TEXAS

Hamilton Distillers, Tucson

PACIFIC OCEAN

Rio Grande

Garrison Bros. Hye
Ranger Creek
San Antonio

M E X I C O

THE USA
▼ Craft distillery

0 — miles — 400
0 — km — 400

MINNESOTA

Panther,
Osakis

WISCONSIN

45th Parallel,
New Richmond

Minneapolis

Lake
Superior

Lake
Michigan

Lake
Huron

Civilized Spirits, Grand Traverse,
Traverse City

Great Lakes,
Milwaukee

MICHIGAN

IOWA

Death's Door, Old Sugar, Yahara Bay
Madison

New Holland,
Holland

Red Cedar,
East Lansing

Aeppeltreow, Burlington
Northshore, Lake Bluff

Detroit

Big Cedar,
Sturgis

Flat Rock, Fairbairn

Templeton

Cedar Ridge,
Swisher

FEW, Evanston

Koval,
Chicago

Quincy Street,
Riverside

Journeyman,
Three Oaks

Ernest Scarano,
Gibsonsburg

Des
Moines

Mississippi River,
Le Claire

INDIANA

OHIO

Middle West, Watershed
Columbus

ILLINOIS

Dancing Tree,
Shade

W. Virginia

Plains,
Indianapolis

Woodstone Creek,
Cincinnati

McCormick,
Weston

Pinkney Bend,
New Haven

Angostura,
Lawrenceburg

John McCulloch,
Martinsville

Kansas
City

Dark Horse,
Lenexa

Mad Buffalo,
Shawneetown Spur

Square One,
St Louis

Barrel House,
Lexington

Alltech

Isaiah
Morgan,
Summersville

Smooth
Ambler,
Maxwelton

MISSOURI

Ohio

KENTUCKY

VIRGINIA

Copper Run,
Walnut Shade

Corsair,
Bowling Green

Piedmont, Madison

ARKANSAS

Nashville

TENNESSEE

Blue Ridge,
Bostic

NORTH
CAROLINA

na City

Arkansas

Memphis

Dark Corner, Greenville

Rock Town,
Little Rock

Prichard's
Distillery Inc.,
Kelso

Ivy Mountain,
Mt.Airy

SOUTH
CAROLINA

in D Witherspoon,
sville

Atlanta

GEORGIA

allas Distilleries,
arland

Cathead,
Madison

Georgia Distilling
Milledgeville

allas

MISSISSIPPI

ALABAMA

e & Robertson,
orth

Jackson

Thirteenth Colony,
Americus

nes,

irits,
e

LOUISIANA

Yellow Rose, Pinehurst

er, Houston

New Orleans

FLORIDA

Tampa

Gulf of
Mexico

Miami

MAINE

Penobscot Bay,
Winterport

Augusta

Sweetgrass,
Union

Green Mountain,
Stowe

New England, Portland

NEW YORK

VT

Saratoga
Galway

NH

Sea Hagg, North Hampton

Ryan & Wood, Gloucester

Nashoba

MA

Bully Boy, Nashoba, Boston

Lake
Ontario

Finger Lakes,
Berdett

Hillrock Estate
Ancram

Bolton

Damnation Alley, Belmont

Berkshire Mountain, Great Barrington

Delaware Phoenix,
Walton

CT

R.I.

Triple Eight,

Catskill, Bethel

Sons of Liberty, Nantucket Is.
South Kingstown

Lake
Erie

Tuthilltown, Gardiner

Long Island, Baiting Hollow

Nahnias & Fils, Yonkers

Tirado, Bronx

New
York

Breukelen Distilling,

PENNSYLVANIA

Mountain Laurel
Bristol

King's County,

Pittsburgh
Distilling

Philadelphia

Cooper River,
Camden

Noble Experiment,
Brooklyn

MD

DE

NJ

Pinchgut Hollow,
Fairmount

Washington, D.C.

Catoctin Creek, Purcellville

W. Virginia
Distilling,
Morgantown

Copper Fox, Sperryville

W.
VIRGINIA

Mount Vernon, Smith Bowman, Fredericksburg

Belmont Farms, Stillhouse, Culpeper

Reservoir, Richmond

VIRGINIA

Virginia Distillery,
Eades Hollow

Appalachian Mountains

Mississippi

ATLANTIC OCEAN

When writing of the burgeoning American craft scene, you need to accept that you're never going to be completely up to date. This constantly shifting, ever-expanding map of distilleries simply changes too quickly. In the time it has taken me to write this sentence, it's possible that another two distilleries have opened. Understanding the thinking behind motivation is more important than simply trying to log what exists.

When the philosophies of these new distillers emerge, you can see that this is not simply a pioneering twenty-first-century approach, discovering what is possible, but also a palimpsest of American whiskey, redressing an imbalance. Craft is breaking new territory by rediscovering what was lost, recasting what whiskey in the USA might have looked like were it not for Prohibition, the Depression, and war.

Here's the country that perfected The Brand now witnessing small-scale revolution, where distillers are establishing new links with farmers, who themselves have existed outside of the agro-industrial system, preserving heritage grains and a holistic relationship with the land. Craft is America asking questions about itself. It can be dismissed as nostalgic, looking at the past through sepia-hued glasses, but if it is true to itself, it is a deep examination of what is possible.

We've already seen the white-whiskey phenomenon (although I'm of the camp that says whiskey is aged spirit), new takes on rye, bourbon, and single malt. There are mixed mashes and new cereals, new smoking techniques and barrel sizes; adapted brewing techniques, different yeasts, the effects of altitude and *solera* aging.

It is similar to craft brewing but different in one significant aspect. "Craft brewing was a reaction to flavorless beers," explains New Holland's Rich Blair. "In distilling, however, we're not up against an inferior product."

It is defined as much by philosophical stance as size. "Craftsmen have to learn their craft," says Chip Tate at Balcones. "That means knowing what people did before you and then adding something to that, rather than simply copying. There is a process you need to undertake. You have to learn from the masters, start as an apprentice, then become a journeyman. Only then, finally, can you become a craftsman. It's a question of discipline."

Inevitably, though, craft can become a lazily (even disingenuously) applied badge. Major distillers are taking note of what the small guys are doing, adapting some techniques to create their own diffusion lines. Some craft operations will be snapped up, as has happened in craft brewing. At the other end of the scale, some small players will continue to claim to be distillers when they are no more than bottlers. In other words, there will continue to be confusion over what is, and isn't, craft.

The ones who will succeed will be those who understand some simple basics about whiskey. It may be craft, but it is also a business. As High West's David Perkins says, "You have to make payroll"— and whiskey takes time.

The other hurdle is distribution. "People don't realize the complexities of the American distribution system," says Anchor's David King. "You can't just develop a whiskey in, say, Colorado and get national distribution. The booze industry is cash-intensive. There will be a lot of fallout because of business reasons, not quality."

Craft is contradictory. It is challenging orthodoxy, which is exactly how things should be. As a result, it is already producing world-class whiskeys. What follows are representatives of a cross-section of what is happening across the country. They are all a hugely welcome addition to the wider whisky family and, like all great distillers, they ask difficult questions.

Challenging orthodoxy is the prerogative of the craft distiller.

Tuthilltown

TUTHILLTOWN • GARDINER • WWW.TUTHILLTOWN.COM • OPEN ALL YEAR; SEE WEBSITE FOR DAYS & DETAILS

Hudson's hand-sized bottles are becoming a familiar sight internationally, thanks to a partnership in 2010 between William Grant & Sons (which now owns and distributes the brand) and Tuthilltown, which makes the whiskey. It is unlikely that it will be the last such merger and solves one of the major issues for the craft producer: distribution.

When Ralph Erenzo got his license in 2003, he became the first (legal) distillery in New York State since Prohibition. He was thus the first to ask, "What is my style going to be?"

"If you ask Dad and Brian [Lee] that, they'll say they didn't know what they were doing, so they created a new way of doing it," says Ralph's son, Gable, Tuthilltown's distiller and brand ambassador. One of their approaches was—and is—to be true to the surrounding area. "We have always worked with local farmers to grow heirloom varieties of corn," he adds. "That remains a huge part of the flavor profile."

The other break with the norm of American whiskey production was the use of small casks. Initially two- to five-gallon casks were used, but as production has grown, their size has increased. "Now the majority are between 15 and 26 gallons," says Erenzo, "and we have a stockpile of 53-gallon casks. They give you a wider spectrum of flavor, but solely using large casks doesn't necessarily fit Hudson's profile, so we are both looking to create consistency through blending different-sized barrels."

Innovations continue. There's a link with a local maple-syrup producer, and a smoked rye (sold as a white whiskey), while even potentially catastrophic occurrences have been turned into opportunities. "When we had a distillery fire in 2012, we had just filled some casks and the ones that survived we'll release as a double-charred whisky," laughs Erenzo. He's also now lecturing on distillery safety for the American Distilling Institute.

He rejects the idea that the partnership with William Grant means Tuthilltown is no longer craft. "As long as we produce Hudson here, we'll be craft," he replies. "Even with our expansion we'll still only be making 60,000 gallons [the limit to "craft" is set at 100,000 gallons per annum]. Working with Grant's has changed our lives for the better because we have access to knowledge, distribution, and over 100 years of distilling experience." His advice to a new distiller? "Work with what you have locally. Don't try to be the next Maker's Mark and a huge national brand."

In other words, you can be happy being small.

TUTHILLTOWN TASTING NOTES

HUDSON BABY BOURBON 92°/46%

Nose: Dry and slightly powdery, moving to corn husk, then sweet popcorn.
Palate: Sweet and ripe to start with, bulging with firm orchard fruit. The the wood gives some structure to the mid-palate.
Finish: Lightly dusty again.
Conclusion: A surprisingly serious baby.

Flavor Camp: Soft Corn
Where Next? Canadian Mist

HUDSON NEW YORK CORN 92°/46%

Nose: Clear—corn whiskey does not need to be aged. Sweet, with popcorn and the wild floral notes that come off corn. Heavy rose/lily and then berry fruit.
Palate: Mashy but has bite and energy. The corn gives this fatness to the palate, which is cut with green corn leaf.
Finish: Nutty, powdery.
Conclusion: Fresh and characterful.

Flavor Camp: Soft Corn
Where Next? Heaven Hill Mellow Corn

HUDSON SINGLE MALT 92°/46%

Nose: Cereal sweetness, grist, and fresh oak. Whole-wheat bread with some dried fruit inside. Lightly citric and a little touch of yeast. With water, more of the mash tun and burlap.
Palate: The oak comes through. Dusty. Malt barns. Some sweetness behind.
Finish: Short and crisp.
Conclusion: A fresh American take on single malt.

Flavor Camp: Malty & Dry
Where Next? Auchentoshan 12yo

HUDSON FOUR GRAIN BOURBON 92°/46%

Nose: Slightly sweeter than Baby Bourbon and even a little grassy. Black butter, fresh corn sweetness, and caramelized fruits.
Palate: Sweet, with bold oak, which balances the almost liqueur-like density. Canned blackberry. Mid-palate is rye-accented, with a fresh green-apple element.
Finish: Lightly dusty.
Conclusion: A fresh, sweet bourbon.

Flavor Camp: Soft Corn
Where Next? Jameson Black Barrel

HUDSON MANHATTAN RYE 92°/46%

Nose: Yew trees. Pine forest with berries in its undergrowth. Sweetness and lightly herbal before black grape and subtly bitter notes appear.
Palate: Lightly oily texture. Big and ripe, with that balancing bitterness on the sides of the tongue.
Finish: Tart.
Conclusion: Characterful.

Flavor Camp: Spicy Rye
Where Next? Millstone 5yo

Kings County

KINGS COUNTY • BROOKLYN, NEW YORK • WWW.KINGSCOUNTYDISTILLERY.COM • OPEN SAT ONLY FOR TOURS

When I was doing a tasting in Brooklyn a few years back, I was given a small bottle of clear liquid from what was the city's first distillery. It seemed both exciting, and kind of strange. The word "craft" is redolent with the idea of the backwoods. Even the uniform—plaid shirts and beards (for the guys)—suggests that. It's not Brooklyn.

Now, however, Nicole Austin, the woman who gave me that bottle, informs me that there are probably 18 distilleries within New York City. The one where she is blender, Kings County, is no longer "the weird one," but part of a trend.

She is a chemical engineer by education, and though whiskey was never suggested as a career option, when the process was explained to her (in a bar) she realized it could be. Fortuitously, her epiphany came just as Kings County was starting up in 2010.

Austin has been a strong advocate of small casks, feeling that not only were they a sensible option in a financial sense, but also that they worked. "People were saying that it was wrong not to use 53-gallon barrels, as that was the only way to produce a mature whisky. We've used five-gallon casks because they make good-quality whiskey as well."

Kings County's size means that there is a narrower margin for error, however.

"If you are a large producer, you can pick the barrels you want," Austin explains. "We can't, so I'm always working within the confines of what barrels we have." Working within such a small scale is also unforgiving, with individual differences being magnified. This intimate focus not only gives greater insights into the nature of maturation, but helps dictate the Kings County style.

"No one could teach us what to do," she continues, "so we had to do what we could. It took a little time to find the sweet spot, but whatever our vision, we're forced to operate in the reality of a market."

It's easy to forget that Austin's "little time" is four years—a nanosecond in whisky history. "I was concerned initially with people saying that you could overextract, and maybe we were more concerned than we needed to be. Part of the process is developing the confidence to trust in our own judgment. I just want us to be established as a high-quality whiskey."

The distillery's expansion with two new stills (from coppersmith Forsyths of Rothes, Scotland) shows that they are on the right path. Their bourbon has been joined by a revelatory rye using local grain, and larger casks are now also being utilized.

Kings County is finding its feet—and doing so quickly.

KINGS COUNTY TASTING NOTES

BOURBON CASK SAMPLE 90°/45%

Nose: Lightly yeasty, with a succulent fruitiness, some citrus fruit (tangerine). Moves into mint/camphor chocolate, light cedar, polished wood, and peppered corn. Lifted and smoothed with water.
Palate: Soft start, then drives forward with crackling rye adding energy and a sour note to offset the inherent sweetness. Sticky and long, with a little lime skin.
Finish: Fragrant bitters.
Conclusion: Young but very promising.

The rapidly expanding Kings County distillery brought distilling back to Brooklyn.

Corsair

CORSAIR • NASHVILLE, TN, & BOWLING GREEN, KY • WWW.CORSAIRARTISAN.COM • OPEN ALL YEAR; SEE WEBSITE FOR DAYS & DETAILS

Strange to think that Corsair, the most innovative, questing distillery in the whiskey world, started with distiller Darek Bell making biodiesel in a garage with his friend Andrew Webber. "While sweating over a batch, Andrew remarked that he wished we were making whiskey," recalls Bell. "Soon we found ourselves studying distilleries and the craft of distilling. We began building stills and making spirits." Soon after, Corsair Distillery was founded. Now there are two: one in Kentucky, the other in Tennessee.

Innovation can mean being different, or a forensic exploration of that question: "What if?" No one has taken that exploration (in whiskey-making terms, at least) as far as Darek Bell.

First came an examination of grains. Every cereal was tried, from barley to quinoa, buckwheat to amaranth, rye to teff. Then came different roastings, distilled beers, then malting and smoking.

"To expand our smoked-whiskey capabilities we had no choice but to build our own malting facility," says Bell. "We've made 80 different smoked whiskeys, utilizing every possible smoke we can get our hands on: from alder wood to white oak and every species in between."

Next came a word not often associated with any American whiskey: blending. "Some types of smoke are great for the nose, some for the palate, and others for the finish, but they rarely work well in all three areas," Bell explains. "A white-oak-smoked malt makes a great base smoke that gives a lot of punch to the palate. Fruit-wood smoke gives

a great nose and pleasant sweetness to the front. Maple wood adds a great finish. By blending these three, you create a whiskey with depth and dimension.

"Then we can blend amaranth whiskey with hickory-smoked malt into a remarkable smoked whiskey. Now that we have this library we can work on new blends at a faster pace. All this allows us more room for creativity and to dial in and refine certain flavors. These individual whiskeys are all-new colors and brushes. The blends are the canvas."

You do sometimes wonder if Corsair is a laboratory or a distillery.

"We have some major attention-deficit disorder," Bell confesses. "We make about 100 new whiskey recipes a year, but we want to create new styles of whiskey: to boldly go where no other whiskey geeks have gone before! From day one we decided to be respectful of tradition but make whiskeys that were anything but."

That's another of those tricky balances.

"I would rather create a new category and be judged differently," he concludes. "How many quinoa whiskeys are we competing with? None."

CORSAIR TASTING NOTES

FIREHAWK (OAK/MUIRA/MAPLE) CASK SAMPLE 100°/50%

Nose: Sweet and slightly leathery smoke, with a little vegetal/green-leaf edge alongside peppercorn. Lightly honeyed and citric behind. Blackberry and incense. With water, more embers.

Palate: Big, dry, smokehouse start that moves to tanned leather. Good spread of flavors, with the sweetness balancing the smoke belch.

Finish: Medium length.

Conclusion: Balanced and fascinating.

NAGA (BARBERRY/CLOVE) CASK SAMPLE 100°/50%

Nose: Aromatic, with rooty purple fruit that hints at licorice and earthy dark fruit. More ash, like a spent bonfire with some smoldering leaves. Dry roots and spices.

Palate: Very dry. Ash smoke allows some orris root to comes through. Light grip.

Finish: Dry.

Conclusion: Same whiskey, different smoke, completely different result.

BLACK WALNUT CASK SAMPLE 100°/50%

Nose: Lifted, with mulberry jam. Rich smoke and subtle fruit. Little touch of cigar ash. Big and powerful.

Palate: Bold distillate and a little more orthodox. Sweet start, mid-palate softness.

Finish: A little short. Smoky.

Conclusion: Has a rich, deep, dark boldness.

HYDRA (BLEND OF SMOKED WHISKEYS) CASK SAMPLE 100°/50%

Nose: Sweet and liqueur-like. Thick honey, some molasses. The smoke is held in check. Very fruity with tobacco leaf. Dry with water.

Palate: An interplay between dry and sweet elements here. A little hint of lanolin and there is some mid-palate richness. Fragrant wood smoke comes in late.

Finish: Smoky and a little dry.

Conclusion: A fascinating experiment.

Balcones

WACO, TEXAS • WWW.BALCONESDISTILLING.COM • OPEN; TOURS BY ARRANGEMENT

Some years ago, the mightily bearded Chip Tate said, "We're not making whiskey in Texas; we are making Texan whiskey." It is a stance that chimes with the more thoughtful distillers around the world: the use of the local, an understanding of what makes you special, taking inspiration from the conditions that arise around you.

Having designed and built his first distillery, Tate was building a new plant at the time of writing. "It was an interesting process because it was the first time I'd put my ideas on paper for engineers. Actually, it's two new distilleries," he adds, "I've taken the chance to rebuild the original. I was tired of not having the still capacity. Now we can fulfill current demand and do the things I've been wanting to work on, which would have seemed self-indulgent in the old plant. I wanted to start a campfire of interest with Balcones, but I've ended up fighting a forest fire."

His whiskies (Balcones is one of the few US distillers to use the "whisky" spelling) are complex, and boldly compelling, yet subtly layered. All are clearly manifestations of Tate's location. The Balcones Blue Corn, made from Hopi atole cornmeal, smells of roasted nachos; Brimstone's aromas (from scrub oak) bring to mind resinous, clinging campfire smoke. This is Texas in a bottle.

"The Texan investigations are progressing well," Tate says. "We use a nonconventional [heirloom] corn that was initially causing some issues over farmers being unable to get insurance for growing it, but now we have a farmer who was an attorney who understands environmental laws.

"Using atole or Texan scrub oak sounded right," he adds. "You have to be open to flavors and smells around you; can I use those big Texan live oaks? How does the Texan climate differ to that of Kentucky and how, then, does that affect maturation? Yes, use science; experiment and work outside the traditional comfort zone, but remember you can't just put lipstick on a pig."

Spend any time with Tate and conversation drifts into these philosophical musings about teleology, craft, and craftsmanship, and his firmly held beliefs about the need to serve an apprenticeship.

"It's like jazz theory," he says. "Learning it is mind-numbingly technical, then you see someone playing intuitively. You taste, you talk, you listen, you feel, you learn. You can learn theory, but it only works when it connects with where it comes from. It becomes intuitive, artistic. It all takes time. Only by understanding all of that will craft distilling progress."

BALCONES TASTING NOTES

BABY BLUE 92°/46%

Nose: Seductive and sweet, with soft oak touches and honey/light corn syrup. The corn husk/cornmeal note is never far off and develops with water, the dryness adding balance.

Palate: Broad and bold, but also sweet and fresh: a tricky balance to achieve. Mouth-filling, with more of the corn coming through.

Finish: Delicately fruity.

Conclusion: A (relatively) gentle introduction to Balcones.

Flavor Camp: Soft Corn

Where Next? Wiser's 18yo

STRAIGHT MALT V 115°/57.5%

Nose: Sensual wood influence. Super-ripe wild berry fruit and a little sandalwood hinting at jamminess. Fresh-planed wood, redwood, and mulch. Mulberry with some Armagnac-like depth.

Palate: Rounded, rich, and silky. Dense and powerful, but there's a velvet glove tempering it all. Fragrant, with a light charred note with water and a little more cereal.

Finish: Long and fruity.

Conclusion: Powerful. New-style Texan malt.

Flavor Camp: Rich & Round

Where Next? Redbreast 12yo, Canadian Club 30yo

STRAIGHT BOURBON II 131.4°/65.7%

Nose: A cherry brandy note to open with. Big-boned and rounded but not aggressive, despite the high proof. Plenty of red and black fruit. Complex, with a hint of dry bark to add some dryness alongside bitter cacao. With water, more scented woods.

Palate: Huge blast of fruit. Balcones is big but doesn't bludgeon you to death. Layered and complex.

Finish: Long and fruity.

Conclusion: Bourbon, yes, but not like you've had before.

Flavor Camp: Rich & Oaky

Where Next? Dark Horse

BRIMSTONE RESURRECTION V 121°/60.5%

Nose: Big and smoky, but with the Balcones dark fruit massed behind. Tarry and resinous. Pitch. Oak fire spitting at you. Clinging, oily, and unctuous. Smoked meats and cheeses.

Palate: Immediate fire, but then the weight and sweetness underpinning the flames.

Finish: Gentian and lightly astringent.

Conclusion: Bold and brave.

Flavor Camp: Smoky & Peaty

Where Next? Karuizawa, Edition Sæntis

New Holland

What started in 1996 as a craft brewery in Holland, Michigan, evolved into a distillery in 2005, when owner Brett VanderKamp's surf bug led him to wonder whether he could make "real" rum in the USA. To turn that dream into reality first meant that he needed to persuade his state legislature to change the law in Michigan, which banned anything other than fruit for distillation.

Today, while the rum is still being made, New Holland's distilling arm is whiskey-oriented, after the team found that their enthusiasm for rum wasn't yet shared by most of their customers. Thankfully, the new distillers also liked whiskey.

"There's a perception that breweries that distill do it just for fun," says New Holland's national accounts manager, Rich Blair, "but it gives us a real advantage financially. As opposed to having to create revenue, the brewery allowed us to do it at a price we wanted to."

Brewing also brought with it an innate understanding of the possibilities of working with malt. "We use our house ale yeast, and have long ferments in closed, temperature-controlled fermenters," explains Blair. "We have a delicate distillate, which is put into cask to add flavor—not to soften any aggression. It means we're finding that it's turning the corner after three years."

Some of the liquid for its rye and bourbon brands has been bought in as mature stock from MGP in Lawrenceburg, Indiana, but increasingly this is a self-sufficient distillery producing in-house brands such as the 100 percent malted

What started out as a rum distillery has become a new whiskey specialist.

barley-based Zeppelin Bend, which spends between ten and 14 days of "thoughtful fermentation" (Blair's words), and Bill's Michigan Wheat, which is made from grains that have been grown and floor-malted by a local farmer.

The distilling arm is continuing to expand. The year 2011 saw the addition of an old applejack still that had lain in a New Jersey barn since the 1930s, before VanderKamp bought it and had it restored by Vendome Copper and Brass Works of Louisville, Kentucky.

"It's very important to innovate," says Blair, "and in that way things are similar to craft brewing. But innovating just for the sake of it isn't good, either. We have a successful pub, which we can use as a test market, and if we mess up every once in a while, we just don't put it out."

What is appearing shows an increasing investigation into that beer/distilling interface.

"We're making a lot of malt," Blair explains. "The US malt market is untapped and we believe that well-aged malt is the next big thing," adding the caveat, "but craft needs time."

Thoughtful indeed.

NEW HOLLAND TASTING NOTES

ZEPPELIN BEND STRAIGHT MALT 90°/45%

Nose: Clean, with hard-cider elements, sawmill, fir, gentle toffee, and white pepper. Opens into stewed Assam tea. Water brings out clean cereal, turmeric, and vanilla.
Palate: Sweet, with a distinct rum-like element: dark fruit, molasses, flamed citrus fruit, blackberry.
Finish: Hint of tight oak but balanced.
Conclusion: Impressive new malt style.

Flavor Camp: **Fruity & Spicy**
Where Next? Brenne

BILL'S MICHIGAN WHEAT 90°/45%

Nose: Bright orange. Highly perfumed, with dried lavender and rose petal. Very spiced, with mace dominating before dark chocolate adds weight.
Palate: Seems young. Fresh, cereal-accented. Tight, with acetone elements. Sugary oak toward the finish. Water gives it more coherence.
Finish: Hot.
Conclusion: Only given 14 months in cask. Well made, butt needs more time to build up complexity.

Flavor Camp: **Fragrant & Floral**
Where Next? Schraml WOAZ

BEER BARREL BOURBON 80°/40%

Nose: Very gentle, laid-back nose with mellow oak notes, old banana, cotton candy, syrup, and dark fruit. With water, more akin to a chocolate brownie.
Palate: Big and soft, and while there's a little youth on show, the spirit has the guts to cope.
Finish: Very spicy, with a little fennel.
Conclusion: Finished for three months in stout barrels, and it works superbly.

Flavor Camp: **Rich & Round**
Where Next? Edition Saentis, Spirit of Broadside

High West

HIGH WEST • PARK CITY, UTAH • WWW.HIGHWEST.COM • OPEN ALL YEAR MON–SUN; BOOKING RECOMMENDED

The high lands of Utah might not spring to mind as a repository of whiskey history, but David Perkins, owner-distiller at the state's High West distillery, is determined to put the record straight. "Was whiskey in the West just cowboys drinking red-eye, or was there something else?" he asks rhetorically. "The Mormons made whiskey here. Sir Richard Burton wrote about it when he came to Salt Lake City to try and convert people to Islam." This, I'm sure you realize, is a book in itself.

His reinvention as a proselytizer for western whiskey came after a career in chemistry, when he saw the parallels between the two industries. If talking of whisky as a biochemical process makes whisky romantics shudder with cold, fear not, it is only part of the story.

Perkins is a whiskey-man who also understands the long-time nature of the business. "It was Jim Rutledge (of Four Roses) who said to me, 'How are you going to make payroll when all your stuff is sitting in barrel?' He advised me to go to MGP [of Indiana] because they make the best rye in the world. I bought it at a price that you can't get new make for these days. I wish we'd bought it all!" The result was that High West started off blending ryes (Rendezvous), bourbon (American Prairie), and bourbon and peated Scotch (Campfire) while its own whiskeys were aging.

As the brands have become established, Perkins has continued to work on his own distillates, starting with yeast.

"We're big yeast people and I can't believe that it's not even considered a significant player in flavor in Scotland," he muses. "We've explored 20 different yeasts." Three of them are used in the rye, which follows an 1840 recipe, is distilled as a full-grain wash, and is released as OMG (which stands for Old Monongahela). Experiments with a rye *solera* are underway, there's an oat whiskey released (as Valley Tan and Western Oat), while a single malt is in the development stages.

"We're very serious about malt," says Perkins," and are currently working from three different recipes." Like the other whiskeys it will be from a non-lautered wash. "The key for a young company is to be different, hence the rye. I love malt whisky and there's a lot of room for innovation."

Ultimately, Utah plays its part. "We're at 7,000 feet, the still boils at a lower temperature, and the altitude and dry climate mean maturation conditions are different."

The past is never far away.

"In 1890 there were 14,000 distilleries in the US," Perkings adds. "We're going back to where we were."

HIGH WEST TASTING NOTES

SILVER WESTERN OAT 80°/40%
Nose: An unaged oat whiskey that's very perfumed and mildly medicinal: ointment meets cut flowers and whipped cream. Tingle of fennel.
Palate: Very light and sweet, with estery confectionery notes and creamy oat drive.
Finish: Pink peppercorns. A little short.
Conclusion: Charming.

Flavor Camp: **Fragrant & Floral**
Where Next? White Owl

VALLEY TAN (OAT) 92°/46%
Nose: Lots of estery notes and very subtle oak. Smells of just-drying rock cut with vanilla, banana skin, light pine needles, and cooked pineapple.
Palate: Sweet, fragrant, and juicy. Slightly hot, but there's a flowery ripple. The oat-driven creaminess develops with water into banana split.
Finish: Lightly dry.
Conclusion: Balanced and very interesting.

Flavor Camp: **Fragrant & Floral**
Where Next? Tullibardine Sovereign, Liebl Coillmor American Oak

OMG PURE RYE 98.6°/49.3%
Nose: Just-baked rye sourdough loaf—you can smell the crumb, the warmth, the spiciness of the crust. Aromatic. Dried flowers, rose petal, and black grape skin.
Palate: Dry to start. Bone-dry, then lifts off into rye flour, then cuts back to heavy spice and oil. Balanced.
Finish: Aromatic.
Conclusion: Pure and clean.

Flavor Camp: **Spicy Rye**
Where Next? Stauning Young Rye

RENDEZVOUS RYE 92°/46%
Nose: Sweet and elegant. Rounded and balanced, which opens into heightened aromatic areas of rose petals, hot gorse, and perfumed face powder.
Palate: The gentleness of the nose gives way to a swaggering palate, where the rye is spiced up to the max. Cardamom shows, as does five-spice and aromatic bitters.
Finish: Green apple and rye dustiness.
Conclusion: A full picture.

Flavor Camp: **Spicy Rye**
Where Next? Lot 40

Westland

WESTLAND •SEATTLE, WASHINGTON • WWW.WESTLANDDISTILLERY.COM • OPEN ALL YEAR, WED–SAT

Emerson Lamb was not yet a teenager when his father sat him down to talk business. The family had been in the Pacific Northwest for five generations, building a successful lumber business, but things were changing. "He told me that no one will buy two by four sheets of paper again, so I grew up with the idea that the family firm couldn't do what it had always done. We had to do something different."

Lamb linked up with high-school friend Matt Hofmann, who had by then studied distilling at Scotland's Heriot-Watt University and was planning to stay in the country to seek employment. "I thought, here in Washington State we have two world-class barley regions, abundant water, and a climate unique in North America. Everything is here to allow us to make a style of whiskey we want to make."

The pair spent eight months traveling the world, visiting 130 distilleries, honing the idea of a fusion between Scottish tradition, American aging, and Japanese whisky-making philosophy. "The Scots told us that we'd screw it up as barley doesn't have the body and complexity to stand up to overoaking." Their solution was tangental. Rather than taking the Scottish approach of once-used casks, they beefed up the spirit with different roasts of malt so it could cope with the full-blown intensity of new oak. The mash bill now utilizes pale, Munich, extra-special, roasted, pale chocolate, and brown malts. A peated variant has recently been added.

Refill casks are also being used because the vision is nothing if not long-term. "The whiskey turns the corner after four or five years," says Lamb, "but not all of this whiskey is coming out that young. We're laying down for 40 years."

Based in downtown Seattle, Westland is not a small-scale operation. "Our goal is to put Washington State on the map as a prime place to make single malt. The distillery might be medium-sized in Scottish terms, but it's sizeable in American ones. To make this work, we need to make 20,000 cases a year."

The generations of watching trees grow is standing him in good stead. "It's expensive to do things on this scale and it takes time, but we're experienced in the latter. You have to have patience."

Growing trees, growing whiskey, and a business. And who knows? A category? The seed has been sown.

WESTLAND TASTING NOTES

DEACON SEAT 92°/46%

Nose: Aromatic. Gentian and chocolate with sweet, polished oak, light pine, and cherry. In time roasted coconut and black cherry. First floor develops with water. Almost Jamaican rum-like molasses.
Palate: Clean, with good feel and citric lift. With water, a more floral note develops, adding strawberry tones. Robust.
Finish: Long and rich.
Conclusion: Only 27 months old and already this is showing maturity.

Flavor Camp: **Fruity & Spicy**
Where Next? Chichibu On The Way

FLAGSHIP 92°/46%

Nose: Light, with apricot blossom and some sweet cereal and squashed raspberries. Expansive, with restrained oak.
Palate: Concentrated fruit. Real sweetness backed with subtly roasted maltiness. Old banana and a hint of tobacco.
Finish: Light pine.
Conclusion: Elements coming together.

Flavor Camp: **Fruity & Spicy**
Where Next? Loch Lomond Single Blend

CASK 29 55%

Nose: Patisserie and sweetness. The most spicy of the range, with some raffia, estery elements, a lick of varnish, and some lemon.
Palate: Mouth-filling, with some charred, roasted elements. Lightly creamy. The citrus fruit and spices work in harmony with the supple feel. With water, there's fruit-chew juiciness.
Finish: Long and zesty.
Conclusion: A more lifted expression which shows promise.

Flavor Camp: **Fruity & Spicy**
Where Next? Glenmorangie 15yo

FIRST PEATED 92°/46%

Nose: Campfire in the woods, behind the distillery character of the roasted malt and citrus fruit. Touches of oatcake and a little hint of medicinal phenols. Lightly oily.
Palate: Minty cool, with a slow release of smoke. Good feel and balance. Dry at the moment but will sweeten.
Finish: Oatcakes. And smoke.
Conclusion: The distillery character already seems fixed.

Flavor Camp: **Smoky & Peaty**
Where Next? Bunnahabhain Toiteach

Anchor/St. George/Other US Craft

ANCHOR BREWING • SAN FRANCISCO, CA • WWW.ANCHORBREWING.COM / ST. GEORGE • ALAMEDA, CA • WWW.STGEORGESPIRITS.COM • OPEN ALL YEAR, WED–SUN / CLEAR CREEK DISTILLERY • PORTLAND, OREGON • WWW.CLEARCREEKDISTILLERY.COM • TASTING ROOM OPEN ALL YEAR MON–SAT / STRANAHAN'S • DENVER, COLORADO • WWW.STRANAHANS.COM • OPEN ALL YEAR; BOOKING ADVISED

Craft continues to boom on America's West Coast with a new wave of distillers following pioneers like Steve McCarthy at Clear Creek, Oregon, or Dry Fly in Spokane, Washington State. There is almost an inevitability that they and others of the early starters are now overlooked as the world looks (too eagerly) for the newest kid on the block with the most outlandish idea. It is time now to reappraise the work done by distillers like them: Fritz Maytag at Anchor in San Francisco, or Lance Winters at St. George in Alameda, California.

"Fritz was trying to prove a point," says Anchor distilleries president David King. "He looked at whiskey from the viewpoint of a historian, and his fascination was what whiskey was like in George Washington's time, when you'd have used your own grains—probably 100 percent malted rye—and sold it at high strength because people wouldn't have wanted to transport water to market. The casks would have been no more than receptacles, and toasted rather than heavily charred. It was nothing to do with creating a modern classic. It was a purist stance."

Old Potrero, launched in 1996, was the result. The single malt is an "eighteenth-century style," aged for one year and bottled at 127.5° proof (63.75% abv), while the oily, spicy Straight Rye was his homage to nineteenth-century whiskeys, with three years in barrel. Both were uncompromising whiskeys, which was ultimately an issue. "It was almost impossible to use the original Old Potrero in a Manhattan and come up with a balanced drink," says King, "so I brought it down to 102° proof (51% abv) to make it more 'user friendly.'"

Functional rather than romantic (but with plenty of room for expansion) the St. George distillery in California.

Both are now aged in charred oak, but have retained their boldness. King describes the eighteenth century as "like a Reuben sandwich," while the straight rye, now at 90° (45% abv), shows a sweeter, wood-influenced aspect. A barrel from each year is always set aside and bottled when well into its second decade as "Hotalings."

"I think Fritz was more interested in being a pioneer than a success," says King. "He was there at the beginning with beer, but was always happy making 80,000 barrels rather than making a huge brand. He was into quality and history: the first dry-hopped IPA, the first London Dry gin, the first 100 percent malted rye."

Maytag retired in 2010, and Anchor Distilling Company is now a partnership between Anchor, Preiss Imports, and Berry Bros. & Rudd. A larger distillery is planned, with more stills and a wider range of spirits. "It will allow us to widen the range and ask those questions about what whiskey is (and other spirits are), and where the future lies."

It's an issue that is never far from the mind of Lance Winters at St. George. The distillery was founded in 1982 by Jorg Rupf as an *eaux-de-vie*/brandy site using Holstein stills before Lance arrived in 1996 with a bottle of homemade whiskey under his arm, asking for a job. A year later, St. George's first whiskey was barreled. What are hailed today as innovations (using different roasts of barley, smoking over beech and alder, aging in refill bourbon, French oak, port, and sherry barrels), all went into this.

Although overtaken in public's consciousness by Hangar One vodka (still distilled at St. George), it remains a compelling introduction to an American take on the barley-based single malt. Holstein stills provide delicacy and floral notes, the different roasts adding sweetness and coffee and, with an ever-widening range of ages to draw from, every batch shows greater layers of complexity.

I was intrigued as to whether Winters was making whiskey in California—or Californian whiskey. "California is known for innovation and reinvention," he says. "Making a Californian single malt is really about applying that philosophy of reinvention to the entire process. I've never had the internal dialogue of 'Hey, how do I make a single malt that's truly Californian?' and I'm pretty sure that if we had started distilling our whiskey somewhere else, it would have been the same whiskey we've made here for the last 17 years.

"Being in California does have the benefit of giving us access to an audience that may be a bit more willing to accept a more innovative whiskey," he admits, "but I don't feel that it has affected what we've wanted to make."

The West Coast. It started here.

ST. GEORGE TASTING NOTES

ST. GEORGE CALIFORNIAN SINGLE MALT 86°/43%

Nose: Lifted and intensely fruity. Pure mango and apricot. Effusive, sweet, and clean with a little touch of smoke underneath.

Palate: The ripe, fleshy, intense aromatics now backed with drier more cereal-driven texture then softens into the center to cream soda.

Finish: Firm yet juicy.

Conclusion: An eye-opening single malt showing the possibilities that exist.

Flavor Camp: Fruity & Spicy

Where Next? Glenmorangie, Imperial

LOT 13 86°/43%

Nose: Classic St. George lift of fragrant, iced tropical fruit mixed with very subtle floral perfume. Touches of moscato, pollen, cut flowers, melon, and green banana.

Palate: Softly honeyed, with good depth. Some cream soda. No water is needed. Spring blossom, but with substance in the center. Wheat-beer accents.

Finish: Light chocolate.

Conclusion: Poised and elegant.

Flavor Camp: Fragrant & Floral

Where Next? Compass Box Asyla

ANCHOR TASTING NOTES

OLD POTRERO RYE 97°/48.5%

Nose: Deeply fruity rye with hot bakery notes and firm oak. A mix of sweetness and spice and an almost smoky edge. Rye flour, caramel, wintergreen, and oak.

Palate: Smooth, pure, and then halfway in the rye ignites into a firework-like dustiness and bittersweet spices. Thick but direct.

Finish: Full-bodied and spicy.

Conclusion: A resolutely old (but paradoxcally new) style.

Flavor Camp: Spicy Rye

Where Next? Millstone 100°

OTHER US CRAFT DISTILLERS

CLEAR CREEK, MCCARTHY'S OREGON SINGLE MALT BATCH W09/01 85°/42.5%

Nose: Grass and smoke to start. Bonfire in the woods, touch of hickory and birch smoke. Gentle and sweet behind. Seems young and fresh. Very lifted.

Palate: Smoke again hits immediately but again the lift of the aromatics is what separates this from a Scotch. Lapsang souchong.

Finish: Smoked cashew.

Conclusion: Iconoclastic.

Flavor Camp: Smoky & Peaty

Where Next? Chichibu Newborn, Kilchoman

STRANAHAN'S COLORADO STRAIGHT MALT WHISKEY BATCH 52 94°/47%

Nose: Crisp and dry initially with roasted notes. Quite understated, then orange, rich malt, cinnamon, and a scented dusty note. Again very lifted. With water, geranium, toffee, and roasted coffee.

Palate: Charred oak giving a lightly sooty note. Fruity with a toffee-ed edge and plenty of sweet spiciness. Moves into cassis/*mures* but always cut with firm oak.

Finish: Zesty.

Conclusion: Balanced and clean. Another new and welcome definition of whiskey.

Flavor Camp: Fruity & Spicy

Where Next? Arran 10yo

CANADA

Canada is the whisky world's sleeping giant. Although it is second only to Scotland in terms of production, it remains curiously overlooked. How does a nation with such volume, heritage, ability, and commercial success come to be dismissed as a mere afterthought?

Could it be because Canadians are the nicest people in the world? They don't like to shout, or make a fuss. They are polite, fun, mellow—and so are their whiskies. In a world where being bludgeoned with flavor is, wrongly, seen as a positive attribute, that can mean being passed over.

It is conceivable that this politeness has also led to misapprehensions about what Canadian whisky is—like the idea that it is made only from rye, that all of it has other liquid blended in, or that it uses different mash bills. All untrue.

Followed by the majority of distillers, the classic Canadian distillery template is the single-distillery blend of a base whisky (usually, but not exclusively, corn) being made alongside flavoring whiskies (usually rye, but also wheat, corn, or barley), which are usually aged separately and then blended.

Each distillery, therefore, has its own personality, and that is where the joy of Canadian whisky lies: in the way in which its distillers and blenders widen those parameters to make complex whiskies. The variety and quality are as great as anywhere in the world.

This is a time of opportunity for all whisky, and Canada cannot afford to continue being sidelined. To avoid that, it has to change the popular mindset. That means fully developing a premium category. Canadian whisky has been sold at too low a price for too long. Even the new top-end expressions are being virtually given away. Maybe the relentless commoditization has made it difficult for distillers to believe that people will take them seriously, but there is a difference between value for money and selling at so low a price that the consumer doesn't believe the product can possibly be good quality.

There are positive signs, however. "The most promising change is the turnaround in the Canadian whisky market at home," says Forty Creek's John K. Hall. "This means that Canadians are discovering and drinking higher-quality whiskies. There are more new releases, more choices, and this is driving innovation in the category. The whisky renaissance that we hoped would happen as younger consumers matured and moved away from flavored vodkas is happening."

Yet, even if the quasi-Prohibitionist Liquor Control Boards would allow it, the country cannot drink all of the whisky it makes. Canada has always relied on its neighbor to take the bulk of its production, yet I cannot help but feeling that the idea of export being no more than keeping the US pipeline full of commodity brands is not in the industry's best interests. There is a whisky-thirsty world out there.

However, there are clear signs of a change in focus. Each of the eight main distilleries is developing a top end, and there are remarkable innovations taking place in terms of blending and distillation. And while wood is generally not as widely explored as it could be, that, too, is only a matter of time. A growing craft-distilling movement is also beginning to build momentum.

Davin de Kergommeaux is a Canadian whisky-writer and commentator who has helped immensely to deepen my understanding of his country's whiskies (and has helped with some of the background

information in this section). For him, the future means, "… a broader range of high-end whiskies with bigger, bolder flavors continuing their expansion into export markets. Just when consumers are becoming more aware of high-quality Canadian whisky, gifted whisky-makers are

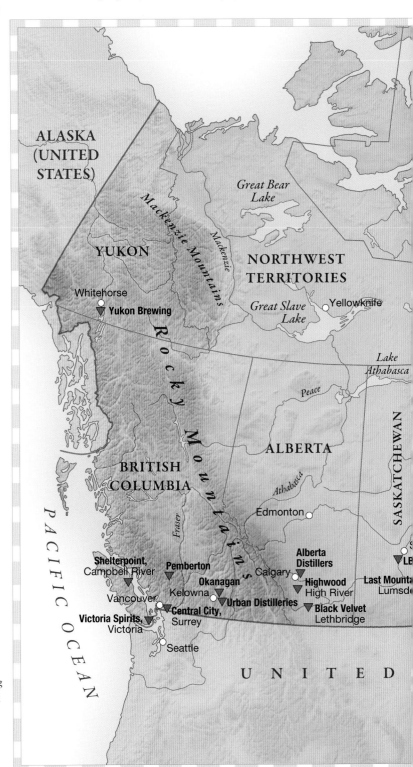

Previous page: Wheat fields in Manitoba—the raw ingredient.

exploring wood management, alternate grains, and flavored whiskies. Watch for new innovative core brands and one-off releases."

By defining their distillery styles, whisky-makers—Canadian and otherwise—are asking what Canadian whisky is. The more

thoroughly that question is examined, the greater the variety of answers will be. So don't look away. These are some of the great whiskies of the world.

Seek them out.

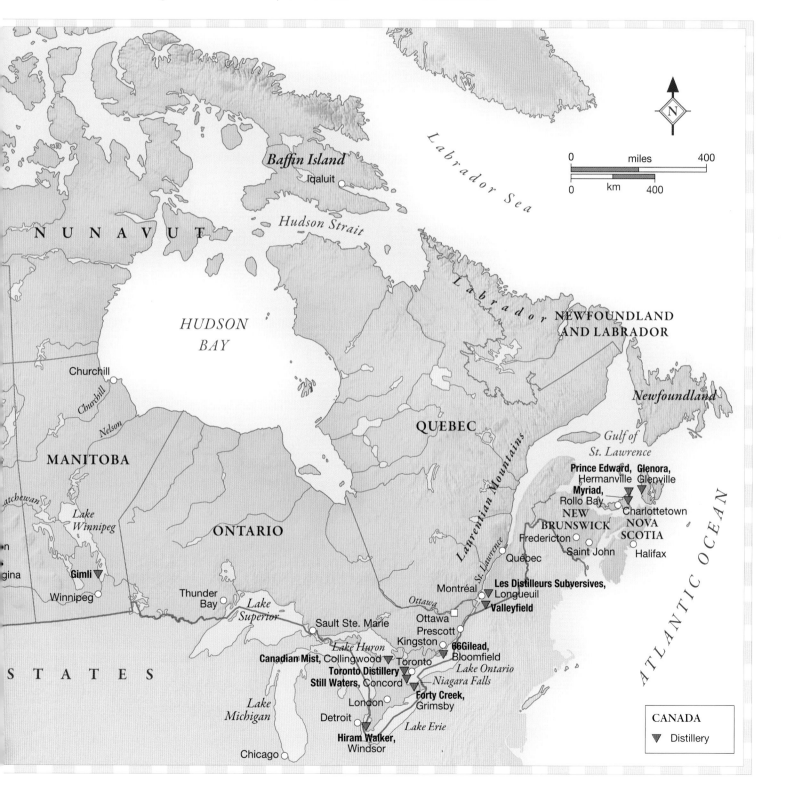

Alberta Distillers

ALBERTA DISTILLERS LIMITED • CALGARY

The decision of Alberta Distillers Limited (ADL) to concentrate on rye was entirely practical. The distillery was built near Calgary in 1946 as an economic development project for a depressed rural area, and rye was the main local crop. Although its immediate surroundings have changed from fields to houses, ADL's principles remain the same. This is the world's greatest rye specialist, making three times more rye whisky than all the straight rye made in the USA.

Why, if Canadian whisky is usually based on corn, is it called "rye"? It's because the use of a small percentage of rye whisky in a blend (instead of in a mash bill), delivers more impact than you'd expect. It's the Canadian signature. Rye-driven, yet not 100 percent rye. Until you arrive here.

Every distiller who works with rye knows how capricious and unruly it is. It's hard to malt, sticky in the mash tun, foams madly in the fermenter. It's as if the prickly, semi-housetrained quality of rye's flavor manifests itself from the start. General manager Rob Tuer got around the problems by isolating a natural enzyme that cuts foaming and viscosity.

Although the bulk of the whisky made here is 100 percent rye, for base, as well as flavoring whiskies, ADL also buys in corn, wheat, barley, and triticale.

Distillation is in the standard Canadian setup of a beer-stripping column, then an extractive column in which water is mixed with the alcohol to separate the insoluble (and unwanted) fusel oils from the desirable compounds. This cleaned-up mixture is then run through a rectifying column and collected at 93.5% abv as the base spirit. The flavoring whiskies are made in a pot-still and collected at 77% abv.

Rye, older rye especially, has long been the key to ADL's blends, but the character of this secret ingredient was only revealed fully first in 2007, then 2011, with the release of 100 percent rye Masterson's and Alberta Premium at 25 and 30 years of age. Complex, spiced, and integrated, they showed pure, mature rye character with none of the dustiness you associate with many American ryes.

Rye is also the future, in the shape of Dark Horse: a mixture of rye base and flavoring, and some old corn just to ease things along.

"Rye gives us an ability to innovate," says production manager Rick Murphy. "There are options here that do not exist with other distilleries."

ALBERTA DISTILLERS TASTING NOTES

ALBERTA SPRINGS 10YO 40%

Nose: Fire orange. Wood, dry grain, baking spices, cedar, with a hint of hot mustard.

Palate: Rich and creamy. Quickly gets hot. Refreshing bitter lemon restrains the toffee, while fresh-sawn wood and the unmalted rye balances the pepper.

Finish: Hot peppermint with hints of wood and citric zest.

Conclusion: Alberta Premium 25yo gets the attention, but this is what the folks at the distillery drink.

Flavor Camp: Spicy Rye

Where Next? Kittling Ridge, Canadian Mountain Rock

ALBERTA PREMIUM 25YO 40%

Nose: Marmalade and toasted vanilla. The freshness of rye is there but with an added elegance of maturation. Some red and black fruit, sweet spice, light caramel toffee. Still fresh.

Palate: Smooth, soft, and elegant. Long and juicy, almost slightly jammy. Mid-palate richness.

Finish: Spiced rye accents.

Conclusion: Mature and elegant.

Flavor Camp: Spicy Rye

Where Next? Jameson Distillers Reserve

ALBERTA PREMIUM 30YO 40%

Nose: More sandalwood and oak. Spicier too, with a more upfront attack. A light oiliness gives some weight.

Palate: Gentle and sweet, with plenty of allspice. Becomes a little fragile and oaked on the back palate.

Finish: Crisp and dry.

Conclusion: Just a little old.

Flavor Camp: Rich & Oaky

Where Next? Sazerac Rye

DARK HORSE 40%

Nose: Black cherry/kirsch, vermouth aromas with some toffee. With water, that green-rye/privet-blossom accent.

Palate: Big, bolder, and slightly caramelized. A touch of cask-derived phenols. With water, it becomes juicy, with hints of morello cherries.

Finish: Fruity, with lightly gripping oak.

Conclusion: A huge, bold rye.

Flavor Camp: Spicy Rye

Where Next? Millstone 100°

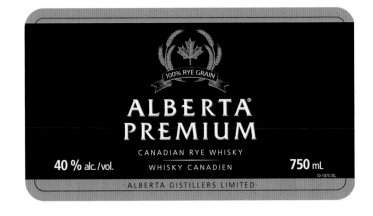

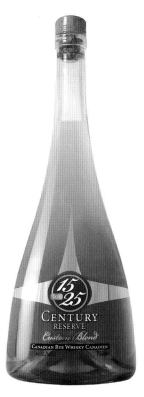

Highwood

HIGHWOOD • HIGH RIVER • WWW.HIGHWOOD-DISTILLERS.COM

It would be easy to miss the Highwood distillery as you drove through the small Alberta town of High River, but by doing so you'd be missing the quirkiest of Canada's eight main producers. It might not have the scale of Hiram Walker, but Highwood is a specialist in seeing gaps in the market, and plugging them immediately. Somehow, 350 different lines come out of here (although we might draw a veil over "Porn Star Bullets"). This is a whisky atlas, after all.

Highwood is a further demonstration that each Canadian distiller approaches whisky-making in its own way. This is a wheat specialist, using nothing but to make its base and flavoring whiskies. In doing so, it is both utilizing local produce and tapping into Canadian whisky's origins, wheat being the grain first used by the country's distillers in the nineteenth century.

A slightly bizarre method of releasing the wheat's starch involves cooking it under pressure, then discharging a jet of slurry at a metal plate, which shatters any whole grains. A 60-hour ferment is then followed by distillation in a beer-column and copper pot-still combination. "It's an old still," says distiller Michael Nychyk. "It works in the same way as an old cast-iron skillet. It just gives the flavor and character we want."

For all the other lines, whisky is becoming the focus, with the creamy carbon-filtered White Owl the biggest seller. The rest are blends, with any rye bought in from ADL (*see* p.272), and the corn components from the Potter's inventory, which Highwood bought in 2004 (Potter's being a British Columbia-based bottler that bought and aged corn whisky).

Highwood's success has come from the speed of its reactions. A focus on whisky, however, necessitates long-term planning—and oak. As with most Canadian whisky, ex-bourbon barrels are used, here located in a warehouse that is so filled with alcohol fumes, you reel after inhaling.

Inside are some remarkable finds, like the deep, caramelized-peach, marmalade, and sandalwood flavors of a 33-year-old corn whisky from the Potter stock and an equally remarkable 20-year-old wheat, which mixes flowers, coconut, and vanilla.

"We're not much different to John K. Hall (*see* p.279)," says sales manager Sheldon Hyra. "Canada needs to focus on premium. It has been undervalued."

HIGHWOOD TASTING NOTES

WHITE OWL 40%

Nose: Very gentle and sweet, with soft fruit whipped up with cream.
Palate: Light but textural, allowing the delicate fruit to hold to the tongue. Quite silky.
Finish: Light and quite short.
Conclusion: This 5yo white whisky is Highwood's top seller.

Flavor Camp: **Sweet Wheat**
Where Next? Schraml WOAZ

CENTENNIAL 10YO 40%

Nose: Light amber. Unusual. Cloves, with hints of flint, dry grain, very ripe black fruit, and cooked green vegetables.
Palate: Weighty. Toffee, pepper, sawdust, and some baking spices, then sweet lemonade with a subtle bite.
Finish: Long but subdued. Fading out on toffee, sweet spices, and pepper.
Conclusion: The softness of wheat whisky but with a bite.

Flavor Camp: **Sweet Wheat**
Where Next? Maker's Mark, Bruichladdich Bourbon Cask, Littlemill

NINETY, 20YO 45%

Nose: Gentle but full with honey/syrup, red fruit, green apple. Touches of cedar (from the long maturation) and green peppercorn.
Palate: Full and soft, with sweet oak giving light grip, black butter, a sprig of mint, some strawberry, and peach.
Finish: Rye spices kick in: plenty of allspice and ginger.
Conclusion: Rye heavy blend.

Flavor Camp: **Spicy Rye**
Where Next? Four Roses Single Barrel

CENTURY RESERVE 21YO 40%

Nose: A toasted-oak start that opens to show some soft, fresh corn, some hay, and a little touch of dry-roasted spices. A little hint of apple mint, then blood orange and caramel.
Palate: A lovely start, with rounded creaminess; toffee syrup and then a burst of lemon-accented citrus fruit. Ripe and full. More citric on the tongue.
Finish: Slightly peppery, with a little oak adding roasted cacao notes.
Conclusion: All corn whisky. Length and depth.

Flavor Camp: **Soft Corn**
Where Next? Girvan Grain

Black Velvet

BLACK VELVET • LETHBRIDGE • WWW.BLACKVELVETWHISKY.COM

Each of Alberta's three distilleries specializes in a different grain, and it seems only appropriate that the one called Black Velvet specializes in the softest cereal of all: corn. While that might not seem surprising, corn being at the base of most Canadian whiskies, it is in Alberta. This is small-grain country.

So why build a corn distillery here? In the 1970s, Canadian whisky was booming in the USA. British-based IDV (owners of the Black Velvet brand), made it, as well as Smirnoff, at the Gilbey's distillery in Toronto. It made logistical sense to build a distillery in Lethbridge, in Alberta, to supply the west with whisky, gin, and vodka.

When the slump came in the 1980s, it seemed likely that the Lethbridge plant would close, but by roping in the town's mayor to plead their case directly to the IDV board in London, it stayed open while the Toronto plant was closed.

A tour around with manager James Mmbando is a tale of dynamism: high pressure, vacuums, injections of enzymes, explosions of starch, backset being fed into the corn slurry, a vigorous fermentation taking place even as saccharification is being completed. A four-column setup gives a 96% abv corn-based whisky, while the corn and rye flavoring whiskies come off the beer column at 67% abv and 56% abv, respectively.

What you end up with is a clean, sweet base; intense, citric, rye-bread-crust characters on the rye; and a punchy, lean, menthol-accented corn.

The blending regime, overseen by Vicky Miller, is complex. The flavoring whiskies are aged separately for between two and six years, adding buttery spices to the rye, and a mixture of flowers and coconut to the corn. These are then blended with unaged base whisky and aged for a minimum of three years. By varying the ratio of flavoring to base spirit, different flavors are created.

The juice ends up in ex-Schenley brands like OFC and Golden Wedding (see p.278), as well as a number of third-party blends, but don't dismiss Black Velvet itself. This is a classic, lush Canadian blend seen at its best when mixed with ginger ale.

Here is another distillery that is dipping its toe in the waters of premium with its aged Danfield's brands. These show complexity and brio: evidence of what this outpost of corn can produce.

A grain truck with two hoppers delivers corn to the Black Velvet distillery in Lethbridge, Alberta.

BLACK VELVET TASTING NOTES

BLACK VELVET 40%

Nose: Lush, soft corn, caramelized apple, lime, raspberry, caramel toffee, and a discreet jag of rye.
Palate: Gentle, quite sweet, a hint of dust, and a little tightening to the end.
Finish: Light and soft.
Conclusion: Very easygoing and eminently mixable.

Flavor Camp: **Soft Corn**
Where Next? Cameron Brig

DANFIELD'S 10YO 40%

Nose: Mature and complex, with good depth. Light oak notes with an almost phenolic edge. Softness abounds, however. Light citrus fruit, baked fruit, and buttered corn.
Palate: Soft and clean, with very light spices in the center. Vanilla bean. Complex but restrained.
Finish: Moves into dusty spices.
Conclusion: Balanced and quite classy.

Flavor Camp: **Soft Corn**
Where Next? Johnnie Walker Gold Reserve

DANFIELD'S 21YO 40%

Nose: Complex but typically discreet. More oak than the 10yo with macadamia and some buttery notes, caramelized fruit, mint, hazelnut, and cocoa/hot chocolate.
Palate: Citric start. Thick, sweet, with *crème caramel* and dry oak.
Finish: Dry-roasted spices. Clean.
Conclusion: Complex and elegant.

Flavor Camp: **Soft Corn**
Where Next? Glenmorangie 18yo

Gimli
GIMLI • MANITOBA • WWW.CROWNROYAL.COM

Distilleries often cluster together, not so much for mutual support, but to be close to markets or for access to a distribution network. As a result, many of Canada's plants were concentrated in its major cities. Not Gimli. Superbly isolated from its colleagues, it sits in Manitoba—932 miles from Calgary, Alberta, and 1,242 miles from Windsor, Ontario. The only other reason for building a distillery is to have easy access to raw material, and that Gimli has. It still uses locally grown corn and rye.

Its presence here also speaks of the 1960s boom, when supply couldn't keep up with demand. Gimli's owner, Seagram, already operated four distilleries in Canada; what harm would one more do?

The Seagram family had started distilling in 1878 in Waterloo, Ontario. In 1928, it merged with the Montreal-based Bronfman family business. The Bronfmans were distillers and highly successful distributors, which in those days was shorthand for making cross-border trips to supply dry-throated Americans.

Buccaneering Sam Bronfman craved respectability. The names of his whiskies illustrate that: Chivas Regal, Royal Salute, and his first monarchic tribute, Crown Royal, which was created in 1939 to commemorate a royal visit.

The slump of the 1980s decimated the Seagram estate, and by the 1990s, only Gimli was left. Today, even Seagram has gone, and the distillery is owned by Diageo. It's a one-brand distillery, and that brand is Crown Royal, Canadian whisky's biggest seller.

Gimli is a perfect case study of the Canadian phenomenon of the single-distillery blend, whose principle is to create as many different flavors as possible on one site. Crown Royal sits on two corn bases.

One of the bases is formed when condensed spirit from a beer-still is redistilled in a pot (the kettle), with the vapor passing directly into a rectifying column. The bourbon and rye are made from a single pass through the beer column, and the remarkable Coffey Rye from a Coffey still.

These streams are then aged in a maturation regime that uses new oak for the flavorings, refill, and Cognac casks. Yeast, grain, distillation regimes, different wood, and time. It's a blender's heaven, set to maximize the flavor options with which to craft variations on the extraodinarily lush, soft, honeyed, Crown Royal signature.

GIMLI TASTING NOTES

CROWN ROYAL 40%
Nose: Huge and sweet, with *crème brûlée* and heady, jammy, red and black fruit, but then come new wood, spice, and orange zest.
Palate: Luscious and honeyed, with some fresh strawberry, a little hint of rye spice.
Finish: Rye and oak comes through to give a light bite.
Conclusion: Soft, gentle, and totally amenable. Impossible not to like.

Flavor Camp: **Soft Corn**
Where Next? Glenmorangie 10yo, Nikka Coffey Grain

CROWN ROYAL RESERVE 40%
Nose: Wood influence and mature stock: *crème brûlée*, hints of sherry, cassia bark, and blackberry, with a sprig of mint adding a top note.
Palate: Fat with overripe mango. Sweet and honeyed before lemon-accented rye and toasty oak give some acidity and grip.
Finish: Light rye accents.
Conclusion: In the sweet, silkily textured house style but with extra grip.

Flavor Camp: **Soft Corn**
Where Next? Tullamore D.E.W. 12yo, George Dickel Rye

CROWN ROYAL LIMITED EDITION 40%
Nose: Amber. Slowly opens to nutmeg, cinnamon, hints of apple juice, toffee, and vague vanilla. Austere.
Palate: Complex mix of barley sugar, rye spices, hot pepper, and grapefruit zest. Good weight. Creamy fruit. Spicy, with a flash of peppermint.
Finish: Medium creamy fade on pepper and wood with citric finale.
Conclusion: Top of the line for Crown Royal.

Flavor Camp: **Spicy Rye**
Where Next? Crown Royal Black Label

Hiram Walker

HIRAM WALKER • HERITAGE CENTER, WINDSOR • WWW.CANADIANCLUBWHISKY.COM • OPEN ALL YEAR;
SEE WEBSITE FOR DAYS & DETAILS

The size of the 33 silos on the shoreline of the Detroit River is a giveaway that the Hiram Walker distillery in Walkerville is a major player. This is the largest distillery in Canada, conceivably North America, making 14.5 million gallons (55 million liters) a year or, looking at it another way, 70 percent of the country's whiskies. The distillates for Canadian Club and Gibson's Finest are made here, but its own brands, like Wiser's, Lot 40, and Pike Creek, are where the real secrets of the distillery lie.

Big it may be, but there's no sense of this being a factory. The questing mind at the controls is blender Dr. Don Livermore. He is part of the generational shift taking place in Canadian whisky. The country's new distillers and blenders are open to the past, but are also asking what they can do to make people sit up and pay attention.

There is a huge range of distillates being made here. They buy in not just corn, but rye, rye malt, barley, barley malt, and wheat. Fermentation takes place in a vast fermenting room, where a technique of adding nitrogen to the fermenters has upped the strength of the wash to 15% abv for corn, and 8% abv for rye. The corn base is a triple-column distillate, while the flavoring whiskies are graded as "Star"

or "Star Special." The former are run through a 72-plate beer-still; the latter are redistilled in a pot-still.

As Livermore says, "The pot-still rye is the pepper on the ear of corn." With two spirits from each of the small grains, the depth of potential components for blending is huge.

If there is one word Livermore uses more than any other, it's "innovation." Every aspect of production is being examined. There's the potential to work with yeast strains dating back to the 1930s, while his ongoing research into small grains includes examination of the potential different flavor profiles that could be obtained from red winter wheat. And with a PhD in wood under his belt, there's little surprise that this is one Canadian distillery where a wood-management program is underway. "This flexibility means we can can do craft style in a large distillery," he says.

It seems an idle boast, but a day in the tasting room with him shows it to be true. Big *can* be pioneering.

HIRAM WALKER TASTING NOTES

WISER'S DELUXE 40%

Nose: Rye leads, but with a honeyed, gentle background. Light sandalwood, blond tobacco, and fennel.
Palate: Maple syrup to open before there's mace, red apple, and a subtle background of oak.
Finish: Dried, sweet fruit.
Conclusion: Easy and comforting.

Flavor Camp: **Soft Corn**
Where Next? Wild Turkey 81°

WISER'S LEGACY 40%

Nose: In the Wiser's style, encasing the the perfume of rye within a smooth toffee/vanilla frame. In time, some pollen, clove, and long pepper, then raspberry jam and light oak.
Palate: The peppery rye leads off, but then there's some peach, dried apricot, light menthol, and a citric edge.
Finish: Clean, spicy rye.
Conclusion: Bigger, more oak-driven, but still Wiser's.

Flavor Camp: **Spicy Rye**
Where Next? Green Spot

WISER'S 18YO 40%

Nose: Orange gold. Fresh-sawn wood, spicy rye, sourdough bread, dry grain, cigar box, and glue stick.
Palate: Complex, richly flavored. Burnt sugar, lumberyard, white pepper, perfumed, dusty rye, dark fruit, baking spices, some pulling oak tannins.
Finish: Long and peppery, fruity sweetness giving way to oak tannins and palate-cleansing bitter lemon.
Conclusion: A cedar box that is filled with sweet and spicy delicacies.

Flavor Camp: **Rich & Oaky**
Where Next? Gibson's Finest 18yo, Alberta Premium 25yo

PIKE CREEK, 10YO 40%

Nose: Red fruit, marzipan, slightly jammy, raspberry coulis. Touches of sweet cinnamon and nutmeg.
Palate: Sweeter and slightly more vanilla-accented. The spices become more bitter and citric: coriander seed in particular.
Finish: Gentle, then a bite of lemon before some red fruit re-emerges.
Conclusion: Note that this is the Canadian release; older than the export and finished in port.

Flavor Camp: **Soft Corn**
Where Next? Chichibu Port Pipe

LOT 40 43%

Nose: Full-on rye attack. Slightly leafy, then rye flour, fresh-baked sourdough. Sweetens into seaside rock, strawberry, green apple/fennel seed. Rich.
Palate: Spicy, with some green olive pit, allspice, and cilantro, light clove. With water, the sweet oak begins to move forward.
Finish: Crackling and clove-like.
Conclusion: Made from 10% rye.

Flavor Camp: **Spicy Rye**
Where Next? JH Special Nougat, Forty Creek Barrel Select

Canadian Club

CANADIAN CLUB • WINDSOR • WWW.CANADIANCLUBWHISKY.COM • OPEN ALL YEAR; SEE WEBSITE FOR DAYS & DETAILS

The continual consolidations, mergers, and takeovers in the twenty-first-century Canadian whisky industry can mean that the stories of its brands can be labyrinthine. Take Canadian Club. When owner Allied Distillers was broken up in 2006, the brand went to Beam and the distillery to Pernod-Ricard. What's left of the legacy of CC's founder, Hiram Walker, are the truly remarkable offices he built for himself in the nineteenth century, which now serve as the brand's heritage center.

Hiram Walker was the whisky industry's Charles Foster Kane. Fall in love with the Pandolfini Palace in Florence? Replicate it as your offices. Need to get home to Detroit but can't wait for a ferry? Build your own terminals and have a private service. Have a country house 45 miles upriver? Build a railway line to take you there. Have a friend called Henry Ford starting out as a car manufacturer? Build a factory in exchange for 30 percent of the business. Have a growing whisky distillery? Build a town for your workers and name it after yourself.

Walker had arrived in Detroit to work in the fur trade but, in 1854, he became a rectifier, filtering, blending, and bottling spirits from local distillers. In 1858, he moved across the river, built his distillery, and

began selling his Canadian whisky back to his countrymen. By the end of the century, his brands were outselling bourbon in gentlemen's clubs. In 1882, Canadian Club was born. If any American distillers thought that stating the country of origin on the label might repel patriotic drinkers, they were wrong. Hiram Walker's style of blend (gentle, light, and sweet) was in line with consumers' palates.

Close proximity to Detroit made this a prime spot during Prohibition. The firm was bought in 1926 by Harry Hatch, by then owner of Toronto distiller Gooderham & Worts (and, in time, of Corby Distillers) and the commander of "Hatch's Navy," which intrepidly crossed the Great Lakes to supply thirsty Americans with Scotch, rum, and Canadian whisky, much of which was magicked across the river by boat under "nun's" habits, maybe through Hiram's old tunnel.

This is hardly a heritage blend, though. It's far too well mannered, too Canadian to swagger, but the quality of the blends, especially at the top end, bear a knowing smile, suggesting that Hiram's vision holds true.

CANADIAN CLUB TASTING NOTES

CANADIAN CLUB 1858 40%

Nose: Very soft and citric: orange peel, orange-blossom honey, barley-sugar candies, apricot jam, gentle corn, and a light jag of rye.
Palate: Medium-weight. Soft corn start, then cocoa butter and white chocolate. Juicy fruit.
Finish: Light rye. Balanced.
Conclusion: Also known as Premium. An extremely sound starting point.

Flavor Camp: **Soft Corn**
Where Next? George Dickel

CANADIAN CLUB RESERVE 10YO 40%

Nose: More rye accents on the nose, which mixes cilantro and long-pepper fragrance. Subtle sweetness behind, with light toffee and a little cereal sweetness. Water brings out an exotic fruitiness.
Palate: Gentle start, with big butter-toffee notes before the fennel-seed kick of rye comes through. With water, there's a balance between light pear, cooked apple, and cinnamon spices.
Finish: A bittersweet note that has ducked in and out comes to the fore.
Conclusion: Rye-accented and quite bold.

Flavor Camp: **Spicy Rye**
Where Next? Tullamore D.E.W.

CANADIAN CLUB 20YO 40%

Nose: Long, complex, and ripe, with a fleshy fruitiness. Apple syrup and fresh-sawn wood. Light, rye-accented spices give some liveliness to its mature depths.
Palate: Oak to start, then some ripe berry fruit that is being constantly jabbed by sharp lemon and allspice from the rye. Water releases spices and brings out canned prune tones.
Finish: Subtle bitterness, with clove and coconut matting.
Conclusion: Mature and complex.

Flavor Camp: **Rich & Oaky**
Where Next? Powers' John's Lane

CANADIAN CLUB 30YO 40%

Nose: Fat and exotically perfumed: a mixture of oak, spices from the rye, and the inevitable oxidation. Ras el hanout/garam masala cut with leather and cigar wrapper and black fruits; almost Armagnac-like depths.
Palate: Soft and fruity and holding the wood at arm's length. Toffee, ripeness, and then that burst of mixed spices.
Finish: Some orange and green peppercorn.
Conclusion: Elegant and rich.

Flavor Camp: **Rich & Oaky**
Where Next? Redbreast 15yo

Valleyfield/Canadian Mist

VALLEYFIELD • MONTREAL
CANADIAN MIST • COLLINGWOOD • WWW.CANADIANMIST.COM

The town of Salaberry-de-Valleyfield has a name that speaks of a lovely *entente cordiale* between the Quebeçois and their English-speaking compatriots. It is harder to say whether its whisky has ever shown any French-Canadian attitude. It did have an American one, however. The Valleyfield distillery came into being in 1945 as part of the Schenley Group and, for a time, made Old Crow and Ancient Age Bourbon, as well as domestic brands such as Gibson's, Golden Wedding, and OFC (Old Fine/Fire Copper; both terms were used). These days it is part of the Diageo portfolio and is home to Seagram's 83 and Seagram's VO (the latter was first made in 1913 in Waterloo, Ontario, for Thomas Seagram's nuptials). Some bases for Crown Royal also hail from here.

Today, two base whiskies are made, both from corn. The lighter goes through a standard multiple-column setup, and the richer, more corn-oil accented one through a kettle-and-column system (*see* p.275). Flavoring whiskies are brought in from Diageo's plant at Gimli.

Canadian Mist, in Collingwood, Ontario, is a relatively modern plant, built by Barton Brands in 1967 to make Canadian Mist for the US market. Now owned by Brown-Forman (owner of Jack Daniel's), it seems initially a pretty straightforward setup: one base whisky made from corn, one flavoring from a mash

bill high in rye. The latter uses the distillery's own yeast and is given a long ferment time to maximize ester creation. Both are distilled in column-stills, which, despite rumors to the contrary, are packed with sacrificial copper.

The Canadian Mist brand is another of Canada's ridiculously amenable whiskies. At times you wonder whether the sheer ease of drinking them (especially long) is one reason why they're ignored by the "serious" drinker. Such are the perils of mass appeal. Brown-Forman has been trying to address this with the launch of Collingwood, a different blend to Canadian Mist, which is then given a period of marrying in vats, into which have been placed toasted maple-wood staves. Now, you can't get much more Canadian than that.

CANADIAN MIST TASTING NOTES

CANADIAN MIST 40%

Nose: Light, fresh, with light dustiness around the edges. Unripe banana, blond tobacco. Delicate, with typical Canadian sweetness.
Palate: Popcorn. Light syrup and green fruit, then some lemon, vegetal notes, and a little touch of ginger.
Finish: Light pepper.
Conclusion: All quite delicate. Would mix well.

Flavor Camp: **Soft Corn**
Where Next? Black Velvet, Canadian Club 1858

SEAGRAM VO 40%

Nose: Light touches of estery fruit, some mashed banana, and a steely rye note.
Palate: Quite firm to start, but water (and even better, ginger ale) allows a softness to be pulled forward.
Finish: Light and spiced.
Conclusion: Made for mixing.

Flavor Camp: **Spicy Rye**
Where Next? JH Rye

COLLINGWOOD 40%

Nose: Estery and lifted. Light with green fennel seed, Chinese green tea, chlorophyll, and some delicate blossom. Fresh.
Palate: Sweetened green tea is all-pervasive. Light jasmine, rhubarb, dried apricot. Delicate honey.
Finish: Floral. Drying. Crystallized ginger.
Conclusion: This will go down well in China.

Flavor Camp: **Fragrant & Floral**
Where Next? Dewar's 12yo

COLLINGWOOD 21YO 40%

Nose: Mature. Immediate soft rye notes with plenty of cracked pepper and cardamom to give lift. Wild herbs and star anise, then it sweetens into liqueur orange, ginseng, chocolate, and mango.
Palate: Succulent and quite floral, with lots of gardenia and rose, hinting at Turkish delight. Lightly powdery before thick sweetness returns.
Finish: Light dusting of cinnamon.
Conclusion: A remarkable one-off. More like this please!

Flavor Camp: **Spicy Rye**
Where Next? Powers' John's Lane

COLLINGWOOD

AGED IN WHITE OAK BARRELS & FINISHED WITH TOASTED MAPLEWOOD MELLOWING. SOME CALL COLLINGWOOD THE SMOOTHEST WHISKY EVER MADE. WE INVITE YOU TO JUDGE FOR YOURSELF • WWW.COLLINGWOODWHISKY.COM

40% alc./vol.   DISTILLED BY DISTILLÉ PAR CANADIAN MIST DISTILLERS, COLLINGWOOD, ONTARIO, CANADA   750mL

Forty Creek

FORTY CREEK DISTILLERY • GRIMSBY • ONTARIO • WWW.FORTYCREEKWHISKY.COM • OPEN ALL YEAR; SEE WEBSITE FOR DAYS & DETAILS

The "Ballad of John K. Hall" has a certain ring to it. It's appropriate, too, since the man behind Forty Creek is no mean musician. The opening verses would tell of a man buying a winery near Niagara in 1993, who decided to make whisky when 15 stills were going silent, who was small when the rest were getting bigger. Him against the giants. Brave John K. Hall, he fought his way to international acclaim, being seen as the founding father of Canadian craft distilling; the man who said, "What if?" The ballad ends happily with him successfully selling to Campari in 2014 for $185 million Canadian.

He's also a man who, by asking what Canadian whisky is, has opened up the possibilities as to what it *could* be. "When I started, Canadian whisky, which had been steeped in tradition, innovation, and excitement, had become stale and tired," Hall says. "It was being left behind."

His response was to take wine-making principles (yeast selection, treating grains as varietals, understanding flavor generation from different charring, toasting, and oak types) and allying them to whisky.

There's no base whisky here, but three distillates: column-still corn, usually aged in heavy char; barley from single passes of two pot-stills with rectifying plates aged in medium toast; and rye from the same pots in light toast. All are aged separately, blended, and married.

Did being the new kid force Hall to break new ground?

"Innovation isn't dictated by size, but by passion," he says. "Passion for your craft, your customers, and for the people who work with you. Hand in hand with innovation is patience. Without patience in whisky, you won't benefit from your innovation."

He sees his approach to the ever-growing Forty Creek range as analogous with music.

"A songwriter's creative process is pretty much done in isolation, the same way barrels of aging whisky sit for a long time. A song needs an intriguing beginning to capture the listener. It needs to have soul, rhythm, and counter-rhythm, and the ending needs to be satisfying. Great whiskies are the same. That is what I try to achieve."

The Forty Creek whiskies continue to significantly demonstrate how this approach can create new flavors that shatter a mindset which, in this case, said: "Canadian whisky can only be this." If the Canadian industry is now innovating, it is in no small way thanks to John K. Hall, the man who also said, "Why not?"

FORTY CREEK TASTING NOTES

BARREL SELECT 40%

Nose: Gentle and very fruity, with oven-baked peach, apricot. Subtle sweet rye creeping in. Slow. With water, some manuka honey and spice.
Palate: Gentle and medium-bodied. The corn is smooth and thick. Well-balanced, mingling toffee and caramel with baked banana.
Finish: Crisps up, with nutmeg and a tightening of rye.
Conclusion: Balanced and relaxed.

Flavor Camp: **Soft Corn**
Where Next? Chita Single Grain

COPPER POT RESERVE 40%

Nose: Big, with more black fruit, caramelized fruit sugars, chocolate-covered macadamia nuts, and some maple syrup. Thick, bold, and sweet. Water brings out red fruit.
Palate: A stickier version of Barrel Select, with more caramel and sweet nuts and a prickle of sweet spices.
Finish: Long and sweet.
Conclusion: Bold, broad, and mouth-filling.

Flavor Camp: **Soft Corn**
Where Next? George Dickel Barrel Reserve

CONFEDERATION RESERVE 40%

Nose: Light, with green apple and oak. Bittersweet with a little varnish and oil. Remains relaxed and sweet in the distillery style, but here there's more acetone and a little tart red fruit.
Palate: Corn leads in thick and slow. Much chewier than the nose suggest. Zesty.
Finish: Green apple.
Conclusion: A slightly lighter expression with more expressive cereal.

Flavor Camp: **Spicy Rye**
Where Next? Green Spot

DOUBLE BARREL RESERVE 40%

Nose: Oak is in charge here. Hint of oak sap, sawn wood mixed with honey and nuts. Needs time to open. Red and black fruit: cassis.
Palate: Complex, moving from cooked citrus fruit to fresh peels to hard candy, to oak, and then honey. Structured.
Finish: Green fennel seed. Crisp.
Conclusion: Layered, oaky, and sweet.

Flavor Camp: **Rich & Oaky**
Where Next? The Balvenie Double Wood 17yo

Canadian Craft Distilleries

STILL WATERS • CONCORD, ONTARIO • WWW.STILLWATERSDISTILLERY.COM • OPEN ALL YEAR; TOURS BY RESERVATION
PEMBERTON DISTILLERY • PEMBERTON, BRITISH COLUMBIA • WWW.PEMBERTONDISTILLERY.CA • OPEN ALL YEAR; TOURS SAT ONLY
LAST MOUNTAIN DISTILLERY • LUMSDEN, SASKATCHEWAN • WWW.LASTMOUNTAINDISTILLERY.COM

If any American craft distillers look north over the border and wonder why there are relatively few following their footsteps, they ought to take a closer look at the conditions Canadian distillers have to work in. As Canadian whisky-writer and commentator Davin de Kergommeaux says, "Restrictive government regulations concerning the production and sale of liquor discourages would-be distillers. There is no single code covering Canada. There's also the question of aging. In Canada, grain spirits must mature for three years before they can be called whisky. However, small producers are taxed at the time their spirit is distilled, not when it is sold.

"Of some 30-odd craft distilleries operating today [2014], eight make whisky spirit and only three regularly bottle whisky they have distilled themselves," says de Kergommeaux. "Still, these are early days. The Canadian craft movement is barely five years old."

One of those who has come through the white-spirit world is Still Waters, in Concord, which started distilling in March 2009 and, as the first craft distillery in Ontario, has had to be the trailblazer in getting the Liquor Control Board to understand what craft distilling is all about. "I soon realized that it's not just whisky-making; it's politics," says distiller Barry Bernstein with a rueful smile.

This neat distillery is now making rye, single-malt, and corn whiskies, the first being the most challenging. "It foams terribly in the fermenter," says Bernstein. "One day we came in and we were ankle-deep in rye. The place was a mess, but it sure smelled great!" Things are considerably more under control now, with their Christian Carl stills with moveable rectification plates allowing different characters and weight of spirits to be made.

The rye is highly perfumed, almost gin-like, with flashes of wintergreen, while the single malt, released as Stalk and Barrel, has some geranium and a little buttery accent. As Bernstein says, "The challenge now is how we make money!"

In Pemberton, British Columbia, Tyler Schramm is taking a more classical approach to his whisky-making. He'd gone to study at Heriot-Watt University in Edinburgh, with the aim of making potato vodka on his return but, as he says, "Within my first week, my plan had grown to include whisky. The passion and tradition surrounding Scottish single malts really hooked me."

A certified organic distillery, Pemberton is very traditional in outlook. "I'd lump myself into the traditionalist category, and I try to make our spirits conform to the way they would traditionally be made in Scotland," he says. "That said, we can have some fun with changing our recipe slightly from year to year. I think our location, our water, the local barley, and our stills will combine to produce whisky that's unique to us."

Still waters is one of the pioneers of craft distilling in Canada.

Last Mountain in Saskatchewan, meanwhile, is also looking locally. Using wheat is a no-brainer when you're on the prairies. "Saskatchewan produces some of the best wheat in the world.," says distiller Colin Schmidt, "so we are focusing on that at this time."

As his whisky matures, he is also sourcing, maturing, and blending sourced-wheat whiskies. "We're learning that blending is truly an art. We can take a three-year-old whisky and drastically change its flavor profile within six months. It's these techniques that we're applying to our own distillate, by using new 10-gallon casks and blending in ex-bourbon barrels. I do believe that the little guy needs to find creative ways to make new whiskies, especially if the supply of used bourbon barrels dries up."

Is this the start of a new Canadian whisky? For Schmidt, definitely. "John Hall [see p.279] is leading the way. He's focusing on crafting complex whisky that is still true to Canadian Whisky." Tyler Schramm wouldn't disagree. "With the growth of microdistilleries here, especially on the West Coast, we're seeing different grains being used. I believe this is going to lead to peoples' ideas changing about what a Canadian whisky is. Many people just assume that Canadian Whisky has to have rye in it. It doesn't."

And what of the father figure, John K. Hall? Schmidt continues: "I think it's great for the industry. In my career I saw the emergence of craft wineries and craft breweries, both benefitting their respective industries. But I also saw the rationalization of the distilling industry. Now, whisky brands, an emerging flavored-whisky category, and fledgling craft distilleries are all creating interest and excitement, and providing customers with an experience which, until recently, was missing from our Canadian whisky fabric."

A multicolored tapestry is being woven. The giant isn't slumbering any longer.

Okanagan's elegant stills are an indication of how varied the new Canadian-whisky world has become.

CANADIAN CRAFT DISTILLERIES TASTING NOTES

LAST MOUNTAIN CASK SAMPLE 40%
Nose: Slightly green, with some celery and grassiness; some warm, mashy sweetness behind. With water, floral with some lime. Young and clean.
Palate: Sweet, gentle, and honeyed, with a little basil, syrup, and a little almond.
Finish: Gentle and short.
Conclusion: Clean and well made.

LAST MOUNTAIN PRIVATE RESERVE 45%
Nose: Darker and more liquorous. Flower petals and concentrated fruit. A little touch of nettle. Water shows its youth but there is substance behind.
Palate: The perfumed/floral character (hibiscus, meadow flowers) is there. Light, dry, a little flour on the end.
Finish: Clean and short.
Conclusion: Developing very nicely.

Flavor Camp: Sweet wheat
Where Next? Last Mountain 45%

STILL WATERS STALK & BARREL, CASK #2 61.3%
Nose: Fresh bread, with marzipan, cranberry, cookie dough, and a little hint of jasmine. With water, there's fresh fig and light cream from the cask.
Palate: Clean with some fresh barrel notes. Slightly grippy with hay and developing estery notes.
Finish: Clean and slightly tight, but has length and a spicy kiss-off.
Conclusion: Well made and though young, showing great potential for longer-term aging.

Flavor Camp: Fragrant & Floral
Where Next? Spirit of Hven

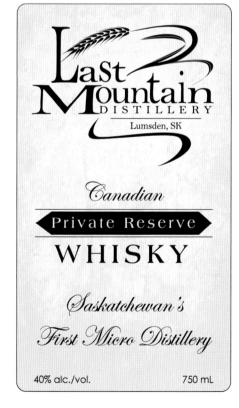

While there are innovations taking place within the classic whisky areas, the whisky-lover must look to the rest of the world to get the full picture of quite how rapidly the scene is changing and how deeply the new distillers are asking themselves that, "What is whisky?" question.

Previous page: **Whisky is now being** made throughout Europe, from the Pyrénées to the Danube, Andalusia to Scandinavia.

What is particularly fascinating is how they are springing from different bases. Many of the whiskies of central Europe come from generations-old expertise in producing fruit spirits. Barley (or whatever cereal is being used) is another option. Even if they sometimes lack mid-palate weight, these spirits open up a new appreciation of what barley (or oats, rye, or spelt) is.

In the Netherlands, Patrick Zuidam's gin heritage makes his take on whisky both ancient and ultra-modern. In the process he has reclaimed rye for the people who first distilled it. In addition, the smokes being used across Europe are being tried because they have been used for centuries with food: be it nettles in Denmark, chestnut in Germany and the Alps, juniper in Sweden, or birch and sheep manure in Iceland. These variations are important not just because they excite geeks like you and me, but because they are challenging orthodoxies.

As Jasmin Haider in Austria says, "It's always important to go your own way. Whiskies are as varied as people's tastes. It's also important to be innovative. First of all, something great can come out of an innovative idea, and when we are mature, it needs the drive of innovation to make sure one always moves forward. It also means being brave and having staying power if you are to take the new idea further. It also doesn't hurt to be a bit mad!"

There is a need to innovate because these whiskies cannot compete with Scotch. Neither should they. The joy of tasting them is that they genuinely show a new approach to whisky, a lack of fear in trying something new—not reacting to Scotch as the enemy, but seeing that its hegemony necessitates other options.

At the same time, these new whiskies have to sell. Quality needs to be paramount, as does consistency. Sure, we should all cut a little slack in early releases, but eventually a distiller has to justify the price of his or her bottle. A whisky-maker isn't judged on the first bottle you buy, but whether you come back for a third.

That means the spirit must be more than just "interesting," it must be compelling. It must tell a story different from that of its neighbors. It cannot be contrived, but has to be honest, open, reflective. The work is more difficult. There is no whisky-making heritage, and nothing to fall back on. New distillers are pioneers. They are all, therefore, exposed.

A new distiller is learning with every cask, which also means accepting that when things do go wrong, it's best to start again instead of covering the mistake in the soiled flag of dubious innovation. The search is always one for consistency (difficult to achieve with single casks), personality, and the fact that it must justify a higher price. As one distiller said to me, "The big boys can afford to sell at €50 ($68). If you want to charge €100 ($135), it must be better!"

The good thing is that the best of the whiskies that follow do just that. They are not Scotch, or bourbon, or Irish. They should not be compared to them. They are new. They are exciting. And yes, sometimes they are also a little mad. Please try them.

The spectacular scenery of the Brecon Beacons shelters Penderyn, Wales's only whisky distillery.

EUROPE

EUROPE
▼ Distillery

N

0 —— miles —— 400
0 —— km —— 400

Faeroe Islands

Shetland Islands

Norwegian Sea

SWEDEN

NORWAY

Oslo

Stockholm

North Sea

DENMARK

Copenhagen

Vänern

Vättern

Öland

Baltic Sea

Dublin

IRELAND

UNITED KINGDOM

▼ **Lakes**

St George's *see inset*

Penderyn ▼

Cotswolds ▼
London Distillery, ▼ **Adnams**
East London
Hicks & Healey's ▼
Liquor Co.

Claeyssens ▼

Northmaen ▼
Warenghem ▼ **Glann ar Mor**

Menhirs ▼

Kaerilis ▼

ATLANTIC OCEAN

Loire

Pays d'Othe ▼

FRANCE

Bay of Biscay

Balthazar ▼

Brunet ▼
Michard ▼

Bordeaux

Garonne

Castan ▼
Toulouse

Pyrenees

ANDORRA

Destilerias Y Crianzas Del Whisky ▼
Segovia

PORTUGAL

Lisbon

Madrid

SPAIN

Douro

Guadalquivir

Granada
Liber ▼

Balearic Islands

NETH.
Amsterdam

Berlin

Hamburg
Elbe

Brussels
BELGIUM
Rhine

Lukembourg

GERMANY

POLAND
Warsaw

Vistula

Prague
CZECH REPUBLIC

SLOVA

Paris

Grallet Dupic ▼
Hepp, Bertrand ▼
Elsasser
Meyer
Holl ▼

Revermont ▼
Rouget de Lisle ▼

Frankfurt

Vienna
AUSTRIA

Bratislava

Budapest
HUNGARY

Ljubljana
SLOV.

Zagreb
CROATIA

Danube

Bern
SWITZ.

LIECH.

ALPS

Rhine

Domaine des Hautes Glaces ▼

Ebro

MONACO

ITALY

Corsica

Mavela ▼

Rome

SAN MARINO

BOS. & HERZ.

Sarajevo

SER

Belgrade

MONTENEGRO

Podgorica

KOSOVO
Pris

Tirana
ALBANI.

Sardinia

Mediterranean Sea

Sicily

MALTA

FINLAND

Lake Onega

Lake Ladoga

RUSSIAN FEDERATION

Helsinki

Tallinn

ESTONIA

Riga

LATVIA

HUANIA

ilnius

Minsk

BELARUS

Moscow

Kiev

Dnieper

UKRAINE

MOLDOVA

Carpathian Mountains

Chisinau

OMANIA

Bucharest

Danube

BULGARIA

Sofia

pje

CEDONIA

Istanbul

Ankara

TURKEY

EECE

Athens

Crete

Nicosia

CYPRUS

Beirut

Damascus

SYRIA

Baghdad

IRAQ

Milk & Honey

Jerusalem

Amman

ISRAEL JORDAN

Volgograd

KAZAKHSTAN

Rostov-on-Don

Praskoveyskoye

Krasnodar

Caspian Sea

Black Sea

GEORGIA

AZERBAIJAN

ARMENIA

IRAN

North Sea

Groningen

Leeuwarden

Den Helder

Us Heit

NETHERLANDS

Amsterdam

The Hague

Vallei, Leusden

Gorter, Schiedam

Utrecht

Rhine

GERMANY

Kampen,

Bruinisse

Rotterdam

Eindhoven

Zuidam, Baarle-Nassau

Antwerp

Filliers,

Gent

Deinze

Brussels

Het Anker, Mechelen

Owl,

Rademacher,

Raeren

Lille

Grace-Hollogne

Liège

BELGIUM

FRANCE

LUXEMBOURG

Diedenacher,

Niederdonven

Luxembourg

miles 100

km 100

England

ST GEORGE'S DISTILLERY • EAST HARLING, NORFOLK • WWW.ENGLISHWHISKY.CO.UK • OPEN ALL YEAR MON–SUN / ADNAMS COPPER HOUSE DISTILLERY • SOUTHWOLD • WWW.ADNAMS.CO.UK • OPEN; SEE WEB FOR DAYS & DETAILS / THE LONDON DISTILLERY CO • LONDON SW11 • WWW.LONDONDISTILLERY.COM / THE LAKES DISTILLERY • BASSENTHWAITE LAKE, CUMBRIA • WWW.LAKESDISTILLERY.COM

That there are two distilleries in the fertile flatlands of East Anglia shouldn't be that surprising. The fact that both are new is perhaps what is more remarkable. The thing is, England just never quite got the whisky-distilling bug. While large distilleries operated in London, Liverpool, and Bristol in the nineteenth century, England's national spirit had become gin.

The situation began to redress itself in 2006, when farmers John and Andrew Nelstrop opened St George's Distillery in Norfolk. The question of what was English whisky is something distiller David Fitt has been addressing since 2007.

The distillery is compact: a one-ton mash tun, three washbacks, and two Forsyth stills. The ferments are long and cool to build up esters, and the stills, with their descending lyne arms, are run at no more than a trickle to give a sweet, gently fruity, nicely layered new make.

All seems orthodox until Fitt opens the warehouse and starts pulling samples, and his training as a brewer comes into play. There's a "grain whisky" made with malted barley, crystal malt, chocolate malt, oats, wheat, and rye aged in virgin oak; a triple-distilled peated malt; Madeira and rum casks. "We can do things differently to Scotland," he say. "You're not constrained here. If they want me to make something mad, I can!"

A similar mindset is being applied 45 miles to the east in Southwold, where local brewer Adnams has joined the English whisky league. Here, brewing expertise is applied to whisky-making. They use their own yeast, get clear wort, and ferment for three days in temperature-controlled vessels at a 52% abv. Two whisky recipes—a 100 percent malted barley and barley/wheat—are run through a beer-stripping column, then into a pot with fixed plates. The new make was recently tweaked down to 85% abv. "At 88%, it was just too clean," says distiller John McCarthy. "You get more congeners just dropping that strength."

That "Why not?" attitude is here as well. Radoux wine casks of American and French oak are used for the two mash bills, beer is being distilled into the Spirit of Broadside, while a rye is currently aging. English rye? "Of course!" says McCarthy. "We can do anything we want!"

England's late-blooming whisky industry isn't restricted to the east. As of January 2014, after a gap of more than 100 years, London has a whisky distillery once more, squeezed into a dockside development on the banks of the Thames River. "The plan is to go back to 1903 and see what single-malt spirit might have been like in those days when London was making spirit," says The London Distillery Company CEO/distiller Darren Rook. "We are starting with the oldest varieties of barley and yeast and moving forward decade by decade. At the end of the process we'll fine-tune and work out which combination gives us the single-malt spirit that best reflects London. We want to make London whisky."

That location is important. "There's a rich heritage here," says Rook. "Chaucer wrote of 'worts distilled' in the 1390s, but people still think whisky came from Scotland. There were distilleries here making everything. We're reviving an ancient tradition."

Back in East Anglia, St George's opened with no windows because the Nelstrops heard rumors a distillery was being built in the Lake District. That plan came to nothing, but at the time of writing another Cumbrian dream is close to being reality. With consultant Alan Rutherford's advice, The Lakes Distillery is trying a "Roseisle" style of interchangeable steel and copper condensers to create different characters. That line of "being able to do what the Scots can't" is used once more by owner Paul Currie. "That said, we don't want to experiment too much," he adds, "because that can end up confusing people. Maybe we'll have a Mad March every year and see what we can do."

It's a common thread. As Fitt says, "English whisky is what anyone wants it to be. I don't want English whisky to have a single identity; I want every distillery to have one." For Rook it's not just having a license to distill, but one to ask questions. With West Country distiller Healey & Hicks quietly maturing its Cornish whisky (*see H&H, below*), it seems as if England is finally becoming a whisky nation.

ENGLAND TASTING NOTES

H&H 05/11 CASK SAMPLE 59.11%

Nose: Light, toasted oak with some light nuttiness, a hint of sweet Calvados in the background. Fresh, but with depth and spiced with mead-like honey.
Palate: Softly honeyed, with mulled fruit, berries, and apples. Good balance. Quite liquorous with an almost Bénédictine-like herbal edge.
Finish: Pears and spices.
Conclusion: Coming on speedily.

EWC MULTI-GRAIN CASK SAMPLE (STRENGTH UNKNOWN)

Nose: Sweet and rich, with some wood oils mixing with creamy toffee and light chocolate.
Palate: The chocolate now dominates, then sandalwood, creamy oats, spruce buds, and light oils.
Finish: Long and gentle.
Conclusion: A mix of different roasts, oats, wheat, and rye. Scotch it ain't!

ADNAMS, SPIRIT OF BROADSIDE 43%

Nose: Aromatic, with dark fruit, plump raisin, stewed damson plum. Roasted tea with lemon. Malty.
Palate: Big, fruity impact with cherry cough drops, damson plum, and blackcurrant. Weighty, showing some fatness in the center.
Finish: Sweet with light oak.
Conclusion: Has weight. An interesting potential direction.

Flavor Camp: **Fruity & Spicy**
Where Next? Armorik Double Maturation, Old Bear

Wales

PENDERYN • WWW.WELSH-WHISKY.CO.UK • OPEN ALL YEAR MON–SUN

Finding your style is always an interesting philosophical adventure for a new distiller. What are your reference points? Do you follow what has gone before, or do you reject your neighbors' approaches and strike out on your own? It's hard enough to find your voice when there are these markers, so what happens when you are really on your own? That was the issue faced by the Welsh Whisky Company (WWC) when, a decade ago, it built its Penderyn distillery in the Brecon Beacons National Park. The fact that there was no other Welsh whisky to compare themselves against was, one would imagine, a daunting challenge, but also a liberation. Welsh whisky was what they said it was.

Why, for example, did they have to mill, mash, and ferment on site when there was Brains brewery close by, which could provide wash to their specification? The advantage, they would argue, is that brewers are yeast specialists and Brains' yeast adds its own fruit-driven personality to the beer.

Neither did they have to install Scottish-looking pot-stills. Instead, the firm turned to Dr. David Faraday's design, which is a pot linked to a rectifying column, allowing spirit to be made in a single pass. The column is split into two, because its original height would have necessitated building a stillhouse to a height that would have contravened building regulations.

The first column is fitted with six plates, the second with 18. Spirit is drawn off at the seventh plate; any vapor rising higher is refluxed back into the first column and the pot. In one way, it is distilling at a single pass. In another, there are multiple distillations taking place. From 660 gallons (2,500 liters) of wash, 53 gallons (200 liters) of focused, chypre-accented, floral new make are collected at between 92% and 86% abv.

A new replica Faraday still was installed in 2013 along with two new pots. These will not just increase capacity but widen the range of spirit styles being made. Plans for a mash tun are also underway. Production is looked after by Laura Davies and Aista Jukneviciute, while maturation has been masterminded by WWC's consultant Dr. Jim Swan, the great guru of wood management. Yet again, convention is flouted. The standard Penderyn (none of the brands carry age statements, and no one has complained) is aged in ex-bourbon and finished in ex-Madeira drums. The Sherrywood is 70 percent ex-bourbon and 30 percent ex-sherry, while there is also a peated expression whose emergence was accidental.

The original intention was never to have smoke intruding into the whisky, and the specification for the refill casks (imported from Scotland) was that they should not previously have held a peaty malt. Some, however, sneaked through. When the whisky was bottled as a once-only special, it sold out. Now it's part of the portfolio.

At the time of writing, Penderyn remains Wales's only distillery, but it surely can only be a matter of time before the whisky-making bug bites here as well.

WALES TASTING NOTES

PENDERYN, NEW MAKE

Nose: Intense and sweet. chypre (bergamot and fresh citrus notes). Mint and fir with perfumed top notes.
Palate: Neat is hot and tense but with water, floral notes, rose, fresh citrus fruit, green fruit, and then a little cereal crunch.
Finish: Fleshy but clean.

PENDERYN, MADEIRA 46%

Nose: Clean, sweet oak. Pine and vanilla. Spring leaves/green bark. Light plum at the background.
Palate: Juicy and clean with lots of apricot nectar and spicy oak relaxing into Lady Grey tea.
Finish: Clean and minty.
Conclusion: The green notes of new make softened and carried forward along with balanced oak.

> **Flavor Camp: Fragrant & Floral**
> **Where Next?** Glenmorangie The Original 10yo

PENDERYN, SHERRYWOOD 46%

Nose: Gold. A clear difference to the standard. Bran this time along with citrus peel, light nuts, and sweet dried fruit (date/fig). With water, some vine flower.
Palate: Has taken the floral notes of new make and deepened them. Similarly juicy to the standard but the fruit more stewed.
Finish: Figgy and sweet.
Conclusion: Light spirit, but balanced here with a complex range of oak-driven flavors. A different take on the new make character.

> **Flavor Camp: Rich & Round**
> **Where Next?** The Singleton of Glendullan 12yo

France

GLANN AR MOR • LARMOR-PLEUBIAN • WWW.GLANNARMOR.COM / WARENGHEM • LANNION • WWW.DISTILLERIE-WARENGHEM.COM / DISTILLERIE DES MENHIRS • PLOMELIN • WWW.DISTILLERIE.FR/EN / DISTILLERIE MEYER • HOHWARTH • WWW.DISTILLERIEMEYER.FR / ELSASS • OBERNAI • WWW.DISTILLERIELEHMANN.COM / DOMAINE DES HAUTES GLACES • RHÔNE-ALPES • WWW.HAUTESGLACES.COM / BRENNE • COGNAC • WWW.DRINKBRENNE.COM

Any discussion with the new generation of French whisky-distillers (now numbering 22) will, at some point, mention the country's distilling heritage. France has expertise in grape spirits: (Cognac, Armagnac); those made from fruit (Calvados, fruit *eaux de vie*); distillations of herbs springing from ancient curative potions (Chartreuse, absinthe); spirits to slake workers' thirsts (pastis); liqueurs to round off the end of a meal.

It might seem reasonable to wonder, with all these national riches, why would whisky even be considered? On the other hand, it is equally justifiable to ask: why not? A cereal spirit completes the set. In any case, this is a whisky-drinking nation. More Scotch is consumed in France than Cognac.

Here, more than anywhere, you delve deep into the concept of *terroir*, that philosophical linkage of product with place, and yet it is dangerous to assume that there is some unified French-whisky style. "Saying that is like saying there's something called 'French wine,'" says Glann ar Mor's Jean Donnay, "whereas in reality you have Bordeaux, Burgundy, and the Rhône, you have Alsace wines and Champagne."

If there isn't a shared approach, might there be a regional style that helps define, say, Breton whiskies from those from Alsace? "No," he says. "Here in Brittany there are four producers making four very different whiskies."

Donnay's distillery, 394 feet (120 meters) from the sea in Pleubian, on the northern Brittany coast, may be new, but it utilizes old whisky-making techniques with a modern maturation regime. Direct-fire, slow-distillation worm tubs give a new make with texture and palate weight aged in first-fill bourbon and ex-Sauternes casks (Donnay was the world pioneer in using the latter).

He is now exploring the effects of the mild maritime climate on barley, with two seasons of crop from fields in front of the distillery having been floor-malted locally. "If you ask whether the location of the barley matters, then yes, it does!" he says. "The new make had more of an earthy, cereal character."

His two whiskies, unpeated Glann ar Mor and smoky Kornog, continue to evolve subtly, both combining expansive mouth-feel with zesty freshness and a distinct salinity.

Donnay's aim is to make Celtic whisky, with Glann ar Mor as a link in a chain that now binds Scotland, Ireland, Wales—and Cornwall (where is the Galician distillery?): a personal project now being reinforced with his construction of Gartbreck, on Islay.

His nearest neighbor, Warenghem, in Lannion, is Brittany's oldest distillery, whose blend WB ("Whisky Breton") was launched in 1987, followed 12 months later by France's first single malt, Amorik. There has been a reformulation of the brands in recent years as a consequence of investment in oak, resulting in a dramatic improvement.

If both follow a Scottish template, then former math teacher, Guy le Lat, dug deep into the native grains of Brittany when he started his

Distillerie des Menhirs, in Plomelin. The grain chosen (technically a grass) was *blé noir* (buckwheat), seen most commonly in *galettes*, the savory crêpes that are one of Brittany's signature dishes. Le Lat soon discovered that even rye is easy compared to buckwheat, which can solidify into concrete in the mash tun. He persevered, however, and Eddu is the spicy, fresh, complex result. Kaerlis, from the southern island of Belle-Île, makes up the Breton quartet.

There are no Celtic considerations in the whiskies from Alsace's five distilleries. This is a region with a long tradition of distilled fruit spirits. As a result, there is more of a shared character with the whiskies from its eastern hinterlands with their purity of character:

lighter, slightly fruity, understated. Here is a focus on the cereal, with wood playing a background role.

The largest producer, Meyer, in Hohwarth, has been making whisky since 2007 and now comprises blends and malts, while the Elsass brand has been made since 2008 by the Lehmann family of Obernai, who have been distilling fruit spirits since the mid-nineteenth century. Their approach is now extending to maturation using exclusively French white-wine casks (Bordeaux, Sauternes, and Coteaux-du-Layon). To see the effect of local wine casks, look for the distillates from Hepp in Uberach, bottled by Dennis Hans under the AWA brand.

Any overview of French whisky takes in a wide range of approaches and flavors. In Corsica, the Pietra brewery and the winemaker/distillers of Domaine Mavela have combined to produce some of the world's most extraordinarily scented whiskies, which come across more like a barley-based Chartreuse after being matured, first in a mix of ex-Malmsey and Patrimonio Petit Grains de Moscatel casks, before being married in ex-*eaux-de-vie* barrels.

A similarly heightened aromatic palette is generated at Michard, predominantly thanks to the use of a singular brewer's yeast. Aging, unsurprisingly, takes place in oak taken from the Limousin forest surrounding the distillery.

Terroir is uppermost in the thinking of Fred Revol and Jeremy Bricka, whose Domaine des Hautes Glaces sits at 2,954 feet (900 meters) in Rhône-Alpes. Founded in 2009, they use organic, locally grown cereals, French oak, and the local tradition of smoking over chestnut wood.

"Our approach is to take the innate French understanding of malting, fermenting, distillation, and coopering and reinterpret these in whisky," says Revol. "We do everything to link the liquid to the soil. We are high, the climate is different, the crops grow on a mix of volcanic soil and limestone. If we did exactly the same thing beside the sea, the liquid would not be the same."

A tentative mention of the theory of barley as fruit is met with enthusiastic agreement. "We consider cereal as a dried fruit," Revol says, "That's why our spirits are very floral and fruity." This is something that is also achieved by not being overly concerned with yields. "If we don't have alcohol [in the wash] we have more esters that help reveal the typicity of the cereal." A remarkable rye aged in Condrieu casks shows this approach at its most intense.

If there is a link among French distillates, it is a similarly gentle use of wood as in wine, where oak is used as structural support, not as an overwhelming contributor to flavor. "If we do everything from the soil, we're not going to make a vanilla infusion," says Revol.

Making whisky in Cognac may seem like a heretical act, but the Brunet family had been distilling grain in the down-time from Cognac production since 2005, and serving it to friends and family. It would have remained unnoticed were it not for whisky proselytizer Allison Patel from New York, who, in her words, was "developing a passion for whiskies from non-traditional countries."

Celtic soul brothers: the Breton coastline is home to a growing number of distilleries.

Soon after starting her own firm to import them to the USA, she was tipped off about the Brunet's whisky. "I was amazed," she recalls. "The stills [the Brunets use the alembic Charentais] and the yeast [a wine yeast] help to bring the fruit forward." Her one change was in maturation. "He had been only been aging in virgin Limousin oak, and

I wondered what it would be like to take it out and finish maturation in really old casks." (This is the standard manner for Cognac maturation.) The Brenne brand now follows that template.

"Maybe the French style is an eclectic one," says Fred Revol, "maybe because there is no tradition."

FRANCE TASTING NOTES

BRENNE 40%

Nose: Light with sweet fruit, some cider vinegar, cooking plums/plum compote and touches of patisserie. Cognac-style floral, fruity lift alongside ripe pear, grape skin, and, with water, celery.
Palate: Immediate coconut and melted white chocolate. Sweet, then comes banana split. Gets sweeter. Water allows sweet fruit and some licorice to come through.
Finish: Gentle and sweet.
Conclusion: The new oak makes its presence felt, but this is clearly a Cognaçais take on whisky.

Flavor Camp: Fruity & Spicy
Where Next? Hicks & Healey (in time)

MEYER'S, BLEND 40%

Nose: Heightened aromatics. Very grapey and reminiscent of Muscat de Beaumes de Venise. Honeyed. Almost sticky to smell and very fruity.
Palate: Highly fragrant with vanillin. Lightly drying toward the back palate. Decent length.
Finish: Quite short.
Conclusion: Sweet but fun.

Flavor Camp: Fruity & Spicy

MEYER'S PUR MALT 40%

Nose: Light and cereal-led. Malt barns and a phenolic (but not smoky) note akin to fire-lighters. With water, garden twine.
Palate: Sweet and well controlled, with length and surprising depth. Slightly sharp on the end as the cereal comes through.
Finish: Roasted cereal.
Conclusion: More central-European style, with airy cereal accents.

Flavor Camp: Malty & Dry
Where Next? JH Single Malt

LEHMANN ELSASS, SINGLE MALT 40%

Nose: Clean, with some cereal. Restrained and light with a touch of bicycle inner tube, then comes honey. Sweet, some fruit, but predominantly cereal-driven.
Palate: The sweetness continues, with some syrup and yellow fruits. Clean with very light oak.
Finish: Tarragon and marzipan.
Conclusion: The lightness of this style needs mid-palate weight, and oak to assist.

Flavor Camp: Malty & Dry
Where Next? Liebl, Coillmor American Oak

LEHMANN ELSASS, SINGLE MALT 50%

Nose: Bigger and fuller, with some dried fruit, black cherry. Drier with more oak and substance. Still a nutty structure.
Palate: Lightly perfumed, touches of grillotines, marzipan; lifted. Seems young. Back to the Muscat sweetness and perfume. Water brings out more chocolate.
Finish: Fruity.
Conclusion: More sweetness on show here, but still maturing as a style and as a whisky.

Flavor Camp: Fruity & Spicy
Where Next? Aberlour 12yo, Teerenpeli Kaski

DOMAINE DES HAUTES GLACES S11 #01 46%

Nose: Very floral and delicately fruity. White fruit and crisp linen—slightly starchy. In time, some hay and meadow blossom.
Palate: Soft pear and apple. Concentrating, but still has the crisp shell of youth, then flowers and sweet grasses. Light minerality.
Finish: Clean and sweet, with light aniseed and exotic spice.
Conclusion: Has presence. The center will fill out. Good potential.

Flavor Camp: Fragrant & Floral
Where Next? Kininvie new make, Teslington VI 5yo

DOMAINE DES HAUTES GLACES L10 #03 46%

Nose: Grassy and hay-like. Restraint and coolness. A little plainer than S11, with more cereal, rock, and earth.
Palate: Light and delicate, with the floral notes again emerging. Wormwood and angelica, even a hint of lavender.
Finish: Tight.
Conclusion: Young, but with potential.

Flavor Camp: Fragrant & Floral
Where Next? Mackmyra Brukswhisky

DOMAINE DES HAUTES GLACES SECALE, RYE, AGED IN A CONDRIEU CASK 56%

Nose: Exotic and perfumed, with fleshiness from Viognier cask cut with spice from the rye. Baked quince. Delicate, with some phenolic notes.
Palate: Sweet and garden-like but more spicy, with a hint of tar and pepper, then menthol. Has silky length, a little fennel, and the thickness of the wine cask comes through.
Finish: Long and fruity.
Conclusion: Already in balance.

Flavor Camp: Spicy Rye
Where Next? Yellow Spot

WARENGHEM ARMORIK DOUBLE MATURATION 46%

Nose: Rich, with some cooked fruit. Light phenols with some espresso coffee, damson, a little cereal.
Palate: Flowing well, with good depth. Assertive, with plums, cooked apples, and integrated oak.
Finish: Medium length and fruity.
Conclusion: Richer than the light, barley-accented standard release. Fleshier, with more weight and a significant step forward.

Flavor Camp: Rich & Round
Where Next? Bunnahabhain 12yo

GLANN AR MOR TAOL ESA 2 GWECH 2013 46%

Nose: Gentle, young, and clean. Yeasty and estery. Freshness abounds.
Palate: Rich and quite thick. Unctuous, showing the worms and direct fire at work. White orchard fruits. Lightly salty.
Finish: Fresh and gentle.
Conclusion: The unpeated variant of the range. Young but impressive.

Flavor Camp: Fragrant & Floral
Where Next? Benromach

KORNOG, TAOUARC'H 48.5%

Nose: Very gentle smoke with a distinct maritime air. Sugared almond, apple, pear.
Palate: Saline, herbal chervil and tarragon; fragrant smoke. Oily, with good central weight, cinnamon, sweet cookie.
Finish: Discreet smoke.
Conclusion: Single-cask ex-bourbon bottling. *Taouarc'h* is Breton for peat.

Flavor Camp: Smoky & Peaty
Where Next? Kilchoman Machir Bay, Inchgower

KORNOG, SANT IVY 58.6%

Nose: Bigger and bolder, with more wood oils and an ozonic freshness cut with grapefruit. The smoke is like distant burning heather alongside real sweetness, just a hint of tar.
Palate: Mashy notes with a lot of energy and drive. Citric and full. Oily.
Finish: Lengthy and discreetly smoked.
Conclusion: Single cask.

Flavor Camp: Smoky & Peaty
Where Next? Chichibu The Peated

Netherlands
ZUIDAM • BAARLE-NASSAU • WWW.ZUIDAM.EU • GROUP VISITS BY APPOINTMENT

Depending on how you look at it, Dutch whisky is either new or centuries old. Consider this. What is whisky? A cereal-based, wood-matured distillate. What is the basis of *genever* (Dutch gin)? *Moutwijn*, a fermented mash of malted barley, corn, and rye, distilled in pot-stills, redistilled with botanicals, blended, then aged. Old-style *genever* and the original (flavored) Irish and Scottish *usquebaugh* were from the same family.

Today, the Netherlands is home to three whisky distilleries: the small Vallei distillery in Leusden, the Friesland brewery/distillery linkup Us Heit, and the best known internationally, Millstone. It is the last that has the closest links to *genever*. Based in the village of Baarle-Nassau, it was built by *genever*-distiller Fred van Zuidam in 2002. His son Patrick now runs the firm, which has increased capacity twice in the past five years.

A hugely talented distiller (he makes *genever*, gin, vodka, and fruit liqueurs as well), Zuidam's approach to his whiskies starts with windmill-ground grain mashed into a thick porridge, which is then pumped into temperature-controlled fermenters and given an extended ferment with different strains of yeast. Distillation, equally slow, is in Holstein stills with *bains-marie* and huge amounts of available copper.

His range is ever-expanding. There is a single malt (with peated variant despite his personal aversion to smoke), but it was his sensual complex, spicy rye that first turned heads. "It's my pride because it's so difficult," he laughs. "It foams—I've been up to my knees in rye mash; it sticks. It's whisky-making on the edge."

There is a "rye-val" for his affection, however. A five-grain (wheat, corn, rye, malted barley, and spelt) mash, fermented for ten days, aged in new oak. "Spelt gives a baby-oil note, there's nuttiness from wheat, sweetness from corn, spice from rye. Together, it's a symphony that is just right at three years."

This young age is unusual here. His whiskies normally start in fresh oak before being transferred for relaxed oxidation in used

Sacks of cereal ground by a windmill at the Millstone distillery.

casks, the general richness of his spirit tending to require long maturation, but each is considered on its own merits.

"We have the freedom and the will to experiment," he says. "In Scotland everyone gets their ass kicked if they're not getting 108 gallons (410 liters of alcohol) per ton. It doesn't matter to me if I get a low yield and the spirit is good. At the end of the day, you have to have freedom to make superior whisky."

NETHERLANDS TASTING NOTES

MILLSTONE 10YO AMERICAN OAK 40%
Nose: Huge mulled-spiced nose that brings in dried orange peel, angelica, pine resin, and some floral notes. Oxidized nuttiness, Christmas spiciness.
Palate: Thick and chewy, moving into burnt orange peel, then pure fruit.
Finish: Lightly bitter, adding a further element of complexity.
Conclusion: Almost Japanese in its control and aromatic transparency.

Flavor Camp: Fruity & Spicy
Where Next? Yamazaki 18yo, Hibiki 12yo

MILLSTONE 1999, PX CASK 46%
Nose: Again, dried citrus-fruit peel is the giveaway here. It is mixed with raisin, old English marmalade, bergamot/Earl Grey tea. Briar-like fruitiness behind adds a soft sweetness.
Palate: Thick and layered, moving deep into forest fruit, dried plump raisin, some blackcurrant and cherry.
Finish: Tobacco.
Conclusion: Hugely ripe and controlled.

Flavor Camp: Rich & Round
Where Next? Alberta Premium 25yo, Cragganmore Distillers Edition

MILLSTONE RYE 100 50%
Nose: Layers of sumptuous red velvet laid on top of rye's feistiness. Still has the requisite spice: allspice especially, with hints of cubeb (tailed pepper) and rose petal, then moves to buckthorn and a thick jamminess that's cut with menthols.
Palate: Prickly start: a Sazerac in a glass. Light maraschino cherry, some tight oak, then a smooth, sweet fruit cut with dried herbs and red fruit.
Finish: Spiced and sweet.
Conclusion: One of the world's greatest ryes, if not *the* greatest.

Flavor Camp: Spicy Rye
Where Next? Old Potrero, Dark Horse

Belgium

THE OWL DISTILLERY • GRÂCE-HOLLOGNE • WWW.BELGIANWHISKY.COM / RADERMACHER • RAEREN • WWW.DISTILLERIE.BIZ

Home to the world's most diverse range of premium beers and repository of much brewing knowledge, why wouldn't Belgium become part of the whisky family? One of its handful of distilleries, Het Anker, took this logical step some years back, distilling its Gouden Carols Tripel into a similarly named whisky, aged for four years. The firm has now moved to a purpose-built site in Blaasveld, near Antwerp.

A different approach has been taken by Radermacher in Raeren in the east. The distillery, which has been producing *genever* and other distillates for 175 years, started making whisky over a decade ago. Its oldest expression is a ten-year-old grain whisky.

The largest producer, however, is The Owl. Since this book's last edition, distiller Etienne Bouillon has moved from the center of Grâce-Hollonge to a large farm on the village's outskirts. His old fruit still is semi-retired and two of the stills from Rothes' Caperdonich distillery (*see* p.78) have been installed.

This change in location and equipment has not meant a change of approach on Bouillon's part; if anything it has allowed him to align himself ever closer to the local *terroir*, which is central to his whisky-making philosophy. "There is a part of the ground that gives flavors and aromas during ferment," he says. "The grain, the minerals, give new, unique flavors. I collect alcohol and flavor linked to the ground." The only barley he uses comes from a geologically specific area that now surrounds the distillery. It has come to the source.

The stills, however, are radically different in size and shape to the original. "I know this can have a significant effect, but after the stills you have the distiller," Bouillon says. "I always cut with my nose and mouth, rather than temperature and time. It took me two weeks to find the parameters, but now the spirit is not much different—just a little more barley but I've kept it fruity and flowery."

Aging, being in first-fill American oak, takes cognisance of the need to preserve this taste of *terroir* and not obscure it behind lashings of vanillin. His only problem has been holding on to it for long enough. "I made this Belgian Owl for Belgians, but we've always been out of stock, so I haven't had an opportunity to age for longer periods. Now with more capacity I have enough product to satisfy the demand."

Maybe the rest of the world can taste this liquid distillation of Belgium.

The rolling hills around Liège are becoming a center of distilling activity.

BELGIUM TASTING NOTES

NEW MAKE, FROM CAPERDONICH STILLS

Nose: Very (insanely) fruity and lifted. Heavy blossom. Peaches and stewed rhubarb. Clean but weighty. Supple with cereal oils.
Palate: Sweet and balanced, with a fine attack. Has ripeness, length, and a full, fleshy feel.
Finish: Gentle.

THE BELGIAN OWL, UNAGED SPIRIT 46%

Nose: Sweet and slightly honeyed, with peach pit, green apricot, peach blossom, and barley.
Palate: Clean and light, with that honeyed quality coming through. Peach skin now.
Finish: Mixing flowers and cereal.
Conclusion: Already soft and well balanced.

THE BELGIAN OWL 46%

Nose: Light and fresh, with a hayloft note underpinning the mix of fluffy spongecake, vanilla cream, and wildflowers. With water, a hit of apricot. Mature.

Palate: Very smooth and silky. This has some heat and a peppermint coolness that opens into sweet cereal and restrained oak. Fleshy fruit.
Finish: Gentle and layered.
Conclusion: Complex and soft.

> **Flavor Camp: Fruity & Spicy**
> **Where Next?** Glen Keith 17yo

THE BELGIAN OWL, SINGLE CASK
#4275922 73.7%

Nose: Big toffee, caramel, and chocolate fudge to open. The ripeness of the distillery character reduces the heat, allowing orchard fruit to come through. Victoria plum jam. Water shows some caramelized edges and little hints of hibiscus.
Palate: Big, sweet delivery. Very hot and lightly spiced. Soft, generous palate with ripe sweet fruit.
Finish: Hints of cereal.
Conclusion: Balanced and gently assertive.

> **Flavor Camp: Fruity & Spicy**
> **Where Next?** Glen Elgin 14yo

RADERMACHER, LAMBERTUS 10YO GRAIN 40%

Nose: Floor polish and banana. Estery and firm, with a little marshmallow (pink).
Palate: Very sweet and perfumed. Fruit cordial. Strawberry and banana.
Finish: Sweet.
Conclusion: A simple grain.

> **Flavor Camp: Fragrant & Floral**
> **Where Next?** Elsass

Spain

LIBER • GRANADA • WWW.DESTILERIASLIBER.COM • OPEN ALL YEAR MON–FRI

For many years, Spain was Scotch whisky's golden market, the country that proved to doubters that young people could enjoy whisky. This era, when brands such as J&B, Ballantine's, and Cutty Sark flowed like water—huge measures poured into ice-filled glasses and topped up with cola—seemed to offer a new way to talk about and drink Scotch. Spain liberated the drink from its book-lined study: it made blended whisky relevant once more. The factors that led to the Spanish explosion are many and complex, and go beyond just fashion, or even flavor. Blended Scotch was a signifier for the new post-Franco Spain: it was a drink that said, "We are democratic, we are European, we reject the old ways."

In the protectionist Franco era, imported whisky was expensive (Franco himself was alleged to have a penchant for Johnnie Walker) and out of the reach of ordinary Spaniards. If they can't get Scotch, thought Nicomedes García Gómez, why don't we make whisky here? Already running an anisette business (aniseed-flavored liqueur), in 1958–9 García acted on his vision and built a massive, multifunctional distillery in Palazuelos de Eresma, Segovia, which encompassed maltings, a grain plant, and a six-still malt site. In 1963, Destilerías y Crianza (DYC) was launched. Demand was such that, in 1973, the firm bought the Lochside distillery in Montrose to supply fillings, although that venture ended in 1992 when the Scottish distillery was closed.

DYC (now part of Beam Global) has remained a multination vatting of Spanish and "Euro" (i.e. Scottish) whiskies, although in recently, 50 years after the first spirit ran from its pot-stills, a 100 percent Spanish single-malt was launched.

It wasn't Spain's first single malt, however. That honor goes to Embrujo, which is distilled at Destilerías Liber in Padul near Granada. Using snowmelt water from the Sierra Nevada, distillation is in two unusual flat-bottomed copper stills, while aging is in, logically enough, ex-sherry casks made from American oak. The brainchild of Fran Peregrino, the whisky is a fusing of Scottish technique with Spanish influence. "I took decisions that would influence how the whisky would taste, the design of the stills, the choice of the barrels for aging," says Peregrino. "But there are other elements which you cannot do anything about, like the water and the climate. Here, we alternate between freezing winters and hot summers, which give our whisky its own character and personality."

The market for Scotch blends in Spain is now crashing as a new generation moves to rum, but the sales of single malts are on the rise. Maybe the Spanish distillers are again in the right place at the right time.

SPAIN TASTING NOTES

LIBER, EMBRUJO 40%

Nose: Youthful and almost grassy freshness matched by rich, nutty sherry notes. Amontillado-style. Green walnut, *madrono* (aromatic fruit related to the mangosteen), then cereal. With water, some malted milk and toffee.

Palate: Roasted malty notes add interest to the dried fruit and nut notes from the oak. The effect is of elements coming together. Clean spirit.

Finish: Light, then a final squeeze of raisin juice.

Conclusion: Still young but has the guts to develop long term.

Flavor Camp: Rich & Round

Where Next? Macallan 10yo Sherry

The Sierra Nevada is the backdrop to Spain's newest whisky distillery, Liber.

CENTRAL EUROPE

Whisky creation is about more than taking a grain and distilling it. If the process is to succeed, there has to be a conscious decision about what is being made. This is an approach that must draw on influences, experience, desires, and —just as importantly—understand what isn't wanted. It can never be copying, but it can be inspired, and hopefully become inspirational.

The approach will always be colored by the back story of alcohol in any particular country. This is perhaps most clearly seen in the whiskies now emerging from Germany, Austria, Switzerland, Liechtenstein, and Italy. What was once too easily dismissed as an interesting oddity today comprises up to 150 distillers.

So just what are the roots of these whiskies? Most clearly, it is the influence of fruit-spirit distillation. Many of the distilleries are family firms with several generations of experience in this area. The stills they use, gently heated with *bains-marie* to stop the thick fruit mash from burning, sometimes with rectifying plates in the neck, produce a light, clear distillate.

This background could also provide a stylistic philosophy. The raw ingredient isn't just a cereal that provides as much alcohol per gallon, but a fruit. The aim of distillation in this instance—usually involving thick mashes—is therefore to try and capture the essence of that fruit. This also allows the distiller to look at a wide variety of starting points—not just barley, but wheat, emmer, rye, oats, corn, and spelt, among others.

A brewing culture, particularly in German whiskies, also has its part to play. Brewers understand different kilning techniques, the importance of yeast, the effects of temperature-controlled fermentation. Wine has given them a supply of top-quality oak, and flavors from local grape varieties. Smoking is mostly over wood (oak, elder, beech, birch) instead of peat. These are a completely different set of conditions, and it's no surprise that the whiskies are different, too.

So are these European distillers more open to new ideas? "Of course we are," says Italy's Jonas Ebensperger. "Even if the orientation is toward Scotland, as it was in Japan, local conditions mean you adapt to suit, and make your own different-tasting products."

This personalized variety is central to the thinking of Jasmin Haider in Austria. "When we started in 1995," she says, "we would never have imagined that not even two decades later such a lively whisky scene would have developed. Variety is the key word. It's always important to go your own way. Whiskies are as varied as people's tastes."

It's also important not to be impatient; that goes for drinkers as well as distillers. Styles take time to forge. National styles, if they exist, take even longer. Although we are still at the start of this journey, it is already an exciting one.

Fields of rye and barley in Saarland, Germany.

Germany

SCHRAML • ERBENDORF • WWW.BRENNEREI-SCHRAML.DE • TOURS BY RESERVATION / BLAUE MAUS • EGGOLSHEIM • WWW.FLEISCHMANN-WHISKY.DE • OPEN ALL YEAR / SLYRS • SCHLIERSEE • WWW.SLYRS.DE • OPEN ALL YEAR MON–SUN FINCH • NELLINGEN • WWW.FINCH-WHISKY.DE / LIEBL • BAD KÖTZTING • WWW.BRENNEREI-LIEBL.DE • OPEN ALL YEAR; SEE WEB FOR DAYS & DETAILS / TELSER • TRIESEN, FÜRSTENTUM LIECHTENSTEIN • WWW.BRENNEREI-TELSER.COM

Germany's whisky history isn't as recent as people believe. The Schraml family has been making oak-aged grain distillates in the Bavarian town of Erbendorf since 1818, when a multigrain mash was distilled, aged, and sold as a "brandy" (a not uncommon term for any brown spirit at the time). "It's possible this 'brown corn' situation arose out of an emergency," says sixth-generation distiller Gregor Schraml. "At that time, cereals such as wheat were not always readily available, and the distillate was put into storage to bridge gaps. We can't assume that the transformative effect of wooden casks on the distillate was actually intended."

Attempts in the 1950s by his father, Alois, to market the "brown brandy" as Steinwald Whisky failed, "…possibly because of the overwhelmingly regional concept and the minimal interest in German whisky." The spirit continued to be distilled, but was sold as "Farmer's Spirit." When Gregor joined the firm in 2004, the whisky project started afresh and Stonewood 1818 Bavarian Single Grain Whisky was launched, aged, with a nod to the past, for a decade in old Limousin oak brandy casks.

The range has since expanded to include a wheat beer-inspired WOAZ using 60 percent malted wheat, 40 percent barley malt, and fermented with wheat-beer yeast, and a "straight" single malt called Stonewood Dra, which is aged for three years in white oak.

With more than 300 breweries, there is no shortage of brewing expertise in Bavaria, so when a customs supervision officer suggested to Robert Fleischmann that he should try distilling a beer mash, it seemed perfectly logical. Fleischmann's Blaue Maus Distillery has been running since 1983, utilizing a number of different malts distilled in the original patent stills and, since 2013, in a new pot-still distillery.

The Stetter family had been making fruit spirits since 1928 in their Lantenhammer distillery, but when Florian Stetter took over the business in 1995, he went on a trip to Scotland because, as Anja Summers, head of marketing at the distillery, tells it, "He discovered numerous similarities—landscape, dialect, independence—between Scotland and Bavaria. He then made a bet with his friends that he could also distill a good whisky at home."

Today his Slyrs whisky distillery produces 20,000 bottles of Bavarian whisky annually. "Everything about Slyrs is Bavarian," Summers adds. "The barley is Bavarian; it's smoked over beechwood; our water is from mountain springs." You can also see that brewing link with the use of temperature-controlled long fermentation.

Farmer Hans-Gerhard Fink started his Finch distillery in Nellingen, Swabia, the same year as Slyrs. "As a cereal grower I am fascinated particularly by the maturation of the cereal distillate," he says. Using only his own cereal (malted barley, wheat, spelt, corn, and emmer, an ancient wheat variety) allows him "to have the whole production chain under my control." His Classic is made from spelt, aged in red-wine cask. The Distiller's Edition is a six-year-old wheat whisky aged in white-wine casks, while Dinkel Port is also made from spelt.

In Bad Kötzting, close to the Czech Republic border, Gerhard Liebl's father was another who started as a fruit-spirit distiller. His son (also Gerhard) branched out into whisky-making in 2006. While at a passing glance it seems as if a straightforward single malt is being made, the use of whole grain puts it in the Bavarian camp, as does the use of fruit stills with their *bain-marie* heating method. "That distilling equipment gives us one of our distinguishing features," says Gerhard Jr. "By this means we aim for a very high purifying effect in the fresh-cereal distillate."

LIECHTENSTEIN

It was a love affair with Scotland that turned Liechtenstein distiller Marcel Telser from fruit-spirit producer (his family firm started in 1888) to whisky-man. He had to wait for eight years before he could distill, because Liechtenstein forbade the production of grain distillates until 1999.

In 2006, he started production. Scotland may be a addiction, but his whisky is resolutely from his homeland. "Commercially, it would be easier to make a Scotch copy, but whisky is clearly linked to region and its characteristics," Telser says. That means techniques like using three different types of malted barley (distilled separately, then preblended before aging), a wholegrain ferment, and distilling in wood-fired, fruit-spirit stills. The aim is for a clean distillate. "If I have two glasses of whisky I don't want a headache," he laughs. "I take a cautious approach and make healthy whisky!"

The influence of this reasoning extends into maturation, with local Pinot Noir casks being used as well as Swiss oak. "It is one of the missing links in oak because the *terroir* gives it different flavors," he enthuses. "It has this subtle, mineralic, almost salty quality."

At 62 square miles, Liechtenstein may be the world's smallest whisky-making country but now, with a dedicated distillery producing up to 26,400 gallons (100,000 liters) annually, its ambitions are huge.

The Holstein still at the Blaue Maus distillery.

GERMANY

▼ Distillery

0   miles   100

0   km   100

SWEDEN

DENMARK

North Frisian Islands

East Frisian Islands

Hamburg   E26   *Müritz*

Bremen

Preussische Whisky ▼
Schönermark

POLAND

Ems

Weser

Aller

Elbe

BERLIN

Oder

Mittelland Canal

Hannover

NETHERLANDS

Bielefeld

E51

▼ **Spreewalder,**
Schlepzig

Rhine

Gelsenkirchen

Essen   Dortmund

Duisburg

Düsseldorf

▼ **Markische,** Hagen
Sonnenschein
Wuppertal

Hammerschmiede,
Eisbach ▼

Leipzig

Elbe

▼ **Augustus Rex,**
Dresden

Uerige

Cologne

▼ **Ziegler,**
Freudenberg

E45

Saale

E40

G E R M A N Y

E51

Ore Mountains

BELGIUM

Birkenhof,
Nistertal ▼

E41

E44

Höhler ▼

Frankfurt

▼ **Faber**

Anton Bischof,
Wartmannsroth ▼

Schraml,
Erbendorf ▼

CZECH
REPUBLIC

Moselle

Wiesbaden

▼ **Obsthof am Berg**

Main

Mößlein ▼

LUXEMBOURG

Nordpfalzer ▼

▼ **Bachgau,**
Schaafheim-Radheim

E45

▼ **Blaue Maus**

Bohemian

Avadis,
Wincheringen ▼

Mannheim

Neckar

Altstadthof, ▼
Nürnberg

E50

Forest

Liebl ▼ ▼ **Drexler**

Danube

Kammer Kirsch, ▼
Karlsruhe

E35

Rieger &
Hoffmeister ▼

Stuttgart

▼ **Roder,**
Aalen-Wasseralfingen

E56

FRANCE

Krabbe-Nescht ▼
Doinich Daal ▼

Rhine

▼ **Hohenheim**
▼ **Sigel**

Theurer ▼

Obst-Korn Zeiser ▼

▼ **Finch Whisky**

Fitzke, ▼
Herbolzheim

Bellerhof, ▼

Augsburg

E52

E52

Bosch Edelbrand, ▼
Gruel, ▼
Owen-Teck

▼ **Badischer**
Whisky,
Biberach

Munich

Sloupitsl ▼

Black Forest

▼ **Lanten-**
hammer

▼ **Slyrs**

AUSTRIA

Steinhauser, ▼
Kressbronn

Lake
Constance

N

SWITZERLAND

LIECHTENSTEIN

GERMANY TASTING NOTES

BLAU MAUS, NEW MAKE

Nose: Fresh and slightly sweet. Dry cereal and hay. Touch of graphite and a slight burnt note. Heavy, malty.
Palate: Hot, with a little putty.
Finish: Toasty and hot.

BLAUE MAUS GRÜNER HUND, SINGLE CASK 40%

Nose: Nougat and polished wood. Some resin and timber-yard characters backed by herbs and cinnamon. Powdery and, with water, some yeastiness and proving bread, some wet dog and leather.
Palate: Green and slightly sappy, mixing green nuts, chestnut flour, and light spice—the cinnamon and allspice are most prominent.
Finish: Sharp and clean.
Conclusion: Sappy and clean.

Flavor Camp: Malty & Dry
Where Next? Hudson Single Malt, Millstone 5yo

BLAUE MAUS SPINNAKER, 20YO 40%

Nose: Very sweet and bourbon-like. Sweet wood and caramel. Toffee apples and nutmeg. Still some green notes and a kernel-like nuttiness.
Palate: Light and cereal-accented. Dry and firm, with the combination of cereal and oak tannins.
Finish: Lightly spiced.
Conclusion: Clean and light.

Flavor Camp: Malty & Dry
Where Next? Macduff

SLYRS, 2010 43%

Nose: Very perfumed and fruity, with notes of quince, yellow plum, and pear. A floral note also develops alongside hot sawdust.
Palate: A slightly dry start, with some heat and low cask influence. The yellow and green fruits continue. Clean and light.
Finish: Fresh and acidic.
Conclusion: Light and bright. Developing.

Flavor Camp: Fragrant & Floral
Where Next? Telser, Elsass Single Malt

FINCH, EMMER (WHEAT), NEW MAKE

Nose: Sweet and perfumed with touches of baby oil. Light cereal; pure, but with some substance.
Palate: Rounded; manages to mix delicacy with a lively mouth-feel.
Finish: Softens slightly.

FINCH, DINKEL PORT 2013 41%

Nose: Pink and fruity, with big impact from the cask. Raspberry and light, sweet cherry That fragrant spelt character shows.
Palate: Sweet; lots of fresh fruit; a hint of sloe. Gentle.
Finish: Soft and gentle.
Conclusion: This is whisky aged in port.

Flavor Camp: Fruity & Spicy
Where Next? Chichibu Port Pipe

FINCH, CLASSIC 40%

Nose: Very candied. Fairground notes: cotton candy, lime jelly. Light oils (there's spelt and wheat in here). With water, it moves into fruit chews.
Palate: That soft texture comes through again. A little more cereal with water.
Finish: Lightly dusty, with the concentrated fruits continuing.
Conclusion: Aromatic and intense.

Flavor Camp: Fruity & Spicy
Where Next? JH Karamell

SCHRAML, WOAZ 43%

Nose: Made from wheat, this has the grain's purity and sweetness, with some candied notes and cake frosting. Very light citrus fruit behind (lemon, mostly), and a dry cereal undertow.
Palate: Sweet and lightly creamy. Precise, with energy, some orange, delicate woods. Energetic.
Finish: Creamy and rounded.
Conclusion: Cereal structure of these whiskies is apparent, alongside wheat's delicate sweetness.

Flavor Camp: Sweet Wheat
Where Next? Highwood White Owl

SCHRAML, DRÀ 50%

Nose: Fine and herbal. Certainly young and in the process of adding in oak. Sweet apples and some grassiness. A little exposed with water but clean spirit.
Palate: Toasted, roasted. Back to the firm cereal spine that's shared by many of these. The hint of red fruit with water indicates promise.
Finish: Lightly peppery.
Conclusion: Fifteen months in oak.

Flavor Camp: Fruity & Spicy
Where Next? Fary Lochan (in time)

LIEBL, COILLMÓR, AMERICAN OAK 43%

Nose: Crisp, cereal-accented. Muesli and cornflakes. Light and pleasant, on the sweeter side of barley. Dry, haystack/chaff with water. Has some sweetness.
Palate: Creamy. Like porridge oats sprinkled with chocolate. Light mid-palate. Green fern.
Finish: Tight.
Conclusion: A pretty definitive style.

Flavor Camp: Malty & Dry
Where Next? High West Valley Tan

LIEBL, COILLMÓR, PORT CASK 46%

Nose: Light pink color. Fruity, with medlar jelly, raspberry, and with water, some fennel pollen, and herbs. Scented in time. Elderberry.
Palate: Sweet with Turkish delight. Alcohol is a little hot. Water fleshes out the middle a little, adding some wild fruit.
Finish: Clean and slightly dusty.
Conclusion: Attractive and open.

Flavor Camp: Fruity & Spicy
Where Next? Finch Dinkel Port

LIECHENSTEIN TASTING NOTES

TELSER, TELSINGTON VI, 5YO SINGLE MALT 43.5%

Nose: Creamily malty and soft, with light cask influence. Quite buttery, but has retained its intensity. Dried apple and sweet peach, green banana.
Palate: Minerality on the tongue. Mouthwatering and intense; hot. Good spices and some soft, sweet fruit.
Finish: Lightly herbal.
Conclusion: Has poise and restraint.

Flavor Camp: Fruity & Spicy
Where Next? Spirit of Hven

TELSER, TELSINGTON BLACK EDITION, 5YO 43.5%

Nose: Soft and sweet, with stone fruit, and almost saline. Lightly dusty cereal and low smoke. Mineral and wild fruit.
Palate: Hot, with spices, curry leaves, and turmeric. Firm and bold, with that minerality coming through.
Finish: Tight and fresh.
Conclusion: Port casks and French oak have aded a fruity, spiced element.

Flavor Camp: Fruity & Spicy
Where Next? Green Spot, Domaine des Hautes Glaces

TELSER RYE, SINGLE CASK, 2YO 42%

Nose: Intense and lifted, with some minerality. A very pure expression of rye on the sweeter, spicier side. Lightly minty.
Palate: Rounded, and showing some supple weight. Well directed. Camphor, allspice, and powder.
Finish: Clean and tight.
Conclusion: Coming together.

Flavor Camp: Spicy Rye
Where Next? Rendezvous Rye

Austria/Switzerland/Italy

HAIDER • ROGGENREITH, AUSTRIA • WWW.ROGGENHOF.AT • OPEN ALL YEAR; SEE WEB FOR DAYS & DETAILS
SÄNTIS • APPENZELL, SWITZERLAND • WWW.SAENTISMALT.COM / LANGATUN • LANGENTHAL, SWITZERLAND
• WWW.LANGATUN.CH / PUNI DESTILLERIE • GLURNS, ITALY • WWW.PUNI.COM

The Austrian approach to whisky-making is summed up by Eva Hoffman from Reisetbauer, which started in 1995 after being "inspired by our home-grown barley and a desire to do something different"—in their case, by using local wine casks, such as Chardonnay and Trockenbeerenauslese.

Elsewhere, in an old customs building south of Vienna, the Rabenbräu Brewery is selling two triple-distilled malts, Old Raven and Old Raven Smoky, while Weutz in St. Nikolai im Sausel has a wide range, including Green Panther, which uses pumpkin seeds in the mash. Rogner in Rappottenstein utilizes wheat, rye, and different roasts of barley, while Granit, in the northeastern Waldviertel region, uses smoked rye, spelt, and barley.

The pioneer of all this experimentation was Johann Haider, who started distilling in 1995 in Roggenreith. The first "J.H." whisky, a rye, emerged in 1999. Now the distillery and its Whisky World attraction attracts 80,000 visitors a year. "We were the first whisky distillery in Austria," says Johann's daughter Jasmin, who took over as distiller in 2011. "With no one locally to compare ourselves to, my father learned the art of distilling just by doing it. We tried to follow our own path."

Rye remains a major focus here, with light- and dark-roasted, and even some peated, all being used. There's also a rye/barley mix, and two single malts, one of which uses different roasts. In common with the wider region's style it is a whole-grain ferment. The next step for Haider is a closer look at maturation: local heavy charred Sessile oak casks have been the mainstay. There's a sense of constant innovation.

"Brightness" was one of the characters Reisetbauer's Eva Hoffman singled out as an Austrian style. It is a word that can be extended across this fast-developing and fascinating whisky zone. Bright in style, and also in thinking.

Because distilling from grain was banned in Switzerland until 1999, its distilleries are relatively new. The best-known brand is Säntis, the distilling arm of the Appenzell's Locher Brewery. In common with many of its Swiss colleagues, maturation techniques are a major focus.

Säntis's singularity comes, aside from their use of local grain and peat, from the use of 60- to 120-year-old beer casks that were originally sealed inside with pitch. When the pitch cracked, beer seeped into the staves, and then the casks were resealed. When the

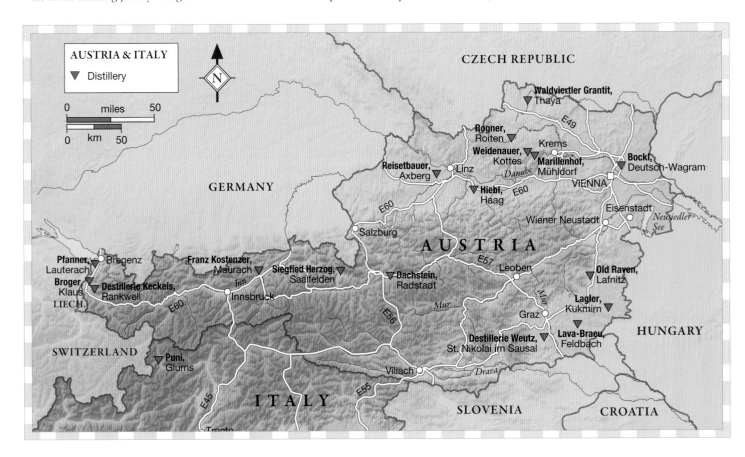

Puni's stunning cube contains one of Europe's most remarkable distilleries.

fermenters that were used to encourage estery notes), and a wide wood remit that includes chestnut, Hungarian, and Swiss oak, and a multiplicity of ex-wine casks.

Brewing links also apply to Langatun, which was started in 2005 by Hans Baumberger, who came home to Langenthal after working in Munich to start a microbrewery. "My vision is to create an independent whisky that is not a Scottish copy," he says, "but one that is convincing through its own multifaceted character." Again, this is rooted as much in cask as in distillate, with its Old Deer aged in Chardonnay and sherry, and the lightly smoked Old Bear in a Châteauneuf-du-Pape cask.

Amazingly, for a country so deeply in love with Scotch, Italy had to wait until 2010 to have its first dedicated whisky distillery. What is now Puni Distillery, encased in a striking terra-cotta cube in Glorenza in the South Tyrol, started as a hobby that soon outgrew the Ebensperger family's home.

As the Vinschgau Valley is rye country, that was tried first, although it was felt to be too flavorsome for the Italian palate, which prefers a light, fruity character.

The result was 130 batches being produced over a three-year period, examining cereals, mashing temperature, fermentation time, and distillation before settling on a mash bill of malted wheat, rye,

casks distillery investigated them as possible maturation vessels, the pitch was removed and it was found that decades of slow ingress had left them saturated with flavorings.

Eflingen's Whisky Castle started in 2002, with a combination of local heritage (smoking over oak), brewing techniques (open-topped

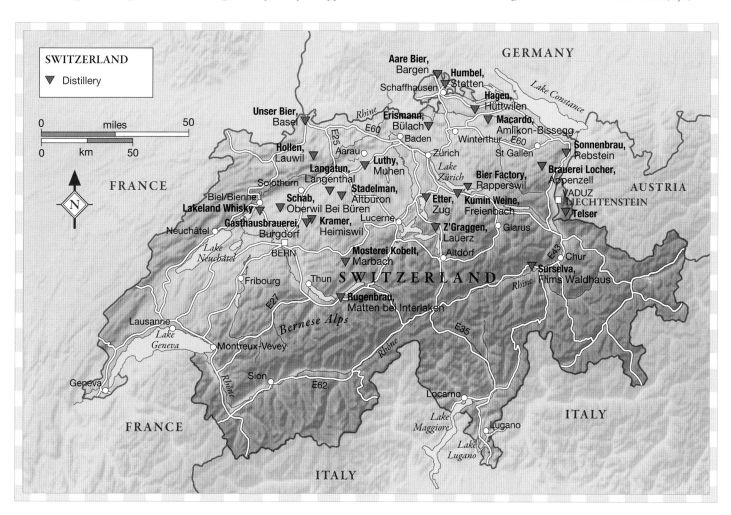

SWITZERLAND

▼ Distillery

and barley and utilizing abandoned World War II bunkers as aging cellars. Nothing has escaped the family's forensic gaze. In distillation, hot-water coils are used instead of steam. "We looked at how different temperatures generated specific flavors and created a distillation plan," says distiller Jonas Ebensperger.

"If we want to run at a specific temperature for a set time, we can. It's slower, more precise; it's *sous vide* distilling!"

Alba, the firm's first release, which is aged predominantly in Marsala casks, shows an extraordinarily heightened perfume, and is a remarkable debut.

AUSTRIA TASTING NOTES

HAIDER, J.H. SINGLE MALT 40%

Nose: Clean, with light sweet hayloft notes. Lightly dusty, with light fruit, and subtly perfumed. Geranium with cereal accents. Felt.
Palate: Sweet, with a *frisson* of spiciness: cinnamon and nutmeg and a little clove. Dries on the sides. Light mid-palate. Clean, with light fruits.
Finish: Ginger and sharpness.
Conclusion: Delicate and fresh.

Flavor Camp: Fruity & Spicy
Where Next? Meyer's Pur Malt, Hellyer's Road

HAIDER, J.H. SINGLE MALT, KARAMELL 41%

Nose: Peppery and herbaceous. Spring-like. Moist earth and green shoots. Cereal-accented. Lots of soft fruits.
Palate: Lifted and perfumed, with more meadow flowers and freesia but also spices. Another that's very "up." Hints of candies in the center. Lightly nutty.
Finish: Acidic, with lightly roasted spices.
Conclusion: Mixes a dry barley theme with perfumed fruits.

Flavor Camp: Fruity & Spicy
Where Next? Finch Classic

HAIDER, J.H. SPECIAL RYE NOUGAT 41%

Nose: Light and quite creamy. Sweet. A little distant but there's some cooking spice and green fennel seed; caraway. Attractive, with green apple and bakery notes.
Palate: Sweet and rounded, with a spicy attack and balanced bitterness. Well balanced. With water, touches of aniseed develop.
Finish: Spicy and clean.
Conclusion: An assured and confident young rye.

Flavor Camp: Spicy Rye
Where Next? Lot 40

HAIDER, J.H. PEATED RYE MALT 40%

Nose: Phenolic, with lots of wild grass notes: lucerne, meadow hay, little hints of pollen, light sooty smoke and creosote, old-fashioned medicine. With water, some rubber.
Palate: Dry, with the rye spices and peat in balance. Good length and clean, with sufficient sweetness to hold the center together.
Finish: Spicy and phenolic.
Conclusion: There are not many peated ryes on the market, but why not?

Flavor Camp: Spicy Rye/Smoky & Peaty
Where Next? Balcones Brimstone

SWITZERLAND TASTING NOTES

SÄNTIS, EDITION SÆNTIS 40%

Nose: Scented with polished oak, deep maltiness, and cooked fruit, moving into sloe and violet, then come hints of geranium and vanilla.
Palate: Equally perfumed, with some Parma violet and a pleasing dustiness that shifts into lavender. Light curry leaf.
Finish: Clean, spiced.
Conclusion: Aged in old beer casks and shows real depth as a result.

Flavor Camp: Fruity & Spicy
Where Next? Overeem Port Cask, Spirit of Broadside

SÄNTIS, ALPSTEIN VII 48%

Nose: Spiced, with lots of tamarind water, cardamom, and the deep fruit of the Edition coming through, allied to some date and fig. Well balanced.
Palate: Mellow and plummy, with mulberry-jam accents and a retention of the exoticism of the nose. Lightly tannic.
Finish: Bright and clean.
Conclusion: A vatting of five-year-old beer cask aged in 11-year-old sherry cask. The most elegant of the range.

Flavor Camp: Rich & Round
Where Next? Balcones Straight Malt

LANGATUN, OLD DEER 40%

Nose: Light, fresh, and zesty, with grapefruit pith and an intense sweet-sour edge that brings to mind tropical fruit mix. Touch of mace and canned pear juice.
Palate: Lightly honeyed. Very up, with fresh, bright acidity and a green vinous quality; Pinot Blanc. Light mid-palate.
Finish: Fresh and vibrant.
Conclusion: Oak in balance. Young and fresh. Sharp.

Flavor Camp: Fruity & Spicy
Where Next? Telser

LANGATUN, OLD BEAR 40%

Nose: Earthy, with cooked plum, ripe orchard fruit. Drier than the Old Deer.
Palate: Hint of smoke comes through; a mix of wood smoke and smoked cheese. Quite firm and young. Red cherry, but still with the light freshness in the middle.
Finish: Slightly dry.
Conclusion: More substance. Showing decent balance.

Flavor Camp: Fruity & Spicy
Where Next? Spirit of Broadside

ITALY TASTING NOTES

PUNI, PURE 43%

Nose: Vegetal, with a hint of artichoke and some zucchini flower. Hothouse, tomato vine. Sweet fruit. Almost syrupy before fresh cereal.
Palate: Bone-dry and chalky, then opens into floral notes. Light and cool, with fresh fruit.
Finish: Drying.
Conclusion: Fragrant and already balanced.

PUNI, ALBA 43%

Nose: Airy and light, with almond and a building and eventually dominant note of rosewater mixed with night-scented stocks and jasmine, dusted with cinnamon.
Palate: Nuanced, sweet, lifted, and scented. Very clean and sweet.
Finish: Nutmeg with rose-hip syrup.
Conclusion: Young, but already seemingly fully formed.

Flavor Camp: Fragrant & Floral
Where Next? Collingwood, Rendezvous Rye

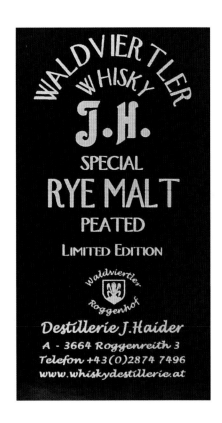

SCANDINAVIA

A deep love of Scotch has led to Swedes and Norwegians becoming regulars in Glasgow's whisky pubs, because, even with travel costs, it's a cheaper to drink there than it is at home. Scotland's distillery shops equally give praise every year to their Nordic visitors.

It was only a matter of time that the Nordic region joined in the rise of whisky distilling. This is, after all, home to the globe's greatest concentration of whisky clubs and festivals, including the largest in the world (Stockholm's epic annual Beer & Whisky Festival). After state control of spirit production was lifted in Sweden, Norway, and Finland, the emergence of whisky distilleries was inevitable. At the time of writing there were 12 in Sweden, seven in Denmark, three each in Norway and Finland, one in Iceland, and more on the way.

Potatoes had been used as the main base for spirits from the late eighteenth century in Sweden and Norway (they were known as "the grape of Scandinavia"), resulting in grain-based spirits being more unusual, and wood-aged examples rarer still. As styles became fixed under the monopolies, the variations on the theme were few and far between, though that's not to say that whisky distilling had never been tried.

In the late 1920s, a chemical engineer named Bengt Thorbjørnson was tasked with finding out whether whisky distillation was possible in Sweden and was sent, in the manner of Masataka Taketsuru (*see* p.212), to Scotland. He came back with an analysis of what was possible and the potential costings, but his report appears to have been shelved. Some whisky was eventually distilled in Sweden in the 1950s, and the Skepets blend was released in 1961 but, even then, production ceased in 1966.

So this is a young whisky industry; actually, that word "industry" seems wrong. Looking at this early stage for a unifying Nordic style is also wrong. Currently, Scandinavian distillers are fully occupied with experimenting, discovering, creating, and digging deep to create their own signature characters.

What is fascinating to observe, however, is the shared belief that while most of these distilleries have been established by Scotch-whisky fanatics, there are determined attempts to root their own Nordic makes in their immediate surroundings.

Scotch (and Japanese) whisky may have been an inspiration, but the majority of these distillers are seeing the benefits that come from a deep reading of the local area, which could be cereals, peat, or other and very different traditional smoking techniques; it could be an understanding of the climate, the oak trees in their forests, and the berries that grow around them, or the spirits and wines that have been made.

This is in a region—Denmark especially—where "the local" has taken on an almost mystical resonance. Now, people are heeding the philosophy of Rene Redzepi of Copenhagen's Noma restaurant, with its belief in the local and the seasonal by "following nature's mood swings through the year ... to sense the world." There is some of that same mindset in the new Nordic whiskies.

"I think the question of a Nordic style will be answered in the next few years," says Mackmyra's master blender, Angela d'Orazio. "There will be one, but it will have branches."

There is a commercial maxim being applied: do not copy. "People have tried to do what Scotch does for hundreds of years," says Ivan Abrahamsen, distiller at Norway's Arcus. "Why do it the same way? In the coming years you will see a Nordic style because we cannot compete with Scotch. You have to tell a story in your whisky. Whatever happens, it's going to be interesting."

Sweden's fertile southern plains (here near Malmö) provide the ingredients for a burgeoning whisky industry.

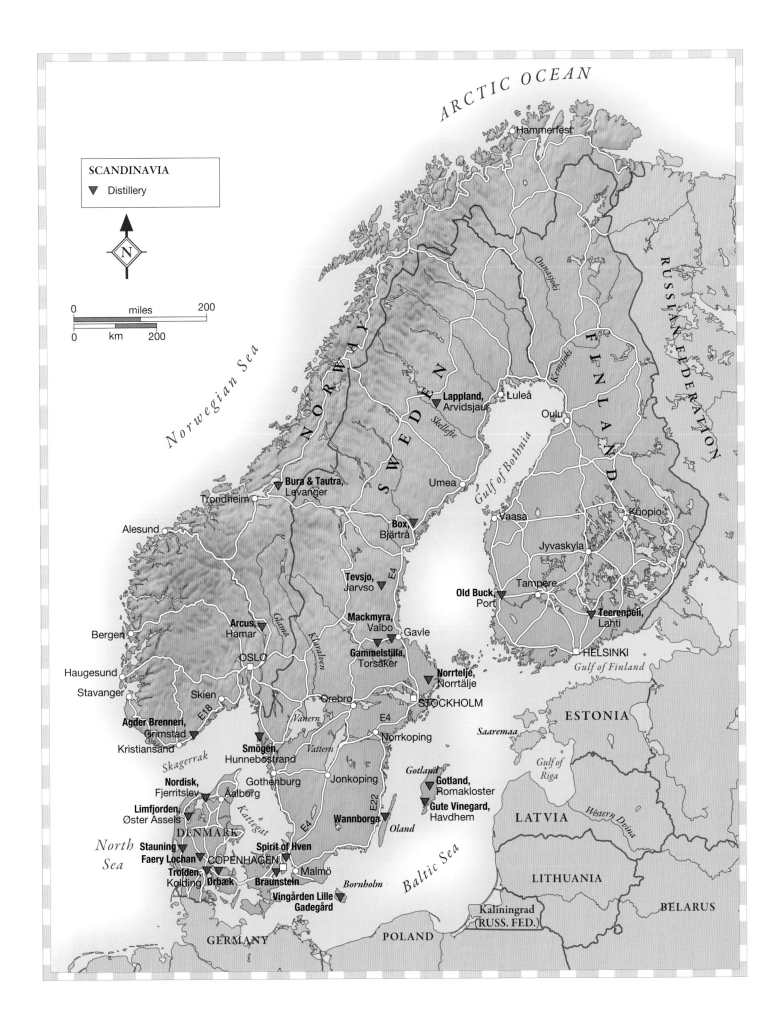

SCANDINAVIA

▼ Distillery

N

| 0 | miles | 200 |
| 0 | km | 200 |

ARCTIC OCEAN

Hammerfest

RUSSIAN FEDERATION

Norwegian Sea

Lappland,
Arvidsjaur

Luleå

Oulu

N
O
R
W
A
Y

S
W
E
D
E
N

F
I
N
L
A
N
D

Ounasjoki

Skellefte

Kemijoki

Bura & Tautra,
Levanger

Trondheim

Umeå

Gulf of Bothnia

Box,
Bjärtrå

Vaasa

Kuopio

Alesund

Jyvaskyla

Tevsjo,
Jarvso

E4

Tampere

Old Buck,
Port

Teerenpeli,
Lahti

Bergen

Arcus,
Hamar

Mackmyra,
Valbo

Gavle

Glama

Klaralven

Gammelstilla,
Torsaker

HELSINKI

Gulf of Finland

Haugesund

OSLO

Norrtelje,
Norrtälje

Stavanger

Skien

Orebro

STOCKHOLM

ESTONIA

E18

E4

Saaremaa

Agder Brenneri,
Grimstad

Vanern

Norrkoping

*Gulf of
Riga*

Kristiansand

Smögen,
Hunnebostrand

Vattern

Gotland

Gotland,
Romakloster

Skagerrak

Gothenburg

Jonkoping

Gotland

Nordisk,
Fjerritslev

Åalborg

E22

Gute Vinegard,
Havdhem

Western Drina

Limfjorden,
Øster Assels

Wannborga

Oland

LATVIA

*North
Sea*

DENMARK

E4

Stauning

Spirit of Hven

Kattegat

Faery Lochan

COPENHAGEN

Troiden,
Kolding

Ørbæk

Malmö

LITHUANIA

Braunstein

Bornholm

Baltic Sea

**Vingården Lille
Gadegård**

Kaliningrad
(RUSS. FED.)

BELARUS

GERMANY

POLAND

Sweden

BOX • BJÄRTRÅ • WWW.BOXWHISKY.SE / SMÖGEN WHISKY • HUNNEBOSTRAND • WWW.SMOGENWHISKY.SE • SEE WEB FOR WHISKY SCHOOL & TOURS / SPIRIT OF HVEN BACKAFALLSBYN • HVEN • WWW.HVEN.COM • SEE WEB FOR TOUR DETAILS

The change in Sweden from whisky consumer to whisky producer has been remarkable and is now spread across 621 miles of the country. Currently, the most northerly distillery is Box, in the town of Bjärtrå, the genesis of which started, somewhat obliquely, with two brothers opening an art gallery. "They soon realized there wasn't that much demand for modern art in the north of Sweden," says Box's ambassador, Jan Groth. Quite how whisky distilling was a logical next step is unclear, but in 2010, with ex-brewer Roger Melander as distiller, they started to make whisky.

Melander hasn't just looked west to Scotland, but east to Japan. "From the start, I had a pretty good picture about how Box whisky should be," he says. "Whether I made the right choice with the new make is a question I can answer in about 15 years. But I'm pretty sure we're on the right path.

"There are no short cuts when you try to make the best whisky in the world," he adds. "Choosing the best ingredients, having the ultimate equipment, and using it with care and understanding are important. We nose every cask before filling and are able to sort out casks that aren't perfect. Most will be filled only once."

The location has an impact. "We have probably the coldest cooling water, giving us clean, pure flavors in the spirit, while the temperature in the warehouses changes a lot during the days and seasons, forcing the spirit to penetrate the oak and develop amazing flavors." Early results show a whisky that is concentrated, high-toned, and fruity.

A more classical Scottish approach has been chosen by Pär Caldenby at the tiny Smögen distillery on the shores of the Baltic, north of Gothenburg. "The inspiration for Smögen's character comes right out of the Isles and the west coast of Scotland," he says, adding, "The place where the spirit is made and matured is what defines its nationality. The fact that we're using Scottish malt does not make our whisky a Scotch."

Although he is such a firm believer in a "Scottish" approach that he feels spirits made in non-traditional pots shouldn't even be called whisky, Caldenby maintains that "using that basic standard doesn't mean you are making a copy. There is still room for variation, if you're clever and resourceful enough." His whiskies already show lifted fruit, light smoke, and chocolate, and that airy clarity that does seem to form a loose link among many Nordic styles.

None of these distillers are hobbyists. "My philosophy is that a whisky has to

have balance to be good, but it also has to have character," says Caldenby. "Otherwise it isn't good, or interesting, and any sales will just be marketing-generated. I'd rather have people exclaim 'I don't like that; it's too strong!' than have the same people say, 'Well, that was ... nice.' At least, that's the idea."

Henric Molin's distillery on the island of Hven, in the Strait of Öresund between Sweden and Denmark, had just opened when the first edition of this book went to print. At that time, Molin said he wanted to create a distillation of "the meadows, flowers, and the barley fields entangled with the sea/ocean beaches, the stone-fruit gardens, and the citric notes from the rapeseed flowers."

And now? His laboratory is being used by other distillers, while he is consulting around the world. A chemist by training, is he moving away from that poetical idea of whisky as manifestation of place? "I wanted to use my chemical knowledge of how to get the most out of the produced stock, to find new paths, and explore new methods," Molin says. "To get this knowledge, you need to allow yourself to test boundaries." The results of this long examination of potentialities is a whisky, Spirit of Hven, with estery lift and that fresh, airy feel mingling with fruit, fragrant flowers, and sea greens.

"Anyone can make a whisky in Sweden," says Molin. "For it to become a *Swedish* whisky, it needs to take a clear influence of the site

Box distillery is housed in an old wood-fired, steam-driven power plant that was abandoned in the 1960s.

of origin. Barley, water, yeast—all make an impact, however small, on the final product. I believe that a Swedish whisky should be made from Swedish raw materials [something Pär Caldenby disagrees with]. Maturation is also affected by site. However philosophical we are, we can see a clear influence of site of maturation in the final whisky." And so, that original intent? "Yes, those answers remain the same! I stand by them."

Is there a Swedish style emerging? It's too early to say.

"I am very anxious that every distillery in Sweden makes a perfect whisky," says Roger Melander. "We need that when we launch the Swedish whisky as a concept on the world market. Therefore we are helping each other. We educate personnel from other distilleries at Box. We are colleagues, not competitors."

This collegiate atmosphere will be a strength as the nations's whiskies develop. Different techniques and philosophies may be employed, but the shrewd belief in making something both Swedish and local unites them all.

Copper stills at Box distillery, Bjärtrå, Sweden. Brothers Per and Mats de Wahl saw the power plant's potential for whisky production and, after a few years of preparation, the first drops of Box Single Malt were distilled on December, 18, 2010.

SWEDEN TASTING NOTES

SMÖGEN, NEW MAKE 70.6%

Nose: Lifted and fruity, with cereal, weight, banana, skin, and smoke. Water brings out putty.
Palate: Intense and hot with good feel. Some oatcake and bran. When diluted, there's sweet dessert apple.
Finish: Dry and clean.

SMÖGEN, PRIMÖR 63.7%

Nose: Clean and slightly nutty: Brazil nut and a little herbal touch and exotic spice. Whiff of enamel paint and light smoke. Burning hay, fragrant grasses.
Palate: Lots of immediate additive oak with coconut milk and dry-roasted spice: nigella especially. Balancing sweet and dry, with a little touch of chocolate.
Finish: Crisp and still tight, with cereal developing.
Conclusion: Good, clean spirit with real potential.

Flavor Camp: Smoky & Peaty
Where Next? Laphroaig Quarter Cask

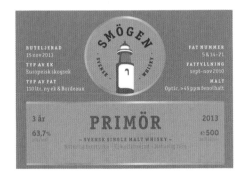

SPIRIT OF HVEN, NO.1, DUBHE 45%

Nose: Rum-like esters, with some pineapple and an open freshness. Very light wood, cypress, and spruce bud. A little hint of redwood bark. Fresh, then dark grains, and malt extract. Water brings out bread-and-butter pudding and white raisin.
Palate: Clean and sweet start, with a tingle of alcohol. The wood is intense and there's more red fruit.
Finish: Young and fresh.
Conclusion: Despite all this complexity massing together, there is still a real freshness. Lots of personality.

Flavor Camp: Fragrant & Floral
Where Next? Westland Deacon Seat

SPIRIT OF HVEN, NO.2, MERAK 45%

Nose: Bright fruit, cherry blossom. Acidic, with a light ozonic, mineral quality. Intense. A hint of white mushroom. Mosses and sea greens. With water, light oil and honey.
Palate: A little discreet to start, with melon and pear. Bubblegum and balanced oak. Very "up." Water adds some honeyed depth.
Finish: Touch of acidity.
Conclusion: Fresh and sweet with succulence developing.

Flavor Camp: Fragrant & Floral
Where Next? Chichibu Chibidaru

BOX UNPEATED CASK SAMPLE

Nose: Tense, concentrated, and high-toned, with fruit chews and estery notes. Delicately yeasty; fresh French-stick (bread) notes.
Palate: Clean and very intense, but with a smooth mid-section with melon, apple, and pineapple.
Finish: Clean and short.
Conclusion: Young, but filled with potential.

BOX HUNGARIAN OAK CASK SAMPLE

Nose: Smoky, with more than a hint of burning mesquite alongside popping brown mustard seeds and light, estery fruit.
Palate: Again, very clean and sweet with smoke, polished oak, and concentrated fruit.
Finish: Long and fresh.
Conclusion: Heightened and intense. One to watch.

Mackmyra

MACKMYRA • GÄVLE, SWEDEN • WWW.MACKMYRA.COM • OPEN; BOOKING ESSENTIAL

You wonder what Bengt Thorbjørnson would have made of Mackmyra. His aim was to take the principles of Scotland and apply them to Sweden. The founders of Mackmyra, who in 1999 put into practice what others had dreamed of, always had a different idea in mind. Yes, they were Scotch-whisky fans but, from the outset, Mackmyra clearly took as much inspiration from Sweden as it did from Speyside.

Before there can be any discussion of a Nordic style, first has to come individual identity, something Mackmyra has always had. Is it from the maturing in the chill of an abandoned mine? Is it the use of Nordic barley varieties, the use of peat from the Karinmossen, or the juniper branches added to the smoky fire (see its Svensk Rök for the effect of juniper scenting)? Could it be Swedish oak casks? All will have an impact, but Mackmyra is also as much about a philosophy of whisky-making.

Even though 170 recipes were tested before the first releases, Mackmyra's whiskies came as a surprise to people weaned on Scotch. They were light, lifted, pure—but not fragile. They had, and still have, a cool restraint, but were never austere.

"It was never meant to be compared to Scotch," says master blender Angela d'Orazio. "People's initial response when it first came out was 'No! Whisky is not meant to be like that!'" She laughs at the memory. In today's fast-evolving whisky world where new flavors and techniques are eagerly welcomed, it's easy to forget how suspiciously anything that challenged Scotch's hegemony on flavor was treated at the turn of the century.

"Scotch is important," she adds. "It's where we come from, but the Mackmyra style was clear, even in those earliest whiskies." Her term is "vivid," which encapsulates accurately the calm intensity of the Mackmyra delivery. Wood offers a calming support. The potent herbal oiliness of Swedish oak is utilized with care: sometimes in casks made entirely from it, but more often in hybrids mixed with American oak.

A new, larger, distillery, which opened in 2011, produces three "classic" styles: "Elegant" and two smoky variants (peat and juniper)—essentially the same spirit with different cut points. D'Orazio's ever-deeper examinations of roots has led to the use of berry wine casks (seen in Skog, Hope, Glöd), experiments with birch wood, and a cask-swap project with pioneering Norwegian craft brewer, Ægir.

"It's great to have traditional whiskies and modern whiskies," says d'Orazio."You don't have to be one or the other."

What you do have to be, however, is true to your vision.

MACKMYRA TASTING NOTES

MACKMYRA VITHUND, NEW MAKE 41.4%

Nose: Light, almost ethereal, with some sweet-pea blossom; pea shoot, even. Lightly vinous (Sauvignon Blanc), with nettles and delicate pear. Honey.
Palate: Sweet and citric. Quite fizzy and lifted, with blossoms. Fruity.
Finish: Delicate and sweet.

MACKMYRA BRUKSWHISKY 41.4%

Nose: Clear progression here. Discreet, cool, and restrained, with very light fruit that bloom with water. Heady florals: lily of the valley.
Palate: More substance than the nose suggests. Light honey, then delicate spice in the background. Quite lacy.
Finish: Gentle and soft.
Conclusion: The "elegant" style lives up to its name.

Flavor Camp: **Fragrant & Floral**
Where Next? The Glenlivet 12yo

MACKMYRA MIDVINTER 41.3%

Nose: Very spiced. Berry-infused. Fruit—blackberry with lots of mint and currant leaf. Cooked, and though it retains discretion, there's plenty of wild fruit on show.
Palate: Sweet to start with; a subtle thickening as the berries come through.
Finish: Lightly jammy. Hedgerows.
Conclusion: Sweet and fruity and fun.

Flavor Camp: **Fruity & Spicy**
Where Next? Bruichladdich Black Art

MACKMYRA SVENSK RÖK 46.1%

Nose: Light, purple fruitiness and delicate smoke in the background. Lingonberry. Water brings out more fragrant smoke.
Palate: Ripe and delicately fleshy, with the smoke all arriving retro-nasally and like hot embers. Quite fleshy.
Finish: Fragrant, subtle smoke.
Conclusion: Not a smoke bomb but discreet and calm.

Flavor Camp: **Smoky & Peaty**
Where Next? Peated Mars (in time)

Whisky from Sweden's pioneering distillery Mackmyra is now available globally.

Denmark/Norway

FARY LOCHAN • GIVE, DENMARK • WWW.FARYLOCHAN.DK / STAUNING • SKJERN, DENMARK • WWW.STAUNINGWHISKY.DK • TOURS BY APPOINTMENT; SEE WEB / BRAUNSTEIN • COPENHAGEN, DENMARK • WWW.BRAUNSTEIN.DK • SEE WEB / ARCUS • HAGAN, NORWAY • WWW.ARCUS.NO • TOURS BY APPOINTMENT; SEE WEB

Though whisky was made briefly in Denmark in the early 1950s, its emergence as a whisky-making nation only took place after the millennium. Now there are seven distilleries, with more planned.

One of those in the first wave comes from the western Jutland town of Stauning, where, in 2006, a group of nine Scotch-loving friends banded together to start to see if they could make whisky. By 2009, they had a converted a farm into a distillery. What they've done since is return to old-school whisky-making principles: floor malting, peat in the kiln, direct fire under the stills. The other key for owner Alex Hjørup Munch is the importance of local ingredients: in Stauning's case, peat, barley, and rye.

In the area of Bøllig Sø, bogs of Middle Jutland have been cut since Neolithic times. It was here that the famous stone-age sacrifice of Tollund Man was found. Today, the peat museum at Klosterlund provides Stauning's requirements.

"Everybody asked whether it was impossible to make whisky in Denmark," he says. "It certainly wasn't. Now everybody from Denmark and other countries wants to see these crazy guys, their floor malting, and their special mash tun. It makes us so proud to see so many whisky people coming."

Three styles are made: a smoked, an unpeated single malt, and (perhaps the most surprising for non-Danes) a malted rye. Rye whisky may be associated with North America, but Jutland is fertile ground for the grain, and as ever, using what is in the immediate vicinity is one way to differentiate yourself.

Floor-malted rye is unusual, however. "It is normally a very difficult grain, but as we make hand-crafted whisky we've developed a special mash tun for the sake of the rye; it's now as easy as working with other types," he says. Even after a scant 18 months in oak, Stauning's Young Rye has built an internal spicy warmth, almost rum-like, with a suitably bittersweet kiss-off. A Statement Whisky if ever there was one.

This theme of whisky-loving Danes becoming whisky-making Danes is carried through into Fary Lochan, established in December 2009 by Jens-Erik Jørgensen. (The distillery name isn't Celtic Twilight feyness, but from the original name of the Jutland village, Ferre, where the still is located.) "I started because I love whisky, and also I have this weakness of wanting to work with anything that's difficult," says Jørgensen. "There was no real history of whisky here."

His inspiration may have been Scotch, but he gave it a Danish twist by shortening the still necks to create an oily, spicy new make. The other surprise is that the smoke used in kilning comes from fresh nettles. "It's a tradition in Fyn [Denmark's middle island] to smoke cheese with nettles," Jørgensen explains. "I thought that if I did everything the same as in Scotland, it might just be a copy. No one likes copies, so nettles it was!"

Braunstein distillery, a microbrewery and whisky distillery in Køge Harbor, Copenhagen.

Although quarter casks have been used for early releases, the majority of the stock is being matured in standard-sized casks. That shows long-term planning.

The Braunstein distillery in Copenhagen's dockside started in 2005–6 as a spin-off from the Poulsen brothers' microbrewery. Holstein stills give two distillates: one rich, the other smoky, with sherry casks being a favored option."I'm a big fan of diversity," says Michael Poulsen, "and believe that everyone should do their own thing. This is small-scale, traditional craftsmanship, and people are now taking us seriously." On the early evidence, Danish whisky is one to watch.

Spirits production in Norway has had a checkered history with: a switch to potatoes from grain; enthusiastic levels of private distillation followed by consolidation in the nineteenth century; Prohibition from 1919–27 and state control on production (mainly the potato-based flavored spirit aquavit); sales and imports from 1928 until 2005. Although the state still controls liquor sales, its monopoly on imports was lifted in 1996. However, independent distillation had to wait until 2005. Since then, whisky distilleries have begun to spring up, such as Agder in 2009.

The state distiller, Arcus, was privatized and in 2009 it diversified from vodka and aquavit into whisky. "From a R&D point of view we wanted to see if we could," says distiller Ivan Abrahamsen. "We are familiar with spirits, but we had never done whisky, so for a year we tried different malts and yeasts, running them through a small pot-still with removable plates."

Now, three German-sourced malts ("Norwegian wasn't good enough") are used: pale barley, pale wheat, and beechwood-smoked barley. "When we started we thought, do we go Scotch, do we go bourbon? But this is Norwegian, so we have to do it our way." That means looking at those different malts, and different casks, including Madeira casks that have previously held *akvavit*.

"We're having fun," says Abrahamsen. "If we don't play around, we'll stop being creative."

It could well be the Nordic motto.

DENMARK TASTING NOTES

FARY LOCHAN, CASK 11/2012 63%
Nose: Light and clean. A light grassiness, vetiver note develops into a warning notes of old bookshops, with a chalky minerality that adds a freshness. Water accentuates the herbal note.
Palate: Young and fresh, with stables, clean wood, wet plaster, and delicate fruits.
Finish: Clean and a little tight.
Conclusion: Smoked over nettles, which might be the herbal character. All positive, coming together.

FARY LOCHAN, BATCH 1 48%
Nose: Highly polished wood that drifts toward beeswax with real sweetness building behind. Hay and herbs again. Hints, with water, of dandelion and burdock and ginger-beer plant. Sappy wood oil.
Palate: Mouth-filling, with subtle oak. Balanced with some aniseed.
Finish: Herbal again.
Conclusion: Precocious and a positive market for the future.

STAUNING, YOUNG RYE 51.2%
Nose: Well-balanced and precise rye notes. Lightly mellow and sweet, with a roasted, almost honeyed note. Clean spices with some caraway behind the grassiness. Complex and rounded, with the required vibrancy of youth.
Palate: Soft start. Butter on a spiced bun, then nutmeg, pepper, and green apple. Sweetens with water.
Finish: Lightly spiced. Long.
Conclusion: This will develop into a world-class rye.

> **Flavor Camp: Spicy Rye**
> **Where Next?** Millstone 100°

STAUNING, TRADITIONAL OLOROSO 52.8%
Nose: Warm graham crackers. Sweet and slightly sugary, with hints of licorice root along with sweet red and black fruit. Concentrated, then white raisin.
Palate: Gentle and slightly dry and dusty. Balanced, with clean spirit and good wood working in congress. Light cinnamon touch.
Finish: Short but fruity.
Conclusion: Also showing great—and rapid—maturity.

> **Flavor Camp: Fruity & Spicy**
> **Where Next?** The Macallan Amber

STAUNING, PEATED OLOROSO 49.4%
Nose: Gentle smoke. Lightly tarry, coal tar, and notes of peat kiln: Ardbeg-like. Hints of grass and good creaminess, adding sweetness. Subtle dried fruits. Quite dense.
Palate: Ripe fruit, black grapes, and raisin mixed with bonfire.
Finish: Liquorous and smoky.
Conclusion: Balanced and richly smoked.

> **Flavor Camp: Smoky & Peaty**
> **Where Next?** Ardbeg 10yo

BRAUNSTEIN E:1 SINGLE SHERRY CASK, 62.1%
Nose: Tight to start. Sweet and soft. Scented. Chestnut flour, and blueberry. Cooked fruit.
Palate: Concentrated with masses of jammy fruitiness. Then comes the dusty cereal and dried fruit. Toffee. Good acidity. Balanced. Polished oak.
Finish: Spicy and fragrant. An exotic element.
Conclusion: An identically aged single cask has more intense mintiness with an appetizing, intriguing wormwood note.

> **Flavor Camp: Fruity & Spicy**
> **Where Next?** Benromach-style

NORWAY TASTING NOTES

ARCUS, GJOLEID, EX-BOURBON CASK 3.5YO 73.5%
Nose: Light, fresh, and clean with a pure, sweet drive. Light touches of confectionary. Focused and balanced, with some citrus fruit. A little touch of cream soda and, with water, a little sherbet.
Palate: Light, with lemon. Holds its high strength well, suggesting integration already. Subtle, clean, with spring-like fruitiness.
Finish: Clean and sharp.
Conclusion: Precocious. One to watch.

> **Flavor Camp: Fruity & Spicy**
> **Where Next?** Great King Street, The Belgian Owl

ARCUS, GJOLEID, SHERRY CASK 3.5YO 73.5%
Nose: Wood smoke and ginger, some cookie warmth. Hot toddy with honey and cinnamon and coffee notes. Honey and fresh mushroom mingling with water. Barley in the background.
Palate: Sweet and rounded, showing the beginnings of fattening out. Young but clean. Balanced, gentle oak.
Finish: Chocolate.
Conclusion: Different casks bring out different aspects of the spirit.

> **Flavor Camp: Fruity & Spicy**
> **Where Next?** Bunnabhabhain (in time)

Finland/Iceland

TEERENPELI • YHTIÖT OY, FINLAND •WWW.TEERENPELI.COM
EIMVERK DISTILLERY (FLÓKI) • REYKJAVÍK, ICELAND • WWW.FLOKIWHISKY.IS

Government control looms large in the sagas of Nordic whiskies. Finland, for example, didn't even permit the importation of Scotch until 1904. A letter discovered by the whiskyscience blog (www.whiskyscience.blogspot.co.uk) shows an enthusiastic journalist writing at the time: "Now the change has come. Now have the doors of whisky-civilization been opened for us, too!"

The enthusiasm was short-lived. The government imposed Prohibition between 1919 and 1932, and, as in Norway after its repeal, production was state-controlled. Although Bengt Thorbjörnson was contacted in the 1930s about possible whisky distilling, he concluded it wasn't possible. Strange, indeed, since Finnish grain was of high quality.

Finnish whisky had to wait until the 1950s, when state distiller Alko made some that was blended into a spiced brand called Tähkäviina, or (unaged) in a Finno-Scottish blend, known as Lion. It wasn't until the 1980s that Alko's first 100 percent Finnish whisky was released. Distillation stopped in 1995, and stocks were eked out in more Finno-Scottish blends, such as Viski 88/Double Eight 88 until 2000.

It was only two years before Old Buck rode to the rescue. Distilled by Beer Hunter's (sic) in Pori in a Holstein still, it is aged in a mix of sherry and Portuguese casks. The same year, Tampere's Teerenpeli beer restaurant also started to distill, and is now the most prominent Finnish brand internationally. Unlike many startups, Teerenpeli has its brewery and restaurant chain to help offset high startup costs.

"I always wondered why there were no whisky distilleries in Finland," says Teerenpeli CEO Anssi Pyssing, "especially since the Lahti region, where we are located, is well known for brewing and malting. Since we'd started brewing in 1995, the next step was logical."

Logical it may have been, but that issue of how to make a whisky redolent with a Finnish approach was also uppermost. "Anyone can produce and sell whisky here," he says.

"However, when you are producing Finnish whisky, there are higher expectations: in quality, in branding, in pride, and the obligations related to the use of the prefix 'Finnish.'"

Designing their own pot-stills was one step. However, when you speak to Pyssing, it is clear that the Lahti location was the key: fresh water filtered through the Salpausselkä esker; local malting barley sourced from no more than 93 miles around the distillery; local peat; and, as Pyssing points out, the Finnish climate.

"The barley grows in the short but intensive Finnish summer, with its long summer days, while the seasonal variation in temperature and humidity differentiates maturation conditions from Scottish ones."

When you look at those variables, all are different. It is Finnish. "Whisky-civilization" has finally arrived.

The question at the back of my mind when talking about Nordic whiskies isn't just how far out can they go to reinforce their sense of place, but how far, physically, can they go north? Norway's Klostergården lies at 63°N, but it is just pipped by Eimverk, in the

Icelandic town of Garðabær, which lies at 64°N, making it, at the time of writing, the most northerly whisky distillery in the world. (However, there are plans to build one on the island of Myken [66°N], off the northern coast of Norway, using desalinated seawater from the Vestfjorden firth.)

There is more to this than just bragging rights. You could, in theory distill at the North Pole, but if you wish to follow the trend to use "the local," then you have to face up to climatic limits. Iceland is right on on the edge of the barley zone, whisky's "Ultima Thule."

This is one reason why a country where brewing was banned from 1915 until 1989, but distillation was allowed (go figure), never made whisky but, instead, specialized in potato-based *brennivín*. Then came Eimverk and its brand, Floki.

"For five centuries, the Vikings grew barley and brewed," says Eimverk's Halli Thorkelsson. "Around the thirteenth century, we entered a period of cooler weather that lasted into the twentieth century, making barley-growing impossible, and resulting in considerable economic hardship. However, for the last 20 years we've had a stable crop."

With the right conditions came whisky. "We started making Floki for the love of the spirit and tradition, which is certainly a big part of our quest. There were five years of experimentation, building our own equipment from scavenged old dairy equipment. Floki is the result of those experiments and is based on recipe number 164."

It is (environmentally speaking) green. The stills are heated with geothermal hot water, the barley grown without pesticides. "We did not set out to make the first "green" whiskey," Thorkelsson says. "It's just one of those things that happens along the way quite naturally with the resources we have at hand.

"We need to select hardy and slower-growing varieties, resulting in lower starch/sugar content than most producers are used to today; there's more barley per bottle! This affects the taste and texture with higher content of oils."

The Icelandic climate and tradition also wreathes itself into the smoke used. There's no peat so, historically, sheep manure has been used to make specialties such as *hangikjöt* (smoked mutton). "We have a head-start in creating a style that's unique just from the climate and environment," says Thorkelsson. "We'd like to see Floki as the starting point and cornerstone of a real whisky industry and tradition in Iceland. Our approach is based on traditions and tastes that are uniquely Nordic."

Maybe that Nordic style is forming after all.

FINLAND TASTING NOTES

TEERENPELI AËS 43%

Nose: Fresh and young, with a malty sweetness that pushes into apples and flowers. Very fragrant and clean. Light whipped cream and apple pie cut with jasmine. Lifted with water.
Palate: Light barley to start, but not skeletal and dry, more warming and sweet, with a floral lift.
Finish: Aniseed.
Conclusion: Showing the sweeter side of cereal.

> **Flavor Camp: Fragrant & Floral**
> **Where Next?** The Glenlivet 12yo

TEERENPELI 8YO 43%

Nose: Broader and slightly drier, with more structure than Aës. Light barley sugar, milk chocolate, and nuts. Balanced.
Palate: Roasted and more toasty malt. Cooked and brassy, with some chestnut. Soft and clean.
Finish: Slightly tight.
Conclusion: Moving into cask-derived flavors.

> **Flavor Camp: Malty & Dry**
> **Where Next?** Auchentoshan 12yo

TEERENPELI KASKI 43%

Nose: Malt loaf, moist and chewy, with some currant and cooked plum and black cherry. With water, a little wood oil.
Palate: Slick, soft, and smooth. Balanced and sweet with honeycomb sugar and dry oak/malt to balance. The plums return.
Finish: Form and cocoa.
Conclusion: The most structured and advanced of the trio.

> **Flavor Camp: Fruity & Spicy**
> **Where Next?** Macduff

TEERENPELI, 6YO 43%

Nose: Gold. Bran. Roasted and nutty. Clean and light oiliness behind that moves into dry grass and flaked almond.
Palate: Very nutt: hazelnut. Young and feisty with some hyacinth.
Finish: Wheat germ.
Conclusion: Clean and fresh. Balanced and nutty.

> **Flavor Camp: Malty & Dry**
> **Where Next?** Auchroisk-style

ICELAND TASTING NOTES

FLÓKI, 5 MONTHS, EX-BOURBON 68.5%

Nose: Sweet, tight, and fresh with light, sweet cereal and a little wild herb/wet-grass note. Chalky and intense and, with water, some pleasant farmyard notes that move into fenugreek and vegetal tones.
Palate: Sweet and needle-sharp. Clean spirit. Fresh and acidic. Water shows a slight youthful austerity.
Finish: Clean and tight.
Conclusion: Well-made, airy and fresh. Worth following.

Flóki's Icelandic single-malt whisky is hand-crafted with pride and distilled in pot-stills made by the distillery.

SOUTH AFRICA

JAMES SEDGWICK • WELLINGTON • WWW.DISTELL.CO.ZA
DRAYMAN'S • PRETORIA • WWW.DRAYMANS.COM

Though best known as a brandy-producing country, whisky has been made intermittently in South Africa since the late nineteenth century, although most companies failed because of legislation that protected the indigenous brandy industry. At one point in the twentieth century, domestic cereal-based distillates (i.e. whisky) were taxed at 200 percent more than brandy.

Whisky, however, was always drunk. South Africa was an important export for Scotch from the nineteenth century onward, but its real boom came post-apartheid, when whisky became the signifier of success for the "Black Diamonds."

The oldest of the country's pair of whisky distilleries is the James Sedgwick plant in Wellington, which started as a brandy distillery in 1886. Just over 100 years later, the distilling equipment from a small R&B distillery in Stellenbosch was transferred here.

Its brand, Three Ships, started as a blend of Scotch and Sedgwick whiskies (the Select and Premium five-year-old still are). Increasingly, though, 100 percent South African whiskies are being used, for the Bourbon Cask Finish blend (given six months marrying in first-fill casks) and the (too) occasional releases of a ten-year-old single malt.

The whisky that has made its name domestically and internationally is Bain's Cape Mountain: a lush single grain specifically aimed at the new whisky-drinking market. "In the past, we've suffered from a perception that whisky (or at least good whisky) can't be made in South Africa," says distiller Andy Watts. "Fortunately, the public is becoming more educated and the perceptions are slowly being changed."

Changing perceptions has been a catchphrase of Moritz Kallmeyer ever since he started Pretoria's first brewpub in the 1990s. He still brews, but the main focus is now his Drayman's High Veldt whisky. Local Caledon barley and (imported) peated malt are fermented to 7% abv with a mix of his own ale yeast and distiller's yeast, for three days. This is then given a two-day rest, helping to create esters and mouth-feel. As Kallmeyer says, "You have to ferment for longer; otherwise you sacrifice distillery character and end up with malt schnapps."

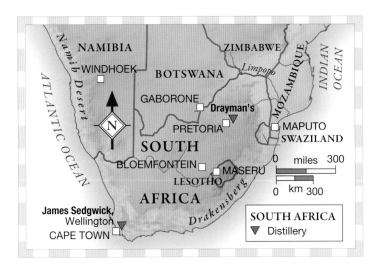

The still is a remarkable assemblage of scrap: a bacterial fermenter for the pot, a neck containing bubble-cap plates, and a high lyne arm/condenser, all packed with sacrificial copper. The spirit is clean and full of personality. No beer schnapps here.

Only re-charred 66-gallon (250-liter) American oak ex-red-wine casks are used. There's also a solera for his Drayman's blend (60 percent Drayman's mixed with bottled imported Scotch.)

"I'd like to make it 100 percent South African, but I can't hit the right price using my own whisky," he says, "although I'm hoping to make grain whisky in a column-still."

Scrap merchants in the High Veldt must be rubbing their hands in gleeful anticipation.

SOUTH AFRICA TASTING NOTES

BAIN'S CAPE MOUNTAIN GRAIN 46%

Nose: Rich gold. Very sweet with a light grassy back note. Fudge, mashed banana, and butterscotch with a piney twang.
Palate: Light but succulently sweet. Quite chewy. Ice cream, soft fruit in the middle then a blast of citrus fruit.
Finish: Cinnamon.
Conclusion: Balanced and characterful. Will appeal to a new (and older) consumer.

Flavor Camp: **Fruity & Spicy**
Where Next? Nikka Coffey Grain

THREE SHIPS 10YO SINGLE MALT 43%

Nose: Soft and sweet. Coconut and some milk chocolate given a zestiness by citrus fruit (kumquat/sour orange), followed by some sweet spice dust: nutmeg, cinnamon then, with water, some dried fruit depth.
Palate: Starts very soft and fruity with dried peach, raspberry, and melon. Light oak tones.
Finish: Fruity still, and well balanced.
Conclusion: Poised and well balanced. Deserves to be bottled more frequently.

Flavor Camp: **Fruity & Spicy**
Where Next? The Benriach 12yo

DRAYMAN'S 2007, CASK NO 4 CASK SAMPLE

Nose: Spicy and clean. Touches of cardamom, cilantro, and straw but also a concentrated persimmon jelly note in the background.
Palate: Very scented and lifted. Rose petal before light cereal comes through.
Finish: Clean and perfumed.
Conclusion: A fascinating range of flavors. One to watch.

SOUTH AMERICA

UNION DISTILLERY MALTWHISKY DO BRASIL • VERANÓPOLIS, BRAZIL • WWW.MALTWHISKY.COM.BR

LA ALAZANA • LAS GOLON DRINAS, PATAGONIA, ARGENTINA • WWW.JAVOODESIGNS.WIX.COM/LAALAZANAIN#!ABOUT-US

BUSNELLO • BENTO GONÇALVES, BRAZIL • WWW.DESTILARIABUSNELLO.COM.BR

Long established as a major region for Scotch-whisky exports—most of the big blenders (James Buchanan especially) established bridgeheads in South America early in the twentieth century—South America is now beginning to enter into the world whisky boom.

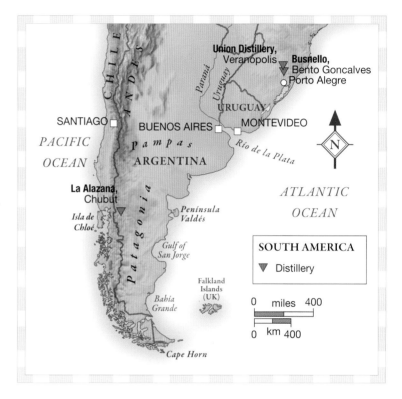

In fact, two of the continent's three distilleries have been making whisky for decades. In 1963, Luigi Pessetto, Antônio Pitt, and João Busnello built a castle in a valleys of Bento Gonçalves. Inside the imposing structure was the Busnello Distillery. And based in Veranópolis, in Rio Grande do Sul, the Union Distillery started in 1948 as a wine producer, but switched to distilling in 1972. Its parent company, Borsato e Cia. Ltda, felt that, given the mountainous location was good for grape-growing, it would be equally amenable for whisky production. From 1987 to 1991 it entered into a technical partnership with Morrison Bowmore. For the next five years, Dr. Dante Calatayud became its consultant.

Locally produced unpeated, and imported heavily peated malts are used. Distillation takes place in copper pots with steep lyne arms that descend into worm tubs to add a fruity weight to the distillate, which comes off the second still at 65% abv.

Initially, the make was sold in bulk as new spirit and mature whisky for admixes, but in 2008 Union Club single malt was launched to commemorate the firm's 60th anniversary. Under Brazilian law it has to be two years old before it can be classed as whisky and can be bottled at under 40% abv. Serge Valentin of www.whiskyfun.com commented that it reminded him of a middle-of-the-road Speysider, with fruit and some nuttiness. He also was enthusiastic about a sample of the heavily peated style.

In 2011, the Brazilian duo were joined by Argentina's first single-malt distillery, La Alazana, which is located in the Patagonian region of Las Golondrinas, close to Piltriquitrón Mountain, which provides it with snow-melt process and cooling water.

Like so many new distillers, Pablo Tognetti and his son-in-law Nestor Serenelli have started as enthusiastic home brewers before deviating into the world of whisky, designing and building the distillery equipment themselves. They use barley grown on the pampas, and in a nice Argentinian twist, the draff is used as horse feed for the animals stabled in their farm's therapeutic riding center.

A single 145-gallon (550-liter) still is used for both distillations, with plans in place for a second to be installed. Their stated aim is to produce a lighter style to suit the local palate, but it is one that is given another local twist in maturation. After all, if you have the possibility to use local wine-quality oak, it would be remiss not to age some of the new make in ex-Malbec casks, as well as the standard ex-bourbon and sherry.

With two other projects are being mooted for Argentina, Patagonia could well become the world's next whisky region.

The beautiful surroundings of La Alazana, the first single-malt whisky distillery in Argentina.

INDIA & THE FAR EAST

India is one of the largest consumers of whisky, yet it hardly drinks any. Confused? You're not the only one. According to World Trade Organization (WTO) rules, whisky can only be made from cereal, but in India "whisky" can also refer to a brown spirit made from molasses, which makes it rum. When you stir in other Indian "whisky" styles, such as unaged, colored neutral grain spirit, blends of molasses and grain/malt, or molasses spirit and Scotch, you can begin to see why trade organizations' lawyers have been tied up in knots for decades.

The refusal of the world to recognize molasses-based spirit as whisky has hardened the Indian government's line on levying high taxes on imported spirits, such as whisky. Although this rate has dropped significantly in recent years, each state within India has the power to raise its own taxes, so the tariff has simply been collected by another revenue office.

This has been especially irritating to the Scotch industry, which sees India as potentially its largest export market. Negotiations continue to move as quickly as Himalayan glacier.

In Asia, the situation is less fraught. Taiwan is emerging as a significant single-malt market that has its own remarkable distillery,

Above: Amrut has established itself in export before launching on its home market.

Below: The hills around Bangalore are home to India's best known single malt—Amrut.

Kavalan, where the complexities of subtropical aging are being forensically examined. Singapore remains both an entry point and a booming market in its own right, while Korea, Vietnam, and Thailand are well established markets for Scotch.

After India, the major prize is China. Producers need to be in a market with such vast potential but have also to rethink the manner in which they enter it. China remains a new market that has a real

taste for imported spirits—and not just whisky. In fact, consumers will happily jump from whisky to vodka to Cognac to tequila. In addition, the cost of entry is high, and the territory is vast. As well as this, a recent *diktat* curbing excessively expensive gift giving has dented the top-end of the whisky market. These issues aside, China cannot be ignored.

It is India, however, that leads as far as production goes.

India

Although there are hundreds of distilleries on the Indian subcontinent, it's well nigh impossible to discover how many of them make non-neutral, grain-based, wood-aged spirit. Pakistan's Murree distillery, claimed to be the only distillery in a Muslim country, certainly does. It's possible that Bhutan's Army Welfare Project in Gelephu does, but most of the country's whiskies are Scotch mixed with local neutral alcohol.

Others that conform to the global definition include Mohan Meakin's Kasauli distillery in the foothills of the Himalayas, and the same firm's Nagar plant in Uttar Pradesh, also home to Radico Khaitan's Rampur plant. All make molasses and grain spirit.

India's largest producer is United Spirits, whose portfolio includes many whiskies of all types, including McDowell's single malt, produced in the distillery of the same name in Goa. The state is also home to the John Distilleries. Although best known for its range of local-style whiskies, (it makes 11 million cases a year) in 2012 it launched its first barley-based Paul John single malts internationally.

Here a Scottish template is in place. The barley is Indian, but any peat is imported from Scotland. Distillation is in pot-stills and maturation exclusively in ex-bourbon barrels. The Goan climate has a significant effect during aging, with high levels of evaporation, resulting in rapid maturation.

The single malts were initially export-only, the aim being to build reputation abroad before launching what will be high-cost whiskies on the local market. It's a strategy that has already been tried since 2004 by Bangalore's Amrut, which is virtually unknown in its home country,

but has a deservedly high reputation with connoisseurs globally. Here's a perfect case study in how location influences character. Amrut's unpeated barley comes from Rajasthan (any peated component is Scottish) and while distillation is standard, it is what happens when the whisky is placed in a mix of new and first-fill American oak casks that sets Amrut apart.

Though Bangalore is at 3,000 feet (914 meters), temperatures range from 68–97°F (20–36°C) in summer and 63–81°F (17–27°C) in winter, and then there's the monsoon season. All impact on evaporation. In Scotland, the "angels" receive on average two percent a year in volume; in Bangalore up to 16 percent of cask volume disappears into the ether each year. These angels (also the name of the firm's oldest whisky) are greedy. Most Amrut is bottled at four years of age.

While accountants love whisky that can be made quickly, distillers need to ensure that the finished product isn't just a mass of oak extract but one that shows complex interaction between cask and spirit, even in a short time. The distiller continues to examine the effects of its climate having, it would seem, a lot of fun in the process.

Fusion is 25 percent peated Scottish malt. Two Continents whisky is taken to Scotland to be finished, while Intermediate starts in ex-bourbon casks, is re-racked to sherry, then goes back to ex-bourbon.

Maybe both distilleries' success may persuade the warring parties that Indian all-malt whisky has a future.

INDIA TASTING NOTES

AMRUT, NEW MAKE

Nose: Sweet mash, linseed oil, saffron, lightly earthy with a fresh corn note and powdered chalk.
Palate: Oily and thick with some red fruit, a sweet pepperiness, and a touch of hyssop and violet. Angular.
Finish: Tight.

AMRUT, GREEDY ANGELS 50%

Nose: Warm, sweet, with persimmon and marzipan mixed with canned pineapple and an intense, lifted perfume. Peach pit and sweet cookies.
Palate: Broad and well balanced. Some heat, but calmed with water, where the mix of cereal and fruit in the center come to life. Ripe and peachy.
Finish: Stone fruits. Sweet.
Conclusion: Has weight and complexity.

Flavor Camp: Fruity & Spicy
Where Next? George Dickel

AMRUT, FUSION 50%

Nose: Very light smoke. Some cheese rind, then sweet cereal and signature sweet cookie. Kiln-like with water; a fresh, wet-grass note, then soft fruits.
Palate: Wood smoke to start; deepens into a latte note before some spiced citrus fruit begins to develop.
Finish: Long and spicy.
Conclusion: Balanced and elegant.

Flavor Camp: Fruity & Spicy
Where Next? Tomatin Cù Bòcan

AMRUT, INTERMEDIATE CASK 57.1%

Nose: Ovaltine and malted milk; sweet cookies. Toffee. Water increases the richness and depth.
Palate: Raisins and plump, ripe stone fruits: very Amrut.
Finish: White raisin and wine-soaked raisin, then vanilla.
Conclusion: Full and ripe.

Flavor Camp: Rich & Round
Where Next? The Glenlivet 15yo

PAUL JOHN CLASSIC SELECT CASK 55.2%

Nose: Very sweet. Barley sugar, preserved lemon macadamia nuts, citrus fruit, ripe melon, mango.
Palate: Continues the sweet, tropical-fruit theme, then a crunch of barley and light oak. Warming.
Finish: Juicy fruits and mint.
Conclusion: Soft and pleasing.

Flavor Camp: Fruity & Spicy
Where Next? Glenmorangie 10yo, Kavalan Classic

PAUL JOHN PEATED SELECT CASK 55.5%

Nose: Heathery smoke to start. Drier than unpeated. Opens into tarriness and cereal. Burning broom.
Palate: Fruits return, with masses of peat smoke. Hot fire, then the soft fruit. With water some maltiness.
Finish: Ember-like.
Conclusion: Big, richly smoked.

Flavor Camp: Smoky & Peaty
Where Next? The BenRiach Curiositas

Taiwan

KING CAR KAVALAN WHISKY DISTILLERY • YUANSHAN, YILAN COUNTY • WWW.KAVALANWHISKY.COM • OPEN FOR TOURS

The days of people being surprised that whisky is made in the subtropical climes of Taiwan are fast receding. The reasons for building Kavalan, Taiwan's first dedicated whisky distillery, in this spot are pretty obvious when you consider that Taiwan is currently the sixth-largest market for Scotch whisky in the world—and that the market itself changed significantly over the past decade as a new generation of drinkers has adopted Scotch single malt.

Construction of the distillery, which is owned by food and beverage conglomerate King Car, started in April 2005, with commissioning (inevitably) by Forsyths of Rothes, which got it up and running by March 11, 2006, "At 15:30!" says blender Yu-Lan "Ian" Chang. It is now both a highly respected producer and a research station in that new field of whisky science: the effects of tropical maturation. Losses here average 15 percent per annum. When you visit, you can almost see the whisky evaporating from the casks, and hear to choirs of angels carousing tipsily in the heavens above.

"The site was chosen for two reasons," Chang explains, "the Shue-Shan Mountains' natural reservoir of spring water, which lies underneath the distillery, and the fact that about 75 percent of the land in Yilan is mountainous, giving clean air that is perfect for the maturation of spirits."

Chang had a clear flavor line in mind from the outset, triggered by the mix of yeasts pitched into the fermenters. "They're a mix of commercial and our own, isolated from wild yeasts growing around the distillery, which help create the fruity character—mango, green apple, and cherry—that is the signature of Kavalan new-make spirit."

After double-distillation, that fruity new make is aged in a complex mix of woods chosen by the man Chang refers to as his mentor, Dr. Jim Swan. The wood mix is based around American oak, but sherry, port, and wine are also used. The key for Chang and Swan is to utilize this accelerated maturation regime while also building complexity. Kavalan's spirit has to sing, not be obliterated by extract.

The waters of Sun Moon Lake may be tranquil, but Kavalan whisky is already making waves internationally.

This is no microdistillery. Kavalan can make .34m gallons (1.3m liters) a year, and there are plans for further expansion. There is also an educative element at work. One million visitors tour the distillery every year, while the firm has established tasting rooms and is now regularly appearing globally at whisky shows.

Kavalan is not a local oddity, but a world leader that has achieved this by a careful investigation into local conditions—not just the climate and yeast, but the wider Taiwanese gourmet culture.

This is not just a whisky from Taiwan, it is *of* Taiwan.

KAVALAN TASTING NOTES

KAVALAN CLASSIC 40%

Nose: Sweet, with tropical fruits galore: guava, mango, and persimmon mixed with orchid and frangipani blossom, vanilla, and coconut.
Palate: Juicy and fruity with central sweetness, ginger, and delicately toasted oak.
Finish: Clean and lightly spiced apple juice.
Conclusion: A perfect introduction to the Kavalan family. Versatile, too.

Flavor Camp: Fruity & Spicy
Where Next? Glenmorangie Original

KAVALAN FINO CASK 58%

Nose: Sherried, certainly, but sweetly so. Light caramel, dark chocolate, espresso, and honey. Behind is dried tropical fruit typical of the distillery.
Palate: Elegant, polished, and full with sweetness and resin (soy) rather than tannic grip. Some red fruit. Citrus fruit.
Finish: Dries slightly.
Conclusion: Balanced and rightly revered as the distillery's finest bottling.

Flavor Camp: Rich & Round
Where Next? Glenmorangie La Santa, Macallan Amber

SOLIST SINGLE CASK EX-BOURBON 58.8%

Nose: Bright gold. Sweet and pure with light corn syrup and soft fruit: mango, melon, and guava cut with ginger and kumqat. Touch of peanut and sandalwood. A hit of sweet sawdust, suggestive of youth.
Palate: Sweet and fruity spirit that's been balanced by classic American-oak flavors of ice cream, *crème brûlée*, and spice.
Finish: Custard-like with canned pineapple.
Conclusion: Sweet and sassy. "New" malt personified.

Flavor Camp: Fruity & Spicy
Where Next? Glen Moray-style

AUSTRALIA

BAKERY HILL • NORTH BAYSWATER, VICTORIA • WWW.BAKERYHILLDISTILLERY.COM.AU • COURSES BY ARRANGEMENT
GREAT SOUTHERN DISTILLING COMPANY • ALBANY, WESTERN AUSTRALIA • WWW.DISTILLERY.COM.AU • OPEN ALL YEAR
LARK DISTILLERY • HOBART, TASMANIA • WWW.LARKDISTILLERY.COM.AU • OPEN ALL YEAR; TOURS BY RESERVATION • CELLAR
DOOR & WHISKY BAR / NANT DISTILLING COMPANY • BOTHWELL, TASMANIA • WWW.NANTDISTILLERY.COM.AU • OPEN
ALL YEAR; TOURS BY RESERVATION / SULLIVANS COVE • CAMBRIDGE, TASMANIA • WWW.SULLIVANSCOVEWHISKY.COM
HELLYERS ROAD DISTILLERY • BURNIE, TASMANIA • WWW.HELLYERSROADDISTILLERY.COM.AU • OPEN ALL YEAR; TOURS,
WHISKY ROAD & VISITOR CENTER

With distilleries scattered across its vast land mass, it would be difficult to try and impose some sort of national style on the new Australian whisky industry. Once you factor in the myriad different approaches taken by its distillers, the task becomes impossible.

The barley tends to be local brewing varieties (and often sourced from brewery maltings), but there are exceptions. Some distillers use local peat, with its own imprint of Australian flora; others remain unpeated. Different yeast varieties are being explored; there is always a way in which to create, and increase, differences, while stills range from Scottish-style pots to John Dore-designed pots, former brandy stills, and old-style Australian stills. All will have an impact.

Then there is the use of different types of casks, with many distillers wisely utilizing ones that had formerly held wine or Australian fortified wine. And that's just where single malt is concerned. There are also distillers who are now trying rye as well as an Australian take on bourbon. All of these factors combine to show that this is an industry where individuals are trying to establish themselves, rather than conforming to some commonality.

What is happening now is also fundamentally different to the old Australian whisky industry, whose low-cost, high-volume ethos finally came to an end in the 1980s. In the relentless search for The New, it's often forgotten that Australia was Scotch whisky's largest export market up until the start of World War II, and that the country had made whisky from the late eighteenth century.

The sands of Albany may soon be the setting for Limeburners' beach barbies.

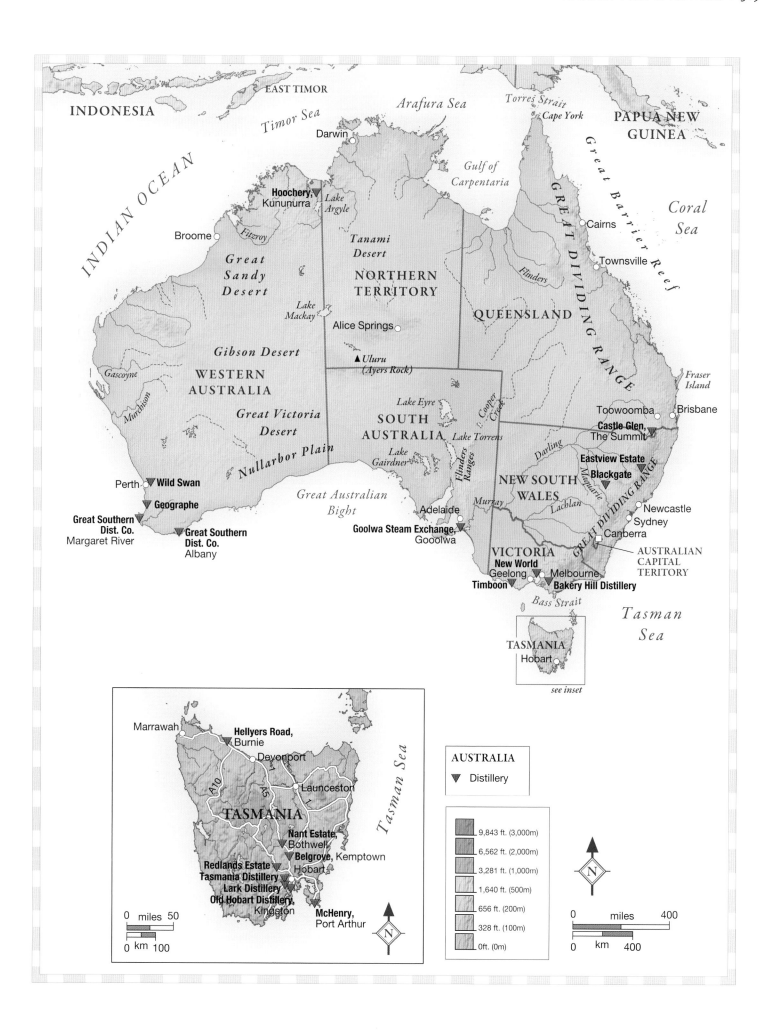

INDONESIA

EAST TIMOR

Timor Sea

Arafura Sea

Torres Strait
Cape York

PAPUA NEW GUINEA

Great Barrier Reef

Darwin

Coral Sea

INDIAN OCEAN

Broome

Hoochery,
Kununurra
Lake Argyle

Fitzroy

Great Sandy Desert

Tanami Desert

NORTHERN TERRITORY

Gulf of Carpentaria

Cairns

Townsville

QUEENSLAND

Flinders

Gibson Desert

Lake Mackay

Alice Springs

▲ *Uluru (Ayers Rock)*

WESTERN AUSTRALIA

Gascoyne

Murchison

Great Victoria Desert

Nullarbor Plain

Lake Eyre

Cooper Creek

SOUTH AUSTRALIA

Lake Torrens

Lake Gairdner

Flinders Ranges

Great Australian Bight

Murray

Darling

Macquarie

Lachlan

Toowoomba
Brisbane

Castle Glen,
The Summit

Eastview Estate
Blackgate

NEW SOUTH WALES

Fraser Island

Newcastle
Sydney
Canberra

AUSTRALIAN CAPITAL TERRITORY

GREAT DIVIDING RANGE

Perth · ▼ **Wild Swan**

▼ **Geographe**

Great Southern Dist. Co.
Margaret River ▼

▼ **Great Southern Dist. Co.**
Albany

Adelaide

Goolwa Steam Exchange,
Gooolwa ▼

VICTORIA

New World
Geelong ▼

Timboon ▼

Melbourne ▼

Bakery Hill Distillery

Bass Strait

Tasman Sea

TASMANIA
Hobart

see inset

AUSTRALIA
▼ Distillery

9,843 ft. (3,000m)
6,562 ft. (2,000m)
3,281 ft. (1,000m)
1,640 ft. (500m)
656 ft. (200m)
328 ft. (100m)
0ft. (0m)

N

0 miles 400
0 km 400

Marrawah

Hellyers Road,
Burnie

Devonport

A10
A5
1

Launceston

1

TASMANIA

Nant Estate,
Bothwell ▼

Belgrove, Kemptown

Redlands Estate ▼
Tasmania Distillery ▼
Lark Distillery ▼
Hobart

Old Hobart Distillery,
Kingston ▼

McHenry,
Port Arthur ▼

Tasman Sea

0 miles 50
0 km 100

N

Australia's burgeoning distilling scene encompasses many sizes and styles.

As Chris Middleton, consultant and historian of this forgotten whisky nation points out, Australia's first grain spirits were made (from wheat) in Sydney in 1791. Although South Australia and Tasmania were distilling in the nineteenth century, it was Victoria that would become the major producer. Dunn's Distillery, producing along Irish lines, was established in Ballarat, Victoria, in 1863, and remained the country's second-largest producer until its closure in 1930. That prime wine-making region, the Yarra Valley, had six distilleries in the nineteenth century, although the state's production was dominated by Federal Distilleries in Port Melbourne, which in 1888 had a total capacity of 1.06 million gallons (4 million liters) a year from pots and columns (cooled by seawater: something the Scottish industry is still trying to crack).

Distilling in the twentieth century was dominated by Corio, built by the Distillers Company Limited (DCL) of Scotland in Ballarat in the 1920s before merging with four other Victorian stills in 1924. Its Corio blend appeared in 1934. London-based Gilbey's branched into whisky blending post-World War II, when it added the Milne distillery in Adelaide to its Moorabbin plant in Melbourne. Both of these UK-owned companies operated a strategy of keeping Australian whisky cheap and young to maintain a price differential between them and their Scotch brands, which at that time were 40 percent more expensive because of protectionist legislation. With the dismantling of tariffs in the 1960s, Scotch prices fell, and the lack of a premium sector

within domestically produced whisky meant that its sales collapsed. By the end of the 1980s, Australia's two whisky distilleries had closed.

This legacy of bulk hung over the industry. When Bill Lark, the father of modern Aussie whisky, tried to start up at the beginning of the 1990s, he found out that the Licensing Act of 1901 stated that stills had to be a minimum of 713 gallons (2,700 liters): almost twice what Lark required, and a size that would make craft distilling pretty much impossible. Undaunted, Lark lobbied the whisky-loving Minister of Agriculture, got the law changed, and set a new chapter in motion, establishing his native Tasmania as the new center of Australian whisky.

Tasmania now boasts nine distilleries, of which the newest include William McHenry & Sons, Mackey's, Shene (making a triple-distilled "Irish style"), and Peter Bignell, who is using his own rye to craft a new style of Australian whisky. As the new arrivals begin to establish themselves, the island state's old guard are moving out into the world, with export an increasingly important element.

Lark still uses Franklin brewing barley, unpeated and smoked, with the latter using Tasmanian peat to add an intense, fragrant aroma of juniper, moss, and gum-tree oil to the spirit. A mix of distiller's and a Nottingham ale yeast are pitched. The spirit, oily and floral as an unpeated new make, scented with the smoke added, is double-distilled in Bill Lark's own design of pots, and aged in 26.4-gallon (100-liter) casks.

The most significant change for Lark has come with the development of Redlands Estate distillery on an old (1819) barley-growing estate and the construction of a floor maltings, where Lark is now sourcing requirements. "This is something I've wanted to do for a long time," says Bill Lark, "and our first half-a-dozen or so batches have been hugely successful. It's Australia's first paddock to bottle whisky!"

Of similar vintage to Lark is Patrick Maguire who, in 2003, bought the Tasmania Distillery in Cambridge, which had been previously producing (with varying success) a brand called Sullivans Cove.

The distillery continues to get wash from Tasmania's Cascade Brewery and distill its fruity, floral spirit in a single ex-brandy still. Aging takes place in ex-bourbon and some ex-Australian "port" French oak casks, which, in an echo of Mackmyra and Puni, reside in a (disused) railway tunnel. A recent partnership with local craft brewery Moo Brew has given an alternative source of wash, a wider yeast regime, and possibilities to broaden the range in the future.

Maguire is trying to balance increased demand from the world; Sullivans Cove is available in Europe, Japan, Canada, and China, with other markets coming on stream. "Export has become important," he says, "while domestically things have kicked in in a big way. The companies are being fully accepted as doing a credible job. After 14 years in production, we are finally in the black."

He admits it has been a learning process. "When Bill and I started distilling, we had no bloody idea what we were doing! We'd read and talked a lot, played around and made a lot of mistakes." Gordon Mitchell, the late and much-missed distiller at Arran and Cooley, consulted

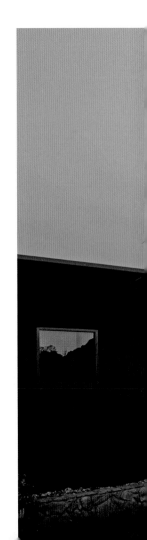

and Maguire has continued to tweak the process in his mission to find the perfect balance. He's clearly doing the right thing. The fact that Sullivans Cove won best single malt in the world in a global competition in 2014 shows how successful his obsession has become.

The days when the distillery had to close in order to allow stocks to come into balance are gone. Expansion is now on the cards. "We're selling all we can make and can double capacity," says Maguire. "It's a good problem to have."

Tasmania is also home to Australia's largest single-malt producer, Hellyers Road. Again, local barley and (Scottish) peat are used, while maturation is in American oak. "The flavor characteristics of Hellyers Road whiskies are uniquely Australian, and very much reflect our region," says distiller Mark Littler. "They provide a succinct and unique taste that embodies crispness and purity." A branching away from standard maturation into Tasmanian Pinot casks has been particularly successful, while the distillery is one of many within Tasmania that has taken a leaf from the wine world and built a cellar-door facility and visitors' center, as well as actively pursuing an export strategy.

Old Hobart Distillery, under the ownership of Casey Overeem who also gives the family name to the brand, started in 2007. Overeem uses dedicated fermenters at Lark and his own yeast and follows the Lark approach to maturation in using cut-down 26.4-gallon (100-liter) French oak casks that previously held Australian "port" and "sherry." Only 8,000 bottles of a bold fragrant, fruity whisky are made a year. Nant, meanwhile, hopes to build its brand in a novel fashion by establishing a chain of whisky bars with plans to take the strategy global.

Hellyers Road—Australia's finest—lies in prime dairy farming country in northwestern Tasmania.

On the mainland, the movement continues to grow, with Southern Coast Distillers and The Steam Exchange in South Australia, Timboon Railway Shed and New World Whisky distilleries in Victoria, and Joadja and Black Gate Distillery in New South Wales all joining more seasoned veterans like Victoria's Bakery Hill, whose owner, David Baker, first lit his still in an industrial unit in Bayswater in 1999.

"From that very first decision that I really wanted to make bloody fine malt, the driving force has been to do things differently, and not to end up as another 'me too,'" he says. "I didn't start out with any preconceived ideas, bar the idea of producing a local product that would appeal to a local palate."

The first thing was testing 40 or 50 yeasts, then working with John Dore, the firm that took over Aeneas Coffey's business in the nineteenth century, to make stills that would give sweetness and a fruity, floral note. A peated expression has changed since its first incarnation. "It was too clean," says Baker. "I wanted a bit of grunge in there, so we cut later to allow that leather, tobacco, and burning wood note to come through."

Finally came an understanding of the effects of local climatic conditions on the mix of ex-bourbon, French-oak wine casks and small barrels he uses. As he says, "If you haven't got the colors on your palette, you won't get a painting." The result is an increasingly elegant single malt, which is gaining traction in the domestic market. "When I started, people told me to go away. Now bars have gone ballistic."

He is concentrating on the domestic market and specifically new drinkers ("particularly women"). "You won't get the old Scotch drinkers, but younger drinkers want to be educated and are prepared to try different styles, so when people behind the bar say 'Why not try an Australian malt?' they say, 'Why not?'"

"Whisky has gone ballistic in Australia, in Melbourne especially," he adds. "But there is still work to be done. We're still getting pushed back because people have been fed that story that Scotland is the only place whisky can be made, but we make some of the best wines and beers here. Both have done the same as whisky: understanding local conditions. That was my starting point.

"Now I want to increase capacity and relocate. It's time to move out of the industrial zone and establish a distillery with cellar-door sales. When people see the distillery, then the penny drops. It is all about education."

In Western Australia, the Great Southern Distilling Company has expanded to include a range of other spirits as well as its Limeburners brand. Based in the cool, maritime climate of Albany, Western Australia (and now with a second plant and cellar door in the wine-growing region of Margaret River) the fragrant, floral Limeburners is made from brewing malt, local peat (this time from the nearby Porongurup Mountain Range), utilizes very long ferments, is distilled slowly in small stills, then aged in a mix of ex-bourbon, ex-Australian fortified wine, and ex-wine casks that have previously held Great Southern's brandy.

With the increased interest has come the start of generic organization. The Tasmanian Whisky Producers Association now comprises ten members, including two independent bottlers. "It means we now have a body that can liaise with the government," says Patrick Maguire. An A$60,000 (US$55,500) grant to develop a marketing program has resulted in the establishment of a whisky trail and a website, while negotiations are underway to establish a legal definition for Tasmanian whisky. "Tasmania is getting a fantastic reputation for food and drink," he adds, "and they want us to be part of the tourism in Tasmania. They are right behind us."

That's a remarkable change of attitude since Bill Lark tried to persuade the same bureaucrats that craft distilling had a future in Oz.

So where is whisky in Australia? "It's tempting to compare Australian wine with what is happening with whisky," says consultant Chris Middleton. "In wine, we've taken European varieties and over time found some *terroirs* to demonstrate their best strengths in a new environment. Our development of modern wine-making techniques in a hot climate has emphasized the fruit flavors. As the world has replicated Australian processes, it can be argued these flavor profiles are being commoditized.

"Perhaps when applied to distillation, national differences may be more apparent. The Australian brandy industry, though in decline for

AUSTRALIA TASTING NOTES

OLD HOBART, OVEREEM PORT CASK MATURED 43%

Nose: Fresh and very fruity, with cake batter, wet canvas, strawberry, and light, jammy fruit.
Palate: Quite perfumed. Vanilla notes mixed with Parma violet and a little lavender. Cinnamon, soft redcurrant, and confectionary.
Finish: Lightly spicy. Hint of cereal.
Conclusion: Sweet perfumed and direct.

Flavor Camp: **Fruity & Spicy**
Where Next? Edition Saentis, Tullibardine Burgundy Finish

OLD HOBART, OVEREEM SHERRY CASK MATURED 43%

Nose: Lightly oxidized. The wet plaster/canvas note again, this time with added layers of citrus fruit, toffee, and those soft fruits (cooked nectarine).
Palate: Amontillado sherry, light almond. Dense red and black fruits, touch of date. With water, some rosemary and lavender.
Finish: Roasted cereal. Bitter chocolate.
Conclusion: Slightly drier and more structured.

Flavor Camp: **Rich & Round**
Where Next? The Macallan Amber

BAKERY HILL, SINGLE MALT 46%

Nose: Fresh, clean spirit with delicate oak and a floral note mixing with bread crumbs, linden blossom, and light apple blossom.
Palate: Soft start, with balanced wood. A clean acidity. Lightly honeyed.
Finish: Milky coffee.
Conclusion: Delicate and fine.

Flavor Camp: **Fragrant & Floral**
Where Next? Hakushu 12yo

BAKERY HILL, DOUBLE WOOD 46%

Nose: Fruit-driven. Strawberry and raspberry to start, then deepening into perfumed blueberry. Picks up richness with water.
Palate: Complex mix of creamy oatmeal and cereal with that dark berry fruit that oozes into plum crisp in the center.
Finish: Light hay.
Conclusion: Well crafted.

Flavor Camp: **Fruity & Spicy**
Where Next? Tullamore D.E.W. Single Malt

BAKERY HILL, PEATED MALT 46%

Nose: Light smoke: wood smoke with honey-nut cornflakes, light orange peel. Water brings out more peat reek.
Palate: Sweet, slightly nutty. Balanced, with light fruit never dominated by smoke.
Finish: Long and gentle.
Conclusion: Well balanced.

Flavor Camp: **Smoky & Peaty**
Where Next? Kilchoman, Machir Bay

Tasmania's unique flora has resulted in peat—here being cut by Bill Lark—that has unique aromatic properties.

over half a century, still has a slightly different Australian sensory profile due to factors like grape variety, climate, and yeast strains."

So can the same be applied to Aussie whisky or are the differences simply too great? That might only become clear in time. As Maguire, Lark, and Baker all pointed out, it takes more than a decade to establish yourself as a business and get your style fixed.

"People are the best place to start," says Middleton.

"There is no one in Australia who has come from a distilling background." he continues. "None of the staff from the earlier whisky period played any role in the craft startup of the 1990s. This can be an asset: no traditions, no ruts, or constricting industry standard to abide by; starting with a clean factory floor. Uninfluenced, they brought different insights and approaches as

they jumped on the whisky learning curve. It wasn't corporate; it was total production, learning from plant to bottle."

In other words, these people with disparate backgrounds: lawyers, surveyors, teachers, and chemists did this because they loved whisky and the idea of making whisky. When you look at the establishing of Australia's wine regions, exactly the same principle applies. They were pioneered by doctors, chemists, and geologists—people with a mindset to do something new.

It is a dynamic shared with the other new distillers around the world. Australia is part of a world movement, not isolated from it. Not only will the approaches be different, they have to be. "Stop looking to Scotland through a whisky straw," as Middleton puts it. Or try to.

"Australians are followers, not leaders," says Patrick Maguire. "They like to have products getting a stamp of approval. You could bottle Scotch in a paper bag and it would sell here. It means we have to try that little bit harder to be noticed, but the world is changing. In Australia they has been a real food revolution, and good-quality food and good-quality beverages go alongside each other. We knew this would take time, but we went to a lot of effort to reach people."

David Baker agrees. "You're only now seeing the beginnings of an industry," he says, adding with a laugh, "It has been a nightmare, but I'm coming through. I was told I couldn't do it—people laughed at me. But I'm here now because of the passion I have for it. I love it."

That—and whisky—is the spirit.

SULLIVANS COVE, FRENCH OAK CASK MATURED 47.5%

Nose: Candied lemon and orange peel mixed with mace and nutmeg. Lightly toasted barley behind. Has weight.

Palate: Mellow start, with chocolate orange the first to come forward. Sweet center where the citrus fruit, some fleshy fruit, and a hint of heavy florals reside. Water brings out light-brown sugar.

Finish: Praline, light char, and some hazelnut.

Conclusion: Balanced and complex.

Flavor Camp: **Fruity & Spicy**

Where Next? Cardhu 18yo, The Glenlivet 21yo

HELLYERS ROAD, ORIGINAL 10YO 40%

Nose: Some bready aromas, whole-wheat spelt flour, lightly nutty grains, then sweet bamboo shoot, hazelnut, and brown rice.

Palate: Tangerine marmalade on brown bread. Light milk chocolate. Toasted, lightly creamy, and balanced.

Finish: Soft and airy, with oak and cereal.

Conclusion: Light, clean, and nutty.

Flavor Camp: **Malty & Dry**

Where Next? Arran 10yo, Auchentoshan Classic

HELLYERS ROAD, PINOT NOIR FINISH 46.2%

Nose: Red fruit: cherry, redcurrant, raspberry, some blackcurrant leaf and citrus fruit. The brown-rice note is there. Clean.

Palate: Toasty and lightly nutty. Clear distillery character but with considerably more spice: light clove notes and slightly drier because of extra oak.

Finish: Fruit and nut.

Conclusion: Soft, but not wine-doped.

Flavor Camp: **Fruity & Spicy**

Where Next? Tullibardine Burgundy Finish, Liebl Coillmor Port

HELLYERS ROAD, PEATED 46.2%

Nose: Dry start. Baked apples on a bonfire. Toasted hazelnut. The smoke becomes aromatic: rose wood and heather.

Palate: Immediate smoke with a little eucalyptus. The smoke and cereal make this quite dry. The middle softens slightly as that bready element returns along with light vanilla.

Finish: Delicately medicinal.

Conclusion: As well-mannered as the rest of the range.

Flavor Camp: **Smoky & Peaty**

Where Next? Tomatin Cù Bòcan

FLAVOR CAMP LISTS

As you have seen, each of the whiskies tasted (bar new makes and cask samples) have been allocated a Flavor Camp rating, allowing you to browse within the style or styles of drams that you particularly enjoy. By looking through these, you can also see how the influence of oak and time can shift a distillery from one Camp into another. Obviously there are variations within these Camps but all the whiskies in each share a dominant commonality of flavor. *See also* pp.26–7 for more detail and the Flavor Map™ on pp.28–9 in the What is Whisky? section at the front of the book.

FRUITY & SPICY

The fruit we are talking about here is ripe orchard fruit, like peach and apricot, maybe even something more exotic like mango. These whiskies will also show the vanilla, coconut, custard-like aromas of American oak. The spiciness is found on the finish and tends to be sweet—like cinnamon or nutmeg.

Scotland *Single malt*
Aberfeldy 12yo
Aberfeldy 21yo
Aberlour 12yo non chill-filtered
Aberlour 16yo Double Cask
Abhainn Dearg
Arran 10yo
Arran 12yo cask strength
Auchentoshan 21yo
Balblair 1990
Balblair 1975
Balmenach 1993
Balmenach 1979
The Balvenie 12yo Double Wood
The Balvenie 14yo Caribbean Cask
The Balvenie 21yo Portwood
The Balvenie 30yo
Ben Nevis 10yo
The BenRiach 12yo
The BenRiach 16yo
The BenRiach 20yo
The BenRiach 21yo
Benromach 10yo
Benromach 25yo
Benromach 30yo
Bowmore 46yo, Distilled 1964
Cardhu Amber Rock
Cardhu 18yo
Craigellachie 14yo
Craigellachie 1994 Gordon & MacPhail Bottling
Clynelish 14yo
Clynelish 1997, Manager's Choice
Dalmore 12yo
Dalwhinnie 15yo
Dalwhinnie Distiller's Edition
Dalwhinnie 1992, Manager's Choice
Dalwhinnie 1986, 20yo Special Release
Deanston 12yo
Glencadam 15yo
The Singleton of Glendullan 12yo
Glen Elgin 12yo
Glenfiddich 21yo

Glen Garioch 12yo
Glenglassaugh Evolution
Glenglassaugh Revival
Glengoyne 10yo
Glengoyne 15yo
Glenkinchie Distiller's Edition
The Glenlivet 15yo
The Glenlivet Archive 21yo
Glenmorangie The Original 10yo
Glenmorangie 18yo
Glenmorangie 25yo
Glen Moray Classic NAS
Glen Moray 12yo
Glen Moray 16yo
Glen Moray 30yo
The Glenrothes Extraordinary Cask 1969
The Glenrothes Elder's Reserve
The Glenrothes Select Reserve NAS
Hazelburn 12yo
Inchgower 14yo
Inchmurrin 12yo
Kilkerran Work In Progress No.4
Kininvie Batch Number One 23yo
Loch Lomond Inchmurrin 12yo
Loch Lomond 1966 Stills
Longmorn 16yo
Longmorn 1977
Longmorn 33yo
Macallan Gold
Macallan Amber
Macallan 15yo Fine Oak
Mannochmore 18yo Special Release
Oban 14yo
Old Pulteney 12yo
Old Pulteney 17yo
Old Pulteney 30yo
Old Pulteney 40yo
Royal Brackla 25yo
Royal Lochnagar 12yo
Scapa 16yo
Scapa 1979
Strathisla 18yo
Tomatin 18yo
Tomatin 30yo
Tomintoul 33yo
Tormore 12yo
Tullibardine Burgundy Finish

Scotland *Blend*
Antiquary 12yo
Buchanan's 12yo
Dewar's White Label
The Famous Grouse

Grant's Family Reserve
Great King Street

Scotland *Grain*
Cameron Brig
Haig Club

Ireland *Malt*
Tullamore D.E.W. Single Malt 10yo

Ireland *Blend*
Cooley, Kilbeggan
Green Spot
Jameson 12yo
Powers 12yo
Tullamore D.E.W. 12yo Special Reserve

Ireland *Single pot still*
Green Spot
Midleton Barry Crockett Legacy
Power's John Lane's

Japan *Malt*
Chichibu Port Pipe 2009
Chichibu Chibidaru 2009
Komagatake Single Malt
Miyagikyo 15yo
Miyagikyo 1990 18yo
Yamazaki 12yo

Japan *Grain*
Miyagikyo Nikka Single Cask Coffey Malt

Japan *Blend*
Hibiki 12yo
Hibiki 17yo
Nikka, From The Barrel

Rest of the World *Malt*
Adnams, Spirit of Broadside *UK*
Amrut, Fusion *India*
Amrut, Greedy Angels *India*
Arcus Gjoleid, Ex-Bourbon Cask, 3.5yo *Norway*
Arcus Gjoleid, Sherry Cask 3.5yo *Norway*
Bakery Hill Double Wood *Australia*
The Belgian Owl *Belgium*
The Belgian Owl, Single Cask #4275922 *Belgium*
Brauenstein e:1 Single Sherry Cask *Denmark*
Brenne *France*

Finch, Dinkel, Port 2013 *Germany*
Finch, Classic *Germany*
George Dickel 12yo *USA*
Haider, J.H. single malt *Austria*
Haider, J.H. single malt, Karamell *Austria*
Hellyer's Road, Pinot Noir Finish *Australia*
Kavalan Classic *Taiwan*
Kavalan Solist, Single Cask Ex-bourbon *Taiwan*
Langatun, Old Deer *Switzerland*
Langatun, Old Bear *Switzerland*
Lehmann Elsass Single Malt (50%) *France*
Liebl, Coillmór, Port Cask *Germany*
Mackmyra Midvinter *Sweden*
Meyer's (blend) *France*
Millstone 10yo American Oak *Netherlands*
New Holland Zeppelin Bend Straight Malt *USA*
Old Holbart, Overeem Port Cask Matured *Australia*
Paul John Classic Select Cask *India*
Säntis, Edition Sæntis *Switzerland*
Schraml, Drà *Germany*
Stauning, Traditional Oloroso *Denmark*
St George Californian Single Malt *USA*
Stranahan's Colorado Straight Malt Whiskey *USA*
Sullivan's Cove, French Oak Cask Matured *Australia*
Teerenpeli Kaski *Finland*
Telser, Telsington VI, 5yo Single Malt *Liechenstein*
Telser, Telsington Black Edition, 5yo *Liechenstein*
Three Ships 10yo *South Africa*
Westland Deacon Seat *USA*
Westland Flagship *USA*
Westland Cask 29 *USA*

Rest of the World *Grain*
Bain's Cape Mountain *South Africa*

FRAGRANT & FLORAL

The aromas found in these whiskies bring to mind freshly cut flowers, fruit blossom, cut grass, and light green fruit. On the palate they are light, slightly sweet, and often with a fresh acidity.

Scotland *Single malt*
Allt-a-Bhainne 1991
anCnoc 16yo
Ardmore 1977, 30yo, Old Malt
   Cask Bottling
Arran 14yo
Arran, Robert Burns
Bladnoch 8yo
Bladnoch 17yo
Braeval 8yo
Bruichladdich Islay Barley 5yo
Bruichladdich The Laddie 10yo
Cardhu 12yo
Glenburgie 12yo
Glenburgie 15yo
Glencadam 10yo
Glendullan12yo
Glenfiddich 12yo
Glen Grant 10yo
Glen Grant Major's Reserve
Glen Grant V (Five) Decades

Glen Keith 17yo
Glenkinchie 12yo
Glenkinchie 1992, Manager's
   Choice Single Cask
The Glenlivet 12yo
Glenlossie 1999,
   Manager's Choice
Glen Scotia 10yo
Glentauchers 1991 Gordon &
   MacPhail Bottling
The Glenturret 10yo
Linkwood 12yo
Loch Lomond Rosdhu
Loch Lomond 12yo Organic
   Single Blend
Loch Lomond 29yo, WM
   Cadenhead Bottling
Mannochmore 12yo
Miltonduff 18yo
Miltonduff 1976
Speyburn 10yo
Speyside 15yo
Strathisla 12yo
Strathmill 12yo
Teaninich 10yo Flora & Fauna
Tomatin 12yo
Tomintoul 14yo
Tormore 1996
Tullibardine Sovereign

Scotland *Blend*
Ballantine's Finest
Chivas Regal 12yo
Cutty Sark

Scotland *Grain*
Girvan 'Over 25yo'
Strathclyde 12yo

Ireland *Malt*
Bushmills 10yo

Ireland *Blend*
Bushmills Original
Jameson Original
Tullamore D.E.W.

Japan *Malt*
Ichiro's Malt Chichibu On The Way
Fuji-Gotemba Fuji Sanroku 18yo
Fuji-Gotemba 18yo
Hakushu 12yo
Hakushu 18yo
White Oak 5yo
Yamazaki 10yo

Japan *Blend*
Eigashima, White Oak 5yo
Nikka Super

Rest of the World *Malt*
Bakery Hill, Single Malt *Australia*
Collingwood, Canadian Mist
   Canada
Domaine des Hautes Glaces S11
   #01 *France*
Domaine des Hautes Glaces L10
   #03 *France*
Glann ar Mor Taol Esa 2 Gwech
   2013 *France*
High West Silver Western Oat *USA*
High West Valley Tan Oat *USA*
Mackmyra Brukswhisky *Sweden*
New Holland Bill's Michigan
   Wheat *USA*
Penderyn Madeira *Wales*
Puni, Alba *Italy*
Radermacher, Lambertus 10yo
   Belgium
St. George Lot 13 *USA*
Slyrs 2010 *Germany*
Spirit of Hven No.1, Dubhe *Sweden*
Spirit of Hven No2, Merak *Sweden*
Still Waters Stalk & Barrel, Cask #2
   Canada
Teerenpeli, Aës *Finland*

RICH & ROUND

There is fruit here as well, but now it is dried: raisin, fig, date, and white raisin. This shows the use of European oak ex-sherry casks. You might detect a slightly finer feel: those are the tannins from the oak. These are deep whiskies, sometimes sweet, sometimes meaty.

Scotland *Single malt*
Aberlour 10yo
Aberlour A'bunadh, Batch 45
Aberlour 18yo
Aultmore 16yo, Dewar Rattray
The Balvenie 17yo Double Wood
Ben Nevis 25yo
Benrinnes 15yo Flora & Fauna
Benrinnes 23yo
Benromach 1981 Vintage
Blair Athol 12yo Flora & Fauna
Bruichladdich Black Art 4 23yo
Bunnahabhain 12yo
Bunnahabhain 18yo
Bunnahabhain 25yo
Cragganmore Distiller's Edition

Cragganmore 12yo
Dalmore 15yo
Dalmore 1981 Matusalem
Dailuaine 16yo
The Singleton of Dufftown 12yo
The Singleton of Dufftown 15yo
Edradour 1997
Edradour 1996 Oloroso Finish
Fettercairn 16yo
Fettercairn 30yo
Glenallachie 18yo
Glencadam 1978
The GlenDronach 12yo
The GlenDronach 18yo Allardice
The GlenDronach 21yo
   Parliament
Glenfarclas 10yo
Glenfarclas 15yo
Glenfarclas 30yo
Glenfiddich 15yo
Glenfiddich 18yo
Glenfiddich 30yo
Glenfiddich 40yo
Glenglassaugh 30yo
Glengoyne 21yo
The Glenlivet 18yo
The Singleton of Glen Ord 12yo

Highland Park 18yo
Highland Park 25yo
Jura 16yo
Macallan Ruby
Macallan Sienna
Macallan 18yo Sherry Oak
Macallan 25yo Sherry Oak
Mortlach Rare Old
Mortlach 25yo
Royal Lochnagar
   Selected Reserve
Speyburn 21yo
Strathisla 25yo
Tamdhu 10yo
Tamdhu 18yo
Tobermory 15yo
Tobermory 32yo

Scotland *Blend*
Johnnie Walker Black Label
Old Parr 12yo

Ireland *Malt/Pot still*
Bushmills 16yo
Bushmills 21yo Cask Finish
Redbreast 12yo
Redbreast 15yo

Ireland *Blend*
Black Bush
Jameson 18yo
Tullamore D.E.W. Phoenix
   Sherry Finish

Japan *Malt*
Hakushu 25yo
Karuizawa 1985
Karuizawa 1995 Noh Series
Yamazaki 18yo

Rest of the World
Amrut, Intermediate Cask *India*
Balcones Straight Malt V *USA*
Kavalan Fino Cask *Taiwan*
Liber, Embrujo *Spain*
Millstone 1999, PX cask *Netherlands*
New Holland Beer Barrel Bourbon
   USA
Old Holbart, Overeem Sherry Cask
   Matured *Australia*
Penderyn Sherrywood *Wales*
Säntis Alpstein VII *Switzerland*
Warenghem Armorik Double
   Maturation *France*

SMOKY & PEATY

These offer a range of aromas, from soot to Lapsang souchong, tar, kippers, smoked bacon, burning heather, and wood smoke. Often slightly oily in texture, all peaty whiskies must have a balancing sweet spot.

Scotland *Single malt*
Ardbeg 10yo
Ardbeg Corryvreckan
Ardbeg Uigeadail
Ardmore Traditional Cask NAS
Ardmore 25yo
The BenRiach Curiositas 10yo

The BenRiach Septendecim 17yo
The BenRiach Authenticus 25yo
Bowmore Devil's Cask 10yo
Bowmore 12yo
Bowmore 15yo Darkest
Bruichladdich Octomore 'Comus' 4.2
   2007 5yo

Bruichladdich Port Charlotte PC8
Bruichladdich Port Charlotte
   Scottish Barley
Bunnahabhain Toiteach
Caol Ila 12yo
Caol Ila 18yo
Highland Park 12yo

Highland Park 40yo
Kilchoman Machir Bay
Kilchoman 2007
Lagavulin 12yo
Lagavulin 16yo
Lagavulin 21yo
Lagavulin Distiller's Edition
Laphroaig 10yo
Laphroaig 18yo
Laphroaig 25yo
Longrow 14yo

Longrow 18yo
Springbank 10yo
Springbank 15yo
Talisker Storm
Talisker 10yo
Talisker 18yo
Talisker 25yo
Tomatin Cú Bòcan

Ireland *Malt*
Cooley, Connemara 12yo

Japan *Malt*
The Cask of Hakushu
Yoichi 10yo
Yoichi 12yo
Yoichi 15yo
Yoichi 20yo
Yoichi 1986 22yo

Rest of the World *Malt*
Balcones Brimstone Resurrection V *USA*
Bakery Hill, Peated Malt *Australia*

Clear Creek, McCarthy's Oregon
  Single Malt *USA*
Hellyer's Road, Peated *Australia*
Kornog, Sant Ivy *France*
Kornog, Taouarc'h *France*
Mackmyra Svensk Rök *Sweden*
Paul John Peated Select Cask *India*
Smögen Primör *Sweden*
Stauning, Peated Oloroso *Denmark*
Westland First Peated *USA*

MALTY & DRY

These whiskies are drier on the nose. Crisp, cookie-like, and sometimes dusty with aromas that remind you of flour, breakfast cereal, and nuts. The palate is also dry but is normally balanced by sweet oak.

Scotland *Single malt*
Auchentoshan Classic NAS

Auchentoshan 12yo
Auchroisk 10yo
Glen Garioch Founder's Reserve
  NAS
Glen Scotia 12yo
Glen Spey 12yo
Knockando 12yo
Loch Lomond Single Malt NAS
Macduff 1984 Berry Bros & Rudd
  Bottling
Speyside 12yo

Tamnavulin 12yo
Tomintoul 10yo
Tullibardine 20yo

Japan *Malt*
Chichibu The Floor Malted 3yo

Rest of the World *Malt*
Blaue Maus Grüner Hund, Single
  Cask *Germany*
Blaue Maus Spinnaker 20yo *Germany*

Hellyer's Road, Original 10yo
  Australia
Hudson Single Malt, Tuthilltown *USA*
Lehmann Elsass single malt (40%)
  France
Liebl, Coillmór, American Oak
  Germany
Meyer's Pur Malt *France*
Teerenpeli 6yo *Finland*
Teerenpeli 8yo *Finland*

RYE-, WHEAT-, AND CORN-BASED WHISKIES

Different production processes and grains mean that different Flavor Camps have been created for North American (or North American-style) whiskeys. Where the whiskey is part of the distillery family, e.g. Jack Daniel's Black Label, the distillery name comes first. Where the whiskey is produced by a specific distillery, e.g. Buffalo Trace produces Blanton's Single Barrel, the distillery name follows the whiskey name.

SOFT CORN

The main cereal used in bourbon and Canadian whisky, corn gives a sweet nose and a fat, buttery and juicy quality on the palate.

Balcones Baby Blue *USA*
Black Velvet *Canada*
Blanton's Single Barrel, Buffalo Trace
  Buffalo Trace *USA*
Canadian Club 1858 *Canada*
Canadian Mist *Canada*
Danfield's 10yo, Black Velvet *Canada*
Danfield's 21yo, Black Velvet *Canada*
Early Times *USA*
Forty Creek Barrel Select *Canada*
Forty Creek Copper Pot Reserve
  Canada
Four Roses Yellow Label *USA*
George Dickel Superior No.12 *USA*
George Dickel 8yo *USA*
George Dickel Barrel Select *USA*
Crown Royal, Gimli *Canada*

Crown Royal Reserve, Gimli *Canada*
Highwood Century Reserve 21yo
  Canada
Hudson Baby Bourbon,
  Tuthilltown *USA*
Hudson Four Grain Bourbon,
  Tuthilltown *USA*
Hudson New York Corn,
  Tuthilltown *USA*
Jack Daniel's Black Label,
  Old No.7 *USA*
Jack Daniel's Gentleman Jack *USA*
Jack Daniel's Single Barrel *USA*
Jim Beam Black Label 8yo *USA*
Jim Beam White Label *USA*
Pike Creek 10yo, Hiram Walker
  Canada
Wild Turkey 81° *USA*
Wild Turkey 101° *USA*
Wiser's Deluxe, Hiram Walker
  Canada

SWEET WHEAT

Wheat is occasionally used by bourbon distillers in place of rye. This adds a gentle, mellow sweetness to the bourbon.

Bernheim Original Wheat, Heaven
  Hill *USA*
Highwood, Centennial 10yo *Canada*
Highwood White Owl *Canada*
Last Mountain Private Reserve *Canada*
Maker's Mark *USA*
Schraml Woaz *Germany*
W L Weller 12yo, Buffalo Trace *USA*

RICH & OAKY

The whiskey picks up all of those rich vanilla-accented aromas from its time spent in barrel, along with coconut,

pine, cherry, and sweet spice. This richness of extract increases in power the longer the bourbon is in cask, giving tobacco and leather flavours.

Alberta Premium 30yo *Canada*
Balcones Straight Bourbon II *USA*
Booker's, Jim Beam *USA*
Canadian Club 20yo *Canada*
Canadian Club 30yo *Canada*
Eagle Rare 10yo Single Barrel,
  Buffalo Trace *USA*
Elijah Craig 12yo, Heaven Hill *USA*
Forty Creek Double Barrel
  Reserve *Canada*
Knob Creek 9yo, Jim Beam *USA*
Maker's 46 *USA*
Old Fitzgerald 12yo, Heaven
  Hill *USA*
Pappy Van Winkle's Family Reserve
  20yo, Buffalo Trace *USA*
Ridgemont Reserve 1792 8yo,
  Barton 1792 *USA*
Russell's Reserve Bourbon 10yo,
  Wild Turkey *USA*
Rare Breed, Wild Turkey *USA*
Wiser's 18yo, Hiram Walker *Canada*

SPICY RYE

Rye can often be picked up on the nose in the shape of intense, slightly perfumed, and sometimes slightly dusty aromas—or an aroma akin to freshly baked rye bread. It appears late-on in the palate after the fat corn and adds an acidic, spiced zestiness that wakes up the palate.

Alberta Premium, 25yo *Canada*
Alberta Springs 10yo *Canada*
Canadian Club Reserve 10yo,
  Canada

Collingwood 21yo, Canadian
  Mist *Canada*
Crown Royal Ltd Edition, Gimli *Canada*
Dark Horse, Alberta *Canada*
Domaine des Hautes Glaces
  Secale *France*
Evan Williams Single Barrel 2004,
  Heaven Hill *USA*
Forty Creek Confederation Reserve
  Canada
Four Roses Barrel Strength 15yo *USA*
Four Roses Brand 12 Single
  Barrel *USA*
Four Roses Brand 3 Small Batch *USA*
Haider J.H. Special Rye 'Nougat'
  Austria
Haider, J.H. Peated Rye malt *Austria*
High West OMG Pure Rye *USA*
High West Rendezvous Rye *USA*
Highwood Ninety, 20yo *Canada*
Hudson Manhattan Rye, Tuthilltown
  USA
George Dickel Rye *USA*
Lot 40, Hiram Walker *Canada*
Millstone Rye 100 *Netherlands*
Old Potrero Rye, Anchor *USA*
Rittenhouse Rye, Heaven Hill *USA*
Russell's Reserve Rye 6yo,
  Wild Turkey *USA*
Sazerac Rye, Buffalo Trace *USA*
Sazerac 18yo, Buffalo Trace *USA*
Seagram VO, Canadian Mist *Canada*
Stauning Young Rye *Denmark*
Telser Rye Single Cask 2yo
  Liechtenstein
Tom Moore 4yo *USA*
Very Old Barton 6yo, Barton
  1792 *USA*
Wiser's Legacy, Hiram Walker
  Canada
Woodford Reserve Distiller's
  Select *USA*

GLOSSARY

Entries in SMALL CAPS are cross-references within the Glossary.

Age statement An age on the label refers to the youngest component. Remember that age is not necessarily a determinant of quality.

ABV (alcohol by volume) The alcoholic content of a whisky expressed as a percentage of the total volume of liquid. By law, Scotch whisky must be 40% abv or more. *See also* PROOF.

Angel's share A cask breathes during MATURATION, so some of the alcohol will evaporate. This is known as the "angel's share." In Scotland, it accounts for a two percent loss of each cask's volume every year.

Backset *See* SOURMASHING.

Barley Barley contains naturally occurring enzymes that, once MALTED, aid in the conversion of starch into fermentable sugars. A percentage of malted barley is therefore added to the MASH of cereals in the production of virtually all types of whisky, while single malt uses 100 percent malted barley.

Barrel Term used to define a 53-gallon (200-liter) American OAK CASK.

Beer (USA) Alcoholic liquid to be distilled, aka WASH.

Beer still (USA) The first still (normally a COLUMN-STILL) in DISTILLATION.

Blended whisky A mix of GRAIN WHISKY with MALT (in Scotland) or BOURBON/RYE (America). Ninety-three percent of the Scotch whisky sold globally is blended.

Bourbon American WHISKEY style, which must conform to the following rules: be made from a MASH containing at least 51% CORN; distilled to a maximum of 80% ABV (160° PROOF); and aged in new CHARRED OAK BARRELS at a strength of no higher than 62.5% ABV (125°) for at least two years.

Butt A 132-gallon (500-liter) ex-sherry CASK used for maturing SCOTCH WHISKY.

Caramel A permitted additive used in many whiskies (but banned in BOURBON production) to adjust the color of the spirit to ensure consistency between batches. Heavy use dulls aroma and gives a bitter finish.

Cask All-encompassing term referring to the different types of OAK containers used for maturing whisky.

Charcoal mellowing This technique, which defines TENNESSEE WHISKEYS, involves passing the new spirit through vats of charcoal prior to aging.

Charring All American BARRELS are charred prior to use, creating a layer of active charcoal that acts as a filter to help remove harshness and other unwanted immature aromas. CHARCOAL MELLOWING accelerates this process.

Clearic *See* NEW MAKE.

Condensing The final part of DISTILLATION where alcohol vapor is turned back into liquid.

Corn The main cereal used in BOURBON production, corn adds a fat sweetness to the final spirit. Also used in Canada and in the production of GRAIN WHISKY.

Corn whiskey American whiskey style. By law, corn whiskey must be made from a minimum of 80 percent corn. No minimum aging requirements.

Dark grains The name for the mix of pot ale (high protein residue after first DISTILLATION) and DRAFF, which is sold as a nutritious animal feed.

Distillation The process that sets spirits apart from wine or beer. Because alcohol boils at a lower temperature than water, if an alcoholic liquid (BEER/WASH) is heated in a still, the alcohol vapor will be driven off in preference to the water, thereby increasing the alcoholic strength and concentrating the flavors contained within the WASH.

Doubler (USA) The simple POT-STILL in which the alcohol from the first DISTILLATION is redistilled to produce the final spirit.

Draff The spent grains that are left after all the sweet liquid (WORTS) has been extracted from the mash tun. It is sold as animal feed.

Dram Though widely thought of as a Scottish term meaning a drink of whisky, "dram" is of Latin origin and refers to a small measure of any spirit.

Drum maltings The most common method of MALTING BARLEY. These huge plants contain large horizontal drums where the green malt GERMINATES.

Esters Chemical compounds created during FERMENTATION. Typically a floral and intensely fruity aroma.

Feints Final alcohols at the end of the second DISTILLATION (aka tails, after-shots).

Fermentation The process by which sugar-rich WORT is converted into alcohol by the addition of YEAST and vital in the creation of flavor.

First-fill A slightly confusing Scottish/Irish/Japanese term, referring to CASKS. When a distiller refers to a barrel as being "first-fill," it means that it is the first time it has been filled with Scotch (or Irish, Japanese etc.) whisky. Because these industries tend to use second-hand CASKS it is not, however, the first time it has been filled. *See also* REFILL.

Floor maltings Traditional way of MALTING barley. The damp grain is spread on a floor and left to GERMINATE, periodically being turned by shovels or plows. Today, floor maltings have been mostly replaced by DRUM MALTINGS. *See also* SALADIN BOX.

Foreshots The first spirit to appear in the final DISTILLATION. Foreshots are high in alcohol, contain volatile compounds, and are redistilled with FEINTS and low wines in the next DISTILLATION (aka HEADS).

Germination Process in which the BARLEY's growth is nurtured during MALTING.

Grain whisky Made from a mix of a small percentage of MALTED BARLEY and either CORN or wheat and distilled to under 94.8% ABV in a column-still. The Scotch Whisky Act decrees that grain must possess the character of the cereal from which it is made.

Heads *See* FORESHOTS.

High wines (USA) The final spirit produced from the second distillation in the DOUBLER (aka doublings).

Hogshead Type of CASK, mostly made from American OAK, with a capacity of 66 gallons (250 liters). (aka hoggies).

Indian whisky A somewhat controversial term because the Indian industry does not conform to the globally recognized definition of whisky being exclusively a cereal-based spirit and permits "whisky" to be made from molasses.

Irish whiskey Although there are only three distilleries operating in Ireland, each makes its whiskey in a different fashion. Cooley uses double DISTILLATION and PEAT. Bushmills uses triple DISTILLATION of unpeated MALTED BARLEY. Irish Distillers produces IRISH POT-STILL whiskey that, though unpeated and triple-distilled, uses a mix of unmalted and MALTED BARLEY in the MASH BILL.

Lincoln County Process The technique that separates TENNESSEE WHISKEY from BOURBON. This involves passing the new spirit through beds of CHARCOAL to remove harsh elements (aka leaching/mellowing).

Liquor (USA) The hot water used in MASHING.

Lomond still A POT-STILL that contains adjustable plates in its neck, which increases REFLUX and gives the resulting spirit a characteristic oily/fruity quality.

Lyne arm/lie pipe Aka swan neck. The top part of a POT-STILL, which leads from the body of the still to the CONDENSER. The angle of the lyne arm will have an impact on the character. An upward angle encourages REFLUX and tends to make a lighter spirit, a downward angle tends to produce a heavier spirit.

Malting The process that makes the starch available to the distiller through steeping the dormant BARLEY in water, GERMINATING it to start growth, and then arresting the barley's growth by drying it in a kiln. This can be done in FLOOR, DRUM, or SALADIN MALTING plants.

Mashing Process by which cereal starch is converted into fermentable sugars.

Mash bill Term used to describe the mix and percentage of different cereals used in whisky-making.

Maturation The final part of the whisky-making process takes place in CASKS and can provide up to 70 percent of a whisky's final flavor (and its color).

Mothballed Term referring to a distillery that has been closed but has not been decommissioned.

NAS Shorthand for a whisky with No Age Statement on the label.

New make An alternative Scottish term for newly distilled spirit. Aka CLEARIC in Scotland and WHITE DOG in the USA.

Oak Legally all Scotch, American, Canadian, and Irish whisk(e)y must be aged in oak BARRELS. During MATURATION, the whisky interacts with the aromatic extractives present in the wood. This interplay between spirit and oak adds to a whisky's complexity.

Peat(ing) Peat plays an important role in the aroma of many whiskies. Semi-carbonized vegetation laid down over thousands of years on wet acidic boggy ground: peat is cut, dried, and then burnt in the kilning process in order to impart a smoky aroma to the final spirit.

Phenols The chemical term for the aromatic compounds given off when PEAT is burnt. They are measured in phenolic parts per million (ppm) and the higher the ppm, the smokier the whisky. The ppm measurement refers to the MALTED BARLEY and not the NEW MAKE spirit. Up to 50 percent of the phenols are lost in the distilling process.

Proof A measurement of alcoholic strength now only used (on labels) by American distillers. American proof is exactly double the ABV (ALCOHOL BY VOLUME) measurement, i.e. 40% ABV equals 80° USA proof.

Pot-still The copper kettle-style stills used in batch DISTILLATION.

Quarter cask Contains 12 gallons (45 liters); its use has been revived recently as a way to inject a large amount of fresh OAK into a young whisky.

Quercus The Latin term for OAK. The most commonly used varieties used in whisky are: *Q. alba* or American white OAK; *Q. robur* or European OAK; *Q. petraea* or *sessile*/French OAK, and *Q. mongolica* or *mizunara*/Japanese OAK. Each has its own range of aromas, flavors, and structure.

Rackhouse American term for a warehouse.

Rancio Tasting term used to describe the exotic, leathery/musky/fungal notes found in very old whiskies.

Refill Term given to CASKS that have been filled once already with SCOTCH WHISKY.

Reflux Technical term referring to the CONDENSING of alcoholic vapor within the still (i.e. prior to it reaching the CONDENSING system), which turns back into liquid and is redistilled. Reflux is one way of lightening the spirit and removing unwanted heavy elements and can be promoted through still shape as well as by the speed of DISTILLATION.

Ricks American term for the wooden supports that whiskey BARRELS lie on during MATURATION. Traditional, tall, metal-sided RACKHOUSES are also called ricked warehouses. Also used to describe the stacks of sugar-maple that are burned to give the active CHARCOAL bed through which TENNESSEE WHISKEY is filtered.

Rye (USA) Cereal used in the production of RYE WHISKEY, BOURBON, and Canadian whisky. Rye gives an acidic, mouthwatering effect, with aromas of sourdough, citrus fruit, and an intense spiciness.

Rye whiskey (USA) Legally a rye whiskey is one made from a MASH BILL containing a minimum of 51 percent rye, which conforms to the regulations governing (USA) STRAIGHT WHISKEY.

Scotch whisky Must be produced in Scotland at a distillery, from MALTED BARLEY (to which other whole cereals can be added) which is then MASHED,

converted to a fermentable liquid through the BARLEY'S own enzymes, FERMENTED with YEAST, distilled to less than 94.8% ABV, matured in Scotland in OAK CASKS not exceeding 185 gallons (700 liters) in size for a minimum of three years and bottled at no less than 40% ABV. Nothing other than water and spirit CARAMEL are permitted to be added.

Saladin box A method of MALTING that sits halfway between a traditional FLOOR MALTINGS and a modern DRUM MALTINGS, in which the GERMINATING BARLEY is placed in a large open-topped box and turned using a screw mechanism.

Single barrel (USA) A slightly confusing term; the whiskey in the bottle comes from a single BARREL, but each batch of a single BARREL whiskey may comprise more than one BARREL.

Sourmash(ing) (USA) The non-alcoholic liquid residue left at the end of the first DISTILLATION, which is then added to the mash in the fermenter. This can make up to 25 percent or more of the total liquid in the fermenter. Adding this souring agent to the mash eases FERMENTATION. Every BOURBON/TENNESSEE WHISKEY is sourmashed (aka BACKSET, spent beer, stillage).

Straight whiskey (USA) Any whiskey made from a minimum of 51 percent of any one grain (corn, rye, wheat) distilled to 160° PROOF (80% ABV), aged at no more than 125° PROOF (62.5% ABV) for a minimum of two years in new CHARRED OAK BARRELS and bottled at a min of 80° PROOF (40% ABV). No CARAMEL addition or flavor enhancement is allowed.

Tennessee whiskey Is controlled by the same regulations as BOURBON, but distillers in Tennessee filter the new spirit through beds of maple CHARCOAL (aka the LINCOLN COUNTY PROCESS).

Thumper Another name for a DOUBLER. The thumper is filled with water through which the low wines pass—a process that helps remove some of the heavier alcohols. As it does, it makes a "thumping" sound.

Toasting Involves heating the staves of the CASK over a fire to make them more pliable. The heat also caramelizes the complex wood sugars in the OAK. It is these sugars that interact with the spirit to produce a complex mature whisky. By varying the level of toasting, distillers can create a wide range of effects.

Uisce beatha/Usquebaugh Scottish/Irish Gaelic terms for whisky; translates as "water of life"—the term that has long been given to distilled spirits. It is widely believed that "uisce" was the root of "whisky."

Vatted malt Archaic term meaning a mix of single malts. *See* BLENDED WHISKY.

Vendome still Type of POT-STILL with a rectifying column in the neck.

Viscimetry The coils and eddies that appear in whisky when water is added.

Wash The fermented liquid (aka BEER) that is distilled into whisky.

Wash-still The first still in batch DISTILLATION, where the fermented WASH is DISTILLED.

Wheated bourbon A BOURBON whose MASH BILL contains wheat instead of rye. This gives a generally sweeter character.

Whiskey/whisky By law Scotch, Canadian, and Japanese whisky are spelled without an E, while Irish and American have an E, though not all American whiskeys conform to this.

White dog American term for NEW MAKE.

Worm (tub) The traditional manner of CONDENSING spirit. The "worm" is a coil of copper that is immersed in a vat of cold water. Because of the lower level of copper interaction that takes place in this method, worm tub whiskies tend to be heavier in character.

Worts The sweet liquid that is drawn off from the mash tun.

Yeast The micro-organisms that convert sugar into alcohol (plus carbon dioxide and heat). Different YEAST strains (types) will have an impact on flavor production.

BIBLIOGRAPHY

BOOKS

Barnard, Alfred, *The Whisky Distilleries of the United Kingdom,* David & Charles, 1969

Buxton, Ian, *The Enduring Legacy of Dewar's,* Angel's Share, 2010

Checkland, Olive, *Japanese Whisky, Scottish Blend,* Scottish Cultural Press, 1998

Dillon, Patrick, *The Much-Lamented Death of Madam Geneva,* Review, 2004

Kaiser, Roman, *Meaningful Scents Around The World,* Wiley, 2006

Gibbon, Lewis Grassic *A Scots Quair* Canongate Books, 2008

Gunn, Neil M., *Whisky & Scotland,* Souvenir Press Ltd, 1977

Hardy, Thomas, *The Return of the Native,* Everyman's Library, 1992

Hume, John R., & Moss, Michael, *The Making of Scotch Whisky,* Canongate Books, 2000

Macdonald, Aeneas, *Whisky,* Canongate Books, 2006

MacFarlane Robert, *The Wild Places,* Granta Books, 2007

MacLean, Charles, *Scotch Whisky: A Liquid History,* Cassell, 2003

Marcus, Greil, *Invisible Republic, Bob Dylan's Basement Tapes,* Picador, 1997

McCreary, Alf, *Spirit of the Age, the Story of old Bushmills,* Blackstaff Press, 1983

MacDiarmid, Hugh, *Selected Essays,* University of California Press, 1970

Mulryan, Peter, *The Whiskeys of Ireland,* O'Brien Press, 2002

Owens Bill, *Modern Moonshine Techniques,* White Mule Press, 2009

Owens Bill, Diktyt, Alan, & Maytag, Fritz, *The Art of Distilling Whiskey and Other Spirits,* Quarry Books, 2009

Pacult, F. Paul, *A Double Scotch,* John Wiley, 2005

Penguin Press & Carson, *The Tain,* Penguin Classics, 2008

Regan, Gary, & Regan, Mardee, *The Book of Bourbon,* Chapters, 1995

Udo, Misako, *The Scotch Whisky Distilleries,* Black & White, 2007

Waymack, Mark H., & Harris, James F, *The Book of Classic American Whiskeys,* Open Court, 1995

Wilson, Neil, *The Island Whisky Trail,* Angel's Share, 2003

MAGAZINES

Whisky Magazine
Whisky Advocate

MUSIC

"Copper Kettle," written by Albert Frank Beddoe, recorded by Bob Dylan on the 1970 album, *Self Portrait*

Smith, Harry *Anthology of American Folk Music,* various volumes

FURTHER INFORMATION

Keep in touch with whisky matters through the net. The vast majority of producers have their own websites these days. Here is a selection of magazines and blogs giving the whisky-lover a broader perspective.

MAGAZINES

www.whiskyadvocate.com
www.whatdoesjohnknow.com
www.whiskymag.com
www.whiskymagjapan.com *in Japanese*

WHISKY SITES & BLOGS

www.maltmaniacs.org, *This should be the first stop for all malt lovers.*

www.whiskyfun.com, *Serge Valentin's daily musings on whisky and music.*

www.whiskycast.com, *Mark Gillespie's weekly podcast.*

www.edinburghwhiskyblog.com & http://caskstrength.blogspot.com, *Two UK-based blogs—both are worth checking regularly.*

http://chuckcowdery.blogspot.com, *Want to find out what's happening bourbon-wise? Check Chuck!*

http://nonjatta.blogspot.com, *The must-visit blog for lovers of Japanese whisky (in English).*

http://drwhisky.blogspot.com, *Sam Simmons was one of the first bloggers and is still one of the best.*

www.irishwhiskeynotes.com, *As it says, this covers Irish whiskey.*

www.irelandwhiskeytrail.com, *Want a tour around Ireland's whiskey related sites? Stop here first.*

www.distilling.com & http://blog.distilling.com, *Keep abreast of news from the world of American craft distilling.*

www.drinkology.com, *Bartender community site that is packed with information.*

FESTIVALS

You can guarantee that as you are reading this there will be one or probably more whisky festivals happening somewhere in the world. The largest global franchise is *Whisky Live!* (www.whiskylive.com). *Malt Advocate* also runs America's largest events, so check its website (*see* above) for details. Also, check the Malt Maniacs' calendar of whisky events on its site (*see* above).

REGIONAL FESTIVALS

Spirit of Speyside, www.spiritofspeyside.com, *Usually the first week of May for one week.*

Fèis Ìle, www.theislayfestival.co.uk, *Usually last week of May for one week.*

Kentucky Bourbon Festival, www.kybourbonfestival.com, *Mid-September.*

INDEX

PICTURE CREDITS

Mitchell Beazley would like to acknowledge and thank all the whisky distillers
and their agents who have so kindly contributed images to this book.

Abhainn Dearg Distillery 177; **Steve Adams** 20bl; **age fotostock** Marco Cristofori 102r; **Alamy** Stuart Black 294r; Paul Bock 62b, 93a; *Bon Appétit* 131a; Cephas Picture Library 52b, 66b, 130b, 163r, 178b, 250–1; Derek Croucher 284–5; Andrew Crowhurst 184; Design Pics Inc. 160–1; DGB 100–1; DigitalDarrell 231; Epicscotland 6; Michele Falzone 210–11; Stuart Forster India 314b; Les Gibbon 20–1; David Gowans 70–1; Simon Grosset 151; Peter Horree 186b, 248; Chris Howes/Wild Places Photography 255l; David Hutt 12–13; Image Management 303; Jason Ingram 136–7; André Jenny 232–3; Tom Kidd 94r; Terrance Klassen 268–9; Bruce McGowan 118r; John Macpherson 56b, 150; mediasculp 308b; nagelestock.com 30–1; Jim Nicholson 152–3; Noble Images 140–1; Oaktree Photographic 124–5; David Osborn 64b; John Peter 34; Rabh images 253a; Jiri Rezac 65a; Mike Rex 35; Scottish Viewpoint 36–7, 53a; South West Images Scotland 24–5, 142–3; Jeremy Sutton-Hibbert 26–7; Transient Light 84–5; Patrick Ward 179a; Margaret Welby 164–5; Wilmar Photography 24; Andrew Woodley 233a; Ian Woolcock 318b; **La Alazana** 313; **Alberta Springs Distillery** 272; **Amrut Distilleries** 314a, 316; **Angus Dundee Distillers** 41, 116; **Arcaid** Keith Hunter/architect Austin-Smith:Lord 90; **Ardbeg Distillery** 154, 155b; **Bakery Hill Distillery** 322; **Balcones Distilling** 262; **Beam Global** 119, 158a, 159b, 203, 204, 244–5; **Ben Nevis Distillery** 139, Alex Gillespie 143a; **The BenRiach Distillery Co** 88–9, 120; **Benromach Distillery Co** 96; **Bladnoch Distillery** 148–9; **Box Destilleri**/Peter Söderlind 305b, 306a; **Dave Broom** 23, 158b, 159a, 227a; **Brown-Forman** 236–7, Brown-Forman Consolidated 278; **Bruichladdich Distillery** 168, 169a; **Buffalo Trace Distillery** 242–3; **Burn Stewart Distillers** 5, 104, 162, 176; **Canadian Club** 277; **Celtic Whisky Compagnie** Glann ar Mor 290; **Chichibu Distillery** 221; **Chivas Brothers** 40, 42a, 43b, 56a, 57, 72, 73ar, 74r, 87, 95, 97, 183r, 193r; **Constellation Brands Inc.** 274a; **Corbis** Atlantide Phototravel 282–3; Jonathan Andrew 198–9; Gary Braasch 22bl; Creasource 22 bcl; Marco Cristofori 7; Macduff Everton 155a, 167a, 201a; Patrick Frilet 295bl; Raymond Gehman 22bcl; Philip Gould 19; Bob Krist 196; Kevin R Morris 240b, 250–1; Studio MPM 22cc; L Nicoloso/photocuisine 22acc; Richard T Nowitz 194–5; Keren Su 22br; Sandro Vannini 46b; Michael S Yamashita 212; **Corsair Distillery** 261; **Daftmill Distillery** 145; **John Dewar & Sons** 60, 61, 74l, 98, 106–7, 109, 114–5, 127, 191, 192; **Diageo** 44–5, 46a, 47a, 48, 50, 51, 54b, 55, 68a, 69, 73al & b, 75b, 83b, 86, 91, 92a, 93b, 110b, 111–13, 128, 133, 138, 144, 146, 156–7, 163l, 178a, 179b, 199l, 254a; Bushmills 200, 201b, 207b; Diageo Canada 275; **Dingle Distillery** 206; **Drinksology.com** 202a; **Echlinville Distillery**/Niall Little 202b; **The Edrington Group** 49, 58a, 59, 108, 182, 183l & c, 190; **Eigashima Shuzo Co** 223; **The English Whisky Co** 288; **Fary Lochan Distillery** 308a; **Finch ® Whisky** 299; **Floki** Egill Gauti Thorkelsson 311; **Fotolia** Tomo Jesenicnik 22ar; Jeffrey Studio 22acr; Kavita 22bcr; Mikael Mir 22al; Monkey Business 22ac; Taratorki 22acl; Vely 22bcr; **Four Roses Distillery** 246; **Getty Images** Best View Stock 317r; Britain on View/David Noton 32; Cavan Images 258; R Creation 224b; David Henderson 135r; Marc Leman 122; Sven Nackstrand/AFP 307b; Warrick Page 8–9; Time & Life Pictures 249; **Glen Grant Distillery** 76–9; **William Grant & Sons Distillers** 62–3, 64a, 65b, 66a, 67,199r, 205; **Glen Moray Distillery** 94l; **Glenmorangie plc** 130a, 131b; **The Glenrothes** 80–81; **Great Southern Distilling Co** 318a; **J Haider Distillery** 302; **Heaven Hill Distilleries Inc.** 240a, 241; **Hellyers Road Distillery**/Rob Burnett 320–1, 323; **Hemis.fr** Bertrand Gardel 291; **High West Distillery and Saloon** 264; **Highwood Distillers** 273; **Ian Macleod Distillers Limited** 11, 102l; **Inver House Distillers** 121, 132, 135l; **Irish Distillers Pernod Ricard** 207–9; **Isle of Arran Distillers** 174; **J & G Grant Glenfarclas** 52a, 53b; **Jack Daniel's Distillery** 252, 253b; **The James Sedgwick Distillery** 312; **Jenny Karlsson** 185; **Karuizawa Distillery** 220; **Kavalan Distillery** 317l; **Davin de Kergommeaux** 274b; **Kilchoman Distillery** 169b; **Kings County Distillery** 260a, Christopher Talbot 260b; **Kittling Ridge Estates Wines & Spirits** 279b; **Langatun Distillery** 300; **Lark Distillery** 322–3; **Last Mountain Distillery** 281b; **Destilerías Líber S.L.** 295a & br; **Loch Lomond Distillers** 103, 189a; **Mackmyra Svensk Whisky** 307; **Maker's Mark Distillery Inc.** 234, 235b; **Morrison Bowmore Distillers** 118l, 147, 166, 167b; **New Holland Brewing Co.** 263; **The Nikka Whisky Distilling Company** 218–9, 224a, 225a; **Okanagan Spirits** 281a; **The Owl Distillery** 294l; **Paragraph Publishing Ltd.**/*Whisky Magazine* 82l, 136a, 225b; **John Paul Photography** 42b, 43a; **Puni Destillerie** 301; **Robert Harding Picture Library**/Robert Francis 228–9; **Will Robb** 2; **Sazerac Company Inc.** 247; **Bernhard Schäfer**/Blaue Maus 296a, 297b; **Shutterstock** konzpetm 296b; Nikolay Neveshkin 193c; Stanimire G Stoev 59a; **Signatory Vintage Scotch Whisky Co**/Edradour Distillery 110a; **Slyrs** 297a; **Smögen Whisky** 306b; **Speyside Distillers** 38; **Spirit of Hven Backafallsbyn** 305a; **Christine Spreiter** 170, 172–3; **Springbank Distillers** 186a, 187–8, 189b; **St George Spirits Inc.** 266–7; **Stauning Whisky** 309; **Still Waters Distillery** 280; **Suntory Liquors** 214–17, 226, 227b; **SuperStock** 222b; **Teerenpeli Distillery & Brewery** 310; **Tomatin Distillery** 126; **Tullibardine Distillery** 105; **Tuthilltown Spirits** 259; **The Welsh Whisky Co. Ltd.** 289; **Westland Distillery** 265; **The Whisky Couple Hans & Becky Offringa** 38c, 54ar, 82r, 180–1, 254b, 255r, Robin Brilleman 39, 68b, 83r, 92b; **The Whisky Exchange** 73a, 75a, 83a, 139l; **Whyte and Mackay Ltd.** 117, 129, 175; **Wild Turkey** 238–9; **J P Wiser's** 276; **Wolfburn** 134; **Zuidam Distillers B.V.** 293.

ACKNOWLEDGMENTS

Scotland Nick Morgan, Craig Wallace, Douglas Murray, Jim Beveridge, Donald Renwick, Shane Healy, Diageo; Jim Long, Alan Winchester, Sandy Hyslop, Chivas Brothers; Gerry Tosh, George Espie, Gordon Motion, Max MacFarlane, Jason Craig, Ken Grier, Bob Dalgarno, The Edrington Group; David Hume, Brian Kinsman, William Grant & Sons; Stephen 'The Stalker' Marshall, Keith Geddes, John Dewar & Sons; Iain Baxter, Stuart Harvey, Inver House Distillers; Ian MacMillan, Burn Stewart Distillers; Ronnie Cox, David King, Sandy Coutts, The Glenrothes; Iain Weir, Iain MacLeod; Gavin Durnin, Loch Lomond Distillers; Frank McHardy, Pete Currie, J & A Mitchell; Euan Mitchell, Arran Distillers; Iain McCallum, Morrison Bowmore Distillers; Jim McEwan, Bruichladdich; Anthony Wills, Kilchoman; Richard Paterson, David Robertson, Whyte & Mackay; Jim Grierson, Maxxium UK; John Campbell, Laphroaig; Des McCagherty, Edradour; George Grant, J & G Grant; Lorne McKillop, Angus Dundee; Billy Walker, Alan McConnochie, Stewart Buchanan, The BenRiach/The GlenDronach; Francis Cuthbert, Daftmill; Raymond Armstrong, Bladnoch; Alistair Longwell, Ardmore; David Urquhart, Ian Chapman, Gordon & MacPhail; Bill Lumsden, Annabel Meikle, Glenmorangie; Michelle Williams, Lime PR; John Black, James Robertson, Tullibardine; Colin Ross, Ben Nevis; Dennis Malcolm, Glen Grant; Stephen Bremner, Tomatin; Andy Shand, Speyburn; Marko Tayburn, Abhainn Dearg.

Ireland Barry Crockett, Brendan Monks, Billy Leighton, David Quinn, Jayne Murphy, IDL; Colum Egan, Helen Mulholland, Bushmills; Noel Sweeney, Cooley.

Japan Keita Minari, Mike Miyamoto; Shinji Fukuyo, Seiichi Koshimizu, Suntory; Naofumi Kamiguchi, Geraldine Landier, Nikka; Ichiro Akuto, Venture Whisky.

The USA & Canada Chris Morris, Jeff Arnett, Brown-Forman; Jane Conner, Maker's Mark; Larry Kass, Parker Beam, Craig Beam, Heaven Hill, Katie Young, Ernie Lubbers, Jim Beam; Jim Rutledge, Four Roses; Jimmy & Eddie Russell, Wild Turkey; Harlen Wheatley, Angela Traver, Buffalo Trace; Ken Pierce, Old Tom Moore; Jim Boyko, Vincent deSouza, Crown Royal; John Hall, Forty Creek; Bill Owens; Lance Winters, St. George; Steve McCarthy, McCarthy's; Marko Karakasevic, Charbay; Jess Graber, Stranahan's; Rick Wasmund, Copper Fox, Ralph Erenzo, Tuthilltown.

Wales Stephen Davis, Gillian Macdonald, Welsh Whisky Company.

England Andrew Nelstrop, The English Whisky Company.

Globally Jean Donnay; Patrick van Zuidam; Etiene Bouillon; Lars Lindberger; Henric Molin; Anssi Pyysing; Michael Poulsen; Fran Peregrino; Andy Watts; Moritz Kallmeyer, Bill Lark, Patrick Maguire, Keith Batt, Mark Littler, David Baker, Cameron Syme; Ian Chang.

The snappers John Paul, Hans Offringa, Will Robb, Christine Spreiter, Jeremy Sutton-Hibbert, and also to Tim, Arthur & Keir and Joynson the Fish for stepping in with photos when distillers admitted they didn't have shots of their products.

Personal Charles MacLean, Neil Wilson, Rob Allanson, Marcin Miller, John Hansell, David Croll, Martin Will; Johanna and Charles, all the Malt Maniacs.

Massive and everlasting thanks to Davin de Kergommeaux for his stepping in when Canada began to look very sticky; Bernhard Schäfer for doing the same with the Central European countries; Chuck Cowdery for all his help with the truth about Dickel; to Ulf Buxrud, Krishna Nukala, and Craig Daniels for contacts; to Serge Valentin for samples and constant good humor; Alexandre Vingtier, Doug McIvor, Ed Bates, and Neil Mathieson for the same.

2nd edition Many thanks to all the distillers, colleagues, friends, and family who pulled out the stops to ensure this was completed on time.

Particular thanks to Davin de Kergommeaux, Lew Bryson, Pit Krause, Jasmin Haider, Philippe Juge, Chris Middleton, and Martin Tønder Smith for all their help in tracking down new distilleries.

To the distillers of said new plants who were willing to spend some time chatting to me: Alex Bruce, Karen Stewart, Francis Cuthbert, Guy Macpherson-Grant, David Fitt, John McCarthy, Marko Tayburn, Oliver Hughes, Daniel Smith, Allison Patel, Jean Donnay, Fred Revol, Patrick van Zuidam, Etienne Bouillon, Michael Morris, John Quinn, Nicole Austin, Chip Tate, Rich Blair, David Perkins, David King, Emerson Lamb, Angela d'Orazio, Ivan Abrahamsen, Roger Melander, Alex Højrup Munch, Gable Erenzo, John O'Connell, Jonas Ebensperger, Marcel Telser, Jens-Erik Jørgensen, and Henric Milon. You are the future.

To Marcin, for driving me around Norfolk and Suffolk while I was driving him mad. To Darren Rook and Tim Forbes, fellow residents of Distiller's Row, for ears, noses, and minds.

To Stephen, Ziggy, and The Major for letting me test out some ideas.

To the fabulous team at Octopus: Denise, Leanne, Juliette, Jamie, and Hilary for not only turning this around, but doing it with such little fuss and a real concern for the quality and accuracy of the copy and design.

To Tom Williams for being a voice of sanity.

Most of all to my wife—and assistant—Jo, for an astonishing job in organizing samples, counting bottles, and doing necessary, but time-consuming, research, allowing me time and space to get on with the writing. How she's put up with me for 25 years I know not.

...and to Rosie for always being able to make me smile.